THE EIGHTH DIVISION
1914 – 1918

By
LT.-COLONEL J.H. BORASTON,
C.B., O.B.E.

and

CAPTAIN CYRIL E.O. BAX

With a Foreword by
FIELD-MARSHALL EARL HAIG,
K.T., G.C.B., O.M., G.C.V.O., K.C.I.E.

PUBLISHED BY
THE NAVAL & MILITARY PRESS

Printed and bound in Great Britain by
Antony Rowe Ltd, Eastbourne

TO THE MEMORY
OF THE OFFICERS
NON-COMMISSIONED OFFICERS
AND MEN
WHO SERVED WITH THE 8TH DIVISION
IN THE GREAT WAR

FOREWORD

By FIELD-MARSHAL EARL HAIG, KT., G.C.B. O.M., G.C.V.O., K.C.I.E.

THE last of the Regular divisions which crossed to France in 1914, the 8th Division then entered upon a career the outstanding exploits of which were to illustrate in most striking fashion one of the historic qualities of British fighting men.

The capacity of the division for successful attack was shown in the capture of Neuve Chapelle in 1915, in the well-planned and executed assault on Bouchavesnes in 1917 and in skilful operations against the Drocourt–Quéant and Rouvroy–Fresnes lines in 1918. Yet these were, comparatively speaking, minor operations. In the major offensives in which it took a direct part the 8th Division, despite unfailing gallantry, was signally unfortunate. Its greatest glories, and those by which it will always be remembered with honour in the annals of the British Army, were achieved in defence.

The capacity to fight a losing battle doggedly and relentlessly against odds, and somehow by sheer grit and obstinacy to wrest victory from defeat, is one which in all ages and in all countries has peculiarly attracted the respect and admiration of mankind. The history of no nation is more rich in instances of this special type of courage than is that of our own British race. The Great War added many fresh examples.

High amongst them is surely the performance of the 8th Division in meeting the great German onslaught of March 1918, and peculiarly the magnificent stand at Rosières when for thirty-six critical hours the division held up the enemy's progress towards Amiens. Not less memorable was the self-sacrifice of the 2/ Devons and the 5th Battery, R.F.A., North of the Aisne on the 27th May 1918, where their heroic resistance, unto death, gained for them the honour of " citation " by our French Allies.

In writing this Foreword to the history of a Regular division which saw its first fighting in the First Army which I then commanded, I am glad to recognize in the recorded actions of all ranks so notable a measure of a quality which I trust will long remain an essential part of British character.

Haig. F.M.

Bemersyde
14th June 1926.

AUTHORS' PREFACE

IN setting themselves to write the story of the part played in the Great War by a division in which they neither of them served, the authors suffered from the start from an obvious handicap. They have also enjoyed one very definite advantage. If they have had to glean their knowledge of the inner life of the division at second hand and thereby, perhaps, have missed some of those personal touches which help to make the atmosphere of a divisional history, they have yet been spared the tendency to regard all the doings of the 8th Division from the standpoint of some particular branch or unit within it. They have been able to look at the actions of all arms and units impartially.

The official records have amply furnished the framework of the story. The generous assistance given by those many former members of the 8th Division who put their private documents and diaries at the authors' disposal, and have clothed the dry bones of officialism with the living tissue of their personal recollections, has made the task of importing atmosphere less utterly impossible than at first it seemed. In this respect, nonetheless, the authors crave the indulgence of those readers who did serve personally with the division.

In another respect the authors feel that they are on surer ground. They conceive that it should be one of the chief objects of a divisional history, not merely to tell the war story of a particular formation, but to tell it in relation to the story of the British Army in the war and of the progress of the struggle as a whole. To record the life and actions of a division as an isolated and individual unit is to tell those who served in it little that they do not already know. It will not help them to understand the reasons for what they did or for the orders given them, nor assist them to appreciate the real value of their successes. More important still, it will not render them such proper consolation for misfortune as may often be gained from a knowledge of the wider effects of those engagements in which they may have suffered reverses.

In the present history an effort has been made to produce a narrative containing the essential details of the actions of the units which from time to time composed the 8th Division, and to enliven—without overburdening—it with personal incident and anecdote; but at the same time to put that narrative in its proper setting and perspective in relation to the successive campaigns on the Western Front, as influenced by the general course of events in all theatres of the Great War. In this way, it is thought that the book will be of special interest to the junior officers and rank and file of the division who, it is common experience, had neither the time nor the opportunity during the war itself to give much thought to what was happening outside their own battery

AUTHORS' PREFACE

or battalion. It is hoped that this history will be the means to enable them in retrospect to take a broader view of the memorable events in which they took so worthy a part eight years and more ago, and to feel, if that be possible, a yet greater pride in the exploits of their old division.

The thanks of the authors are especially due to General Heneker, who put a mass of valuable material at the authors' disposition; and to General Davies and General Hudson, who, with General Heneker, read the typescript of the history and made many suggestions which are incorporated in this book; to General Anderson, General Coffin, General Pinney, General Montgomery, Colonel J. D. Mitchell, Major J. H. T. Priestman and Captain J. H. Dyer for material; to Colonel E. H. L. Beddington and Colonel C. C. Armitage for material and for invaluable assistance in connection with the chapters dealing with the periods when they were respectively G.S.O.1 of the division; to Captain S. Rogerson for reading the typescript and for a great part of the account of the Aisne battle; to Captain P. Triefus, Major H. Ramsbotham and Major J. Wedderburn-Maxwell for reading portions of the typescript and proofs and for numerous suggestions; and to many others for help for which the authors are most grateful.

J. H. B.
C. E. O. B.

CONTENTS

	PAGE
FOREWORD BY FIELD-MARSHAL EARL HAIG, KT., G.C.B., O.M., G.C.V.O., K.C.I.E.	vii
AUTHORS' PREFACE	ix

CHAP.
- I. EARLY DAYS AND WINTER NIGHTS — 1
- II. NEUVE CHAPELLE — 16
- III. FROMELLES AND AFTER — 31
- IV. BOIS GRENIER — 45
- V. LINE AND RESERVE — 55
- VI. THE SOMME BATTLE: OVILLERS — 65
- VII. THE SOMME BATTLE: LE TRANSLOY — 84
- VIII. BOUCHAVESNES AND THE GERMAN RETREAT — 96
- IX. THE CAMPAIGN IN FLANDERS IN 1917: WESTHOEK RIDGE — 121
- X. THE CAMPAIGN IN FLANDERS IN 1917: THE HANEBEEK — 141
- XI. AUTUMN AND WINTER, 1917 — 156
- XII. THE GREAT GERMAN OFFENSIVE — 169
- XIII. VILLERS-BRETONNEUX — 199
- XIV. THE BATTLE OF THE AISNE, 1918 — 216
- XV. RECONSTRUCTION — 241
- XVI. THE FINAL OFFENSIVE: DOUAI — 248
- XVII. THE FINAL OFFENSIVE: MONS — 268
- XVIII. VICTORY — 276
- APPENDIX I. COMPOSITION OF HEADQUARTERS — 283
- APPENDIX II. ORDERS OF BATTLE — 286
- APPENDIX III. TABLE OF SECTORS, ENGAGEMENTS AND CASUALTIES — 295
- APPENDIX IV. HONOURS AND AWARDS — 297
- INDEX — 347

LIST OF ILLUSTRATIONS

	FACING PAGE
GENERAL SIR FRANCIS JOHN DAVIES, K.C.B., K.C.M.G., K.C.V.O.	6
NEUVE CHAPELLE: SCENE OF GERMAN STAND AT NORTH CORNER OF VILLAGE	22
FROMELLES FROM ROUGE CROIX	31
GENERAL SIR HAVELOCK HUDSON, K.C.B., K.C.I.E.	44
WINTER ON THE LYS FRONT	60
OPPOSITE LA BOISSELLE	62
EIGHTH DIVISION LIMBERS GOING THROUGH LONGUEVAL, AUTUMN 1916	86
LIEUT.-GENERAL SIR WILLIAM C. G. HENEKER, K.C.B., K.C.M.G., D.S.O.	96
GERMAN RETREAT, MARCH 1917.	
TREES FELLED ACROSS A ROAD NEAR PERONNE	
A VILLAGE IN THE DEVASTATED AREA	112
YPRES 1917.	
THE MENIN ROAD	126
A GERMAN "PILL BOX"	130
WINTER 1917–18.	
YPRES SALIENT: A DUCK-BOARD TRACK	
THE ROAD TO PASSCHENDAELE	160
TANKS	
BRITISH "MALE" TANK	
BRITISH WHIPPET TANK	
GERMAN TANK	204
THE BOIS L'ABBE, APRIL 1918, STRETCHER BEARERS, 24TH INFANTRY BRIGADE, CROSSING THE RIDGE THAT SCREENS AMIENS, ON THE WAY TO VILLERS-BRETONNEUX	206
OPPY WOOD FROM VIMY RIDGE	248
DOUAI: GRANDE PLACE, OCTOBER 1918	248
THE KING'S VISIT, TOURNAI, DECEMBER 1918	276

LIST OF MAPS

	FACING PAGE
THE FIRST ATTACK AT NEUVE CHAPELLE, 18 DECEMBER 1914	10
NEUVE CHAPELLE, 10–14 MARCH 1915	28
FROMELLES, 9 MAY 1915	37
ACTION BEFORE BOIS GRENIER, 25 SEPTEMBER 1915	47
BATTLE OF THE SOMME, 1 JULY 1916	68
LE TRANSLOY, 23 OCTOBER 1916	90
BOUCHAVESNES, 4 MARCH 1917	105
THE GERMAN RETREAT, SPRING 1917	108
THE BATTLE OF YPRES THE FIRST ASSAULT, 31 JULY 1917	138
THE ATTACK FROM WESTHOEK, 16 AUGUST 1917	152
PASSCHENDAELE RIDGE, 1–2 DECEMBER 1917	166
THE GERMAN OFFENSIVE, 1918	194
THE SOMME FRONT, MARCH 1918	198
VILLERS BRETONNEUX (1) SITUATION 3.45 A.M. 24 APRIL 1918	208
(2) SITUATION 6 P.M., 25 APRIL 1918	214
THE BATTLE OF THE AISNE (1)	230
(2)	240
ROUVROY–FRESNES LINE, 7–8 OCTOBER 1918	262
DIVISIONAL BOUNDARIES AND STAGES OF ADVANCE, OCTOBER–NOVEMBER 1918	274

CHAPTER I

EARLY DAYS AND WINTER NIGHTS

ON the 19th September 1914 a small group of officers took up their quarters at the Polygon Hotel, Southampton, and with their accompanying clerks, orderlies and type-writers established their offices in the big lounge built on to the hotel on the right of the main entrance. This room, with its wide-arched ceiling dimly prophetic of future Nissen-hutted offices, had already been used for a like purpose by the Headquarters of the 1st, 2nd, 3rd and 7th Divisions. Now in turn it gave shelter to Maj.-General F. J. Davies, C.B., one time Director of Staff Duties at the War Office, and the Headquarters of the Regular division which he had been appointed to command. The story of the 8th Division in the Great War had begun.

Within a week of the arrival of Headquarters at the Polygon Hotel, the first troops of the division, the 23rd Infantry Brigade, which had been brought back post haste from Malta, commenced to assemble, under command of Brig.-General F. A. Adam, C.B., in camp on Baddesley Common. With the exception of the Northamptonshire Yeomanry, the Wessex (Territorial) Field Ambulance and the Signal Company, the division was to be composed of Regular troops. All its infantry battalions and engineer units (the Signal Company excepted) had been serving in stations abroad when the war broke out and were hurried homewards across the seas to the scene of the great conflict. In these circumstances, it was inevitable that the concentration of the division should take some little time.

By the 2nd October, however, the first brigade was complete, and on that day moved with Divisional Headquarters to Hursley Park, near Winchester, there to await the arrival of the rest of the division. Hursley Park had been placed voluntarily at the disposal of the division—this was, of course, long before the days of D.O.R.A.—by its owner Sir George Cooper, Bt. All ranks, and especially those officers for whose wives Lady Cooper found house room during their husbands' last days in England, owed much to Sir George Cooper's patriotic action, and to the generous hospitality which accompanied it. To-day, a monument set up by Sir George outside the park gates marks the spot past which the division marched to embark at Southampton.

Meanwhile three weeks of fine weather gave an opportunity all too brief for the division to find itself, and for the new units as they successively arrived to settle down into their allotted places in the divisional organization. The process of assimilation was greatly assisted by the fact that officers and men were for the most part Regulars; yet even so all ranks necessarily felt the lack of opportunity for the combined training so urgently required

EARLY DAYS AND WINTER NIGHTS

if a division is to become something more than a mere agglomeration of units. Those, too, who had joined the division from Eastern stations suffered from the further handicap that they could be given no proper time for acclimatization. Indeed it may be doubted whether at this stage of the war the need for acclimatization was properly understood. Men from India and Singapore found themselves, after a few short strenuous weeks in England, sent straight out to face the rigours of a winter of trench fighting in Flanders. It was small wonder that the sick lists of the division during this first winter were grievously high.

Even before leaving Hursley Park, the division was given an inkling of the trials in store for it. Towards the end of October the fine weather broke, and by the time the last battalion joined up on the 30th of the month,* the mud which pervaded the camp and its approaches afforded a foretaste, mild by comparison yet sufficiently unpleasant, of the conditions which awaited the troops in Flanders.

They were soon to see the real thing. On the 4th November the first five battalions marched out of camp for Southampton, where they embarked. Next day the remainder of the division followed and during the night of the 5th/6th November, over a calm sea, the 8th Division crossed to France.

That quiet night crossing, in which the peaceful stillness of the elements made contrast with the object of the journey, was a strange introduction to the long series of desperate encounters and grim, hard-fought battles which destiny had ordained to be the career of the 8th Division in the Great War. No division in the British Army was to be more buffeted by the tempest of war than the one now borne upon a peaceful autumn sea. Nor had the division long to wait before the commencement of its ordeal. Havre was reached on the morning of the 6th November, and, after a disembarkation made slower than it need have been by a lack of adequate arrangements for unloading heavy vehicles and horses, by the evening of the 7th November the division was temporarily established in rest camps outside the town. Next day it began entraining.

Meanwhile, General Davies and certain officers of the divisional staff had motored to Abbeville for instructions, and thence had gone on to St. Omer, where Sir John French's Headquarters had been established since the 12th October. They received orders for the division to proceed to the neighbourhood of Merville, a small town South-East of the Nieppe Forest and destined to become famous through misfortune in the last year of the war. Divisional Headquarters were installed there on the 9th

* For composition of Headquarters and Order of Battle at this date, see Appendices I and II.

INTO LINE

November, on which day the first units of the division began to arrive by train from Havre. By the 12th November, the day following the last great German assault in the first battle of Ypres, the concentration of the division had been completed and on the same day the 2/Devonshire (Lieut.-Colonel J. O. Travers, D.S.O.) went into line North of Ploegsteert Wood, in support of our hard pressed forces covering Ypres. For this purpose the Devons, together with the rest of the 23rd Infantry Brigade (Brig.-General R. J. Pinney), were placed temporarily under the orders of the Cavalry Corps.

Though to the Devons, therefore, belongs the honour of having been the first troops of the division to face the enemy in line, they did not gain the privilege by much. Two days later, the 14th November, the 24th and 25th Infantry Brigades (Brig.-Generals F. C. Carter and A. W. G. Lowry Cole, C.B., D.S.O.) marched to Estaires, and at dusk on the same day took over from the Lahore division the sector of the British front extending from Rue du Bois to Fauquissart, relieving the 8th and 14th Infantry Brigades (3rd and 5th Divisions), then temporarily attached to the Lahore Division. Each brigade had two battalions in line. These two brigades, which on the preceding day had been strengthened by the addition of two territorial battalions, the 5/Black Watch going to the 24th Infantry Brigade and the 13/London to the 25th Infantry Brigade, being now in the Indian Corps area, were placed temporarily under the orders of the commanders of the adjoining Indian divisions.

It was, therefore, as chance would have it, under strange command that the infantry of the 8th Division had their first experience of the warfare of the trenches; for, while the 23rd Infantry Brigade were still detached with the Cavalry Corps, on the 15th November the Indian Corps became engaged on the whole front from la Bassée to Armentières. At mid-day the sector of the 25th Infantry Brigade was subjected to heavy bombardment and a portion of the trenches held by the 2/Lincolnshire (Lieut.-Colonel G. B. McAndrew) was blown in. The same evening, between 5.30 p.m. and 6.30 p.m. a similar outburst of firing blazed up opposite the 2/Northamptonshire (Lieut.-Colonel C. S. Prichard, D.S.O.), but was replied to with such vigour that the attack, if attack was intended, failed to materialize. The division had incurred the first of its long roll of battle casualties; but the damaged trenches of the 2/Lincolnshire were re-occupied and the troops settled down quietly and determinedly to the work before them.

On the 15th November also the divisional artillery, under command of Brig.-General A. E. A. Holland, D.S.O., M.V.O., moved into position, covering the front held by their infantry;

EARLY DAYS AND WINTER NIGHTS

and the divisional Ammunition Column, Field Ambulances and Train arrived in the divisional area. That night the 24th and 25th Brigades took over from the Ferozepore and Jullunder Brigades, Lahore Division, the responsibility for the front from Rue du Bois to Tilleloy, and at 10 a.m. on the 16th November the G.O.C. 8th Division assumed command of the sector. Next day the 23rd Infantry Brigade rejoined, and the 8th Division as a complete unit stood for the first time face to face with the enemy. The front held by the division at this date was some 8,000 yards in length, and the division now formed part of the IV Corps, commanded by Sir Henry Rawlinson. At the end of the year the IV Corps was to become the left Corps of Sir Douglas Haig's First Army.

The arrival of the 8th Division in line, in a part of the front which, with minor shiftings to North or South and occasional transfers from one Corps of the First Army to another, was to be its home without relief for the next twelve months and more—surely a record for the war—offers a good opportunity to pause in the divisional narrative and to consider for a moment what was the general position of affairs on the Western Front when the 8th Division was being so hurriedly rushed into the struggle.

At the date at which this story opens, namely the 19th September 1914, the movement which has been called "The Race to the Sea," but was in fact an endeavour upon the part of each of the belligerents to turn the other's western and northern flank, had already been begun by the northward extension of the left of General Maunoury's Sixth French Army on the right bank of the Oise. The forward rush of the Allied Armies which had followed the victory of the Marne was spent, and East of Soissons the British Expeditionary Force, lately reinforced by the 6th Division, was entering upon the stage of trench-warfare. West of Soissons, Maunoury's efforts to envelop the German right flank had been checked before Noyon; but the movement, once begun, continued rapidly and almost automatically. The Seventh and Tenth French Armies under de Castelnau and Maud'Huy built up the Allied front northwards, till by the 2nd October, the date when the 8th Division commenced its concentration at Hursley Park, the opposing lines already stretched unbroken to the neighbourhood of Lens. The contest on the Western Front was beginning to assume the appearance which three years of trench warfare were to make so familiar. Yet North of Lens to the coast, except in so far as it was covered by the presence of the Belgian forces in Antwerp or filled by bodies of German cavalry, there still remained a wide gap; and the constant extension of the fighting front was trying to the utmost

"THE RACE TO THE SEA"

the ability of our Allies to provide in time sufficient troops to hold the lengthening line.

Before the close of September, Sir John French had obtained General Joffre's consent to the gradual transfer of the British Expeditionary Force from the Aisne, where it then was, to the position on the left of the Allied line which, strategically as well as politically, was the obvious and proper place for it. The rearrangement had been begun with the withdrawal from line on the nights of the 1st/2nd and 2nd/3rd October of the II Corps which, with the two British cavalry divisions, reached the northern area early in the second week of the month and began to move on Bethune. The III Corps followed, and was directed towards Bailleul and Armentières. Finally, the I Corps detrained at Hazebrouck on the 19th October and thence began to move towards Ypres.

The movement of the British forces eastwards on this new front had encountered and driven before it the screen of mounted troops which the Germans had flung to the West and North of the drive of their main armies. By the 11th September British cavalry had cleared the Nieppe Forest and were in touch with French cavalry to the South. French and British troops were still in Ghent. It was thought that a continued advance in the direction of Lille and Tournai, even though too late to save Antwerp, would deny the enemy direct access to the Channel and turn the flank of the main German positions stretching from the Aisne to Lens. At first the British Army and the French troops operating with them in this advance had made rapid progress, and a number of localities destined later to become familiar to all divisions of the British Army, and not least to the 8th Division, were rescued from the enemy. Gough's 2nd Cavalry Division had attacked and captured the Mont des Cats on the 12th October, had gained Mont Noir on the 13th, and on the 14th had taken Kemmel and pushed advanced detachments as far East as Warneton. On the 12th October Bailleul and Meteren had fallen to the infantry of the III Corps, and the II Corps had reached the line Annequin-Festubert. By the 15th the III Corps had reached the Lys.

Meanwhile, the Belgian Army had been falling back, covered by Rawlinson's IV Corps, till at this date they had reached the shelter of the Yser. The 7th British Division had retired from Ghent via Æltre, Thielt and Roulers and was now East of Ypres, with the 3rd Cavalry Division covering it to the East and in touch with Gough's cavalry. Then had come a check. The German resistance on the la Bassée front stiffened and became too great to be overcome. Though we were able to secure Givenchy and establish a line northwards to Armentières, which latter place

EARLY DAYS AND WINTER NIGHTS

was taken on the 18th October, troops which on the same day had crossed the Layes to the South-East of the town were first held and then driven back across the river. The offensive perforce came to a halt and was transformed to a desperate defence. The first phase of the Battle of Ypres, that in which the Allies made successive attempts to develop a great turning movement round the German right flank, had ended in failure. The second phase, in which the Germans in great force strove to drive in the thin Allied line covering Ypres, was about to begin.

The storm centre of this great struggle lay, however, North of Armentières. In the British sector South of that town to the la Bassée Canal there was, indeed, heavy fighting in the latter days of October, and the arrival of troops of the Lahore Division, the first instalments of General Willcocks' Indian Corps, provided a very welcome addition to the British resources on this front. Hard put to it though our troops were, the enemy's constant pressure was unable to overcome our defence. Even before the end of that month the front from the la Bassée Canal to Armentières had already begun to stabilize on a line which was to see no change of more than a local character till the spring of 1918.

North of Armentières, where the roads to Calais converged upon the little town of Ypres, under the impulse of successive German drives the line fluctuated violently for the better part of a month. It was in the early stages of this struggle, on the 27th October, that General Rawlinson and his Headquarters were sent back to England to supervise the preparation of the 8th Division, destined to form part of the re-formed IV Corps which, under General Rawlinson's command, was to come to the aid of the much-tried British Army as soon as the 8th Division could be equipped and sent to France. Though at the date when the division began to embark at Southampton the first and greatest crisis of the battle on the Ypres front had already been reached and passed, the danger was by no means over, and the position on the Ypres front was still serious when the 23rd Infantry Brigade was detached and sent to the assistance of the Cavalry Corps.

This brief review of facts now world famous will serve to explain the haste with which the units of the 8th Division were brought together, despatched to France, and hurried into the line. Under the tremendous German assaults which marked the close of October and the first fortnight of November 1914, the Allied front before Ypres had held together by a miracle—a miracle largely made possible by the splendid fighting qualities of the British Regular Army, reinforced by a few no less gallant Territorial units. With the needs of the moment so urgent, it was not to be expected that a Regular division, even though

PLATE I

GENERAL SIR FRANCIS JOHN DAVIES, K.C.B., K.C.M.G., K.C.V.O.

THE COLD OF THE TRENCHES

composed of battalions but lately returned from foreign stations and having had no proper opportunities for combined training, would long be left out of the fight. Yet, as it happened, by the 16th November the enemy had made his last great effort for the year, and the entry of the 8th Division into line coincided with the gradual settling down of both combatants to the first winter of trench warfare. It might fairly have been considered, however, whether to troops so recently returned from warmer climates the conditions of the Lys Valley in winter might not prove almost as exhausting as battle fighting.

A glance at the general position will complete the setting of the stage upon which the 8th Division had just entered. The front of the British Army at the date when the division took its place in the line extended from the la Bassée canal on the South to the Ypres battle area on the North, where French and British troops were fighting side by side. A few days later, the British troops in the Ypres salient were relieved by French divisions and by the end of November the left of the British Army marched with the French at Wytschaete. The British forces then held a front of some 21 miles, with the Indian Corps, IV, III, and II Corps in line and the I Corps and Cavalry in reserve. South of the British area, French Armies guarded the long line past Arras, Albert, Roye, Soissons and Verdun to the Swiss frontier. To the North, French and Belgian units held the Salient and watched the line of the inundations behind which the Belgian Army was commencing to re-organize. From the Swiss frontier to the sea there had already been drawn the 400-mile double line of trenches which, growing stronger, deeper and more intricate from month to month, was for the next three years to be the governing factor in the war on the Western Front.

The remainder of November was passed by all ranks of the division in accustoming themselves as best they could to a new and uncomfortable way of life, made more trying by snow and by a frost which was for the time of year unusually hard. The troops, as was only to be expected, suffered extremely. Hurriedly extemporized braziers burning coke or charcoal could do little to bring relief from the bitter cold of the trenches, and within a week of their arrival in line many men began to go down with sore and frost-bitten feet. It was the beginning of an experience which all the early divisions went through, but from which no white troops suffered more severely than did the unacclimatized battalions of the 8th Division. The winter of 1914/15 was to prove exceptionally wet, and the hardships and discomforts of the troops in the trenches can scarcely be realized by those who came to France later in the war. The appliances which were brought into use in succeeding years to combat mud and water

EARLY DAYS AND WINTER NIGHTS

and make the trenches more habitable were at this date unknown. Trench life and trench warfare were entirely new, even to the comparatively old soldiers of which the division was mainly composed. Everything concerning the new type of warfare had to be learnt by actual and often bitter experience. Everything had to be improvised, from trench-mortars to trench-boards. Necessity once more proved the mother of invention, and to the division belongs the credit of the first utilization of wooden trench tramways for the supply of the troops in line. The idea originated with Lieut.-Colonel H. M. de F. Montgomery, D.S.O., who had succeeded Colonel Hoskins as A.A. and Q.M.G. to the division. Having observed similar tramways in use for agricultural purposes on farms in the neighbourhood, he had realized the military use to which they might be put. Later the practice spread to all armies on the Western Front.

Nor was this period devoid of those minor incidents which lend excitement to trench life. There was much protective wiring to be done; the trench lines themselves were incomplete and not yet organized for defence; a watchful eye had to be kept on the enemy. Eight days after the arrival of the division in line, Lieut. E. H. Impey and eight men of the 2/Lincolnshire carried out the division's first embryonic raid. Draped, with attention to practical rather than artistic effect, in white sheets and ladies' nightdresses, the party advanced over the snow-covered ground to a trench junction in the German line from which the enemy had been enfilading an elbow known as "Red Lamp Corner" in our own front. The first shot from Lieut. Impey's revolver brought the German garrison tumbling out till the trench swarmed like an angry wasps' nest, the raiding party opened rapid and effective fire upon easy targets showing black against the snow and then, aided by the way in which their own unconventional apparel blended with the white background, withdrew without loss. So happy an exploit soon found its imitators. In the early morning of the 27th November, Lieut. P. Neame and a party of Royal Engineers under escort of 2nd/Lieut. L. M. Kerr and nine men of the 2/West Yorkshire went across to the German lines and blew up the farmhouse, known as "The Moated Grange," from which snipers had caused us several casualties. At its second attempt, the idea of the raid was beginning to take more definite shape.

During the afternoon of the 1st December the King, accompanied by President Poincaré and General Joffre, visited the division, and was received by a Guard of Honour formed by the 2/Lincolnshire, who only that morning had come out of the trenches. All ranks of the division were much heartened and encouraged by receiving so early a proof of the interest taken by

A LOCAL OPERATION

His Majesty in the welfare of his troops and the success of their efforts. The visit was a good introduction to the first demand made upon the division to take part in combined offensive operations.

DECEMBER 1914

Old though the year already was when the enemy's first attempts to force a passage at Ypres finally broke down, General Joffre decided that the Allied Armies should themselves end it upon the keynote of attack. The advance of winter, which on the Western Front offered the obstacle of endless mud to any considerable offensive, on the Russian front opened a new campaigning season, when once the alternate snows and thaws of autumn yielded to winter's binding frosts. It was hoped that continued activity in the West, besides improving the Allied positions there, and particularly in the coastal sectors, would bring relief also to the Russian Armies by preventing the transfer of German troops to the East.

Accordingly in the month of December was begun a series of local operations, nowhere attended by very much success, but intended to gain ground, though not on any very extensive scale, at a number of points ranging in the northern battle area from Albert to the sea at Nieuport. Among these operations, and intended to develop the recent French success at Vermelles, was an attack by the 58th French Division against the German positions immediately South of the la Bassée Canal, supported North of the Canal by the Lahore Division opposite Givenchy. The rôle allotted to the 8th Division was the comparatively minor one of containing the enemy on its front during these operations, so as to prevent as far as possible help being sent to the threatened portions of the German line. This task, though a secondary one, entailed greatly increased activity on the part of both infantry and artillery from the morning of the 14th December onwards till the 18th December. On the afternoon of the latter day this activity culminated in infantry attacks at two points along the divisional front against selected portions of the German trench system.

Verbal instructions for the attack, which was to be directed against Neuve Chapelle and the German forward trench covering the village, were given by the G.O.C. IV Corps at midnight on the 17th/18th December. Short as was the time for preparation, the assault of General Pinney's 23rd Infantry Brigade upon the trenches covering the village was duly launched at 4.30 p.m. on the 18th, after fifteen minutes' preparatory bombardment. The troops delivering the attack were two companies of the 2/Devonshire of which the right company under Capt. C. A. Lafone, supported by troops of the 2/West Yorkshire who in the event took a decisive part in the fighting, passed successfully over the

9

EARLY DAYS AND WINTER NIGHTS

small German trenches fronting the Moated Grange,* and rushed the main German front trench which lay East of the farm. In spite of the increased activity of the preceding days, the enemy did not appear to have been expecting attack at that time and many Germans were bayoneted in their dug-outs. The 2/West Yorkshire, under Lieut. F. J. Harington, then bombed the enemy out of a further portion of trench, enabling a third company of the Devons, under Capt. G. I. Watts, to follow up the success. The left of the attack, however, was less fortunate. Here Major W. M. Goodwyn's company found its way of advance barred both by our own wire and the enemy's, and suffered heavily under the German fire. Only a few men of this company reached their objective, with the result that our new positions lay uncomfortably open to counter-attack from the left. After personal reconnaissance, General Pinney decided that the hope originally entertained of continuing the attack to the German second line was impossible of realization, and accordingly ordered Colonel Travers to hold the 150 yards of German trench which his battalion had won.

Meanwhile, the two companies of the 2/West Yorkshire, and a party of Royal Engineers who had followed closely after the attacking troops, at once commenced to dig communication trenches from our lines to the nearest German saps. Shortly after 8.30 p.m., the enemy's fire, which throughout the operations had largely been kept under by our artillery, commenced to die down yet further and advantage was taken of this to carry out the relief of the Devons by the West Yorkshire (Lieut.-Colonel G. F. Phillips). So the position remained during the night; but at about 7.30 a.m. on the 19th December the enemy began bombing at the North-East end of the captured trench, using small round bombs which were apparently fitted with some sort of time fuse and could be thrown 40 yards. Our bombs at this time consisted of old jam tins with a fuse which had to be lighted before the bomb was thrown. Once the fuse was ignited the bombs went off well; but lighting them was a difficult process, and nearly a whole platoon was knocked out by the German bombers while our men were vainly endeavouring to get the fuses of their own bombs to burn. The enemy was making steady progress down the trench and matters were beginning to look very serious for the whole garrison of the captured position, when Lieut. P. Neame, who had come up in charge of the Royal Engineer party, found a way to light the jam-tin bombs. Then standing on the parapet of the trench he counter-bombed the enemy so effectively, as long as the supply of bombs held out, that the rest of our men were able to get clear. For this gallant

---

* See sketch map opposite. The farmhouse shown in No Man's Land in "C" sub-sector is the Moated Grange.

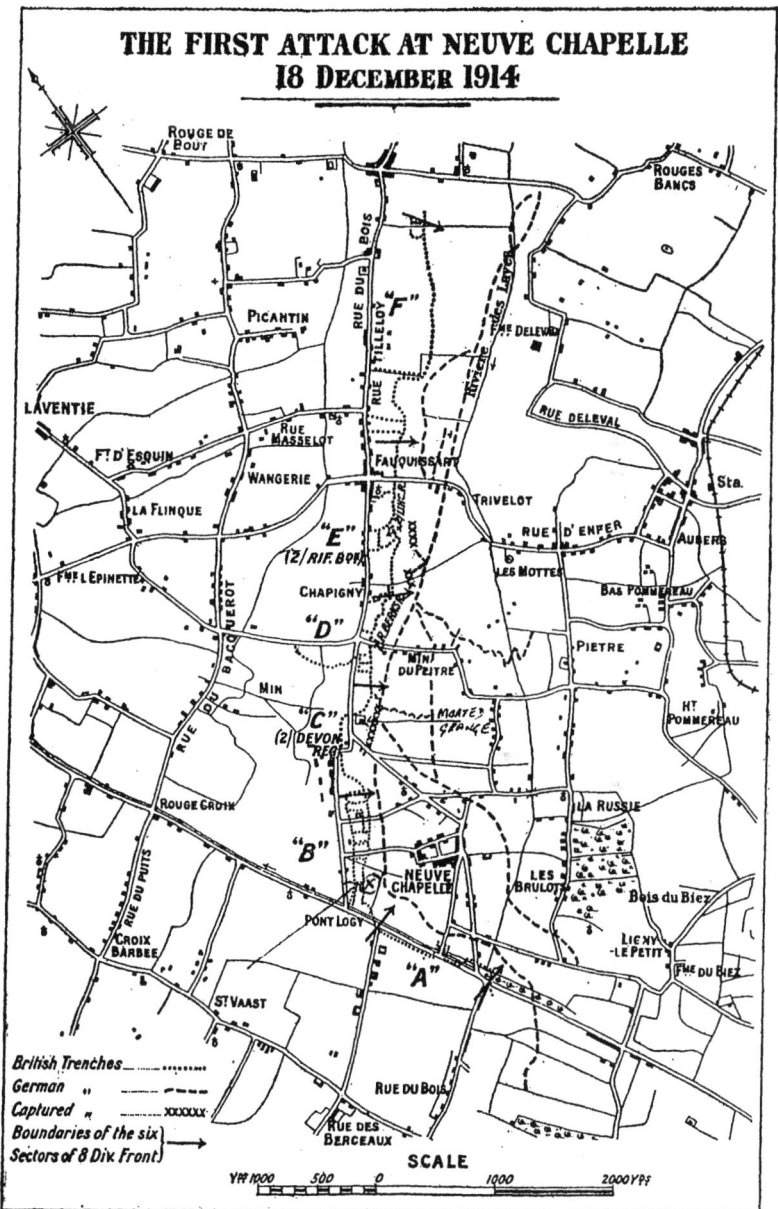

EARLY DAYS AND WINTER NIGHTS

exploit Lieut. P. Neame gained the Victoria Cross, the first awarded in the division.

In the event, it was necessary to withdraw right back to our old line, for water from the moat had got into the new trenches which we had dug to join up with the captured trench, and rendered them untenable. The operation of the 18th December, however, should not be judged only by its immediate local results. Desirable from a tactical point of view as an improvement of our position opposite Neuve Chapelle undoubtedly was, the action of the 8th Division from the 14th December onwards had been subservient to the immediate interests of the French attack South of the Canal, and to the general interests of the wider scheme of operations. The harassing tactics of the preceding four days had been admirably calculated to keep the enemy on the alert and distract his attention from other sectors; but had not been of sufficient weight or intensity to serve as an effectual preparation for an assault. The attack itself had been ordered at very short notice. There had been no opportunity properly to instruct junior and non-commissioned officers in the tasks they were to perform, no time to cut the enemy's wire, or even, as the left of the attack discovered so disastrously, to arrange proper gaps in our own defences. Inadequate time for preparation and explanation, and the inferior quality and scarcity of our bombs, were facts amply sufficient to account for the inability of the 23rd Infantry Brigade to hold the ground which the attacking companies had so gallantly won. Yet the division could find some consolation in the reflection that their allotted task of occupying and distracting the enemy had been conscientiously performed. South of the la Bassée Canal the French attack had enjoyed a certain measure of success and had gained an advantage of some local importance. It was here that the division could look for the concrete reward of their endeavour.

Moreover, the division had gained valuable experience in a style of fighting new to them. Against their own losses of 48 killed and 188 wounded or missing, they could set casualties inflicted on the enemy estimated at over 100 in killed alone, and in addition 24 prisoners were brought back to our lines.

While the attack opposite Neuve Chapelle was proceeding, the 25th Infantry Brigade (Brig.-General A. W. G. Lowry-Cole) had engaged the enemy all along the line with rifle and artillery fire, and had moved out four platoons of the 2/ Rifle Brigade to the advanced German trenches opposite the centre of the brigade sector. These trenches had been occupied and held until the situation on the front of the 23rd Infantry Brigade had declared itself, and here also useful experience had been gained and the task of holding the enemy accomplished. The division had no

A CHRISTMAS TRUCE

need to be unduly disappointed with the results of its opening essay in offensive operations.

After this attack, the division settled down once more to the dreary ordeal of its first winter in the line. There was plenty of work to be done. The milder weather which had followed the frosts of November had reduced the trenches to a deplorable condition. Fighting the water became more difficult than fighting the enemy. The part of the line occupied by the division was so low-lying that it was impossible to carry off the water by drainage. All that could be done was to block off certain sections of the trenches and pump out the water into adjacent portions. This entailed isolating the garrisons of the parts of the trenches so pumped out, for it was impossible to keep the communication trenches from flooding, and the only access to the front line was over the open in full view of the enemy. Mud and water accumulated everywhere, the sides of trenches fell in, and life became a heart-breaking round of revetting, pumping, draining, wiring, varied though not relieved by the construction of new defences, trench lines and communications.

As Christmas approached, special vigilance was ordered, as a rumour was current that the enemy intended to celebrate the ending of the old or the opening of the new year by starting a fresh offensive. These rumours proved baseless. A Christmas Day of hard frost was marked by an unofficial truce which was utilized by both sides for burying their dead. The troops, both English and German, came out of the trenches, kicked footballs about, exchanged cigarettes and other small articles, and—more curious still—lent one another implements for reinforcing each other's wire entanglements. The incident was part of a strange tribute which on this first Christmas of the war was paid at many points along the fronts of the contending armies to the spirit of peace and goodwill among men. It was never repeated.

Again rain followed the frost, and the condition of the trenches became steadily worse. Before the end of the month, the water was $2\frac{1}{2}$ feet deep in many places, and the utmost efforts of the pumps were needed to keep the level from rising above the fire-steps. Wagon loads of brushwood and planks brought up to lay along the bottoms of the trenches were swallowed up in the mud almost as soon as they were laid. Throughout January the wet weather continued, and the depth of water increased until many lengths of trench were wholly untenable. It became necessary to construct breastworks in rear of these trenches, in order to enable the line to be maintained. Yet even in the midst of increasing labour on defences, the duty of maintaining a proper offensive spirit among the troops was not forgotten. At 7.45 p.m. on the 3rd January Lieut. F. C. Roberts with a party of 25

EARLY DAYS AND WINTER NIGHTS

men of the 1/ Worcestershire carried out the first genuine raid to be undertaken on the British front. During the preceding night the enemy had dug a new trench opposite "B" sector * to within 40 yards of our lines. Lieut. Roberts and his party entered the western end of this trench, took the enemy completely by surprise, bayoneted 30 Germans, and returned to our lines with the loss of 2 men missing and 1 wounded. The whole operation took not more than four minutes.

Still the rain continued. The Lys flooded its banks, and wide tracts of country became submerged. The Germans suffered equally with ourselves, and on one occasion were caught by our rifle and machine-gun fire while standing on their parapets baling water from their trenches. Towards the middle of the month conditions became so bad that they could only be met by special dispositions of the troops. It was arranged that those portions of the front line which could still be occupied should be held by day very lightly, and at night only strongly enough to delay any attack till supports could come up. The supports themselves were stationed in rear of the trenches, in such shelter as could be made available; while the rest of the front-line garrisons were held in reserve yet farther back. Machine-gun positions were selected to cover possible approaches and everything was done, by lighting fires in the trenches and maintaining steady sniping by the few men left in the front line, to deceive the enemy as to the nature of our dispositions. Nature was forcing the division to adopt thus early something very like the elastic system of defence which technical considerations forced upon the whole army at a later stage.

The organization of the sector, so as to give greater depth and strength to the defence, was, indeed, pushed on steadily, despite the demands of the front line. Arrangements were made for the construction of what were then called "Pivot Points," with definite garrisons allotted to them, in rear of the first line and designed to lend support to it in case of attack. The advantage of such points was one of the lessons learnt from the attacks which the enemy made on the 25th January at Cuinchy and Givenchy, where the resistance of such strong points enabled our French Allies and our own 2nd Brigade to dislodge the enemy by counter-attack from the footing which his first assaults had established in the Allied lines. By the middle of February, the majority of these supporting points in rear of the front line trenches had been constructed. Fifteen closed works capable of all-round defence were approaching completion in what was known as the G.H.Q. line, and behind this line a series of similar works were being built by civilian labour to form a third system

* See map opposite page 10.

EXPEDIENTS OF EARLY DAYS

of defence. Our defences in this area were already taking the shape which assisted the First Army to stem the great German attack of 9th April 1918.

FEBRUARY 1915

Throughout all this period, the sufferings of the troops from exposure in the trenches, and especially from "trench feet," had been very great. The various precautions and remedies dictated by experience, and rigorously enforced, had been quite unable to prevent heavy lists of casualties from this cause. In common, also, with the rest of the Army, the division had felt the urgent need of a more powerful and more numerous artillery, more plentifully supplied with ammunition; of better and more numerous trench mortars and an adequate supply of efficient bombs both for mortars and hand-throwing. It was the day of expedients; jam-pot hand-bombs, petrol-tin mortar-bombs, catapults and bronze cannon. A serviceable type of trench mortar, throwing a jam-pot bomb, was manufactured by the divisional R.E. out of gaspipes. Everything that could hurl destruction over the short distance separating the opposing lines of trenches was pressed into use, till more adequate weapons could be made available. In the meantime, these crude or antiquated weapons helped to keep up the spirit of our troops and to prevent them from feeling that the enemy was having things all his own way.

In the later stages of trench warfare it became possible and usual to withdraw from the line for a substantial period of rest and special training divisions with which it was intended to carry out an attack. There was little opportunity for anything of this kind in the spring of 1915, and, when the approach of the new fighting season brought the need for fresh Allied offensives, the task of renewing the assault upon Neuve Chapelle was entrusted as a matter of course to the troops who had spent the whole winter in the water-laden trenches opposite that place. The best that could be done for the division was to allot to it a new Territorial battalion, which would so far strengthen it as to enable the attacking brigades to be withdrawn from the line for a few days prior to the assault.

The 4th Battalion Cameron Highlanders joined the division on the 22nd February, and was attached to the 24th Infantry Brigade. On the same day died in hospital at Estaires a very able and gallant officer, General John E. Gough, V.C., of wounds received two days earlier from shell fire while visiting the trenches held by a battalion of his old regiment, the 2/ Rifle Brigade, 8th Division. By his death the British Army was deprived of the services of an officer of a type which no army can afford to lose.

CHAPTER II

NEUVE CHAPELLE

FROM the first moment when the 8th Division had come into line, Neuve Chapelle in German possession had been the open sore in the divisional sector. Until a short time before the division's arrival the village had been in British hands, and its loss was a misfortune the extent of which all ranks were soon made to realize. Its houses were at this date still mostly intact and were full of snipers. The troops in " A " lines on the right of the divisional front had a particularly bad time of it, for German snipers were able to shoot straight into our trenches. Aided by German shelling from the Aubers ridge and " overs " from our own line further East, they contrived to make the sub-sector a most uncomfortable and unhealthy one.

Thoughts turned naturally, therefore, to plans for re-taking the village, and as early as the 3rd January instructions from IV Corps Headquarters had emphasized the fact that the capture of Neuve Chapelle was the first task in front of the division. Meanwhile, the German garrison was to be harassed constantly by artillery, rifle and machine-gun fire. Though the effect of these instructions was somewhat spoiled by the fact that the available supply of artillery ammunition was totally inadequate to carry them out, the division none the less did what it could in preparation for an early attack. The water-logged condition of the ground made it impossible to contemplate the opening of offensive operations on this front before March; but on the 20th February General Davies submitted his first scheme for the capture of the village; the general idea being for an attack by two brigades between Sign Post Lane and Moated Grange, where the German trenches were weakest, followed on the second day by an assault upon the village from the North, taking the village defences in flank.

The Army Commander, however, intended the operation to be carried out by larger forces than one division, and after a conference at Army Headquarters a fresh scheme was submitted, whereby the attack from Pont Logy southward was to be undertaken by the Indian Corps and the northern portion of the attack by the IV Corps; the whole to be treated as one day's operation. The enlargement of the plan entailed a reconsideration of methods, and ultimately the advantages of greater simplicity and easier co-operation with the Indian Corps led to a decision in favour of direct attack upon the village, thereby avoiding the risk of the breakdown of some essential detail in a more complicated scheme.

On the 28th February, therefore, " A " lines (Port Arthur

PREPARATIONS FOR ATTACK

to Pont Logy) were taken over by the Dehra Dun Brigade, Meerut Division, in relief of the right of the 24th Infantry Brigade, and next day " E " and " F " lines on the further flank were taken over from the 25th Infantry Brigade by the 22nd Infantry Brigade, 7th Division. On the same day the 24th Infantry Brigade with the divisional mounted troops, cyclists, and the 4/ Cameron Highlanders took over " C " and " D " Lines, and the 25th and 23rd Brigades thereupon went back to La Gorgue and Merville to rest and get fit.

FEBRUARY–MARCH 1915

The arrival of additional artillery, detailed for the operation from other divisions, commenced on the 2nd March and when this concentration was completed General Holland, C.R.A. 8th Division, and General Uniacke, commanding the 2nd Group G.H.Q. Artillery, had 202 guns at their disposal, including one 15-inch gun. The latter, which was manned by naval officers, was the first 15-inch gun to be used in France and was commonly called " Granny." The Indian Corps had about as many guns to support its share of the attack.

The work of preparation proceeded rapidly; but there was much to be done. An elaborate scheme of artillery co-operation, containing the germ of future developments in later battles, had been worked out. Artillery positions had to be prepared for wire-cutting and bombardment, and a solution found for the lack of suitable observation posts. Capt. Langley of the 5th Siege Battery got over this difficulty by constructing a " crow's nest " on the Rouge Croix—la Bassée road and the 33rd Battery (Major L. C. L. Oldfield) adopted the same plan. Certain straw stacks near the Rue Tilleloy were carefully hollowed out and used for the same purpose ; but suitable positions were few, and at one time during the battle no less than 30 artillery observation officers were using the same house at Pont Logy.

Then there were the infantry places of assembly to be got ready, emplacements to be built for machine guns and trench mortars, and extra communication trenches to be dug. Provision was made for supplies of food, water and ammunition to be available close up to the front. Engineer depots were formed in the Rue Bacquerot and Rue Tilleloy and additional stores were placed in readiness in dug-outs just in rear of the forward trench lines. Colonel Montgomery's wooden tramways proved invaluable in this all-important matter of supply and were run up close in rear of " B " lines; extra lengths of rails being prepared and stored well forward, so that the tramways could be continued to Neuve Chapelle as soon as the progress of the attack permitted.

Apart from all this new work, those parts of our old front line trenches which had been abandoned when the water forced

NEUVE CHAPELLE

the division to take to breastworks had now to be reclaimed. Steps had to be cut in the front parapet to enable the assault troops to get out readily, and the existing communication trenches required to be reconditioned or improved. Where our trenches were still flooded, portable bridges were constructed to enable them to be crossed; others were provided to assist our troops to cross the German trenches. A certain number of ladders were also made for getting over breastworks; but in the event these proved to be death-traps, as the enemy shot down our men in turn as they appeared above the parapet. The experience served as a lesson that arrangements for assault must be such as to enable all the assault troops in each bay to get over the parapet simultaneously. Finally, on the night before the attack the troops of the 24th Brigade in line cut the wire in front of our own trenches, leaving " knife rests " only in position, and sawed gaps where necessary in hedges.

The troops of the 23rd and 25th Infantry Brigades meanwhile were exercising in route-marching, running drill, physical training and in advancing in extended order across ploughed fields; though the 25th Brigade, which was the nearer to the line, had at the same time to furnish large working parties to assist the C.R.E., Lieut.-Colonel P. G. Grant, with the work of preparation. Special instruction was given to bombers, machine-gun detachments, and wire-cutting parties. Other parties were detailed to construct " blocks " in certain trenches, indicated to them by air photographs; so as to secure the flanks of the attack. All officers visited their places of assembly and the trenches from which they were to assault, and studied carefully their lines of advance. Everything, in short, was done to make all ranks thoroughly acquainted with every detail of the task before them.

The operation had become something more than a local attack by the division in line to improve its own tactical situation. At another conference held at Army Headquarters on the 5th March, Sir Douglas Haig indicated that a serious offensive was being undertaken, with the object of breaking the German line. The keynote to the whole undertaking was offensive action, and if all went well the Aubers Ridge was to be gained and progress made beyond. The date ultimately selected for the attack was the 10th March, and as the day approached the troops intended for the assault were gradually concentrated forward, both the 23rd and 25th Infantry Brigades being crowded not without difficulty into the little village of la Gorgue.

On the night of the 9th/10th March the troops marched into their positions, the 23rd Infantry Brigade (Brig.-General R. J. Pinney) moving forward via le Drumez till its head had

MOVING UP

reached the Rue du Bacquerot, where the men found cookers and water-carts waiting for them and were given a hot meal and filled their water-bottles. After an hour's halt here, the brigade moved across country by battalions at quarter-hour intervals to the assembly trenches and breastworks North of Sign Post Lane. The men had the rest of the day's ration and one iron ration in their haversacks, and carried two extra bandoliers of ammunition and two empty sandbags. They were without packs, but wore greatcoats, the skirts in front fastened back in French fashion.

MARCH 1915

In like manner the 25th Infantry Brigade (Brig.-General A. W. G. Lowry Cole) had halted with its head at Rouge Croix for a hot meal and to fill water-bottles, and then, similarly equipped, had moved forward by battalions to Pont Logy, and so into its assembly trenches and breastworks on the right of the 23rd Brigade, South of Sign Post Lane. The 24th Infantry Brigade (Brig.-General F. C. Carter) thereupon withdrew into divisional reserve; less the 2/ Northamptonshire who, with the 5/ Black Watch and certain R.E. Units, were left under command of Lieut.-Colonel C. S. Prichard, D.S.O., to garrison the "B" lines and to provide parties for escorting prisoners and carrying up stores. The garrison of "C" and "D" lines was provided by the 4/ Cameron Highlanders and divisional mounted troops, the whole under command of Lieut.-Colonel H. Wickham, Northamptonshire Yeomanry.

The accompanying map * shows the southern boundary between the 8th Division and the Indian Corps on its right, the dividing line between the 25th and 23rd Brigades, and the northern flank of the original assault. Farther North, well beyond the Moated Grange, which was included in our objectives by a natural extension of the northern flank of the operation, can be seen the boundary, prior to the attack, between the 8th and 7th Divisions. Later the boundary between these two divisions would lie farther to the South, as their respective lines of attack converged. The 25th Infantry Brigade had the 2/ Royal Berkshire (Lieut.-Colonel E. Feetham) and 2/ Lincolnshire (Lieut.-Colonel G. B. McAndrew †) in front line, the 2/ Rifle Brigade (Lieut.-Colonel R. B. Stephens) and 1/ Royal Irish Rifles (Lieut.-Colonel F. G. Laurie ‡) in support and the 13/ London (Territorials) under Lieut.-Colonel F. G. Lewis and two mountain battery sections in reserve. The battalions in line on the 23rd Brigade front were the 2/ Scottish Rifles (Lieut.-Colonel W. M. Bliss §) and 2/ Middlesex (Lieut.-Colonel R. H. Hayes). The 2/ Devonshire (Lieut.-Colonel

* Opposite page 28.   † Killed.   ‡ Killed, succeeded by Major O. C. Baker.
§ Killed, succeeded by Lieut.-Colonel C. B. Vandeleur.

NEUVE CHAPELLE

J. O. Travers) and the 2/ West Yorkshire (Lieut.-Colonel Barry Drew), the latter with one mountain battery section, were in support and reserve respectively.

At 6 a.m. on the 10th March the last of our batteries to get into position fired a few ranging shots. By 7.30 a.m. registration was to be completed and at that hour was opened the bombardment preliminary to the attack. Trench mortars and heavy fire from rifles and machine guns supplemented the effort of our artillery, the task of the machine guns including that of protecting the flanks of the infantry advance by sweeping special arcs of fire assigned to them for that purpose. Their way prepared in this manner, at 8.5 a.m. the four battalions in front line left their trenches and went forward to the attack, the troops in support and reserve moving up successively behind them.

On the right, the attacking companies of the 2/ Royal Berkshire and 2/ Lincolnshire led by Capt. Harris * and Capt. Fraser,* Capt. Eager * and Capt. Bastard and closely followed by the companies in immediate support, gained the enemy's front line without much loss, despite a pretty hot fire. Capt. Bastard was the first man in, but soon the whole length of trench was in our hands and the troops of both battalions pressed on to the German trenches which marked the line of our first objectives. Here more serious opposition was met with ; but the position was none the less captured without a check and blocking parties of the Berkshire under Lieut. Gordon * and of the Lincolnshire under Capt. Peake,† provided with flags to indicate their position to our troops, were at once directed to make good the German trenches leading off to the right and left flanks. Holding his blue flag high above his head, Capt. Peake led his party rapidly along the trench to the left, driving out and capturing some 30 Germans whose retreat was stopped by throwing bombs behind them. In like fashion, the Berkshire bombing party cleared the trench to the right, driving the German garrison into the arms of the Indian Corps. Already large numbers of the enemy had been killed or forced to surrender. Our own men were elated by their success and showed a heartening eagerness to push forward. Lce.-Corporal Perry of the Lincolnshire went on with his men although he had been hit three times and had been ordered to go back, and the spirit he showed was typical of that displayed by all ranks. Knowledge of the gallant conduct of his men would surely have brought comfort to Colonel McAndrew,‡ who with his leg shattered by a shell lay propped up

---

* Wounded. † Killed.

‡ Colonel McAndrew was succeeded in command by Major Howley, who was killed on the morning of the 11th March. Command was then taken by Major S. Fitz-G. Cox.

"HAVE THEY TAKEN THE TRENCHES?"

against a parapet, watching the assault with dimming eyes and asking with dying breath, "Have they taken the trenches?"

Meanwhile, the artillery had switched on to Neuve Chapelle itself, and for thirty minutes had subjected the village to an intense concentrated bombardment. After their first success the infantry had delayed only to re-organize their leading units, and to permit the 2/ Rifle Brigade and the 1/ Royal Irish Rifles to move into position in rear of the captured line. That accomplished, at 8.35 a.m. these two battalions took over the attack. Moving through the 2/ Royal Berkshire and 2/ Lincolnshire they reached at about 9 a.m. the line of the road running through Neuve Chapelle, from the central cross-roads on the right northwards to the point where the road forks (2/ Rifle Brigade), and then along the left-hand road to the cross-roads on the brigade boundary in Sign Post Lane (1/ Royal Irish Rifles). Opposition on the front of the right battalion was comparatively slight; but, like the Lincolnshire before them, but in greater degree, the Irish Rifles encountered heavy machine-gun fire from the left flank and suffered severely. Of the four company commanders, Capt. Biscoe, Capt. O'Sullivan, Lieut. Graham and Lieut. Burgess, the last was killed and Capt. Biscoe and Lieut. Graham were wounded.

Despite their losses, the Irish Rifles pushed on gallantly with the attack, and making a partial wheel to the right, reached and gained the Chateau at the North end of the village and made good the line of the Chateau road as far North as the brigade boundary, holding their position with their left echeloned back to guard against attack from the North. The precaution was well taken, for at about 10.50 a.m. the enemy counter-attacked at this point, but was beaten off. This advance completed, in substance, the capture of the second objectives of the 25th Brigade; for the right battalion had already cleared the portion of the village on its front and had established touch with the Bareilly Brigade, Indian Corps. Detachments of the Royal Engineers with tools and material were sent forward to consolidate the captured ground.

The attack of the 23rd Infantry Brigade, though launched with equal courage and determination, had been much less fortunate. The right battalion, the 2/ Scottish Rifles, succeeded in entering the German line; but the 2/ Middlesex were unable to do so. The batteries detailed to deal with the German trenches opposite this battalion had come out direct from England and had not got into position until midday on the 9th March. The time left for them in which to acquaint themselves with the ground and register their targets had been much too short for accurate shooting, and the preliminary bombardment, which

NEUVE CHAPELLE

on the rest of the front of attack had been peculiarly effective, here completely failed to destroy the enemy's defences and left the German garrisons unshaken. As soon, therefore, as the Middlesex left their trenches to assault, they were mown down by intense and well-directed machine gun and rifle fire. Three of the four company commanders and the Adjutant were shot down at once; but none the less the gallant battalion three times attempted to move forward, only to be driven back each time with heavy loss.

The holding up of the Middlesex had its inevitable effect upon the attack of the Scottish Rifles. Constantly exposed to a severe and searching fire from their left flank and resisted with obstinacy on their own front, they too lost very heavily. No less than 10 of the battalion's officers found graves between the opposing lines of trenches. The troops had gained, however, a precarious foothold in some hundred yards of the German front line North of Sign Post Lane, and refused to be dislodged. Closely and fiercely engaged, by stubborn and determined fighting they maintained their hold until General Pinney had had time to bring up the 2/ Devonshire to their support. The Devons were directed to advance via Sign Post Lane and work northwards towards the left of the brigade front, and at the same time a request was sent to Divisional Headquarters for a fresh bombardment.

The request reached the division at 9.40 a.m. and the necessary orders were given at once, but on this occasion the bombardment was carried out by batteries familiar with the ground. It was extremely effective; so effective, indeed, that an officer and 64 men of the Jager garrison left the German trenches and surrendered to escape the devastation caused by our guns. About the same time, namely at 10 a.m., the 2/ East Lancashire (Lieut.-Colonel C. L. Nicholson [*]), of the 24th Infantry Brigade were ordered to move up to the Sign Post Lane cross-roads, where the holding up of the 23rd Brigade had left the northern flank of the 25th Brigade dangerously exposed to counter-attack. Though the battalion came under machine-gun fire from the West, it successfully carried out this movement and closed the gap between the two brigades.

Notwithstanding that these two measures had been successfully taken, the fighting in the German trenches North of Sign Post Lane continued to be of the fiercest description and for some time of doubtful issue. Both the 2/ Scottish Rifles and the 2/ Devonshire were now hotly engaged, and were hard pressed to hold their own. The last available battalion of the Brigade, the 2/ West Yorkshire, was in course of being put into

* Wounded, succeeded by Major H. Maclear.

PLATE II

NEUVE CHAPELLE: SCENE OF GERMAN STAND AT NORTH CORNER OF VILLAGE

OUR OBJECTIVES GAINED

the fight. For a time the situation was critical, and that ultimately it was saved and our attack in this sector successful was due to the skill and resolution of General Pinney, admirably seconded as he was by the great gallantry and determination of the troops engaged. By using the ground already gained as a pivot for further attack, and by employing bombing parties of the West Yorkshire and the Devons along the German trenches, the tide of battle was turned and the enemy driven back step by step; until by midday he had been forced to abandon the whole of his positions West of the road running from Sign Post Lane cross-roads to the Rue Tilleloy.

MARCH 1915

Realizing the difficulties of the 23rd Brigade's task, the Divisional Commander had authorized General Pinney to call upon the 24th Infantry Brigade for support if necessary. Accordingly, at General Pinney's request, the 1/ Worcestershire (Major E. Wodehouse *) of the latter brigade had been sent forward and on their arrival in line the forward movement was continued. The orchard South of the Moated Grange was carried at 12.30 p.m., on the heels of an unsuccessful German counter-attack, and all along the front of the brigade our troops were making steady progress. By 1 p.m. the brigade was in possession of the whole of its second objectives and had cleared also the German trenches lying between the left flank of its advance and Moated Grange. This line it at once proceeded to put into a state of defence, the Moated Grange sub-sector being allotted to the 4/ Cameron Highlanders (Lieut.-Colonel A. Fraser) allocated from the 24th Brigade as part of General Pinney's command.

At this hour (1 p.m.) the 25th Brigade was entrenching on a line which ran from the most easterly houses of Neuve Chapelle just South of the divisional boundary, where it was in touch with the Garhwal Brigade, along the eastern edge of the village to the road junction North of the Chateau, whence its left flank bent back along Sign Post Lane to join up with the 23rd Brigade at the farm South-East of the cross roads. The division had successfully accomplished the first stage of the operation in which it was taking the central part ; the time had come for that larger development of the attack which aimed at a definite rupture of the German battle line.

Except for two companies of the 1/ Worcestershire at the Orchard and the 2/ East Lancashire, whose movements have been described above, the 24th Infantry Brigade was at this time distributed in rear of " B " lines and was available for continuing the attack. Accordingly, at 1.30 p.m. this brigade was ordered to assemble as rapidly as possible, two companies of the

* Killed, succeeded by Major G. W. St. G. Grogan.

NEUVE CHAPELLE

2/ Lincolnshire relieving the two companies of the 2/ East Lancashire which had been detached to reinforce the 1/ Royal Irish Rifles. Orders to advance were received by the brigade from IV Corps at 3.10 p.m., the immediate objective being the collection of houses to be seen on the map about half a mile East of the Orchard. The attack was to be supported by artillery fire and by flanking fire from the 25th Infantry Brigade.

The area over which the attack was to be made was intersected by trenches and deep ditches, and beyond the trench system East of Sign Post Lane Farm was wholly open and exposed. From the moment when the advance began at 4.20 p.m. progress was slow and the troops soon came under a withering fire from German infantry and machine gunners holding the line of the road. Encouraged by the success of the other two brigades, the advance was none the less doggedly continued and the 1/ Sherwood Foresters (Major C. R. Mortimer *), gradually working their way forward with their right on Sign Post Lane, reached the road junction and the southern end of the trench system in front of the group of houses which formed the object of the brigade's attack. On their left the 2/ Northamptonshire (Lieut.-Colonel C. S. Prichard †) got within 300 yards of the houses themselves, only to find that the enemy was holding in strength a prepared position covering them.

The evening had brought rain, and with the rain early darkness. The attacking troops had suffered severe punishment in the course of their long and exposed advance, and in the crossing of the numerous intersecting dykes had been thrown into some confusion. The difficulties of command were further increased by the presence of units of the 7th Division which had crossed the front of the brigade and intermingled with its troops. Though gallant efforts were made in the growing darkness to organize a further attack, they were not successful, and eventually the brigade dug in for the night on the line it had already gained.

The hope of exploiting the initial success had not yet, however, been abandoned. Although in the light of events and the knowledge they brought with them the project may well have seemed to have been hopeless, in the early hours of the 11th March orders were issued by the division for the advance to be continued at 7 a.m. against the Aubers ridge. Accordingly at that hour the attack in the left brigade sector was renewed; but the preliminary bombardment which was to have dealt with the German defences in and around the group of houses had fallen beyond them, and our troops were once more met by an intensity of fire too great to be withstood. Though the bombardment was renewed later in the morning, communication between Bri-

* Wounded.   † Wounded, succeeded by Major L. St. H. Morley.

FURTHER PROGRESS STAYED

gade Headquarters and the battalions in front line had largely broken down. Telephone lines were cut and cut again faster than they could be repaired, and the constant fire which swept the open spaces over which the troops had advanced with so much courage and determination on the previous day made it almost impossible for runners to get through. Correctly interpreting the intentions of their Brigade Commander, the 1/ Sherwood Foresters and 2/ Northamptonshire made every effort to gain ground; but the fierce and accurate fire from the houses and from the loopholed breastworks covering them could not be subdued. So the day passed, until early in the afternoon the 1/ Worcestershire, who had been sent forward under command of Major Wodehouse, made with the support of the remnants of the battalions in line yet another attempt to get forward. This attack, however, was no more successful than those which had preceded it, our men being mown down by concentrated rifle and machine-gun fire as soon as they stepped out of their trenches.

Nor had the day been more fortunate on the front of the right brigade. There in the course of the morning the 23rd Brigade had relieved the 25th Brigade, with the idea that the latter might be free to support the 24th Brigade attack. At 2.10 p.m., however, a message had been received at Divisional Headquarters from the Meerut Division to the effect that the Dehra Dun Brigade was about to assault. As no information had been received regarding the progress of the 24th Brigade, it was decided to employ the 25th Brigade to co-operate with this attack. Orders were issued; but the same difficulty was encountered in getting them down to the units concerned as was experienced on the 24th Brigade front. Telephone communication between division and brigade and brigade and battalion was practically non-existent. The message from the division did not reach the 25th Brigade Headquarters till 3.20 p.m.; and when General Lowry Cole then went forward personally to the headquarters of his right battalion, beating his own messenger by a comfortable margin, he found on arrival that the attack of the Dehra Dun Brigade had been unable to make progress and that no further action was contemplated.

At the end of the second day of the battle, therefore, the whole line of the 8th Division rested, with but minor alterations, in the position reached at the close of the first day's fighting and, though the struggle was continued for another thirty-six hours, the result remained unaffected. The story of many future battles of position found here its first example, and long years of fighting were to pass before the lessons it implied were fully understood. The change which came over the face of the battle

NEUVE CHAPELLE

in the course of this day was emphasized on the morning of the 12th March by a series of German counter-attacks, extending along the front of both brigades. With the loss of the momentum which preparation, artillery concentration and the element of surprise had given to the first stage of the offensive, the advantage afforded by superior organization, easier communications, better knowledge of the terrain and readier means of reinforcement had begun to weight the balance in favour of the defence. There was on this day a noticeable increase in the volume of German artillery fire.

The German re-action commenced before daybreak on the 12th March with an attack against the 2/ Rifle Brigade, which was decisively repulsed with the loss of more than 100 German dead. At about the same hour a more serious assault was made upon the 1/ Sherwood Foresters just North of Sign Post Lane. The enemy attacked in considerable force and after severe fighting drove back the Sherwood Foresters to their support trenches. Following up his success closely, he was then caught under the enfilade fire of the 2/ West Yorkshire South of the road, and his discomfiture was completed by the gallant action of the right company of the 1/ Worcestershire to the North of his thrust. The officer commanding this company drew back his right flank as the Germans advanced and, having first poured in a heavy fire, charged the attacking column with the bayonet, flinging it back in confusion and with great loss. The Sherwood Foresters, though they had already suffered heavily, then resumed the offensive in their turn with great vigour and by 7.15 a.m. had regained possession of their front-line trenches. A further attempt in this sector made by the enemy in two successive waves against the West Yorkshire was wiped out by the steady fire of our men.

The northern counter-attack against the 2/ Northamptonshire ended even more successfully for the defence; for, having stopped the enemy's advance, this battalion and the 1/ Worcestershire followed up their advantage so promptly and vigorously that they were able to drive the enemy from the southern portion of the trench system covering the houses which had been their objective on the previous day.

Though these counter-attacks were an indication that the enemy had recovered from the shock of our opening assaults and, once more strongly posted and supported by a powerful artillery, was well prepared to resist any further advance, they did not in fact lead to any immediate alteration either in the general British plan or in the programme for the day's operations. A more decisive factor was the thick mist which forced a postponement of the preparatory artillery bombardment from 10

GALLANTRY UNREWARDED

a.m. until noon. Even at that later hour the result of the bombardment was once more unsatisfactory. Our batteries which, with one conspicuous exception, had bombarded the German lines at the opening of the battle with absolutely devastating effect, in the subsequent stages experienced the greatest difficulty in accurately locating the centres of enemy resistance. Despite the gallantry of the forward observation officers, whose devotion to duty is evidenced by the fact that out of 30 engaged in the battle 6 were killed and 5 wounded, the bombardments intended to prepare the way for our infantry assaults were rarely effective. On this occasion the misfortunes of the infantry were increased by the fact that the orders postponing the assault failed to get through to the 24th Brigade in time to prevent the attack beginning at the hour originally fixed, with the result that the troops came under our own postponed bombardment and had to fall back. None the less, at 12.30 p.m. another attempt was made by both brigades, while all through the afternoon and far into the night repeated efforts were made by the 25th Brigade to gain the German trench lines between the Layes River and Sign Post Lane, and by the 24th Brigade to capture the houses which they had already so nearly reached.

The utmost courage and devotion of officers and men were unavailing. Our bombardments, more than once repeated, could not locate the German positions or keep down the deadly machine-gun fire which swept our advancing lines. Though the troops went forward time after time to the attack and parties of the 1/ Worcestershire and 2/ East Lancashire even reached some of the coveted houses and the orchards to the South of them —only to be shelled out by our own guns—spirit and determination could not prevail against the leaden hail which swept the bare ground of their advance.

Recognition of the inevitable had to come. It came more slowly perhaps than the situation required, because of the breakdown of communications and the difficulty of obtaining a true knowledge of conditions in the fighting line, with which to correct earlier and no longer accurate reports as to the condition of the enemy's moral. Neuve Chapelle and the Rue Tilleloy were under constant and heavy shell fire ; telephone lines could not be kept intact ; runners lost their lives in the attempt to get messages across the fire-swept zone. Gradually the conditions in the fighting line became known. All units had lost heavily ; the casualties of the 24th Brigade alone numbered 75 officers and over 1,600 other ranks. The troops were greatly intermingled, no less than five units of the 7th Division being interspersed among the battalions of the 8th Division. Dead and wounded lay everywhere on the sodden ground, the packs of the

NEUVE CHAPELLE

7th Division contrasting with the great coats of the 8th.* The living were well-nigh dead from physical exhaustion. At every halt, men fell fast asleep from sheer overmastering fatigue and could only be aroused by violence. Yet when at 4.30 p.m. the order came through from IV Corps announcing, to troops who knew too well the contrary, that the enemy was in a state of demoralization and that all available troops were to advance regardless of loss, again an attempt was made to respond to the appeal.

After a short preliminary bombardment, the 25th Brigade attacked at 5.15 p.m. with the 1/ Royal Irish Rifles and the 2/ Rifle Brigade, only to be met by devastating machine-gun fire which cut our men down as soon as they had clambered out of their trenches. In the northern brigade sector the attack took longer to organize; although General Pinney, who as senior brigadier had been placed in general command, at once sent for commanding officers and pointed out to them their objectives on the ground, while their battalions were being collected ready to be moved into position. Originally ordered to take place at 11 p.m., it became necessary to postpone the assault until 1.30 a.m. on the 13th March, and even at that hour only two out of the four attacking battalions had succeeded in reaching the positions assigned to them. The 2/ Devonshire and 2/ Scottish Rifles found the enemy holding in strength a position well covered by wire and blackthorn hedges and could make no progress. A second assault was in course of preparation when word came that the attack of the 7th Division had been postponed, and that the 8th Division was to consolidate the positions it then held. The battle had ended.

The positions ultimately won, as the result of three days and nights of almost incessant fighting in which a division that had spent the whole winter in line furnished both the assault battalions and their supports and reliefs, are shown approximately on the accompanying map. They were held by the 25th and 23rd Brigades, to which latter brigade the 4/ Cameron Highlanders were attached. The 24th Infantry Brigade withdrew before daylight on the 13th March into divisional reserve ; but on the 14th took over again from the 23rd Infantry Brigade on the extension of the divisional front northwards to Chapigny, in relief of the right of the 7th Division.

Looking back over four long years of war and reviewing the mighty battles which from 1916 onwards mark the story of the 8th Division, Neuve Chapelle with its four or five hundred guns

---

* Splendid indeed throughout the battle was the work of the Wessex Field Ambulance. It earned and deserved the special commendation of General Pinney.

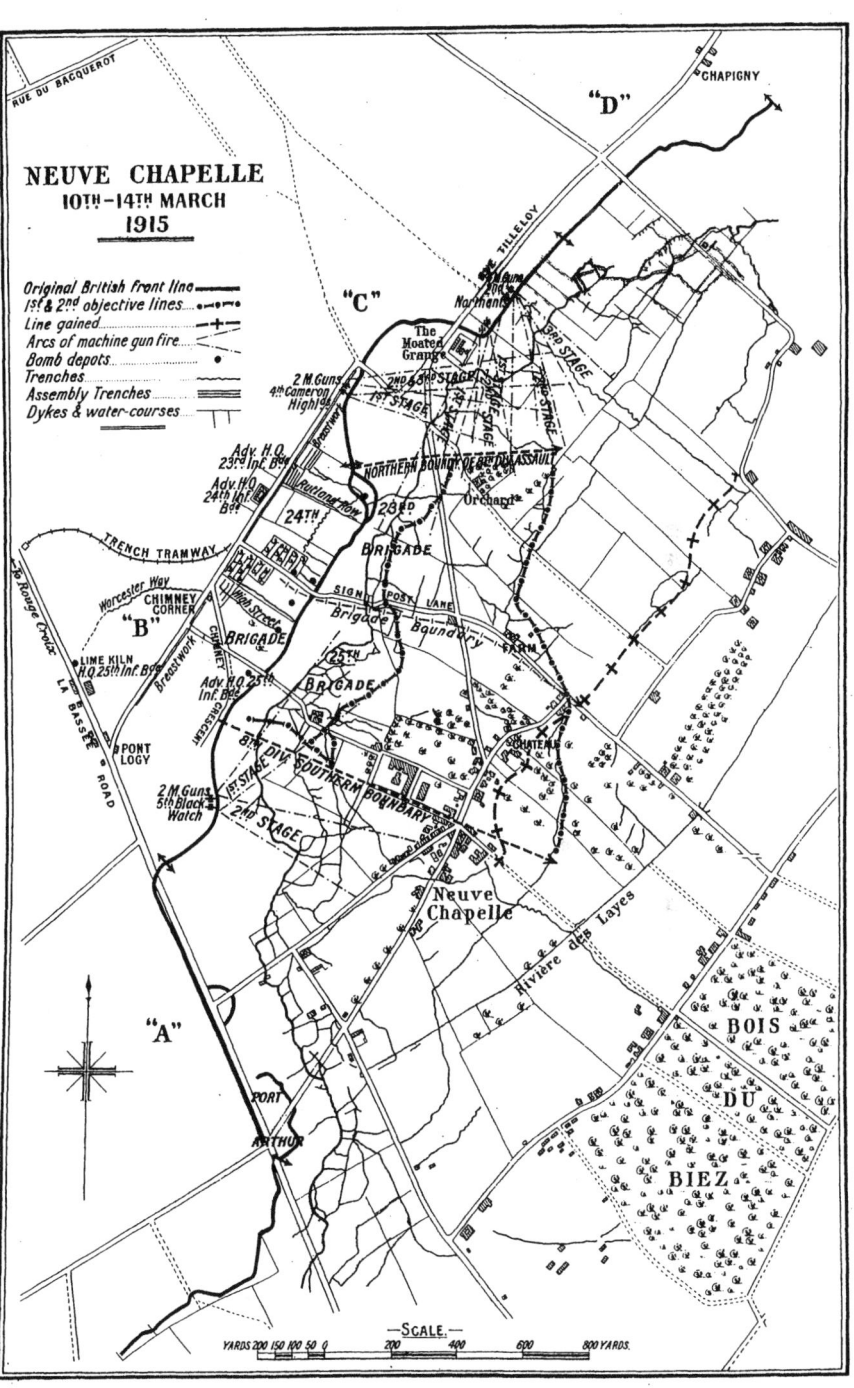

A LEGEND BROKEN

and front of four brigades is apt to be overshadowed and its meaning and importance overlooked. Yet it was a remarkable achievement; bought, it is true at heavy cost, for the casualties of the 8th Division alone exceeded 4,800 officers and men ; but charged with significance to those who looked ahead and understood. In this case, at least, a contemporary view gives a clearer and juster picture of the battle than has been formed by many whose attention has been held by the vaster conflicts which succeeded it. " For the first time the British Army has broken the German line and struck the Germans a blow which they will remember to the end of their lives. The importance of our success does not lie so much in the capture of the German trenches along a front of two miles, the killing of some 6,000 Germans and the taking of 2,000 prisoners. It is the revelation of the fact that the much-vaunted German army-machine on which the whole attention of a mighty nation has been lavished for four decades is not invincible."* A legend had been broken, and in its breaking the 8th Division had performed the central and decisive part.

MARCH 1915

* *The Times*, 19th April, 1915.

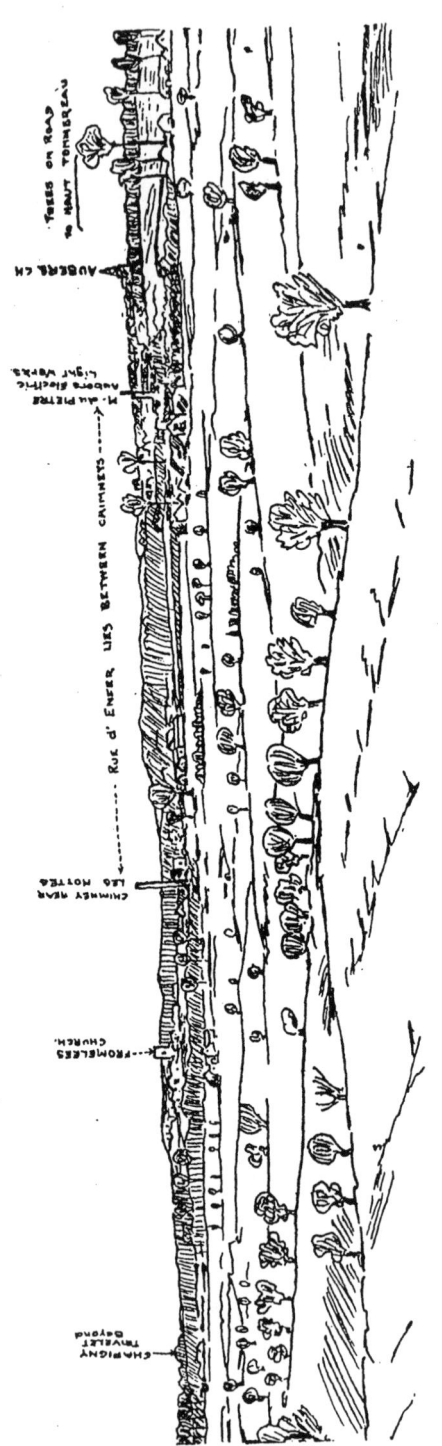

FROMELLES FROM ROUGE CROIX.

CHAPTER III

FROMELLES AND AFTER

AFTER so long a period in line, during which the wearying strain of winter was succeeded by the sharp stress of battle, the division was urgently in need both of rest and reinforcement. The demands of the general situation denied it rest, giving instead a change of scene and the near prospect of a new conflict; but reinforcement it obtained.

On the 15th March, described in the operations reports as " a much quieter day "—evidence, it may be, that the enemy was no less exhausted than were we—the 7/ Middlesex (Lieut.-Colonel E. J. King) joined the division and was posted to the 23rd Infantry Brigade. A week later the same brigade was further strengthened by the arrival of the 6/ Scottish Rifles (Lieut.-Colonel W. M. Kay). The 24th Infantry Brigade, indeed, lost the 4/ Cameron Highlanders on the 8th April and was left with the 5/ Black Watch as the only addition to its original four battalions ; but the 25th Infantry Brigade was made up to six battalions by the arrival of the 1/ London (Lieut.-Colonel E. G. Mercer) on the 13th March.

A comparatively uneventful week had been spent in clearing the battlefield and strengthening our new defences when, on the 22nd March, the division was ordered to withdraw from the sector it had held so long and directed to move North to the line then occupied by the 1st Canadian Division in the Fleurbaix sector, extending from Petillon in the neighbourhood of Rouges Bancs to the neighbourhood of la Boutillerie. These moves were carried out during the period 23rd to 26th March, and at 10 a.m. on the 27th March General Davies assumed command of the new area, Divisional Headquarters being transferred from Estaires to Sailly.

The change of scene was not of a marked character, neither was there any noticeable alteration in the nature of the division's activities. From one offensive successfully concluded they passed forthwith to preparation for another. The Higher Command had decided to strike again and so to complete the work begun by the battle of Neuve Chapelle. The new operation would combine also with the great French offensive against the Vimy Ridge and Notre Dame de Lorette, with which our Allies followed up on the 9th May and far into June their earlier efforts in Alsace and at St. Mihiel.

Already on the 1st April, on this occasion in very truth an ill-omened day, the First Army had issued a general scheme which is referred to by Sir John French in his Despatches in the following terms: " In pursuance of a promise which I made to

FROMELLES AND AFTER

the French Commander-in-Chief to support an attack which his troops were making on the 9th May between the right of my line and Arras, I directed Sir Douglas Haig to carry out on that date an attack on the German trenches in the neighbourhood of Rouges Bancs (N.W. of Fromelles) by the IV Corps and between Neuve Chapelle and Givenchy by the 1st and Indian Corps."

The plan was, in fact, considerably more ambitious than could be stated in this contemporaneous description. The Anglo-French offensive, timed originally to co-operate with the resumption of active operations on the Russian front, but in the event made more than ever necessary as a measure of relief to the Russian Armies hard pressed by Mackensen's victorious attacks, was designed on a grand scale. Its primary aim was to break the German line South of Lille and gain possession of that town, an advance which it was hoped would produce decisive results. "The operations contemplated aim at gaining a decisive victory, and not merely a local success. The entire First Army will therefore be called upon to fight a violent and continuous action lasting for a considerable period of time."*
The immediate objectives of the allied attacks were, on the French front the Vimy Ridge, and on the British front the Aubers ridge. The main British attack was to be made in the vicinity of Neuve Chapelle by the I and Indian Corps. The IV Corps was ordered to co-operate by means of a subsidiary attack delivered by the 8th Division and a portion of the 7th Division, and directed against the northern portion of the Aubers Ridge at Fromelles.

The preparations of the 8th Division were pushed forward with a will, for time was short, and during the earlier part of April proceeded under conditions of abnormal quiet. "No hostile shelling" figured in the reports on a number of these days. The work inevitably followed the same general lines as that which had preceded the Neuve Chapelle battle; with such improvements and additions as the experience of that action suggested, and such alterations as local peculiarities of ground demanded. The front line trenches were amply provided with steps to enable the attacking troops to get out quickly and together; splinter proofs were prepared for use as report centres for infantry brigades; foot-bridges for crossing the River Layes and ditches on the line of advance were made in large quantity; and two mine galleries were run out towards the German trenches. The wooden tram-lines which had already proved so useful were again brought into service.

The roads serving the new battle area were improved and

* *Notes on Prospective Operations.* H.Q. IV Army Corps, 24th April 1915.

GERMAN ACTIVITY INCREASES

added to, new gun emplacements were built, and ammunition and supply dumps formed. Meanwhile, the infantry selected for the attack had been undergoing special training, which included route-marches, physical drill, and extended order work, and the places of assembly and trenches from which the assault was to be made had been visited and studied by all officers and section commanders. In the limited time at their disposal, all ranks of the division were strenuously busy.

APRIL 1915

There is little doubt that as time passed the enemy became aware of our unusual activity. His artillery fire grew decidedly brisker as the month wore on, and an increasing number of casualties were suffered from this cause both by the troops in the line and by engineer and infantry working parties. The German Higher Command had been busy, also, in other directions, and on the 22nd April had launched on the Ypres front, against the French and against those Canadians whose old sector the 8th Division had taken over, the first gas attack of the war. Though he thereby contravened all the accepted usages of war, the heroism of the Canadians and his own failure to foresee the extent of his opportunity foiled the enemy in his new attempt to break through the Allied line. The series of violent and desperate encounters known officially as The Battles of Ypres, 1915, dragged on with varying intensity until May was almost over; but the threat to the Allied line was safely met and parried, nor was the danger sufficient to prevent the launching of the Allied May offensive.

In spite of short notice and the increased shelling, the preparations of the 8th Division proceeded well up to time, a welcome improvement in the weather assisting materially. Already, on the 28th March the West Riding Division had taken over sections 3, 4, 5 and 6 of the 8th Division line, leaving in charge of the 8th Division only sections 1 and 2 from which the attack was to be delivered. These two sections were garrisoned by the 2/ and 7/ Middlesex, commanded respectively by Lieut.-Colonel R. H. Hayes * and Lieut.-Colonel E. J. King. During the first week of May, preparations were intensified and the final touches given, including the instruction of junior commanders in the plan of battle.

Briefly the plan was as follows : the 24th and 25th Brigades (Brig.-Generals R. S. Oxley † and A. W. G. Lowry Cole) of the 8th Division were to combine in three separate but co-ordinated attacks, the main thrust to be delivered on a three-battalion front astride the Sailly–Fromelles road, the 2/ East Lancashire

---

* In general command of the trench garrison.

† General Oxley had taken over command of the 24th Infantry Brigade on the 16th March, *vice* General Carter who had been invalided.

FROMELLES AND AFTER

(Major H. MacLear), 24th Brigade, operating West of the road and the 2/ Rifle Brigade (Lieut.-Colonel R. B. Stephens), and 1/ Royal Irish Rifles (Major O. C. Baker), 25th Brigade, to the East of it. Of the two subsidiary assaults, that on the right, separated from the central main attack by a space of about 500 yards and launched ten minutes later, was to be delivered by the 2/ Northamptonshire (Major C. R. J. Mowatt), 24th Brigade, against an exposed salient (point 372) in the German lines. The left subsidiary attack was to be undertaken by the 13/ London (Lieut.-Colonel F. G. Lewis, T.D.) immediately following the explosion of two mines and was directed against a sector (point 882) about 200 yards East of the main attack.

The general idea of the IV Corps' operation was to effect a preliminary break in the German line on the front of the five battalions engaged in the opening assault, when the remaining troops of the 24th and 25th Brigades were to push on southwards to the Aubers Ridge between Aubers and Fromelles. In this part of the attack, the 24th Brigade would capture Deleval Farm and the Rue Deleval and secure the right flank of the advance, while the 25th Brigade would take Fromelles itself and make good the left flank from the village back to our old line in the neighbourhood of la Cordonnerie Farm. In the succeeding stages, the 23rd Brigade (Brig.-General R. J. Pinney) and a brigade of the 7th Division, moving forward closely in rear of the two brigades which had opened the attack, would pass through the gap made by them and advance upon Aubers village from the North-East, capturing that place and ultimately joining hands with the Indian Corps at la Cliqueterie Farm, a short mile South of Aubers.

The attack had originally been arranged for the 8th May, and on the evening of the 7th the troops were actually on parade when orders were received postponing the operation for twenty-four hours. On the evening of the 8th May, therefore, in perfect weather, the troops moved up to their positions of assembly, and in the small hours of the following morning all were in readiness without mishap. Advanced Divisional Headquarters had been opened at Rue du Quesnes on the 8th May.

At 5 a.m. on the 9th May our artillery bombardment opened, the first ten or fifteen minutes being devoted to wire-cutting and the remainder of the bombardment prior to the commencement of the infantry assaults to the destruction of the trenches to be attacked. In this bombardment and in the subsequent fighting brass mortars dating from 1840 were pressed into service and a battery of them under Lieut. D. Uzielli did particularly good work. So great was our need of artillery. The number of our guns, indeed, proved utterly inadequate for the accomplishment

THE GROWING NEED OF GUNS

of their tasks in the time allotted. Even at the height of the bombardment of the hostile trenches, the volume of effective fire was not sufficient to compel the German garrisons to keep under cover.

MAY 1915

That this was so, was shown conclusively by the experience of the 2/ East Lancashire on the right of the central attack. At this point, the opposing lines of trenches lay some considerable distance apart, and the original intention had been to launch the attack of the battalion from a trench to be dug immediately West of the Fromelles road, in the position marked " A "— " A " on the map overleaf. The new trench had been begun under supervision of the Engineers; but the water-logged condition of the soil and the close proximity of the enemy had made it impossible to complete it to an extent sufficient for it to be useable. In these circumstances, 200 men had been assembled in two short lengths of reclaimed trench, " B "—" B ", just in front of our line and the rest of the battalion had been retained as long as possible behind our breastwork, " C "—" C ". At 5.20 a.m., therefore, the East Lancashire moved out from sally ports in their breastwork, with the idea that under cover of our guns they might take up a position in No-Man's Land within assault distance of the German line, ready for the main attack to be delivered. No sooner had they left the protection of the breastworks, than they were met by heavy rifle and machine-gun fire, which seemed to be entirely unaffected by our bombardment and caused many casualties and some disorganization among the attacking troops.

The inadequacy of our artillery preparation and support, indeed, and its failure either to destroy the enemy's defences or to subdue the fire of his infantry decided the fate of the whole operation. It did not check, however, the ardour of the attack nor prevent it, despite grievous losses inflicted by a murderous fire, from effecting a lodgment in the German trenches in all three sectors.

The losses which the East Lancashire suffered in getting out to their assault position did not stay them from launching their attack at 5.40 a.m. in conjunction with the other battalions of the 25th Infantry Brigade. Their task, however, was especially difficult; for the sector of the German front allotted to them, between points 375 and 884, lay at an angle to the battalion's position of departure and in consequence the troops had to make a change of direction to their left in the actual course of their advance. Already weakened by the fire to which they had been exposed as they issued from the cover of the breastworks, the attacking companies were swept anew by heavy enfilade fire from machine guns in emplacements in the German parapet,

FROMELLES AND AFTER

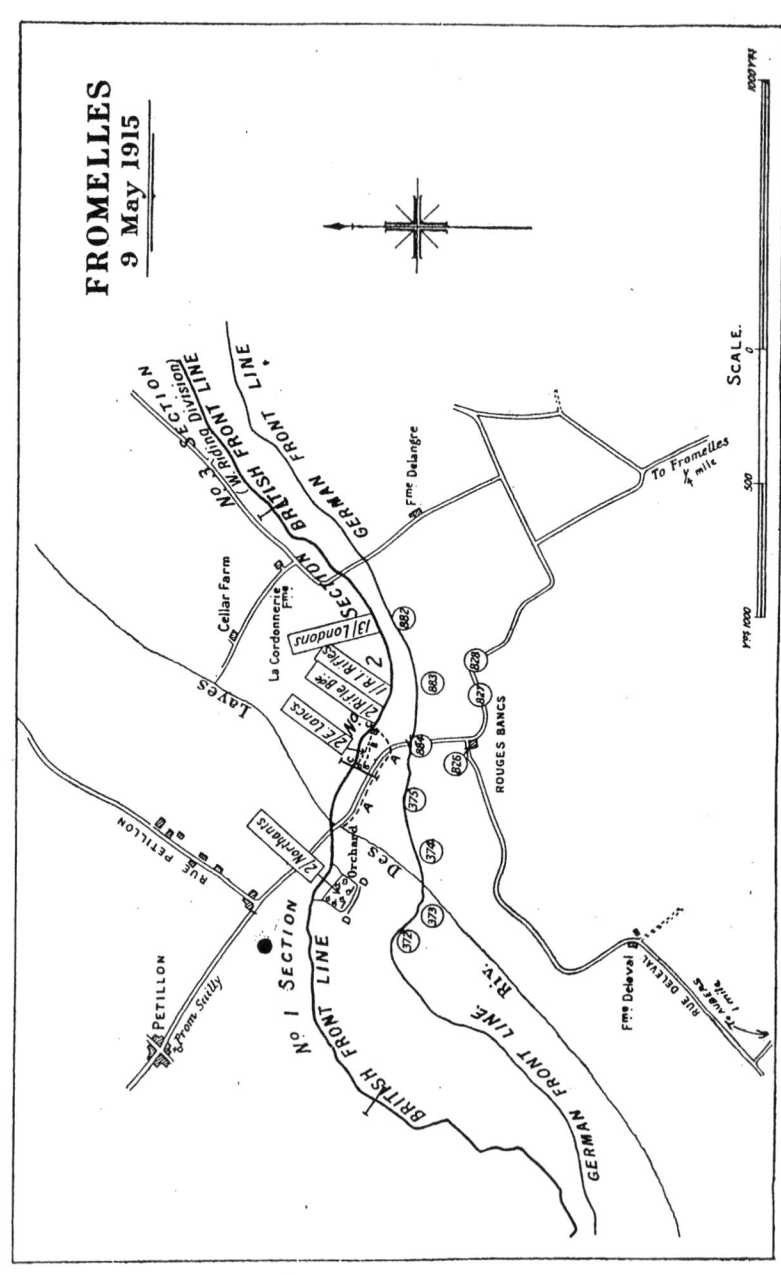

ENFILADE FIRE

or mounted under cover of shields on the top of the parapet itself. Progress became impossible, and the survivors made their way back with difficulty to the line of the Sailly–Fromelles road.

Meanwhile, in accordance with the main idea of the operation, the essence of which was the maintenance of a continuous forward movement with fresh troops, the battalions in rear had begun to advance and considerable congestion and some admixture of units took place in the front trenches, now the target of continuous artillery and machine-gun fire. Despite the difficulties and confusion thereby caused, the leading platoons of the 1/ Sherwood Foresters (Major L. St. H. Morley) crossed our breastwork at 6.10 a.m. and, finding the survivors of the East Lancashire held up in front of them, changed direction half-right and advanced against point 373. This new attack got close up to the German wire, only to find that much of it was sunk beneath the ground level and that our guns had failed to make any practicable gap. Here also—inevitably—the attack broke down, and by 7 a.m. the whole movement in this sub-sector had come to a standstill.

The subsidiary attack by the 2/ Northamptonshire, starting ten minutes later than the central assault, was largely dependent upon the success of the main effort. The two attacking companies left in due time the assault trench " D "—" D " which they had dug during the night in front of the orchard where the battalion had assembled; but the misfortunes of the East Lancashire then had their effect and the Northamptonshire became exposed to enfilade fire from the German trenches about points 374 and 375. In spite of this, the two attacking companies pushed forward resolutely across the wide belt of No-Man's Land which separated them from the German trenches. " A " Company on the left felt the full force of the enfilade fire from across the Layes and was almost completely wiped out ; but " D " Company under Lieut. O. K. Parker, aided by the fire of two field guns of the 104th Battery, XXII Brigade R.F.A., which had been brought forward under Capt. Hon. B. J. Russell to within 350 yards of the opposing lines, reached the breach which the guns had blown in the German parapet and established itself precariously in the shattered trench.

It proved impossible, however, to exploit the success so gallantly won. The two support companies, sent forward at 6 a.m. and 6.30 a.m. respectively, came under severe enfilade machine-gun fire immediately they left the shelter of the Orchard and were unable to reach their comrades hard pressed in the German line. No-Man's Land was now impassable. One volunteer—Private Lapham—alone succeeded in getting through to "D" Company and back with a message which revealed the desperate situation of Lieut. Parker and his men. The right attack had been brought to a dead stop, and "D" Company was cut off.

East of the Sailly–Fromelles road, the central and left attacks met at first with a greater measure of success. The attacking troops both of the 2/ Rifle Brigade and of the 1/ Royal Irish Rifles carried, under heavy fire, the German front line, between points 884 and 883 and continued their advance to the line of the road on the northern edge of Rouges Bancs, from point 826 to point 828. On their left, the leading companies of the 13/ London, following on the explosion of the two mines which had been fired at point 882 simultaneously with the lifting of our barrage, moved forward rapidly in lines of platoons. Not without loss, they made good their position in the crater; but advanced parties who had got as far as the Rouges Bancs–Fromelles road, were outflanked and gradually forced back. The support companies followed the leading companies across, although by this time the enemy had recovered from the shock of the explosion and his fire had greatly increased in intensity.

News that a lodgment had been effected in the enemy's lines on the front of both attacks was received at Advanced Brigade Headquarters at 6 a.m., and on this information General Lowry Cole decided to get into closer touch with his attacking troops. He arrived at our breastwork at 6.20 a.m., to find that all forward movement had ceased, and that the ground between our trenches and those of the enemy was being swept by a heavy rifle and machine-gun fire which appeared to come from both flanks.

What in fact had happened was that the German garrisons on both flanks of the advance, protected by parapets 15 and even 20 feet thick which our artillery had for the most part been unable to breach and well provided with bomb-proof shelters capable of keeping out all but the heaviest shell, had realized that their own fronts were not seriously threatened. They had thereupon turned their whole attention to containing those of our troops who had broken into the German line and to preventing reinforcements from reaching them. Deprived of the supports they so badly needed, and counter-attacked in flank and even in reverse, the advanced parties of the 2/ Rifle Brigade and the 1/ Royal Irish Rifles who had reached the outskirts of Rouges Bancs were driven back to the German front line trench, having lost the greater part of their number and almost all their officers. Here they found Colonel Stephens who had brought his Headquarters across with the second wave of his battalion. Under his energetic leadership our hold on this short length of captured

DEATH OF GENERAL LOWRY COLE

trench, extending from about 50 yards West of the Sailly–
Fromelles road to the neighbourhood of point 883, was strengthened and maintained.

Realizing the situation, General Lowry Cole ordered Major S. Fitz-G. Cox to send the two companies of his battalion, the 2/ Lincolnshire, which had not yet crossed our breastwork * to work down the sap which led to the new mine crater and endeavour to work westwards so as to clear the German front line between the 13/ London and Colonel Stephens' command.

At this instant, a number of our men were seen to come streaming back over the German parapet. An order to retire had been given by some unauthorized person, and the movement spread rapidly among the troops immediately East of the Sailly–Fromelles road. In order to stop the retirement Brig.-General Lowry Cole leapt up on to our parapet, and by voice and gesture and the prompt and effective orders he gave to those around him, succeeded in turning the troops. By his courageous action and personal example he regained control of a perilous situation, but all efforts to renew the advance were frustrated by the growing intensity of the enemy's fire. While still standing on the parapet urging on his men and encouraging them by his example, the Brigade Commander was mortally wounded and died shortly afterwards.

Lieut.-Colonel Stephens, upon whom the command of the brigade devolved, was isolated with his battalion in the German front line, so Major Cox of the 2/ Lincolnshire temporarily assumed control. Meanwhile the two companies of the Lincolnshire which had been ordered forward by General Lowry Cole had pushed along the crater sap under command of Capt. B. J. Thruston and had successfully reached the German line; but had struck it at a point to the westwards of the 13/ London, and so brought no relief to that hard-pressed battalion. Nor were they able to join hands with Colonel Stephens' force, though they worked some 200 yards along the German line in that direction and were able to hold the ground they had made. The general features of the situation, therefore, remained unchanged. The troops which had entered the enemy's trenches were still holding out precariously in isolated sectors of the German line. The two leading companies of the Lincolnshire, after having been held up in No-Man's Land as already recorded, had taken part in the unauthorized retirement, until stopped by the example of General Lowry Cole. Thereafter they had been reorganized by Major Cox, and now made another attempt, after a second bombardment, to close the

---

* The two leading companies of this battalion had already gone to the support of the Irish Rifles, but had been held up in No-Man's Land.

gap between points 883 and 882. They found that the volume of German rifle and machine-gun fire was little reduced and were again unable to make headway.

Such was the position at 8 a.m. when Colonel W. H. Anderson, G.S.O.1 to the division, went forward to 23rd Brigade Headquarters to direct General Pinney to take command of all troops East of the Sailly–Fromelles road. In order, if possible, to clear up the situation and bring relief to the detachments in the German lines, a further general bombardment was ordered; the fire of our guns East of the road being directed upon the German second line, so as to avoid harm to our troops in the enemy's front line. Following upon this bombardment, the 24th Brigade was directed to renew the assault at 9 a.m., while General Pinney was to endeavour to push forward supports to the assistance of our leading troops on his front.

Neither at this time, however, nor yet later in the day was General Oxley, whose available reserves were reduced to one battalion, the 1/ Worcestershire, able to report that his brigade was in a condition to renew the attack with any prospect of success. It had suffered too greatly, not only in the opening assault, but also, subsequently, from continuous shell fire in crowded trenches. The orders for advance on this flank were therefore cancelled, which was perhaps as well; for at about 1 p.m., the second hour selected for the renewal of the advance, the German artillery, heavily reinforced, opened a concentrated and prolonged bombardment of our lines and assembly positions. Even as it was, our troops suffered severely.

Meanwhile, on the old 25th Brigade front General Pinney had sent the 2/ Scottish Rifles forward to the support of the 13/ London, who had already sent back a message that their stock of bombs was running low and that they had exhausted every available reinforcement. Access to the German front line at this point was now only possible by crawling in single file up a shallow and much battered trench, over which rifle and machine-gun bullets whined and cracked incessantly. Yet a party got across with bombs and a machine gun, and turning East reached the survivors of the London battalion. The assistance they could bring, however, was not sufficient to provide material relief, and at 10.45 a.m. a message came back that casualties were increasing and that without support it would be impossible to hold on against another attack.

By this time, the intermixed units on the 25th Brigade front had been to some extent sorted out, and shortly after 11 a.m. a party of some 200 men of the 2/ Royal Berkshire (Major R. P. Harvey) were collected under Capt. C. Nugent and began to crawl forward man by man along the crater sap. The process was

THE STAND OF THE RIFLE BRIGADE.

a long and dangerous one, and Capt. Nugent at the head of his men was about three parts of the way across when the 13/ London were heavily attacked under cover of trench mortar fire and driven out.

Shortly after midday, a similar attempt to reinforce the forward troops of the 2/ Rifle Brigade was made by a party of 50 men of that battalion, who in the process of re-organization had been collected together under 2nd Lieut. Gray. The party formed up in an abandoned trench opposite point 884, and then amid a hail of bullets rushed across the intervening space. Lieut. Gray and some 20 men alone joined their comrades in the German line. More than half the gallant band were shot down before they could reach the shelter of the trench.

It had become quite evident that any further attack by daylight was doomed to failure, and before nightfall orders were issued by the IV Corps Commander that the 7th Division would renew the assault on the following morning and that meanwhile no further effort to advance was to be made. Accordingly, since it was clearly useless to attempt to hold permanently the isolated position on the extreme right, at 8 p.m. under cover of dusk Lieut. Parker and the remnants of " D " Company, 2/ Northamptonshire, were withdrawn to our own trenches. For similar reasons, General Pinney had decided to evacuate the short length of trench, still held by Capt. Thruston and his detachment of the Lincolnshire, West of point 882, and at about 7.30 p.m., in the midst of a German counter-attack, the survivors of this party also had been brought back to our lines.

There remained the sector of German trench astride the Sailly–Fromelles road held by the troops under Colonel Stephens. With the assistance of a captured machine gun which Lieut. Gray had succeeded in putting into working order, a fresh attack made by the enemy at about 7.50 p.m. was successfully beaten off, and thereafter the struggle on this front temporarily quietened down. At about 8.30 p.m., therefore, Colonel Stephens handed over command to Lieut. Newport, 1/ Royal Irish Rifles, and went back to our lines to take over command of the brigade; finding time, however, on his way to collect and send up some 70 men of his own battalion with two machine guns, as well as two bombing parties of the Berkshire, to strengthen the garrison he had left behind him. Numerous attempts were made later in the night to send up further help, for the enemy counter-attacked unceasingly. To this end the 15th Field Company, R.E., under Major P. K. Betty, commenced to dig a communication trench towards the captured line.

The relief of the 8th Division during the night was found to be impracticable owing to the heavy shell fire and the fact that

FROMELLES AND AFTER

the 7th Division were unacquainted with the trenches. It was decided to postpone the movement till daylight, and the change of plan entailed the abandonment of the proposal for a renewal of the attack on the following morning. Meanwhile, the defence of the 8th Division's line was taken over by the 23rd Infantry Brigade and the 1/Worcestershire (Major G. W. St.G. Grogan), of the 24th Brigade and the rest of the division, except the troops under Lieut. Newport, was withdrawn.

While these changes of disposition were being carried out, and while a detachment of the 7th Division was stumbling slowly through battered and unfamiliar trenches in a further effort to relieve Lieut. Newport and his men, the last remaining of our hard-won gains was lost. At about 2.30 a.m. the enemy launched a new counter-attack, bringing up large forces against the front of our position and bombing heavily from both flanks. Despite the stops we had erected in the captured trench, both flanks were gradually driven in. Our own supply of bombs had given out, and though our machine guns were fought very gallantly and were thought to have caused the enemy heavy loss, by about 3 a.m. the trench had become untenable and those survivors of the garrison who had escaped death or capture fell back to our former line. Some two hours later all that was left of the 2/ Rifle Brigade, 3 officers and some 195 men, marched back to billets near Sailly.

So far as the 8th Division was concerned, the battle had ended. It had ended in failure; but the failure was not due to any lack of the most splendid courage and resolution on the part of the troops engaged. They had been set, as the event proved, an impossible task. The enemy's defensive system had been found to be infinitely stronger than had been expected, and very different from that which had been overcome at Neuve Chapelle. His 20-foot thick breastworks and bomb-proof shelters, furnished with a parados of corresponding strength behind them, had successfully resisted our artillery bombardment, and the protection they afforded enabled the German garrisons to line their parapets with rifles and machine guns the moment our bombardment lifted. In such circumstances, the fact that our troops had broken into the German lines at all was a noteworthy achievement. They had, indeed, gone as far as human endeavour could go to accomplish the impossible. The measure of their efforts and of their great gallantry in attack is given by their losses.

The remnants of the 1/ Royal Irish Rifles—they had lost 477 officers and men—marched back to billets under the regimental sergeant-major. Not a single commissioned officer of this battalion came through the ordeal unscathed. The casualties of the 2/ Rifle Brigade were 21 officers and 571 other ranks.

THE COST OF THE ATTACK

The two other battalions of this brigade, the 2/ Lincolnshire and the 2/ Royal Berkshire, each lost over 300 officers and men. The 24th Infantry Brigade suffered scarcely less severely. The 2/ East Lancashire lost 19 officers and 435 other ranks; the 2/ Northamptonshire 12 officers and 414 other ranks; the 1/ Sherwood Foresters 347 officers and men.

Nor were the attacks of the I Corps and the Indian Corps any more successful. The attempt upon the Aubers Ridge had broken down, and the general plan of the First Army operations had to be modified in consequence. "On the evening of the 10th," says Lord French in his Despatch, "I sanctioned Sir Douglas Haig's proposal to concentrate all our available resources on the southern point of attack. The 7th Division was moved round from the IV Corps area to support this attack.... It was decided that the attack should be resumed on the night of the 12th inst., but the weather continued very dull and misty, interfering much with artillery observation. Orders were finally issued, therefore, for the action to commence on the night of the 15th inst." Thus opened the ten days battle of Festubert, a battle which, though it was not a "decisive victory" producing strategical results, did at least obtain a certain measure of tactical success. It may well be that the efforts of the 8th Division, and the concentration of German forces which the division drew to its front, were not without effect upon that result.

Apart, however, from artillery co-operation, the 8th Division took no active part in this second battle, although despite its heavy losses, it did not go wholly out of the line. On the 11th May, indeed, a number of units went for a short time into billets in the neighbourhood of Estaires and Laventie; but opportunities for rest were limited. Four days later, the 1/ Worcestershire and 1/ Sherwood Foresters (24th Infantry Brigade) and the 1/ London and 2/ Lincolnshire (25th Infantry Brigade), the whole under command of Brig.-General R. S. Oxley, relieved the 146th Infantry Brigade in the "Ducks Bill" sector, "C," "D" and "E" lines, on the right of the 23rd Infantry Brigade in "F" lines. The normal life of trench warfare recommenced, broken only by certain changes in command and in the composition of the division, and on the 14th and 15th June by "demonstrations" designed to assist the abortive operation against Givenchy which took place on the night of the 15th/16th June; "demonstrations" which were carried out to the accompaniment of the sullen and continuous reverberations of the mighty battle at Lorette.

Meanwhile, on the 20th May, the 13/ London left the division and was transferred to General Headquarters as line of communication troops. On the 31st May, owing to a

FROMELLES AND AFTER

reorganization of the First Army, the 8th Division came once more under the orders of the Indian Corps (Lieut.-General Sir James Willcocks). On the 2nd June the 6/ Scottish Rifles left to join the 51st (Highland) Division, their place in the 23rd Infantry Brigade being taken, on the 21st June, by the 8/ Middlesex, with which the 7/ Middlesex was amalgamated. At the end of June the 8th Division was transferred to the III Corps (Lieut.-General Sir W. P. Pulteney) and side-stepped to the North, taking over the adjoining sector previously held by the 49th Division.

In this new sector extending from Picantin to le Bridoux the division remained throughout July and August, enjoying a period of comparative quiet, which was the nearest approach to rest the troops had experienced since the division had come out to France. It lost on the 18th July, on promotion, its C.R.A. Brig.-General A. E. A. Holland, D.S.O., M.V.O., who had formed the divisional artillery and had commanded it with marked ability. His place was taken on the 21st July by Brig.-General G. H. W. Nicholson, C.M.G.

During this period the division said good-bye also to its first Divisional Commander. Maj.-General Sir Francis Davies, under whose care the division had come into being and gone out to France, who had commanded it for ten months of service in the line, broken only by pitched battles, and had led it to the capture of Neuve Chapelle, had been accorded the promotion which his services had won. He left on the 27th July to take over the VIII Corps of the Mediterranean Expeditionary Force, a command which was to prove the stepping stone to further advancement. He left behind him many friends and took with him the respect and affection of his troops. His place in the command of the division was taken on the 1st August by Maj.-General H. Hudson, C.B., C.I.E., Brig.-General R. S. Oxley having held command of the division temporarily during the intervening days.

PLATE III

GENERAL SIR HAVELOCK HUDSON, K.C.B., K.C.I.E.

CHAPTER IV

BOIS GRENIER

THE Summer of 1915 had been a disappointing period for the Allies. By the end of August their general position, though to some extent screened from the public view by the web of political camouflage, was far from satisfactory. The Russian " steam-roller " conception had been exploded and the slow forward movement of the Russian Armies at the opening of their campaign had been turned into a retreat, conducted at a pace which not even the sprightliest of steamrollers could hope to emulate. Russia was not yet, indeed, out of the fight; but the rapid success of the German counteroffensive was alarming, and its progress had not ceased.

Nor was the outlook more cheerful on other fronts. In the Dardanelles, the Suvla Bay operation had failed to bring relief to the situation in Gallipoli, where the open beaches of the Peninsula and the passing of the calm seas of summer were already pointing to the inevitable conclusion of a daring but ill-fated enterprise. In France itself, early hopes, born of the accession of Italy and of a consciousness of growing strength, had not been realized. An Allied superiority in men and guns * had not sufficed to prevent Germany from turning upon Russia and rending her; while the partial successes which the Allies had won in the West were gained at a cost in lives which was to have a lasting effect upon the fighting capacity of their armies. Bulgaria was on the point of joining forces with the enemy. The danger to Serbia was imminent. Only in Mesopotamia were our forces meeting with ephemeral success—a success which before long was to be shrouded in the Siege of Kut.

In all these circumstances it was to be expected that the high commands in France should decide to make another effort before the close of the campaigning season to gain some more definite advantage in their own theatre of war and, if possible, to bring some effective measure of help to stricken Russia and gravely-threatened Serbia. Hence the great French offensive in Champagne and the renewal of the French efforts South of Lens. Hence Loos with its startling promise of success, a promise which was not grasped and so remained unfulfilled. Hence, too, subsidiary to Loos, the action of Bois Grenier which was the contribution of the 8th Division to the general whole.

Immersed though the 8th Division was in the routine detail of trench warfare, varied by the preparation of defence schemes and by the instruction of attached units of the 20th Division,

---

* The numerical superiority in guns was not yet apparent in practice on the British front, where ammunition had to be used with the greatest economy.

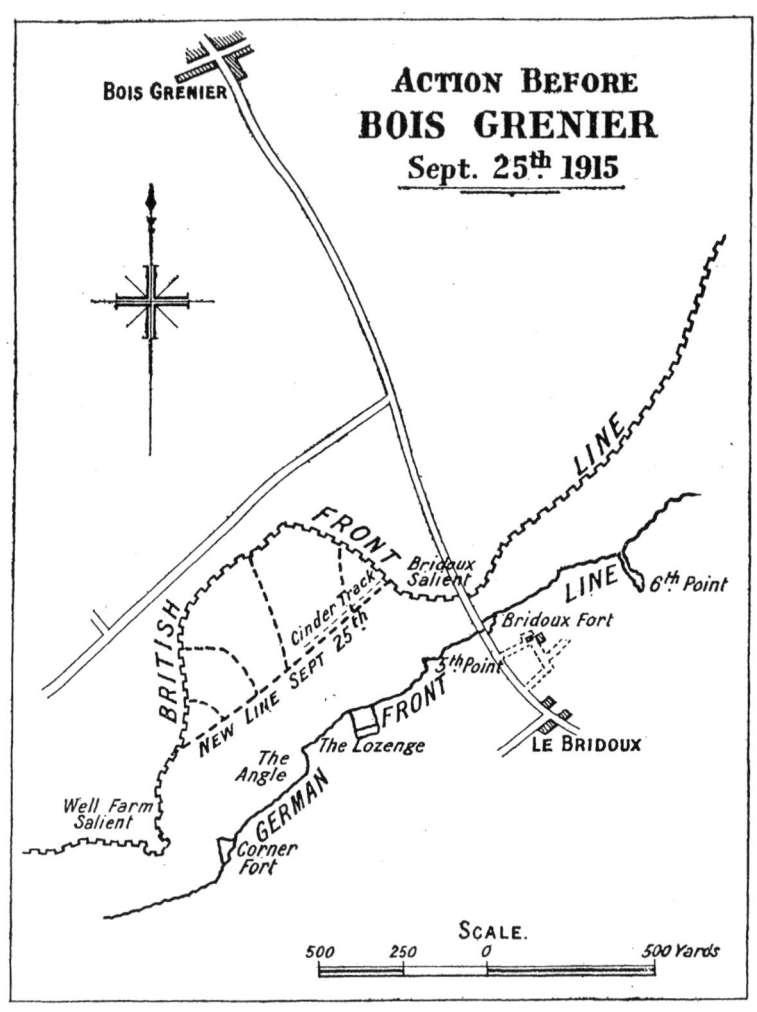

THE ALLIED AUTUMN OFFENSIVE, 1915

the troops in line were yet not left wholly ignorant of happenings in the world outside. With commendable promptitude and a generous desire to instruct, the Germans on the 7th August had erected a board in a conspicuous position in their front line announcing that " Warsaw has been fallen." Other indications of the course events were taking nearer at home, and of the part the division was to play in them, came in due time in the shape of operation orders, and in the first days of September preparations for an attack near Bois Grenier were already under way.

It had been decided to loose the whole offensive force of the Allied Armies in the West on one day, the 25th September. The chief effort of the Allies was to be made by the French Armies in Champagne, their objective being Vouziers and their design the breaking of the German lateral communications running East and West along the Aisne. The attack of the 10th French Army against the Vimy Ridge and the British main thrust at Loos were to be subsidiary to the Champagne offensive. They had, nevertheless, important aims; for the capture of the high ground to the South and North of Lens would have isolated that town and opened up the plain of the Scheldt. Subsidiary again to these northern Allied attacks were a series of minor British operations, one at Givenchy, another against the Aubers Ridge just North of Neuve Chapelle, the third the 8th Division operation against the Bridoux Redoubt, and the fourth an attack upon the Bellewaarde Ridge, East of Ypres.

It will be seen, therefore, that the part allotted to the 8th Division was but a small one in the general scheme of the offensive; but it offered considerable local advantages, quite apart from its contribution to the success of the larger plan. Our line in the sector selected for the attack, between the Well Farm salient and the le Bridoux Road salient, ran back in an almost complete semi-circle. Across the mouth of this deep re-entrant lay a disused ditch, dry in summer, but flooded and wet in winter, which Brig.-General R. B. Stephens, whose 25th Brigade had been selected for the attack, reported would make a suitable jumping-off place. The object of the operation was to capture about 1,200 yards of the German front line system opposite the re-entrant and link them up with our own line at the Well Farm and Le Bridoux salients, thereby both shortening and strengthening our position.

The troops detailed by General Hudson for the assault were the 2/ Rifle Brigade (Major F. H. Nugent) on the right, the 2/ Royal Berkshire (Lieut.-Colonel E. P. Hunt) in the centre and the 2/ Lincolnshire (Lieut.-Colonel S. Fitz-G. Cox) on the left; all from Brig.-General Stephens' 25th Brigade. Holding the trenches on the left of the assault were the 1/ Royal Irish Rifles

BOIS GRENIER

(Lieut.-Colonel R. A. Daunt, D.S.O.), while the remainder of the brigade, the 1/1 London (Lieut.-Colonel E. G. Mercer) and 1/8 Middlesex (Lieut.-Colonel P. L. Ingpen) formed the brigade reserve. The 24th Infantry Brigade (Brig.-General R. S. Oxley) was in support, the 2/ East Lancashire (Lieut.-Colonel T. S. Lambert) and the 1/ Sherwood Foresters (Lieut.-Colonel C. R. Mortimore, D.S.O.), being detailed under the general command of Colonel Lambert to hold the trenches on the right of the attack; where they were to assist the actual assault by demonstrating, holding themselves in readiness to follow-up any weakening of the enemy opposite them. The remainder of the 24th Brigade was to be in general support in rear, and the 23rd Infantry Brigade (Brig.-General H. D. Tuson, C.M.G.) formed the divisional reserve.

Four days prior to the assault a powerful artillery bombardment was opened, adding its share of din and tumult to the continuous, uneven roar of sound which swelled and sank and swelled again all along the Allied front. The task of the artillery allotted to the 8th Division attack was to destroy the enemy's defences and demoralize his garrisons and, there being insufficient guns to cut the whole, to blow gaps in selected portions of the German wire. For the first two days, the enemy's retaliation was not very serious; but on the third day his shelling became so much more severe that it was thought that several fresh batteries of heavy guns had been brought into action. Yet the battalions in line reported that our own gunners were making excellent practice and doing great damage to the German wire and parapets, damage which the infantry strove to keep unrepaired by sweeping the areas of destruction with rifle fire at night. In the early hours of the 24th September the severity of the bombardment was increased as though to herald an assault, and maintained at full intensity for a slightly longer period than that which was to precede the actual attack.

That same evening, the troops of the 25th Infantry Brigade, who had been given a few days out of the line to prepare themselves for the strain of battle, moved forward to their positions of assault. By 3.30 a.m. on the 25th September all units of the division were in their allotted places. Six 18-pounder guns, dug into our front line parapet and well masked from view, were ready to join in the covering bombardment and blast the German trenches at point-blank range. Preparations had been made for smoke discharges to cover the flanks of the advance; but an unfavourable wind made it impossible to carry out the smoke programme in its entirety. Two shallow mines, one in front of each of the two salients, were to be exploded at the moment of assault, with the idea that their craters might be converted into

CORNER FORT CAPTURED

communication trenches; but here also the result was not wholly satisfactory, as the charges did not break the surface of the ground sufficiently for the purpose intended.

At 4.25 a.m. an intense artillery bombardment was opened on the German first and second line trenches, while other guns barraged the flanks of the advance. The 18-pounder guns concealed in our front line joined in with devastating effect. Two of these guns, one of the 1st Battery R.F.A., under Lieut. F. R. F. Lankester, and the other of the 5th Battery R.F.A., under Lieut. J. Wedderburn Maxwell, had been dug in on the actual front of attack and contributed materially to the initial success of the infantry, blowing great gaps in the German parapet and scattering his sand-bag defences in all directions. Under cover of this bombardment the attacking infantry crept forward towards the German line and, when the guns lifted five minutes later, leapt to the assault.

The attack of the 2/ Rifle Brigade on the right was delivered by " C " Company, under Capt. the Hon R. Brand, followed by 80 specially trained bombers under Lieut. F. E. Young. So skilfully did these troops make use of the covering artillery fire that they reached the front trench of their objective, Corner Fort, almost at the very moment when our guns lengthened range. The German front trench was seized immediately, and the way opened for " A " Company (Capt. C. W. Wolseley Jenkins) who brought four machine guns with them. Capt. Jenkins took his company along to the right of Corner Fort, bombing his way forward and building blocks as he advanced. He was killed at the head of his company ; but, before he fell, his gallant and skilful leadership had firmly secured his gains. Command of both " A " and " C " Companies was then taken over by Capt. H. L. Riley, D.S.O., who had gone forward with " A " Company, and the troops continued to make ground, until by 6 a.m. the German second line trench on the front of their attack was in their hands.

Meanwhile, the centre attack delivered by three companies of the 2/ Royal Berkshire, had also made good progress; although they had found the enemy opposite them more upon the alert. As the attackers crept forward, under cover of the bombardment, up went a number of flares, and a small searchlight was turned upon the right company which soon found itself under so hot a fire that it was impossible to get on. The two other companies successfully forced their way into the German lines; though not without loss, for Lieut. R. H. G. Trotter, commanding the centre company, was killed in mounting the enemy's parapet and Capt. R. Oke of the left company was wounded no less than three times. Once in, however, both

BOIS GRENIER

companies made short work of the defenders, using the bayonet in grim and deadly fashion. Bombing parties, followed by the second wave of attack, then proceeded to work their way outwards on the flanks of the breach; until at about 8 a.m. the left party under Lieut. G. F. Gregory,* who although wounded continued to direct the fight, gained touch with the 2/ Lincolnshire.

The latter battalion had attacked on the left with two companies, their objective being Bridoux Fort and the German trenches immediately South of it. As soon as our bombardment lifted, " Z " Company had dashed across the short 100 yards which separated them from the German trenches and captured the forward defences of the Fort in the first rush of their assault. Bombers were then sent forward to take the second line and within ten minutes of the opening of the battle the whole position was in our hands. Thereupon " X " Company on the right moved forward in turn, and entering the German trench immediately South of the Fort, bombed their way along it till they met the 2/ Royal Berkshire.

By 8 a.m., therefore, the greater part of our objectives had been gained, and our position seemed fairly secure except that the gap of some 200 yards between the Rifle Brigade and the Berkshire could not be closed. This was a definite source of weakness, as it covered one of the enemy's main communication trenches, up which he at once began to send forward reinforcements. On the rest of the battle-front, also, as soon as the first shock of our assault was over, his troops began to react vigorously and in increasing strength.

Already, at about 6.30 a.m., the Rifle Brigade had found it impossible to maintain their hold on the enemy's second line, and had withdrawn the troops there to the German front line. Here a firm position was established, strong blocks being built on both flanks. At all points, however, great difficulty was experienced in getting up an adequate supply of bombs, and our misfortunes in this respect were increased by the rain which made matches and fuses damp and rendered the bombs unusable. Yet handicapped as they were, bombers of the Berkshire led by Sergt. A. Johnson, who took over the command after yet another officer, 2nd Lieut. B. Russel, had been killed, captured the German work known as the Lozenge in the centre of the attack. Thereafter for some hours, though a fierce bombing encounter had already developed on the right, the position of this battalion, shortly afterwards reinforced by half a company of the 1/ London, remained substantially unchanged. On the right flank, indeed, the Germans, fed from their uncaptured communi-

* He was unfortunately killed later in the battle.

THE LOSS OF BRIDOUX FORT

cation trench, strove time after time to push northwards along their old front line, but were as many times stopped and driven back. Lieut.-Colonel E. P. Hunt had reached the German line before 5.30 a.m. and had taken control of his troops there, sending back Capt. Sawyer, who had been wounded by a bomb, to have his wound dressed and to give a personal report to the Brigade Commander.

In the left sector of the attack, developments subsequent to the successful opening assault of the 2/ Lincolnshire were not so promising. Making full use of the many covered approaches (orchards, communication trenches, ditches and the like) which led up to Bridoux Fort from the South-East, the enemy rallied strongly and the pressure upon " Z " Company became severe. The arrival at about 7.40 a.m. of two companies of the 1/ Royal Irish Rifles had eased the situation for a time; but the shortage of bombs and bombers continued to be acute. At this date, no less than twelve different varieties of bombs were in simultaneous use and great numbers were wasted because in the supreme excitement of action the men forgot how the different types were to be treated. Apart from those spoiled by the rain, many bombs of the time fuse type, which required to be lighted, were thrown unlighted and so failed to explode.

The danger was realized, and in order to meet it the three Grenadier platoons of the 24th Infantry Brigade (1/ Worcestershire, 2/ Northamptonshire and 5/ Black Watch) were sent up at about 8 a.m. to reinforce our troops throughout the length of the captured trenches. Despite this further reinforcement, the situation in Bridoux Fort again became serious as the morning advanced. In the midst of yet another counter-attack the supply of bombs gave out entirely, and, fighting desperately but in vain, our men were gradually driven from the fort. For a further space of time they hung on doggedly under shelter of the German parapet; but such a position could not be maintained for long. Touch with the battalion on their right had long since been lost, and by 2 p.m. the survivors of the two attacking companies of the Lincolnshire and their reinforcements had been forced back to our own lines.

The result of the German progress at Bridoux Fort had been to expose the 2/ Royal Berkshire and other troops in the central sector to vigorous attacks on both flanks, pressed continuously by an enemy who had evidently been strongly reinforced. Finding that the position was rapidly becoming untenable, Colonel Hunt shortly before 2 p.m. gave the order for his battalion and attached troops to withdraw to our own trenches along certain ditches which afforded them some small protection. The movement was carried out steadily and without serious loss, under cover of a small rearguard which stayed on with Colonel Hunt in the German trenches until the enemy were within 20 yards on either side of them and the last serviceable bomb had been thrown. The whole retirement across the wide area which separated them from our old line called for the utmost coolness, intrepidity and good judgment and was executed in a manner creditable to all ranks, however unsatisfactory a conclusion it might be to a gallant and successful assault.

In the meantime, the 2/ Rifle Brigade in the right sector of the attack had been giving proof, if proof were needed, that if serviceable bombs were forthcoming in reasonable quantities our troops were fully a match for the German bombers. In this sector, the opposing lines approached each other comparatively closely and it had been possible with the help of the engineers to establish secure communication with Well Farm salient. In addition to the Grenadier platoon of the 1/8 Middlesex which had been sent to the assistance of the troops in Corner Fort, two companies of the same battalion had been employed as carrying parties to take up bombs, water and ammunition to the captured position. Two trench mortars were also brought up and did good service. The result of these measures was that, though constantly engaged by bombing attacks delivered from both flanks and from the German second line trench, our troops had firmly consolidated the position they had won, and had already reversed some of the captured trenches. They had done more, for a certain amount of fresh ground had been gained towards the 2/ Royal Berkshire. A big effort to join hands with them was in course of preparation, when the news came through that both the left and centre had retired.

In these circumstances, the 2/ Rifle Brigade had no alternative but to withdraw also; for their gains in and around Corner Fort obviously could not be maintained as an isolated position. Under the skilful direction of Capt. Riley, this retirement also was carried out in a most orderly and methodical manner and with comparatively few casualties. By 4 p.m. the whole of the morning's gains had been evacuated and all along the line our troops were back in our own trenches.

Throughout the operation the weather was bad and grew worse as the fight progressed. Mist and rain made it most difficult to see what was happening and rendered artillery observation almost impossible. In spite of this, the artillery support was splendid. In the desperate fighting at Bridoux Fort the aid given by our guns was of the utmost value, as Lieut.-Colonel S. Fitz-G. Cox testified in his official report: " Before the fort finally fell, at least six attempts were frustrated by the close co-operation afforded me by the artillery and the excellent com-

A TRIBUTE TO THE ARTILLERY

munication that existed between the guns and their liaison officers attached to me. This enabled me to nip these attacks in the bud." The preliminary work of wire cutting had also been well and thoroughly done, and the final artillery bombardment before the assault was extraordinarily effective and well aimed. The six field guns which had been installed in our parapet undoubtedly contributed in no small degree to the initial success of the operation. Their moral effect was enormous, even more decisive, indeed, than the material damage they caused. It is significant that The Angle, which was the one place where the infantry failed to get in, was also the one place where the attack was not supported by a parapet gun.

A fair number of prisoners—about 3 officers and 120 other ranks—were taken and the nature of the operation made it easy to ascertain that the enemy's other casualties were severe. Our own losses were by no means light, the total for the division being 56 officers and 1,342 other ranks, of whom 38 officers and 1,121 other ranks were from the attacking brigade. A satisfactory feature of the operation, and a tribute to the discipline of the troops, was that few if any of our wounded were left behind in the German trenches.

After dusk, all the battalions of the 25th Infantry Brigade, except the 1/ Royal Irish Rifles, were relieved by the 24th Infantry Brigade, and in the course of the night the relieving brigade commenced the construction of a breastwork along the course of the ditch which formed the chord of the re-entrant between Well Farm and the Bridoux salient. The new work was thoroughly wired by the Home Counties Field Company, Royal Engineers, and incorporated as a permanent part of our front line which it shortened by some 400 yards. In this way, the desired improvement in the local position was effected, even though it had not been possible to retain our hold upon the German trenches.

Gallantly and well as it had been carried out by all arms, the operation had failed to secure its immediate material objectives; even as the larger Allied scheme of which it formed a very minor part failed also to gain more than local and indecisive successes. The German barrier held, and the great and costly effort in Champagne could not bring effective help to Russia nor save Serbia from her fate. Yet as a contribution to the general scheme of the Autumn offensive on the Western Front, the work of the 8th Division had been well done. Even before the attack was launched, the severity of our preparatory bombardment and his fears for what might come had compelled the enemy to strengthen his artillery and to relieve his troops in line with a fresh division; though the British division confronting them had been in line continuously for a year. For all that he had done the German troops in line had given way before our assault, and in order to regain the ground which had been lost, the enemy had been compelled to engage reserves which might otherwise have been available for service elsewhere. Had the British main effort at Loos gone only a little more favourably, the necessity of defending his line against serious attack at Bois Grenier and in the three other sectors where minor operations had been undertaken might have cost the enemy dear.

To that extent, the action of Bois Grenier may quite properly be regarded as a successful operation; for it had resulted locally in an improvement in our tactical position, which the enemy would certainly have resisted strenuously in whatever fashion it had been attempted, while strategically it had amply accomplished the purpose for which the 8th Division had been sent into the fight. The division received the commendation of the Commander-in-Chief for the manner in which it had fulfilled its task.

CHAPTER V

LINE AND RESERVE

THOUGH rumours of yet further offensives continued to circulate and preparations were actually commenced for a fresh attack in November, Bois Grenier was to prove the final engagement of the prolonged period in line which had been the 8th Division's introduction to modern war. It was all the more satisfactory that this last effort should have filled its part so well in the general scheme, and all the more gratifying to all ranks to find that their action had won the approval of their Commander-in-Chief.

Two months later, on the 25th November, Field-Marshal Sir John French was to have inspected the division, then just out of the line, and to have addressed it with reference to its share in the fighting of the 25th September. Exceptionally bad weather prevented the inspection from taking place; but the Field-Marshal sent a message which reached the troops in the form of a Special Order of the day, and was read out to all units on parade. In it " he expressed his complete satisfaction with the manner in which the operations on that day (the 25th September) had been carried out and spoke in terms of high praise of the gallantry and thoroughness with which the attack had been delivered. The results precisely fulfilled his wishes and expectations, for the attack distracted the enemy's attention from the main point threatened, compelled him to withhold and expend his reserves, prevented his moving his artillery, and finally inflicted considerable loss. Such results could not have been attained had the attack not been pressed home with vigour and determination."

This heartening message came to the division when it was at last out of the line; but that welcome and well-deserved change did not occur until some weeks after the fight. So long as there was any possibility of further attacks being launched before the conclusion of the year, the 8th Division could not be left out; and, indeed, on the night of the 27th/28th September the front for which it was responsible was extended somewhat, ground being taken over on the right from its neighbour the 20th Division. The 8th Division was now disposed with two brigades in the trenches and one in divisional reserve. Conditions on the divisional front had quietened down, and the ordinary routine of trench life recommenced.

Opportunity was taken during this period for a temporary re-sorting of the units of which the division was composed, the idea being to facilitate the training and acclimatization to war conditions of the troops of the new armies, now beginning to come out to France in ever-increasing numbers. On the 18th

LINE AND RESERVE

of October, therefore, the 24th Infantry Brigade changed places with the 70th Infantry Brigade of the 23rd Division, and, with the idea of assimilating the less-experienced troops of the newer division with the older and more seasoned soldiers of the regular division, a further interchange of units within the division itself was carried out as soon as the 70th Brigade arrived. The new brigade was ordered to detach two of its battalions, the 8/K.O.Y.L.I. and the 11/Sherwood Foresters, and send them to the 25th Infantry Brigade, receiving two regular battalions, the 2/Lincolnshire and the 2/Rifle Brigade, from the latter brigade, in return. Nor did the scheme of amalgamation stop there; for the transferred battalions were themselves split into halves and two companies of the new troops united with two of the older companies, so as to form blended battalions composed in equal proportions of tried and untried troops.

In this way the new material was readily absorbed and by the 9th of November the process of acclimatization was considered to have been completed and the transferred battalions returned to their own units. The 24th Infantry Brigade was used in similar manner to leaven the remaining formations of the 23rd Division; but in this case the exchange, temporary though it was always intended to be, lasted in fact until the middle of the following July.

During the month of October a great deal of hard work was accomplished by the division not only in the strengthening of the front line trenches by thickening the parapets and in other ways, but also in the preparation of winter accommodation both in and behind the lines. The abortive preparations for a November attack added considerably to the work to be done. Facsimiles of the German trenches which were to be the division's objectives were carefully laid out behind our lines, and the battalions of the 23rd Infantry Brigade carried out a number of practice assaults upon them. The Germans opposite us seemed to be expecting to be attacked, for at the end of the month they shouted across to our trenches asking when we were coming over, and whether it was to be the 6th of November. They were, indeed, very conversationally, not to say amicably inclined; objecting strongly to our retaliation to their trench mortars, expressing regret for the sinking of the *Lusitania*, and promising not to fire if we would not. These friendly overtures, however, were freely interspersed with, and somewhat marred by, peculiarly insulting remarks about Glasgow. So our own men, particularly those hailing from North of the Border, were in no way tempted to abandon the customary aggressiveness of British troops in line, or to alter their usual practice of making things consistently as uncomfortable as possible for the other side.

REST AT LAST

Fortunately, perhaps, for the division, which had already achieved and suffered so much, the projected attack was countermanded. The primary reason for its cancellation, no doubt, was the complete break in the weather, which in the early days of November became nothing less than abominable, the change being heralded by forty-eight hours of continuous rain. On the 16th November, however, the welcome news that relief was at hand came in the shape of preliminary instructions for the withdrawal of the division into rest billets. Yet before they left the front, the troops had one last fling at the enemy. An artillery offensive, consisting of a timed bombardment supported by bursts of machine-gun and trench-mortar fire, was carried out on the 20th November. The object of the operation was to destroy mine shafts and do as much damage as possible to the enemy's personnel and material. The result was satisfactory. Numerous hits were made by 9·2-inch howitzers on the German front line, one of which caused a considerable secondary explosion. Our field artillery and trench mortars also made good practice. The enemy's reply was slight, and quite ineffective.

Four days later, at 10 a.m. on the 24th November, General Hudson handed over command of his sector to the 20th Division and the 8th Division was withdrawn for its first period of rest since it came to France. It had completed a year and twelve days of continuous service in the line. Divisional Headquarters were transferred on the same day from Sailly-sur-la-Lys to Blaringhem, a village about 8 miles South-East of St. Omer. Surrounding villages—Lynde, Sercus, Morbecque, Steenbecque and Wittes—gradually accommodated the units of the division, and before the end of the month training was in full swing. The division while in rest was in Army and General Headquarters Reserve. A staff change which had taken place before the division left the line remains to be noted. Colonel G. W. H. Anderson, G.S.O.1. to the division, had on the 25th October left to take up the appointment of B.G.G.S. XI Corps. Lieut.-Colonel H. Hill, M.V.O., D.S.O., Royal Welsh Fusiliers, succeeded him as G.S.O.1. of the division.

The bad weather which had led to the cancellation of the Commander-in-Chief's visit on the 25th November continued throughout the first three or four weeks of training, which were devoted principally to company and battalion exercises. During this period, on the 19th December, Field-Marshal Sir John French relinquished his command of the British Armies in France and was succeeded by General Sir Douglas Haig, under whose leadership, as commander of the First Army, the 8th Division had fought its opening battles. Sir John French's Special Order of the day on giving up command was announced to the division on the 18th December.

The course of training culminated with large scale divisional manœuvres which took place in the First Army training area from the 20th to the 23rd December. The same dates were selected by the powers responsible for the weather for a culmination in keeping with the long series of mild wet days which had already done much to rob the troops of the full benefit which they expected to obtain from their well-earned period of rest. During practically the whole of the manœuvres the rain poured down incessantly, and this, coupled with the fact that most of the country was under seed, restricted movement to a great extent to the roads. The discomfort caused to the troops is too obvious to need emphasis, though the comments of the troops themselves were often emphatic enough.

None the less, a considerable area of country was covered in the course of the manœuvres, and valuable lessons were learned by all ranks concerning the technical difficulties to be overcome and practical problems to be solved by a division in moving warfare. Perhaps more important still, a useful if brief opportunity was given to shake the division together. The exercise, with its general and special ideas and concealed orders, its entirely fictitious co-operating units and almost equally imaginary enemy represented by white flags and a few men, must have recalled to many of those who took part in it the army manœuvres which they had attended in the spacious days of peace. Yet in how poignant a contrast with those remembered days, when the heather of Frensham Common was murmurous with the song of bees beneath the warm summer sun, when manœuvres were an agreeably strenuous summer expedition, when the war was still far away, was the material setting of the present exercise amid the dreary winter landscape of Northern France, under grey and weeping skies, low hung with cloud and heavy with the distant sound of guns.

The guns were again calling. Already on the closing day of the manœuvres instructions for the relief of the 20th Division in line on the opening day of the New Year had been received at Divisional Headquarters. Scarcely, therefore, had the troops returned to their former rest billets, when divisional orders were issued for the projected move. On the 29th December, however, came fresh orders announcing a postponement, and the first days of the New Year were spent after all under conditions which permitted occasional games of football to be combined with a resumption of training and the work of clearing up the area. In carrying out the latter task, the divisional engineers at least found the work of levelling practice trenches and clearing demonstration barbed

TRAINING THE YOUNG IDEA

wire entanglements to be little less laborious, if less exciting, than that of constructing the real thing.

JANUARY 1916

On the 9th January 1916 began the move back to the Lys front, familiar but unlovely and unloved; and hopes, cherished but unsubstantial, of transfer to Egypt or Salonika vanished into the bleak and watery air of Flanders. Next day the 25th Infantry Brigade (Brig.-General R. B. Stephens) took over the left brigade sector, the 70th Infantry Brigade (Brig.-General H. Gordon, D.S.O.) going into line on its right on the night of the 11th January. On the 12th January, on which day Divisional Headquarters opened again at Sailly-sur-la-Lys, General Hudson assumed command once more of the right, or Fleurbaix, divisional sector of the III Corps' front. The condition of the trenches proved better than had been expected; the weather continued mostly fine and mild and the river Lys was reported to be falling rapidly.

During this tour of duty, which lasted till the latter end of March, there were further developments in the wise policy of acclimatizing newly arrived divisions, and increasing their war efficiency, by bringing them into contact in the trenches with the seasoned regular troops who might already fairly be considered to be veterans in France. On this occasion there was no attempt at amalgamation of units; but each incoming battalion was allotted to one of the infantry brigades of the division and was then directed to attach one of its companies to each of the four regular battalions of that brigade. The course of training was progressive. The new soldiers were sent into the trenches first as individuals supernumerary to the regular trench garrisons. When in this way they had begun to find their way about, they went in as platoons with definite if limited responsibilities of their own, next as companies and finally as complete battalions with a sector of their own to defend.

The first to join the division for this purpose, on the 26th January, were the headquarters and two battalions—1/ and 2/ Tyneside Scottish—of the 102nd Infantry Brigade, 34th Division. Brigade Headquarters and the 2/ Tyneside Scottish went to the 25th Infantry Brigade; the first battalion to the 23rd Infantry Brigade. A week later the 3/ and 4/ Tyneside Scottish came up in their turn, and were attached to the 23rd and 70th Infantry Brigades in front line. The 103rd Infantry Brigade, 34th Division, sent two battalions for a week's instruction on the 8th February. Before its turn of duty in line had ended the 8th Division had also acted as instructor to a part of the Headquarters Staff of the 39th Division as well as to a number of units of that division, namely: the 116th and 117th Infantry Brigades; two Field Companies R.E.; one howitzer and two 18-pounder

59

LINE AND RESERVE

Brigades, R.F.A.; the pioneer battalion (15/ Gloucestershire) and the Divisional Ammunition Column. The experience which the 8th Division had gained, arduously and at no light cost, in the course of its first long period in the line, was used, therefore, to full advantage, and employed to help in the preparation of our citizen armies for the work which was to be theirs in the coming years. Meanwhile, the three territorial battalions, the 1/1 London, 1/7 Middlesex, and 1/8 Middlesex, which had been attached to the 8th Division since the Spring or early Summer of 1915 and had already shown in the fighting of the 25th September 1915 of what sterling stuff those citizen armies were composed, were withdrawn on the 8th February and sent to rejoin the 56th (London) Division.

The presence of the different units attached for instruction brought a new interest and, what was perhaps even more appreciated, gave increased opportunities for reliefs to the troops of the division. The Sailly Empire, "Variety and Cinema," had started its career in November 1915, under the general management of Lieut. P. Triefus and the direction of a committee composed of Colonel F. W. Boteler, Lieut.-Colonel C. Hull and Major P. J. Harris, and on the 5th and 6th of that month had celebrated the first birthday of the division in France with Grand Gala Performances. The venture, the first of its kind, met with great success and a number of imitators. Now that the division was once more back in the Sailly area, with some small leisure on its hands, the Empire, where at the end of January Charlie Chaplin had been "featuring," was again well patronized.

Even when on the 15th February the division was given an additional sector to defend—that of the 3rd Guards Brigade on its right—it was still found possible to keep one brigade in divisional reserve. In the trenches, the weeks passed without special incident; for the vagaries of the weather in a Flanders winter had ceased to surprise, though they could still draw curses; and the enemy showed no special enterprise, despite the rumours of an early German offensive which originated no man knew where. It was, indeed, no time for offensive action in Flanders. The fine dry spell with which the year had opened could not and did not last. Though motor pumps were installed near Dead Dog Farm, with a view to lowering the water level in the front line system by pumping from the main draining ditch into the River Layes, and did very useful work whenever they could be induced to work at all, heavy rain and snow during February and March soon reduced the trenches to a condition painfully reminiscent of the first winter of the war.

It was, therefore, a not unwelcome rumour which ran through the division at the end of the third week in March and, on this

PLATE IV

WINTER ON THE LYS FRONT: PUMPING WATER FROM THE TRENCHES

Copyright: Imperial War Museum

SOUTH TO THE SOMME

occasion, proved to be well founded. On the 24th March the story that the division was to be relieved and sent to another part of the front seemed to be confirmed by the taking over by the 34th Division of the left sector of the divisional front. The very next day, indeed, certain units of the division began to move South. The attached troops of the 39th Division were returned post-haste to their own command and by the 28th March the 8th Division was on its way to join the II Corps (Lieut.-General Sir C. Fergusson, Bt., K.C.B., M.V.O., D.S.O.) of General Sir Henry Rawlinson's Fourth Army. On that day General Hudson handed over his sector to the 35th Division.

Great events were in prospect, had indeed already begun. The German February offensive, rumours of which had reached the trenches of the 8th Division on the Lys, had burst out in fury unparalleled at Verdun. The French were soon locked fast in the long and desperate struggle which was to go far towards the accomplishment of the enemy's ambition—the first steps towards which had been taken at Notre Dame de Lorette and in Champagne—of bleeding their nation white. To relieve the pressure on the French front, the Russians had opened in the middle of March a new offensive at Lake Narotch, and about the same time the Italians had renewed their attacks on the Isonzo front. Neither counter-measure, however, had been attended by much success. The violence of the German attacks at Verdun remained undiminished, and over Italy the clouds were gathering for the Austrian attack in the Trentino.

The British armies were growing steadily in numerical strength; but despite measures such as those in which the 8th Division had lately taken part both in reserve and in line, the training of the new troops was still far from being complete. The interests of the British armies, it was clear, would best be served by postponing as long as possible the commencement of the joint offensive on the Somme which the French and British higher commands had planned for the main Allied operation on the Western Front. Every week gained for training meant an increase in efficiency. Each improvement in efficiency would carry with it a reduction of losses and a more rapid and complete development of any success that might be won.

The strain at Verdun, however, was still maintained. In May it was to become yet greater, in addition to which the situation of the Italian Armies was to grow critical under the threat of the Austrian southwards thrust. At the date when the 8th Division moved down by train from the familiar northern area to Flesselles, where Divisional Headquarters opened on the 29th March, it was already becoming clear that the great offensive in which the division was to join might have to be launched earlier

MARCH 1916

than the condition of the British reinforcements could fully warrant. It behoved the division to make good use of all the time that might be given it, in which to prepare for the mightiest offensive in which it, or any British troops, had yet been engaged.

By the 30th March all the troops of the division had arrived in the Fourth Army area, and were billeted around Flesselles, some 9 miles North of Amiens. They were not left there long. On the 4th April General Hudson's Headquarters moved to Henencourt Château, and next day the division took over from the 32nd Division the la Boisselle–Thiepval sector, overlooking the River Ancre and the German lines in front of those villages.

The new front was a great change in every respect from the one the division had just left. In many ways it was more comfortable. The trenches were for the most part dry, and provided with fine deep dug-outs. From many points a good view could be obtained of the German defences opposite; but this carried with it the corresponding disadvantage that the enemy could overlook equally well some of our own positions. Ovillers Post, for example, was in view of the German lines from two points, and the division had not been in line two days before " The Glory Hole " was being well " strafed " by " oil-cans " and other delights, although no sign of life could be seen in the German trenches. On the 11th April the Royal Irish Rifles were raided there, after a bombardment with lachrymatory shell, and lost a number of prisoners.

The enemy, indeed, was much more active than he had been during the winter months in the North. Even during the march to Albert on the way up to the line it had been necessary to take the troops forward in open order, so as to avoid German shelling. On the other hand, billets were comparatively good, and the enemy's guns were not yet so active as to prevent occasional riding lessons being given surreptitiously in Aveluy Wood to enterprising individuals who had no real right to horses. That such a place could be used for such a purpose will illustrate perhaps as well as anything could do the extent to which the launching of the offensive was to alter conditions on the Somme front.

As the weeks passed and the Allied preparations for the offensive progressed and became intensified, so grew the activity and watchfulness of the enemy. The accepted methods of attack, with their vast massing of material and prolonged preliminary bombardments, made it impossible to conceal the fact that a powerful offensive was in course of preparation. Only in the date and time of the assault and the limits of the sectors against which its main weight was to be launched was there any room for the element of surprise.

At first with two brigades in line and later, after the 10th May,

PLATE V

OPPOSITE LA BOISSELLE

Copyright: Imperial War Museum

PREPARATION

with one brigade only on the actual front of assault, and under ever-increasing harassing fire from the German guns, the work of getting ready was pushed steadily forward. Before the end of April the engineers had commenced to push out towards the enemy's trenches "Russian" saps, shallow covered ways intended to act as communication trenches when the German front line had been won. Work on dug-outs, assembly positions and bomb depots, and in the construction of concrete shelters, observation posts, and dressing stations was pushed on daily in the forward area; while behind the lines the troops detailed for the attack and its support practised at musketry, at throwing the new "Mills" bomb and at the rapid erection of barbed wire defences with folding "knife rests" and other entanglements. The divisional sector seethed with purposeful activity, which yet did not prevent the final of the divisional football competition being played out to a finish on the 23rd May.

Certainly, the enemy had ample notice of our intentions, and he kept his information up to date by occasional raids. He commenced a methodical shelling of the square at Albert, and at times his general artillery and trench mortar activity swelled into deliberate bombardments, to which our own guns replied vigorously. Busy as the gunners were, the opportunity was taken during the first half of May to reorganize the divisional artillery. The CXXVIII Howitzer Brigade R.F.A. Headquarters were disbanded, and the 55th and 57th Batteries each detached a section to form a third 4-gun howitzer battery, "D" Battery. At the same time, the Battery Ammunition Columns were merged into the Divisional Ammunition Column. After these changes, the divisional artillery under Brig.-General Nicholson consisted of mixed artillery brigades of three 6-gun 18-pounder batteries and one 4-gun 4·5-inch howitzer battery, as follows :—

V Brigade R.H.A.; Lieut.-Colonel A. T. Butler, C.M.G. ; "O" and "Z" Batteries R.H.A.; and "D" 4·5-inch Howitzer Battery.

XXXIII Brigade R.F.A.; Lieut.-Colonel T. St. A. B.-L. Nevinson ; 32nd, 33rd and 36th 18-pounder Batteries R.F.A.; and 55th 4·5-inch Howitzer Battery R.F.A.

XLV Brigade R.F.A.; Lieut.-Colonel H. W. Hill; 1st, 3rd and 5th 18-pounder Batteries R.F.A., and 57th 4·5-inch Howitzer Battery R.F.A.

8th D.A.C.; Bvt.-Colonel F. W. Boteler.

The reduction of the divisional front to a single brigade sector afforded extended opportunity for special training of the infantry out of the line. By the end of May, attack practices on a large scale were being carried out in the corps' training area, in conjunction with the neighbouring divisions, over ground specially

LINE AND RESERVE

prepared to represent, so far as possible, the features and defences of the sector to be attacked. In line, our engineers and working parties were out nightly, interrupted at times when the enemy's guns and trench mortars became too active; but sometimes undisturbed, despite the no small noise of hammering, sawing, digging and talking—probably because the enemy was equally engaged with his own preparations.

So the busy days passed swiftly and the date of the great attack drew nearer.

CHAPTER VI

THE SOMME BATTLE : OVILLERS

JUNE with its lengthening summer days wore on, and, as the climax of the year approached, brought closer the fateful moment of that other climax for which the 8th Division had been so long and so strenuously preparing. It was, indeed, on Midsummer Day itself that our artillery bombardment opened, and with the crashing chords of that stupendous and devastating overture was ushered in the heroic drama of the Somme.

It was time. The long-drawn struggle at Verdun had continued since February with deadly and unchanging purpose ; until at last Sir Douglas Haig, anxious though he was to secure the utmost period of training for the young and inexperienced troops of his new divisions, had promised General Joffre that the British attack should not be further delayed. Impelled by the urgent need of Italy, Brussilov had already launched the Russian Summer Offensive. In two days he had taken Lutsk, while further South other Russian Armies overran the Bukovina. For a time our Allies on the Eastern Front carried all before them in both theatres of their offensive. Their victories came at a good time for Italy, and undoubtedly contributed to the success of her counter-offensive in the Trentino in the middle of June, which left her free to turn her attention once more to preparations for the renewal of her offensive at Gorizia. Both the obvious strategic advantage to be gained for the Allies by simultaneous attacks on all fronts, and the urgent need of relieving the pressure at Verdun, pointed to the early launching by the Western Armies of their projected joint offensive.

The original project had, indeed, been planned long before the Verdun offensive had begun, and had presupposed that the British Army would grow in strength with sufficient rapidity to enable it to undertake powerful preparatory attacks early in the year. These, when the German reserves had been partially exhausted, were to have been followed up by a great French offensive on the British right, in which the British would join with all the remaining forces at their disposal. The scope of this offensive, and the relative parts which it was intended that the French and British Armies should play in it, are shown by the fact that the front of the attack as originally proposed was to extend from the neighbourhood of Lassigny (West of Noyon) to Gommecourt. On this combined front of over 45 miles the French were to employ a force of thirty-nine divisions on a front of 30 miles. The remaining 15 miles were to be allotted to the British, who were to employ there as many divisions as they could make available, up to a possible maximum of twenty-five divisions.

OVILLERS

This great scheme had gradually been whittled down as the year advanced; and as it became evident, first that the numbers and condition of the British reinforcements would make it impracticable for the British Army to undertake preparatory attacks of any weight if they were to play an effective part in the main battle, and secondly that the losses of the French at Verdun would sadly curtail the share which our Allies could take in it. Their original proposal of an operation by thirty-nine divisions on a front of 30 miles, steadily dwindled; until ultimately it became an attack by five divisions in line on an effective front of 6 miles astride the Somme from Fay to Maricourt, in support of a British attack by thirteen divisions in line on a front of $15\frac{1}{2}$ miles from Maricourt to Gommecourt. The whole conception of the combined offensive had been reversed. Instead of being engaged in an operation subsidiary to a far more powerful and extended French drive, the British found themselves called upon to shoulder the main burden of the offensive.

This shifting of the balance of responsibility had necessarily caused a modification of the larger objectives of the offensive. The original plan contemplated a comparatively rapid advance eastwards, until the French had gained the rising ground beyond the Somme and Tortille Rivers, and the British Army held the semicircle of high ground beyond the upper valley of the Ancre, having Bapaume approximately at its centre. Thereafter, the scheme was to direct the pressure of the Allied armies outwards, the French to the South-East and the British to the North-East, so as to roll up the German trench systems on either side of the breach, while French and British cavalry covered the operations of the main armies.

Verdun had eaten up the reserves which the French had destined for their part of the joint operation; but the British programme stood. It was hoped that the assistance which the French could give, limited though it would of necessity be at first, would grow greater as the battle progressed and the cessation of the German attacks at Verdun set free additional French divisions. Yet it was realized that the abandonment, or postponement, of the larger complementary movement by the French would increase the resistance which the British would have to overcome, and perhaps force them to limit their ambitions for that year to the nearer Morval–Thiepval ridge, South of the upper Ancre Valley. Even so, they would be behind the flank of the German trench systems to the North of them, and would have won a favourable position for the renewal of the joint offensive in the following year. In any event, they would be co-operating effectively with the Russian and Italian offensives, and

THE EFFECT OF VERDUN

would give relief to a situation at Verdun which at the end of June was becoming desperate.   JUNE 1916

So radical a change, however, in the plan of battle had a direct and decisive effect upon the fortunes of the 8th Division, and indeed upon those of all the British divisions employed in the attack from the village of la Boisselle northwards. Knowledge of the losses suffered by the French at Verdun led the enemy to believe that the French share in the offensive would be limited to the narrow sector held by them North of the Somme, and that the main thrust would be made by the British astride the Ancre. His misreading of the situation led him to neglect the sector South of the Somme, where on the 1st July the French attack took his troops by surprise and gained striking successes, and to concentrate his available reserves of men and guns opposite the northern half of the British front. On this northern portion, the greater part lying beyond the bounds of the principal Allied thrust which in fact was laid between the Somme and Ancre Rivers, his precautionary measures proved adequate and the Allied advance during the opening stages of the battle was confined to the sectors extending from la Boisselle southwards. The 8th Division, therefore, found at and around Ovillers an alert enemy, fully prepared for their attack and provided with powerful artillery support.

The British artillery bombardment which opened on the 24th June was to have continued, according to plan, for five days and nights without cessation. In the event, a spell of wet weather deferred the attack for forty-eight hours and so for this additional period also the preliminary shelling was continued. The delay was unfortunate, for the amount of ammunition available for the British gunners was not sufficient to enable the bombardment to be maintained at the same intensity for the extended period. There had to be a certain slackening, with the result that the enemy was given an unexpected and, to him, invaluable opportunity to get food, water, and reinforcements through to his front line garrisons. Yet this bombardment was impressive. Dwarfed though it may be in retrospect by the stupendous artillery concentrations of later days, no such weight of metal had hitherto been brought together in any British battle. Men's ears sang again with the clanging of the hammers of war and at night the whole countryside was lit up by the flashes of the guns.

Hope ran high that the result would be so to pulverize the enemy's defences that a legitimate chance would be given to the infantry to press forward to success. So far as the infantry themselves were concerned, all had been done that experience could suggest or ingenuity and foresight could devise. The

OVILLERS

expectations of the troops of the 8th Division were increased by a successful raid carried out by the 2/ Royal Berkshire on the night of the 25th/26th June. To be sure, the deep dug-outs in the enemy's lines were found full of Germans singing and apparently in good spirits notwithstanding our bombardment; but confidence and concert alike were violently dispersed by the raiders' bombs. It did not, indeed, seem too much to expect that, when the day of the great attack came, the division would succeed in gaining, or at least nearly approaching, its objectives on the further edge of Pozières ; and so would take a prominent and effective part in the realization of the general objectives of the British Army.

Powerful as our bombardment was, however, the Germans had found to it, as the event proved, a counter-stroke which staunch and well-trained troops might make effective. Although trenches and barbed-wire entanglements, no matter how intricate and elaborate, might be pounded to pieces, it was still possible to construct on these high and undulating uplands, which offered so striking a contrast to the level water meadows of the Lys Valley, deep underground chambers which no artillery could altogether destroy. It is to the existence of these dug-outs, sunk 30 feet and more below the surface of the ground, and to the fact also that the " creeping barrage " had not yet come into general use, that one must look for the explanation of what occurred on the northern half of the Somme battle-front on the 1st July.

On this northern front astride the Ancre, where the enemy was expecting the principal blow to fall and had made his preparations accordingly, no division was more difficultly placed than the 8th Division. Except for a short space in the centre of the divisional sector, No-Man's Land was everywhere exceptionally wide. Particularly was this the case on the right, where both our own and the German lines were to some extent recessed. Here the 23rd Infantry Brigade had before it an appalling stretch of No-Man's Land to negotiate before it gained contact with the enemy's trenches. Furthermore, the advance of the right brigade lay up a valley dominated to the left by the higher ground of Ovillers and on the right even more dangerously threatened by the German salient at la Boisselle. If all went not well elsewhere, it was obvious that both from Ovillers and from the la Boisselle spur a deadly flanking fire could be brought to bear on our troops as they struggled up that desolate valley towards their distant objective. Nearer the centre of the divisional front, though the lines lay closer together, the village of Ovillers was a solid and terrible obstacle to the progress of the 25th Brigade. On the left, the opposing lines again drew farther apart, and here

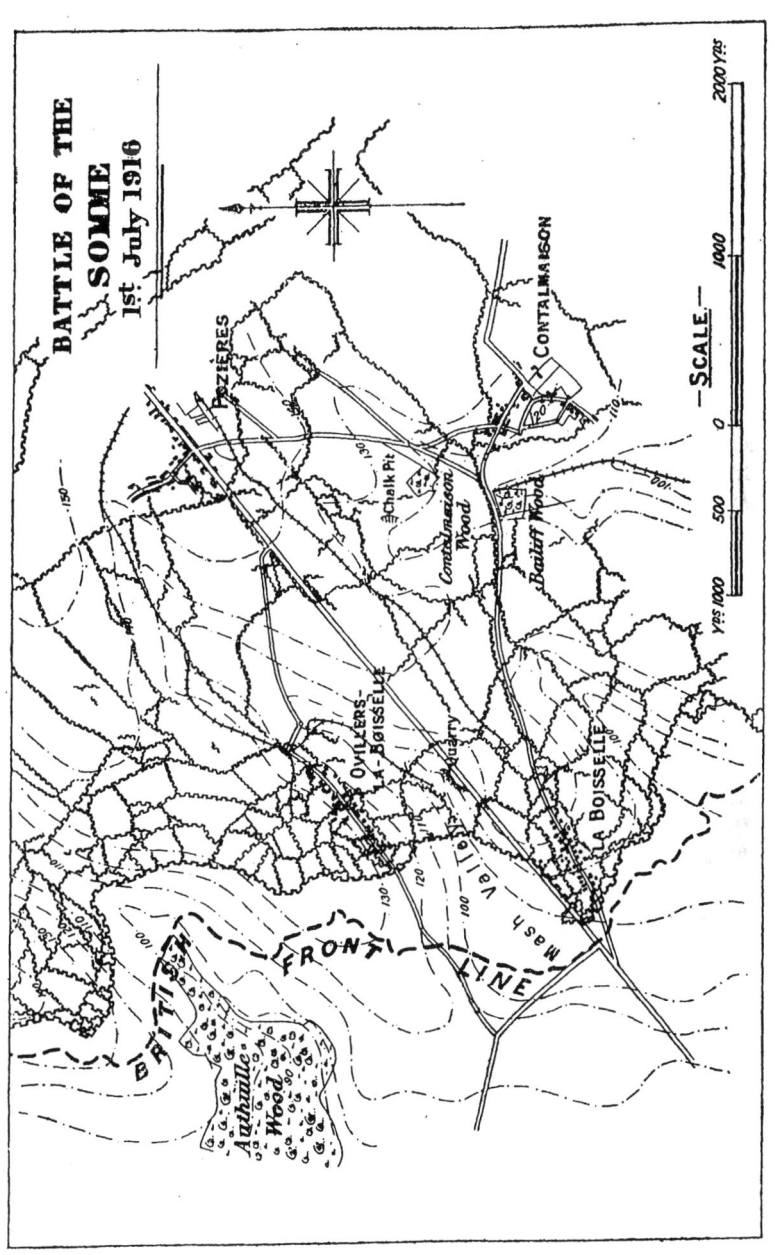

OVILLERS

the attack of the 70th Brigade lay beneath the southern spur of the Thiepval salient, which jutted far into our lines and commanded in enfilade every inch of the ground over which our infantry would have to advance. It will readily be appreciated that unless the results of the final intense bombardment covering the assault were such that the defence was for the time being put almost completely out of action, and unless the progress made by the troops on either flank was rapid and successful, the 8th Division was likely to find its task beyond the power of human accomplishment.

Meanwhile, however, the preliminary arrangements went smoothly forward to the thunderous accompaniment of the guns. On the 26th, 27th and 28th June smoke was discharged along the divisional front and on the 27th a large and, as far as could be judged, successful discharge of gas was also made. The destruction of the enemy's trenches and the cutting of his wire were steadily continuing. All along the curving battle front a score or more of our balloons could be seen directing the fire of our guns.

In the air we were dominant. A gunner officer gives the following graphic account illustrative of our complete supremacy. "On the opening day of the bombardment, I think it was, our planes flew along the line of German observation balloons and destroyed them all with the new rocket apparatus. From my battery position 1,000 yards or so from Thiepval we saw gas bag after gas bag burst into flames. Our new Sopwith biplanes also were let loose during this time. I did not see a German plane or balloon in the air from the first day (24th June) until we, the R.A. of the 8th Division, were pulled out of the line some ten days later. The enemy was fighting blind!"

During the night of the 29th/30th June the infantry of the division, which was now the left division of the III Corps (Lieut.-General Sir W.P. Pulteney), moved into their assembly positions. The 23rd Infantry Brigade (Brig.-General H. D. Tuson) on the right had the 2/ Middlesex (Lieut.-Colonel E. T. F. Sandys) and the 2/ Devonshire (Lieut.-Colonel A. J. E. Sunderland) in line, the 2/ West Yorkshire (Lieut.-Colonel L. Hume Spry, D.S.O.) in support and the 2/ Scottish Rifles (Lieut.-Colonel V. C. Sandilands) in reserve. In the centre the attacking battalions of the 25th Infantry Brigade (Brig.-General J. H. W. Pollard, C.M.G.), were the 2/ Royal Berkshire (Lieut.-Colonel A. M. Holdsworth) and the 2/ Lincolnshire (Lieut.-Colonel R. Bastard, D.S.O.); the 1/ Royal Irish Rifles (Lieut.-Colonel R. A. C. Daunt, D.S.O.) being in support and the 2/ Rifle Brigade (Lieut.-Colonel the Hon. R. Brand) in reserve. On the left, the 70th Infantry

THE ASSAULT

Brigade (Brig.-General H. Gordon, D.S.O.) attacked with the 8/ K.O.Y.L.I. (Lieut.-Colonel H. E. Trevor, D.S.O.) and the 8/ York and Lancaster (Lieut.-Colonel M. L. Hornby, D.S.O.), and kept the 9/ York and Lancaster (Lieut.-Colonel A. J. B. Addison) in support and the 11/ Sherwood Foresters (Lieut.-Colonel H. F. Watson, D.S.O.) in reserve. By the evening of the 30th the enemy's wire on the front to be attacked was reported to be well and sufficiently cut by the artillery. Lanes had been cut in our own wire and blocked temporarily with moveable *chevaux de frise*. Every detail had been carried out and every preparation made: it remained only to put this vast and elaborately organized adventure to the test.

During the final trying period of waiting, those who had opportunity and inclination sought where they could in the early morning hours a short snatch of uneasy sleep, troubled by the continuous whistling and rushing sound of heavy howitzer shells passing overhead and by the faint pervading smell of lachrymatory gas.

The dawn broke fine, but misty, and at 6.25 a.m. there burst forth in supreme and concentrated violence the preliminary bombardment which was to herald the infantry attack at 7.30 a.m. At 7.22 a.m. our Stokes mortars joined in with a hurricane of fire directed upon the enemy's front line.

Shortly before " zero " the assault troops of the 23rd Brigade (2/ Middlesex and 2/ Devonshire) left their assembly positions and crawled towards the German front-line trenches: during this manœuvre, and notwithstanding the intensity of the covering bombardment, they were subjected to a searching fire from rifles and machine guns and sustained many casualties. As soon as our barrage lifted at 7.30 a.m. the two battalions got up and went forward in waves to the assault. The first wave of the Middlesex was caught immediately by yet heavier machine-gun fire and again suffered serious losses. As the succeeding waves came under this fire they doubled forward and before the German front line was reached the original wave formation had ceased to exist. None the less, about 200 of all ranks succeeded in reaching the German positions. Passing over the first line of trenches they entered the second; but after a short fight, during which about half their number became casualties, the remainder were forced back to the German front line. Here under the leadership of Major H. B. W. Savile an attempt was made to consolidate; but though 3½ companies of the 2/ West Yorkshire were sent forward in support of the brigade attack, No-Man's Land had become a death-trap and, except for a few men of " B " Company who joined Major Savile's troops, none lived to reach the German lines. The survivors of the Middlesex held

OVILLERS

on until 9.15 a.m., at which hour those who were still unwounded were compelled to retire to shell-holes outside the enemy front line, where they remained until darkness enabled them to regain our trenches.

The danger from la Boisselle had proved only too real, for the attack of the adjoining 34th Division had failed to reach that village, though immediately to the South of it good progress had been made. The flanking fire from numerous enemy machine guns sited in deep emplacements or tunnels dug into the slopes of the hill on the la Boisselle side of the valley had sealed the fate of the Middlesex attack. Nor were the Devons on the left in better case. They also were caught as they advanced by a terrific machine-gun fire from the front and from both flanks. Few of them reached the German lines; yet, those who did, broke into the hostile trenches and put up a desperate and determined fight there till overpowered by overwhelming odds.

The position on the 23rd Infantry Brigade front shortly after 9 a.m. was that the remnants of these three battalions were out in No-Man's Land, while the 2/ Scottish Rifles had moved forward to take the place of the 2/ West Yorkshire in the forward assembly trenches. At about 9.15 a.m. the artillery barrage was brought back on to Ovillers and the 2/ Scottish Rifles were ordered to stand fast until the situation was cleared up.

In the centre opposite Ovillers both attacking battalions of the 25th Infantry Brigade went forward to the assault with three companies in the front line and one in support. The 2/ Royal Berkshire on the right were at once met by an intense rifle and machine-gun fire and only a small party on the left of the battalion succeeded in entering the German trenches. They were too few to hold their position and were eventually bombed out. By 7.45 a.m. both the Commanding Officer, Lieut.-Colonel A. M. Holdsworth, and the Second in Command, Major G. H. Sawyer, D.S.O., were wounded (the former mortally), and the Acting Adjutant, 2nd Lieut. C. Mollet, took over command. But the battalion had lost too heavily to be able to renew the attack; by 9 a.m. its available fighting strength was little more than a couple of platoons.

The 2/ Lincolnshire got their first two waves over the parapet shortly before " zero," and the third and fourth at " zero " hour. These evolutions were excellently carried out, no hitch occurring, although casualties from machine-gun fire were fairly heavy. As soon as the barrage lifted the three companies assaulted, and though met as they advanced by very severe rifle fire which appeared to come chiefly from the German second line, and by machine-gun fire from the left, succeeded in reaching the enemy's front line. This was found to be thickly manned by

A HURRICANE OF FIRE

troops erupted from the cellars of Ovillers, who greeted the attackers with showers of bombs; but shortly before 8 a.m. our men had captured, after a very hard fight, about 200 yards of the front German trench. Precarious and uncertain touch was gained with parties of the K.O.Y.L.I. (70th Brigade) on the left.

JULY 1916

By this time the support company of the 2/ Lincolnshire, though it had suffered severely from shell fire on its way up to our front line, had joined up with the attacking companies, and the few officers who were left gallantly led their men over the German trench to attack the second line. This valiant attempt failed under the increasing rifle and machine-gun fire, and the battalion thereafter found that the whole of its strength and attention was required in the attempt to consolidate the captured front trench. One frontal attack from the German second line was repulsed; but enfilade machine-gun fire, continual bombing attacks and lack of support gradually rendered the position untenable. At about 9 a.m. the remnants of the battalion fell back as best they could to our own front line, where Colonel Bastard collected together as many men as he could and made a most gallant effort to renew the attack in conjunction with the support battalion, the 1/ Royal Irish Rifles. By this time, however, the hurricane of machine-gun and rifle fire which swept across No-Man's Lane from front and flank made progress utterly impossible. At 10 a.m. Colonel Bastard reported that he had only about 30 men in hand.

Both the 1/ Royal Irish Rifles and the 2/ Rifle Brigade in brigade reserve had moved forward meanwhile in support of the two leading battalions. The leading company, indeed, of the Irish Rifles succeeded in entering the German positions and even pushed forward two platoons to the second line. The remainder of this battalion, as also the reserve battalion, suffered very severely indeed on their way to our own front line from the heavy and accurate barrage which the enemy was then putting up against our forward positions. Progress was made most difficult by the wrecked condition of our trenches, blocked too, as they were, by dead and wounded men and by stragglers from the assault battalions who had been unable to go forward or had been driven back. Of the two rear companies of the Irish Rifles, only about 50 men were able to get as far as our own front line. The 2/ Rifle Brigade was obstructed to an even greater degree and ultimately was ordered to remain *in situ* until a decision was come to regarding its employment.

The course of affairs on the 70th Brigade front on the left had proceeded in very different and, at first, more hopeful fashion. The hostile barrage opened with less intensity and the assaulting battalions, 8/K.O.Y.L.I., and 8/ York and Lancaster, had com-

OVILLERS

paratively few casualties in their first dash across, except on the extreme left where machine-gun fire was heavy. The German wire was found completely cut, offering no obstacle, and within a few minutes of " zero " the German first line trench was captured along the whole front of both battalions. On the extreme left the attacking troops were unable to get further forward, owing to intense machine-gun fire; but in the centre and on the right the attack continued to make progress. The second, or support, line was taken in due course and in the centre our troops reached the enemy's third, or reserve, line in considerable numbers.

These later stages of the attack met vigorous resistance, and the K.O.Y.L.I. on the right had a very severe fight for the second trench, which several times changed hands. The persistence of our troops had been rewarded and some of them had even penetrated the German third line, when, at or soon after 8.30 a.m., the retirement of the centre brigade, already recorded, led to a mistaken idea, possibly even originating with the enemy, that an order had been given for the withdrawal of the K.O.Y.L.I. also. The bulk of the battalion, therefore, together with a number of the 2/ Lincolnshire, fell back to our parapet. There, however, they were collected together and linked on to the 9/ York and Lancaster, who were now coming up in support. The enemy was by this time putting down an intense barrage behind our front line and the supporting battalion had already suffered severely. One company, indeed, lost 50 per cent. of its effectives before leaving its assembly positions. The battalion now encountered severe machine-gun fire which swept No-Man's Land both from right and left; but, together with the re-formed troops of the K.O.Y.L.I. and the Lincolnshire, it pressed onwards and, having joined up with the 8/ York and Lancaster in the centre, advanced there to the second German line, while on the right it recaptured the first line trench.

Thus an hour and a half after the commencement of the assault the position on this brigade front was as follows. The centre of the brigade was fighting in the second and third German lines; but both flanks had been thrown back and were not in advance of the first German line. Each flank was completely exposed. Machine guns from Ovillers and from Thiepval were bringing a cross-fire—momentarily growing more intense—to bear on the captured positions and on No-Man's Land. The enemy's artillery barrage was heavy upon our forward and support trenches. Our own artillery barrage had moved on to the divisional objective and the Heavy Artillery barrage had been lifted for over an hour from the valley. The German infantry and machine gunners who were now unmolested on the flanks, where our other infantry attacks had failed, were

OUR ASSAULT TROOPS ISOLATED

able to remain in their trenches and take deliberate measures for defence.

JULY 1916

The dangers of the position were obvious. Shortly before this hour the brigade reserve battalion, 11/ Sherwood Foresters, were getting ready to leave our trenches; but news having been received from the 25th Brigade that their battalions were back in our own trenches, Colonel Watson was given orders to consolidate the first German trench and hold on to this only. Even this limited task had passed by now beyond the range of possibility. Machine-gun fire, in particular from the Thiepval spur on the left flank, was now so intense and accurate on No-Man's Land that the first two waves of the battalion were only able to advance at all by crawling forwards on hands and knees. Colonel Watson then took his Battalion Headquarters forward, and walking diagonally across the front, collecting men as he went, gave a fresh impetus to the attack by his personal example. But coolness and courage, however splendid and self-sacrificing, could not avail against the hail of lead which beat down incessantly on No-Man's Land. Colonel Watson himself and the officers who accompanied him were wounded, and the attack died out for want of men before the German line was reached.

By 10 a.m. all communication with the troops of the 70th Brigade in the German trenches had been completely cut off. No-Man's Land was impassable everywhere on the brigade front and every telephone line which had been laid across it had been broken. The whole of the brigade was over the front line parapet and our trenches were empty; except for 100 men of the 9/ York and Lancaster on the extreme left who had been prevented by the severity of the German fire from going forward with the rest of their battalion. Nor was the position happier on the rest of the divisional front. On the right the remnants of the 2/ Middlesex, 2/ Devonshire, and 2/ West Yorkshire, were lying out in No-Man's Land, sheltering as best they could in shell-holes or other accidental cover. The 2/ Scottish Rifles and half a company of the 2/ West Yorkshire were in our forward assembly positions and were losing men steadily from the enemy's artillery fire. In the centre, those that were left of the 2/ Royal Berkshire, 2/ Lincolnshire, and two companies of the Royal Irish Rifles, were for the most part similarly isolated in shell-holes in No-Man's Land; save for some few that had got back to our own trenches and certain small parties, perhaps, which it was thought were still holding on in the German front line. Two other shattered companies of the 1/ Royal Irish Rifles and the 2/ Rifle Brigade garrisoned our own front line under the constant punishment of the German guns. To the right la Boisselle, unconquered, still dominated the valley to the North of it. Beyond the

OVILLERS

left of the divisional sector the enemy still held firmly all but the extreme southern point of the Thiepval salient, and from his positions on the higher ground swept the valley beneath and the slopes leading to Ovillers.

It was evident that nothing further could be done without fresh artillery preparation and both General Pollard (25th Infantry Brigade) and General Tuson (23rd Infantry Brigade) had already asked that the artillery barrage might be brought back on to the enemy's third line and Ovillers. The Brigade Commanders were instructed to arrange between themselves the hour at which they wished the new bombardment to commence, and accordingly shortly after 11 a.m. Brig.-General Pollard visited 23rd Brigade Headquarters. As the result of their consultation, reported in due course to III Corps Headquarters, General Pulteney placed the 56th Infantry Brigade (19th Division) at General Hudson's disposal, and orders were issued from 8th Divisional Headquarters for a fresh attack at 5 p.m.

Meanwhile, there was no direct news as to the position of the battalions of the 70th Infantry Brigade who had entered the German lines. At midday General Gordon had reported to Divisional Headquarters that he thought that the 8/ York and Lancaster had got on well, though it was likely that their losses had been heavy, and that the 8/ K.O.Y.L.I. were probably in the German front trench, with the 9/ York and Lancaster somewhere in front of our line and the 11/ Sherwood Foresters either in the German front-line trench or just outside it. To do any good, a fresh attack would have to be made with fresh barrages; but he did not think that it could be delivered by his own brigade nor, indeed, at all until the German machine guns on his left flank had been put out of action. Till this had been done, he could neither communicate with the German front line nor withdraw troops from there.

During the course of the afternoon it became increasingly doubtful whether any of our troops still held on in the German trenches. Artillery observers in the 70th Brigade sector stated that movement in the enemy front line had practically ceased. There was no sign of any British occupation. Rifle fire on the other hand was being directed at one of our aeroplanes from the enemy lines and our wounded men crawling in from No-Man's Land were being continuously sniped. Reports elsewhere were, however, contradictory and on that account there was a considerable disinclination to open a bombardment on the German front line. In view of all the circumstances the G.O.C. III Corps finally cancelled the order for the fresh attack and gave instructions that the 56th Infantry Brigade which had now come up was to be used for holding our front line while the troops of the 8th

COUNTING THE COST

Division re-organized. It was not, however, found necessary to use the 56th Infantry Brigade for this purpose and it was kept in support, the front line being held by the remaining troops of the 8th Division.

JULY 1916

In the meantime the 19th Division was ordered to use its two remaining brigades to attack la Boisselle, in order to form a defensive flank between the 8th and 34th Divisions. These troops as they moved forward through the trench system of the 34th Division were much hampered, as the support troops of the 8th Division had been earlier in the fight on their own front, by the fact that all avenues of approach were still blocked by killed, wounded, and carrying parties. The attack was in consequence delayed and was not delivered till late that night. Some progress was made during the night hours; but la Boisselle remained intact. It was not until the afternoon of the 2nd July that the village itself was entered; it was not until the 4th that it was finally cleared.

While the preparations for this attack were in progress, orders were received—shortly before 7 p.m. on the 1st July—for the relief of the 8th Division by the 12th Division. The relief was carried out during that night and before 6 a.m. on the 2nd July was reported to be complete. The 8th Division Artillery and certain Royal Engineers' units remained in action for some time longer and came under the orders of the 12th Division. The rest of the division withdrew to positions in the rear, the 23rd Infantry Brigade to Millencourt, the 24th and 25th Infantry Brigades to Long Valley.

For the 8th Division, as indeed for all divisions on this northern portion of the battle front, the experience of this day had been bitter, and its losses terrible. In the 23rd Infantry Brigade the 2/Devonshire lost in killed 7 officers and 43 other ranks, and in wounded or missing 9 officers and 372 other ranks. The 2/West Yorkshire sent into action 21 officers and 702 other ranks; 5 officers and 212 men came out. Of the 23 officers of the 2/Middlesex who took part in the assault only one returned unwounded to our lines; out of 650 other ranks 50 alone answered to their names in the early morning of the 2nd July. In the 25th Infantry Brigade the casualty percentages were as follows: 2/Royal Berkshire 53 per cent., 2/Lincolnshire 62 per cent., 1/Royal Irish Rifles 64 per cent., 2/Rifle Brigade (reserve battalion which took no part in the assault) 18 per cent. The casualties to the 70th Infantry Brigade were even more dreadful. The 8/K.O.Y.L.I. lost 24 officers (all who went into action except the M.O.) and 548 other ranks. The 8/York and Lancaster similarly lost all officers who took part in the attack, 18 being killed or missing and 5 wounded. Both the Commanding Officer

OVILLERS

and the Adjutant were among the killed. Among the men the losses reached the appalling figure of very nearly 90 per cent. The 9/ York and Lancaster had 22 officers casualties and 556 among the N.C.O.'s and men. The corresponding figures for the 11/ Sherwood Foresters were respectively 21 and 508. Such figures are the most eloquent testimony to the difficulties of the attack and of the courage with which it was delivered.

Dependent as it was, by the very nature of the terrain, upon the simultaneous success of the divisions on either flank, the task allotted to the 8th Division had indeed been one of the utmost difficulty. The odds against success were yet further weighted, as the event showed, by lack of experience in dealing with the deep German dug-outs, with their underground communications and many exits, and in the proper control of the artillery barrages. As General Pollard cogently remarked in his report of the action of the 25th Infantry Brigade " a bombardment on some given line may be of value in damaging the enemy's defences and preventing supports from being sent up; but if the line in question is 1,000 yards behind the line from which our assaulting troops are being held up, as was the case on July 1st, the position is very far from being satisfactory. To prevent reinforcements from reaching the enemy is but of minor value, if we are ourselves unable to maintain our hold upon the enemy's front line. . . . I consider that, in principle, no barrage should lift, until the infantry concerned have notified that they are ready for it to do so." The knowledge of the proper co-ordination of artillery and infantry in attack was to come; but it was knowledge that was dearly bought.

The troops of the 8th Division were not alone in their misfortune. From all along the battle line to the North of them came stories of experiences exactly similar to theirs; of gallant attacks which in many sectors had pierced deeply into the German positions, there to fail for want of artillery protection and infantry support. Nor in their own sector can they be charged with having failed where other troops might have succeeded. The attack by the 12th Division against Ovillers on the 2nd July, though more limited in extent and aided by the better progress made at la Boisselle, failed as their own attack had done, and in almost identical fashion. It was not till la Boisselle had been taken, and the way cleared for simultaneous assaults from the South as well as from the West, that a foothold in Ovillers was won and gradually extended. Even so, it was not until the night of the 16th July that the last remaining strongholds in the village were captured by the 28th Division and our line carried North and Eastwards towards Pozières.

The failure of the 8th Division on the 1st July was not due to

TEAM WORK

any lack of quality in the fighting troops. "The men went in high spirits, and came out with regret; they are only waiting for our next chance." Such was the verdict of one of their brigade commanders. Nor was their effort wasted, or their sacrifice in vain. They might regret their failure to attain the objectives set them, the many comrades they had lost. If the part they played in the battle as a whole be looked at in its right perspective, there is no need for those who to-day look back upon the action to allow bitterness to colour their regrets.

If " team work " is an essential of successful war, as it most surely is, then all members of the team, whether they themselves got through or merely made the way for others, are entitled to share in the credit of the common victory. Fatal as the day had proved for the divisions on the northern half of the British battle-front, yet from the very cause of their misfortunes the southern portion of the combined attack had reaped swift advantage. The German defence on both banks of the Somme had suffered by the preference in men and guns given to the northern sectors of the threatened front; and while the 8th Division and the divisions to the North of them were fast locked in the enemy's foremost trenches, from beyond Fay to North of Fricourt the Allies were sweeping victoriously across the German lines.

The results of the day's fighting on the whole British battle-front, short though they fell of our highest hopes, none the less represented by far the biggest material gains which had yet fallen to the lot of our armies. The German positions had been carried to a depth of more than a mile on a wide front and the way opened for future successes which, costly as they were in the lives of our gallant but inexperienced troops, yet brought the enemy before the end of the campaign to the lowest ebb he was to touch till the final collapse. The effect upon the Verdun battle was immediate. Within a few days of the launching of the Somme offensive the danger at Verdun had ceased, the initiative had passed to the Allies and the first of their larger objectives had been gained. The divisions which fared so badly on the Ancre front can fairly claim a share in the credit of these considerable achievements.

The infantry brigades of the 8th Division had, on their relief on the night of the 1st/2nd July, retired to positions in the rear of the line at Millencourt and Long Valley. On the 2nd came further orders, in consequence of which the division entrained at Dernancourt and Mericourt and moved via the Ailly–Picquigny area and the Hangest–Molliens–Vidame area to its ultimate destination in the I Corps, First Army. On the 6th July the area behind the Somme, still unspoiled by war and gay with roses though the bombardment thundered in the East, was left behind and the division travelled North by train to the slag heaps of

OVILLERS

Bruay. On the 8th July Divisional Headquarters opened at that town and the division went into billets in the Bruay–la Pugnoy–Allouagne area.

The division remained here—resting and training—for a week when orders were received to take over the Cuinchy sector from the 39th Division, on the night of the 14th/15th July. The relief was completed by 6 a.m. on the 15th July, at which hour General Hudson assumed command of the sector with Divisional Headquarters at Bethune, the 23rd Infantry Brigade and one battalion of the 25th Infantry Brigade in line and the remainder of the latter brigade in reserve in Bethune and Beuvry. On the previous day the division had parted company with the 70th Infantry Brigade which had been ordered to stand fast in the Bruay area, and thence had left to join the 23rd Division. In its place, the 8th Division welcomed back the 24th Infantry Brigade, which had arrived on the 13th July. The complete reassembling of the division was postponed, however, for a few days longer by the detachment on the 14th July of the divisional artillery which on that day was transferred to XI Corps to assist in the operations carried out by that Corps on the 19th July opposite la Cordonnerie Farm. While performing this task, the divisional artillery unfortunately sustained considerable casualties from hostile shelling.

On the 22nd July, in consequence of the withdrawal from line of the 15th Division, the 8th Division took over the Hohenzollern Redoubt sector in addition to the Cuinchy sector, and continued thereafter to maintain two brigades in the line and one in reserve. Divisional Headquarters moved to the Château des Prés, at Sailly la Bourse. The new front was once more a complete change from anything the division had previously encountered.

In the Lys Valley, the division had grown used to waterlogged breastworks, on the Somme to deep trenches searing a rolling countryside still comparatively undefiled; but here the troops found themselves in an area which from an early period of the war had been a cockpit of battle. It had seen the sanguinary French attacks around Vermelles in December 1914 and later the battle of Loos and its many subsidiary operations.

The front was a maze of trenches, old and new, German, French and British; trenches blown in and disused or abandoned and derelict; British fire trenches which had once been German communication trenches; trenches ending in saps 20 yards from the enemy's lines; salients, re-entrants and fortified mine-craters —all reeking of death and stagnation. Any attempt to dig new lines was a task gruesome in the extreme. Bodies were turned up at almost every yard. In many places—notably the captured

"KEEP YOUR EYES IN THE AIR"

Kaiserin Trench—the parapet was largely reveted with corpses, thinly concealed by rotting sandbags through which at night the rats fled squealing from their ghoulish repasts.   AUGUST 1916

Close together though the front lines were, they were often out of sight of each other, the continual struggle of mine and counter-mine having reared great crater mounds of gleaming chalk high along the narrow No-Man's Land. Observation could be kept up only by wretched sentry posts perched at the end of shallow saps on the British lip of the craters, where the sentries crouched to gain the shelter of the crumbling soil, their eyes glued to periscopes pointed at their German counterparts some few feet away. Ever and again a rifle-grenade or a bomb would fall accurately and a post would be wiped out.

At the end of the first week in August there took place a further re-organization of the I Corps' front, as a result of which the Cuinchy sector was handed over to the 32nd Division and the 24th Infantry Brigade, released from Cuinchy, moved to the Quarries sector. A fortnight or so later the responsibilities of the division were increased by the addition of the Hulluch sector, and from this time until the division returned to the Somme in October all three brigades were in the front line.

The Somme battle, indeed, was drawing to itself all the men and guns that could by any means be set free from the remainder of the British line, with the result that the divisions on the defensive fronts were stretched to the utmost. Not that this meant any decrease of activity. As far as possible, the enemy had to be prevented from stripping his own front to reinforce the Somme. Throughout August and September, therefore, the 8th Division carried out many raids; and although in some cases the Germans sought to avoid loss by evacuating their front line, they were not always quick enough to escape our troops, so that in the course of the two months and more a good number were killed and some prisoners taken.

A highly active trench warfare—in all its various manifestations—was, in fact, maintained throughout. Artillery, trench mortars and machine guns were rarely silent; rifle grenades and aerial darts were projected; bombs were thrown; gas was discharged. "Keep your eyes in the air" was the old soldiers' advice to new recruits. Equally unpleasant were the pertinacity, enterprise and accuracy of the German snipers. They made movement in the open dangerous even at a distance of 1,000 yards from the front line, while in the more forward areas their unwelcome activities were helped considerably by the haphazard character of the trench system, many parts of which could be directly enfiladed from the German line. The G.S.O.1 of the division, Lieut.-Colonel H. Hill, M.V.O., D.S.O., fell a victim to

OVILLERS

one of those snipers, being shot dead while inspecting the front line trenches on the 10th September.* The enemy, indeed, had the best of the observation generally; and where the black mass of the Hohenzollern Redoubt rose abruptly from the plain he completely dominated the situation.

Underground warfare also never ceased and mines were sprung by one side or the other almost daily. On one occasion as many as five mines were fired in the course of twenty-four hours; two being blown by us at The Hairpin at 10 a.m.; another at the Hairpin by the enemy at 10.42 a.m.; a large mine by us at Border Redoubt at 3 p.m., and a fourth at the Hairpin by the enemy at 7.35 p.m. By this time, the enemy's early supremacy in this dangerous and nerve-racking form of warfare was being seriously challenged, a challenge which provoked him to many furious raids in the endeavour to blow in our mine-shafts. Even in trench mortar fighting, in which the enemy had long had matters nearly all his own way, the arrival of better weapons in greater numbers, Stokes guns and 2-inch mortars, enabled our batteries gradually to contest the superiority of the German heavy "minenwerfer."

One morning the enemy opened a particularly severe systematic bombardment of our forward lines with his largest type of minenwerfer, in an attempt to silence the British medium and Stokes mortar batteries which were worrying him increasingly. The " shoot " started at about 8 a.m. and went on till lunch, and some idea of the number of rounds fired may be gathered from the fact that over a hundred of the big 180-lb. bombs fell within the frontage of one company of the 2/ West Yorkshire. Considerable damage was done, but the moral effect was not great. The pithiest observation on the bombardment was the remark of a lance-corporal that he pitied " the Boche working-parties who had to carry all those ' minny-woffers ' up the line ! "

So the time passed, full of minor incident but without event of special interest, until the 6th October, when a combined trench mortar and gas attack was delivered all along the divisional front, under cover of which the 2/ Devonshire and 1/ Sherwood Foresters carried out a raid on a larger scale than usual, in the course of which many of the enemy were killed and valuable identifications were secured. This proved to be the closing incident of this period in line; for the next day came orders for relief and on the 12th October the 8th Division handed over the Quarries and Hohenzollern sectors to the 21st Division and the Hulloch sector to the 40th Division. On the 13th October

* His place as G.S.O.1 was taken on the 17th September by Lieut.-Colonel R. E. H. James, Loyal North Lancashire.

BACK TO THE SOMME

Divisional Headquarters moved back to Bethune and the division commenced its move southwards via Abbeville to the Fourth Army, and so to its second entry into the great battle. On the 20th October Divisional Headquarters opened at Bernafay Wood.

OCTOBER 1916

CHAPTER VII

THE SOMME BATTLE: LE TRANSLOY

GREAT changes had taken place in the three and a half months which had elapsed since the division had left the Somme. The attacks of the first three weeks of July had gained for the Allied Armies North of the river a line extending from East of Hem to East of Hardecourt (French) and thence North of Longueval and the Bazentins to the southern borders of Pozières and the old British front North of Ovillers. This advance of over a mile on the French portion of the front and of 2 miles and more in the British sectors had been followed by six or seven weeks of bitter, obstinate, local fighting which on the northern flank had at length given us Pozières and the crest of the ridge to High Wood; had brought our right to Guillemont and the French to beyond Maurepas.

During these latter weeks of slow and stubborn progress the French, entirely relieved of their anxieties at Verdun, had gradually been strengthening their forces on the Somme. The British infantry strength had been maintained by reinforcements from home, and the supporting artillery substantially increased. It had been possible, therefore, in a September of better weather to resume in brilliant fashion the large scale attacks with which the offensive had commenced. Assisted on the British front by a new instrument of war, the tank, the Allies North of the Somme had overwhelmed the fresh system of defences which the enforced delays of August had enabled the enemy to construct. Bouchavesnes, Morval, Gueudecourt, le Sars and Thiepval had been taken, and by the end of September the enemy had everywhere been driven off the ridge which lies between the Tortille stream and the River Ancre. His resistance had begun to weaken, and on our eastern flank there remained but one strong system of trenches in his possession, that which covered the villages of le Transloy and Beaulencourt and the town of Bapaume. It seemed as though, if the weather would only hold, the Allied thrust might yet break through to open country and enable the later development of the offensive to be undertaken against the German entrenched positions to the North of the battle-front.

In the result the situation was saved for the Germans by the advance of winter. The weather broke—and broke so badly that it became impossible to exploit the situation with the necessary rapidity. The delay in our advance gave the enemy time to reorganize his forces, to construct new trenches, and again to stiffen his resistance. In the meantime the condition of the trampled and shell-torn battlefield went from bad to worse. Movement was slowed and was ultimately stopped. So the whole great enterprise of the Somme came to an end, drowned in a sea of mud and rain.

THE CREEPING BARRAGE

It had been to assist in the movement against the le Transloy line that the 8th Division had been brought back to the Somme; but before ever they had left their northern sector the weather had definitely turned. The 19th of October, when the 25th and 24th Infantry Brigades went forward from reserve positions in and about Bernafay and Trônes Woods to relieve two brigades of the 6th Division in the line, was a day of dismal and incessant rain. The tracks were for the most part impracticable and the roads were deep in liquid mud and crowded with traffic. Owing to these conditions the process of relief was a lengthy one; but it was completed during the night of 19th/20th October. At 9 a.m. on the 20th General Hudson assumed command of the front les Bœufs–Gueudecourt, being the left sector of the XIV Corps (Lieut.-General the Earl of Cavan). On the night of the 21st, the 23rd Infantry Brigade took over a portion of the 4th Division's front on the right of the 25th Infantry Brigade, and the whole division was once more in line.

The new sector fronted a long tongue of rising ground which covered the village of le Transloy and was itself dominated by the still higher ground about Saillisel. This latter village formed the key to the whole le Transloy position. Throughout October and well into November, whenever a temporary improvement in the weather offered opportunity for local operations, the French strove to take Saillisel, the British co-operating with them. The neighbouring village of Sailly Saillisel had been reached and gained by the French by hard fighting on the 12th and 18th October. The arrival of the 8th Division in line, accompanied as it was by an all too short interval of better weather with bright days and frosty nights, coincided with the preparations for a fresh attempt on the 23rd October, in which the British XIV Corps (4th and 8th Divisions) was directed to assist by attacking on the French left.

The motive of this operation was to prepare the way for an attack on le Transloy from the South-West at a later date. The tactical objective of the XIV Corps, therefore, was to advance the Corps front to within assaulting distance of le Transloy. The preliminary artillery bombardment was already in progress when the 8th Division came into the line.

Assaulting troops had, by this date, one great advantage in their favour which had been lacking (and so disastrously lacking) when the battle opened on the 1st July. Co-operation between artillery and infantry had in the meantime been greatly perfected and the principle of the creeping barrage had been put into effective operation. The guns no longer fired with a series of lifts, worked according to a pre-arranged time-table and independent of the progress which the infantry happened to have made.

LE TRANSLOY

Instead, the preliminary bombardment by heavy artillery was followed at "zero" hour, not only by a standing barrage on the objectives to be attacked, but also by a creeping barrage beginning close in front of the assault positions of the attacking infantry and going forward at a fixed rate per minute. The new plan demanded a high degree of skill on the part of the artillery, and great confidence in that skill on the part of the attacking troops; but granted that skill and confidence, the infantry clearly stood a much better chance of gaining their objectives.

It was with the benefit of these new artillery developments that the 8th Division made its second entry into the Somme battle; but under conditions of ground and weather which went far to nullify the advantages they gave. Exposure to the wet and cold of the trenches told upon the vitality and stamina of the troops, and movement of any kind in the deep mud and slime in and about the trenches called for great physical effort. To cover a distance of 1,000 yards in going round the line might take an officer nearly two hours of hard going. Fifty yards a minute was the rate decided upon for the creeping barrage in the approaching operation. In such circumstances it was none too slow.

In spite of these difficulties and the labour of getting stores of food and ammunition forward, the arrangements for the attack proceeded steadily. Additional communication trenches were dug during the nights of the 21st/22nd and 22nd/23rd October, and on the latter night the troops detailed for the attack took up their positions. "Zero" hour had been fixed for 11.30 a.m. on the 23rd, but owing to fog it was ultimately decided to postpone the assault until 2.30 p.m.

On the right the 23rd Infantry Brigade (Brig.-General E. A. Fagan) attacked with the 2/ Scottish Rifles (Lieut.-Colonel V. C. Sandilands, D.S.O.) and the 2/ Middlesex (Lieut.-Colonel H. W. E. Finch); their objectives being Zenith and Orion Trenches, and to establish a line beyond. The 2/ West Yorkshire (Lieut.-Colonel J. L. Jack) were in support and the 2/ Devonshire (Lieut.-Colonel A. J. E. Sunderland) in divisional reserve. The 25th Infantry Brigade (Brig.-General J. H. W. Pollard, C.M.G.) occupied the centre with the 2/ Lincolnshire (Lieut.-Colonel R. Bastard, D.S.O.) and the 2/ Rifle Brigade (Lieut.-Colonel the Hon. R. Brand) in line, the 2/ Royal Berkshire (Lieut.-Colonel R. Haig, D.S.O.) in support and the 1/ Royal Irish Rifles (Lieut.-Colonel E. C. Lloyd) in reserve. The objectives of this brigade were to capture the remainder of Zenith Trench and then similarly to establish a line beyond it in touch with the 23rd Infantry Brigade.

PLATE VI

Copyright: Imperial War Museum
EIGHTH DIVISION LIMBERS GOING THROUGH LONGUEVAL, AUTUMN, 1916

FERGUSON'S GALLANT EXPLOIT

OCTOBER 1916

The share of the 24th Infantry Brigade (Brig.-General A. J. F. Eden, D.S.O.) in this operation was limited to the capture by the left battalion (2/ East Lancashire, Lieut.-Colonel G. E. M. Hill, D.S.O.) of Mild Trench and the straightening out of the salient already held by the right battalion (2/ Northamptonshire, Lieut.-Colonel C. G. Buckle, M.C.). The 1/ Worcestershire (Lieut.-Colonel G. W. St.G. Grogan, C.M.G.) were in support and the 1/ Sherwood Foresters (Lieut.-Colonel R. L. Sherbrooke) in reserve.

By 1.30 p.m. the fog had cleared and the attack started to time in much improved weather. The first wave of the 2/ Scottish Rifles was held up temporarily by machine-gun fire; but on the arrival of the second wave the whole went forward and after stiff fighting captured the allotted portion of Zenith Trench. The success was due in a large measure to the great gallantry of three men, 2nd/Lieut. J. Ferguson, Sergt. Hawkins and Pte. Murray. These three bombed their way along the German trench, 2nd/Lieut. Ferguson being responsible for the destruction of three German machine guns. After clearing almost the whole front opposite the battalion this gallant officer was unfortunately killed. Meantime, the attack of the 2/ Middlesex on the left of the 23rd Brigade had been a complete success. Following closely behind our creeping barrage, the troops advanced without check to the German front line and carried it by hand-to-hand fighting in which they inflicted great loss on the enemy. Having captured their respective sectors of Zenith Trench, both battalions pushed on according to programme and by 3.45 p.m. were establishing themselves on a line from 100 to 150 yards beyond it, the Scottish Rifles having also occupied Orion. Two weak counter-attacks, delivered at 3.15 p.m., and 4.15 p.m., were easily repulsed. Efforts were made by the Middlesex to bomb along Zenith Trench towards the left, in order to join up with the troops of the 25th Brigade; but, for reasons which will shortly appear, they failed to gain touch with anyone except a small party of the Lincolnshire on their immediate left.

The assaulting troops of the 25th Infantry Brigade in the centre of the attack had a less happy experience and were only partially successful. At about three-quarters of an hour before "zero" the enemy in the sector opposite the 2nd Lincolnshire could be seen working his way in considerable numbers along Zenith Trench towards his right; his object evidently being to avoid our attack by retiring via Eclipse Trench. Eclipse Trench, however, had been blocked by our fire and, exit being impossible, the German front trench opposite the 2/ Lincolnshire was, as a result, very thickly manned when at "zero" hour the assault began. More unfortunately, the bulk of the battalion found it

LE TRANSLOY

impossible to keep up even with a creeping barrage moving forward at the slow rate of 50 yards a minute, and so gave opportunity for one of those individual deeds of gallantry which even in modern battles so often decide the fate of an attack. The troops had made but little progress across the open when a German officer, with consummate bravery and supreme disregard for death, jumped up and ran along his own parapet ordering up his men. They responded quickly to his appeal and, standing shoulder high above the parapet, met the advancing Lincolnshire with bursts of rapid rifle fire. Except for the one section on the right which, as already described, entered Zenith Trench and managed to join up with the Middlesex, the first wave of the Lincolnshire was cut down by this fire. Their second wave was assailed by both rifle and machine-gun fire, the latter coming principally down a valley from the direction of le Transloy. They, also, did not succeed in reaching Zenith Trench.

The objective of the 2/ Rifle Brigade on the left was a line running from Misty Trench to the angle formed by the junction of Zenith and Eclipse Trenches. The assembly trenches in which this battalion had passed the previous night were newly made and had no dug-outs. No fires had been allowed and the night had been bitterly cold. Nevertheless, the two leading waves advanced in good order close behind the creeping barrage. The right platoon failed to take the strong point at the junction of Zenith and Eclipse trenches; but the check to the 2/ Lincolnshire was no doubt to some extent responsible for their misfortune here. The remainder of the battalion succeeded in gaining and consolidating a line of shell holes running from Misty Trench for about 130 yards in the direction of Eclipse. They had thus gained the major portion of their objectives; but attempts later in the day to bomb southwards so as to close the gap left by the Lincolnshire proved unsuccessful.

In the meantime, the isolated attack by the 2/ East Lancashire on the extreme left of the 8th Division's front had narrowly escaped premature disaster; for information that " zero " had been postponed did not reach Battalion Headquarters until a few moments after the hour originally fixed. Fortunately, the Company Commanders concerned had had some intimation from an artillery F.O.O., and they were actually in consultation as to whether they should attack or not when the hurried message announcing the postponement was received from the battalion. Having escaped this mischance, the assaulting troops went forward at 2.30 p.m. with great dash and, keeping close behind the creeping barrage, entered and captured Mild Trench before the garrison had time to use their rifles. Many Germans were killed in the trench itself, and those of the remainder who escaped

HOIST WITH HIS OWN PETARD

capture fled into our barrage under a hot fire from rifles and Lewis guns.

OCTOBER 1916

Though the German strong point at the junction of Sunray and Cloudy Trenches remained untaken, the second attacking wave of the East Lancashire followed closely on the first and, passing through the latter, attempted to establish themselves on a line beyond Mild Trench. Communication with these advanced troops was, however, very difficult, as they were out of sight over the crest line. Runners invariably became casualties, and when ultimately it was discovered that the two companies were not in touch with each other or with the troops on either side of them, and that they had only one officer left unwounded, Colonel Hill withdrew the survivors to Mild Trench and gave orders that that trench should be consolidated. This was done without any counter-attack by the enemy, other than bombing attacks at the blocks which we had made at the open ends of Mild and Stormy Trenches. These attacks were repulsed by our bombers who, thanks to their knowledge of the mechanism of the German bomb, great quantities of which were found in the captured trench, were able to repulse the enemy with his own weapon.

The situation on the divisional front at about 5.30 p.m. was as follows. The attacks of the flank brigades had been substantially successful; but that of the centre brigade had partially failed, leaving an awkward gap which threatened the safety of our gains. Moreover, the uncaptured portion of Zenith Trench had been strongly reinforced and the supporting battalion of the 25th Infantry Brigade (2/ Royal Berkshire, then in Gusty Trench) had reported that a renewal of the attack was impracticable without a further bombardment. General Pollard reported accordingly to Divisional Headquarters, and, while preparations were in progress for a fresh bombardment, two companies of the 1/ Sherwood Foresters were placed at his disposal from divisional reserve, the remnants of the 2/ Lincolnshire being ordered back to Rose Trench to reorganize.

The enemy also had not been idle. At 6.30 p.m. Colonel Sandilands reported that the Germans were massing for counter-attack in the sunken road on the right flank of the 2/ Scottish Rifles. The enemy was assisted in this manœuvre by the fact that the left brigade of the 4th Division had not succeeded in occupying Dewdrop Trench, although it had advanced and dug in close thereto. Shortly afterwards came a further report that the enemy were shelling Orion so heavily that our men had been obliged to evacuate it. Our own artillery was turned on to both the sunken road and Orion, and General Fagan ordered up his supporting battalion (2/ West Yorkshire) to re-take the lost work. Later in the evening this operation was cancelled and the 23rd

LE TRANSLOY

Infantry Brigade was ordered, on Corps instructions, to make no further attack but to consolidate what they had gained.

Our own arrangements for a renewal of the attack on the 25th Infantry Brigade front were duly completed, and the preliminary bombardment opened at 1 a.m. on the 24th October. "Zero" hour for the infantry assault was fixed for 3.50 a.m., the troops employed being the 2/ Royal Berkshire and the 1/ Royal Irish Rifles in line, two companies of 1/Sherwood Foresters in support, and the 2/ Lincolnshire in reserve. The 2/ Rifle Brigade were to co-operate by renewing their attack on the strong point at the angle of Eclipse and Zenith Trenches.

Unfortunately, on the evening of the 23rd October the weather had again changed and rain fell steadily throughout the night. Realizing that movement was rapidly becoming more and more difficult the assault troops commenced to leave their trenches before "zero," hoping thus to make certain of being close behind the creeping barrage. The manœuvre was without avail. The condition of the ground was so bad that it was impossible to keep pace with the line of bursting shells, slowly though it moved, and the attack was stopped by rifle and machine-gun fire after advancing for about 70 yards. Casualties were, unfortunately, very severe.

All that day the rain continued without a break and though preparations for yet a third attack had been put in hand immediately, its prosecution was for the moment out of the question. Additional troops were detailed to General Pollard and came under his orders as from midday on the 25th October; but the bad weather persisted or grew worse and the date of the attack had continuously to be postponed. Ultimately, after the choice of 3 p.m. on the 29th had proved the signal for another heavy downpour which began at 8 a.m. and lasted all day, the attack was postponed indefinitely. On the same day orders were issued for the relief of the division. During the nights of 29th/30th and 30th/31st October, therefore, the place of the 8th Division in the line was taken by the 17th Division, although the 8th Divisional Artillery remained in action. The weather on the 30th was deplorable and the troops left the line, as they had come into it, to the accompaniment of heavy and persistent rain.

The order postponing the attack of the uncaptured sector of Zenith Trench had stated definitely that, although the attack would not be delivered by the 8th Division, all necessary preparations were to be pressed on, in order that the relieving division might carry out the project at an early date. It was satisfactory to the troops of the 8th Division, in Corps rest area around Treux and Meaulté, to learn that, with the aid of the preparations they had made and in an interval of rather better weather, the work

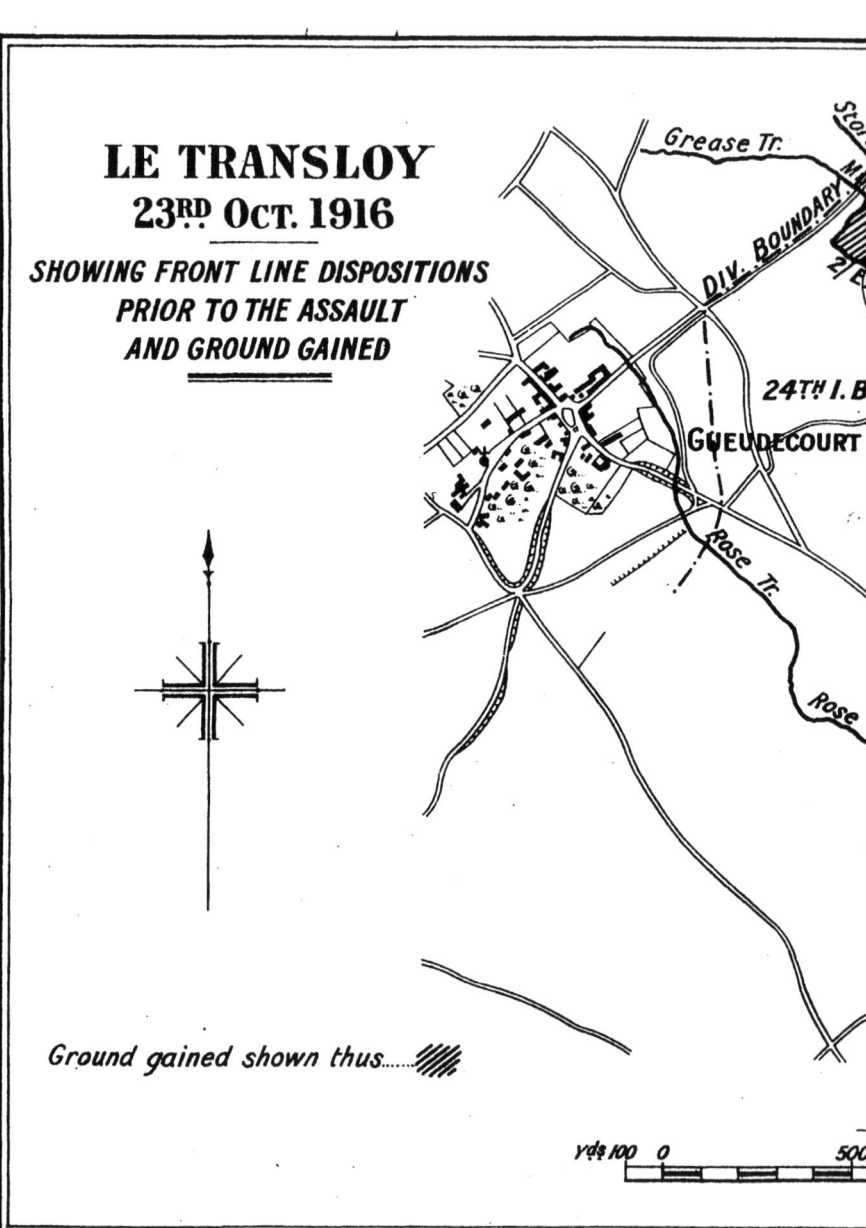

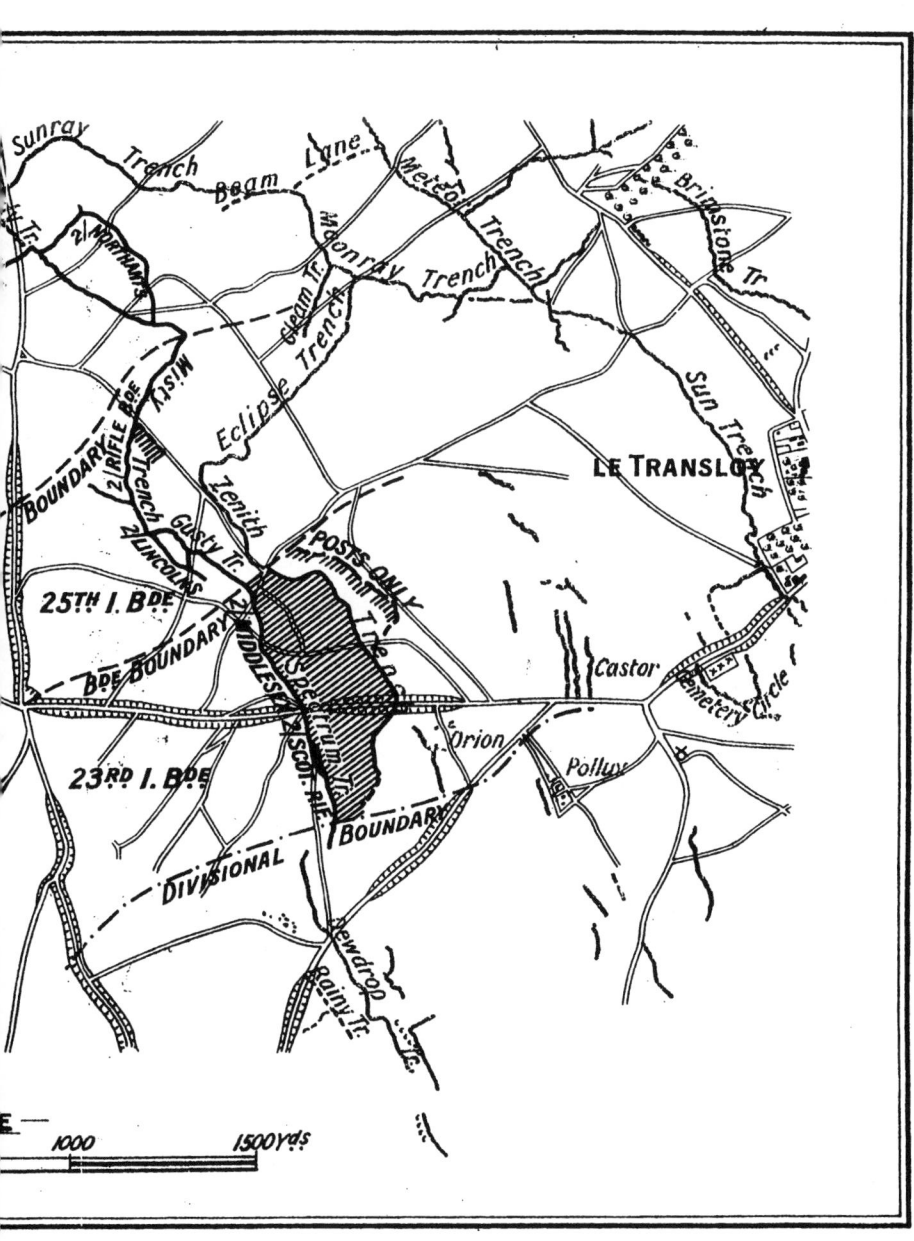

THE WEATHER DECIDES

they had commenced was completed by a successful surprise attack at dusk, without artillery support, delivered by troops of the 17th Division on the 2nd November. The remaining sector of Zenith Trench was captured and, though found to be in deplorable condition, incorporated with our line, and a new trench dug to connect with the shell-hole line to Misty Trench.

NOVEMBER 1916

Although by this date it was only too clear that the larger development of the Somme offensive had become impossible, and indeed that the time had passed for anything in the shape of successful major operations on the main battle front, there still remained the possibility of a more limited exploitation, before winter finally set its seal to the campaign, of the favourable situation of the British forces astride the River Ancre. Here on the 13th November, in a short period of better weather and over somewhat less damaged ground, the battle flared up again in one final, surprising blaze of victory; earnest of what might have been accomplished had more stable weather conditions rendered possible the more rapid and persistent prosecution of the Allied plan of attack.

Until this concluding stroke had been played, the 8th Division remained in the battle area. On relief it had marched back to the XIV Corps reserve area, where on the 2nd November the 2/Rifle Brigade had the honour of being inspected by H.R.H. the Duke of Connaught. Divisional Headquarters were reopened at Treux. After a week's rest the division returned to the line, going on this occasion to the right sector of the XIV Corps in front of les Bœufs. General Hudson took over command from the 33rd Division on the morning of the 8th November, having the 18th French Division on his right and the 17th Division on his left. The 23rd and 24th Brigades were in line, the 25th in reserve.

An interesting and vivid account of a battalion relief carried out at this time, written by 2nd/Lieut. M. McConville, M.C., of the 2/West Yorkshire, gives a graphic picture of the conditions on the Somme front at this date.

"Camp 34 it was called, for no reason as far as we could see other than to fix its position in the monotonous featureless mudscape that lay about Fricourt. Camp it certainly was not—unless one might thus euphemistically flatter the few forlorn groups of rude tarpaulin-sheet shelters which huddled closely together, as though they shrank from the surrounding desolation. One or two bell tents there were, it is true, here and there, but even they looked as unhappy as if they knew themselves to be but insecurely at anchor in the rising sea of mud. Camp 34 was, in fact, little more than a position on the map. Of comfort, in any ordinary sense, it could not even pretend to boast. And yet, it had been comfort enough for the weary battalion that, a few mornings before, had stumbled down from the trenches, worn out as much by the night-long journey as by the previous seventy-two hours of standing waist-deep in the slush of the front line. It had been enough for them

LE TRANSLOY

to know that here at least was a place where a man might throw himself down in luxuriant surrender to the long-denied sleep of exhaustion; where a man might find, on waking, hot food and hot drink; where a man might even, in the daytime, of course, take off his boots.

"In those days, our standard of comfort must have been very largely comparative. If any feeling at all could be said to have arisen above the chronic indifference with which we had come to look upon the possible vagaries of fortune, it was with a certain regret that we quitted the chilly hospitality of Camp 34 and turned our faces once more towards the line.

"The first part of the journey, to Ginchy cross-roads, was comparatively simple. At Ginchy we were to pick up guides from the outgoing battalion, who were to conduct us to Headquarters in the Sunken Road near les Bœufs. Another relay of guides from the companies in the line was to meet us in the Sunken Road.

"An hour or so before dusk on the afternoon of the 10th, the first Company, 'A,'* began to file out. 'B' Company followed at an interval of ten minutes, with Rogerson commanding, and Hall and myself as his subalterns. The other two companies † came behind us at about the same intervals.

"With any luck we had hoped to reach Ginchy cross-roads before the wintry twilight gave place to night. But, owing partly to the waterlogged state of the narrow country lane along which we had to pass, and partly to the volume of traffic bent upon the same purpose, nightfall had overtaken us of 'B' Company more than an hour before we got to the cross-roads. Even then, we found 'A' Company still there.

"The guides had not arrived!

"Not that this was very surprising. Of Ginchy itself literally not a brick remained. Having blown most of it away before its capture, our gunners had carried off the bricks and timber to make their gunpits when they moved up to the new positions. Obliteration of landmarks after this painstaking manner went on all over the Somme at that time. Maps were thereby rendered of no great assistance even in daylight; by night they were worse than useless. Roads could not be distinguished among the numerous tracks ploughed up in the mud; the little villages were often completely blotted out; woods discovered themselves only, as a rule, when one stumbled among their mangled stumps. Small wonder, therefore, when to these difficulties were added mazes of disused trenches, stretches of old tangled barbed wire, desultory but persistent shelling, and over all, the inky blackness of a cloud-laden winter sky—small wonder it was that the unfortunate guides should fail to find, punctually to the minute, a village that had no existence in actual fact.

"That they turned up at all, as they did, not quite two hours late, was an achievement deserving congratulation rather than the lurid abuse with which they were received.

"'A' Company, headed by its guide, set off at once, followed as before, at short intervals by the other three companies.

"Now, to lead a party from Ginchy to les Bœufs was, at that time, a matter of considerable anxiety even in daylight. Men moving in those areas fell naturally into single file mainly because it was the only formation possible in that waste of mud. And such mud! Mud that squelched, and that gurgled, mud that gripped round the ankles like a vice, mud that very often soaked the boots off a man's feet, mud that made movement a painful dragging labour, thin mud, thick mud, neverending incredible mud. Picture it at night. Burdened with heavy equipment, harassed by shell-fire, sliding and slithering in and out of shell-holes and old trenches,

---

* 2nd/Lieut. A. E. Skett commanding.

† "C" Company, Capt. F. H. Hawley; "D" Company, 2nd/Lieut. D. Sankey.

A BATTALION RELIEF

every man in the straggling line straining his whole energy on keeping in sight the vague blur of the man in front, and all, ultimately, following blindly a guide who had only the haziest notion of his whereabouts. Picture the state of mind of the Company Commander who knew himself responsible for the safe arrival of every single member of the party panting somewhere behind him; who, when he 'ducked' for a shell-burst, feared more the cry of 'stretcher-bearers' 'stretcher-bearers' which would mean that one of them was hit and would have to be carried somehow; who shared their distrust of the so-called guide, but for their sakes as well as his own, must feign confidence; who must have neither regard for his own fatigue, nor consideration for their distress, but must use every faculty to get them to the appointed place in the shortest possible time. Now and again when a man sank up to the middle in some unseen hole, the exasperating cry 'Halt in front,' 'Halt in front; man stuck' would hold up the line until he had been hauled out. More often, the guide, giving way perhaps to an uneasiness that had been forcing itself upon him, would come to a standstill, peering anxiously about him; whereupon the line of men, their eyes over-strained in piercing the darkness, would telescope one on top of the other, and, fluently indignant, jostle the harassed guide into moving on somewhere, anywhere, that he might not, by standing still, add to the existing hopelessness the final crowning despair of being 'lost.'

"No man who reached the Sunken Road that night could tell by what ways he had come. It is extremely unlikely that any man was troubled by curiosity on that idle point. Most of us were sufficiently thankful to have emerged at all from the enveloping terror of that wilderness of trackless mud.

"With good reason it was considered unhealthy to linger in the Sunken Road itself. The men were led out some distance to lie about in the sporting safety of the open, while the officers were reporting their arrival to the Colonel.

"Battalion Headquarters was in one of the dug-outs with which the sides of the road were honeycombed. Colonel Jack was already there, having gone on some time ahead of the battalion. It was characteristic of the man that even in that low filthy dug-out, crowded to twice its normal capacity by two sets of occupants, he still preserved an atmosphere of dignity and ordered control.

"The wisdom of avoiding the treacherous shelter of the Sunken Road received unmistakable proof before we moved off again. The Hun dropped along it sudden vicious salvoes of heavy high explosive. The havoc a direct hit would surely have wrought among men crowded together in a narrow space may readily be imagined. As it was, a few were wounded slightly by falling splinters.

"The new guides had by this time attached themselves to their companies. Splitting up into smaller parties of about a platoon each, the battalion set off once more, Arthur * going, as before, with the first party of 'A.'

"This last thousand yards would in the ordinary way have been provided with communication trenches; but the ground had only recently been captured and even if the sodden state of the approaches had not made digging almost impossible, there had not been time to make trenches. We moved up over the open.

"Some enterprising Engineer had laid along the mud a line of white tape. Many a silent prayer of gratitude must have gone up to that unknown benefactor from the men who, following its slender guidance, groped their way through the shell-scarred maze. It is improbable that anyone at the time spared a breath to put a blessing into so many words.

"The atmosphere of that valley behind the front line was significant enough to inspire even the most stolid with respectful haste. It was not altogether the dead, whom the hurrying eye noted, unconsciously, sprawling in the grotesque attitudes in which they had fallen; nor yet the impressively new shell-holes which the accus-

NOVEMBER 1916

---

* 2nd/Lieut. Skett.

LE TRANSLOY

tomed nose registered immediately by the pungent reek of fresh lyddite. It was not altogether the sudden flaring glow of the Verey lights, suspiciously vigilant over No-Man's Land; nor yet the staccato bark of an occasional machine-gun, startling the crowded stillness, its unnaturally bold rat-tat-tat stealing hastily away in subdued, stealthy, listening echoes into the silence which closed in more heavily oppressive than before. It was some of these things and all of them. The night was dark, so dark that a man was invisible at a few yards' distance, and yet for all their haste men crouched low along the tape as though they felt a hundred baleful eyes to be upon them. In that valley, deserted but for their own presence and yet filled with a nameless dread, men had a vividly stifling sense of unbearable crowding.

"My own party of 'B' reached the Support line with only one mishap. A solitary random whizz-bang caught the head of the party from the flank. Whizzing into the ground it went off with a smothered phutting burst. One would have thought it a dud, but that my platoon Sergeant † rose bodily in the air and fell back dead—killed by concussion. His weight, cramping the burst, had collected the whole force of the explosion. We had taken the papers from his body and moved off again before the last man of the party had time to close up and learn the meaning of the temporary stoppage.

"'A' Company lost three men and 'B' had one other killed in the passage of the valley. At about nine o'clock we slid into the Support Trench, and by ten we were in position in the front line.

"The relief had taken nearly seven hours!"

The 8th Division remained responsible for this portion of the front until the 18th November, the line being held by two brigades with the usual alternation of reliefs, and the work of repair and consolidation of the trench system being carried on continuously amid alternate rain and frost. There was no infantry action, except the patrol encounters which formed a normal part of trench warfare; but as may be judged from the foregoing narrative, the condition of the trenches was in itself enough to put an immense strain upon the stamina of the troops. Apart from an unwelcome visit on the afternoon of the 14th November from a squadron of 12 German aeroplanes, which flew backwards and forwards low down over our lines and fired with machine guns at our trenches, the chief incident during this period was the staging of a "Chinese Attack," in order to assist the operations of the Fifth Army against Beaumont Hamel, to which reference has already been made. At the "zero" hour of that attack—5.45 a.m. on the 13th of November—and as part of a general scheme to disguise our precise intentions, an intense artillery bombardment with all the paraphernalia of a creeping barrage was opened by every available gun of the XIV Corps. The barrage was maintained at the utmost intensity for twenty minutes, and thereafter gradually died down during a like period. It produced very little retaliation.

On the nights of the 16th/17th and 17th/18th November the division was relieved in the line by the 29th Division, command

---

* Sergt. (Acting C.S.M.) Chamberlain.

BACK TO REST

of the sector passing at 10 a.m. on the 18th November. The division left the line with the assurance that the infantry at any rate—the divisional artillery were less fortunate—were to enjoy at least a month's rest and training, a respite which had been thoroughly earned.

NOVEMBER 1916

CHAPTER VIII

BOUCHAVESNES AND THE GERMAN RETREAT

AS from midnight of the 19th November the 8th Division came under the orders of the XV Corps (Lieut.-General Sir J. P. du Cane, K.C.B.) and the 19th and 20th were spent in entraining and moving into the XV Corps' back area. Divisional Headquarters were opened at Belloy St. Leonard at noon on the latter day and the units of the division were assembled in the vicinity. The new area was behind the Somme about 16 miles West of Amiens.

The division, part of its artillery excepted, as noted below, remained here resting and training for a period of six weeks. It was a change well earned and, truth to say, much needed. The Somme offensive had left its mark on all divisions that had taken part in it; but on none more than those which on the 1st July had delivered the unsuccessful attacks on the northern half of the battle front. Among them, the troops of the 8th Division had suffered as grievously as any in that first day's fighting. From it they had gone, with the sense of disappointment and failure still heavy upon them, to a long and anxious tour of duty in the trenches; holding a sector which was over-stretched deliberately, in order that other troops might be set free to carry on the struggle on the Somme. No proper opportunity had been given to train and assimilate the drafts with which their depleted ranks had been filled up. The division had had no time to find itself, when it was hurried back to its share in the last and perhaps most trying phase of the advance. Fate had given the troops no direct part in the victories of the Somme; but had dealt out to them a full measure of its bitterest and darkest hours.

It was not then to be wondered at if the move to Belloy St. Leonard found the morale and temper of the division at a low ebb. Few divisions there were in France which at one time or another did not go through a similar experience. Yet there were none—and nothing speaks more for the innate fighting qualities of the British soldier—that failed to respond, and respond quickly and completely, to treatment such as that which the 8th Division now received. Six weeks were no long period of rest after the year which had been gone through; but despite the inclemency of a cold and wet December, they were enough to turn the scale and set the division once more upon the upward grade. All ranks now enjoyed a short interval of real rest, with opportunities for football and other forms of recreation, and later for that systematic training which is impossible while in line, and without which a division cannot hope to become a really effective fighting unit.

The reorganization was thorough and complete; entailing changes in a divisional command and staff worn out by strain and

PLATE VII

LIEUT.-GENERAL SIR WILLIAM C. G. HENEKER, K.C.B., K.C.M.G., D.S.O.

CHANGES IN COMMAND

responsibility passing the limits of human endurance, as well as the incorporation of reinforcements and the re-equipment and training of the completed units.   DECEMBER 1916

On the 4th December, Lieut.-Colonel E. H. L. Beddington, M.C., 16th Lancers, was appointed G.S.O.1, vice Lieut.-Colonel R. E. H. James, and on the 10th, Maj.-General W. C. G. Heneker, D.S.O., A.D.C., took over command of the division from Maj.-General H. Hudson, C.B., C.I.E., who had been appointed Adjutant-General in India. On the 3rd January Brig.-General H. G. Lloyd was appointed C.R.A. of the division vice Brig.-General G. H. W. Nicholson. Changes were also made in brigade commands. On the 11th January Brig.-General C. Coffin, D.S.O., R.E., succeeded Brig.-General Pollard, C.M.G., as G.O.C. 25th Infantry Brigade; on the 14th January Brig.-General H. W. Cobham, D.S.O., took over the 24th Infantry Brigade from Brig.-General Eden, D.S.O.

Early in December, as part of the arrangement whereby the British front was extended southwards to the Amiens–Roye road, the XV Corps had relieved the French in the sectors opposite Bouchavesnes and Saillisel. The front was taken over by the 33rd and 4th Divisions, but each of the four divisions comprising the XV Corps sent two artillery brigades into line. The 8th Division contributed the XXXIII and XLV Brigades R.F.A. (Lieut.-Colonels T. St. A. B. L. Nevinson and C. A. H. Campbell) and three sections of the Divisional Ammunition Column (Bvt.-Colonel F. W. Boteler). On the 19th December orders were issued for the 8th Division to relieve the 4th Division in the left sector of the XV Corps during the nights of 29th/30th and 30th/31st December. The necessary forward moves followed and at noon on the 31st, General Heneker assumed command of this portion of the front with Divisional Headquarters in dug-outs near the Maurepas Ravine. The brigades sent into line were the 23rd in the right (Priez) sub-sector, and the 25th in the left (Saillisel) sub-sector. The 24th Infantry Brigade were established in shelters and huts at Bronfay Farm.

The new front was, in more senses than one, in a very fluid condition, as may be judged from the following account by the 25th Infantry Brigade: "The front line of the sector consists of a series of 'posts' not connected up and with only a little wire out. The ground is a swamp of shell holes and any length of trench dug at once caves in, in spite of revetment. The support line consists of two bits of trench; ... Blue Avenue, the only communication trench, is impassable. Reliefs are carried out across the open. There are two main duckboard walks to the front line. Machine-guns are right forward. Betty Support has a little wire and the next line behind is well wired. The enemy is in

BOUCHAVESNES

very much the same position. He is quite inactive, but carries on intermittent shelling on back areas and roads."

Remedial work was at once put in hand. The front line posts were improved and rendered reasonably dry, many new duckboard tracks were made, and much additional wire put out to complete the very inadequate system which had been found on taking over. The division's spell in line was on this occasion of short duration, the 25th Infantry Brigade being relieved on the 3rd January by the 61st Infantry Brigade, 20th Division, while on the 10th January the 2nd Guards Brigade, Guards Division, took over from the 23rd Infantry Brigade; but short as their time had been, the troops had not wasted a minute of it. The really remarkable improvement they had effected in the condition of the sector earned the express commendation of the XIV Corps Commander, Lieut.-General Cavan, and a very gratifying message of thanks from the Commander of the Guards Division, Maj.-General Fielding, for the "lot of work, and very good work" which the 8th Division had done. Proof of the improving discipline of the division and evidence of the effectiveness of the steps taken to better the condition of the trenches were furnished by the comparative immunity of the troops in line from cases of "trench feet," despite the rigours of the weather.

Upon completion of the reliefs the division, less the 23rd Infantry Brigade, retired again for a further fortnight's training in the neighbourhood of Belloy St. Leonard, Divisional Headquarters being reopened at that place on the 11th January. The 23rd Infantry Brigade moved back only as far as Vaux and Sailly-le-Sec (on the Somme between Amiens and Péronne). Here it was employed in providing working parties (at railheads, etc.) for the XV Corps, a necessary but arduous and thankless task. On the 23rd January Divisional Headquarters again moved forward, this time to Chipilly, preparatory to a return to the line, and during the nights of the 26th/27th and 27th/28th January the division once more took over the left sector of the XV Corps' front, relieving the 40th Division in line. While the division had been in rest, however, the XV Corps had side-stepped to the right, and the 24th Infantry Brigade in the southern sub-sector now found itself with its right at Bouchavesnes with the 25th Infantry Brigade on its left in the Rancourt sector. The 23rd Infantry Brigade remained in divisional reserve. Divisional Headquarters were established in an old French "poste de commandement" just North of Hem Wood.

A very keen frost had set in towards the end of January and it continued practically without intermission during the whole of this tour of duty. All ranks greatly preferred the cold to the never-ending struggle with the mud which had marked their

PRELIMINARY RECONNAISSANCE

previous period in line; but the ground was so hard as to make digging very difficult. On the other hand, movement was facilitated and it became possible to carry up much-needed material without undue difficulty. Opportunity was given, too, for careful and thorough reconnaissance, in which the Divisional Commander and G.S.O.1 took personal part, of the high ground overlooking Bouchavesnes from the East, which the Corps Commander had told General Heneker it would be the duty of the 8th Division to attack and take at an early date. The operation, if successful, would give observation into the German positions about Moislains and the Tortille River, and would in any event have the effect of damaging the enemy and drawing his attention to our portion of the front. With a view to a final training of the troops for this attack, on the 10th and 11th February the division was again relieved and went into General Headquarters reserve with Divisional Headquarters at Corbie on the Somme.

On the southern wing of the old Somme battle-front the opening weeks of the new year had passed in comparative quiet; the northern flank had from the first days of January been the scene of constant and increasing activity. The successful attack astride the Ancre River, by which in November 1916 Gough's Fifth Army had captured Beaumont Hamel and the German defences in that neighbourhood, had left the British forces there in a favourable position for systematic exploitation of the tactical advantages which their advance had given them. Although, therefore, the supersession of Joffre by Nivelle in command of the French Armies had modified the scheme originally agreed upon between Joffre and Haig for the renewal of the Allied offensive in 1917, and in particular had postponed indefinitely the resumption of French attacks on the southern shoulder of the Somme salient, the corresponding British attacks on the northern shoulder astride the Ancre had proceeded according to plan.

In the terrible cold and wet and mud of the early part of January, amid conditions which the troops of the 8th Division who had had experience of the trenches opposite le Transloy could readily appreciate, the operations of the Fifth Army had begun. Step by step, it had triumphed over both the forces of inclement nature and the resistance of a stubborn enemy. Position after position had been gained by the skilful use of ground and close co-operation of artillery and infantry. As our troops progressed, they were heartened by a growing conviction that their action was anticipating and hastening the decision of the German Higher Command to evacuate a wide area of territory and retreat to what was already becoming known as the Hindenburg Line.

On the night of the 23rd/24th February, while the 8th

BOUCHAVESNES

Division was in rest, the enemy, following the Fifth Army's attack of the 18th February opposite Miraumont, began on a front stretching from Gueudecourt to Gommecourt his first movement of retreat; but long before this date, despite the persistent incredulity of their Allies, the British Command had become persuaded that a far greater withdrawal was in course of preparation. Holding this opinion, and realizing the difficulties which would ensue were the enemy allowed to postpone his retreat until the eve of the main Allied offensive planned to take place in April, it was natural that the British Command should desire that everything possible should be done to hustle him and prevent him from carrying out his projected movement at his leisure and in his own time. The utmost activity on the part of all the British forces on the Somme front became all the more important when it was found that our Allies refused to credit the possibility of a German retreat.

It was this need for exerting pressure on the enemy, even more than the improvement of our local position, that provided the reason for the projected offensive of the 8th Division. The ten days in reserve were devoted to careful preparations in which the long hours of reconnaissance, spent in crawling and lying in the open amid the snow, bore fruit. A faithful reproduction of the German trenches was marked out in the training area, and the attack under an artillery barrage (represented by flags) was rehearsed by battalions, brigades and by the division. Forming-up on tapes was practised both by day and during darkness.

A considerable amount of preliminary work in our own front-line sectors had been necessary; for example, two Brigade Headquarters, two Battalion Headquarters, battery positions, aid posts, platoon dug-outs, etc., had to be constructed, the 60 cm. railway extended for some 600 yards, and gun emplacements prepared at closer range for wire cutting. A beginning had been made by the division during its previous tour of duty, and the work was carried on with energy and skill by the 4th Division which took over on the 11th February. The good work done by this division was of real assistance, for the severe frost was a very serious handicap to any work involving digging. Then on the 20th February came the thaw, rain following it, with the result that work became even more difficult. So bad was the condition of the ground that several men of the 4th Division were drowned in the course of their relief, when the 8th Division moved back into line on the 21st February. The final preparations were much hindered, and in consequence the attack which had been originally fixed for the 27th February had to be postponed until the 4th March. Even so, it was not possible to complete entirely the preparatory work.

SANS BREECHES!

The deadly adhesiveness of the mud was such that many instances occurred, not only of single men, but even of small parties, getting completely stuck and often not being found until too late. On one occasion—a fine sunny morning—two or three senior artillery officers came up to the Headquarters of the infantry battalion in line to observe. They went up to what was called the support line, but were warned before they set out that the communicating trench was impassable. Movement in the open was of course out of the question. In a short time they came back, having been literally pulled out of their boots and with their feet cut and bleeding. On another occasion, a private soldier walked into Battalion Headquarters late at night, minus boots, socks, trousers and pants! He had fallen off his " island " in the trench and had to be cut out of his nether garments before he could be rescued!

As already indicated, the tactical objective of the operation was to gain the German positions on the " hog's-back " overlooking Bouchavesnes which would give us a wonderful view over the Moislains Valley up to Nurlu, and over the whole of the enemy's back areas in that district. At the same time, we should deny to the enemy the close observation he now enjoyed over the Bouchavesnes Valley and the valley that runs North-East of it towards Rancourt. To secure these results it was necessary to take two lines of trenches on a front of about 1,200 yards, East and North-East of Bouchavesnes.

The improvement of the local position was not, however, the only advantage which would follow from the capture of these trenches. They formed part of the powerful system against which the French attacks had worn themselves out at the end of 1916. A breach made in them could not fail to affect the security of the German defences North of Péronne, and so hasten the preparations which the enemy was believed to be making for the evacuation of the whole Somme area.

Two infantry brigades were detailed to carry out the operation. On the right, the 25th Infantry Brigade (Brig.-General C. Coffin, D.S.O.) with a frontage of about 300 yards and one battalion (2/ Royal Berkshire, Lieut.-Colonel R. Haig, D.S.O.) in the front line; on the left, the 24th Infantry Brigade (Brig.-General H. W. Cobham, D.S.O.) with two battalions (1/ Worcestershire, Lieut.-Colonel G. W. St. G. Grogan, C.M.G., and 2/ Northamptonshire, Lieut.-Colonel C. G. Buckle, M.C.) on a front of about 800 yards. The 2/ Lincolnshire (Major J. A. A. Griffin) and the 1/ Sherwood Foresters (Lieut.-Colonel R. L. Sherbrooke) were detailed to provide " moppers-up " and carriers to both brigades. No intensive preliminary bombardment was undertaken, as the destruction of the trenches to be attacked

BOUCHAVESNES

was not desired. They were to be held after capture. The artillery, provided from outside as the 8th Division artillery was at this date in action on another part of the front, had none the less plenty to do. Besides wire-cutting, strong points in the enemy's trench system, trench junctions, machine-gun emplacements and the like, were dealt with by our guns for several days prior to the attack. The strength of the division in machine guns was increased by the addition of the 120th Machine-Gun Company, 40th Division, which in conjunction with the three companies of the 8th Division put down a most effective barrage on the front and flanks of the assault.

Owing to the climatic difficulties it had not been possible to construct assembly trenches in the time available. The two leading waves of assault had, therefore, to form up in our front and support line posts and the remainder on five parallel lines of tapes. " Zero " hour had been fixed for 5.15 a.m. on the 4th March, and by 3.15 a.m. the attacking troops were correctly formed up on their tapes in complete silence. A novel experiment was the issue to the assault troops of chewing gum which seemed not only to stop the men from coughing as they waited shivering on the tapes, but also to give them something to distract their minds. The moon was nearly full and did not set until half-past four; but there was fortunately a slight mist which must have been sufficient for the purpose of concealment, for both artillery and infantry on the German side were very quiet until " zero " hour. The going, too, had been greatly improved by a slight frost.

Aided, no doubt, by these circumstances, but as a result, chiefly, of the care and foresight displayed in its planning and preparation and in the orders and instructions issued,* the attack went forward with vigour and confidence from the start and achieved complete success. Slightly before 5.15 a.m. the barrage descended, and lifted five minutes later. Following close behind the creeping barrage, the assaulting troops captured their first objective (Pallas Trench) with little loss in strict accordance with schedule. A small section of trench, at the junction of the two brigades, which had been overlooked in the assault, was taken with 20 prisoners by the 2/ Northamptonshire battle patrol platoon under Lieut. Jarvis before the reverse fire opened by its garrison on " C " Company 2nd Northamptonshire (Lieut. Bird) could do much damage. Leaving Pallas Trench to be consolidated by the " moppers-up," the attacking troops continued their advance and with similar success gained the second

---

* So excellent were the instructions and orders issued by the G.S.O.1 of the division deemed to be by G.H.Q. that at a later date, when the Americans entered the war, the division was called upon to send complete copies to the United States for the use of the U.S. Staff Training College.

SUCCESS SWIFT AND ASSURED

objective (Fritz Trench on the right, Pallas Support on the left). So splendid was the dash and vigour of the attack that in one place, where Pallas Support had been so destroyed by our artillery as to be no longer easily recognizable in the half light, part of " B " Company, 2/ Northamptonshire (Capt. Fergusson) swept past it and on to the next German line (Fritz Trench). Here they killed several of the enemy, captured a machine gun and bombed a dug-out and then, discovering from the position of our barrage the error they had made, withdrew in good order to Pallas Support.

MARCH 1917

Swift as our success had been, the enemy fought stubbornly, and but for the excellent co-operation and determined fighting of the 1/ Worcestershire and 2/ Northamptonshire at the key of the position, called " The Triangle," the result might have been very different. Seeing that Lieut. Bird's company had lost too heavily to be able to hold the whole of this important point, the left company of the Worcestershire immediately extended their line to the left and took over a part of the defence. The attack of " C " Company was also materially assisted by an act of conspicuous gallantry performed by Lce.-Corporal Pickard and Pte. Ette of that company. These two rushed an enemy machine gun which was holding up the attack, putting the gun out of action and killing or capturing the gun team. Another act of great gallantry was performed by Pte. H. Bamford of " B " Company, 2/ Northamptonshire. In the fight for the last strong point holding out on the front of this battalion, Pte. Bamford while working his Lewis gun was struck in the face by a shell splinter and lost the sight of one eye; but he refused to leave his post and half-blinded and in great pain, worked his gun for two hours after he was hit, until wounded a second time.

Nothing could stop troops attacking with such spirit, and the excellence of the arrangements for their support ensured that their gains should not be lost. A German battalion assembling for counter-attack in the wood North-West of Moislains was broken up by the machine-gun barrage, losing some 400 killed or wounded, and meanwhile the arrangements made for " mopping-up " had dealt faithfully with any Germans overlooked by the assault troops. The whole of our objectives having been taken without failure or hitch at any point, the work of consolidation was put in hand at once, and with a minimum of that temporary confusion and uncertainty which so often opens the way to counter-attack and so mars an otherwise successful operation.

In the course of the day some five counter-attacks were in fact launched by the enemy across the open; but the speed with which our troops had established themselves, and the excellent observation obtainable from Fritz Trench, allowed all of these

BOUCHAVESNES

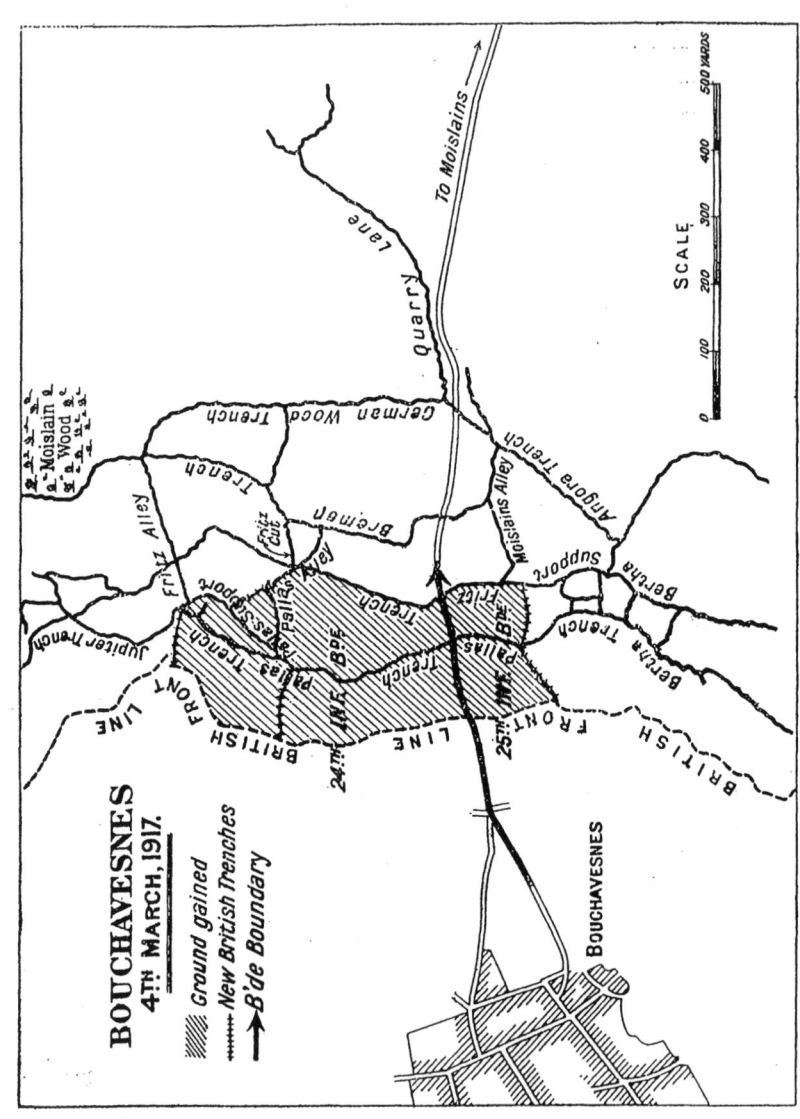

GALL BLADDER CUT

to be dealt with and beaten off by machine gun, Lewis gun and rifle fire. The enemy also made several vigorous attempts to re-enter his lost positions at points where German communication trenches led away from Fritz Trench. These were defeated in the same resolute manner in which our attacks had been made. Sergt. Parker of " D " Company, 2/ Northamptonshire (Capt. Lane, M.C.) distinguished himself by holding a post on the extreme left for half an hour single-handed, until relieved by a party of the Sherwood Foresters. At another point, where a German post existed close up to the line of the captured trench, much hard fighting took place throughout the day, repeated bombing attacks being launched by the enemy. As soon as the situation had become clear, our artillery was turned on to the German communication trenches which led up to the disputed area. The strong point being thus isolated, its garrison was soon dealt with and by dusk the enemy, at length thoroughly beaten, gave up the struggle for the day.

In addition to these unsuccessful infantry reactions, hostile shelling of the captured trenches, No-Man's Land, our former front line and of the area between that and Bouchavesnes village, was carried on steadily throughout the day, and it was to this that we owed the greater part of our casualties. It caused, also, much difficulty and delay in maintaining communication between forward battalions and Brigade Headquarters. The weather conditions preceding the attack had made it impossible to lay down lines of buried cable and in consequence telephone lines were constantly being cut and could not be repaired fast enough. In these circumstances, carrier pigeons were of great assistance and proved a most valuable means of communication. Communications were further assisted, and the situation of our troops in the captured area greatly improved and strengthened, by the construction during this day of two communication trenches from our old front line to Pallas Trench. These trenches were dug by the 22/ Durham L.I. (Pioneers) (Lieut.-Colonel C. B. Morgan, D.S.O.) under heavy fire; but, despite this, the work was thoroughly well done; a very notable performance. One of these communication trenches was known as Gall Bladder Cut, and Colonel Morgan, who came through his hazardous experience untouched, afterwards caused much amusement in the division by describing how he had suffered this "cut" without harm.

Shelling continued during the night of 4th/5th March, causing the garrison of the captured trenches considerable loss. The prolonged activity of the enemy's artillery was followed shortly after 4 a.m. by a powerful infantry attack directed against the extreme right of our line. The assault succeeded in capturing

BOUCHAVESNES

the block which protected the southern limit of our line, together with about 100 yards of Fritz Trench to the North of it, the German infantry attacking both up the trench from that part of it beyond our block and also across the open. During this attack Capt. A. H. Hanbury Sparrow, D.S.O., who had been in command of the assault troops of the 2/ Royal Berkshire and had shown conspicuous gallantry throughout the operation, was wounded for the second time and had to withdraw.

The enemy was not allowed to enjoy his triumph long. A counter-attack was immediately organized by the Berkshire and was carried out with complete success by " C " Company (Lieut. H. E. W. Prest) who, supported by Capt. Cahill with rifle grenade fire from Pallas Trench, bombed their way along Fritz Trench and recovered the whole of the lost ground.

The enemy's artillery fire continued to be heavy throughout the 5th March, and at 7.30 p.m. he was seen to be forming up for a further attack against the right of the 25th Infantry Brigade. An " S.O.S." call was sent up to our guns and the threatened attack was dispersed by our artillery and machine-gun barrages before the Germans had left their own trenches. No further infantry action was taken by the enemy and, after further heavy shelling on the 6th March, the activity of his artillery gradually died away. Thereafter he acquiesced in his defeat, having, it may fairly be assumed, made in his plans for a general withdrawal the readjustments necessitated by our successful action. Certainly the violence and persistence of his attempts on the 4th and 5th March to recover the ground which we had taken from him make it evident beyond question that it was no part of his plan to retire at this juncture from his powerful positions opposite Bouchavesnes. By forcibly driving him from them the 8th Division had seriously disarranged his programme.

The operation had been completely successful in achieving its immediate objects, to deprive the enemy of his close observation over our own positions and gain for ourselves wide observation over the German trenches and gun positions in the Moislains valley. At a cost of casualties, most of them incurred from shell-fire subsequent to the attack, amounting to 56 officers and 1,081 other ranks, we had captured 3 officers and 214 other ranks and 7 machine guns. Furthermore, the losses inflicted on the enemy had been exceedingly heavy, as was evidenced not only by the bodies found in the captured trenches, but by the large numbers of German dead found within the area covered by our barrages, when at a later date we followed up the enemy in his retreat.

In addition, we had broken through an important trench system that had defied the attacks of our Allies at the close of

WELL-EARNED CONGRATULATIONS

1916, and our position astride it was a direct menace to the defences of Péronne and to the river line South of that town. The new situation was bound to have its effect upon issues far wider than those involved in the comparatively small area that had passed into our possession. Taken in conjunction with the continued successes of the Fifth Army, which on the 10th March captured Irles and so came in contact with the defence system known as the Loupart line, which formed the northern continuation of the line that the 8th Division had just pierced, it brought the enemy under the necessity of an immediate decision. Either he would have to stand and fight at the risk of being involved in a general engagement, or he must break away at once and proceed with his major scheme of withdrawal at least a fortnight before he had intended to do so.

MARCH
1917

For its contribution towards this important result the division obtained the merited award of a message of congratulation from the Commander-in-Chief. In forwarding it to XV Corps, General Rawlinson, the Army Commander, added also his own congratulations and continued: " The very careful preparations that were made and the gallantry of the three battalions engaged, coupled with the effective barrages and counter-battery work, reflect great credit on all concerned in the planning and execution of the enterprise."

The effect of this operation and of the more prolonged and considerable offensive of the Fifth Army rapidly made itself apparent. The conclusions which the British Higher Command had drawn from the facts and indications before them were to prove well founded, and the capital which we had invested in the Somme adventure in the previous summer and autumn was now to receive a deferred dividend. Not, it is true, so convincing a payment as would have been secured had we been able to enforce it at the time—for the enemy was now retiring with his forces intact, having had the winter season in which to make his preparations. He was now conducting his retreat under the best possible conditions of weather; leaving behind him a thawed and swamped battle area in exchange for conditions of terrain which improved progressively the farther he moved East. None the less it was a payment which did result in the abandonment of hundreds of square miles of French territory, and one which heartened those who regarded the struggle solely in the terms of painful inches measured on the map into a belief that it heralded the beginning of the end. It was, moreover, thanks to the active and continued pressure of the British Army, in which the 8th Division had so successfully played their part, a payment made not in the enemy's own time but under instant threat of execution. The gain to the British Army, now mounting its main Arras

THE GERMAN RETREAT

offensive, in having the situation declared and stabilized well before its preparations were completed, can hardly be overestimated.

On the night of the 7th/8th March the 23rd Infantry Brigade relieved the 121st Infantry Brigade of the 40th Division in the trenches, and with three brigades now in the line (25th Infantry Brigade in Quarry Farm sector, 24th Infantry Brigade in Bouchavesnes North sector, and 23rd Infantry Brigade in Rancourt sector) the 8th Division began to feel its way forward. The enemy was definitely in retreat on the whole front from the neighbourhood of Soissons to Arras. The attack of the Fifth Army on the Loupart line, intended for the 14th March, was never delivered. On the night of the 12th/13th March patrols of the Fifth Army found the powerful trench systems opposite them unoccupied and the whole Allied line, the French now alive to the situation, shook itself into motion to follow up and press upon the retreating enemy.

On the 8th Division's front patrols were out constantly, feeling for the enemy, and the first indications of withdrawal were instantly followed up. The trenches leading East from those recently captured were first occupied (on the 14th March); and on the following day two further lines of trenches—Bremen and German Wood—came into our possession. In the new northern sector of the divisional front our troops worked their way right through the southern portion of St. Pierre Vaast Wood to its eastern limit. Progress continued steadily in the wake of the patrols and by the 18th our troops had advanced to the line of the Canal du Nord, having gone through the town of Moislains which the enemy had vacated.

On this day at dawn the 2/ West Yorkshire (Lieut.-Colonel J. L. Jack, D.S.O.) moved out of their trenches to take up the position of outpost battalion. " After all the weary months in line, the order to move forward as outpost troops and co-operate with the Wiltshire Yeomanry was a tonic indeed. The bonds of trench warfare were burst and as the battalion moved in fours over the old No-Man's Land between Rancourt and St. Pierre Vaast Wood there was not a man who did not feel a thrill of elation, increased by the cheering which broke out as we passed the front line trenches still manned by the division. The strength of the battalion was only 17 officers and some 280 other ranks; but what did that matter? We were after the enemy in the open, for the first time, so far as we were concerned, in the war. There was little time to take stock of the ground as we moved forward; but the briefest glance was enough to show the terrible slaughter which the French had suffered at the end of 1916. The wide No-Man's Land up to St. Pierre Vaast Wood was carpeted with

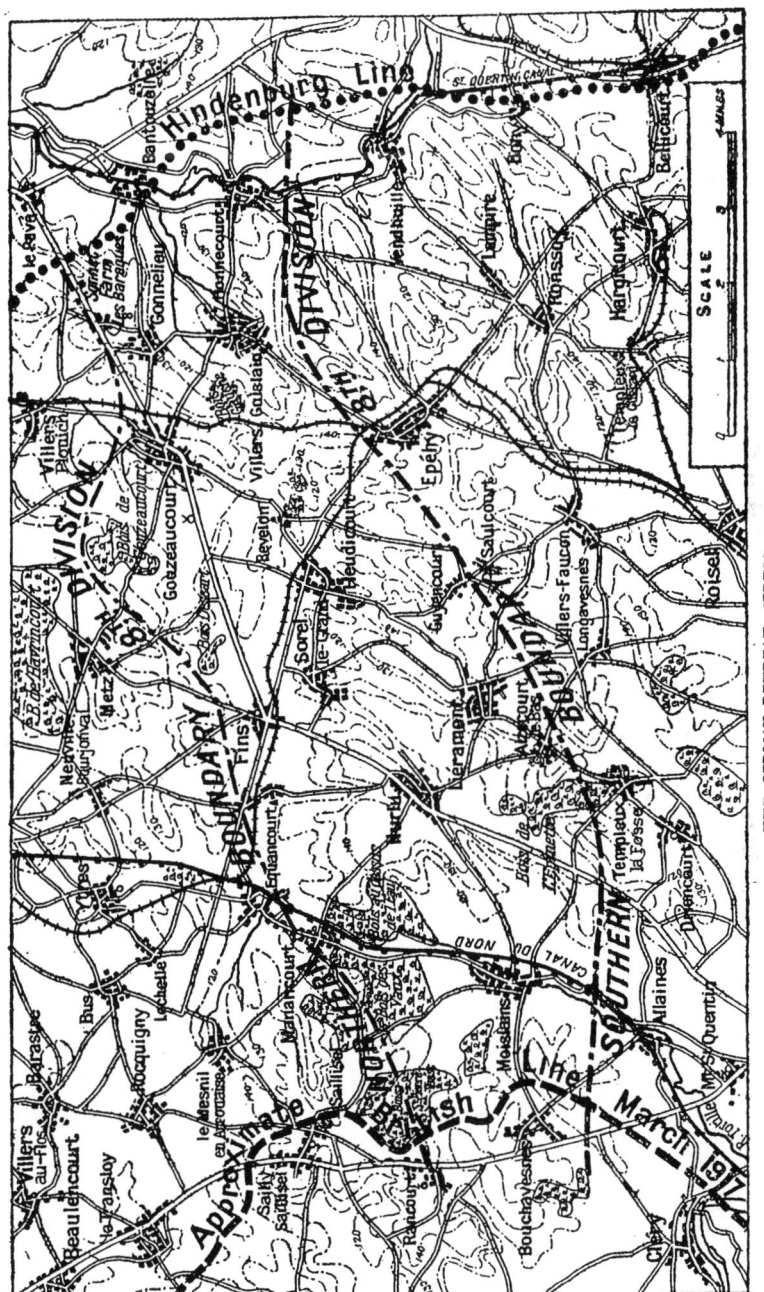

THE GERMAN RETREAT, SPRING, 1917.

THE GERMAN RETREAT

horizon-blue uniforms as far as the eye could see."* On the following day the whole of the divisional outpost line was entrusted to one brigade only, the 23rd,† the 25th Brigade being held in support.

The advance was continued on the 20th March in this new formation, and at dawn on that day the 2/ West Yorkshire entered Nurlu and found it empty. Aizecourt-le-Bas was occupied on the 22nd by an advance post of the 2/ Devonshire under 2nd/Lieut. L. Pertwee and on the 23rd we obtained proof that we were pressing inconveniently closely upon the enemy's heels; for on that day he made a resolute but unsuccessful attempt to regain the village. Next day, the 5th Canadian Cavalry Brigade (Brig.-General the Rt. Hon. J. E. B. Seely) arrived on the divisional front and acted, with conspicuous success, as an advanced screen to the infantry. By skilful use of ground and cover and with bold flanking movements, often carried out at the gallop, the mounted troops ousted the enemy from positions in which he sought to stand and pressed him still more closely. On the 26th the cavalry attacked and occupied Equancourt, subsequently handing it over to the 25th Infantry Brigade, who had relieved the 2nd Guards Brigade in that sector two days previously. Pursuing the same tactics, the Canadians occupied on the 27th the villages of Liéramont and Guyencourt, taking the latter village and ridge at the gallop. Liéramont they gave over to the Devons and Guyencourt to the 2/ Scottish Rifles, whose good work in support of the cavalry received the special thanks of General Seely.

On the same day the 2/ Lincolnshire repulsed with heavy loss a German counter-attack upon Equancourt. The enemy, in fact, was now drawing near to the Hindenburg line—in the northern sectors, indeed, the troops of the Fifth Army had already reached its outer defences—and he was beginning to cling to his positions with more determination. Counter-attacks multiplied along the whole front of advance and on the 28th and 29th our reconnoitering parties found the villages of Heudicourt, Sorel-le-Grand and Fins held strongly.

It was, therefore, decided that a combined attack should be launched by both brigades against these places on the 30th March. From the centre of our outpost line about 1,000 yards South of Sorel, a fine view could be obtained over the country in

---

* Capt. S. Rogerson, 2/ West Yorkshire.

† The 23rd Infantry Brigade had on the 12th March changed its Commander, Lieut.-Colonel G. W. St. G. Grogan, C.M.G., commanding the 1/ Worcestershire, being promoted to the Brigade Command *vice* Brig.-General E. A. Fagan, D.S.O. General Grogan was later succeeded in the command of the battalion by Lieut.-Colonel G. M. C. Davidge.

SOREL-LE-GRAND

front. Fins, Sorel-le-Grand and Heudicourt could be seen lying in a basin, on the far side of which the ground rose to a clearly defined rim. Along the skyline could be made out Jacquenne Copse to the eastward, and further North two other small woods and Revelon. On the northern edge of the basin Dessart Wood was clearly outlined. It was evident that the way to take the villages was to capture the rim of the basin first and then proceed to collect what it contained.

MARCH 1917

Adopting this idea General Grogan's and General Coffin's brigades, assisted by the XV Corps Cavalry* under Lieut.-Colonel the Hon. E. Thynne, were ordered to carry out the operation on the 30th March with the 2/ Devonshire and 2/ Middlesex (Lieut.-Colonels A. J. E. Sunderland and J. H. Hall) and the 2/ Rifle Brigade and 1/ Royal Irish Rifles (Lieut.-Colonels the Hon. R. Brand and E. C. Lloyd). Each infantry brigade commander was allotted four sections of 18-pounders and one section of 4·5-inch howitzers, as well as 24 machine guns. These guns were to provide covering fire, and it was arranged that Verey lights fired by the attacking troops should be the signal for them to lift their fire. The remainder of the divisional artillery, with the CLXXXI Brigade R.F.A. (40th Division) attached, the whole under Brig.-General H. G. Lloyd, co-operated. The 20th Division on the North made arrangements to protect the left flank of our advance, and the 48th Division on the South were to keep the northern and western ridges of Pezière and Epéhy under artillery fire.

The attack was opened at 4 p.m. on the 30th March, when the 2/ Rifle Brigade debouched against Dessart Wood from the northern outskirts of Fins, which village had been rushed by them at dawn. Covered by the fire of their guns, the troops soon broke down the resistance they encountered and cleared the wood, the enemy taking to their heels. Sending up their Verey lights to tell the guns to lengthen range, the infantry established posts along the eastern edge of the wood, in touch with the 20th Division.

As soon as the Rifle Brigade had reached the edge of Dessart Wood the 1/ Royal Irish Rifles, who at dawn had rushed Sorel-le-Grand in like manner to that in which Fins had been taken, attacked and captured the plateau 1,500 yards to the South-East of the wood, covered by their artillery and by the fire of the 2/ Rifle Brigade.

In the meantime, the cavalry had advanced from the shelter of Guyencourt and, covered by the fire of two Hotchkiss guns, took Jacquenne Copse, which they handed over to a platoon of the 2/ Scottish Rifles, and advanced to the sunken road beyond,

* The Canadian Cavalry had left this part of the front on the previous day.

THE GERMAN RETREAT

where they were checked by artillery and machine-gun fire. By 4.30 p.m., however, the attack of the 25th Brigade had progressed sufficiently to warrant the launching of the assault upon Heudicourt, the East and West sides and southern half of which was being barraged by our guns. The 2/ Devonshire approaching from the South-East and the 2/ Middlesex from the West had crept up as close to the barrage as possible and fired their Verey lights. The guns lifted on to the northern end of the village and the infantry rushed in. The advance was too rapid to be stayed by the wild and erratic fire of those of the garrison who awaited the coming of our men, and, the guns having lifted once more in response to their signals, the two battalions pushed through the village and joined hands at its northern extremity.

Capt. Clayton, of the Middlesex, then pushed out skirmishers towards Revelon to which the guns had already turned their attention, and covered by the artillery the rest of Capt. Clayton's company followed the skirmishers by short rushes. Revelon and the neighbouring copse were captured after stiff fighting in which a large number of Germans were killed. This enabled the cavalry and a company of the Devons to advance against and capture Railton,* and thereafter to push on to the second copse which they entered from the South at the moment when the Middlesex reached it from the North. The German garrison was taken between the hammer and the anvil, and streamed out of the wood in a north-easterly direction under the fire of our 18-pounders. By 7 p.m. the whole of our objectives were captured, with 28 prisoners and 5 machine guns, and our line had been advanced over 6,000 yards on a front of 3 miles, at a cost to our own troops of 12 killed and 56 wounded. The German killed numbered at least 200.

The success of the troops engaged in adapting themselves after so many months of trench warfare to what was in the nature of an open warfare attack was extremely gratifying, and earned the warm commendation of the Divisional Commander.

The beginning of April found the Fifth Army well up to the main Hindenburg line defences at all points, the capture of the last of the enemy's covering positions in the sectors extending from Doignies to Hénin-sur-Cojeul being completed on the 2nd of the month. The ground was already cleared for the main British spring offensive opposite Arras and the Vimy Ridge, and thanks to General Gough's unceasing pressure, assisted as it was on the Fourth Army front by such successful operations as that of the 8th Division at Bouchavesnes, it had been cleared in time for our offensive to be mounted by the scheduled date. South of

* 700 yards South of Revelon.

PLATE VIII

Copyright: Imperial War Museum
GERMAN RETREAT, MARCH, 1917
TREES FELLED ACROSS A ROAD NEAR PERONNE

Copyright: Imperial War Museum
GERMAN RETREAT, MARCH, 1917
A VILLAGE IN THE DEVASTATED AREA

FURTHER SUCCESSES

Doignies, however, the enemy still held a number of villages and covering positions in advance of the main Hindenburg system. In order to assist our troops engaged in the main battle astride the Scarpe, it was important that these should be reduced and the enemy kept under constant threat of attack in this southern area also.

APRIL 1917

During the month of April, therefore, the 8th Division, in common with the other divisions of the Fourth Army, undertook a number of further advances in which fresh successes were gained. In the early afternoon of the 4th April the 25th Infantry Brigade made an attack on Gouzeaucourt Wood, the main object of the movement being to protect the right flank of the 20th Division then attacking Metz-en-Couture. The battalions employed were the 2/ Rifle Brigade on the right and the 2/ Royal Berkshire on the left. Winter that year was slow to relax its grip. Snow had fallen on the 2nd April and on the day of the attack there was another heavy snowstorm which much interfered with visibility and co-operation. Launched at 2 p.m. after a postponement due to the weather, the attack developed into a series of stubborn fights in which the background of snow gave all the advantage to the defenders; but before dawn the high ground South-West of Gouzeaucourt which formed our objective had been taken, and the task of covering the operations of the 20th Division in their successful advance on Metz-en-Couture was satisfactorily accomplished. Another congratulatory message from General Rawlinson recompensed the troops engaged for an exhausting and hard-fought day.

Four days after the completion of this advance our troops were cheered by the news of the successful launching by the Third and First Armies on the 9th April of the great Arras–Vimy Ridge offensive with its, till then, unprecedented tale of captures in ground and prisoners and guns. Three successive German systems of defence, including a wide sector of the famous Hindenburg line itself, had been pierced and the British half of the Allied spring offensive had been brilliantly begun. Since the enemy would strain every nerve to hasten additional divisions to the point of danger and to re-establish his defences there, it was more than ever incumbent upon the divisions of the two southern British armies to co-operate with the principal attack by maintaining pressure upon the German troops opposed to them.

There could be no remission, therefore, of the efforts of the 8th Division to get at grips with the enemy's main line of defence, and the next objective in its path was the village of Gouzeaucourt itself. Intelligence reports had suggested that hostile infantry opposition would not be very serious: in order to counteract that of his artillery, General Heneker decided on a night advance, to

THE GERMAN RETREAT

be carried out by the 2/ West Yorkshire (Lieut.-Colonel J. L. Jack) and 2/ Scottish Rifles (Lieut.-Colonel V. C. Sandilands) of General Grogan's brigade and the 2/ East Lancashire (Lieut.-Colonel A. A. Sharland) and 1/ Sherwood Foresters (Lieut.-Colonel R. L. Sherbrooke) of General Cobham's brigade. The ground of advance was carefully reconnoitred beforehand by all leaders and compass bearings taken, to be carefully back-checked during the advance itself. This was commenced at 7.45 p.m. on the 12th April, the troops, covered by patrols, moving forward by short bounds in artillery formation. The weather was again unkind, a heavy storm of snow and sleet raging for some hours before the attack and still continuing at its commencement; but it was blowing, fortunately, in the direction of the advance. A number of Germans were killed and several prisoners secured, sharp fighting taking place in Gouzeaucourt itself and at certain other points; but the chief difficulties encountered arose from the difficulty of keeping direction and touch. That these were overcome was due to the forethought with which the operation had been planned and to the methodical care with which it was executed. No little credit should be given to the artillery, which burst shells with great accuracy on fixed positions as marks by which to guide the troops. The right company of the Scottish Rifles, which had started to consolidate too far to the North and West of its objective on the eastern edge of Gauche Wood, was brought into correct position at midnight by Major C. R. H. Stirling, second in command of the battalion; but with this exception the whole of the troops engaged had established touch on their correct line of objectives by 9.45 p.m.—an extremely fine performance having regard to the very adverse nature of the weather.

The following message from the Commander-in-Chief was received by the Corps Commander and published in a special Divisional Order of the Day:

"I congratulate you and all concerned on the successful operations carried out by the XV Corps on the 12th inst. Please convey this message to 8th Division."

The operation just described had brought the 23rd Infantry Brigade close up against the village of Villers Guislain. At dawn on the 14th April the 2/ Devonshire had attempted to enter it; but were checked by the thickness of the protecting wire and by heavy fire from its garrison. On the night of the 15th/16th patrols of the 2/ Middlesex succeeded in cutting large gaps in the German entanglements, and next day the artillery bombarded the village and completed the destruction of the enemy's wire. Finally at 4.25 a.m. on the 18th, after a hot meal in billets at midnight, troops of Colonel Jack's West Yorkshire battalion,

THE CAPTURE OF GONNELIEU

well led by Capt. J. P. Palmes, M.C., attacked and took the village, killing 60 Germans and capturing 18 prisoners and 5 machine-guns. Our own casualties are believed to have been limited to one man who, like the unfortunate Mousqueton on two celebrated occasions, had the misfortune to be wounded in that portion of his anatomy which ought not strictly to have been turned towards the enemy.

APRIL 1917

During the 19th and 20th April wire-cutting and other necessary preparations were carried out for the taking of Gonnelieu, the capture of which was imperative, as the village overlooked the whole of the new positions of the division. General Coffin was ordered to attack this place on the 21st April, the 23rd Infantry Brigade co-operating and advancing their line. The 40th Division on the left were also attacking at the same hour, their advance being directed against the spur which lies to the North of the village. The attack was launched at 4.20 a.m. by the 2/ Lincolnshire (Lieut.-Colonel R. Bastard) preceded by a creeping artillery barrage and assisted by standing barrages by artillery and machine-guns. The 2/ Rifle Brigade (Major G. M. A. Ellis)* were in support. No difficulty was experienced in getting through the wire except on the extreme right, where a platoon of the Lincolnshire under Lieut. F. F. Davies was held up by unusually strong wire, and heavily fired upon. Lieut. Davies skilfully withdrew his platoon, reformed it some 50 yards in rear and went through more to the left, following his neighbouring platoon. In the village there was some fairly heavy fighting, but at 5.15 a.m. a succession of Verey lights indicated that the Lincolnshire had reached its eastern edge and the Rifle Brigade advanced in their turn. The latter battalion was held up for a time by machine-guns from Gonnelieu Château to the North of the village. This opposition was eventually overcome by flanking attacks and the enemy, being then almost surrounded, was forced to surrender.

In the meantime the 23rd Infantry Brigade had pushed forward their posts all along the line, while further to the left the 40th Division gained also all their objectives. In the whole operation the 8th Division captured over 90 prisoners, in addition to a number of machine-guns and trench mortars. Another congratulatory message from the Commander-in-Chief marked this successful operation.

The advance of the XV Corps was now rapidly approaching its logical conclusion; for our troops were already in touch either with the Hindenburg line itself or with outpost defences so

---

* The Battalion Commander, Lieut.-Colonel the Hon. R. Brand, was at this date on a Course at Fourth Army School. During the attack Major Ellis was wounded, and his place taken by Major Hon. E. Coke.

THE GERMAN RETREAT

closely linked with the main position that the enemy could confidently be expected to fight with determination to retain them. Meanwhile, the course of the general Allied offensive had disappointed early hopes. The broad outline of the plan which General Nivelle had substituted for that originally agreed upon by Joffre and Haig was that the assault of the British Third and First Armies at Arras on the 9th April should immediately be followed, on the 12th April, by a great French offensive in Champagne. This latter was to be the main stroke, which it was hoped would prove conclusive. The rôle of the British Armies at Arras, mighty as was our effort there, was intended as a subsidiary operation, to exhaust the enemy, engage his reserves and draw divisions to the Scarpe front from the sectors where the French Armies were to deliver the decisive blow.

General Nivelle's plan, his new *recette de Victoire* which he had based upon a brilliant but limited success at Verdun in the autumn of 1916, had caught the imagination not only of his countrymen, but of certain members of the British War Cabinet as well, who recoiled from the terrible necessities of the " war of attrition." At Verdun in 1916, a dove-tailed offensive based on a very elaborate pre-arranged time-table, and dependent absolutely for its success on the maintenance and smooth working of that time-table, had succeeded admirably in a local tactical offensive, definitely limited in scope and provided with ample artillery resources. Nivelle saw no reason why the same method should not be applied to a vast strategic offensive, designed to produce a definite break through on a comprehensive scale, with all that that implied. The offensive was to be launched on the Aisne front in Champagne, clearing the Chemin des Dames and the heights North and East of Rheims. Laon was expected to fall as a result of the first day's fighting. Joffre's plan for a combined Allied offensive, commenced early in the year by operations against both shoulders of the Somme salient, went by the board and the British Army was relegated to a secondary rôle. Optimism in France was raised to a dangerous pitch.

The British Armies had performed the task allotted to them in the new plan with a success which had already resulted in a gain of 4 miles of territory and the capture of more than 13,000 prisoners and over 200 guns. On the 12th April, however, the French offensive was not ready, and when ultimately loosed on the 16th April the enemy had had four extra days in which to take stock of the situation. Almost from the moment of assault it became apparent that Nivelle's grandiose conception was not to achieve its ambitious results. The attack at once fell behind the time-table, and thereafter any hope of a definite break through was gone. Some progress, indeed, was made, but at terrible cost,

A FINAL RAID

and the rapid fading of too buoyant hopes had an immediate and disastrous effect, both on French opinion in political and civilian circles, and upon the morale of the French Armies. The failure of the great French offensive necessarily had its effect also upon the operations of our own armies. The Arras battle was maintained as long as active fighting on the French battle-front continued; but the hope of big developments was gone and the concluding British attacks, though delivered on wide fronts, were deliberately limited in scope. The new condition of affairs was reflected on the front of the 8th Division, where, following the operation of the 17th April, there was for a fortnight a period of comparative quiet.

MAY 1917

There was, indeed, but one village remaining in German hands in front of the Hindenburg Line in its sector, namely the village of la Vacquerie. Orders were issued at the beginning of May that on the 5th of the month, coincident, that is, with a final effort by the French on the Aisne front, and two days after the last of our own major attacks in the Arras battle, the la Vacquerie position was to be captured by the 8th and 40th Divisions and incorporated in our front system of trenches. Subsequently these orders were countermanded in favour of a large-scale raid, intended merely as a demonstration and to damage the enemy's defences.

The operation in the 8th Division's sector of attack was carried out by the 23rd Infantry Brigade, employing the 2/ Middlesex, the 2/ Scottish Rifles and one company of the 2/ West Yorkshire (under Lieut. E. Myers, M.C.). The raiders started at 11 p.m., in a night black with cloud in place of the full moon which had been relied upon, and with a cold driving rain beating in the faces of the attackers. Worse followed when the troops reached two sunken roads which ran diagonally across the front of attack. Giving way to a natural tendency, which ought to have been provided against but was not, they lined the eastern banks of these roads before continuing the advance, and lost direction in consequence. Despite all their difficulties, " B " Company of the Middlesex did reach their objectives at Sonnet Farm, and in a sharp fight with its garrison killed several of the enemy and brought back a wounded prisoner. Certain sheds on the Gouzeaucourt–le–Pavé road were blown up also; but the operation was an expensive one, our own casualties numbering 191 killed, wounded and missing.

This raid was the last operation of any magnitude that was undertaken by the 8th Division on this front. It may well be regretted that it did not meet with better fortune; but it was after all but a single semi-failure to set off against a long series of successes which had earned the division the frequent commend-

THE GERMAN RETREAT

ation of the higher commands. Commencing on the 2nd March, the troops of the division had gone resolutely and rapidly forward, meeting and overcoming skilfully all the difficulties in their way, gaining steadily in knowledge and experience, and in that quiet confidence in themselves and their leaders without which the best work of a division is impossible. In the end, the morale of all ranks had been raised to a pitch which made them feel that there was nothing they could not accomplish.

The events were already in train which were to carry the troops of the 8th Division to a trial where all their courage and resolution would be needed. For all its brilliant opening on the Arras front, the Allied spring offensive had proved abortive and the decision to transfer the main conduct of offensive operations in the West to the British Armies, and the scene of operations to Flanders, had been taken. Henceforward, fighting on the Arras front was directed only to local improvements of position and to diverting attention so far as possible from our preparations in the North.

With the adoption of the new plan of campaign, Petain succeeded Nivelle in the command of the French Armies and immediately devoted himself to the task of restoring discipline and fighting spirit to his discouraged troops. The period was a critical one; for if the enemy had been able to develop a serious counter-offensive against the French at this juncture, he would have found our Allies in no condition to resist him and the consequences would have been beyond foretelling. It was essential, therefore, that at all costs the enemy should be kept fully employed, a task which the British Army alone was at this time fit to undertake.

On other fronts, moreover, the outlook for the Entente was no brighter. The Russian Revolution was already leading to the disintegration of that unhappy country. The Italian offensive was delayed and when it was delivered at the end of May fell short of anticipations. The Rumanian campaign had long since ended in disaster. Sarrail's projected spring offensive from Salonika came to nothing. The one bright spot was the entry on the 5th April of America into the War; but it was quite certain that American assistance could not make itself felt for many months to come. It was, therefore, only too clear that it was solely upon Haig and the British Armies in France that the main burden of supporting the Entente during the summer of 1917 was to fall. As a result, our Flanders offensive became the culminating military adventure of the 1917 campaign. Its chances of complete success were for that very reason correspondingly reduced; for with no simultaneous offensive either developing or even threatening elsewhere, the German reserves

BACK TO THE NORTH

could all be diverted to the Flanders front. The struggle developed once again into a terrible battle of attrition on either side, in which the British Army was pitted almost unaided against the massed resources of Germany.

MAY 1917

In this great contest the 8th Division was destined to play its part. On the 15th May General Heneker handed over command of his sector of the XV Corps front to the G.O.C. 40th Division, and the 8th Division passed into XV Corps reserve in the neighbourhood of Nurlu and Moislains and other surrounding villages. The march back, as also the march out of the area a fortnight later, gave a most valuable opportunity to instil really good march discipline; and to strengthen, with the *esprit-de-corps* and pride of membership which march discipline most surely promotes, the splendid fighting spirit of which the division had already given such signal proofs. The fortnight spent in Corps Reserve was also turned to excellent account, being the first opportunity for consistent training which the division had enjoyed for four and a half months.

At the end of May the division was ordered North and marched away across the old Somme battle-front. The route, traversing, as it did, a terrain only just released from the stranglehold of years of trench-locked war, was of extraordinary and tragic interest. Lieut.-Colonel J. L. Jack, D.S.O., O.C. 2/West Yorkshire, described it in the following graphic note: "Latter part of route through the devastated, shell-swept, smoking and still-covered-with-débris battleground of two years. The villages recognizable by a few bricks lying here and there; the woods a few bare shell-blasted poles; the ground a mass of shell-holes where the position of one side or the other had drawn intense shell fire. The old front line trenches distinguishable still by the remains of the rust-brown wire entanglements; unexploded shells everywhere; everywhere scattered graves, marked not at all or by broken crosses, the French with a tricolour rosette."

Having traversed this area of desolation the division commenced on the 2nd of June entraining for the Second Army Area.

It had earned good opinions on the Somme and took with it to the North the following fine tribute:

"Before the 8th Division leaves the Fourth Army I desire to express to all ranks my appreciation of the good services they have rendered during the past seven months.

"Their capture of Zenith Trench in October 1916 and of Pallas and Fritz Trenches in March 1917 were operations requiring careful preparation and bold leadership. The success attained on both these occasions deserves high praise.

"The successful operations carried out during March and

THE GERMAN RETREAT

April 1917, including the capture of Heudicourt, Fins, Gouzeaucourt and Gouzeaucourt Wood, Villers Guislain and Gonnelieu, were conducted with a gallantry and skill which was wholly admirable and show that the division has been brought to a high state of fighting efficiency.

" I regret that the division is leaving the Fourth Army, but I hope that on some future occasion I may again have the good fortune to find them under my command.

(Sgd.) " H. RAWLINSON,
" General.

" H.Q. Fourth Army.
21st May 1917."

Such a testimonial spontaneously given by so high and competent an authority was one of which the division might indeed be proud.

CHAPTER IX

THE CAMPAIGN IN FLANDERS IN 1917: WESTHOEK RIDGE

WHILE the 8th Division was still resting and training in the Nurlu area, the British preparations for the northern offensive were being hurried forward with all possible speed. It was already late in the season for the commencement of a fresh campaign, and the amount of preliminary work necessary was, of course, gigantic. Something, it is true, had been done even before 1917, on the general principle of endeavouring to be ready for every eventuality, and more precise preparation had been undertaken as soon as the results of the French offensive in Champagne made it doubtful whether the Arras battle could be persisted in profitably. Yet much still remained to be done when the decision to break off the southern battle was definitely taken.

So far as the British plans were concerned, it would have been possible to have stopped the Arras battle with advantage at the end of the first week's fighting, and thereupon to have transferred to the northern theatre the troops, labour and material required to complete our preparations there.* Had this been done, an invaluable three weeks of good campaigning weather would have been gained and the results upon the course of the Flanders battle might well have been far-reaching. In the event, the necessity of continuing the Arras battle until the failure of the French offensive had declared itself made this course impossible. It was with the knowledge that the time before them was all too short for the accomplishment of their designs, that the British Higher Command turned their undivided attention and the full resources of the British Armies to the northern campaign.

The reasons for choosing this theatre for the British effort were overwhelming. Throughout the area of the German retreat our communications were in no condition to feed a sustained offensive and it would take many months to re-establish them. On the Arras front the German divisions were now heavily massed. Further progress there would be slow and difficult, and without the assistance of a successful French offensive to the South, this front offered no strategic objectives which could possibly be attained in the time at our disposal. From Lens to Armentières a thickly populated mining district, with its large towns and long streets lined with buildings, presented many obstacles to an advance and frequent opportunities for stubborn resistance. In the northern sector, however, conditions of terrain, provided the weather were favourable, were less difficult. Moreover, a strategic objective of immense value lay near at hand in

---

* Cf. *Haig's Despatches*, Dent's Edition, p. 95.

WESTHOEK RIDGE

the clearing of the Belgian coast and the destruction of the German submarine bases at Ostend and Zeebrugge. During 1917 the German submarine campaign reached its height and our Admiralty had become anxious regarding our cross-Channel communications. Seeing that the safety of the whole Allied cause demanded that the enemy should be fought hard and continuously by the British, until the Armies of our Allies were in better shape, everything pointed to Flanders as the scene of operations.

The general plan of the Flanders offensive of 1917 was to drive forward eastwards from Ypres, until we had gained and consolidated the line of the ridge which runs in a north-easterly direction from Wytschaete to Passchendaele and Staden. The Fifth Army had been moved North from the Somme area for this purpose. When the ridge had been won, the line of advance was to swing to the left and to be continued north-eastwards, in co-operation with an attack by the Fourth Army along the coast in the Nieuport sector and the landing in the neighbourhood of Ostend of a strong force of infantry and tanks. By these methods it was hoped both to clear the Belgian coast and to cut off and capture large German forces. With our left flank resting on the Dutch frontier, we should not unduly have lengthened our own line; we should, on the other hand, have gained new lines of cross-Channel communication and at the same time have turned from the North the whole position of the main German Armies in France.

Such a scheme, given sufficient time and good weather, was by no means impossible of realization; but, for the reasons explained above, time was uncomfortably short and, before the main offensive East and North of Ypres could be launched, it was necessary to secure the high ground about Messines and Wytschaete which flanked and overlooked the ground whence our principal attack would be delivered. The task of capturing the Messines-Wytschaete salient was entrusted to the Second Army and was carried out with conspicuous success on the 7th June; a few days, that is, after the arrival of the 8th Division in the Second Army area.

Divisional Headquarters had been opened at Merris on the 2nd June and by the 4th the concentration of the division (less artillery and pioneers) in the Merris area was complete and training had begun. The division was in Army Reserve during the Messines battle as part of the XIV Corps, and on the 7th June all ranks remained in their areas ready to move forward if required. The ground over which the division might have to operate had been carefully reconnoitred and other measures taken to ensure that its intervention would be effective. By the following day, however, it was clear that the services of the division would not

INTO THE SALIENT

be wanted; the order directing all ranks to stand by was cancelled, and training was resumed.

On the 11th June the 8th Division was transferred from the Merris area to the Caestre area—a move of a few miles only—and next day came under the orders of the II Corps (Lieut.-General C. W. Jacob) of the Fifth Army, preparatory to taking part in the opening of our main offensive. General Jacob found the occasion to visit each of the brigades and to talk to each officer, an example of personal interest which was very deeply appreciated. Divisional Headquarters was opened at Caestre on the 11th June.

From Caestre the division moved forward into the line in the Ypres salient and relieved portions of the 30th and 55th Divisions in the sector astride the Menin Road at Hooge, command passing to General Heneker on the 15th. The relief was carried out by the 24th and 23rd Infantry Brigades, both having their headquarters in the Ypres ramparts; but on the 18th of the month the 23rd Infantry Brigade took over the whole of the divisional front, the 24th Infantry Brigade withdrawing into divisional reserve. Thereafter the brigades relieved each other in rotation, the 24th Infantry Brigade replacing the 23rd in line on the nights of the 28th/29th and 29th/30th June and itself being in turn relieved by the 25th Infantry Brigade on the night of the 6th/7th July. All units were thus given an opportunity to make themselves acquainted with the ground over which they were to attack; work was facilitated and the conditions made easier for the brigade in reserve.

During this period a proposal was put forward by the Fifth Army Commander for a preliminary operation by the 8th Division to take Stirling Castle; but after discussion General Gough accepted the Divisional Commander's views and decided to include this position in the main operation. The division was spared the losses which even a successful attack must have caused, but the enemy's artillery was very active and casualties due to his heavy shelling were serious. Traffic up and down between Zillebeke Lake and the Ramparts met with great difficulties even from our own batteries. So closely were the guns packed that arrangements had to be made for the northern half of our massed artillery to fire during one portion of the night and the southern half during another; otherwise it would have been impossible for traffic to have got through. The amount of traffic can be gauged from the fact that on the 8th divisional front alone some 2,000 men were engaged nightly as working parties, employed in the final preparations for the attack,—burying cable, constructing dug-outs for Brigade Headquarters at Half-way House, and carrying forward stores to the various dumps.

WESTHOEK RIDGE

A violent artillery duel had rapidly developed, in which all advantages of position and observation were with the enemy who on the 12th July sprang a surprise upon us by heavily bombarding Ypres and our artillery positions and troops in back areas with " mustard " gas. The flat and open nature of the countryside about Ypres and the observation which the enemy enjoyed from the ridge meant that practically all work and movement, the going forward of guns and troops and the getting up of stores and ammunition, had to be carried out at night. Even so, the avenues of approach, both East and West of Ypres, were few and the enemy had every yard of road and track " taped " by his artillery. The corduroy road to Zillebeke was constantly broken by direct hits, and as often methodically repaired by the patiently enduring road gangs. Abandoned wagons, corpses of men, dead and wounded horses and mules lined the scene of their labours; limbs and bodies sticking in rigid and grotesque pathos out of the mud of the shell-holes were the grim companions of their toil.

The Ypres–Poperinghe road, straight and narrow as the way to heaven, to those who ran the gauntlet in the shell-riven darkness seemed rather the road to hell. Nor did the German guns confine their attention to the roads. Other likely targets were marked down with the same deadly sureness. Divisional Headquarters at Winnipeg Camp were shelled so persistently on the night of 18th/19th June that on the following and subsequent nights they were moved a mile or so back to Scottish Camp, returning during the day to their former quarters. A few days later they were transferred definitely to Scottish Camp. Even here, the German bombing planes found them, and the wise " counter-sank " their beds beneath the ground level.

On the nights of the 8th/9th and 9th/10th July the 25th Infantry Brigade was relieved in the line by the 7th Infantry Brigade and on the morning of the 10th command of the sector passed to the 25th Division. " B " Company and one platoon of " C " Company of the 2/ Royal Berkshire remained in the line, however, for a night raid on Hooge. " Zero " was fixed for 1 a.m. on the 11th July and punctually at that hour the barrage fell. Its exact position had been carefully demonstrated beforehand to all the officers of the raiding party by Major Duncan, R.F.A., and the excellent co-operation between artillery and infantry contributed greatly to the success of the operation.

Under the personal supervision and leadership of Colonel Haig, the troops moved forward so close to the line of bursting shells that some men (50 per cent. of the company had never been in action before) were wounded by our own guns. The enemy showed fight in every instance and a machine gun brought up from a dug-out, the entrance to which had been overlooked in

INTENSIVE TRAINING

the darkness, caused some difficulty till the team was knocked out by Sergt. Sturgess. The enemy's resistance was so stubborn that it was difficult to secure prisoners. Only one was taken, a German who, after firing at Pte. Bauden at short range and failing to do more than graze the latter's arm, immediately put up his hands. Exercising considerable self-restraint, Pte. Bauden, who knew how badly identifications were wanted, accepted the German's surrender and brought him in. Their tasks accomplished forty-four minutes after " zero," the raiders withdrew in good order to our lines, having killed 70 or 80 Germans and secured the coveted identification at a cost of 5 killed or missing and 31 wounded, most of the wounds being slight. The men were deservedly pleased with their success and returned in high fettle. They were rewarded by a congratulatory telegram from General Gough.

The division had been withdrawn from the line for a period of intensive training with a view to the coming offensive. It was consequently taken well back from the line, Divisional Headquarters being established at Bomy and the infantry brigades billeted in the vicinity. All ranks were soon hard at work. Exercises in attack on trenches, specially flagged to represent the German system which would form the objective in the battle, were diligently and carefully practised. The ground over which the division was to attack was thoroughly reconnoitred by all commanders and staffs. The enemy's territory opposite the II Corps and our own route and method of advance were closely studied by all officers and N.C.O.'s, with the aid of an exceptionally large scale map and a big raised model in which the features of the ground and the position of the German defences were faithfully reproduced. By these means, the incidents and obstacles to be met with were foreseen and prepared for so far as was humanly possible.

Both Sir Douglas Haig and his Chief-of-Staff, General Kiggell, paid visits to the division during these exercises and expressed themselves pleased with the results attained. Lectures by specialists of all kinds formed another and important part of the course of training. In particular, all ranks drew no little amusement and much very valuable instruction from the bloodthirsty exhortations of Colonel Campbell at certain of whose lectures the Commander-in-Chief unobtrusively assisted, sharing in the general enjoyment of Colonel Campbell's grim and intensely practical humour.

After ten days spent in this way, the division began to move back to the line. Divisional Headquarters reopened at Scottish Camp on the 21st July, and two days later the 23rd Infantry Brigade went into the trenches. General Heneker took over

WESTHOEK RIDGE

command of the left sector of the II Corps' front astride the Menin Road on the following morning.

The return to the front line was signalized by a successful daylight raid near Bellewaarde Farm, carried out by three platoons of the 2/West Yorkshire under 2nd Lieut. M. McConville, in the early afternoon of the 24th July. Five prisoners of the 89th Grenadier Regiment were captured and about 15 other Germans killed. A less extensive raid undertaken by a detachment of the 2/Devonshire (2nd Lieut. A. E. Titley commanding) at 5 o'clock on the afternoon of the 26th found the German front line trench unoccupied, but the support trench held in strength. The object of these raids, and of others carried out at frequent intervals along the whole front of the Fifth Army, was both to secure identifications and also to keep constant touch with our opponents. It was thought that the enemy intended to evacuate his forward positions prior to the assault; in order to save his own troops from our bombardment and to enable him to turn his guns upon his own front-line trenches.*

Our own guns were by this time already hard at work on a methodical and comprehensive programme of bombardment and wire-cutting. The artillery supporting the attack of the 8th Division alone comprised, in addition to the divisional artillery † under General Lloyd (the XXXIII Brigade, R.F.A., Lieut.-Colonel T. St. A. B. L. Nevinson and the XLV Brigade, R.F.A., Lieut.-Colonel E. L. Wheeler), the 25th Divisional Artillery, the CCXXXII, XXXVIII and " X " Army Brigades, R.F.A., a counter-battery group consisting of the LXXXVIII H.A.G. (6-inch, 8-inch and 12-inch howitzers) and the LXXIII H.A.G. (60-pounders and 6-inch guns) and a double bombardment group consisting of the LVII H.A.G. (6-inch and 8-inch howitzers) and the XXIV H.A.G. (6-inch, 9·2-inch and 15-inch howitzers). To this mass of artillery were added six batteries of 2-inch trench mortars, three Newton 6-inch trench mortars and two old and two new 9·45-inch trench mortars. All had regular programmes and targets and systematically bombarded every yard of ground within the German positions.

The swelling discord of the guns, persisting both by day and by night, heralded the imminent approach of " zero." It was a time of great trial for all the troops and not least for the artillery.

---

* On the 27th July, the day originally chosen for the launching of the offensive, the enemy did in fact evacuate his trenches West of the Canal on the XIV Corps front, and also retired temporarily from his forward trenches in wide sectors in other parts of the Fifth Army front, but these latter he reoccupied. The postponement of the attack was due to the fact that the First French Army was not ready.

† The artillery of the British Army had been reorganized during February and March on a 6-gun battery basis, as a result of which the V Brigade, R.H.A., left the 8th Division to become an Army Brigade.

PLATE IX

Copyright: *Imperial War Museum*

YPRES OFFENSIVE, 1917: THE MENIN ROAD

THE PLAN OF ATTACK

Casualties from shell-fire mounted up, and among them the JULY division lost an exceptionally fine officer in its divisional trench- 1917 mortar officer, Capt. W. G. J. Walker, M.C. No one who passed through it will forget the utter discomfort and incessant nervous tension created by the continuous bombardment.

The main burden of the great attack was to be borne by the Fifth Army on a front of some 7½ miles from the Zillebeke–Zanvoorde Road to Boesinghe. The Second Army was to co-operate on its right, making no great advance, but extending the area of attack as far South as the Lys River and thus forcing the enemy to distribute his artillery fire. On the left of the Fifth Army General Anthoine's First French Army was to advance its right in close touch with our forces, thus securing them from counter-attack from the North. The Fifth Army consisted of four Corps, II, XIX, XVIII, XIV, disposed from the right in the order given. The II Corps had three divisions in line, the 8th Division being on the left of the Corps front.

The design of the attack was a methodical series of advances in three stages, at any one of which a halt could be called if necessary, while a further line was given for exploitation purposes should success warrant such action. The plans and objectives of the 8th Division in this operation can be most easily appreciated by a glance at the attached map (opposite page 138). It will be seen that the II Corps' front included the difficult area of broken and wooded ground where the Menin Road strikes across the main ridge, and that its task took the form of a frontal assault upon a strong and easily defensible position. It will be noticed, too, that following the general line of the ridge the depth of our principal objectives increased rapidly from right to left, and that the 8th Division, with what was in fact the widest front of attack of any division in the battle, was located at the point where the objective line turned southwards and the depth of our objectives was greatest. It will be less easy to realize from any map the peculiar difficulties, due to the nature of the ground and lack of cover, which were encountered in moving forward and forming up for the attack. To meet these difficulties special underground chambers of huge size had to be made as shelter for the troops, in particular for the accommodation of the reserve brigade. The good work done by the Tunnelling Companies and by the Field Companies under the C.R.E. of the division, Lieut.-Colonel C. M. Browne, D.S.O., deserves special mention in this regard.

The several stages of the advance were to be worked as follows. The 24th and 23rd Infantry Brigades (General Cobham and General Grogan) were to deliver the assault on the first two objectives, known respectively as the Blue and Black lines. Two battalions from each brigade were to capture the Blue line, then

WESTHOEK RIDGE

after a short pause the remaining two battalions of each brigade were to advance to the second objective. A section of 4 tanks was to co-operate with each of these brigades. After the Black line had been captured, the 25th Infantry Brigade, to which had been allotted No. " C " Company " A " Tank Battalion (twelve tanks, under Major Keating), would go through to attack the third objective, or Green line. Thereafter if all should go well General Coffin was to push out a battalion, assisted by Tanks and " B " Squadron 1/1 Yorkshire Dragoons, towards the Red line, the line of exploitation. The 25th Infantry Brigade was to be supported in its attack by General Grogan's brigade which, in order to be available for this purpose, would hand over its portion of the Black line to General Cobham. The 30th Division, II Corps, was to attack on the right of the 8th Division as far as the Black line, whence the advance would be carried on by a brigade of the 18th Division going through. The 15th Division of the XIX Corps was on the 8th Division's left. The 25th Division was behind the 8th Division ready to go through after the capture of the Red line, if circumstances required.

Hostile shelling on the night of the 30th/31st July was below the normal—it had on previous nights been exceptionally heavy—and the move to assembly areas was carried out, despite the peculiar difficulties presented by the ground, in due accordance with the careful arrangements made and without undue casualties. Punctually at 3.50 a.m. on the 31st July, the attacking troops left their trenches and advanced under cover of artillery and machine-gun barrages which crept forward at the rate of 100 yards in four minutes. The morning was very dark—faint streaks of light in the East served but to show where the dawn would come—and companies had to move by compass bearings. Though this led in some places to a certain amount of confusion in the torn and crater-strewn area of No-Man's-Land, the troops went forward everywhere with great spirit and were soon inside the German lines on the whole front of both brigades.

Having surmounted the Hooge spur, the 1/ Worcestershire (Lieut.-Colonel G. M. C. Davidge) on the right passed on rapidly to their objectives, overrunning all opposition. One platoon per company acted as " moppers-up " and successfully bombed a number of dug-outs in their prescribed areas. The tunnel under the Ypres–Menin Road was expected to give a great deal of trouble; but in the result it proved no very serious obstacle and yielded 41 prisoners. After Ignorance Support had been taken " A " and " B " Companies passed through to attack James Trench and captured it, although they found it strongly held. The communication trenches leading from James Trench to the top of the Bellewaarde Ridge were next cleared, and the battalion

COLYER-FERGUSSON'S V.C.

proceeded to dig in on the line of its objectives (the Blue line) on the forward slope of the ridge overlooking Westhoek. JULY 1917

The 2/ Northamptonshire (Lieut.-Colonel C. G. Buckle) had a harder task, the hardest perhaps of the day, but went forward at " Zero " hour in fine style. " The barrage came down with a tremendous roar and the battalion, lying on the parapets of Kingsway and Kingsway Support, advanced under its cover. Perfect order prevailed, the battalion keeping its formations as if on the practice trenches back at Bomy."* Nearly half of their front was covered by the obstacle of the Bellewaarde Lake; so that most of the left half of the battalion had to skirt the eastern edge of the lake and then, having deployed on the northern edge of it, attack and capture the highest point of the Bellewaarde Ridge which seemed to tower over them. South of the lake lay Château Wood, a mass of fallen trees and wire, in the path of the right half of this battalion. Through Château Wood, parallel to the front of attack and full of water, ran a ravine which drained the high ground about Clapham Junction into the Bellewaarde Lake. The whole formed an extraordinarily difficult piece of country, and that the Northamptonshire took it all and gained their objectives speaks volumes for the spirit of the men and the leading of the junior commanders. Ploughing through the mud and water, this fine battalion, keeping in touch with the Worcestershire, finally won clear of both Bellewaarde Lake and Château Wood and began their deployment to the left.

It was here that Capt. T. R. Colyer-Fergusson, Commanding " B " Company, 2/ Northamptonshire, gained his V.C. The difficulties of deploying and forming-up were very great. The mass of the Bellewaarde Ridge loomed in front some 100 yards away, and the barrage was beginning to move forward. To lose the barrage meant almost certain failure. This gallant young officer grasped the situation, and collecting some 10 men, amongst whom were Sergt. W. G. Boulding† and Pte. B. Ellis,† his orderly, pushed on under the barrage and without further assistance gained a footing in Jacob Trench on the crest of the ridge. Almost as soon as the trench was captured a company of Germans was seen advancing in mass formation against them, and a bare 100 yards away ! Capt. Colyer-Fergusson and his picked men knocked out 20 or 30 of them with rifle fire and the remainder put up their hands. The men of his own company were beginning to come up, when Capt. Colyer-Fergusson saw a German machine gun in action near him. He left his company to hold the trench and, assisted by his orderly only, attacked and

* W.D. 2/ Northamptonshire, July, 1917.
† Awarded the D.C.M. for their great gallantry on this occasion.

WESTHOEK RIDGE

captured the machine gun. He then turned it on to another group of the enemy, killing a large number of them and driving the remainder into the hands of an adjoining British unit. Later, assisted only by Sergt. Boulding and Pte. Ellis, he attacked and captured a second machine gun. He had now been joined by the rest of his company and had begun to consolidate his position when, hearing that Colonel Buckle had arrived, he went to him to report. Five minutes later Capt. Colyer-Fergusson was shot through the head by a chance machine-gun bullet; a grievous loss not only to his battalion but also to the Service.

Second Lieut. Frost of the adjoining " C " Company on the right exhibited similar qualities of dash and leadership. Encountering a German post of about 50 men who were shooting down the Worcestershire, he rushed them at the head of his men, killing a German officer and 14 other ranks. Other Germans who were lurking in two large concrete shelters were blown up. One of these shelters apparently contained a store of bombs and Verey lights, for a bomb thrown into it caused a large explosion and a fire by which eight or nine of the enemy were killed. Before 5.30 a.m. Jacob Trench had been captured on the front of both companies and the troops moved on to dig a line of posts some 150 yards forward of it. The Blue line had been secured.

The 23rd Infantry Brigade on the left made equally good progress. The 2/West Yorkshire were unfortunate in losing at the outset of the attack their commanding officer, Colonel Jack, who was wounded by a shell one minute after "zero." The command devolved upon Major R. J. McLaren. Despite the darkness of the morning and the roughness of the ground, the battalion had a clear run through and captured the Blue line, including Ziel House, without serious loss. A line of small posts was immediately dug on the Blue line, and the battalion was then collected and companies were reorganized.

The 2/Devonshire (Colonel Sunderland) on the left also reached their objective with slight opposition, except for two strong points which were overcome by riflemen and bombers working round the flanks under cover of rifle-grenade and Lewis-gun fire. Some sniping from undergrowth and shell-holes on the left flank was effectively dealt with by Lewis-gun fire and, though shortly afterwards subjected to a heavy searching fire from 4·2's and 5·9's, the battalion proceeded to consolidate its position.

Thus the first stage had been successfully accomplished all along the divisional front. The capture of the Black line—the second stage—was hardly less successful. It was only on the extreme right that it failed of complete accomplishment, and the partial failure there was due to circumstances which were quite outside divisional control. The 23rd Infantry Brigade on the

PLATE X

YPRES OFFENSIVE 1917: A GERMAN "PILL BOX"

Copyright: Imperial War Museum

THE CAPTURE OF THE "BLACK LINE"

left went forward to an unqualified success and it will be convenient to deal with this stage of the battle in reverse order from left to right and to reserve the account of the more chequered fortunes of the 24th Infantry Brigade until later.

JULY 1917

The 2/ Middlesex (Colonel J. H. Hall, D.S.O.) on the left of General Grogan's brigade had followed closely behind the 2/ Devonshire, thereby avoiding the enemy's barrage. At 5 a.m. the battalion was assembled West of our own protective barrage, where it remained for 29 minutes until the barrage lifted. During this time many parties of the enemy were observed to be retiring. At 5.29 a.m. the battalion advanced with the barrage and at 5.41 a.m. captured the Black line. At 5.45 a.m. a line 100 yards East of the Black line was occupied. No serious opposition had been met with during the advance.

Lieut.-Colonel C. R. H. Stirling, commanding the 2/ Scottish Rifles, was also wounded at the opening of the attack and the battalion experienced some little difficulty in crossing the craters in No-Man's-Land. Once the German front line had been passed matters improved, the enemy's barrage being quickly left behind. Some opposition was encountered from machine-gun fire on the right flank and from snipers in shell holes; but once more rifle grenadiers and Lewis-gun sections were brought effectively into action. The opposition was overcome and many of the German snipers killed or taken prisoner. Passing through the 2/ West Yorkshire on the Blue line, the Scottish Rifles advanced simultaneously with the 2/ Middlesex. No resistance was encountered at Jaffa Trench, their immediate objective; but machine-gun and rifle fire was directed against the advancing troops from houses on the Ridge at Kit and Kat and North of Westhoek. This caused a temporary check. Fire from rifle grenades and Lewis guns directed by observers pushed out in front was again brought into play, enabling the infantry to surround and capture these houses and isolated posts and by 9 a.m. to establish their position firmly on the Black line just East of the crest.

Meanwhile on the left of the 24th Infantry Brigade Colonel Sherbrooke had formed up the 1/ Sherwood Foresters without difficulty behind the Bellewaarde Ridge, whence he took them forward through the 2/ Northamptonshire. During this stage the battalion was heavily fired upon by machine guns from the high ground on the right about Surbiton Villas and Clapham Junction, as well as from strong points in front. This fire to some extent delayed the troops and increased their distance from the barrage. They continued, however, to push forward and, overcoming the German resistance at The Snout and Westhoek cross-roads and other strong points on their front, succeeded in

WESTHOEK RIDGE

establishing themselves on the forward slope of Westhoek Ridge —in their appointed position on the Black line.

The 2/ East Lancashire (Lieut.-Colonel A. A. Sharland) on the right had a harder task and were, as was natural, still more impeded by the machine-gun fire from the high ground. The explanation of this galling fire was not at first understood. Later it was found that the adjoining battalions of the 30th Division had been held up and had been unable to capture the high ground about Clapham Junction and Glencorse Wood, which overlooked the whole of the right sector of the 8th Division. In spite of the heavy fire which took them in flank and even in reverse, the East Lancashire worked their way forward, throwing out Lewis-gun sections to cover their right, and succeeded in occupying their allotted sector on the Ridge. The 1/ Worcestershire worked men along Jabber Drive to keep touch, and at about this time the two battalions of the 18th Division detailed to carry on the attack on the 30th Division front, pushed forward and made a gallant but unsuccessful attempt to capture Clapham Junction. The failure of this attempt left the right flank of the 8th Division entirely in the air. The flanking fire grew steadily in volume, raking our line of advance as far back as Château Wood, where the Brigade Major, Capt. A. Holmes Scott, R.E., was shot dead at General Cobham's side as Brigade Headquarters were moving up to Jacob Trench. Colonel Sunderland of the Devons was also killed about this time. He had gone forward towards Kit and Kat with some other officers, including the Adjutant of the Middlesex, Capt. E. Baker, in order to reconnoitre, and was shot while standing up looking at a map.

The action of the 25th Infantry Brigade in its attempt upon the Green line remains to be considered. The fact that the 30th Division had not got forward was not known until just before the time when General Coffin's brigade was due to pass over Westhoek Ridge. In consequence, the brigade was committed to the attack with its right flank unprotected from the outset. As soon as news was received that the Black line had been captured, General Coffin had moved forward with a small advance party to fix the position of Brigade Headquarters and to carry out a preliminary reconnaissance with the four battalion commanders. It became immediately apparent that the situation on Westhoek Ridge was not what had been anticipated. It seemed doubtful whether it would be possible to carry out the attack as planned; but a change of plan at so late an hour involved obvious dangers of its own. To try to clear up the position, General Coffin went back to the Scottish Rifles Headquarters at Ziel House. Here he found 23rd Brigade Headquarters and received the more reassuring informa-

THE FORTUNES OF THE 25TH BRIGADE

tion that the Scottish Rifles had overcome the opposition from Kit and Kat and the North Westhoek houses. Accordingly, he decided that the lesser risk was to proceed with the original scheme and orders to this effect were issued to battalions at about 9.20 a.m.

The three attacking battalions, 2/ Lincolnshire (Lieut.-Colonel R. Bastard, D.S.O.), 1/ Royal Irish Rifles (Lieut.-Colonel A. D. Reid, D.S.O.), and 2/ Rifle Brigade (Lieut.-Colonel Hon. R. Brand, D.S.O.), went forward in fine style over Westhoek Ridge and observers of the 18th Division, who from the right could see their line of advance, reported that they were "going strong." In order to counter so far as possible the danger from the exposed situation on the right flank, a company of the reserve battalion (2/ Royal Berkshire, Lieut.-Colonel R. Haig, D.S.O.) was ordered to fill immediately the gap South of the Lincolnshire, the remainder of the battalion following in support ready to form a defensive flank if necessary.

This endeavour to protect the right flank was a proper and necessary precaution, and indeed the only one that could be taken; but it was not enough. The Rifle Brigade, being farthest from the danger point, were able to advance a considerable distance and their right company established a post near Hanebeek Wood. Casualties, however, were heavy, including every officer of the company in question, and a gap developed between it and the Irish Rifles which left the right flank of the Rifle Brigade in the air. In consequence, the troops at Hanebeek Wood had to retire and ultimately the battalion was forced to take up a line which was slightly forward of the Black line on its left and thence fell back towards Kit and Kat.

The centre and right battalions naturally suffered far more severely from the enfilade and reverse fire from Glencorse and Nonne Bosschen Woods. The effort made by them, and particularly by the Irish Rifles, was all the more splendid. The latter battalion attacked with great spirit, advancing under a withering fire in perfect order until close up to our barrage. There, in spite of many gallant efforts to get forward, the right company was definitely checked. It proceeded to consolidate, despite the fire to which it was continuously subjected, and drove off several counter-attacks. The centre company got the farthest forward, fighting its way up to the Hanebeek Stream. A gallant few even crossed the stream and made some progress up the western slope of the Anzac spur to within measurable distance of the Green line. Weeks of desperate fighting were to pass before British troops could master this position. Finding that they were unsupported, and that the enemy was working round the right flank, the company was compelled to retire, falling back

WESTHOEK RIDGE

until each flank was again in touch with the companies on the right and left.

The 2/ Lincolnshire had gone forward under command of 2nd Lieut. K. Young, both Colonel Bástard and the Adjutant, Lieut. H. Ingoldby, having been wounded before the order to advance had been given. The battalion came at once under the full force of very heavy machine-gun fire from the exposed right flank. The 30th Division barrage was falling beyond these machine guns which in consequence were able to dominate the situation so effectually as to prevent further progress of any sort. It was decided to consolidate the reverse slope of the Ridge and to hold the crest with Lewis-gun posts. The line finally taken up ran along Jabber Trench and just forward of it; some short distance West of the original Black line.

With the holding up of this attack and the increasing strength of the German reaction, the situation had grown critical and it had become a question whether the weakened line would be able to hold what had already been gained. The tanks, though handled with the greatest gallantry, had found the ground conditions too much for them and had practically ceased to exist as a force. The infantry could look to them for no further help than their crews could give with their dismounted Lewis guns. Yet any further falling back would have had consequences which might have been most serious, for it would have uncovered the flank of the 15th Division to the North and the whole of the substantial advance made by the centre and left of the Allied Armies.

It was at this point that General Coffin's example proved the salvation of his men. With a coolness and intrepidity which put new life and resolution into all he met, he went about from shell-hole to shell-hole, organizing the defence of the position gained and urging on his troops to new and willing efforts. Walking about in the open, with supreme disregard of the fact that he was at all times under fire, he seemed to bear a charmed life. His control was everywhere and his spirit irresistible. During the afternoon he himself carried up ammunition to the front line. No spot was too exposed for him to visit, no task too laborious for him to share. By his magnificent courage and calm behaviour he inspired all ranks.

The work of consolidation proceeded. Local counter-attacks, delivered by the German troops on the spot, had developed before midday, but these had not proved formidable and had been driven off. Two attacks of a more serious nature were launched by the enemy more or less simultaneously shortly after 2 p.m. and were pushed home with much determination. They were directed against the right and the centre battalions and were

OUR GAINS CONSOLIDATED

supported by a barrage which fell upon the Bellewaarde Ridge, the valley West of Westhoek and our own front line. The Lincolnshire on the exposed right gave ground at one or two points and the enemy reached the trench held by the centre company of the Irish Rifles. Vigorous counter-attacks were immediately launched and the enemy were driven out, leaving many dead. In the result no ground whatever was lost. Thereafter the right and the centre were left unmolested by any infantry attack and were able to continue without interruption the consolidation of their positions.

JULY 1917

The situation on the left remained for some hours yet not altogether reassuring. The gap between the Irish Rifles and the Rifle Brigade was closed by bringing the Middlesex slightly forward, while the Rifle Brigade slightly withdrew their right in order to gain touch with them. Even so the enemy from 5 o'clock onwards continually threatened the Rifle Brigade's position to the South of the railway. To meet this danger, the 2/ Royal Berkshire were ordered to send up the remainder of the company in reserve to support the Rifle Brigade, and the artillery were asked to draw in their barrage by 300 yards. These measures proved efficacious and the enemy lost heavily from our rifle, machine-gun and Lewis-gun fire while attempting to form up at the bottom of the Hanebeek valley. Night fell with the position unchanged.

It was indeed a fortunate circumstance for the fate of the right half of the main assault that the troops of the 8th Division were thus able to maintain their hold upon the ground they had won; for, had they failed, the comparative success of the German reaction in the Menin road sector would inevitably have extended northwards and the gains of our centre and left have been endangered. Even as it was, the right division of the XIX Corps (the 15th), which, on the far side of the Ypres–Roulers railway, forming the boundary between the two Corps, had pushed out to the Green line, was forced by counter-attacks during the afternoon to draw back till it was in touch with the 8th Division. The left of the XIX Corps, however, remained in touch with the XIV Corps on the Green line, and from that point north-westwards all our objectives were taken and even exceeded. The result of the first day's fighting on the Fifth Army front, therefore, was complete success on the left and left centre and a partial success on the right, where the 24th and 30th Divisions were either on or just short of the Blue line, with the 8th Division acting as a link holding the two halves of the advance together.

The importance of the feat which the 8th Division had accomplished was accentuated by circumstances over which neither combatant had control. From the opening of the battle rain

WESTHOEK RIDGE

had been threatening, and in the course of the afternoon there began a downfall which for four days and nights continued without appreciable intermission. The effect upon the shell-tormented battle ground is known only to those who saw it with their own eyes, for it cannot be described in words. It was to prove the decisive factor in the offensive. For the moment, however, the 8th Division had done their part, or had nearly done so. During the night of the 31st July/1st August the 25th Infantry Brigade, other than the 2/ Royal Berkshire, was withdrawn and the front taken over by the Royal Berkshire and 2/ West Yorkshire, under command of the 24th Infantry Brigade, and by the 2/ Middlesex and 2/ Devonshire, 23rd Infantry Brigade. Next day and in the course of the night which followed it (1st/2nd August) the 8th Division was relieved by the 25th Division.

The division moved back to the Steenvoorde area to refit and train. It had come through a very trying ordeal in a manner which reflected the greatest credit upon all concerned. Its position in the battle line was, as has been pointed out, one of critical importance. It had proved to be the pivot on which the whole forward movement to the North depended and, in the face of acute difficulties and dangers for which the 8th Division was not responsible, the vital pivot had held. Maj.-General Heneker in a congratulatory message to those under his command summed up the division's achievements in words which deserve to be placed on record.

" I wish to thank all troops for their splendid efforts yesterday. The infantry formed up well and attacked magnificently. Eye-witnesses report the advance as being carried out with the greatest precision and dash. The Blue and Black lines were taken without a hitch. Observers of another division reported that the advance of the 25th Infantry Brigade over the Black line towards the Green line was splendid and was going strong. It was then that our southern flank became exposed to the concentrated fire of enemy machine guns. A defensive flank being formed, the infantry held on splendidly to the ground won, and so enabled the other divisions on our northern flank to push on and secure their objective. Had we failed, others on our left would have been exposed. The Army Commander recognizes this and desires me to convey to all ranks his appreciation of our action and of the way the infantry held on to the ground which had been gained.

" I desire also to thank the R.E., Signal Service, Pioneers, Machine Gunners and R.A.M.C., for the several parts they have played. Last but not least, I desire to thank the Royal Artillery. The Royal Artillery have been in action now for some six weeks,

THE TASK OF THE ARTILLERY

and in spite of the constant shelling to which they have been
subjected, and in spite of the severe casualties which they have
suffered, they rose to the occasion on the 31st, and the infantry
speak in high praise of their barrage and of their shooting generally."

JULY
1917

Narratives of battles must of necessity confine themselves
principally to the deeds of the infantry. The concluding paragraph of the Divisional Commander's message comes, therefore,
as a fitting reminder of the essential share borne by the other
arms and services in this long-drawn and terrible struggle. It
was, indeed, the peculiar character of this offensive that,
except during the actual progress of an assault, the back areas
of the battlefield were even more dangerous than the front
line.

While others passed perilously through these areas, the
gunners, and those responsible for the maintenance of communications, lived there. The Royal Artillery had been in action for
some six weeks before the battle began, and when the infantry
battle opened, had already suffered heavy losses. During the
two months spent in the Ypres salient from June to August 1917,
the 8th Division R.A. actually suffered greater casualties than
they had incurred in the whole of the preceding period since their
landing in France in 1914! The localities in which the guns were
crowded for such shelter as some slight movement of ground
afforded reeked with mustard gas. The very soil itself was contaminated, and digging parties were overcome by fumes which
rose around them as they worked. It was small wonder that
throughout the battle the percentage of casualties was higher
among the artillery than among the infantry. The wonder was
that, in spite of conditions so adverse, the support given by the
guns to the infantry was at all times so excellent. The artillery
barrage on the 31st July was extremely effective. The infantry
reports stated, indeed, that it could not have been better. Equally
good was the way the artillery co-operated with the infantry in the
later stages of the fight. On many occasions during the day,
when the enemy was seen to be massing on the high ground
beyond the Hanebeek or advancing down the valley, the guns
caught and crushed the attack before it could be developed or
pushed home. In this way the artillery, assisted according to the
nature of their arms by the trench mortar batteries and machine
guns, were able to do as much to help the infantry in their difficult
task of maintaining the ground which had been won as they had
originally done in helping them to win it.

Two of the divisional machine-gun companies (the 23rd and
24th, Capt. J. Bourke and Capt. A. M. Pratt) had been actively
engaged since the night of the 23rd/24th July. From that time

WESTHOEK RIDGE

until the 31st July harassing fire was maintained each night by eight guns in conjunction with the artillery; fire was opened by day on the occasion of practice artillery barrages, and support was given as required to the raids both of the 8th and of adjoining divisions. During this period all machine-gun emplacements were shelled by the enemy; but as the guns were always in action in shell-holes some distance away, casualties were minimized. Both companies were almost continually employed with very little opportunity for rest.

For the attack itself four machine-gun companies were available, the 23rd, 24th, 25th (Capt. A. Simonds), and the 218th (Major S. C. Houston). These companies had been detailed to move forward from their assembly points between fifteen and thirty minutes after "zero," and to take up successive barrage positions in the captured territory, in order to cover the various advances from one objective to another. This programme was carried out in its entirety until after the Black line was captured. Thereafter, while owing to the casualties which they had suffered two batteries remained in the first positions, the remainder proceeded with their programme. The barrage lines were thus to some extent broken up and the forward batteries near Westhoek were therefore used as batteries of "opportunity," being switched on to various suitable targets with excellent promptness and effect. In the evening these guns were brought into close defensive positions in the Blue and Black lines.

The excellent work of the artillery and machine guns in covering and supporting the infantry advance could not have been performed had it not been for the splendid efficiency of the Divisional Ammunition Column (Bvt.-Colonel F. W. Boteler). Nothing could be more horrible than the conditions under which the Ammunition Column had to carry out duties always arduous, but in this battle laborious beyond description. Reference has already been made to the dangers that had to be faced during the weeks of preparation. Each yard of the advance multiplied the hardships and the perils of the task, yet the guns were kept supplied and the stupendous artillery duel never faltered for lack of ammunition.

The Royal Engineers (Lieut.-Colonel C. M. Browne, D.S.O.) and the Pioneers (22nd D.L.I., Lieut.-Colonel C. B. Morgan, D.S.O.) were employed on the construction of the special dug-outs required for places of assembly, and also on the construction of tracks, without which progress over ground of the nature of the Ypres battle area was impossible. Both tasks were very heavy, and although, owing to the limited nature of the advance, the entire programme of track construction could not be completed, the task of maintaining the tracks in practicable condition

BATTLE OF YPRES 1917
THE FIRST ASSAULT 31 JULY 1917

German front line .... — — — —
1st Objective (Blue line) ⊢•⊣•⊢•⊣
2nd   "   (Black   ") ▬▬▬▬
3rd   "   (Green   ") ✕—✕—✕—

15TH DIVISION

Divisional

Railway Wood

23RD INF. BDE ASSEMBLY AREA

23RD INF. BRIGADE

Idiot Row
Idiot Dr.
Bellewaarde Lake

Sentry T.
Idiot Tr.
Inter

8TH DIV.

25TH INF. BDE ASSEMBLY AREA

Birr X Rds

24TH INF. BDE ASSEMBLY AREA

Ignorance

ENTRANCE TO TUNNEL

Zouave Wood

Divisional

30TH DIVISION

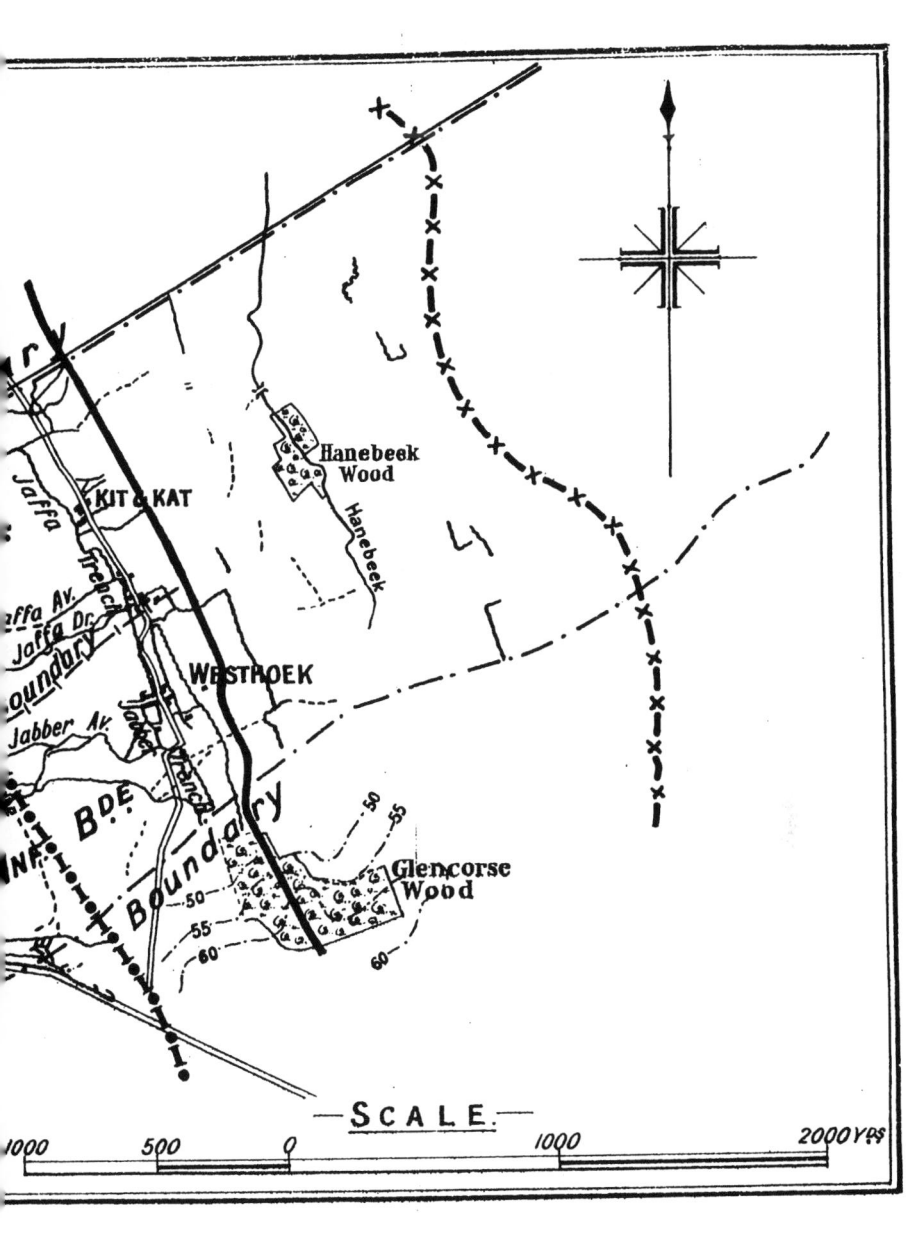

TRANSPORT AND MEDICAL ACHIEVEMENTS

under continuous shell-fire taxed to the utmost the courage and endurance of all ranks.

A word too must be said on behalf of the Divisional Train (Bvt.-Colonel C. R. I. Hull, D.S.O., A.S.C.) and transport generally, which performed in an equally admirable manner the indispensable task of getting stores forward. These troops, too, knew the peril of the "taped" roads, and of the constantly lengthening timber and duck-board tracks. They had to contend with shell-damaged roads and tracks congested past belief by reinforcements, lorries, ammunition wagons, ambulances, parties of prisoners and returning wounded. The incessant shelling caused severe casualties both to men and pack animals. The tracks were continually being broken, and to leave them meant a fair chance of being drowned. Work was at all times carried out under conditions of great risk, as well as of immense difficulty and discomfort; yet somehow it was performed.

Both the enemy's shelling and the mud added also to the difficulties and dangers of the R.A.M.C. (Lieut.-Colonel G. J. A. Ormsby, D.S.O.). None the less, two hours after "zero" a service of ambulance cars was started to Birr Cross-roads and this was maintained—with occasional interruptions owing to shell-fire—throughout the operations. The evacuation of forward casualties was for the reasons mentioned no easy task, but the regimental aid posts were cleared before relief. About 1,700 wounded passed through the divisional dressing stations on the 31st July/1st August.

The success of the division in perhaps the severest test to which it had yet been subjected was, indeed, due to the splendid team work of all arms and services, and to the spirit which inspired all ranks. As a factor which contributed to that spirit, there should not be forgotten the inspiration and example of the Rev. A. Stafford Crawley, M.C. He never spared himself, and acted at all times on the principle that his place was with the men whose welfare he had so much at heart. So much so, that the G.S.O.1 of the division was constrained to post a sentry over his dug-out to prevent him from going over with the leading waves of infantry.

In this battle, the 8th Division took over 600 prisoners, out of the 6,100 prisoners captured by the ten British divisions which took part in the attack. Its own casualties had not been light. Of the commanding officers in the infantry, Lieut.-Colonel Sunderland of the 2/Devonshire and Lieut.-Colonel A. D. Reid of the 1/Royal Irish Rifles had been killed, and Lieut.-Colonel Jack, 2/West Yorkshire, Lieut.-Colonel C. G. Buckle, 2/Northamptonshire, Lieut.-Colonel R. Haig, 2/Royal Berkshire, Lieut.-Colonel R. Bastard, 2/Lincolnshire, Lieut.-Colonel Hon.

WESTHOEK RIDGE

R. Brand, 2/ Rifle Brigade, and Lieut.-Colonel C. R. H. Stirling, 2/ Scottish Rifles, had been wounded. In the artillery, Major C. T. S. Paul, commanding 36th Battery R.F.A., and Major A. F. Nash, commanding 1st Battery R.F.A., were killed, and Lieut.-Colonel T. St. A. B. L. Nevinson, commanding XXXIII Brigade, R.F.A., was wounded. The total losses of the division in killed, wounded and missing were 160 officers and 3,000 other ranks. Apart from the heavy shelling, the factor which contributed most to the losses suffered was the deadly enfilade fire from beyond the southern flank of the division; a fire made possible by the fact that the critical positions on the high ground around Stirling Castle could not be taken. In the event, these positions on the flank of the main attack of the 31st July were not to be secured until they were included as the central portion of the Second Army attack on the 20th September.

Heavy as the 8th Division's casualties had been, it must not be thought that it went out of the fight so shattered and broken as to be incapable of further service. Far from it. It went back to refit with the knowledge that it had come out of the fight with honour and that only a short relief was either needed or contemplated. After the briefest spell of rest and reorganization the division was ready to go in again, and to make a valiant attempt to complete the work which it had so gallantly begun.

CHAPTER X

THE CAMPAIGN IN FLANDERS IN 1917: THE HANEBEEK

THE division was not left long in doubt as to the nature of its next task. On the 2nd August, the very day on which it left the line, a divisional order was issued to the effect that as soon as the remainder of the Black line had been taken by the II and XIX Corps the 8th Division would co-operate in a general attack upon the Green line. Accordingly, the succeeding days were spent in energetic efforts to reorganize the division and to restore it to a fit condition to take its part in an early renewal of the offensive.

The extent of the work to be done in the short time available can be gathered from the fact that between the 2nd and 16th August reinforcements to the number of 48 officers and 2,213 other ranks joined the division. The absorption of drafts on such a scale in the space of a fortnight was in itself no mean undertaking and the difficulty of accomplishing it was increased by the necessity of making good no less than eight casualties among infantry commanding officers. Re-fitting, training, and special preparation for the coming operation were pushed on with the utmost vigour, and the troops soon began to respond to the attention given to them. The following is a typical extract from a battalion diary at this time: "August 11th: Companies carried out a parade attack in turn, practising formations and advancing under barrage, also procedure on reaching objective. The exercise was carried out without a hitch" and later in the same day "officers took their N.C.O.'s to see model of ground and objectives of the new attack."

Soon after its arrival in the Steenvoorde area where this training was carried on, the Fifth Army Commander, General Gough, and the II Corps Commander, Lieut.-General Jacob, came to see the division and congratulated and thanked all ranks for the part they had played on the 31st July. The troops did not escape their share of the attention of far less welcome visitors. On the night of the 10th August, in particular, as though in retaliation for the fact that on that day the work commenced by the 8th Division had been successfully completed,* low-flying German aeroplanes dropped bombs at 20-yard intervals right across the camp alongside Divisional Headquarters. Two huts occupied by the 2/Middlesex received direct hits which caused 66 casualties. Another bomb struck the hut occupied by Major C. C. Bryan, D.S.O., R.E. (T.), commanding

---

* On the 10th August "a successful minor operation carried out by English troops (18th and 25th Divisions) gave us complete possession of Westhoek" (*Haig's Despatches*, Dent's Edition, p. 117).

THE HANEBEEK

the 490th (Home Counties) Field Company R.E., killing him instantly. Two other officers of this Company, 2nd Lieut. S. U. Baily and 2nd Lieut. A. J. Kennedy, and 6 other ranks were wounded in the same raid.

The bad weather which had set in on the afternoon of the 31st July had already had a most unfortunate effect upon the development of the offensive. Whereas the successful working out of the Allied scheme depended upon an orderly but rapid series of attacks, each blow falling upon the enemy before he had had time to recover from the stroke which had preceded it, poorness of visibility and difficulty of movement imposed a heart-breaking period of delay. For many vital days major operations were brought to a complete standstill and it was not, as has been seen, until the 10th August that even the preliminary work of consolidating the Black line at Westhoek could finally be accomplished. Every day during which our troops were held up was a day gained to the enemy, in which to recover from the shock of our opening attack, to strengthen his defences and to increase his reserves. The slight improvement in the weather which took place towards the middle of August was, therefore, instantly seized upon for a renewal of the advance. The date selected was the 16th of the month, and on the 15th, in order to give the enemy something to think about on a different part of his front, the Canadian Corps launched their long-prepared attack at Loos and captured Hill 70 with over 1,100 prisoners.

The 8th Division had already returned to the line, having on the nights of the 12th/13th and 13th/14th August relieved the 25th Division in the left sector of the II Corps front between Westhoek and the Ypres–Roulers railway. General Coffin's brigade and General Grogan's brigade were in line and were to open the assault. The troops found the condition of the sector far worse than when they left it, although even then it had been bad enough. All shell-holes were full of water and movement and supply had become difficult in the extreme. The Hanebeek stream which lay across the front of their advance and in July had been almost dry was now a formidable obstacle, and it was clear that the eighty portable bridges which had been prepared for assisting the attack across marshy ground would speedily be called into use.

"Zero" hour on the 16th was fixed for 4.45 a.m., and the attack of the Fifth British Army, on a front extending from Inverness Copse to St. Janshoek, was to be supported, as on the 31st July, by a similar attack by the First French Army on the British left. The method of attack was once more an advance by stages, the intention being to keep the infantry well under the protection of our guns. It will be noticed that the whole battle lay to the

DANGER ON THE RIGHT

North of the Menin road, so that the high ground about Inverness Copse and Glencorse Wood, which had given so much trouble on the 31st July, and constituted probably the most formidable obstacle on the Ypres front, was only partially included in the assault, and that part only on the extreme right flank of the attack. As the general tendency of the ground North of Clapham Junction, where the line gained on the 31st July crossed the Menin Road, is a gradually descending slope past the East face of Westhoek to the marshy valley of the Hanebeek, this meant that any failure or even delay on the extreme right would again expose the troops advancing down the slopes North of the Menin road to a devastating cross-fire from the higher ground to the South of them.* The fortunes of all the troops engaged South of the Ypres–Roulers railway depended, therefore, in large measure upon the rapidity and completeness of the success of the battalions on the extreme right of the battle. These latter battalions started to the assault of a most formidable position under the serious handicap which is almost invariably attached to the task of troops located on the flank of a battle-front. This circumstance was to have an important influence upon the course of the fighting on the whole front of the II Corps.

AUGUST 1917

The attacking battalions of the 25th Brigade were the 2/ Royal Berkshire (Lieut.-Colonel A. A. H. Hanbury-Sparrow, D.S.O., M.C.), with their right on the Westhoek–Zonnebeke road in touch with the 56th Division, and the 1/ Royal Irish Rifles (Lieut.-Colonel H. W. D. McCarthy O'Leary, M.C.). The 2/ Lincolnshire (Lieut.-Colonel E. F. O. Richards) were holding the Black line prior to the assault and had suffered heavily from shell-fire during the previous night, on the occasion of a German counter-attack against the adjoining 167th Infantry Brigade. The 2/ Rifle Brigade (Major J. J. B. Cole) were in reserve about Westhoek. In the 23rd Infantry Brigade sector, the 2/ West Yorkshire (Lieut.-Colonel H. St. J. Jeffries) and the 2/ Middlesex (Major A. G. Cade, M.C.) were detailed for the assault, the Black line being held by the 2/ Scottish Rifles (Lieut.-Colonel W. F. Somervail, M.C.) with the 2/ Devonshire (Lieut.-Colonel A. Tillett, M.C.) in reserve about Westhoek. Two companies of the latter battalion were told off to provide "moppers-up" for the 2/ Middlesex. The left flank of the division rested on the Ypres–Roulers railway, which once more formed the Corps boundary, in touch with the 16th Division. The 24th Infantry Brigade had one battalion (2/ East Lancashire, Lieut.-

---

* The danger had been pointed out by General Heneker in a memo to II Corps dated the 12th August 1917, wherein he had urged, in vain, that the attack of the 56th Division on the higher ground should be delivered shortly before the 8th Division's attack, and should be supported by a special concentration of artillery.

THE HANEBEEK

Colonel A. A. Sharland) located just West of the Westhoek Ridge, ready to take over the defence of the Ridge after the assaulting brigades had gone forward, another battalion (2/ Northamptonshire, Major S. G. Latham, M.C.), on Bellewaarde Ridge at the call of the G.O.C. 25th Brigade, and the remaining battalions (1/ Worcestershire, Lieut.-Colonel C. M. G. Davidge, and 1/ Sherwood Foresters, Major T. H. Watson, M.C.) in divisional reserve in Railway Wood and Ypres.

The attack was again provided with powerful artillery support, six brigades of field artillery, organized in three groups of two brigades each under the general command of Brig.-General H. G. Lloyd, D.S.O., being allotted to the 8th Division's front. Ninety 18-pounders were detailed to form the creeping barrage, and thirty-six 4·5-inch howitzers and eighteen 18-pounders to form the standing barrage. The machine-gun companies (23rd Machine-Gun Company, Capt. F. W. Robinson; 24th Machine-Gun Company, Capt. A. M. Pratt; 25th Machine-Gun Company, Capt. A. Simonds, and 218th Machine-Gun Company, Lieut. E. Tall) were grouped to fire on two barrage lines, the one along the Zonnebeke Redoubt line and the other on a line extending from the north-east edge of Polygon Wood to a point south-west of Zonnebeke village.

Owing to the darkness of the night and the broken nature of the ground, the attacking troops on both brigade fronts found it no easy matter to make their way up to the assembly positions; despite the fact that guides had reconnoitred the way both by day and night and small posts or tapes had been laid out by the Royal Engineers to assist in keeping direction. This difficult task had been admirably executed under the direction of Lieut. Wilkins, 2nd Field Company, R.E., on the 23rd Infantry Brigade front, and of Lieut. Chiswell, 490th (H.C.) Field Company, R.E., on the 25th Infantry Brigade front. By 4.15 a.m. or soon after all troops were in position, including a company of the 2/ Rifle Brigade (under Capt. Curtis) which had been sent to act as "moppers-up" to the 1/ Royal Irish Rifles who had lost a number of men from shell-fire while moving up to their assembly positions.

Punctually at 4.45 a.m. the artillery barrage fell. It came down with admirable intensity and precision and the attacking battalions, moving forward in splendid fashion close behind it, made good progress all along the line of the division. The ground West of the Hanebeek was occupied without difficulty, and the 2/ Royal Berkshire reported the capture of about 50 prisoners during this advance. The 2/ West Yorkshire found two German machine-guns in Hanebeek Wood still hot from firing, with their detachments lying about near them killed or

GERMAN "PILL-BOXES"

wounded by our barrage. It was noticed that these guns had AUGUST
been fired without tripods, being merely rested on the top of the 1917
parapet. The hand bridges, accurately placed in position by
carrying parties of the 22/ D.L.I. (Pioneer Battalion) under
Major J. D. Mitchell, enabled the Hanebeek Stream to be
crossed without a check and progress was successfully continued
up the Anzac Spur towards our objectives on the Ridge (the
Green line).

Meanwhile, the German " pill-boxes " and strong points at
Sans Souci, in Hanebeek Wood and near the railway embankment, were being scientifically reduced by the troops detailed for
that purpose. The front waves of the attack had swept over these
points, leaving them to the " moppers-up," who dealt with them
with smoke bombs and mills grenades as only trained experts
could do. Clouds of smoke, obscuring the landscape, soon
began to pour from the interior of these isolated concrete forts,
till the survivors of their garrisons were smoked out and compelled to surrender.

The protective barrage put down by the German artillery
fell at about two minutes after " zero " on the crest and western
slopes of the Westhoek Ridge. It therefore just missed our
support battalions, 2/ Lincolnshire and 2/ Scottish Rifles, which
were able to move up to the original front line as arranged without suffering many casualties. So far, everything was going
well.

The first check came at about 5.5 a.m. on the front of the 2/
Middlesex, whose left company, having outstripped the troops of
the adjoining brigade of the 16th Division, found itself exposed
to enfilade machine-gun fire from the railway embankment and
from German strong points to the North of it. The approach of
the 48th Infantry Brigade towards Potsdam Redoubt eased the
situation temporarily and enabled the left of the Middlesex to
resume its advance; but, having reached a line running due South
from the railway at a point approximately opposite Potsdam, its
progress was again held up by the same cause. There seems,
indeed, little doubt that few, if any, of the British troops North
of the railway were able to pass East of Potsdam, with the result
that the German garrisons there were left free to command the
situation South of the railway with machine guns posted in the
Redoubt and on the higher ground beyond it.

This first check, due to factors beyond the control of the
division, found its parallel, in yet more serious circumstance, on
the right flank of the division. The doubts which the Divisional
Commander had expressed in the memorandum already referred
to proved only too well founded. The 56th Division and the 18th
Brigade on its right were forced to acknowledge, after many

THE HANEBEEK

gallant efforts to get forward, that the task of clearing the wooded sector North of the Menin road was beyond them. Local defences, most formidable in themselves, were reinforced not only by machine-gun fire from Inverness Copse, but also by a powerful concentration of artillery from the South-East, and provided a barrier which proved unbreakable. The tanks detailed to assist the attack in this sector discovered at an early stage that progress across the mud and brimming shell-holes was a mechanical impossibility. Their undaunted crews laboured to get them forward till, one after another, they stuck fast and immovable. Not one succeeded in coming into action. Terribly handicapped as they were, parties of the 56th Division infantry reached the western and north-west outskirts of Polygon Wood, but they were in far too small force to withstand the German counter-attacks.

It soon became clear to the officers of the 2/ Royal Berkshire on the spot that no protection for their flank could be looked for from the troops to the South of them. Having re-formed his battalion, therefore, after its successful advance across the Hanebeek, Colonel Hanbury-Sparrow detailed one company to guard his right flank and with two other companies continued the attack as soon as our barrage lifted. Though impeded by heavy enfilade fire from German machine guns in Nonne Bosschen and Polygon Woods, the Berkshire succeeded in capturing the greater part of Iron Cross Redoubt and the defences to the North of that place, where another 50 prisoners were taken. On their left, the 1/ Royal Irish Rifles and 2/ West Yorkshire had naturally been less immediately affected by the failure of the right of the II Corps and, after passing through Hanebeek Wood, had swept forward up the ridge. Anzac and Zonebeke Redoubts were captured in spite of a strenuous and prolonged resistance, Anzac Redoubt falling as the result of skilful flanking movements in which the left company of the Berkshire, under Capt. J. A. Cahill, M.C., co-operated ably with the Irish Rifles. Consolidation was at once begun, and covering parties were pushed forward down the farther side of the ridge, some even getting as far as the next ridge overlooking Zonnebeke.

The enemy's first counter-attacks were dealt with successfully, and here in the centre of the 8th Division attack, with our troops already settling down on their final objectives, the local outlook at about 7 a.m. was distinctly promising. Unfortunately, from the point where at Iron Cross Redoubt the 2/ Royal Berkshire were facing the enemy on two fronts to the point where beyond Zonnebeke Redoubt the 2/ Middlesex were forming front to the North, the 8th Division was a full 1,000 yards in

PERIL FROM THE FLANKS

front of the divisions on either side of it. A number of frontal counter-attacks, delivered in greater strength, were driven off as the earlier attacks had been; but more serious trouble came from the flanks, and came quickly. Particularly heavy fighting took place round Zonnebeke Redoubt, where our troops were attacked simultaneously on three sides, and along the whole front the line began to grow very weak as the result of the unceasing sniping and enfilade machine-gun fire. From the 56th Division sector on the South, there developed a powerful German reaction which, despite the stubborn gallantry of the covering party of the Berkshire, threatened to cut off a great part of the 8th Division troops in the forward areas of their advance. When, shortly before 8 a.m., the enemy regained possession of Anzac and forced back the 1/ Royal Irish Rifles to the line of the road West of the Redoubt, leaving the forward companies of the 2/ Royal Berkshire in turn exposed on both flanks, the situation became desperate.

At about 9 a.m., Colonel McCarthy O'Leary, severely wounded in the shoulder and exhausted from loss of blood, arrived at 25th Brigade Headquarters accompanied by his Adjutant Capt. G. H. P. Whitfield to report in person on the position of his battalion. He told how the enemy were counter-attacking in great force on the left of the Irish Rifles, and that his forward companies, without a single commissioned officer remaining, were putting up a stubborn fight against overwhelming odds and were gradually giving ground. The Berkshire were also fighting practically without officers. Acting upon this report, General Coffin sent two companies of the 2/ Lincolnshire to support the Berkshire and a company of the 2/ Rifle Brigade to the help of the Irish Rifles. The situation, however, was not relieved and all units were becoming very mixed up.

The retirement of the Irish Rifles left the 2/ West Yorkshire in almost equally desperate case. It was no longer in touch with the 25th Brigade, nor yet with the 2/ Middlesex, who were finding the increasing pressure from beyond the railway more than they could withstand. For another hour the West Yorkshire hung on to their positions and then, reluctantly accepting the necessity of safeguarding their own position, called in their outposts on the forward slope of the Green line ridge and withdrew to the West side of the crest.

In these circumstances, at about 9.30 a.m. the enemy launched along the whole front of the division a series of powerful and determined counter-attacks in which he employed large numbers of fresh troops, brought up in buses from the direction of Passchendaele. The masses of low cloud which had rendered the night so dark and made the forming up of our troops for the

THE HANEBEEK

assault so difficult, now impeded our aeroplanes in their work of indicating targets to our guns. Though the de-bussing of the German reinforcement could be clearly seen by our forward troops, the thickness of the weather made it impossible for ground artillery observers to discern or answer the " S.O.S." signals which the infantry sent up. Deprived of the protection of their artillery, exhausted and thinned in numbers by a difficult advance and by five hours' continuous fighting under heavy flanking fire, and with their rifles in many cases clogged and useless with mud, the men were unable to hold their ground against the assault of the enemy's counter-attack divisions. Our front was driven in and there was a general retirement.

Grievously handicapped as our troops were, they were still fighting with the utmost gallantry, and the retirement was stubbornly contested. In the right battalion sector General Coffin, who had gone forward to reconnoitre the position in person, himself rallied the retiring line and succeeded in checking the enemy's advance. A composite force composed of all available troops was got together under Colonel Hanbury-Sparrow and a fresh stand was made on a line running from a point on the divisional boundary about midway between the Hanebeek stream and Iron Cross Redoubt north-westwards to Hanebeek Wood. Here were already established, under command of Major J. B. B. Cole, M.C., all that were left of the 1/ Royal Irish Rifles and of the two attached companies of the 2/ Rifle Brigade, in touch with the 2/ West Yorkshire who had fallen back to the Hanebeek after disputing with dogged determination every foot of the ground yielded. To the North of the West Yorkshire the 2/ Middlesex continued the line to the railway at a point some little distance West of the stream, with a defensive flank aligning the railway itself.

The right flank of the division was still very much in the air and exposed to continuous machine-gun fire from Nonne Bosschen Wood; but the position was held without change for several hours. To stiffen our line on the right, the two remaining companies of the Rifle Brigade were sent up to reinforce Colonel Hanbury-Sparrow's command and shortly after 11 a.m. Capt. C. E. Blake and two companies of the 2/ Northamptonshire were ordered to get into touch with the 167th Infantry Brigade (56th Division) and to find out the exact position of its forward troops.

It was not until the afternoon that the enemy made any further attack in force; but at 2.45 p.m. the 2/ Royal Berkshire reported that the Germans could be seen to be reinforcing strongly on the right, in evident preparation for a counter-attack. A green Verey light (the " S.O.S." signal) was fired to summon

GEN. COFFIN SAVES THE SITUATION

the assistance of the artillery; but in the mist and rain it passed unnoticed and the enemy was enabled to assemble in large numbers without artillery molestation. An hour later the attack was delivered in strong force all along the 25th Brigade front and made steady, if slow, progress. The enemy did not attempt to close with our troops, but worked his men forward in small parties from shell-hole to shell-hole, occupying first of all the ground to our flanks and then as we retired the ground vacated. In this way he continued to gain ground with methodical persistence, pressing back our troops to the under-features at the foot of the Westhoek Ridge.

So menacing, indeed, did the situation become that General Coffin, whose energy, resource and daring had once more become the soul of the defence, decided to put Brigade Headquarters personnel into the line. This reinforcement, scanty though it was, sufficed to bring temporary relief. All accepted readily enough the opportunity to take a direct part in the actual fighting, and the Brigade Signalling Officer, Lieut. Cohen, R.E., was found by the Brigade Commander shooting away very happily and putting carefully into his pocket the empty cases of cartridges with which he had scored a hit.

Meanwhile, Capt. Blake, commanding the two companies of the Northamptonshire mentioned above, had found that the most advanced troops of the adjoining 167th Brigade were some 100 yards behind the 2/ Royal Berkshire, while the majority of them were still further back in the neighbourhood of Jabber Reserve. The two Northamptonshire companies were now ordered forward from their positions in Jaffa Trench by General Coffin in person and they moved up with great resolution through a heavy barrage which wounded Capt. Blake and also 2nd Lieut. Frost, the officer commanding " C " Company. Second Lieut. J. M. Bailey, although himself wounded in four places, immediately took command and conducted the advance with the greatest coolness and intrepidity. Under his leadership, the two companies pushed on, drove back the enemy and with the remnants of the other battalions stabilized the line on the forward slopes of Westhoek Ridge. The arrival of these two companies had the further result of releasing the personnel of Brigade Headquarters for their proper duties, and also made it possible to fill up the gap which had arisen between the 2/ Royal Berkshire and the adjoining 167th Brigade. The remaining two companies of the 2/ Northamptonshire were ordered forward to the positions in Jaffa Trench vacated by the two former companies.

The line of the 25th Brigade was once more steady when the climax of the German reaction came. During the afternoon

THE HANEBEEK

further German reinforcements had been brought up by bus and were collected and formed up, apparently, in the valley beyond the Anzac Ridge. These were now seen advancing in a series of lines over the crest of the ridge and down its western slopes, bidding fair by their very numbers to drive back still further the exhausted and depleted battalions opposed to them and perhaps to take Westhoek Ridge itself. At this moment the massed batteries of the Divisional Machine-Gun companies (Major J. M. Mood, M.C.), situated on the western slopes of the Westhoek Ridge, saw and seized their opportunity. As the dense waves of German infantry surged down the open slopes towards the Hanebeek, the machine guns opened a furious barrage over the heads of our own infantry. The Artillery F.O.O.'s also saw their chance, and a few minutes later the artillery joined in. It was a perfect bit of work. The counter-attack hesitated, halted, and then melted away.

There can be no doubt that, as in similar circumstances on the 31st July, the remarkable courage and coolness shown by General Coffin, in face of the violent bombardment and a most critical situation, had a very high moral effect on his troops and was an important factor in restoring the fortunes of the day. Despite the extreme difficulty of communication and the confusion resulting from the heavy loss of officers and mingling of units, he succeeded in maintaining an effective control over the forces under his command, and on more than one occasion turned the scale by his personal intervention. The Victoria Cross which was awarded to General Coffin for his consistent gallantry and skill both on this day and in the opening battle was most thoroughly earned. Stirred by his example and confident in his leadership, heartened too by the disaster which they had seen befall the German counter-attack, the troops of the 25th Brigade now offered so firm a front that the enemy showed no inclination to attempt any further advance. The crisis on this part of the front had been successfully overcome.

In co-operation with the attack just described the enemy had also advanced at about the same time against the 23rd Infantry Brigade, whose two forward battalions had until this time maintained themselves in the positions described above. The exposed flank of the 2/ Middlesex had been strengthened early in the afternoon by a company of the 2/ Scottish Rifles and touch had been gained with isolated mixed groups of two battalions of the adjoining 48th Infantry Brigade. These troops had no officers and were found to be no further forward than the line of the road running immediately West of the railway dump.

The renewed attack against the 23rd Brigade had come mainly from the direction of the Zonnebeke Redoubt Ridge,

THE GUNS TAKE A HAND

where also the enemy had been seen massing in large numbers during the early part of the afternoon. At 4.45 p.m. his troops began to pour down the forward slope; but fortunately Major H. C. H. Smith, 2/ Scottish Rifles, who with two companies of his own battalion and two companies of the 2/ East Lancashire was holding the northern part of the Black line, was from his Headquarters in direct visual communication with the guns. In response to his call a powerful and effective barrage, in which the machine-gunners again joined, was promptly put down on the slope leading down from the Zonnebeke Redoubt. It caught the enemy's infantry in full descent and practically annihilated them. Here, too, the attack was completely wiped out.

AUGUST 1917

The withdrawal, however, of the 25th Brigade to the foot of the Westhoek Ridge had left the right flank of the 23rd Brigade unduly exposed and the 2/ West Yorkshire were in consequence compelled to move back some distance further to the West of the Hanebeek, a movement to which the 2/ Middlesex conformed in due course. Later in the same evening, as it appeared to be useless to continue to hold an exposed line in the Hanebeek Valley, the brigade was ordered back to approximately the original Black line and touch was established with the 25th and 48th Brigades on either flank.

During the night the battalions which had borne the main burden of the day's fighting were relieved. On the 25th Brigade front the line was taken over by the 2/ Northamptonshire and the 1/ Sherwood Foresters, the latter battalion being temporarily attached to that brigade for the purpose. The 2/ Rifle Brigade remained in support, and the rest of the brigade (except the 1/ Royal Irish Rifles who went right back to Birr cross-roads*) withdrew to Jacob Trench. The line of the 23rd Brigade was held after relief by the 2/ Scottish Rifles and the 2/ East Lancashire, with the 1/ Worcestershire (attached from 24th Brigade) in support on the western edge of Westhoek Ridge and the 2/ Devonshire in reserve on Bellewaarde Ridge. The 2/ West Yorkshire and 2/ Middlesex were withdrawn to Railway Wood.

The night and following day passed quietly, no counter-attacks developing. Infantry movement on the 17th was, indeed, confined on both sides to the collecting of wounded. Artillery fire on the forward area was only slight, and the work of consolidation was carried on without interruption, until the relief of the division on the night of the 18th/19th August.

The battle ended, therefore, as far as the 8th Division's front was concerned, in a return practically to the *status quo*. It had started with a fine promise of success, with steady and

* Their strength on retirement was 1 officer and 60 men! A few more men were collected during the night.

THE HANEBEEK

uninterrupted progress all along the front of attack and a very considerable booty in prisoners, of whom at least 300* had been received by the 2/ Northamptonshire on the Bellewaarde Ridge and passed back under escort to the divisional cage quite early in the morning. But the early promise could not be maintained. To the obvious danger on the right had been added early in the day an unexpected danger on the left. Here the two divisions of the XIX Corps, after pushing on rapidly—too rapidly, perhaps, for they left unreduced strong points in their rear—at the first German reaction at about 9 a.m. came back almost as rapidly to their line of departure. With both flanks in the air, and exposed on both flanks to enfilade machine-gun fire which searched their positions continually from higher ground, the attacking battalions of the 8th Division yet contrived, not only to make a very considerable advance during the opening stages of the battle, but to hold a substantial portion of their gains until well into the afternoon. Their depleted ranks had then been exposed to determined counter-attacks carried out by large numbers of fresh troops. Though for the most part deprived by adverse weather conditions of the aid they had looked for from the artillery, they had fought in their enforced withdrawal as stubbornly and tenaciously as in their original advance. They had punished the enemy heavily with their rifle fire, and at the end of the day still held North of Westhoek one of the only two small gains recorded for this battle on the whole front South of St. Julien.

North of St. Julien, though the XVIII Corps had been forced by the failure of the 16th and 36th Divisions to throw back their right to that village, our troops on this day took Langemarck and reached substantially the whole of their objectives. There can be little doubt that if the troops of the XIX Corps had been more successful in resisting the German counter-attacks on their front, the 8th Division could have maintained the major part of its own advance and the results of the whole battle would have presented a far more encouraging picture.

Though no more than a half-success, the attack of the 16th August is interesting as affording a good example of the enemy's new methods of defence. For to meet our new method of step by step advance he had been forced to find once more a fresh antidote. In the battle of the Somme he had, it will be remembered, devised a means of counteracting the destructive effects of our preliminary bombardment by the construction of deep underground chambers which no artillery could destroy, whence the defenders could emerge when the destructive storm had passed.

---

* The total number of prisoners taken on this day by the nine British divisions engaged was 1,600. The 8th Division, therefore, did particularly well in this respect.

Black line .... ─────
Approximate Front line ....
Objective (Green line) .... ─x─x─x─

16TH DIV.

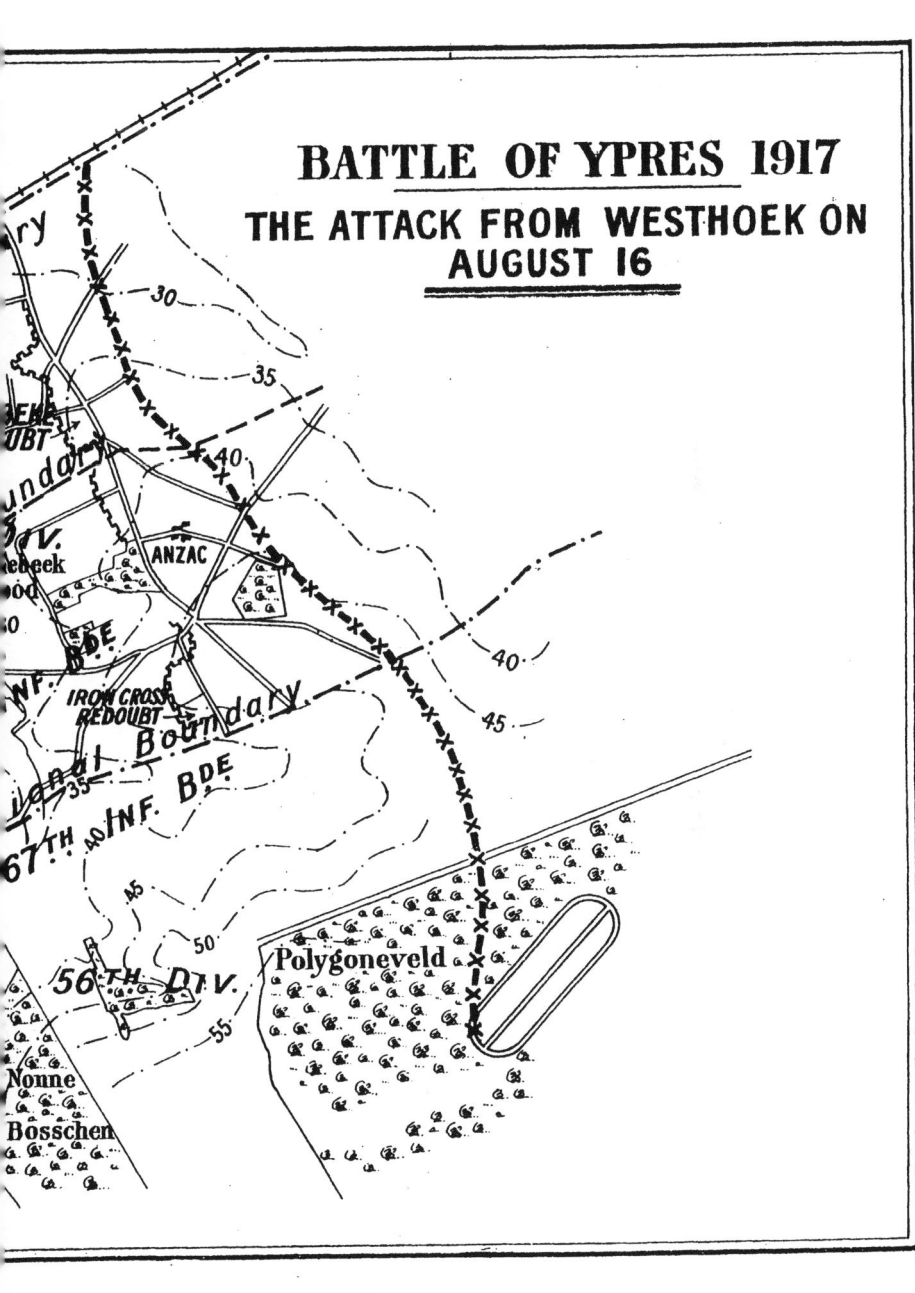

THE DEFENCE IN DEPTH

The weight of metal fired by our artillery had been enormously increased by the passage of a year, and the construction of underground chambers was, moreover, in most cases quite out of the question in the mud flats of Flanders. Some new plan had had to be devised, and the enemy had solved the problem by adopting the defensive in depth. The front lines which received the full weight of our projectiles were only lightly held: the bulk of his forces were kept in close reserve, ready to deliver immediately powerful and premeditated counter-attacks which were designed to neutralize the advance which, it was conceded, would have been made by the attackers. In other words, our troops were to be counter-attacked on carefully prepared lines, while they were still tired and disorganized by their advance and before they had had time to consolidate. In this way it was hoped that the positions which had been overrun might speedily be recovered.

AUGUST 1917

Another device had been adopted to strengthen this method of defence. This was the so-called "pill-box," a small fort or shelter built of reinforced concrete, so thick as to be impervious to anything but direct hits by heavy artillery. These were distributed in depth throughout the fighting zone and, being heavily armed with machine guns, were very serious obstacles to progress. The constant mention during the course of this narrative of the Ypres fighting of machine-gun fire from the flanks, and the extent to which it was responsible for the limitation of our gains on the 31st July and for the partial failure of the 16th August, clearly indicate what powerful instruments of defence these "pill-boxes" were. Yet the account of the fighting of the 8th Division on the latter day, and the capture of Iron Cross, Anzac and Zonnebeke Redoubts, show that these obstacles could be overcome by skilled and resolute troops.

In these two first battles of the Flanders offensive of 1917 the 8th Division was certainly unlucky in having adjacent to it on its right a sector so difficult that twice it proved too big an obstacle for the troops of the adjoining division. On each occasion its task on its own front was only less hard—if indeed its difficulties can fairly be said to have been less—than that of the troops attacking on its right. On both occasions its disappointment was the greater and its misfortune emphasized owing to the fact that advances which its own gallantry had won were nullified by events for which it was not responsible. The lack of success of the XIX Corps on the 16th August was an additional disaster and left the forward battalions of the 8th Division in a situation which no troops could have maintained against resolute attack. There seems, indeed, to be no reason to doubt that the 8th Division would have completed its allotted tasks with unqualified

THE HANEBEEK

success, but for these untoward circumstances over which it had no control.

That the gallant effort made by the division in this Ypres fighting was understood and appreciated by the Higher Command is shown by the exceptionally large number of honours and awards issued to all ranks in connection with these operations. They included 2 V.C.'s, no less than 9 D.S.O.'s, 54 M.C.'s, 2 Bars to the Military Cross of which one fell to the Rev. A. S. Crawley, 52 D.C.M.'s, 198 M.M.'s, and 9 Bars to the Military Medal.

The 8th Division remained in the line, as has already been said, until the evening of the 18th August. During that night it was relieved by the 47th Division and moved back to Ypres and neighbouring camps, command of the sector passing at 10 a.m. on the 19th August. Twenty-four hours later the division was transferred from the II Corps Fifth Army to the Second Army reserve and moved back, chiefly by motor omnibus, to the Caestre area, Divisional Headquarters being opened at Caestre. The division was once more sadly reduced in numbers. Its casualties in this last encounter amounted to 81 officers and 2,074 other ranks and when the infantry were inspected by Sir Douglas Haig on the 21st August the full strength on parade numbered no more than 3,950 all ranks. The Commander-in-Chief gave the division many words of encouragement and thanks, inspiring all ranks by his generous appreciation of what they had done. About a week was spent in resting and training, and the opportunity was taken to make up the depleted units with some 1,293 drafts. On the 23rd August the division began its move South to the II Anzac Corps (Lieut.-General Sir A. J. Godley).

The departure of the 8th Division from the II Corps provided the occasion for the receipt by the Divisional Commander of very gratifying congratulatory messages, from the Fifth Army Commander, General Sir H. de la P. Gough and from the II Corps Commander, Lieut.-General Sir C. W. Jacob. In congratulating General Heneker and the division on the splendid and very gallant fights which they had fought on two occasions, General Gough pointed out that it was no fault of theirs that they failed to retain all the ground won on the 16th August, and that their fine success in going forward over all difficulties of ground was due to their great spirit and their good discipline and training. The message from General Jacob was also couched in the most cordial and appreciative terms, and this chapter cannot be concluded more appropriately than by reproducing it verbatim. It ran as follows:

"On the conclusion of the operations of your division which began on the 31st July and ended on the 18th August, I wish to

GENERAL JACOB'S THANKS

offer my congratulations to the whole division on the success which has invariably attended their efforts.

AUGUST 1917

"The division is well commanded, staffed and trained, and by its excellent discipline and training has shown that it can successfully attack, go through and capture any system of enemy defences no matter how strongly fortified and prepared.

"The gallantry and dash shown by all ranks was the admiration of us all and great credit is due to the brigade and battalion commanders for the way they led their units in the hard fighting which was before them.

"It is with great regret that I have received orders for the transfer of the division from the II Corps. My best wishes to you all for the future. A hearty welcome will await you if you return to the Corps."

CHAPTER XI

AUTUMN AND WINTER 1917

AFTER its two hard-fought battles, the 8th Division both had earned and required a rest; but the strain to which the British Armies were subjected in the Ypres offensive did not permit it to be left long out of the line. On the 25th and 26th August, therefore, the 24th Infantry Brigade was moved forward by bus to the Romarin area and by the morning of the 27th August had relieved the 1st New Zealand Brigade in the sector opposite Warneton. Brigade Headquarters were established at Rue du Sac.

At 10 a.m. on the 27th August General Heneker took over command of the right (Ploegsteert) sector of the II Anzac Corps, with Headquarters at Steenwerck. The movement of the infantry was completed at the end of the month, when the 24th Infantry Brigade extended its left northwards to the line of the River Douve in relief of the 13th Australian Brigade, 4th Australian Division, and the 23rd Infantry Brigade came into the line on its right, taking over from the 4th New Zealand Infantry Brigade. The artillery reliefs took place a few days later.

The front for which the 8th Division was now responsible extended for a distance of some 7,000 yards from the point where the River Lys crossed our front line—between Houplines, a suburb of Armentières, and the village of Frelinghien—on the South, to the line of the River Douve on the North. On the right the 23rd Infantry Brigade held during the whole period of this tour of duty a front of some 5,200 yards covered by the river Lys. In the less comfortable northern portion of the divisional front the 24th and 25th Infantry Brigades relieved one another in turn.

The new sector formed the most southern portion of our gains in the great victory of the 7th June, which had flattened out the Messines–Wytschaete salient. It was all fresh ground, wet and muddy, with its defences still incompletely organized. But hostile shelling was not heavy, except at times in la Basseville and to the North of that place, and it was possible to reorganize the division and even to train and absorb the new drafts. Meanwhile, the II Anzac Corps, which in the June attack had captured the positions for the defence of which the 8th Division was now partly responsible, had been detailed to take its turn in the larger battle from which the 8th Division had just come. On the 2nd September, therefore, the VIII Corps (Lieut.-General Sir Aylmer G. Hunter-Weston) took over command of the II Anzac Corps' front.

Quiet though the new sector was by comparison with the scenes which the 8th Division had just left, the absence of infantry

GAS ATTACKS AND "DEMONSTRATIONS"

action did not mean that the enemy was left alone. During the month of September, on the nights of the 8th/9th, 12th/13th, 13th/14th and 18th/19th, a series of highly successful gas attacks were carried out by " L " Special Company, Royal Engineers, by means of Liven's projectors, a weapon which had been introduced by us for the first time in preparation for the Arras battle of this year. Many hundreds of cylinders, equivalent to several tons of lethal gas, were projected on to targets which included Duriez Farm, Inden Rooster Cabaret and the German trenches in the neighbourhood of Warneton. The main episode of the month was, however, the " demonstration " on the VIII Corps' front which took place on the 20th September. That day marked the resumption in force of our advance on the principal battle front further to the North. The infamous weather which had prevailed during the latter part of August had prevented any major operations since the attack in which the division had taken part on the 16th of that month. The battle of the 20th September was, therefore, the third large scale attack in the course of the Ypres offensive.

The operation was a remarkably successful one, resulting among other gains in the capture of the whole of the bitterly contested ground astride the Menin Road which had played so large and unfortunate a part in the two attacks of the 8th Division to the North of it. It is, therefore, of interest to note that the plan of attack was changed in a material particular. The active front was extended southwards to the Ypres–Comines Canal, and the whole attack from the canal to the neighbourhood of the Ypres–Roulers railway was entrusted to the Second Army which thus had the difficult Menin Road sector in the centre of its assault. The enemy was at last driven from the positions from which on the 31st July and 16th August he had raked the advancing troops of the 8th Division, and the 2nd Australian Division, who on the 20th September attacked where the 8th Division had so stubbornly fought on the 16th August, were able to conduct their advance without experiencing a devastating cross-fire from the right flank.

Though other troops were thus to complete the work which the 8th Division had begun, the division still had its part to play in aid of the success which had been denied to its own efforts. For the object of the demonstration on the VIII Corps' front was to assist the real attack by inducing the enemy to believe that an assault was to be delivered along the whole of the VIII Corps' front North of the River Lys. " Zero " hour for the demonstration—5.40 a.m.—synchronized with the " zero " hour of the real attack, and at that hour a heavy barrage, both artillery and machine gun, was put down on the German positions. The

AUTUMN AND WINTER 1917

brigades in the line—now the 23rd and 25th—co-operated by creating a dense cloud of smoke by means of 1,200 smoke candles, and by sending up groups of special rockets. Dummies constructed by the 2nd Field Company Royal Engineers (Major A. H. Brown, M.C.) had been laid out along the front of the 25th Infantry Brigade. By an arrangement of cords, these were raised suddenly at " zero " hour, so that through the smoke it appeared to the enemy's observers that our infantry had left their trenches to assault the German lines. The enemy was undoubtedly deceived; for he put down a strong barrage on our front and support lines and also fired heavily with machine-gun and rifle fire at the dummies, most of which he knocked down. He subquently reported that a British attack had been repulsed!

For the remainder of the month and also throughout October activity on the divisional front remained normal, with the ordinary artillery, trench mortar, and machine-gun fire and patrolling on either side, varied by the usual air fighting and at times by the bombing and machine gunning of our roads and trenches by enemy airmen. One may pick out as worthy of special notice a raid attempted by the enemy on two posts of the 2/ Rifle Brigade at 10.30 p.m. on the 23rd September. There was no preliminary artillery bombardment, but small trench mortar bombs were fired on the posts for fifteen minutes before the raid commenced. Then suddenly a Verey light discovered the enemy in and about our wire and a sharp fight with bombs, rifles and revolvers followed. Owing to the smoke of the bombs it was difficult to see the details of what occurred; but the Germans were successfully driven off without casualties to the defenders and, when the confusion was over, it was found that they had left seven dead (2 Unter-offiziers and 5 other ranks) behind them.

The chief interest of the division, as of the whole British Army outside the battle area, was centred during this period upon the work of our troops in the Ypres salient whence in the concluding weeks of September and the opening days of October came news that cheered all who heard it. Yet even the small change of daily trench warfare was not without its piquant and exciting incidents. Take, for instance, the adventure which befel an unnamed officer and N.C.O. of the 1/ Royal Irish Rifles when out on patrol on the night of the 25th/26th October. These two became detached from their patrol and being uncertain of their position, although they knew that they were somewhere on the German line, were forced to take cover in what appeared to be a sniper's post. A sniper's post, indeed, it was, and with the dawn there came along the German occupier. Quite unsuspicious, and not unnaturally, of such unlikely tenants, he blundered straight on—into the path of a revolver bullet. Whereupon the

PASSCHENDAELE

two made off at top speed in the glimmering dawn and despite the noise of the shot succeeded in getting clear. At about 11 o'clock they managed to regain our lines where they had long since been given up, and indeed had been officially reported as missing.

During the latter days of October rumours had reached the division that it was to be sent to Italy under Lieut.-General the Earl of Cavan, to form part of the British Army of Italy afterwards commanded by General Plumer. These rumours, as rumours have a way of doing, came to nothing; but early in November a definite intimation was received that the division was to move to a much less attractive theatre. On the 6th November a warning order was published stating that the 8th Division would shortly be relieved in the line by the 3rd Australian Division. The relief began with the arrival on the 9th of the Australian Artillery and on the following day the 8th Divisional Artillery marched to Ypres, coming under the orders of the Canadian Corps. The interchange of infantry units followed and the relief was completed by the 14th November.

The division left the Ploegsteert sector in far different condition from that in which it had entered it. Two months in a reasonably quiet sector had done wonders to restore its capacity as a fighting machine. Drafts had been assimilated and support troops, machine gunners, Lewis gunners, bombers, etc., had been carefully and thoroughly trained to their special duties. Opportunity had been found for horse shows, football, and sport and recreation generally, and the result showed itself in the high spirit and excellent morale of all ranks.

When the Australians had taken over, Divisional Headquarters moved to Watou and the units of the division were assembled in the Berquin and Lamotte areas to the South-East of Hazebrouck. The destination of the whole division was the Ypres front once again and on the 16th November the 25th Infantry Brigade moved from the Berquin area by route march to Caestre, thence by train to Ypres, and thence by route march again to St. Jean and Wieltje on the Ypres-Passchendaele road. Here they relieved the 8th Canadian Infantry Brigade group in support and on the following day took over from the 7th Canadian Infantry Brigade in line just North of Passchendaele. On the next day (the 18th November) the 8th Division completed the relief of the 3rd Canadian Division in this sector which formed the extreme limit of our gains in the Ypres fighting. Passchendaele itself had only been captured by the Canadians on the 6th November. The front taken over was a single brigade front only, with the 24th Infantry Brigade in support in the Wieltje area and the 23rd Infantry Brigade in reserve in the Brandhoek

AUTUMN AND WINTER 1917

area due West of Ypres. Divisional Headquarters were transferred to Ypres.

The division arrived when the great battle, which had cost so much in blood and suffering to the British troops engaged, had ended; but to the troops fresh from their two months on a comparatively quiet front there was little evidence that the conclusion of the mighty contest had already come. Nor was it intended that there should be such evidence; for, as will shortly become apparent, it was important that the enemy should think for a few days longer that our dogged and insistent struggle against a stubborn foe and a scarcely less hostile season was still continuing.

During the absence of the division from the active battlefront, much had been accomplished. The interval of fine weather which had marked the month of September had for a brief space given the British Armies an opportunity to put into uninterrupted execution the plan of a series of methodical advances, carefully though rapidly prepared and individually limited in scope, by which it had been hoped to achieve the primary strategic object of the campaign—the clearance of the Belgian coast. Late though the season was when the advance had been resumed in force on the 20th September, the success of our efforts then and in the subsequent battles of the 26th September and 4th October had for a moment raised hopes high. It had been proved that, given reasonably favourable weather, the plan of campaign was sound and could accomplish all that had been claimed for it. In each of these three great battles our full objectives had been gained substantially at all points without undue difficulty, and with comparatively little loss. With the better communication and co-operation between our infantry and artillery made possible by the clearer weather, the enemy's new system of defence by counter-attack had definitely broken down, and on the 4th October in particular had involved him in appalling casualties. In the course of this splendid fortnight, eloquent of what might have been accomplished had the weather been kinder in August, our front had been carried forward from 2 to $2\frac{1}{2}$ miles and our line firmly established on the western slopes of the main ridge East of Ypres. The morale of the German infantry was strained to breaking-point and the enemy was beginning to be short of troops with which to feed the battle, when once more the weather came to his rescue. The battle of the 9th October was fought in the old stormy conditions after two days of continuous rain. That of the 12th October was, perforce, broken off half-fought in consequence of the extreme violence of the weather.

With the abandonment of this attack vanished all hope of achieving in 1917 the larger strategic purpose of the offensive. The clearing of the Flanders coast had become for the present

PLATE XI

Copyright: Imperial War Museum
WINTER, 1917-18
YPRES SALIENT: A DUCK-BOARD TRACK

Copyright: Imperial War Museum
WINTER, 1917-18
THE ROAD TO PASSCHENDAELE

AN UNEASY FRONT

impossible; but there remained a lesser object to be achieved in the Flanders theatre, namely, that of securing for our troops a safe and reasonably comfortable line for the winter and one from which, if opportunity offered, the offensive might one day be resumed. The immediate purpose, therefore, of the fighting which took place on the Ypres front after the 12th October was to gain if possible before winter the remainder of the ridge to Passchendaele and Westroosebeke, from which latter place a winter line could be established on reasonably dry ground westwards to Houthulst Forest. When the 8th Division arrived upon the front this hope also had been disappointed. On the 10th November the last engagement of the offensive had been fought and Passchendaele had proved the limit of our advance along the ridge.

Yet there remained a further purpose to be served by maintaining activity on the Flanders front. The second great purpose of the whole offensive, if, indeed, it should be reckoned second, was to occupy the attention of the German Armies and prevent an attack upon the French during the period of intense discouragement which followed the breakdown of their spring offensive. The fighting for Passchendaele and Westroosebeke had had the further merit of assisting the French in their attack at Malmaison on the 22nd October and of diminishing to some extent the disaster which two days later befell the Italian Armies at Caporetto.* So now, apart from local improvements in our line in the Passchendaele sector which it was still desirable to effect, the continuance of infantry and artillery activity on the Ypres battle front was required in order to distract the enemy's attention from our preparation for the surprise attack with tanks opposite Cambrai, carried out by General Byng's Third Army on the 20th November.

Indeed, although our big offensive had come to an end, the new line East of Ypres had by no means settled into quietude. The front was restless, just as the ocean is restless with continued heave and swell after the violence of the storm has passed. The enemy was palpably nervous and his state of mind was revealed by the activity of his aircraft and the intensity of his artillery fire —which latter took the form, ever and anon, of a definite barrage.

The shelling of the forward areas at this time was indeed more severe than any which the division had yet experienced, while the mud and water and discomfort of life East of Ypres were indescribable. To get from Ypres to the front line entailed a

---

* As a result of our insistent pressure at Ypres, two German divisions which were on their way to Italy were diverted to Flanders. Cf. Ludendorff, *My War Memories*, Vol. II, p. 491.

AUTUMN AND WINTER 1917

walk of several miles along duck-boards. One step off the duck-boards meant sinking to the knees in mud from which it was impossible to extricate oneself unaided. Men got into this mud in the dark, and, after many hours of exposure, died of cold and exhaustion despite every effort made by rescue parties to save them. The old battlefield was one vast tormented bog, seamed by narrow lines of corduroy or duck-board tracks which, marked down by the enemy's artillery, were swept with high-explosive and shrapnel by day and night. The mere work of repair kept large numbers of men continuously employed, both in the huge workshops where the 6-foot lengths of duck-boarding were made and in the more arduous and dangerous task of restoring the gaps blown by the enemy's shells. Brigade and Battalion Headquarters were housed in huge captured concrete "pill-boxes" capable of resisting 6-inch shells and containing, some of them, three rooms, each 8 feet high and 12 feet by 14 feet in area. They were often hit, in one case at least as many as seventeen times in a single night, the terrific jar of the impact compelling their inmates to keep standing as the best way to lessen the concussion. Our own artillery lived and fought in conditions of constant physical distress. Guns sank in the mud till they became useless and ultimately disappeared beneath the surface; till our battery positions were dotted with little red flags marking the positions where guns had sunk from view.

Yet through it all, our policy of maintaining a show of threatening activity continued and did nothing to restore the enemy's confidence. His infantry dispositions were indeed highly favourable for the exploitation of minor openings for aggression by our junior commanders. His troops were distributed between a forward line of outposts for observation; an intermediary, or covering, line through which the forward troops would drop back, their retreat covered by its fire; and finally a main line of resistance to which both the former lines would eventually retire. The forward line, consisting of isolated posts, held in some cases by half a dozen men or less and well in advance even of the second or covering line, offered obvious opportunities and these were not neglected. The capture of two or three prisoners became an almost regular feature of the daily reports. Each brigade took its turn in this occupation, the 24th Infantry Brigade relieving the 25th on the night of the 19th/20th November, and themselves handing over to the 23rd on the night of the 23rd/24th November.

Shortly after midnight on the 24th/25th November our line was advanced by a small operation of a more formal character, carried out without any barrage by the 2/Devonshire and the 2/West Yorkshire. A temporary hitch on the right of the Devons,

A LOCAL OPERATION

caused by a German machine gun which took full advantage of the bright moonlight, was overcome by the action of Capt. H. H. Jago, M.C., who took charge of the troops there and with the assistance of the West Yorkshire worked round to the back of the gun position and forced the enemy to abandon it. A considerable number of Germans were killed and 5 prisoners passed back for identification, and a new line was dug on the crest of the ridge with an uninterrupted view for about 400 yards. The enemy retaliated at about 6 a.m. on the 30th November with an organized attack, complete with barrage and aeroplane co-operation; but the division was ready for some such counter-move. The 2/Devonshire in line opened fire immediately with rifles and Lewis guns, causing many casualties, and a very good and effective artillery barrage which came down promptly on receipt of the " S.O.S." signal completed the enemy's discomfiture.

DECEMBER 1917

Meanwhile, on the 20th November a warning order had been issued that the 14th Division would relieve the 8th Division at the beginning of December, the 8th Division moving on relief to the Wizernes area. Notice had been received on the 19th, however, that before this relief took place there was to be another and rather more considerable local operation, in which troops of the VIII and II Corps would be engaged. Our line to the North of Passchendaele village at this date formed a pronounced salient of which the apex was held by the 8th Division. On the right and to the South of the 8th Division troops, the 33rd Division faced East along the line of the ridge; on their left and to the West slightly in rear, the 32nd Division (II Corps) faced due North. The object of the attack was to open out the West side of the salient and at the same time carry our line sufficiently far northwards along the ridge to give us observation into the valleys running up to the Passchendaele plateau from the North and East. The 8th Division was to be represented by the 25th Infantry Brigade which accordingly on the night of the 30th November/1st December took over the line from the 23rd Infantry Brigade. The major part of the operation was to be undertaken by the 32nd Division. The rôle of the 33rd Division was to assist by demonstrating.

It had been learnt from captured documents that the enemy had issued orders for his artillery, if we attacked, to barrage our front line at once and a few moments later to withdraw the barrage on to his own outpost line. To escape this fire it was necessary to get forward into his main position as soon as possible. Accordingly a surprise attack unaccompanied by any opening barrage was decided upon, in the hope that our infantry would be able to cross the dangerous area and reach the enemy's main position before his barrage could come down. " Zero " hour was arranged for 1.55 a.m. on the 2nd December and our barrage was not to open till " zero "+8', i.e. 2.3 a.m.

The plan was not without its dangers. The moon was only three nights past its full and it was, therefore, by no means unlikely that the enemy might catch sight of our advancing troops and open upon them with machine-gun and rifle fire between " zero " and " zero "+8'. General Heneker was much concerned about this possibility and advocated that either the artillery barrage should open earlier—at " zero "+6' or even " zero "+4' — or alternatively that arrangements should be made for an " S.O.S." signal to be sent up by a conveniently placed observer—the O.C. 2/ Lincolnshire, Lieut.-Colonel N. M. S. Irwin, M.C., from his Headquarters at Mosselmarkt was chosen for the part—should the occasion demand it. In the opinion of the Divisional Commander hostile machine-gun fire from prepared positions on a bright moonlight night was more to be feared than any artillery barrage. The progress of events would certainly seem to show that this opinion was justified. Both suggestions, however, were overruled, as the 32nd Division considered that it was impossible to organize an effective creeping barrage to cover the infantry advance on their front; because that attack was to be delivered from South to North, whereas their guns would be firing from West to East. The barrage would, therefore, perforce be in enfilade, and experience had shown that such a barrage was difficult to manipulate, was often inaccurate and tended to mislead the infantry as to their direction. The original plan was accordingly left unchanged.

The battalions detailed for the 25th Brigade attack were as follows: 2/ Royal Berkshire (Lieut.-Colonel C. R. H. Stirling, M.C.) on the right, 2/ Lincolnshire (Lieut.-Colonel N. M. Irwin, M.C.) in the centre, and 2/ Rifle Brigade (Lieut.-Colonel Hon. R. Brand, D.S.O.) on the left. Owing to the bright moonlight, the forming up of the assaulting troops had to be done inside our outpost line which was to be held at the moment of assault by a half-company of the Berkshire, one company of the Lincolnshire and one company of the Rifle Brigade, in front of the remainder of their respective battalions.

The company of the Lincolnshire which had been detailed to hold the outpost line in the centre was unfortunately heavily shelled on the way up and arrived only 20 strong. One company of the original garrison of the 1/ Royal Irish Rifles (Major T. H. Ivey) was, therefore, ordered to remain in the front line, its place in brigade reserve being taken by a company of the 2/ West Yorkshire under Capt. Scott. The frequent gaps which shell-fire had made in the duckboard tracks made the move forward very difficult and many men became completely stuck in the mud.

SOUTHERN REDOUBT

Some casualties also were sustained from the enemy's guns, while the Rifle Brigade were unlucky enough to lose their C.O., Colonel Brand, who was wounded by a rifle bullet while reconnoitring the forming-up line. Lieut.-Colonel G. H. G. Anderson, M.C., took over command of the battalion in his place. The journey was, however, ultimately accomplished and, once they had arrived, the troops, assisted by Lieut. O. S. Francis, M.C., Brigade Intelligence Officer, succeeded in getting into their correct forming-up positions without further difficulty.

The objective on the 8th Division front was a section of the German main defensive line containing two redoubts, Southern Redoubt and Venison Trench. This line was covered by the usual outposts and, as our attacking troops moved forward under a bright moon, machine-gun fire was opened almost immediately. On the left, indeed, heavy fire commenced the moment our men left their forming-up positions and on the right and centre, where the shadow of a passing cloud momentarily veiled the front, within three minutes of " zero." By " zero "+ 5' machine-gun and rifle fire was intense along the whole front of attack, and the enemy was thoroughly on the alert, sending up lights of various colours and designs in large numbers. Our guns opened fire at " zero "+ 8' according to plan, and the enemy's artillery barrage did not come down until a minute later; but owing to the delay caused by the machine-gun fire already encountered the support platoons were not all clear of the barrage zone and suffered considerable casualties. The Company Headquarters of " B " Company 2/ Royal Berkshire were blown up, and the Company Commander, 2nd Lieut. Giddings, was knocked over and dazed.

The 2/ Royal Berkshire reached their objectives none the less, and " D " Company dug themselves in on a line extending to the south-east edge of Southern Redoubt. On their right " C " Company (Capt. Flint), detailed to form the defensive flank, had succeeded in their task without much difficulty; though in getting into touch with " D " Company their left platoon under 2nd Lieut. Smith had some brisk fighting and took 30 prisoners. Despite " B " Company's initial misfortune, No. 5 Platoon (Sergt. Sturgess) entered Southern Redoubt itself and very heavy fighting took place there with bomb and bayonet. Many Germans were killed and our own casualties were not light. Unfortunately, the left platoons of " B " Company, in an endeavour to keep touch with the 2/ Lincolnshire who had not succeeded in reaching the main German line, bore too much to the West and so opened a gap just North of the Redoubt. No. 5 Platoon in the Redoubt was thus left without sufficient support, and after losing its platoon commander, was forced out, the survivors ultimately digging themselves in on a line to the South-West. The

AUTUMN AND WINTER 1917

evacuation of the Redoubt exposed the left of " D " Company; but our troops there succeeded in maintaining themselves none the less and repelled minor attacks by which the enemy attempted to dislodge them.

Meanwhile, the left platoons of " B " Company under 2nd Lieut. W. A. Upton had captured a portion of the German trench connecting the two redoubts, killing many Germans and taking three machine guns. Although isolated on either flank, they succeeded in establishing themselves in this trench which was actually on the front of the 2/ Lincolnshire. The attacking companies of this latter battalion had suffered severely from the enemy's machine-gun and rifle fire in the first stages of their advance. All their officers became casualties, and after overrunning many forward shell-hole positions, they were compelled by the intensity of the enemy's fire to dig in about 30 yards short of the main German trench line.

On the left of the attack, the 2/ Rifle Brigade had an even more unpleasant experience. In addition to their full share of the German machine-gun and rifle fire on their front, they were much impeded by enfilade fire from a strong point known as Teal Cottage on the front of the 32nd Division. It had been arranged that the 32nd Division was to take Teal Cottage prior to the attack and that the forming-up tape of the 2nd Rifle Brigade should be laid out with its left at this post. At the last moment, however, it was found that the strong point was still in the enemy's possession, and the battalion was compelled at once to throw back a defensive flank to face it. As a result of this combination of misfortunes, the attacking companies never succeeded in reaching Venison Trench and, when over 50 per cent. of their effectives had become casualties, including 10 officers out of 12, the survivors dug themselves in about 100 yards in advance of their original line.

Thereafter, the position on the 8th Division front remained substantially unchanged and a number of minor attempts to drive in our new posts were repulsed without difficulty. At 4.10 p.m., however, the enemy's shell-fire became intense and the " S.O.S." signal was sent up by the 32nd Division. It was repeated on the 8th Division front and our artillery opened fire at once. Large numbers of the enemy advancing East of Southern Redoubt were thoroughly caught and scattered and the counter-attack, as far as the 8th Division's front was concerned, faded away completely. By 5 o'clock the enemy's barrage was dying down and unusual quietness prevailed. At dusk Colonel Stirling took the opportunity of withdrawing 2nd Lieut. Upton's party from the isolated position on the 2/ Lincolnshire's front which it still maintained. On withdrawal it filled up the gap

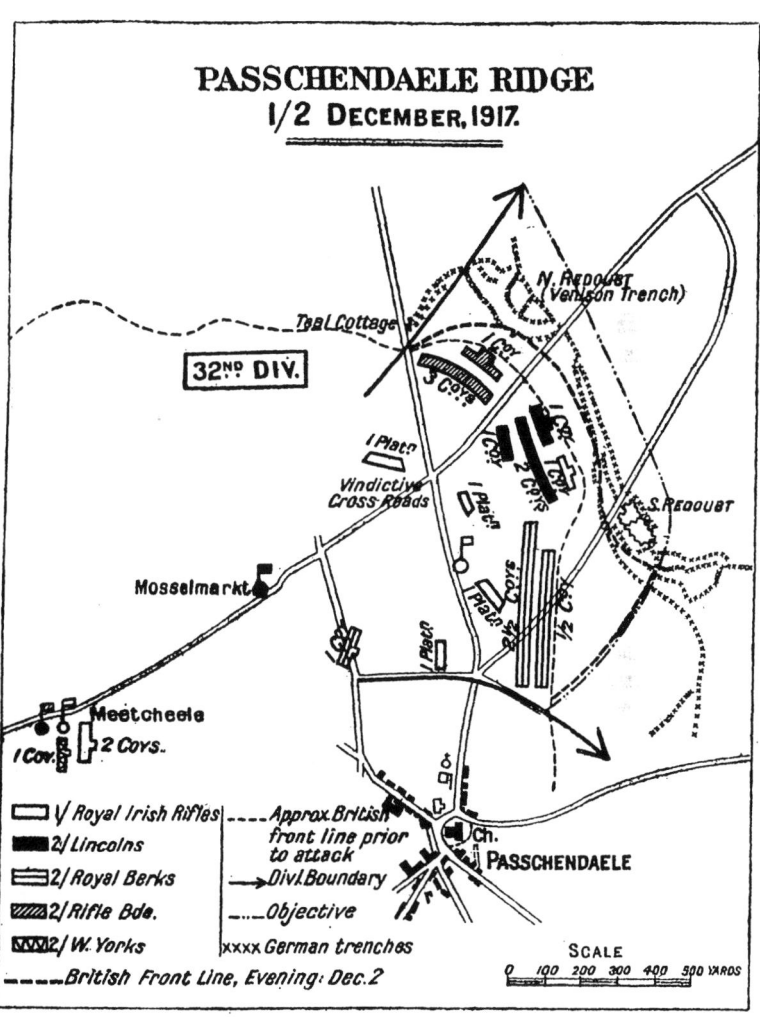

A QUALIFIED SUCCESS

between the Lincolnshire and the Berkshire and thus formed the whole of our front into a continuous and connected line. The engagement by that time was definitely over and during the night General Coffin's brigade was relieved, in accordance with previous arrangements, by the 41st Infantry Brigade, 14th Division.

The operation can only be regarded, at best, as a qualified success. For, although about 150 prisoners and 4 machine guns had been captured and a certain amount of ground had been gained, the main purpose of this attack—the capture of the two redoubts and the gaining of observation down the valleys they commanded—had not been accomplished. The noise inseparable from forming up for the attack among such trying conditions of mud and water had put the enemy on his guard; thereafter the brightness of the moonlight and the absence of a protecting barrage during the first critical eight minutes were responsible for all that followed. It was evidently possible for the enemy to see our men, moving forward in bodies, at a distance of 200 yards. Assuming that he could do that and that he made proper use of his opportunities, failure was inevitable. In the circumstances the infantry of the 8th Division, in particular the 2/Royal Berkshire, had done remarkably well; though casualties had not been light. Lieut.-Colonel A. Tillet, commanding the 2/Devonshire, was mortally wounded on this day and the total losses of the division amounted to 40 officers and 584 other ranks. It only remains to add that the 32nd Division had been even more unfortunate; for, though some ground was won at the opening of the assault, all its gains were lost in the afternoon counter-attack to which reference has been made.

After completion of its relief by the 14th Division, the 8th Division moved to the Wizernes area, South of St. Omer, Divisional Headquarters being opened at that place on the 3rd December. On this day, too, Lieut.-Colonel E. H. L. Beddington, M.C., who had been G.S.O.1 of the division for exactly a year, left on promotion to be G.S.O.1 of the Fifth Army. His place as G.S.O.1 of the division was taken by Lieut.-Colonel H. S. Adair (The Cheshire Regiment). The division remained in the Wizernes area resting and training for a clear three weeks. Training facilities were good and a great deal of useful work was accomplished, of which lectures by specialists formed an important part. All good things, however, have an end. It was actually on Christmas Day—in traditional Christmas weather, with snow and frost—that the move back to the line was commenced. The division returned once more to the Passchendaele sector, relieving the 14th Division at the very point of the salient, and took over on the 27th December, 24th Infantry Brigade (Brig.-General R. Haig, D.S.O.) being in line, 25th in support

AUTUMN AND WINTER 1917

and 23rd in reserve. Divisional Headquarters were established at The Dead End, in the Canal Bank at Ypres. Conditions in the line were normal, though the weather was very cold with a good deal of snow. Elaborate precautions were taken, with success, to prevent trench feet and the health of the troops was good. They were cheered by a New Year's Message from their Corps Commander, in which Sir Aylmer Hunter-Weston recalled the fact that he had visited every infantry unit and placed on record his appreciation of the efficiency of the division.

So in bleak and bitter weather the year ebbed away with the battle lines still locked, mile after dreary mile from Switzerland to the sea, in their deadly and seemingly purposeless embrace. The experience of the 8th Division in each of the three engagements in which it had taken part in the Flanders offensive had been harsh and disappointing. Endeavour had been dogged by misfortune, and effort brought to naught by circumstance. As had been the case with the great offensive itself, the immediate objectives for which the troops had striven had constantly eluded them.

Yet in actual fact the British Ypres offensive had played an essential rôle in the long struggle in the West. It had secured a period of repose for our Allies and enabled General Petain to achieve his arduous task of restoring confidence, discipline and heart to the French Armies. In that greater rôle the 8th Division in its more restricted sphere had played its own part right worthily; but considerations of such a kind could scarcely be expected to be present to the minds of the fighting rank and file of the division fresh from the mud and suffering of Flanders. To them at that time, tactical successes at ruinous cost seemed still to be the sum of achievement that could be produced by either side on the Western Front. The conclusion of the year seemed to add but another term of accomplished time to a struggle which was apparently at once unending and incapable of being ended. Both the hazards and the victories of the coming year, concealed in the womb of time yet begotten in the bitter Flanders struggle, were imperceptible to the eyes of the men who suffered and endured in trench and dug-out, in order that the deadlock might be maintained.

CHAPTER XII

THE GREAT GERMAN OFFENSIVE

THE situation on the Passchendaele front remained very much as it was when the 8th Division had left that sector at the beginning of December. The two redoubts and the trench system connecting them, which the 8th Division had vainly essayed to capture on the 2nd of December, were still in German hands and the enemy appeared to be working hard on his defences there. At this period of the year defence, and not attack, was necessarily the main concern of either combatant; but this did not prevent considerable activity on the part of both artilleries and in the air. Hostile aeroplanes were much in evidence.

The weather continued to be very trying. Alternate periods of extreme cold and sudden thaw, varied by heavy falls of snow and hail, maintained a seesaw of intense discomfort; until on the 15th of January a warmer spell was ushered in by a terrible storm, the wind blowing with gale force and the rain coming down in torrents. Towards evening on that day the consequences of the violence of the elements became serious, plank roads being washed away and duckboard walks disappearing. On that very night the 25th Infantry Brigade were relieving the 23rd in the line, and the sufferings of the troops of both brigades were great. Men sank deep into ice-cold clinging mud and had to be dug out. When the 23rd Brigade finally reached camp after relief all ranks were in a state of complete exhaustion.

Nor were conditions any more cheerful in the line itself. Battalion Headquarters which were chiefly in " pill boxes " were all flooded and had to be pumped out with infinite labour. Most of the accommodation for the men at Brigade Headquarters was in a like condition and could only be cleared gradually. Though the weather subsequently improved, the 25th Infantry Brigade had a most trying experience throughout its whole tour in the trenches. Many men collapsed from exposure and exhaustion; several were partially buried in mud and shell-holes and were extracted with great difficulty. Even Divisional Headquarters itself was not immune. It was located on the Canal Bank, and by the morning of the 16th the water in the canal had risen until it had flooded all the lower dug-outs and was endangering the bank, which showed signs of landslide in several places. Some of the dug-outs were entirely destroyed and others were much damaged. The whole division found once more, as it had found in the first winter of the war, that life in Flanders trenches in mid-winter could be dangerous (let alone discomfortable) enough, even if the enemy were left entirely out of account.

After nearly three weeks of purgatory, the division was

THE GREAT GERMAN OFFENSIVE

relieved by the 29th Division, command passing on the 19th January. A spell out of the line had certainly been earned and was even more than usually welcome. Divisional Headquarters were opened after relief at Steenvoorde, with the units of the division in the surrounding area. Two battalions of the 24th Infantry Brigade (1/ Worcestershire and 1/ Sherwood Foresters) were, however, left at Poperinghe for work in the Army Battle Zone. The remainder of the division at once settled down to training, the first few days being devoted to cleaning up, drill and general organization, the later period to the training of specialists and to instruction in the consolidation of shell-hole positions. For the latter purpose each brigade blew a series of shell holes with gun-cotton. These were then drained and worked upon to form defended posts.

At the end of the month important changes took place in the composition of the division, in connection with the reduction of infantry brigades from a 4-battalion to a 3-battalion basis. This reorganization had been forced upon the Higher Command by the exigencies of the man-power situation, and it affected every infantry division of the British Army, with the exception of the Dominion divisions. The 8th Division, being composed of Regulars, did not have to contemplate the suppression of any of its battalions; but the transfer of three of them to other divisions became necessary. The battalions selected to leave the division were: 2/ Scottish Rifles, 23rd Infantry Brigade—transferred to 20th Division; 2/ Lincolnshire, 25th Infantry Brigade—transferred to 21st Division; 1/ Royal Irish Rifles, 25th Infantry Brigade—transferred to 36th (Ulster) Division. To complete the 25th Infantry Brigade the 2/ East Lancashire were transferred to it from the 24th Infantry Brigade. These moves were ordered on the 31st January and took place on the 3rd February.

The division remained in Corps reserve until the 9th February when the move back to the line to relieve the 29th Division was begun, command passing on the 12th February. During this tour of duty there took place certain changes of command, both inside and outside the division. On the 20th February General Sir H. S. Rawlinson gave up command of the Fourth Army, of which the 8th Division now formed part, on appointment to the War Council at Versailles. He was succeeded by General H. C. O. Plumer, who had returned from Italy after the establishment of the Allied line on the Piave. Four days later General Coffin* left to take temporary command of the 50th Division, handing over the 25th Infantry Brigade to Lieut.-Colonel A. H. S. Hart-Synnot, East Surrey Regt., attached from

* He returned to the command of his brigade on the 15th March.

A MENACING OUTLOOK

the 29th Division. On the last day of February Lieut.-Colonel MARCH
C. C. Armitage, D.S.O., joined the division as G.S.O.,1 vice 1918
Lieut.-Colonel Adair.

Apart from these changes, the ordinary routine of trench life was broken by a little adventure undertaken by the 2/ Middlesex (Lieut.-Colonel C. A. S. Page, M.C.). At 6 o'clock in the evening of the 3rd March two complete platoons moved out under cover of a mixed barrage of smoke and shrapnel, their objective being to raid the enemy's defences in the vicinity of Teal Cottage (see p. 166. previous chapter). The enterprise was a complete success. The enemy's line was entered at the point intended and all Germans encountered were either killed or captured. Six prisoners were brought back, and the whole undertaking was carried through at the cost of one man slightly wounded by a splinter from one of our own trench-mortar bombs.

A few days later the division was again relieved by the 29th, command passing on the 8th March. As they left the line the troops of the 8th Division were taking, though they knew it not, a final farewell of the Ypres front. They went again to the Steenvoorde area, Divisional Headquarters being opened at Abeele. A comprehensive programme of training was immediately commenced, the scheme being to devote the greater part of the time at first to musketry and elementary exercises in extended order work. More advanced tactical schemes by battalions and brigades were to come towards the conclusion of the training period. But the training period was never completed. Before a fortnight had passed the division was summoned South—to the greatest episode of its career in France.

Since battle fighting had died away late in the previous Autumn, a very marked and menacing change had come over the general situation. The final collapse of Russia had set free thousands of German troops from the Eastern Front. Throughout the winter division after division had been railed across the continent, until numerical superiority on the Western Front lay once more with the enemy. The Italian disaster at Caporetto at the end of October, which made it necessary to reinforce that front with both French and English divisions sent from France, accentuated the discrepancy in the enemy's favour. The initiative, in a word, had passed once more into his hands. He would only be able to retain it temporarily; the steady arrival of American troops made that certain. Yet until the Americans had arrived and, still more important, had been trained in adequate numbers, the balance of power was his. Nothing was more likely than that he would use that balance—while still he had it—in a vigorous attempt to bring the war to a satisfactory and a victorious conclusion.

THE GREAT GERMAN OFFENSIVE

These facts were sufficiently recognized at General Headquarters and everything had been done that could be done to prepare for the adoption for a time of a defensive instead of an offensive rôle. But the strenuous efforts made in 1917 " had left the Army at a low ebb in regard both to training and numbers,"* and the political authorities at home turned a deaf ear to the repeated requests of the British Command in France for adequate reinforcements. The enormous flood of reinforcements from home which was released *after the blow had fallen* is in itself evidence, incontrovertible enough, that thousands upon thousands of troops sufficiently trained for service overseas had been retained in England in deference to the bogey of German invasion. Had these thousands been sent out earlier, the great German thrust could have been held and parried long before it had developed into the mighty onrush which brought the Allied Armies within measurable distance of decisive defeat in the field. It would have been stopped, too, at far less cost to the gallant divisions of the Fifth and Third Armies, the 8th Division among them, which, outnumbered as they were, yet contrived by their own sacrifice to stave off irreparable disaster.

However, as things were, it was inevitable that some part of our long line—a line extended moreover in January by the taking over of an additional 28 miles from the French—should be lightly, too lightly, held. The danger of weakening it to the North, where there was so little rearward room for manœuvring that a successful German thrust might drive us all too quickly back upon the sea, was obvious. If ground had to be given up, it was better that it should be yielded in the Somme area where an equal loss would not have such serious consequences. It was, moreover, a legitimate hope that the scarred and tormented nature of that stricken field would act, to some extent, as a check upon the exploitation of any break in the defensive line.

The general situation remained, however, at best both doubtful and menacing. The imminence of a German offensive on a most ambitious scale was logically clear enough to have been convincing, one must suppose, not merely to highly placed officers at General Headquarters but to almost any man of intelligence and vision throughout the armies. In many a camp or dug-out the question was, no doubt, discussed and re-discussed and speculations raised. To the 8th Division, sharing with the 29th the task of holding the Passchendaele sector of the Ypres front, the question seemed at first merely of academic interest. For in that sodden and muddy theatre an attack so early in the year was hardly likely; although already new defensive lines, about Wieltje and yet farther back, were nearing completion; to which

* *Haig's Despatches*, Dent's Edition, p. 178.

the Fourth Army might fall back in order to shorten its line and set free divisions should they be required elsewhere.

MARCH 1918

Quite suddenly, however, the outlook changed. After the division had been in rest for only two or three days its brigades were ordered, one by one, and day by day, to move from the Steenvoorde area to the Tilques area. Divisional Headquarters followed, being transferred from Abeele to Wizernes, and on the 13th March the definite order was issued that the division had been placed in General Headquarters reserve and was to be prepared to move at twelve hours' notice. The new area, adjacent to the railway junction of St. Omer, made the division conveniently placed for immediate entrainment.

The question of the German attack, and of its time and place, had become for the 8th Division a matter of cardinal interest and importance. For under existing conditions it was practically inevitable that any division placed as the 8th Division now was would be involved, sooner or later, in the coming battle. The brigade units carried on with their training in the new area according to programme; but for the staffs there followed a period of strenuous activity. Every possibility had to be explored and every preparation made, in order that the division might be immediately ready whenever the expected order to move by strategical trains should be received. Hence there flowed forth a perfect spate of contingent orders and instructions, and one has visions of staff officers sitting weary-eyed at their tables far into the watches of the night.

For the move of a division *en bloc*, at short notice and without loss of time, cannot be carried out without the most painstaking and detailed preliminary arrangements. The allotment of trains and entraining stations and the determination of the precise manner and order in which each train would have to be filled were in themselves a highly complicated piece of work, and involved a whole host of subsidiary problems. Where horses should be watered; how many days' rations would be required for issue to units in advance, and what proportion should be carried on the man; the allocation of cookers and teams to the different trains in such a way that all should be in order on arrival; the precise number of wagons which could be allotted to D.A.D.O.S.; the ultimate disposition, even, of the divisional laundry—such were the kind of problems which had to be thought out in advance, the proper solution discovered, and the necessary orders and instructions issued accordingly. The move of the division in the circumstances contemplated—going perhaps straight from disentrainment into battle—made it necessary to eliminate all unnecessary impedimenta, and another set of instructions was therefore issued regarding the establish-

THE GREAT GERMAN OFFENSIVE

ment in St. Omer of a divisional surplus kit store. Much prevision and a vast amount of detailed hard work was, indeed, called for from the staff and administrative officers of the division and freely and efficiently given by them.

So the days passed, the staff busied with these problems and the fighting units preparing themselves for battle, until on the 21st March the German blow was struck. General Headquarters had been closely watching events, and at 9 o'clock on the same morning a telegram was issued ordering all units of the division to be in readiness to move at five hours' notice. At 6 o'clock that evening came the definite instruction: " 8th Division will entrain on March 22nd and 23rd. . . . First train for Infantry will leave St. Omer at 3 a.m. and first train for Artillery will leave Hopoutre or Godewaersvelde at 5 a.m. on March 22nd." The Divisional Commander and G.S.O.1 were ordered to proceed immediately by car to Fifth Army Headquarters at Nesle to report to General Sir Hubert Gough for orders at 6 a.m. on the 22nd March.

The hours mentioned for the entrainment of the troops had subsequently to be altered, for the great attack had thrown a tremendous strain upon the British railway system at all points; but the first infantry train left at 6 a.m. on the 22nd March and the first artillery train at 11.45 a.m. Throughout the day trains departed at approximately three hourly intervals from each of the three principal entraining stations. The journey was a long one and few of the trains took less than a dozen hours to accomplish it. As they rumbled their slow way southwards, the battle front to which their living freight was being directed was becoming hour by hour more fluid and less stable. By the time the journey was ended, what would be the limit of its westward yield? None could say; but as the hours passed and rumour and conjecture gave place to more certain knowledge of events, the high importance of the task which the division would shortly be called upon to perform became more and more apparent.

The detrainment of the various groups took place at Nesle, Chaulnes and Rosières during the evening and night of the 22nd; but concentration prior to going into line was never completed. The division had been allotted to the XIX Corps (Lieut.-General Sir H. E. Watts) and late on the previous evening, at 11.30 p.m., divisional orders had been issued giving a *support* line some 5 miles East of the Somme, which infantry brigades were to be prepared to occupy at short notice. On his arrival, however, at Fifth Army Headquarters, General Heneker had been ordered by General Gough to make at once a personal reconnaissance East of the Somme of the switch line Voyennes–Monchy Lagache–Tincourt; and had been told that until the general situation had

ADVENTURES OF A BILLETING PARTY

developed further, no indication could be given to him as to the rôle which his division would be called upon to fulfil.

MARCH 1918

General Heneker and Colonel Armitage went off at once by car, but before they had completed their reconnaisance found themselves in the fighting zone. The roads along which they passed were a distressing sight—stragglers, wounded, guns, transport and vehicles of every description all moving westwards; while the roar of battle drew nearer every moment. General Heneker and his G.S.O.1 returned to Army Headquarters, then at Villers-Bretonneux, at about noon and reported what they had seen. Later they went to Villers-Carbonnel, where they found General Watts and the XIX Corps Headquarters, and learned that the 8th Division was to take up a position on the western bank of the Somme. Orders to that end were given by the XIX Corps to the different units of the division as they reached their detraining stations, with the result that the division went into action piecemeal as each train arrived. In one case a complete machine-gun company was taken by the XVIII Corps and was not seen again by the division till the battle was over. No opportunity was given for the infantry commanders and staffs to choose their defensive positions and dispose their troops to the best advantage, or to conduct that thorough preliminary reconnaissance which would in all probability have enabled the line of the Somme to have been defended for an even longer period than in the event proved possible.

Events had been moving only too quickly. The 24th Infantry Brigade had received orders, when they were *en route*, that the brigade on arrival at Nesle would proceed by march route to Athies where they would be billeted in reserve positions. But Athies lies East of the Somme (see map) and so well to the East of the line which they were now being called upon, with all urgency, to defend! One of the units of this brigade—the 2/Northamptonshire,—had, indeed, sent a billeting party forward in advance on the night of the 22nd/23rd March, and it had duly arrived at the village. " The party had already provided accommodation for the battalion in Athies, but owing to the enemy's rapid advance it had to fight its way out and find billets in Licourt."* A startling and ominous experience for a peaceful billeting party!

Before proceeding with our account of the 8th Division's fighting and fortunes in the Great Retreat, it will be well to turn back for a moment in order to give a brief *resumé* of the sequence of events on the Fifth Army front since the commencement of the battle. It had opened at about 5 a.m. on the 21st with an intense bombardment of gas and high-explosive shell from

* W.D. 2/ Northamptonshire, March 1918.

THE GREAT GERMAN OFFENSIVE

artillery of all natures. The assault of the German infantry had been delivered at about 9.45 a.m. A dense white fog, which lasted till 1 p.m., favoured the attackers; for the defence of our lightly held forward zone depended largely on the cross-fire of carefully sited machine guns and forward field guns. The lack of visibility rendered these guns more or less useless and so to a great extent destroyed the defensive scheme. Not only so, but the detachments holding the forward positions were in many cases overwhelmed or surrounded before they had even realized that the hostile assault had been delivered and before, therefore, they had been able to pass back information concerning the attack.

Favoured by this fortuitous advantage and with practically the whole of his striking force—carefully selected and for months specially trained for the shock offensive—committed to the one great battle against our Third and Fifth Army fronts, the enemy on the first day had gained ground to greater or lesser extent nearly all along the line—which, indeed, he had been expected to do. At three points, however, one on the extreme right of the Fifth Army front opposite la Fère, the second in the sector South of St. Quentin, and the other in the Cologne valley East of Péronne, not far from the junction of the Fifth and Third Armies, he had made more serious progress and in each of these localities had broken into our battle zone.

On the 22nd, the enemy renewed his attacks in great strength all along the line. There was again a thick morning mist, and although at this stage it was probably a handicap to the attack as well as to the defence, he succeeded in exploiting the advantage which he had gained in the sectors South of St. Quentin and in the Cologne Valley; until, during the late afternoon and evening, the centre of the Fifth Army, assailed by a tremendous concentration of German divisions and now deeply outflanked to South and North, was also compelled to give ground. By the evening of this day the enemy had crossed the St. Quentin Canal at Tergnier opposite la Fère and had established a bridgehead there after sanguinary fighting. The remainder of the Crozat Canal line was still held by the III Corps; on their left the XVIII Corps had commenced under orders the withdrawal from the battle zone opposite St. Quentin, and were finding it impossible to maintain a continuous fighting line over the greatly extended front which, as a result of the withdrawal, they were called upon to defend. On the left of the XVIII Corps the battered line divisions of the XIX Corps were retiring through the 50th Division which, strung out on a front of over 10,500 yards from Villéveque to Boucly, was being attacked at both extremities of its long line and had lost touch with its neighbours. Farther North, the

GENERAL GOUGH'S DECISION

troops of the VII Corps, greatly overstretched by reason of the progress the enemy had made along the Cologne valley, were with the utmost difficulty maintaining connection with the right of the Third Army.

The situation was uncommonly serious, in view of the fact that all available reserves at the disposal of the Fifth Army had already been thrown into the battle; while the Third Army was also fighting for its life and had not a man to spare. Our third and last defensive zone had been breached, and an immediate retreat to the bridgehead positions East of the Somme, covering Ham and Péronne and linking with the Third Army on the Nurlu plateau, appeared to be the only course open to the Fifth Army. Orders to this effect were given by the Army Commander late on the night of the 22nd March; but later General Gough, being under the impression that the Crozat Canal line had already been forced at Jussy, revised even this decision and came to the conclusion that it was no longer safe to offer further battle at all on the eastward side of the Somme. His troops were so exhausted that to do so would be, he thought, to run the risk of a decisive defeat; and a decisive defeat, with no reserves behind, would lead to a real and definite rupture of the line with all which that implied. Such a disaster must at all hazards be avoided. The line must continue to bend and to yield, to yield and to bend, to retreat and to retreat; the inevitable fissures must somehow, by possible or impossible means, be patched up; but it must at any cost be kept in being. Rupture, complete and definite, would mean irreparable disaster.

Such were the reasons which led General Gough to the decision to retreat at once to the western bank of the Somme. It is hard to criticize that decision, even in the light of the fuller knowledge of events now available, for it was crowned by success. Yet in fairness to the 8th Division it is only right that proper attention should be drawn to its immediate and inevitable results. It meant that, instead of being given some period of time in which to put the Somme river line into a state of defence under cover of the resistance, however short-lived, which the 50th Division and other troops might find it possible to offer East of the river, the troops of the 8th Division were called upon to undertake the active defence of the river line directly they had arrived upon it. No time was given them to acquaint themselves with the details of the position they were so suddenly required to defend, to ascertain and guard against its weaknesses or to turn its advantages to the best account. They went straight into the battle, fortified only by the knowledge that upon them depended the fate of the Fifth Army.

This then is the explanation of the sudden and hasty orders

THE GREAT GERMAN OFFENSIVE

direct to the Brigadiers concerned from the XIX Corps, on whose front the division was to operate. The 50th Division, and the remnants of the worn and exhausted divisions which had been engaged since the opening of the battle, were to come back across the bridges and go through the 8th Division into reserve positions in the rear, there to reorganize. The bridges were then to be blown up, and behind the protecting barrier of the water another desperate attempt was to be made to stem the German avalanche.

The sector of the river frontage allotted to the 8th Division ran from the river d'Ingon, at its junction with the Somme in the South, to Eterpigny in the North. This represented a front of about 15,000 yards, or $2\frac{1}{2}$ times the length of line normally allotted to a division in the defence of an organized trench system. The southern sub-sector from the river junction to Pargny Wood was given to Brig.-General Coffin and the 25th Infantry Brigade; the 24th Infantry Brigade (Brig.-General R. Haig) was in the centre holding a front from Pargny Wood to St. Christ bridge; Brig.-General Grogan with the 23rd Infantry Brigade held the left from St. Christ bridge to Eterpigny. The troops retiring through this line in the northern part of the area were the 50th Division with remnants of the 66th and 39th; to the South they were those of the 24th Division.

The 24th Infantry Brigade, to whom Colonel Armitage had been dispatched post haste to divert them from their march to Athies, were the first in position, at a very early hour on the 23rd March. General Heneker had himself gone to Chaulnes, where he had found General Grogan detraining, the darkness of a pitch-black night lit up by columns of red sparks from the shunting engines, and by a huge bonfire blazing in front of an American Red Cross hospital marquee. The air was heavy with the droning of German aeroplanes and shrill with the whistling of falling bombs. Two burst on the marquee, killing seventeen of the inmates and wounding many others. The troops and the trains mercifully escaped with scarcely any casualties; but the detraining took time and the 23rd Infantry Brigade were not completely established at their posts until the afternoon. The 25th Infantry Brigade, to whom General Heneker next went, had received no orders direct from XIX Corps and were in position even later. It was, indeed, found necessary to retain the 1st Cavalry Division to cover the river crossing at Béthencourt until the 25th Infantry Brigade should arrive. It was night before the cavalry were withdrawn.

At about 1 o'clock in the afternoon, before, that is to say, the 8th Division were fully in position, the first elements of our retiring infantry began to trickle back across the bridges. The guns and transport had already crossed. By 4 o'clock their rear-

THE SOMME RIVER LINE

guards had all passed over and the work of blowing up the bridges (which had been prepared for demolition long before the arrival of the 8th Division) was immediately put in hand. It had to be carried out, under orders of the Fifth Army, with undue haste and the results were not altogether satisfactory. A number of our tanks arrived to find the bridges already impassable and had to be burnt out and abandoned East of the river. On the other hand, the charges which had been laid in readiness proved in many cases insufficient to cause complete destruction and the hurried retreat left no time for further demolition. Most of the bridges remained to a greater or a lesser extent still passable, at any rate for infantry.

The disadvantages of the direct retreat from our rear system of defence to the Somme line were making themselves felt. The German infantry, with field batteries and trench mortars in close attendance, followed hard upon our retiring troops and, instead of being obliged to wait until dawn on the 24th March before advancing to the river, were able to take up their position on the East bank before nightfall on the 23rd. During the night the enemy made several attempts to cross at different places on the fronts of all three brigades. Although certain of the 8th Division troops had reached the West bank no sooner than the enemy had arrived opposite them, these attempts were all repulsed with complete success, such few Germans as succeeded in crossing being either killed or driven back again or rounded up.

The defence of the river line did not, however, depend only on the maintenance of the 8th Division's front. It has been pointed out that already, on the 22nd March, the river line had been crossed on the extreme right of the Fifth Army at Tergnier, and that the rapid widening of the front during the night retreat to the Somme had opened gaps in the XVIII Corps line. In the early morning of the 23rd the enemy, profiting by one of these gaps, had reached the river at Ham and had found the railway bridge East of the town intact. By 10.35 a.m. German troops had crossed the river in the Ham sector in strength and had begun to press back our troops. At about the same time he established an effective bridgehead West of the canal at Jussy. Thereafter he began to push forward on the whole front from the Oise River to beyond Ham, endeavouring at the same time to widen his attack by thrusting northwards along the West bank of the Somme, so as to roll up from the South the river line of defence.

When, therefore, at dawn on the 24th March, the enemy renewed his attacks and succeeded, by felling trees across the river and by the use of rafts, in making effectual crossings at three places on the front of the 25th Infantry Brigade, the position of that brigade was already gravely compromised by the

THE GREAT GERMAN OFFENSIVE

progress he had made on its right flank. Heavy fighting developed, all the brigade reserves being ultimately thrown into the struggle. With the southern flank crumbling, however, the task was more than any troops of their number could be expected to perform. By 10 a.m. the enemy had taken Béthencourt and was well to the westward of it. The left flank of the brigade was now also in difficulties, as the enemy had crossed at Pargny and was working round behind the left battalion (2/ Rifle Brigade, Lieut.-Colonel H. S. C. Peyton, M.C.), pressing them back and frustrating their endeavours to regain touch with the right battalion (1/ Worcestershire, Lieut.-Colonel F. C. Roberts, D.S.O., M.C.), of the adjoining brigade. The 2/ Rifle Brigade had also lost touch temporarily with the adjoining battalion of its own brigade (2/ East Lancashire, Major D. W. Hollingsworth commanding), on its other flank. Brigade Headquarters reported that they had no further troops in hand, except one Field Company, all the remainder having been used up in trying to maintain touch.

Meantime the brigade had to make the best of the situation with what troops it had. The Field Company in question (490th Field Company, Major D. L. Herbert, M.C., commanding), which had arrived as reinforcement during the morning, was ordered to take up a position astride the Morchain–Pertain road to act as a rallying point. The rest of the brigade after further severe fighting, during which Lieut.-Colonel Peyton was killed and Lieut.-Colonel C. R. H. Stirling, D.S.O., M.C., commanding 2/ Royal Berkshire, was dangerously wounded, gradually fell back on this position; and by about 2.15 p.m. the brigade was holding a line of trenches astride the Morchain–Pertain road and West of Potte.

In response to General Coffin's appeal, General Heneker had placed his only divisional reserve, the 22/ D.L.I. (Pioneers), Lieut.-Colonel C. B. Morgan, D.S.O., commanding, at General Coffin's disposal. The battalion arrived at Pertain early in the afternoon and two companies were immediately sent into the line South-West of Potte. The third company, together with the 490th Field Company, was sent to gain touch with the 20th Division (XVIII Corps) on the right. This they succeeded in doing in the neighbourhood of Dreslincourt. Touch had also been regained at about 3.30 p.m. on the other flank, and thus by about 6 o'clock, although the brigade had been forced back from the river line, the position on its front was once more comparatively stable.

The retirement of the 25th Infantry Brigade had, of course, affected the adjoining (24th) Brigade on their left. On taking up its positions along the river this latter brigade had been disposed

THE SOMME STILL HELD

as follows: 1/ Worcestershire (four companies in the line) on the right; 2/ Northamptonshire (three companies in the line, one in support) in the centre; 1/ Sherwood Foresters (four companies in the line) on the left. As the 25th Brigade was pressed back, the Worcestershire had perforce to form a defensive flank, the support company of the Northamptonshire being added, by single platoons as and when necessary, to continue the extending line. The Worcestershire " owing to the bravery and dash of Lieut.-Colonel Roberts, their Commanding Officer, in counter-attacking and clearing the South end of Epénancourt,"* brought considerable assistance to the 25th Infantry Brigade in their retirement. But the right flank continued to be a source of danger and, as has been seen, touch with the 25th Infantry Brigade was for a time completely lost. By 5 o'clock, when infantry action on this front had ceased for the day, the right flank of the brigade had been bent back considerably. The two right companies of the centre battalion (2/ Northamptonshire, Lieut.-Colonel S. G. Latham, M.C., commanding) had also become involved, and had had to retire to conform to the withdrawal of the Worcestershire.

By evening the 24th Brigade line left the canal bank about a mile South of St. Christ crossing, and ran thence in a south-westerly direction until it joined up with the 25th Brigade at a point about a mile South-South-East of Licourt. As will be seen from the map (p. 198) the left battalion (1/ Sherwood Foresters) still maintained itself stoutly in its original position; but it had suffered a sad misfortune in the loss of its Commanding Officer—Lieut.-Colonel T. H. Watson, M.C.—who had been killed by a machine-gun bullet during one of the enemy's nocturnal attempts to establish himself across the river.

On the left of the 8th Division, the 23rd Infantry Brigade, with the 2/ Devonshire (Major A. H. Cope) and 2/ West Yorkshire (Lieut.-Colonel A. E. E. Lowry, M.C.) in line and the 2/ Middlesex (Lieut.-Colonel C. A. S. Page, M.C.) in support in trenches North-West of Villers Carbonnel, successfully maintained their positions along the canal bank throughout the day. The stability of the Sherwood Foresters secured their right flank and a gap on the other flank which had been discovered in the early morning had been filled by moving forward a battalion of the 50th Division. The enemy did not leave them alone, but all his attempts to cross the river were successfully repulsed. During the night the Middlesex relieved the West Yorkshire in line.

The general situation at the close of the day's fighting on the Fifth Army front on the 24th March was that the retreat was continuing on both flanks; while in the centre, where was the 8th Division, some 6 miles of the river line was holding firm. To

* W. D. 2nd/ Northamptonshire, March 1918.

THE GREAT GERMAN OFFENSIVE

the North the westward bend of the Somme still offered some security to the flank of the troops holding the river defences; but their southern flank lay open, and it was clear that, unless the river line to the South of them could be re-established, it would only be a matter of time before they too were compelled to fall back. Accordingly, Divisional Headquarters at Foucaucourt received telephone instructions from XIX Corps during the night that at 8 a.m. on the following morning an attack was to be delivered by the French on the right, the 24th Division in the centre and the 8th Division (24th and 25th Infantry Brigades) on the left, with the object of regaining the Somme line. At 2.10 a.m. on the 25th March divisional orders were issued accordingly, and in order to clear the way for the 24th Division the flanking troops who were protecting the 25th Infantry Brigade right at Dreslincourt (see p. 180 *ante*) were withdrawn at 5.30 a.m. by order of the XIX Corps. The withdrawal was well intentioned, but unfortunate; for at daybreak the French, without whose newly arrived divisions counter-attack was impossible, asked for a postponement of the operation for three hours as their troops were not in position. Three hours passed, but the French attacking troops were still not in position and upon inquiry it was discovered that no definite orders for attack had been issued to them. In consequence the counter-attack never took place, and the gap at Dreslincourt remained open.

The attack, indeed, came from the side of the enemy. Early in the morning he delivered a very determined assault against the right of the 24th Infantry Brigade, and forced it back a considerable distance. As a result the 25th Infantry Brigade, against whom the enemy were advancing also, became exposed on this flank as well as on the other. A general retirement on this part of the front became necessary. By 9.0 a.m. the enemy had marched into Dreslincourt (there was no one to stop him) in strong force, and he proceeded to debouch thence to the West and in a northerly direction towards Pertain.

The enemy's advance against the right of the 24th Infantry Brigade was also continuing. The G.S.O.1 of the division, Lieut.-Colonel Armitage, who had ridden out from Divisional Headquarters at 10 a.m., found Brig.-General Haig in Marchélepot, on his way back to new Brigade Headquarters just East of Ablaincourt. Our troops were retiring. Lieut.-Colonel Armitage went on and rode to the eastern end of Marchélepot and along the Licourt road for a short distance. He noted that the Germans were advancing from direction of Licourt, but in no great strength; though there was a certain amount of hostile machine-gun fire and sniping. Parties under General Rees (G.O.C. 151st Infantry Brigade, 50th Division) and Capt. Rollo

ST. CHRIST BRIDGE

on the eastern side of Marchélepot were holding firm and securing the right flank. Eventually a line was formed on the railway immediately West of Marchélepot, and this was held during the afternoon and until night.

On the 25th Infantry Brigade front Pertain had to be abandoned; but at midday the remnants of this brigade, in conjunction with the 17th Infantry Brigade (24th Division), were still holding the eastern outskirts of Omiécourt. Brigade Headquarters, which had fallen back to that village at 10 a.m., retired yet further, to Chaulnes, in the early afternoon. Here General Coffin visited the G.O.C. 17th Infantry Brigade in order to discuss the situation, and it was decided between them that all the troops of the 25th Infantry Brigade which could be collected—300 or 400 only—should be kept in reserve North of Chaulnes and behind the left flank of the 17th Infantry Brigade. This was done, the 25th Infantry Brigade troops being placed under the command of Major J. D. Mitchell (22/ D.L.I., Pioneers).

In the meantime what of the fortunes of the rest of the division; and what, first, of the 1/ Sherwood Foresters, left battalion of the 24th Brigade, still holding, when last we heard of them, their original positions along the Somme, still keeping the St. Christ bridge inviolate? They continued to do so! At half-past three o'clock on that afternoon of the 25th March they were still there! " Soon after dawn "—so the record in their diary runs—" the troops on our right withdrew under orders leaving the right flank of the battalion ' in the air.' "* The Sherwood Foresters remained unperturbed. Had it not been written in divisional orders: " the line of the Somme will be held *at all costs* and there will be *no* retirement from it " ? " To remedy this," to quote their own laconic words, " a defensive flank was formed."* But a defensive flank cannot be extended indefinitely by the spare troops of a single battalion. It was inevitable that there should come a gap. Their comrades of the 24th Brigade were being forced back and back, until they finally stood on the railway behind Marchélepot 2½ miles away from the river. How, indeed, could a gap be avoided? It came, and with it came danger—danger in the form of German parties advancing northwards on the lucklessly named village of Misery, and threatening to take in rear, not only the Sherwood Foresters themselves, but the whole of the 23rd Brigade as well. It was, indeed, only the rapid development of this menace that ultimately forced withdrawal. At 3.45 p.m. General Grogan of the 23rd Brigade telephoned to 8th Division Headquarters as follows: " 1st Sherwood Foresters of 24th Infantry Brigade right of 2nd Devons are not in touch with their own brigade and are in danger of being

* W. D. 1/ Sherwood Foresters, March 1918.

THE GREAT GERMAN OFFENSIVE

surrounded. I have ordered them to fall back on the line Licourt–Villers Carbonnel." At 4 p.m. consequently "the battalion under orders withdrew through Misery having to fight its way out, the enemy being directly in its rear."* St. Christ and its bridge had been gallantly defended.

The 23rd Infantry Brigade was no less staunch. Quite early—at or before 8 o'clock in the morning—the enemy succeeded in crossing the river North of Eterpigny, at a point on the 50th Division's front immediately beyond the left flank of the brigade. The enemy came over in strong force and worked round behind " C " Company of the 2/ Middlesex, who were holding the village and bridge of Eterpigny. Mindful of the order to hold out at all costs without retirement the company held on until completely encircled, when the O.C. company, Capt. A. M. Toye, leading a forlorn hope, succeeded in cutting his way out with a mere handful of men. Out of all the four platoons of this company only ten individuals succeeded in getting away. The rest either perished at their posts or were captured. Having got clear of the village, Capt. Toye successfully rallied some 70 men of the 7/ D.L.I. (Pioneers), 50th Division, led them in a brave and bold counter-attack and held on across the Eterpigny–Villers Carbonnel road until assistance came. But for his prompt and energetic action the whole of our remaining positions along the river would have been turned.†

Assistance came from the 2/ West Yorkshire, in support, two of whose companies were at once ordered by Brigade Headquarters to counter-attack and fill the gap between the Middlesex and the battalion to the North of them. They went forward at 9.30 a.m. The gap was successfully filled, but owing to heavy machine-gun and rifle fire the West Yorkshire were unable to push their attack home or to drive the enemy back across the river. Accordingly, a defensive position was organized on the ridge and was held against severe and sustained assaults throughout the day. The Middlesex also continued to battle all day against desperate odds. Hostile troops poured across the river at Eterpigny and above, and the weight of the enemy's attacks grew with each hour. The two companies, " B " and " D," defending Brie Bridge were subjected to the severest pressure both from frontal attacks and by parties coming down our own (West) bank of the river from Eterpigny. From 7 o'clock in the morning until nearly 7 o'clock at night they held on. At last, at 6.45 p.m., orders to withdraw came through from the brigade. The orders

---

* W. D. 1/ Sherwood Foresters, March 1918.
† For his gallantry on this and subsequent occasions during the battle Capt. Toye was awarded the V.C.

THE STAND OF THE MIDDLESEX

arrived too late. Acting on the direction to resist at all costs and make no withdrawal, three platoons each of " B " and " D " companies and one platoon of " A " company had fallen at their posts. The remainder of " A " company on the right were not seriously attacked during the day and withdrew with the Devonshire in the evening. Thus no less than eleven platoons—four of " C " company, three each of " B " and " D " companies, and one of " A " company—of this gallant battalion in obedience to their orders resisted to the end and paid the utmost penalty.

One has a final picture of the remnants of the battalion—the Headquarters' party, one platoon of " D " company, details and so on—carrying out from the higher ground behind the river (whence they had since 11 o'clock been stalling off the Germans who had crossed) the order to withdraw. The Commanding Officer, Lieut.-Colonel Page, was, like the captain of a doomed ship, the last to leave. At 7.15 p.m. he sent off Major C. D. Drew and the Adjutant (Capt. W. Evans) with half the party to a covering position. The remainder he sent back in batches up the trench. Finally Pte. Burgess (the C.O.'s servant) and Pte. Allen of " D " company were left with the C.O., each firing rapid to cover the retirement and helped also by a single Vickers gun under Capt. Robertson, M.G.C. At 7.25 p.m., when the light had begun to fail, the C.O. sent back his comrades and after a final five rounds rapid, the last of over 200 he himself had fired, followed them up the trench. The Germans occupied the trench about three minutes after Colonel Page left it and sent up Verey lights from it to signal their presence to their friends, and to discover if possible the source of the obstinate resistance that they had encountered. So ended a day's fighting during which the 2/Middlesex had nobly sustained the reputation of their regiment and had covered themselves with glory.

The right battalion of the 23rd Brigade on this day was the 2/Devonshire. Being secured on either flank the battalion had not been so severely tested as the Middlesex had been, and it had successfully maintained its sector intact until the order to withdraw was received. This does not mean, however, that the enemy had not done his best to drive the battalion from its position, and when the time came to withdraw it found that its line of retreat was intercepted by small parties of the enemy. By means of a resolute attack with the bayonet against such of the enemy as barred the way, it opened a line of withdrawal with complete success and with but few casualties.

The failure of our Allies to deliver their promised attack in the Nesle sector and the continued progress of the enemy North of the Somme, where the command of the VII Corps passed on

THE GREAT GERMAN OFFENSIVE

this day to the Third Army,* had left at the point of a pronounced salient the troops of the 8th Division who were still on the river line. It had been decided, therefore, during the afternoon of the 25th that a general retirement to a new line had become necessary. Eighth Division Headquarters had accordingly received orders from the XIX Corps at 4.15 p.m. for withdrawal to the general line Hattencourt–Chaulnes–Ablaincourt–Estrées–Assevillers–Herbécourt–Frise; the sector to be taken over by the 8th Division being that from Chaulnes to Estrées, with the 24th Division on the right and the 50th Division on the left. The withdrawal was to commence at dark. The movement was carried out successfully and in good order, the retirement of the 23rd Infantry Brigade being covered by the 2/ West Yorkshire. It was powerfully assisted by the action of General Lamont, C.R.A. of the division, who placed single guns in front of the infantry line to sweep likely approaches. Though these guns had to be abandoned later, they did remarkable execution.

At 6 a.m. on the 26th March Divisional Headquarters (which had itself during the night withdrawn from Vermandovillers to Harbonnières) was able to report to Corps Headquarters that the new line was complete, with both flanks in touch with neighbouring divisions. The 8th Division's dispositions were as follows: 24th Infantry Brigade on the right (Brigade Headquarters: Vermandovillers), 23rd Infantry Brigade on left (Brigade Headquarters: Soyécourt), 25th Infantry Brigade in divisional reserve at Lihons. The 24th Infantry Brigade had the following units (from right to left): 6/ D.L.I.,† 2/ Northamptonshire, 1/ Worcestershire, all that was left of the 150th Infantry Brigade, and 8/ D.L.I.† in front line—observe the intermixture of troops—and the 1/ Sherwood Foresters in reserve. The 23rd Infantry Brigade had their three battalions in the front line and the 2nd Field Company, Royal Engineers, in reserve. Early in the morning the enemy attacked the new positions in considerable force, but was driven off with heavy loss.

Despite this success, however, orders were received from XIX Corps at 10 a.m. for a further gradual retirement in a south-westerly direction to the Rouvroy–Proyart line, reasons for the order being amply provided by events in other sectors. Severe enemy pressure on the right of the battle line—threatening a breach between the French and British forces—and the

---

* General Fayolle, commanding the French Northern Army Group, had assumed responsibility for the whole of the Fifth Army front as far North as the Somme river on the morning of the 25th March.

† Both these battalions belonged to the 151st Infantry Brigade.

ROSIÈRES

rapid German advance North of the Somme where the Ancre line had already been reached, made imperative a further straightening of the battle front. The withdrawal commenced on the left, the 50th Division on the left flank starting to go back at about 10 a.m. and the 23rd Infantry Brigade taking up the movement some half-hour later. The 25th Infantry Brigade was left till the last moment at Lihons to cover the retirement of the 23rd and 24th Infantry Brigades. The 8th Divisional Artillery again did splendid work in covering the infantry during retreat.

Some general details can be gathered once again from the report of Lieut.-Colonel Armitage. " On receipt of information from 50th Division that withdrawal had commenced, I motored,'' he writes, " with C.R.A. to Soyécourt and Vermandovillers and warned 23rd and 24th Brigades and Royal Artillery to conform. Then proceeded to Divisional Headquarters at Harbonnières and went out from there mounted to see how the withdrawal was being carried out. . . . Went up to Headquarters 25th Infantry Brigade at Lihons and saw General Coffin and found everything quiet. The enemy did not appear to be advancing, though Lihons was being shelled, but was reported in Chaulnes. Rode North-East and met General Haig with his brigade and also units of the 23rd Infantry Brigade who were all withdrawing in good order and were not being molested. Returned to General Coffin, reported to him progress of 23rd and 24th Infantry Brigades. Thence rode southward. There were no signs of any Germans, but elements of troops of other divisions were in positions between Lihons and Meharicourt waiting for orders to withdraw. Rode to position to be taken up by the division from Rosières southwards. From that time onwards troops arrived gradually and in perfect order on their positions. . . ." By about 4.0 p.m. all were in their new positions and in touch on right (24th Division) and left (50th Division).

The Rosières position was held on the right by the 24th Infantry Brigade which, in addition to the units enumerated above, had now assimilated also—on its extreme right—the 20th Entrenching Battalion*, on the left by the 23rd Infantry Brigade. The Sugar Factory was the inter-brigade boundary. Headquarters of both brigades were at Caix. At 5.30 p.m. the 25th Infantry Brigade (with them the 22/ D.L.I.) and the artillery withdrew from their covering positions East of Lihons, the infantry going into divisional reserve immediately to the West of Rosières. During the afternoon Divisional Headquarters again went back, retiring from Harbonnières to Marcelcave. The enemy followed up the movement of the division without loss of time and in the evening our patrols came again

* This unit was already in position when the 8th Division arrived.

THE GREAT GERMAN OFFENSIVE

into touch with his. The day ended with the receipt of the following message from the Corps Commander:

" Under instructions from French Commander-in-Chief* to Fifth Army, the XIX Corps will maintain at all costs the line we are now on until the arrival of French troops who are on their way to relieve us. For this purpose every available man will be put into the fight, and the Corps Commander looks to all ranks to make one more supreme effort and maintain to the last the magnificent fighting qualities and endurance already displayed throughout the battle."

The test was not long postponed. In anticipation of a struggle as desperate as it would be vital, the headquarters of all three infantry brigades had already been moved forward and established together at the West end of Rosières, and General Coffin had been placed in command of all the infantry of the division. At about 8 o'clock in the morning of the 27th March the opening blow came, a determined attack being delivered all along the new line.

The attack was pressed most severely on the right (24th Infantry Brigade front), where, after the first two waves had been wiped out by artillery fire, the third wave got into our lines on the extreme right. The 20th Entrenching Battalion and the 6/ D.L.I. holding this sector were driven back and the 2/ Northamptonshire and 1/ Worcestershire were obliged to readjust their line in conformity with the new situation. The 1/ Sherwood Foresters were promptly thrown in from reserve to counter-attack. Advancing with great spirit, they succeeded in driving off the enemy and re-established the 6/ D.L.I. and the Entrenching Battalion in their original line. The 1/ Worcestershire and 2/ Northamptonshire were prompt to seize their opportunity and, advancing in their turn, also re-occupied their original positions. At no other point on the divisional front did the enemy succeed in endangering our positions, and after an engagement in which he had lost heavily and to no purpose, he withdrew to a considerable distance. Nor did he show any inclination to renew the attack.

The task of the division did not end, however, with the successful defence of its own front. At 11 o'clock in the morning a telephone message was received by the division from XIX Corps stating that the position in the North in the direction of Proyart† was serious, and that troops were urgently required to restore the situation. This meant that there was danger of the enemy breaking through along the line of the main road to Amiens, the use of

---

* Foch had been appointed Generalissimo on this day, the 26th, at the Doullens meeting.
† 39th Divisional sector.

A GALLANT COUNTER-ATTACK

which would enable him to make rapid progress behind the flank of the Rosières positions. As the front of his own division now appeared stable, General Heneker readily agreed to detach Major Cope with the 2/ Devonshire (then in reserve to the 23rd Infantry Brigade) and three companies of the 22/ D.L.I. (Pioneers) for this purpose and meanwhile despatched his G.S.O.2, Major R. M. Weeks, D.S.O., M.C., to Harbonnières to find out the situation there. At 1.0 p.m. these two battalions reached Harbonnières, deployed North-East of that village, and attacked in a north-easterly direction. Despite the effort of a hurried march and the accumulated weariness of days of continuous fighting and retreating, the attack was delivered with a spirit which made light both of their own fatigue and of the enemy's opposition.* The advancing German troops were driven back with the loss of many prisoners to a distance of 1,000 yards. Their progress about the Amiens road was stopped and a serious threat to the safety of the British line removed. Our own casualties were comparatively light, but Lieut.-Colonel C. B. Morgan, commanding the D.L.I., was mortally wounded and died in a Rouen hospital two days later. The detached troops remained with the 39th Division until the following morning.

In the meantime further trouble had been brewing on, or rather immediately to the left of, the main divisional front. At about 2.0 p.m. the 50th Division, who were here posted, were forced to give ground and it became necessary to use all remaining reserves (including personnel of 23rd, 24th and 25th Infantry Brigades Headquarters) to restore the situation on this flank by prolonging the 8th Division's left towards Harbonnières. For this purpose, the 1/ Sherwood Foresters were brought from the other flank across the full breadth of the divisional front, and with the 15th Field Company (Major R. M. Taylor) and 24th T. M. Battery (Capt. W. B. Greensmith), were thrown into the fight at the new danger-point. Here the latter unit, temporarily abandoning its special weapon for methods more suited to a desperate occasion, distinguished itself by a bayonet charge which killed a considerable number of the enemy and effected the capture of some 30 prisoners and 3 machine guns. By these means the situation here also was restored and, though fighting continued, the extended front (shown by a dotted line on the map) was firmly held until late at night, when the sector was again handed over to troops of the 50th Division.

At the close of the fighting of the 27th, therefore, the British front South of the Somme, largely owing to the successful efforts of the 8th Division, had held, and the rapid German advance had

---

* " A very gallant and successful counter-attack carried out with great dash by 2/ Devons and 22/ D.L.I."—*Haig's Despatches*, Dent's Edition, p. 209.

THE GREAT GERMAN OFFENSIVE

here encountered a definite check. The general situation on the Army front was not, however, satisfactory. To the South, despite the arrival in line of a number of French divisions, the Allied front had fallen back with disturbing rapidity. On the previous day, the 26th March, ground had been yielded to the enemy to a depth of over 10 miles, and on the 27th the retreat continued. On the evening of the 25th March the Allied line had rested on the Libermont Canal. By nightfall on the 27th it was to be well to the West of Montdidier.

Neither was comfort to be found on the northern flank. Here, owing to the misinterpretation of an order, the right of the Third Army North of the Somme had during the evening of the 26th retired too far. Instead of continuing to stand, as had been intended, on the line Bray-sur-Somme–Albert which it had successfully defended, it had fallen right back to the line of the Ancre below the latter town. Though a hurried attempt to rectify the mistake had succeeded in checking the withdrawal before it had been wholly completed, on the morning of the 27th March the right of the Third Army rested on the Somme at Sailly-le-Sec. Thus, while the Fifth Army still held the South bank of the Somme North of Proyart, the Third Army instead of carrying on the line through Bray were some six miles further West. " The left flank of the Fifth Army, therefore, was dangerously uncovered, being protected merely by the obstacle of the river and an improvised force of 350 men with Lewis guns and armoured cars which had been sent up to hold the crossings."*
Throughout the 27th March the enemy had been seeking to exploit this advantage, and at 8 o'clock in the evening Divisional Headquarters received information from XIX Corps that the Germans had crossed the Somme at Cerisy and were advancing southwards. Leading enemy troops had reached Warfusée Abancourt and hostile patrols were reported in Bayonvillers. The situation was uncommonly serious, and at a conference held at Cayeux at about midnight between the General Officers Commanding 8th, 50th and 66th Divisions it was agreed that, unless a retirement was ordered at once, the greater portion of what was left of these three divisions would be outflanked and cut off in rear. The question was referred to XIX Corps, who referred it in their turn to Fifth Army. The Army got on the telephone to General Foch, rousing him out of bed to answer; and at 3.30 a.m. instructions for the inevitable withdrawal were at last obtained.

The line to be taken up ran in a north-westerly direction as follows: 8th Division, Vrély to Caix; 50th Division, Caix to Guillaucourt; 66th Division, Guillaucourt to Wiencourt. The 24th Division was in Vrély, and on their right on this evening

* *Haig's Despatches*, Dent's Edition, p. 208.

OUTFLANKED

of the 27th the remnants of the 20th, 30th and 36th Divisions were struggling heroically and without artillery support to maintain a front to the enemy across the Roye–Amiens road in the neighbourhood of Arvillers. Beyond them the French line ran South-West to Mesnil St. Georges, West of Montdidier.

MARCH 1918

The 8th Division commenced withdrawing to the new line at about 8 a.m. on the 28th March; and the 24th Infantry Brigade were in position on the right by 11 a.m., the 23rd Infantry Brigade, on the left, by midday. The 25th Infantry Brigade again covered the withdrawal and then went into reserve. At about 1 p.m. some of the 24th Division's units were forced back and the right of the 24th Infantry Brigade fell back to conform. They took up a strong position, consisting of deep trenches well wired, to the South of Caix. Here they maintained themselves until subsequently ordered to withdraw.

Developments on the other flank were more serious. In the early afternoon the 50th Division West of Caix retired, under pressure of the German outflanking movement on the North bank of the Somme; and the Germans coming down from the North entered Caix, outflanking the 23rd Infantry Brigade. The whole division was indeed in danger of being surrounded. Orders from the division to retire on Mezières and Moreuil were received at 3 p.m. and immediately thereafter the withdrawal commenced. The 24th and 25th Infantry Brigades got clear without difficulty and proceeded to Moreuil by march route. 23rd Infantry Brigade were not so fortunate. The position in that quarter had already become so critical that the greatest difficulty was experienced by the brigade staff in communicating the order to retire to the various units. In some cases the order was never received; and the unit concerned finally on its own initiative fought or attempted to fight its way out. The majority of the 2nd Field Company (Major A. H. Brown, D.S.O., M.C.) and of the 2/West Yorkshire were either killed or captured in such circumstances. Lieut.-Colonel Lowry of the West Yorkshire himself fell into the hands of the enemy, but later on managed to escape.

This escape was indeed an astonishing adventure and one which no one, perhaps, except this gifted soldier, whose indomitable courage was matched only by his imperturbable *sang froid*, could have brought to a successful issue. He had been sending remnants of his battalion in small parties to the rear, until he alone with two other ranks were left. When their turn came to try and rejoin their comrades, a party of Germans and a machine gun so unequivocally barred the way that surrender was inevitable. As a prisoner Colonel Lowry was deprived of his trench coat, revolver and other personal belongings, but a Boche

THE GREAT GERMAN OFFENSIVE

private's waterproof cape given in exchange at once suggested possibilities to his fertile brain. The enemy seems to have been somewhat careless in dealing with the large quantities of prisoners which he was taking, and later in the day the group to which Colonel Lowry was attached was left quite unguarded. It was then dusk. Colonel Lowry seized the chance, slipped across the road and hid himself behind a potato heap on the opposite side. Here he stayed until it was dark when, having acquired a German steel helmet, he sallied forth and boldly joined the stream of German transport which was flowing down the main Villers Carbonnel–Villers–Bretonneux road—a German private whose knowledge of the German tongue amounted literally to two words, " Nicht Wahr! " But the confidence of his bearing covered this linguistic defect. No one seems to have taken any notice of him and he accompanied the stream of wagons down the road until he reached the cross-roads near Villers–Bretonneux. Here he knew that traffic control men would most probably pierce his very unsubstantial disguise, so he left the highway and, making admirable use of his knowledge of the country, regained our lines after a long detour. During the hours he had been behind the enemy lines he had made notes of gun positions and troop movements. On rejoining his own people he went straight to Army Headquarters and reported the results of his enforced reconnaissance to the Army Commander as coolly as if the whole episode had been a matter of ordinary routine.

The 2/ Middlesex, being on the brigade right, were in a position slightly less evil than that of the West Yorkshire; but they also lost heavily. By a skilfully organized retirement they managed to retain themselves as a fighting organization; but in cutting their way out they completely lost touch with both brigade and division, finally coming to a halt and snatching a few much wanted hours' sleep at Berteaucourt. There the C.O. (Lieut.-Colonel Page) with great difficulty at last got news of the division at Moreuil, and on arrival at that town found that his battalion had been reported captured.

During the night of the 28th/29th March the units of the division were collected together at Jumel. Both the 23rd and 24th Infantry Brigades remained in billets in this place throughout the following day (29th March), a very welcome rest. The division had now been fighting and retreating for nearly a week without cessation, and some rest and the chance to obtain a certain amount of consecutive sleep were essential. The two brigades were in fact so utterly exhausted that they were for the moment quite unfit to move. In a written account, in which successive incidents are necessarily recorded in a comparatively ordered and methodical sequence, it is quite impossible to convey

STUBBORN REAR-GUARD ACTIONS

anything at all of the perpetual strain and harass and worry of these unending days, and above all of the appalling physical fatigue and exhaustion which the ceaseless programme of march and fight and dig, dig and fight and march, produced and continued to produce. One man needed the strength of ten and had to do the work of ten.

Thus even on this day it was still necessary to call upon the 25th Infantry Brigade, who were ordered to hold a portion of the wood North of Moreuil. On arrival there, however, General Coffin found that this line was already occupied by French troops. He therefore kept his brigade in reserve in the vicinity of Moreuil, and when at about half-past five in the afternoon the French were seen to be retiring from the South through Moreuil, the 2/ Royal Berkshire were sent to move East-South-East to hold the wood immediately West of the town. They found that the enemy was already there, and ultimately the troops of this brigade, fighting once more a stubborn rear-guard action to protect the right of the XIX Corps, established themselves on the high ground* immediately to the North of the big wood North-East of Moreuil.

Late in the evening of this day (the 29th) orders were issued for the 23rd and 24th Infantry Brigades to march northwards early on the morrow, in order to relieve the 24th Division who were holding a support line North of Berteaucourt. During the night, however, these orders were cancelled and the brigades were ordered, instead, to proceed at once to Castel to hold the Avre river crossing at that place. They started to move thither early—between 5 and 6 o'clock—in the morning.

In the meantime the 25th Infantry Brigade, in conformity with the decision of a French regimental commander† to retire via the Castel bridge to the left bank of the Avre, had at 4.30 a.m. on the 30th March commenced to fall back on the river. General Coffin had intended to hold a bridge-head at Castel if necessary. Once more he found French elements already in position, and as the other two brigades of the 8th Division had not yet come up he moved on to the neighbouring village of Rouvrel. Here cookers and rations were found and the brigade re-formed, fed and obtained a brief spell of much needed rest.

During the morning of this day the division was cheered by the news that the 2nd Cavalry Division had crossed the Avre and that a brilliant counter-attack carried out by the Canadian Cavalry Brigade supported by the 3rd Cavalry Brigade had driven

---
* Shown on the accompanying map by a ring contour.
† This officer was in command of two French battalions which were in proximity to the ring contour North of Moreuil Wood. These battalions had been at Villers aux Erables earlier in the day (29th March).

THE GREAT GERMAN OFFENSIVE

the enemy from Moreuil Wood. The German infantry, however, had not yet given up the struggle. Though from this date the Allied line South of the Somme commenced to stabilize, as the British line North of the river had already done some four days earlier, the 8th Division was once again called upon to take a share in the fight.

The 2/West Yorkshire, who numbered now but a hundred men, had already been sent up to the assistance of the Canadian Cavalry Brigade in Moreuil Wood, and at 3 o'clock in the afternoon the XIX Corps ordered the rest of the division to move up at once to relieve the Cavalry Division. In pursuance of this order, the Divisional Commander directed General Grogan to take command temporarily, while General Coffin had the food and rest for lack of which he was on the verge of a collapse, of the 23rd, 24th and 25th Infantry Brigades and to proceed at once to take over from the 2nd Cavalry Division the eastern edge of the wood North-East of Moreuil. The 23rd and 24th Infantry Brigades were to be in front line and the 25th Infantry Brigade in reserve East of Castel bridge. General Grogan would have the 20th Division on his left and French on his right, and he was informed that the situation in Moreuil was obscure.

The obscure situation in Moreuil quickly resolved itself into the fact that the Germans were in possession of the village, and the British line North of it was found to run along the western and not the eastern edge of the wood. The relief of the Cavalry Division was none the less successfully completed by about midnight, one cavalry brigade remaining in support of General Grogan's troops. During the remainder of the night the situation on the divisional front was quiet; but by the morning of the 31st our patrols, who had pushed out eastwards through the wood, were being held up by hostile bodies. Later in the morning information came that the enemy was massing for attack and the Field Artillery opened on him. Despite the fire of our guns, the Germans were not to be denied, and shortly after 1 p.m. attacked with such violence as to break through on the left of the divisional front, the 2/Devonshire (23rd Infantry Brigade) being driven out of Moreuil Wood. The 24th Infantry Brigade, however, on the right managed to maintain their positions by throwing out two companies of the 1/Worcestershire as a defensive flank to the North, and the 25th Infantry Brigade was ordered at 2.30 p.m. to counter-attack. The 2/East Lancashire (less one company) and 2/Royal Berkshire, both under command of Major J. A. Griffin of the latter regiment, were hurried forward. Their attack was successful and our line was restored. The "head"[*] of the Wood was reoccupied and the elements of

[*] The projecting copse shown on the map at the north-west end of the wood.

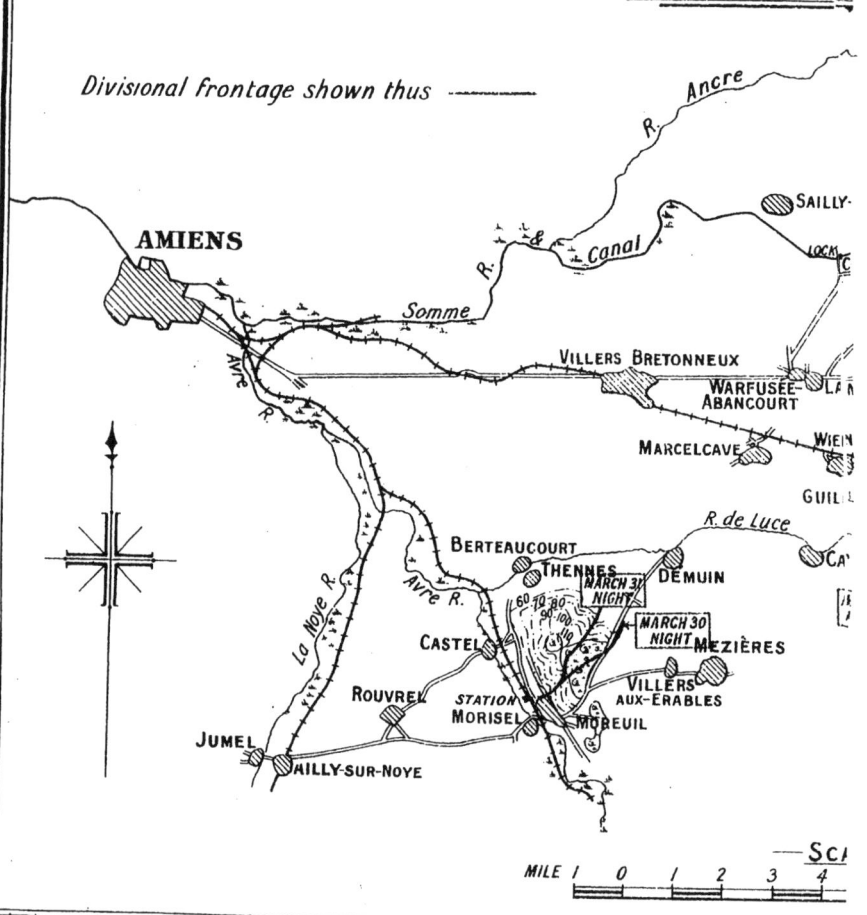

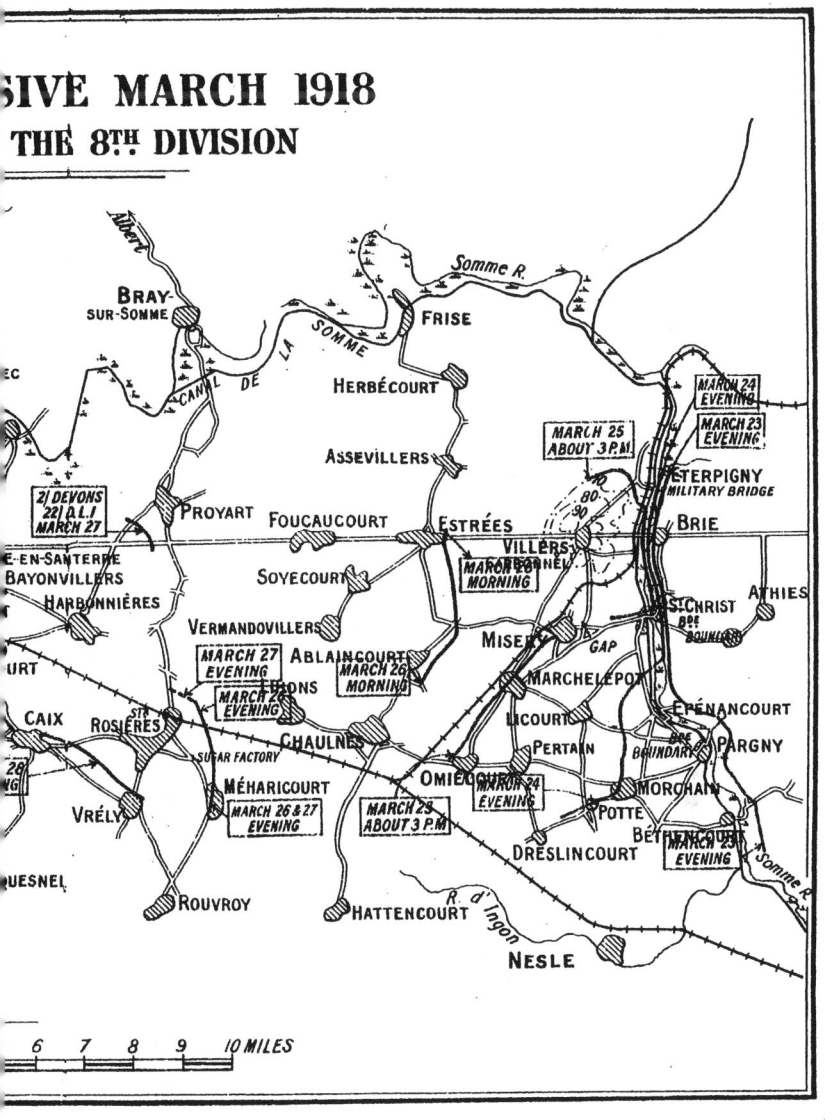

"A QUIET DAY ON THE WHOLE"

the Berkshire penetrated into the wood proper; but later in the evening our troops in the larger wood were withdrawn, as General Heneker had arranged to bombard it during the night as a preliminary to a further counter-attack early on the following morning. Opportunity was accordingly taken to relieve Major Griffin's men, who were by now very wet and tired, with troops of the 23rd Infantry Brigade. At 8 p.m. General Coffin again took over command of all three Infantry Brigades.

Once more the night passed quietly, and on the morrow, the 1st April, at 9 a.m., the projected counter-attack was duly made by the 2nd Cavalry Division. The assault, which was delivered to the North of the Moreuil Wood and from the direction of Thennes, immediately to the left of the front held by the 8th Division, provided another example of the success with which mounted troops can be used in the concluding stages of a protracted battle. A large number of the enemy were killed, many prisoners captured, and valuable territory regained. The advance enabled the left flank of the 23rd Infantry Brigade to be pushed forward several hundred yards to conform to the new line, and this forward movement also eased the position for the 24th Infantry Brigade, whose troops had previously been troubled by machine-gun fire from the left flank. It would seem that the counter-attack, coupled with the effective bombardment of the wood during the previous night, had taken the spirit out of the enemy, and for the first time since the opening of the battle a unit of the 8th Division, the 1/Worcestershire, were able to report " a very quiet day on the whole." How quiet may be judged from the following charming little incident recorded by the 2/Northamptonshire. "During the late afternoon Corpl. Scrivener and Pte. Pepper took possession of two cows that had been wandering for some time in the forward position. They were milked and sent back to the transport." But alas! owing to transport shortage they had next day to be abandoned. None the less a grateful and homely touch to mitigate the shells and the bullets and the beastliness of war.

In the afternoon information was received that the whole division would be relieved the same night by the 133rd French Division. The relief commenced at midnight and was completed without incident at 4.15 a.m. on the 2nd April. During the course of this day the division moved by bus and march route to the Cavillon area (behind Amiens). By 10 o'clock at night they were there concentrated. They were definitely out of the battle at last.

Indeed, the battle itself was almost over. This 2nd of April, when the remnants of the 8th Division were marching away, was the first day since the offensive had been opened on which there

THE GREAT GERMAN OFFENSIVE

was no attack on the British front South of the Somme. The enemy also was nearing the end of his tether. He made two more final efforts, one on the 4th April, the other on the 5th, to set the Allied line once more in movement. On both days, although he made some further progress of a local character, he lost heavily and his end was not achieved. Our resistance had definitely stiffened, while the offensive spirit of his troops was for the time being spent. Amiens was saved, and the front crystallized once more into the locked warfare of the trenches.

So concluded what was perhaps the most perilous chapter for the Allied cause of any throughout the whole history of the war. A chapter which very nearly ended in irreparable disaster; which indeed must so have ended, but for the superhuman qualities of courage and endurance exhibited by the overworked and outweighed defenders on the spot. Among them the 8th Division had a record second to none. The only British reinforcement to the Fifth Army, it had proved sufficient. Time and again during these critical days the 8th Division had held the breach; but at no time more splendidly or more conspicuously than in the critical days of the 26th and 27th March, when the rest of the Allied line South of the Somme had become fluid, and the 8th Division alone stood like a rock at Rosières.

On the 26th Foch had taken command of the Allied Armies, prepared, as Haig had urged so insistently upon the French Command, to sacrifice everything to the supreme task of maintaining unity between the French and British Armies, and to this end to throw in, if necessary, all the French reserves. The orders for the transfer of the French divisions had been given. Could they arrive in time? On the answer to that question depended the fate of the Allied Armies and the future of the Allied nations. The answer was given by the 8th Division; supported with heroic gallantry by the battered regiments of the divisions of the Fifth Army that had borne the first brunt of the assault, supported by a wonderful display by our airmen of the capacity of air forces to co-operate in ground fighting; yet primarily by the troops of the 8th Division whose stubborn defence of Rosières for forty vital hours barred the way to Amiens, and gave heart and encouragement and hope to those who fought beside them.

When the 8th Division finally came out of the battle, shattered in numbers, worn out in body, but unconquered in spirit, it had covered itself with glory.

The message addressed to his troops by the Divisional Commander on withdrawal will serve admirably to sum up the necessarily long and somewhat detailed narrative which has already been recorded in this chapter.

"On being withdrawn from the front line to rest and

A GLORIOUS RECORD

reorganize after the strenuous 9 days of fighting in which the division has taken such a distinguished part, I desire to convey to all ranks my admiration of their behaviour and fighting spirit.

"While every day and hour was full of heroic deeds, and it is perhaps invidious to refer to any particular unit by name when all have done so well, I feel that I should like to record certain outstanding operations.

"(1) The holding of the line of the Somme on a 9-mile front for nearly 2 days and the beating off of the attacks of 9 German divisions until the flanks of the division were turned.

"(2) The withdrawal, under orders, from the Chaulnes-Estrées line, when 23rd and 24th Infantry Brigades gallantly supported by the 8th Division Artillery gave the enemy a rough handling, and then covered by 25th Infantry Brigade at Lihons, withdrew in perfect order, as if on parade, and took up the Rosières–Vrély line.

"(3) The action of 2nd Devonshire Regiment and 22nd D.L.I. in moving North from the Rosières–Vrély line and counter-attacking towards Vauvillers and Proyart, thus restoring the line on a front of 8,000 yards North of the real front of the division. These two battalions held this new line, together with the elements of other divisions into which they had infused new life by their counter-attacks, for some 12 hours, when they withdrew in perfect order under instructions.

"(4) The holding of the Rosières-Vrély line by all units in spite of determined enemy attacks. In connection with this, the holding of the Station by 2nd Field Company, Royal Engineers, and the counter-attacks made by nearly all units and by the brigade headquarters of all brigades, should be recorded.

"(5) The defence of the Caix–Vrély line by the 2nd West Yorkshire Regiment, 2nd Middlesex Regiment, and 2nd Field Company Royal Engineers, when they held on until practically surrounded.

"(6) The counter-attack by 2nd Royal Berkshire Regiment and 2nd East Lancashire Regiment at Moreuil Wood.

"A special word of praise is due to the artillery of the division for their boldness and close support of the infantry, and I can assure them that when, by superior orders, they were taken from me* and given another front to cover, we felt their absence severely.

"It is impossible for me adequately to express my admiration for the action of the 22nd D.L.I (Pioneers), and the Field Companies, Royal Engineers, of the division. They were all thrown into the fight as infantry and acted as such during the

* This happened on the 29th March.

THE GREAT GERMAN OFFENSIVE

whole of the operations, earning the unstinted praise of the Brigadiers to whom they were attached.

"The newly formed, and barely organized, Divisional Machine-Gun Battalion must be included with the other units of the division who distinguished themselves.

"I wish to thank the Signal Service for their hard and efficient work, also the Field Ambulances and the remainder of the Administrative Services in the division.

"In conclusion, I must express my thanks to Brigadier-General C. Coffin, V.C., D.S.O., who during the latter part of the fighting was in command of the infantry of the division, which he handled with the greatest skill, and to the staffs of the division and of infantry brigades for their untiring energy and able assistance.

"*The magnificent fighting qualities and discipline displayed by the troops themselves*, have earned for the 8th Division a reputation second to none in the British Army."

That the work and the value of the work done by the 8th Division was not unappreciated or unrecognized may be proved by the following messages which were received from the Army and the Corps Commanders. The first from Sir H. Rawlinson* was as follows:

"I desire once more to thank my old friends the 8th Division for the invaluable services they have again rendered, and to express to them my sincere congratulations. They have had a very strenuous time and I trust the situation may now permit of them being given a well-earned rest."

The Corps Commander, Sir H. E. Watts, wrote thus:

"Please accept and convey to all ranks my thanks and congratulations for the splendid work since joining the XIX Corps. The fighting spirit and power of endurance shown have been admirable and have been of invaluable assistance to XIX Corps in carrying out its task."

A message—"Heartiest congratulations on the magnificent work the 8th Division is doing for the Empire"—was also received from Sir A. Hunter-Weston, the Division's former Corps Commander; and another from the Italian 8th Division ran as follows:

"The Italian 8th Division warmly congratulates the British 8th Division on its magnificent behaviour in the great battle in Picardy and hopes soon to be able to follow the glorious example of its British sister in the fight against the common foe."

In these tributes there was no hyperbole. It is unnecessary to add anything to them here.

---

* Sir H. Rawlinson had taken over command of the Fifth Army front from Sir H. Gough on the 28th March.

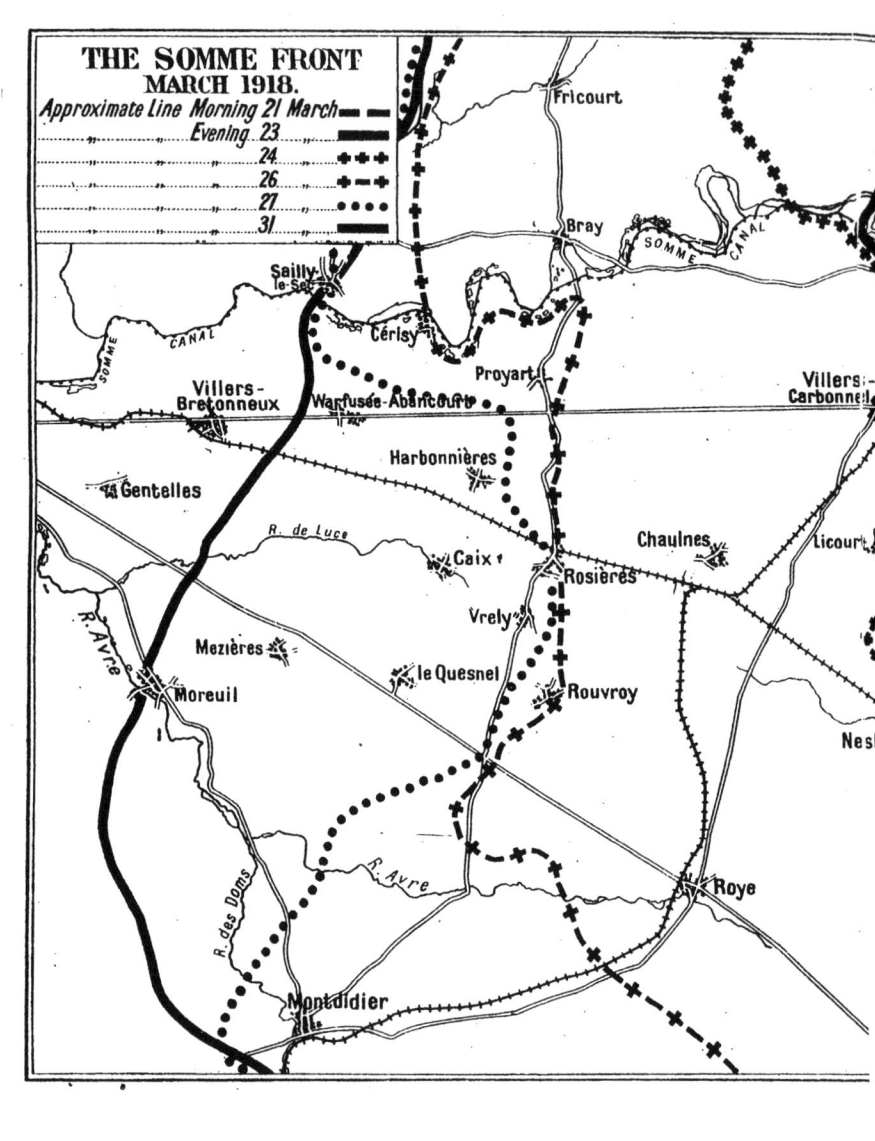

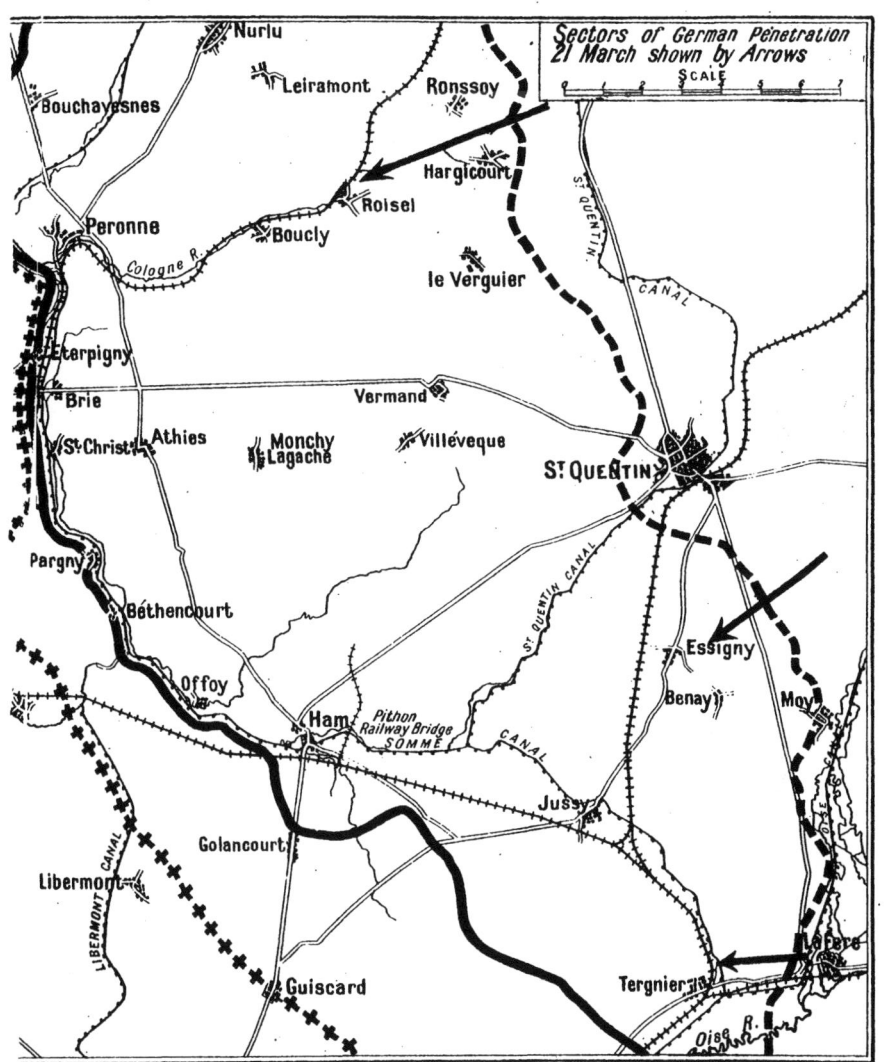

CHAPTER XIII

VILLERS-BRETONNEUX

THE 8th Division after leaving the battle had, as already noted, been withdrawn to the Cavillon area. Here it remained for a full week, resting, reorganizing, and assimilating and training the very large drafts which were necessary to fill up its sadly depleted ranks. The divisional casualties had been terribly severe, the total figures being 250 officers and 4,693 other ranks. The two battalions which had suffered most were the 2/ West Yorkshire and the 2/ Middlesex, and during its short period of rest the former battalion received no fewer than 11 officers and 700 odd other ranks. The drafts to the Middlesex were but little less. Fortunately both battalions still retained their Commanding Officers (Lieut.-Colonel A. E. E. Lowry and Lieut.-Colonel C. A. S. Page) and this proved of great assistance to them in dealing with so large an influx. The work of absorbing and training the new men was taken in hand by all units with great energy, for time was short and all ranks felt that at any moment they might be called upon to take part in another big battle.

At one time it seemed that the call would come even sooner than it did. The last gusts of the great tempest in the South had not blown themselves out when indications reached British General Headquarters that the storm centre was shifting rapidly from the Somme to the North. The line which the 8th Division had done so much to save had definitely stabilized, and some weeks must necessarily pass before the enemy could re-establish across the battle area communications adequate to the renewal of the offensive there on any considerable scale. Meanwhile, in order to retain the initiative in his hands and prevent any reaction by the Allies against the long southern flank of his advance, he must continue to attack. April was still young when the German Higher Command released—on the Lys front—the second of their shock offensives.

The blow fell on the 9th April and already on the morrow Divisional Headquarters found it necessary to issue a warning that the division would probably be required to move North by tactical trains in two days' time. On the 11th the move North was cancelled and the division was ordered instead to join the Anzac Corps under General Sir W. Birdwood. Next day the project revived and another warning order was issued by wire that the division (less artillery) might be required to entrain for another Army, commencing on the morning of the 13th April. Later in the same day came the following amendment: "Move postponed one day," and on the 13th, "Movement of 8th Division (less artillery) by rail on April 14th is now cancelled."

VILLERS-BRETONNEUX

These orders and counter-orders are evidence of the anxiety caused by the rapid progress once more made by the enemy in the opening days of his attack, and of the safe passing of the first crisis of the battle. On the 13th April the British line on the southern half of the Lys front, aided by the gallant defence of Givenchy by the 55th Division and the heroic action of the 4th Guards Brigade and other troops East of Nieppe Forest, had begun to stiffen, and the area of danger to move northwards where French troops were already arriving behind the 2nd Army. There was no need, therefore, to call upon the 8th Division to go to the succour of the old sector in which it had seen its first fighting in France.

Though it remained in the South, the division was not for that reason destined to escape its ordeal. The Battle of the Somme had one further, final flare up—brief but very violent —and it was the 8th Division which bore the brunt of it.

The transfer to Australian Corps Reserve entailed a move, Divisional Headquarters leaving Cavillon on the 12th for Bertangles, a village some five miles to the North of Amiens. On the same day the 23rd Infantry Brigade moved to the Saleux area, and the 24th to the Querrieu area, the former place being to the South-West and the latter East-North-East of Amiens. The 25th went to the area of Rivery, which is a northerly suburb of the city itself. Training in the new areas was energetically continued.

As from midnight on the 17th April the division, transferred again, came under the orders of the III Corps, with a view to taking over forthwith a sector of the line. The front in question was astride the main Amiens–Foucaucourt highway immediately East of Villers-Bretonneux, then held by troops of the 58th Division and the 5th Australian Division. The 24th Infantry Brigade went in on the night of the 19th/20th April, relieving the left (174th) brigade of the 58th Division, and thus becoming responsible for the right of the new divisional sector. The 25th Infantry Brigade on the following night relieved the 14th Australian Infantry Brigade, 5th Australian Division, and so occupied the left. At the same time the 2/Devonshire took over the Villers-Bretonneux defences from the 33rd Australian Infantry Battalion and the rest of the 23rd Infantry Brigade relieved other Australian battalions in positions in the reserve system. Command of the new sector passed to General Heneker at 9 a.m. on the 21st April, and at this hour the following artillery came under divisional orders: 20th Division Artillery (XC and XCI Brigades R.F.A.) and CCXCI Brigade R.F.A., the whole under command of Brig.-General H. W. A. Christie, C.R.A. 20th Division. The 8th Division's own artillery had only just been released from working with the French about Domart and

MUSTARD GAS

along the line of the Luce River, and was back at Pont Remy, refitting and training.

APRIL 1918

Divisional Headquarters had in the meantime, on the 19th April, been moved to Glisy, a small village to the East of Amiens. " It was a noisy spot, especially after dusk, for the enemy's planes were over every night bombing, and his guns were also active. To add to the noise, two long-range French guns mounted on railway carriages were in position on the railway just behind the town. These fired the whole time, and at almost every discharge slates fell off the roofs and the glass of the windows cracked and fell out. There was little sleep the first night."

The line taken over by the division—a total frontage of about 4,000 yards—may be seen on the attached map. The 58th (London) Division was in line on the South. To the North the division joined hands with the 2nd Australian Division on the high plateau which overlooked the German lines about the Bois de Vaire. It will be noticed that just South of the Amiens–Chaulnes railway the line bent back sharply westwards making an abrupt and narrow salient with sides facing East and South.

During the days which immediately preceded the arrival of the division in the line both the village of Villers-Bretonneux and the woods to its rear (Bois l'Abbé and Bois d'Aquenne) had been heavily shelled with Yellow Cross gas shell which had caused numerous casualties among the troops of the 58th Division holding the Villers-Bretonneux defences. The occurrence was ominous, for it recalled the drenching of Armentières with " mustard " gas which had preceded the opening of the Lys battle. On the 20th the gas shelling of the village ceased, but the woods were still attacked and were continuously filled with gas. As a result, it was impossible to hold the line along the eastern edge of the woods, which was designed to cover the western exits of the village. For a similar reason the use of the wood as a covered means of approach to the village or the front trenches beyond it was to a great extent denied to our troops. Despite all the precautions taken, gas casualties in the division rapidly became considerable.

It had been anticipated for some time that a strong local attack would be made to take Villers-Bretonneux, Cachy and Gentelles, with the high ground in the vicinity of these villages, as being the key to another big offensive against Amiens which these positions overlooked. Information confirming this opinion had been obtained on the 16th April from a prisoner of the 16th Bavarian R.I.R. captured before Villers-Bretonneux, and on the 22nd April came more definite information of impending attack from a sergeant-major of the 4th Guards Division who was taken during that morning by the 1/Sherwood Foresters. The

VILLERS-BRETONNEUX

prisoner stated that his division had relieved the 9th Bavarian Reserve Division expressly in order to take part in an attack on Villers-Bretonneux, which was timed for 3 o'clock the next morning. Accordingly all ranks were warned to be on the alert, and our artillery put down a counter-preparation on the German lines. In the event, no attack took place that night, although gas shelling of the woods and of our artillery positions continued to be fairly constant.

On the next day, the 23rd April, indications of attack began to accumulate. Other prisoners and a deserter confirmed the story of their fellow-countrymen that an attack was imminent. They stated that it would take place very early in the morning; probably on the day following. Substantiation for this view was provided by reports both from the front line and from the air, which stated that the Germans were moving troops forward and that their front lines were already very strongly held. Our heavy artillery was at once turned on and counter-preparation of exceptional intensity by guns of all calibres was carried out. The field artillery batteries fired as many as 100 rounds per gun, and so heavy a fire must have greatly hampered the enemy's preparations for attack and caused him considerable casualties.

The measures taken did not, however, succeed in checking the development of the German plan, for on the following morning (the 24th April) the attack opened on a front of about 8,000 yards from Hangard Wood on the 58th Division's front in the South to the left flank of the 8th Division in the North. It was carried out by no less than five German divisions in front line.

The enemy's plan of operations on the 8th Division's front was for the 228th Division and part of the 243rd Division to attack Villers-Bretonneux from the East, while the 4th Guards Division was to capture the south-western portion of the town and then advance westwards to the Bois d'Aquenne. The 228th Division, after entering Villers-Bretonneux on its eastern face, was to wheel northwards and clear the northern edge of the town in conjunction with the 243rd Division. As soon as these objectives had been gained, the attack on Hill 104 (North-East of Villers-Bretonneux) was to be undertaken by the 228th Division.

Prior to the infantry attack, a tremendous bombardment descended at 3.30 a.m. upon the Allied front and support lines, extending from Moreuil on the South to the right of the Australian Corps opposite Vaire Wood. Mixed gas and H.E. shells were poured out continuously over a wide area, large numbers of trench mortars supplementing the efforts of the German guns. It was, indeed, the heaviest bombardment that the division had yet experienced, and lasted at its fullest intensity for more than two hours. From information which has since been obtained

GERMAN TANKS

from an officer captured by the enemy early in the attack, it appears that there was a long line of heavy guns drawn up axle to axle just West of Marcelcave, and that these guns were being fired at the utmost possible speed, the gunners stripped naked to the waist and reliefs standing by. The bombardment lifted from our front line after about $2\frac{1}{4}$ hours; but it remained on our reserve positions in varying volume throughout the day.

During the previous evening the 23rd Infantry Brigade had relieved the 24th in the right sector of the divisional front, the relief being completed by 11.45 p.m., and it was against this brigade, as has been seen, that the German attack was principally and most successfully directed. All units had already suffered very heavy casualties from the German bombardment, when at about 6.30 a.m. the enemy began to put down smoke all along the front. The morning was very misty and the natural and the artificial fog combined made it difficult for men in the front line to see more than 20 yards ahead.

Suddenly at about 7 a.m., looming large and terrible out of the clinging wall of fog, enemy tanks were discerned close up against the fronts of the 2/West Yorkshire (Lieut.-Colonel A. E. E. Lowry) and the two southern companies of the 2/ Middlesex (Major C. D. Drew), holding respectively the South and East faces of the railway salient. An eye-witness, describing the advance of one of these monsters, states that as it came forward " it emitted long jets of lachrymatory gas." A modern and terrible form of dragon, indeed, breathing from its nostrils not fire but an element with which it was no less difficult to contend! The tanks were followed closely by the infantry of the 4th Guards Division, who took full advantage of their moral and material support. The five British companies, despite the furious bombardment they had undergone, opened heavy fire with rifle and machine guns; but with little apparent effect. The tanks kept on their way unchecked, until they had gained a position astride our trenches which they proceeded to rake with enfilade machine-gun fire, so covering the assault of the German infantry. The three forward companies of the 2/West Yorkshire were in this way completely overwhelmed.

On the front of the 2/ Middlesex the same combination of artillery, tanks, and a vastly superior infantry produced a similar result. "On the right immediately the barrage lifted, two enemy tanks approached our line, firing their machine-guns. Owing to the liberal use of smoke shells they could not be seen until they were about 30 yards from the trench. They got into position to enfilade the trench, causing further heavy casualties. They were followed by another tank and infantry with *flammenwerfer*. Rifle fire was opened, but could not stop their progress."

VILLERS-BRETONNEUX

All three tanks, followed or accompanied by their infantry, passed over our front line; the last of the tanks, turning towards the support trench (whence fire was being directed upon it) and traversing that also, caused many casualties in the support company. To avoid the tanks the remnants of this company retired into the railway cutting. The cutting, however, was heavily shelled and more casualties were caused. Finally the officer commanding the company, Capt. Brodie, with about half a dozen men, the sole survivors, made his way under heavy fire through Villers-Bretonneux to Battalion Headquarters. Thus both the right front line companies, as well as the support company of this battalion, were crushed and the village of Villers-Bretonneux, with the 2/ East Lancashire defending it, awaited the assault of the enemy.

Owing to the gas shelling to which the village had previously been subjected, it had been found necessary to place the garrison of Villers-Bretonneux around its outskirts. Here the three companies of the 2/ East Lancashire (Lieut.-Colonel G. E. M. Hill, D.S.O.) which were extended in a semicircle round the southeastern edge of the village, were in their turn overwhelmed, with the result that the company holding the northern portion of the village defences was outflanked. After suffering severe casualties the remnants of this battalion fell back, and by 9.30 a.m. had taken up a line on the falling slope West of the village to prevent the enemy debouching therefrom.

Already before this hour the enemy's advance had turned the flank of the support company of the 2/. West Yorkshire, compelling them to fall back to the North to their Battalion Headquarters, where Major H. Ingham, M.C., organized a new line of defence. There was a gap of about half a mile between them and the 2/4 London of the adjoining 58th Division. The extemporized line was held for some time, until Major Ingham became a casualty.* Then finding that their right flank was again being turned, the company and a number of stragglers whom they had rallied to them took up a fresh position on the railway West of Villers-Bretonneux. Working further westwards along the railway, they finally gained touch with the East Lancashire and formed a defensive flank from the railway to the main Amiens road. Very heavy machine-gun fire was brought to bear upon this position which was now overlooked by the enemy in the village. Many casualties were suffered and the remnants of the West Yorkshire were again forced back, this time to the North of the railway. The few men still fit to fight had now no ammunition left and at 10.30 a.m. Lieut. R. Kennington, in

* He was wounded and was later killed on his way back to the advanced dressing station.

PLATE XII

BRITISH "MALE" TANK

BRITISH WHIPPET TANK

Copyright: Imperial War Museum

GERMAN TANK

OUR FRONT LINE CRUSHED

command, decided to bring them back to the reserve line in the Bois l'Abbé.

The driving in of the front line troops had uncovered the 2/ Devonshire (Lieut.-Colonel R. H. Anderson-Morshead, D.S.O.) who formed the support and counter-attack battalion of the 23rd Infantry Brigade and were located just forward of the road Cachy–Villers-Bretonneux and just to the rear of the road Domart–Villers-Bretonneux. As none of the West Yorkshire had withdrawn through the Devons, the first intimation the latter received of the success of the German attack was the unwelcome sight of a German tank which came right up to Battalion Headquarters from the South, blew away the parapet and then moved off. This occurred shortly before 8 o'clock in the morning. After the first tank had vanished three more appeared, followed immediately as the others had been by overwhelmingly powerful infantry supports. These drove in the two left companies of the Devons, already weakened by their losses during the bombardment, and over-ran their whole position. The right two companies of the Devons and the two companies of the 1/ Worcestershire (Lieut.-Colonel G. M. C. Davidge, D.S.O.) on their right again, were, however, successful in maintaining their positions in the Cachy Switch. The left battalion of the 58th Division had also been driven in by infantry and tanks—seven machines in all appear to have been employed in this attack—and had been forced back south-westwards on the general line Hangard Wood–Cachy.

The success of the hostile attack against the right of the divisional front and beyond had its necessary reaction on the troops further to the North. When the two southern companies of the 2/ Middlesex had been overwhelmed, the enemy worked round the right and rear of the northern company and practically destroyed it, although it put up a desperate fight. The few survivors withdrew in a north-westerly direction. The enemy thereupon employed the same enveloping tactics against the two right companies of the 2/ Rifle Brigade (Lieut.-Colonel H. S. C. Richardson) of the 25th Infantry Brigade North of the Villers-Bretonneux–Warfusée road. Unobserved owing to the dense mist and the smoke barrage, he pushed his way northwards between the battalion's front and support lines and also in rear of the latter. "A" and "C" Companies in front line were taken unawares from behind by greatly superior numbers of the enemy, and, though the course of the battle showed that they must have put up a most gallant resistance, the whole of the two companies with few exceptions were killed or captured. Very little could be ascertained as to the exact fate of these two companies; but it is known that one platoon of "D" company in support, which was caught in the same movement, fought to their last man and was

VILLERS-BRETONNEUX

completely wiped out. Second Lieut. J. Doyle, dangerously wounded while commanding this platoon, was found in the night of the 24th/25th during the counter-attack by the Australians and brought back the story of the gallant end his men had made. The scanty remnants of these three companies of the Rifle Brigade, reinforced by Battalion Headquarters details, fell back to the North-West. Here they got into touch on the right with the support battalion, the 2/ Royal Berkshire who had also swung back their right. On the left they continued the line across the southern face of Hill 104, to form a defensive flank to " B " company, the northern company of their own battalion. This latter company of the Rifle Brigade maintained its original position throughout the day. By the accuracy of its fire it caused the enemy many casualties and with the rest of its battalion and the Berkshire successfully prevented the enemy from developing his attack northwards and so gaining the important area of high ground between Villers-Bretonneux and the Somme.

As the morning wore on and the fog cleared it was possible to ascertain with some degree of accuracy the extent of the German penetration. The enemy had gained possession of Villers-Bretonneux and was holding its northern, western and southern edges, and had installed machine-guns round the perimeter. North of the main high road which runs from Amiens straight through Villers-Bretonneux to Warfusée and Foucaucourt, his advance took the form of a semi-ellipse running westwards from the point where " B " company, 2nd Rifle Brigade, still held its original position, until it dropped in a southerly direction to touch the high road just where the railway crossed it. Our troops—the balance of the Rifle Brigade, all four companies of the Berkshire and remainder of the East Lancashire—held a containing line which conformed to this figure, with their right resting on the railway. South of the road the enemy held in strength the line of the railway which, swinging away to the South-East, forms a boundary line round this sector of the town. In addition he had pushed a party forward in front of this position through the eastern edges of the Bois d'Aquenne. The tank attack which had flattened out the two northerly companies of the 2/ Devonshire had opened the way for this irruption. Further to the South the remaining two companies of the Devons and two companies of the 1/ Worcestershire still maintained their positions in the Cachy Switch, though the Germans in the Bois d'Aquenne were well behind their flank. Meanwhile the left of the 58th Division had been forced back from a front line which had crossed the Villers-Bretonneux–Demuin road South of Monument Wood, to a position about 1,000 yards to the East of Cachy.

During the latter part of the morning an attempt was made

PLATE XIII

Copyright: *Imperial War Museum*

THE BOIS L'ABBÉ, APRIL, 1918

STRETCHER BEARERS, 24TH INFANTRY BRIGADE, CROSSING THE RIDGE THAT SCREENS AMIENS, ON THE WAY TO VILLERS-BRETONNEUX

TANK *VERSUS* TANK

by the 1/ Sherwood Foresters (reserve battalion 24th Infantry Brigade, allotted for the purpose of this operation to 23rd Infantry Brigade) to clear the Bois d'Aquenne of the enemy. The battalion moved in artillery formation along the southern edge of the wood and then turned northwards into it. Here they encountered the enemy in some strength and drove him towards its eastern edges. At this stage, however, the Commanding Officer (Lieut.-Colonel R. F. Moore, M.C.) was wounded. Deprived of his leadership at a critical juncture, and losing direction in the wood, the battalion was unable to push home its attack and commenced to dig in on the road which runs diagonally in a north-north-easterly direction through the wood. While digging in here it came under a very heavy 5·9-inch barrage and suffered severely.

This local counter-attack, though not completely successful, had the effect of checking any further attempt on the part of the enemy to advance through the Bois d'Aquenne. Although with the aid of his tanks and a powerful concentration of artillery and infantry he had captured Villers-Bretonneux, he had failed to push on to the secondary ridge which at the northern end of the Bois l'Abbé crosses the line of the road and railway and blocks from Villers-Bretonneux the open view down the Somme Valley to Amiens. In other words he had failed, though not by much, to attain the main object of his operation. His force of tanks had been employed in the sector lying between Hangard Wood and Villers-Bretonneux, where the nature of the ground was particularly well suited to their use and the sharp salient in our line offered favourable opportunities for assault. He had achieved the initial success which throughout the war attended well supported tank attacks under such conditions; but, while the stubborn fighting of our own infantry had limited his success and prevented its exploitation, later in the morning our own tanks came into action.

As it happened, the first British tanks to meet the enemy's machines were either the light, fast " whippets," or " female " tanks, each armed only with machine guns. These could do little damage to the heavily armoured German machines and certain of them were put out of action by the small calibre gun carried by their opponents. When, however, British " male " tanks arrived upon the scene, heavier metal at once told and all German tanks encountered were put out of action or driven to retreat. Not that the " whippets " failed to do admirable service; for, moving faster than an armed man can run, in the afternoon they caught two German battalions in the act of deploying, charged and utterly destroyed them and returned to our lines their sides splashed high with blood.

VILLERS-BRETONNEUX

More important still, our artillery, gallantly holding their positions, were continuously sweeping the northern and northwestern exits from Villers-Bretonneux with direct fire. In this way they gave the infantry invaluable assistance in preventing the enemy from exploiting his initial success. An eye-witness relates how he saw one field gun, unfortunately unidentified, come into action on the railway bridge itself, the gun team pulling down the parapet of the bridge to enable their gun to open fire at point blank range upon the German infantry crowded in the railway cutting beneath them. A great number of our guns and batteries were under machine-gun fire, but refused to withdraw and suffered heavily. Early in the afternoon some of the more forward of them were moved back under orders to positions which were less accessible to direct machine-gun fire, but from which the exits of the town could be as effectively swept. The gunners continued their splendid work and their fire was so admirably maintained as to form, in conjunction with our machine-gun and rifle fire, a barrier against which the enemy was quite unable to advance. The situation remained until nightfall as has been described above.

This, however, was not enough. It was imperative that Villers-Bretonneux should not remain in German hands. For it is situated on the very spear-head, pushed out westwards, of a high plateau, and within a few hundred yards of the spur from which the road to Amiens is laid bare and the whole city and its environs come under direct observation. Acquiescence in the permanent German occupation of this commanding position could not be thought of. Counter-measures had inevitably to be taken and for such a purpose the 13th Australian Brigade had already, during the morning, been placed under General Heneker's command. On the other hand, in view of the very large number of machine-guns which the enemy had brought up and posted in the captured positions, a counter-attack carried out in daylight across the open slopes which led to our old lines would almost inevitably break down with the most terrible casualties.

Such was General Heneker's opinion and he communicated it both to Corps and Army. He reported further that he felt confident that he could hold the enemy during the remainder of the day, and suggested that the proposed counter-attack should be postponed until after sunset and should then, after all details had been carefully worked out, be launched as a night operation, assisted by moonlight. This proposal was approved and after some discussion the following plan was decided upon and orders were issued at 5.30 p.m. by III Corps. The attack was to be carried out by the 54th Infantry Brigade (58th Division) on the right, by the 13th Australian Brigade (temporarily under the

VILLERS BRETONNEUX (Nº 1)

SITUATION 3.45 A.M. 24TH APRIL 1918.

⌐ *Indicates 1 Company (unless otherwise stated)*
----- *Contours*
xxxx *Indicates 2nd Line Trenches*
ARROWS *Show direction and extent of German penetration.*

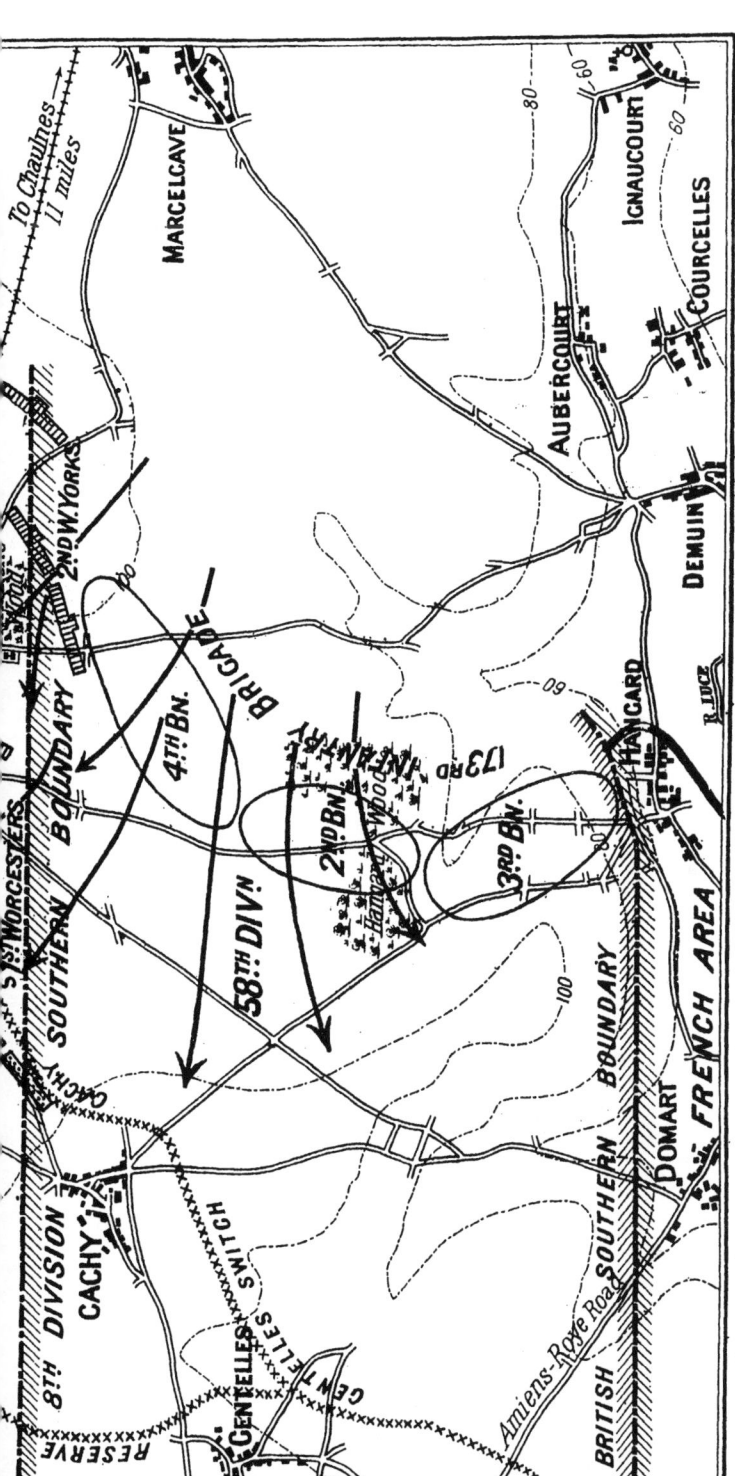

THE COUNTER-ATTACK

command of the 8th Division) in the centre, and by the 15th Australian Brigade (5th Australian Division) on the left. The 54th Infantry Brigade was to recapture the original front line on the 58th Division front East of Cachy. The 13th Australian Brigade forming up South of the Bois de l'Abbé was to advance due East, leaving Villers-Bretonneux on its left. The 15th Australian Brigade forming up on the plateau to the North of the town, where the Australian Corps had not been directly attacked, was to advance in a south-easterly direction leaving the town on its right, its objective being our original front line in the vicinity of the Villers-Bretonneux–Warfusée high road. One battalion (22/ Durham L.I.) of the 8th Division was allotted to the 15th Australian Brigade, and another battalion (2/ Northamptonshire) to the 13th Australian Brigade, for the purpose of clearing the town of Villers-Bretonneux as the attack went forward on each side of it. The rest of the 8th Division was to hold the reserve lines, in order to secure the present positions should the counter-attack not prove successful. All three attacking brigades were placed under General Heneker's orders for the actual operation.

APRIL 1918

Such a plan was not without its risks. To launch a counter-attack on a large scale, at night, and without previous reconnaissance, over country which would necessarily be strange to the attackers, was a bold policy, and one which could clearly only be entrusted to troops of the highest quality whose officers and men inspired the fullest confidence. Even so it would be a hazardous undertaking. Yet the situation was one which called for a desperate remedy. Moreover, a bold and prompt counter-measure which would find the enemy still to some extent disorganized after his advance of the morning offered the greatest chances of success.

It was essential that the counter-attack should be put in at the earliest possible moment, in order to forestall any possible enemy attack, and so " zero " hour had been fixed for 10 o'clock*; but the time available for preparation and for the forward movement of the attacking units had been short. The artillery bombarded the town and other selected localities; but there was no creeping barrage, so that an absolutely accurate and synchronous advance was not indispensable. On the other hand it had been arranged that the standing barrage which the artillery was to place on the railway South of the main road and also on the western edge of Monument Wood, should lift forward at " zero "+one hour. Consequently the delay in starting deprived the attacking troops of some artillery protection. Moreover, there was considerable discrepancy between the starting times of the two

* Originally 8 p.m.; but altered on representations from the division.

VILLERS-BRETONNEUX

brigades. The 13th on the South got off practically to time; the 15th on the other hand were about an hour late. This meant not only a certain loss of co-operation as between the two attacking brigades, but also that the 13th, which started first, received more than its fair share of attention from the enemy.

The 13th Australian Brigade had, indeed, by far the harder task. Its path lay across a stiff northward falling slope, and troops moving over such a terrain have an almost inevitable tendency to crowd together in the direction of the slope. Further, a belt of wire in front of the Cachy Switch ran diagonally across its line of advance: and in a night operation barbed wire thus disposed is the most formidable of obstacles. It renders the maintenance of correct alignment and direction a matter of the utmost difficulty. None the less the brigade successfully moved across the steeply sloping ground and got through the wire without deviating from its true course; a notable achievement in any case, but one which was rendered the more remarkable because it was accomplished under very heavy fire. The achievement constitutes a fine tribute to the skill of its commander, Brig.-General T. W. Glasgow, and to the training, discipline and fortitude of the troops engaged.

The attacking battalions had come under severe machine-gun fire from the railway immediately they had started to advance. Casualties from this cause were heavy; but the gallant Australians would not be denied, and overcoming all obstacles— the scattered enemy posts being attacked and disposed of in their stride—they pressed on until their leading troops had entered Monument Wood. Here a very heavy enfilade machine-gun fire was met with from Villers-Bretonneux; for the " mopping up " of the village, where cellars and houses afforded ample cover, had as yet made no progress. The flanks of the brigade, too, were dangerously exposed; for the 15th Australian Infantry Brigade had not yet come up and the 54th Brigade on the right was in difficulties. These two factors made it impossible to retain the ultimate line which had been gained. Accordingly the brigade withdrew a short distance to dig in on a line which ran between the roads leading from Hangard and Domart to Villers-Bretonneux, just to the South of the fork at which these two roads join.

The 2/ Northamptonshire had advanced behind the 13th Australian Brigade. As soon as they started, they came under very heavy artillery fire which caused serious casualties to the Battalion Headquarters party, the C.O., Lieut.-Colonel S. G. Latham, M.C., being killed and the Adjutant, Capt. H. Essame, being wounded almost immediately. Major H. T. Forster took over command and after clearing the southern edge of the Bois d'Aquenne the battalion swung to the left towards the southern portion of the village. When within 500 yards of the railway they were met by fierce machine-gun fire directed from that position down the steep bare slope which formed a natural glacis in front of it, and were unable to get on. Their casualties here were very severe. Finally side-stepping to the right, they got into touch with the left of the Australian troops and formed a defensive flank to the Australian left, to the South of the village and facing North.

The attack of the 15th Australian Infantry Brigade (Brig.-General H. E. Elliot) did not get under way, as has been said, until 11 p.m. Once started, it went forward very smoothly and successfully and without meeting any very serious opposition; although checked slightly on the North of the village owing to machine-gun fire. The attack was planned in two bounds and at 12.40 a.m. information came back that the first objective had been taken. The following extract gives some indication of the method of advance: " The enemy was using a lot of flares and these assisted our men in a large measure in locating the positions and posts occupied by him. Our men would watch for the places from which the flares were coming and would then rush and capture them at the point of the bayonet. Buildings on fire in the village also assisted in giving direction. The night itself could not have been better for a night operation; for, although movement could be seen up to about 200 yards, there was not sufficient light to sight a machine-gun. There was very little shelling, because the enemy was not sure of the position of his own troops."* The brigade carried on until it had successfully attained the second objective and at about 4.30 a.m. Brigade Headquarters was able to report to 8th Division that its battalions were in position on the old front line,† and that 60 prisoners and 3 machine guns had been captured. The 15th Australian Infantry Brigade had not yet, however, been able to gain touch with 13th Australian Infantry Brigade, and Villers-Bretonneux was still full of the enemy's troops.

Like the 2/ Northamptonshire, the 22/ D.L.I. (Lieut.-Colonel B. C. James) found the enemy's positions in Villers-Bretonneux itself too easily defensible and too strongly held for direct attack to be successful, and they did not succeed in accomplishing their task of " mopping-up " the town during the night. There was for some time considerable doubt as to the battalion's whereabouts, and as to how far it had been able to proceed with the work allotted to it; but it was at any rate certain that strong

* H.Q. 15th Australian Infantry Brigade W.D., April 1918.
† The line actually taken up was from a few hundred yards up to 1,000 yards West of the old British front line.

VILLERS-BRETONNEUX

forces of the enemy were still in active occupation of the village. On receiving at 4 a.m. information to this effect, General Heneker ordered General Coffin to send forward the 2/ Royal Berkshire, 25th Infantry Brigade, to attack and enter Villers-Bretonneux from the North.

The 2/ Royal Berkshire (Lieut.-Colonel J. A. A. Griffin) moved forward to the attack at about 6.30 a.m. and advancing with great dash they soon made their presence felt. " B " Company, 57th Australian Infantry Battalion co-operated in the movement, clearing a considerable area and capturing a number of prisoners; and with the coming of daylight the 22/ D.L.I. also succeeded in effecting an entrance from the North-West. The brilliant work of the 2/ Royal Berkshire in this engagement was acknowledged by a message from the 5th Australian Division. " Well done Royal Berks."

The combined efforts of all these troops produced the most excellent results. Though parties of the enemy resisted stubbornly and held out for some hours, these isolated " pockets " were reduced one by one, until some 400 prisoners and over 100 machine-guns had been captured. At the same time the Bois d'Aquenne was finally cleared of the enemy by the joint action of parties of the 2/ Middlesex, the 2/ West Yorkshire and the 1/ Sherwood Foresters. One officer and 73 men were captured here in addition to a number of machine guns and trench mortars, a battery of heavy trench mortars being included among the latter.

Thus by midday there had come a very marked and welcome change in the general situation. The enemy's gains of the day before had already been to a great extent recovered and a large number of prisoners and much material had passed into our hands. Villers-Bretonneux had been cleared, except for a small portion round the railway bridge at its south-eastern corner. Early in the afternoon four tanks were allotted to the division for the clearing up of this last point of resistance. These tanks never reached the town, but already before this the 2/ Northamptonshire by a courageous dash across exposed ground had occupied the railway station and the railway in its vicinity. During the course of the afternoon the remainder of this German " pocket " was cleared by the 22/ D.L.I.

There remained but one further task to complete the operation. Owing to hostile machine-gun fire the 13th Australian Infantry Brigade could not advance their left to join up with the 15th Australian Infantry Brigade, and it was feared that the enemy was dribbling men up under cover of the railway embankment and was massing for an attack at dusk. Capt. B. C. Pascoe, M.C., Brig.-Major 25th Infantry Brigade, was therefore ordered to

OUR LINE RESTORED

take two platoons of the 2/ Rifle Brigade and clear up the situation. This he did with great gallantry and judgment, driving off the enemy and completely reorganizing the defence of this locality. When night had fallen a firm line had been established linking up the two brigades into a solid and united front.

Though the front had been made secure, Monument Wood and certain territory to its South were still in German hands and it was arranged that the French Moroccan Division (which had relieved the 54th Infantry Brigade) should make an attack at 5.15 on the following morning (26th April) to improve our position on this part of the line. The right battalion of the 13th Australian Infantry Brigade was to co-operate. The attack was duly launched, but owing to heavy machine-gun fire from Monument Wood the attempt to enter the wood was a failure and our line on this part of the front was not advanced. Further to the South the French did succeed in recapturing a certain amount of ground.

The remainder of this day was fairly quiet, and the enemy, who seemed to have had his fill of fighting, showed no inclination to make any fresh attack. Machine-gun fire from Monument Wood continued, however, to be very troublesome and plans were made at Divisional Headquarters for another attempt to be made to retake this position the same night by the 1/ Sherwood Foresters and 1/ Worcestershire. Later it was found that these battalions had already suffered too severely to be in a fit state to undertake an operation of this nature, and it was finally decided that the project must be abandoned.

On the following morning (27th April) orders were received that the division would be relieved that same evening by the 4th Australian Division. The relief took place accordingly. After relief the division was assembled in the near vicinity of Amiens, Divisional Headquarters moving to Vaux en Amienois, half a dozen miles to the North-West of the city, the 23rd Infantry Brigade to Quevrieux, the 24th to Camon and the 25th Infantry Brigade to Boutillerie. These were to be only temporary resting places and it was intimated that the division would shortly move elsewhere for a real opportunity to recover from the arduous times through which it had passed. A period of rest, recuperation and reorganization was, indeed, essential, for once again the division had suffered very severely. Hardly in fact had the wastage of the March battle been made good, the necessary reinforcements received and the work of assimilation commenced, when they had again been consumed in the furnace of battle.

The total casualties suffered during the action of Villers-Bretonneux were as follows: officers, 133; other ranks, 3,420. Of the infantry battalions the three which had been in the front

VILLERS-BRETONNEUX

line when the attack was launched had all suffered heavily, the West Yorkshire and the Middlesex, against whom the hostile tanks had had full play, having once more the worst figures. The 2/ Middlesex had lost 13 officers and 539 other ranks, the 2/ West Yorkshire had lost 16 officers and 406 other ranks. Thus the misfortunes of war had decreed that the same two battalions which had lost most heavily in the March battle should again be the severest sufferers on this occasion. The 2/ Rifle Brigade with 14 officers and 380 other ranks casualties was not in much better case; and, of the others there were no less than six battalions, of which the 22/ D.L.I. (Pioneers) was one, which had lost more than 350 men.

These losses were certainly grievous; but there was some consolation in the knowledge that in the whole operation German losses must undoubtedly have been heavier than our own. The following is extracted from a Fourth Army Intelligence Summary published shortly after the battle: " Though no very definite figures have been obtainable as to the enemy's losses during the fighting of the 24th April and subsequently, there can be no doubt that the divisions (243rd, 228th, 4th Guard, 77th Reserve Division) engaged opposite this front suffered very heavily indeed. The evidence goes to show that the 77th Reserve Division was completely broken up: this is confirmed by its relief by the 19th Division until a fresh division (109th) could be brought up. This applies in a lesser degree to the 243rd Division which was similarly relieved by the 9th Bavarian Reserve Division."

More important from the larger point of view was the fact that the spirit of our troops in line had not been broken in this, their first, encounter with German tanks attacking in force and at close quarters. At their initial onset the tanks, assisted by appropriately powerful infantry bodies, had, it is true, overrun our front and support lines and opened the way to Villers-Bretonneux; but thereafter our troops had successfully re-established the defence, bringing the enemy to a halt before he had succeeded in penetrating our rear lines of defence. The action as a whole was not dissimilar to that undertaken by us at Cambrai in 1917. It was of course on a much smaller scale, and on this occasion the reaction of the defensive was more rapid and far more successful. But in both there was the surprise tank attack gaining a sudden success which could not afterwards be maintained. The initial attack of the Germans on the 24th April, fog and tanks combining as its chief assets, had certainly met with considerable success: but the dangerous situation produced by the capture of Villers-Bretonneux was faced and tackled with the utmost promptness and resolution. Neither our infantry nor our artillery had allowed their spirit of resistance to be quelled by the formidable forces

VILLERS BRETONNEUX (N° 2)

SITUATION 6 P.M. 25TH APRIL 1918.

☐ Indicates 1 Company (unless otherwise stated)
— Contours
▬▬ Limits of German Advance
xxxx Indicates 2nd Line Trenches
ARROWS Show Method and Direction of British Counter-attack during night of 24/25 April.

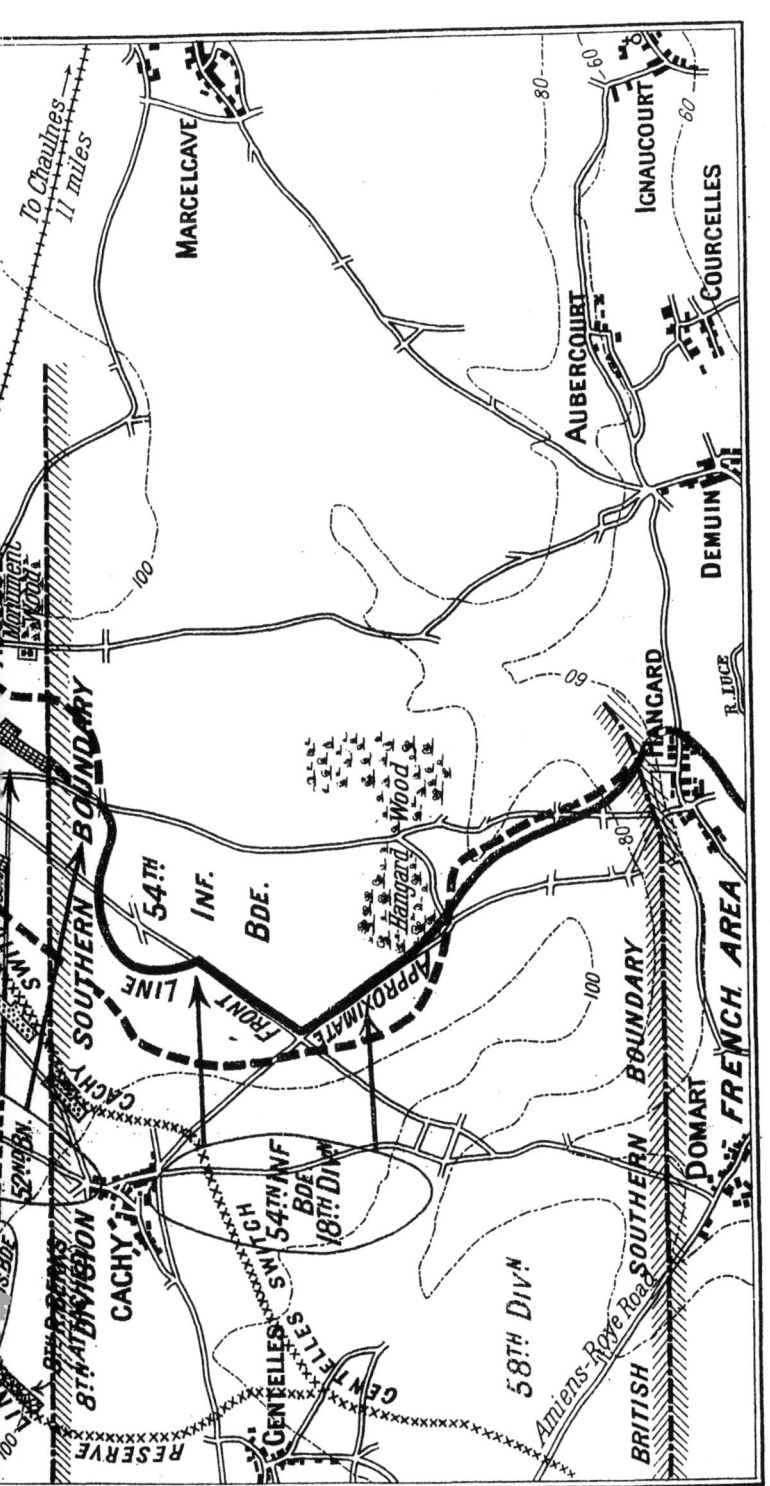

THE BATTLE REVIEWED

brought against them. Tank had been met with tank—hostile tanks in conflict for the first time in history—and already by the afternoon the enemy was held. On the same night our counter-attack, boldly and resolutely planned and carried out with the like qualities—without them it could not have succeeded—turned the tables with a completeness which the Germans at Cambrai had been unable to achieve.

The enemy's last desperate thrust towards Amiens had been definitely foiled. Though it was the splendid fighting qualities of the Australian troops which turned him out of the positions he had gained, it was the 8th Division, on whom the full weight of the blow fell, who stopped his advance before its purpose had been accomplished.

CHAPTER XIV

THE BATTLE OF THE AISNE, 1918

BY the end of April the Lys battle had burned itself out as the great Somme offensive had done, leaving the enemy in possession, as the result of his second adventure, of a flat and exposed salient dominated by our guns. The intervention of French divisions on the Kemmel front, following so soon after their active participation in the southern battle, had largely exhausted the available reserves of our Allies. It was accordingly decided that certain British divisions should be sent South to take the place of French divisions transferred to the Lys. These British divisions, although reconstituted after the trials that they had undergone on the British front, could not yet be considered fit for further battle fighting. It was therefore originally intended that they should be kept in reserve for a time, and that when they did go into the line it should be in some sector which was not thought likely to be the scene of active operations.

The 8th Division was selected to be one of these divisions, and at the beginning of May was transferred from the Fourth Army (Australian Corps) and sent South to form part of the IX Corps, attached to General Duchesnes' Sixth French Army on the Aisne.

Entrainment commenced on the 3rd of the month and on the following day Divisional Headquarters were opened at Chèry Chartreuve, South-West of Fismes and some 3 miles due South of the Vesle river. The units of the division were comfortably established in huts and villages in the surrounding neighbourhood.

As a result of the heavy fighting described in the two previous chapters, the division was, of course, in no condition to take part in major operations and was in urgent need of rest, training and reorganization. The extent to which it had suffered may be most easily expressed by the following plain statement of figures. Since the 23rd March it had lost in casualties 390 officers and 8,210 other ranks and had received 329 officers and 7,567 other ranks as reinforcements. No division in the British Army had more thoroughly earned a rest; but when it and the other battle-worn divisions (21st, 25th and 50th) which had been allotted to Lieut.-General Sir A. Hamilton Gordon's IX Corps had been but a few days in the French area, they were directed by the French Army Commander to take over a sector of the front line. It was represented to General Hamilton Gordon that the front was so quiet that rest and training could still be continued and, since the opportunity to recuperate fully behind the line was denied them, the course proposed seemed to be the next best thing.

Yet it was essential that the sector to be taken over should be

RUSTIC PEACE

really quiet, and on this point there was considerable difference of opinion between the French and British Commands. Since the successful operation by the French at Malmaison in October 1917, the Chemin des Dames front now held by General Franchet d'Esperey's Group of Armies, had undoubtedly been markedly peaceful. It was also of great natural strength. On the other hand, it had long been very lightly held, and seeing that the bulk of the Allied reserves had at this date, as a result of the heavy fighting on the Somme and the Lys, been drawn towards the North, it seemed to the British by no means unlikely that the enemy's next blow would fall on the southern flank of his March drive. Representations to this effect were duly made to our Allies as soon as their intentions with regard to our divisions became known; but the British view did not win their approval; and, the matter being largely one of opinion, the British Command, despite its own misgivings, had no option but to accept the dispositions which our Allies had made.

MAY 1918

Instructions were received on the 7th May that the 8th Division was to relieve the 71st French Division, and six days later the division went into line in the Berry-au-Bac sector, holding a front of about 10,000 yards. Divisional Headquarters were established at Roucy. " The front on arrival," says one witness, " was certainly the most peaceful the division had ever been in. It was seldom that a shell was heard." Moreover, the weather was remarkably fine. The country, much more naturally attractive than the flatter and less varied areas farther North, looked at its best in the full glory of spring and sunshine. It is a wide and rolling type of landscape, the uplands for the most part consisting of bare and breezy stretches which are a little reminiscent of our Sussex Downs; the hollows where the streams run are in many cases pleasantly shaded by groves of trees.

An officer attached to the Headquarters of the 23rd Infantry Brigade* gives the following admirable description: " To the battered, battle-weary troops, whose only knowledge of France was based on their experience of the northern front, the Champagne country in the full glory of spring was a revelation. Gone was the depressing monotony of Flanders, drab and weeping, with its mud and its mists, its pollards and its pavé: gone the battle-wrecked landscapes of Picardy and the Somme, with their shattered villages and blasted woods. Here all was peace. The countryside basked contentedly in the blazing sunshine. Trim villages nestled in quiet hollows beside lazy streams, and tired eyes were refreshed by the sight of rolling hills, clad with great

* Capt. S. Rogerson, 2/West Yorkshire, to whom the authors are indebted for those subsequent passages of this chapter which are printed between inverted commas, but not otherwise acknowledged.

THE BATTLE OF THE AISNE

woods golden with laburnum blossom; by the soft greenery of lush meadowland, shrubby vineyards and fields of growing corn. Right up to within 2 miles of the line civilians were living, going about their business of husbandry as if ignorant of the close proximity of war.

"Nor was this illusion of rustic tranquillity shattered by the trench area itself, although this had been the scene of the great French offensive of 1917—one of the bloodiest battles of the whole campaign on the Western Front.

"The ground was everywhere pitted with shell-holes, honeycombed with dug-outs and littered with tangles of barbed wire. Here were concrete 'pill-boxes'—super 'pill-boxes'—resembling square forts and all bearing the marks of artillery fire; there, in a line, the remains of seven or eight French tanks—a grim memento of the first use of these. But whereas only a year ago it had been an area of death and destruction, in May 1918 Nature had reasserted herself and hidden the grosser evidences of battle under a mantle of green. Only the actual front line trenches, dug in the chalk, seared the landscape with white scars. The woods had been blasted by the shell-fire of the previous year; but now each shattered tree stump had covered its wounds with a wealth of close foliage. In the shell holes grass had grown and water plants; near the gun emplacements in the reserve line grew lilies of the valley, forget-me-nots, larkspur and honeysuckle. The whole battle area had become a shrubbery, a vast garden fashioned by artillery.

"In places coils of rusty wire showed redly through the grass while the derelict tanks and shattered 'pill-boxes' still resisted all Nature's attempts to conceal the evidence of battle. Occasionally, too, a shell would break the summer silence and wake echoes in the sleeping hills. But even the shells seemed tired, arriving in a leisurely sort of way and exploding apologetically without injury to anyone."

To the worn-out division it must, indeed, have been a welcome and a wonderful change; here, at last, they might legitimately expect to find and to enjoy the rest which had been so thoroughly earned. But it was not to be. Here also the division was doomed, like some unlucky magnet, to attract the storm; before the month was out it was to experience yet once again the full shock of a violent offensive. After but a very few days in line there came a subtle change in the situation. The enemy's artillery fire grew gradually in volume and his whole attitude became more aggressive. "There was no shelling as we had become used to it, but there was an increase in the steady methodical 'crumping' of battery positions, one shell at a time. This was the more significant as the suspicious observer could only put it down to

SINISTER SIGNS

ranging or to calibration of new guns." By the 20th May rumours were already circulating that attack in this region was possible; but there was still nothing in the Intelligence reports to suggest that any such attack was likely. Even as late as the 25th the situation was quiet and there seemed to be no indication on our front that anything unusual was contemplated by the enemy. On this very day, indeed, a message was received at IX Corps Headquarters from French Headquarters to the effect that in the opinion of the French Command there were no indications that the enemy had made preparations which would enable him to attack on the morrow.

MAY 1918

The noon reports of the 26th May, however, told a different story. Greatly increased movement was seen behind the enemy's lines and there had been much noise and sounds of hammering at night. What appeared to be black notice boards—direction boards, it was suggested, for tanks—were seen at daybreak in the German lines opposite the 25th Infantry Brigade front. Battle stations were ordered in the division and the wisdom of this step was confirmed when in the afternoon a telephone message was received from IX Corps, stating definitely that the enemy was expected to attack on the 27th May and that the 8th Division front would probably be involved. The Corps orders to take up battle stations followed at about 6 p.m. Two prisoners, captured by the French on the previous night, had both given independent but coinciding evidence that an attack was to be launched on the morrow. There was left no reasonable room for doubt. Divisional Headquarters were moved to the high ground above Roucy from which the whole of the ground North of the river could be overlooked.

The arrival at 23rd Infantry Brigade Headquarters at about 3.45 p.m. of the orders to take up battle positions is thus described by Captain Rogerson: " Millis, the Brigade Major, was stretching himself in the sun outside the dug-out. A signaller approached, saluted and handed him the little pink telephone form: ' The enemy will attack on a wide front at 01.00 hours to-morrow, 27th inst. aaa ' then followed instructions as to dispositions. In a flash the world seemed altered. The landscape smiled no longer. It was all a grinning unreality, a mockery, the earth decked in spring finery so that hopes aroused might be more completely dashed."

As will be seen from the map, the sector occupied by the division formed a right-angled salient pushed out into the German positions. The right flank of the division rested on the Aisne itself at the village of Berry-au-Bac. This sub-sector was held by the 25th Infantry Brigade (Brig.-General R. H. Husey, D.S.O., M.C.) with the 2/ Rifle Brigade (Lieut.-Colonel H. S. C.

THE BATTLE OF THE AISNE

Richardson) and the 2/ Royal Berkshire (Lieut.-Colonel J. A. A. Griffin) in line and the 2/ East Lancashire (Lieut.-Colonel G. E. M. Hill) in the main line of resistance. The eastward face of this sector was protected from surprise attack by the northerly continuation of the river and of the canal. The Miette stream, which was about 20 feet wide, deep and with very marshy banks, divided the 25th Infantry Brigade area from that of the 24th Infantry Brigade (Brig.-General R. Haig, D.S.O.) which latter brigade held the centre of the divisional area with the 2/ Northamptonshire (Lieut.-Colonel C. G. Buckle) in line, the 1/ Worcestershire (Major J. B. F. Cartland) in the main line of resistance and the 1/ Sherwood Foresters (Lieut.-Colonel R. F. Moore) in reserve South of the Aisne. The 23rd Infantry Brigade (Brig.-General G. W. St. G. Grogan) held the left with the 2/ West Yorkshire (Lieut.-Colonel A. E. E. Lowry) in line, the 2/ Middlesex (Lieut.-Colonel C. A. S. Page) in the main line of resistance, and the 2/ Devonshire (Lieut.-Colonel R. H. Anderson-Morshead) in reserve. The 8th Battalion Machine Gun Corps (Lieut.-Colonel E. M. Beall) was disposed with eight guns in each sub-sector and eight guns in reserve. South of the Aisne the high ground round Gernicourt, which overlooked the river, was an important tactical feature, forming part of the battle zone and covering the right flank of the division. Protected by the river and situated on a cliff-like eminence arising immediately therefrom, it was a position of great natural strength. The Gernicourt defences were held by a permanent garrison composed of the 22/ D.L.I. (Lieut.-Colonel B. C. James, D.S.O.) and the 11th/23rd French Territorial Battalion (less one company). A certain amount of French artillery and some French machine-gun companies and anti-tank guns were also under the command of the G.O.C., 8th Division.* The 8th Division occupied the central position on the IX Corps front, with the 21st Division holding a front of 7,500 yards on its right and the 50th Division holding a front of 8,000 yards on its left. The 25th Division was held in Army reserve.

The defensive positions occupied by the division consisted of an Outpost Line some 1,000 to 1,500 yards in depth, in touch with the enemy, and a Battle Zone immediately in rear, some 1,500 to 2,000 yards in depth; all North of the Aisne. The orders from the French Command were that not a yard of ground was to be given up. The Outpost Line was to fight to the last. The Battle Zone was to be held at all costs, and all reserves were

---

* 1 Group, 203rd Regiment French Field Artillery (75 mm.); 122nd and 125th French Batteries of Anti-Tank Guns; 11th, 162nd and 313th Companies of 26th French Machine-Gun Battalion; 24th and 25th Companies of 25th French Machine Gun Battalion.

A FAULTY METHOD OF DEFENCE

to be put in to retake any portion of this zone which might be lost to the enemy. These directions meant that the main infantry strength of the division was committed to the defence of these two zones, and that to support them the greater part of the artillery* at the disposal of the 8th Division was posted North of the River Aisne. This was necessary in order that the front of the outpost zone should be covered, and in view of the fact that the range of our 18-pounder gun was more limited than that of the French 75 mm.

Dispositions for defence so markedly at variance with all the experience of the British armies in the March and April battles naturally aroused the serious criticism of the British commanders. General Heneker, General David Campbell, commanding the 21st Division, and General H. C. Jackson, commanding the 50th Division, all protested energetically against the placing of the bulk of their troops in front of the natural obstacle of the Aisne. It was pointed out that it was suicidal to ignore the lessons of the earlier battles, and that the French method of defence would result in the bulk of the troops North of the Aisne being wiped out by the enemy's trench mortar and artillery bombardment. It was urged that the positions on the right bank of the Aisne ought to be held lightly by an outpost line which, when the attack opened, could be withdrawn to the main defence line South of the river, so that the British artillery and machine guns from positions on the South bank could barrage in depth the forward zone over which the German infantry would advance to the attack of the river line. Such a method would give ample time for the systematic destruction of such bridges† as would require to be left for the service of the lightly-held zone, North of the river.

Although General Foch had previously given orders that the British experience on the Somme and Lys should be used to determine the method of defence to be adopted on the Aisne, the local French Command concerned overrode the objections of the British Generals and disregarded their advice. Not an inch

---

* 8th Division Artillery (Brig.-General J. W. F. Lamont): XXXIII Brigade R.F.A. (Lieut.-Colonel H. G. Fisher); XLV Brigade R.F.A. (Lieut.-Colonel J. A. Ballard); CX Brigade R.F.A. (25th Division Lieut.-Colonel H. R. Phipps). Attached, 24th, 28th and 29th Batteries French Field Artillery (le Capitaine Paul); No. 7 and No. 8 French Heavy Batteries (le Capitaine d'Ainval); 122nd and 125th Batteries, 176th Régiment d'Artillerie.

† It seems evident that the number of bridges was too many to allow of their destruction being left with safety till the last minute, and that a system of defence which would have permitted some of them to have been destroyed prior to the opening of the attack was urgently required. General Heneker pressed, in particular, for the immediate destruction of the main three-arch stone bridge which crossed the Aisne at Berry-au-Bac, but his request was not granted.

THE BATTLE OF THE AISNE

of the sacred soil of France was to be given up, and the orders to hold the northern zones in force stood unaltered.

The troops of the 8th Division were, therefore, occupying the positions described above in accordance with the orders thus explicitly and forcibly given. Such were their dispositions on that golden afternoon of the 26th May when, filtering down from higher formations to lower, came those little presaging pink messages which made of the gold a mock, and turned to futility the peaceful quiet in which the long summer day waned slowly to its close. " With the coming of night an uncanny silence settled over the countryside, a silence such as can only prevail in crowded places." But at 9 p.m. in view of the impending attack our artillery started to carry out counter-preparations and harassing fire. "All along the line batteries gave tongue, the sharp bang of 18-pounders mingling with the hoarse reports of the field howitzers. Behind the river the few French heavies coughed asthmatically now and again, while the intermittent rattle of machine guns came as a staccato punctuation.

" Yet the feeling of silence persisted. Not a shell came from the enemy, and his quietness removed any lingering doubts as to his intentions.

" How that evening dragged! The time crept slowly on towards zero hour till only a few minutes were left. . . . Suddenly two German gas shells burst close at hand, punctual heralds of the storm. Within a second, a thousand guns roared out their iron hurricane. The night was rent with sheets of flame. The earth shuddered under the avalanche of missiles . . . leapt skyward in dust and tumult. Ever above the din screamed the fierce crescendo of approaching shells, ear-splitting crashes as they burst . . . all the time the dull thud, thud, thud of detonations . . . drum fire. Inferno raged and whirled round the Bois des Buttes.* The dug-outs rocked . . . filled with the acrid fumes of cordite, the sickly-sweet tang of gas. Timbers started: earth showered from the roof: men rushed for shelter, seizing kits, weapons, gas masks, message-pads as they dived for safety. It was a descent into hell. Crowded with jostling, sweating humanity the dug-outs reeked and to make matters worse Headquarters had no sooner got below than gas began to filter down. Gas masks were hurriedly donned and anti-gas precautions taken —the entrances closed with saturated blankets, braziers lighted on the stairs. If gas could not enter, neither could air. As a fact both did in small quantities and the long night was spent forty foot underground, at the hottest time of the year, in stinking overcrowded holes, their entrances sealed up and charcoal braziers alight drying up the atmosphere—suffocation rendered more

* 23rd Infantry Brigade Headquarters were here located.

A TERRIBLE BOMBARDMENT

complete by the gas mask with clip on nostrils and gag in teeth."

It was at 1 o'clock in the morning of the 27th May, punctual to the predicted time, that the German bombardment was loosed. The whole of the IX Corps front and many back areas—railheads, ammunition dumps and the like—were drenched with gas shell. Outpost lines were assailed in addition by trench mortars of every calibre, and the Battle Zone received the terrible bombardment from artillery of all natures which has just been so graphically described. Our artillery positions were also violently attacked with gas shell and H.E. and had area shoots carried out upon them; with the result that by 6 a.m. most of our guns North of the river were out of action. A mist which rose into being with the opening of the bombardment, as though evoked at the will of the German Higher Command and in fact accentuated by the enemy's gas and smoke shells, grew steadily thicker as the night proceeded and made the task of defence additionally difficult. It was, indeed, almost uncanny how in this spring of 1918 the luck of the weather favoured the Germans in attack. On each preceding night spent on the new front the weather had been clear and when, for the third time, the troops of the division found their defence hampered by a dense blanket of fog, men and officers began firmly to believe that the enemy had discovered means to put down a mist whenever it was wanted.

The first infantry attack, assisted by tanks which flattened out the wire, was delivered, it is probable, at about 4 o'clock in the morning, against the angle of the salient in our right sub-sector (25th Infantry Brigade). Owing to the dense mist and to the fact that nearly all units in the Outpost Zone were cut off to a man, it is difficult to reconstruct precisely the sequence of events. It is only at intervals that a clear message comes back out of the chaos and confusion which the fog necessarily produced. Even such a message only serves to emphasize the assistance which the lack of visibility and the exposed position of our troops in the salient gave to the enemy in his attack. Take, for instance, the following pigeon message, timed 5.15 a.m., which was received at Divisional Headquarters at 6.5 a.m.: "H.Q. 2nd R. Berks. Regt., consisting of Lieut.-Colonel Griffin, Capt. Clare, R.S.M. Wokins, Sergt. Trinder, Corpl. Dobson, Ptes. Stone, Gregory, Slee, and Quartermaster, surrounded. Germans threw bombs down dug-outs and passed on. Appeared to approach from right rear in considerable strength. No idea what has happened elsewhere. Holding out in hopes of relief."

Such hopes, alas! were vain. The attack swept forward, and although our troops resisted stubbornly for a time in the Battle Zone and caused severe losses to the enemy on this line, the

THE BATTLE OF THE AISNE

defence was overwhelmed by weight of numbers. Brigade Headquarters had been early involved in the fighting, being practically surrounded before it was known that the front line had gone. It was near here that the Brigade Major, Capt. B. C. Pascoe, M.C., Rifle Brigade, was killed while making a gallant stand. General Husey and what remained of his Headquarters staff fought their way out and moved back to Gernicourt to organize its defences. At 6.30 a.m. General Husey reported to Divisional Headquarters that he was holding the river line there with the remnants of his brigade. At 7.15 a.m. he further reported that all the bridges East of the junction of the Miette and Aisne had been blown up* and that he was holding the high ground West of Gernicourt. Later in the morning General Husey, who had only taken over command of the brigade front (vice General Coffin, promoted to a divisional command) on the 7th May, was badly wounded and gassed, and he died a few days after in German hands.

Meanwhile the fortunes or misfortunes of the other two brigades remain to be considered. These two brigades do not appear to have been seriously attacked until about 5 a.m. The front-line battalion of the 24th Infantry Brigade (2/ Northamptonshire) was then gradually driven back to the Battle Zone. Tanks do not appear to have been used on this front; but as the light increased enemy aeroplanes were observed flying low over our forward system and firing into the trenches. Colonel Buckle, whose conduct and example had been an inspiration to his men, was killed outside his Battalion Headquarters; but his battalion fought on and in the Battle Zone in this sector the enemy's advance was definitely checked. The position here was very strong and repeated attacks were beaten off both by the 2/ Northamptonshire and the 1/ Worcestershire.

The last message sent by Colonel Buckle to his front line companies a short time after the German bombardment started, is recorded in tribute to a very gallant officer, and as an example of the spirit in which the defence was made. It ran:

"All Platoon Commanders will remain with their platoons and ensure that the trenches are manned immediately the bombardments lifts aaa. Send short situation wire every half-hour aaa. No short bombardment can possibly cut our wire and if sentries are alert it cannot be cut by hand aaa. If they try it shoot the devils aaa.

"C. G. BUCKLE, Lieut.-Col."

---

* There were twenty bridges, including both river and canal bridges, in this sector. R.E. evidence goes to show that thirteen of these were destroyed and two partially destroyed. As to the remaining five no evidence was available owing to the fact that the personnel detailed for their destruction were missing.

TAKEN IN FLANK AND REAR

This message was found pinned on the wall of the Battalion Headquarters dug-out by Colonel Buckle's father, who visited the spot after the Armistice. He found his son's grave close to the entrance, and on each side of the grave a German had been buried. Those who knew Colonel Buckle felt sure he would fight to a finish and never surrender.

MAY 1918

The position here was, as has been said, so strong that our troops might well have held out indefinitely against any frontal assault, but the enemy was able to profit by his success on our right. At 5.45 a.m. large numbers of Germans were suddenly observed from 24th Brigade Headquarters approaching along the line of the Miette Stream which they had crossed South of the Battle Zone. The main line of defence was taken by this movement in flank and rear and its defenders were cut off and surrounded. Major Cartland, commanding the 1/ Worcestershire, was killed in the trenches with his men and, at 6 a.m., Brigade Headquarters was itself attacked from the rear. The Staff Captain to the brigade was taken prisoner, and General Haig, and his Acting-Brigade-Major (Capt. F. C. Wallace, M.C.) both of whom were suffering from gas, had great difficulty in getting clear. A few others, including the Signalling Officer, Intelligence Officer and some of Brigade Headquarters personnel, managed to fight their way back to la Pêcherie bridge, the defence of which they organized under Capt. Pratt, M.C., 1/ Worcestershire. The Germans, however, were seen shortly afterwards to have worked round behind Capt. Pratt's party and appear to have cut them off. Soon after 9 o'clock in the morning the collected remnants of this brigade, *now numbering 3 officers and 68 other ranks only*, were holding a trench on the north-east side of Roucy.

The 23rd Infantry Brigade had been attacked at about the same time as the 24th Brigade. The enemy were held for a short time by the forward battalion (2/ West Yorkshire) who were then forced back to the Battle Zone, where, with the 2/ Middlesex they held their ground against all attacks. The 2/ Devonshire maintained their positions in the Bois des Buttes with equal stubbornness. The enemy brought up tanks against these troops, but these were destroyed by the French anti-tank guns. At 7 a.m. these battalions were still holding out. Once again, however, the gallant frontal defence was of no avail. The turning movement which had got round the flanks and rear of the 24th Brigade was continued against the 23rd Brigade, and not only so but a breach had been made in the right front of the 149th Infantry Brigade (50th Division), the neighbouring brigade on the 8th Division's left. As a result of this double thrust the unfortunate West Yorkshire and Middlesex were taken in rear from both flanks and cut off.

THE BATTLE OF THE AISNE

Here is an account of the receipt, turn by turn, of these disastrous tidings at Brigade Headquarters. "Dawn began to break, but no news came of any infantry attack. The Brigade Intelligence Officer reported that a heavy ground mist rendered observation impossible, but shortly afterwards sent the amazing message : 'Enemy balloons rising from our front line.' Hot upon this came another from 24th Brigade : 'Enemy advancing up Miette Stream. Cannot hold out without reinforcements.' Such news was startling in the extreme; but worse was still to come, for at about 5.30 a.m. the 149th Brigade on the left reported : 'Enemy has broken our battle-line and is advancing on Ville au Bois.' Thus before word had come of the brigade front being assaulted, the enemy had turned both flanks and was advancing on the Bois des Buttes."

The 2/Devonshire here posted were soon in desperate straits. Heavily attacked in front and on both flanks, the battalion slowly fell back towards Pontavert. When some distance North of the town the gallant Commanding Officer, Lieut.-Colonel R. H. Anderson-Morshead, D.S.O., refused to retire further and called upon his battalion to take up a position and protect the crossing. This they did, but the enemy coming in from the East along the river finally got into Pontavert itself and thus surrounded them and cut them off. The fact that the Germans were behind them made no difference to the dauntless spirit of the Devons. There they remained, an island in the midst of a sea of determined enemies, fighting with perfect discipline, and, by the steadiness of their fire, mowing down assault after assault. A battery commander, who was an eye-witness, gives the following account of this action:

"At a late hour in the morning I, with those of my men who had escaped the enemy's ring of machine guns and his fearful barrage, found the C.O. of the 2nd Devon Regiment and a handful of men holding on to the last trench North of the canal. They were in a position in which they were entirely without hope of help, but were fighting on grimly. The Commanding Officer himself was calmly writing his orders with a perfect hail of H.E. falling round him. I spoke to him and he told me that nothing could be done. He refused all offers of help from my artillerymen, who were unarmed, and sent them off to get through if they could. His magnificent bearing, dauntless courage and determination to carry on to the end moved one's emotion."

Refusing to surrender and preferring to fight to the last, this glorious battalion perished *en masse*, its losses comprising the C.O., 28 officers and 552 N.C.O.'s and men. In fit acknowledgment of its splendid choice the battalion was " cited " in French

THE ORDEAL OF THE ARTILLERY

Army Orders and awarded the Croix de Guerre.* Its self-sacrifice enabled Brig.-General Grogan to organize, with the remnants of his brigade,† a defensive position on the high ground about la Platrerie, due South of Pontavert and across the river, to which he had moved his Headquarters. The command of such troops as were left was entrusted to Capt. Clive Saunders, Adjutant of the 2/West Yorkshire.

MAY .1918

Thus, by early morning, the remnants of the division were all across the river ‡ and the enemy, rapidly following up, was crossing the river also. Before continuing the further narrative of the battle it will, however, be convenient to consider what had happened to our artillery during the progress of the initial attack.

There can be no doubt that our battery positions were known to the enemy and when his artillery was loosed at 1 a.m. all our gun positions were heavily shelled, at first with gas shells and later with H.E., or with mixed H.E. and gas. " H.E. and gas in mixed doses followed the preparatory gas," says one battery report, " and the enemy shooting seemed uncannily accurate." Under these conditions it was, in many cases, impossible to carry on the counter-preparation and harassing fire which was to have been continued all night; but it was maintained whenever possible and for as long as possible. The 5th Battery (XLV Brigade) for instance, continued to fire throughout the night until, at about 6.30 a.m., the enemy appeared on the battery position. Many guns, however, were early put out of action by direct hits. The three guns at the main position of the 57th Battery (Major B. W. Ellis) of the same brigade had been absolutely wrecked by 2.30 a.m. and the fourth pit (which was unoccupied) had been set on fire. The 1st Battery (Major M. T. Bargh), also of the XLV Brigade, similarly had three guns put out of action by hostile shell-fire.

The 8th Divisional Artillery's dispositions when the battle opened were as follows: The zone of the 25th Infantry Brigade, on the right, was covered by the French Group Paul, under Commandant Paul. This Group of 75 mm. guns was located South of the Aisne. The 24th Infantry Brigade, in the centre, was covered by the XXXIII Brigade, R.F.A. (Lieut.-Colonel H. G. Fisher, D.S.O.) while the XLV Brigade, R.F.A. (Lieut.-Colonel J. A. Ballard), covered the zone of the 23rd Infantry

---

* The citation is set out in full at the end of this chapter.

† " Hardly a soul had escaped—Colonel Lowry of the West Yorkshire with a bullet wound in his foot; a corporal of the same regiment; a mere handful of the Middlesex; two or three of the Devons and a few gunners completed the tale of the survivors."

‡ It is doubtful whether the total strength of all ranks who succeeded in crossing the river exceeded or even reached a thousand.

THE BATTLE OF THE AISNE

Brigade. Both these brigades of 18-pounder guns were North of the river. Owing to this circumstance and as a result of the rapid German penetration which has already been described, the personnel of the two British brigades became involved, between 6 and 7 a.m., in hand-to-hand fighting, and such guns as had not previously been destroyed were ultimately captured by the enemy. The 1st Battery was completely surrounded by 7 a.m. Breech blocks were taken out to render the guns useless to the enemy and the men fought with rifles and Lewis guns; but of the whole battery only 2 sergeants and 6 men succeeded in breaking their way through and getting back to the wagon lines.

When the enemy in like manner approached the position of the 32nd Battery (XXXIII Brigade) Major A. G. Ramsden, the Battery Commander, had one of his guns run out of its emplacement, so as to give it a wider arc of fire, and with it kept the enemy off at close range, the remaining gunners and N.C.O.'s assisting with Lewis gun and rifle fire. The gun was eventually placed on a small railway truck; and, after all maps, records, kits, etc., which could not be moved had been burnt and the other guns had been rendered useless by the removal of breech locks and sights, Major Ramsden retired down the Miette Valley fighting a rearguard action with his one gun. Although nearly surrounded and ultimately forced to abandon his gun, he was finally able to get the remaining personnel of his battery across the canal.

A detailed account has been compiled from survivors' statements of the heroic action of the 5th Battery (XLV Brigade), already mentioned, and it may be quoted fairly fully here as a typical example of the appalling trials which our gunners on this night had to undergo, and of the magnificent spirit with which they were met.

The battery was carrying out its counter-preparation work when the deluge from the enemy's guns broke over it. " Gas masks were instantly adjusted and about ten minutes later the rocket sentry reported S.O.S. rocket on the front. The call was immediately responded to by our gunners, Capt. J. H. Massey controlling the fire of the battery, while Lieut. C. E. Large and 2nd Lieut. C. A. Button commanded their sections. To continue to serve the guns indefinitely during such a terrific bombardment was a physical impossibility for any one man, and Capt. Massey, realizing this, organized a system of reliefs, two gunners and one N.C.O. manning each gun. The remainder of the personnel took cover until their turns came round to take their places at the guns.

" After the customary period of fire on the S.O.S. lines, guns were once more laid on ' counter-preparation ' lines and a steady rate of fire was continued during what seemed an interminable

THE 5TH BATTERY R.F.A.

night. Lieut. Large and 2nd Lieut. Button frequently took their places with the gunners in the reliefs, while Capt. Massey kept moving from pit to pit and dug-out to dug-out and then to the detached sections, encouraging the detachments and telephonists and reminding them of the splendid traditions of the Royal Regiment.

MAY 1918

"By about 5 a.m. No. 4 gun had been put out of action owing to a shell splinter tearing up the guides. The detachment was withdrawn and sent in to reinforce the other detachments.

"The strain on all concerned was terrific, but at last at about 6.45 the enemy's barrage lifted clear of the position. Instead, however, of the expected respite, large numbers of German infantry and gunners came into view less than 200 yards from the battery position. A few rounds were fired at point-blank range, but it was then reported that Germans were coming up in rear. There was nothing left but to resort to rifles and the Lewis guns. Capt. Massey, realizing the situation a little earlier, had called for volunteers and pushed off with 4 gunners and a Lewis gun to a small eminence to the eastward in an endeavour to protect the flank. Nothing more has been heard of Capt. Massey* and his men. Lieut. Large, although wounded in the foot, took the other Lewis gun, 2nd Lieut. Button, after having destroyed all maps, papers and records, was last seen moving off with a rifle to assist Capt. Massey. The remainder of the battery fought to the last with their rifles till overwhelmed by sheer weight of numbers." †

Only three gunners, who were unarmed and were ordered to retire, and one with a rifle who fought his way out, survived. Of the two F.O.O.'s, 2nd Lieut. C. Counsell and 2nd Lieut. H. Reakes, and their telephonists nothing was heard again. The 5th Battery shared with the 2/ Devonshire the honour of being "cited" in French Army Orders and awarded the Croix de Guerre.‡

Many a similar conflict, carried to the same grim, gallant and inevitable end, must have been fought in the dim and misty dawn on that tract of country North of the Aisne, where were collected on the night of the 26th May the fighting troops of the 8th Division.

To continue now with the main story. By 6.30 a.m. the right of the line rested on the Gernicourt position, but between this and the right of the 24th Infantry Brigade there was a gap. The battalion in divisional reserve (1/ Sherwood Foresters) was ordered to move forward and fill it, and succeeded in preventing

---

* All three officers were officially reported killed in action.
† An account compiled from the statements of survivors.
‡ The citation is set out at the end of this chapter.

THE BATTLE OF THE AISNE

the enemy from crossing the river on its front in the vicinity of la Pêcherie bridge. Elsewhere, however, he was getting across and, well covered by artillery (of which the 8th Division now possessed none), he outflanked and drove back General Grogan's party (23rd Infantry Brigade), which was holding the high ground above la Platrerie. The enemy drove forward thence and the Sherwood Foresters and the other defenders of the Gernicourt position were ultimately cut off. The great natural strength of the position, which must have made it a most serious obstacle to a direct assault, was thus of no avail. It was turned from the South-West and the battle passed it by. The garrison, including the French Territorial troops, appear to have put up a good fight; but they were surrounded and, later in the morning, were overpowered. All the French 75's and the guns of the CX Brigade R.F.A. which were in action in this neighbourhood were lost.

In view of the rapid advance of the enemy the Divisional Commander decided, shortly after 10 a.m., to use his remaining reserves—some 600 men from the Lewis gun school,* men from the transport lines, etc.—to hold the second position. This ran along the northern slopes of the high ground South of the river Aisne on the general line Bouffignereux–Roucy–Concevreux. Troops of the 25th Division were already moving up to this line in accordance with Corps orders. At 1.20 p.m. the 75th Infantry Brigade, which had originally been ordered forward from 25th Division in reserve to fill a gap between the remnants of the 8th Division and what was left of the 50th Division, was put under General Heneker's orders and the line about this time was held generally as follows. On the right front, isolated and surrounded, remnants of the 22/ Durham L.I. and 1/ Sherwood Foresters were still holding portions of the Bois de Gernicourt. The 75th Infantry Brigade was holding the second position from Bouffignereux to Concevreux as follows: on the right, from Bouffignreeux to Roucy, the 2/ South Lancashire with remnants of the 24th and 25th Infantry Brigades; on the left, from Roucy to Concevreux, the 11/ Cheshire, with remnants of the 23rd Infantry Brigade. The 8/ Border Regiment was in close support behind Roucy. On the divisional right the forward swell of the hill on the right of Bouffignereux was occupied by the 7th Infantry Brigade of the 25th Division; on its left at Concevreux was the 74th Infantry Brigade.

During the afternoon there was a lull in the fighting. " The day was extremely hot, the sunshine brilliant and, but for the deep drone of heavy shells winging their way rearwards, all sounds of battle were temporarily stilled. Viewed from the hills

* These Lewis gunners had been withdrawn for training upon the advice that no hostile attack need be expected!

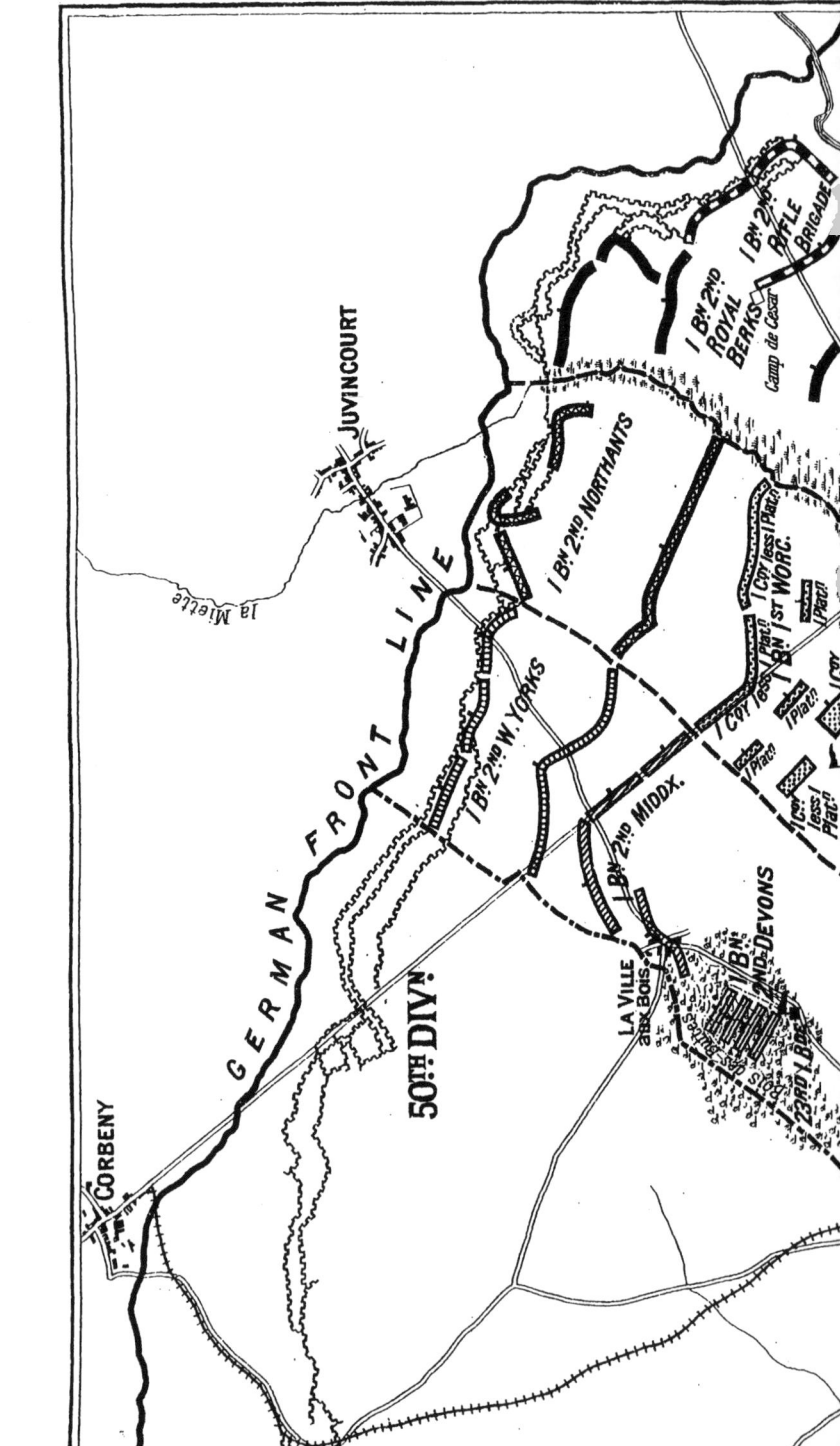

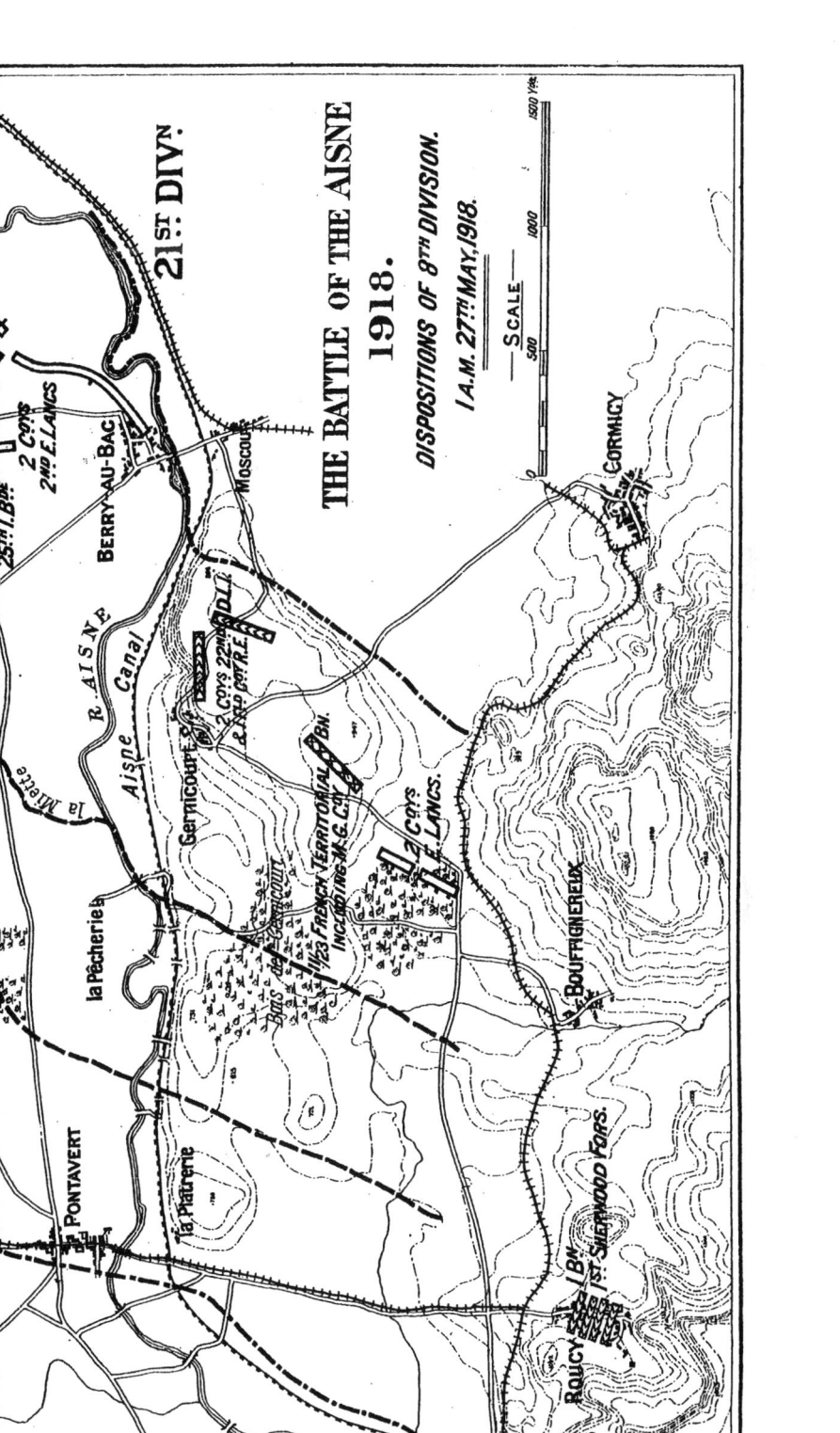

OUR LINE FORCED BACK

above Roucy the battle area presented a vivid spectacle. The MAY 1918 Aisne and its attendant canal glittered like silver ribbons in the sun, while in the vacated trench area beyond hung a pall of haze and dust, which lifting at intervals revealed the roads thick with marching regiments in field grey, with guns, lorries and wagons. Above, like great unwinking eyes, rode observation balloons, towed along by motor transport." These balloons were brought up very close and the German preparations for a fresh assault continued methodically and with hardly any molestation.

Between 4 and 5 o'clock in the afternoon, under cover of heavy fire from trench mortars and machine guns, the attack was renewed all along the line. Our line on the right, at the point of junction with the 7th Infantry Brigade, was pierced and the village of Bouffignereux was captured. This success was vigorously exploited and our whole line forced back. By 7.15 p.m. it had been pushed back some 3,000 yards and ran along the tops of the hills separating the valley of the Aisne from the valley of the Vesle. The G.O.C. 75th Infantry Brigade (Brig.-General H. A. Kennedy) was calling urgently for reinforcements and ammunition. The latter was sent at once. To meet the former demand, General Heneker sent out officers to collect all the stragglers they could find and these, supplemented by his Headquarters Guard and the personnel of his Headquarters—a total force of some 500 men—were sent forward under his A.D.C., Major G. R. Hennessy and were handed over to General Kennedy at 10 p.m. Our line, often out of touch with adjacent formations, continued to fall back and, before midnight, Ventelay and Bouvancourt were in the hands of the enemy. So rapid was the enemy's advance that in the latter village the entire 25th Field Ambulance was captured. The village was surrounded before the Ambulance knew that any danger existed! Subsequently the O.C., Lieut.-Colonel T. P. Puddicombe, D.S.O., and another officer, Lieut. Kelly, an American doctor, managed to escape and to regain our lines.

Divisional Headquarters, which had already at 5 o'clock that afternoon fallen back to Montigny-sur-Vesle, were opened at 11.30 p.m. at Branscourt to the South of that river; but during the night the enemy succeeded in turning our right flank, our troops were forced to fall back to the line of the river Vesle, and Divisional Headquarters had again to retire, opening at Faverolles at 9.45 a.m. on the 28th May. Meanwhile General Grogan, G.O.C. 23rd Infantry Brigade, was ordered, at 6 a.m., to assume command of all troops in the vicinity of Jonchery and to hold a front on the river Vesle extending 1 mile on either side of that town. General Kennedy was ordered to continue the line on the right of this front with the 75th Brigade and to join with the left

THE BATTLE OF THE AISNE

of the 21st Division. On arrival at Jonchery, General Grogan found elements of the 25th, 50th and 8th Divisions pouring South across the bridge there and the enemy in possession of the Montigny heights and pressing forward to the river. He at once took steps to arrest this stream of stragglers and, having collected all available men, he formed a firing line along the Vesle, aligning the men on the railway embankment. By 10 a.m. a strong and fairly well-organized line had been established, with the bridge-heads well guarded. A good deal of sharp fighting took place, but up till 1 p.m. our line was maintained and heavy losses had been inflicted on the enemy as he attempted to attack.

Shortly before that hour, however, the enemy had broken through the 50th Division line about 2 miles to the West of Jonchery and General Grogan's force was, therefore, compelled to fall back. "All the morning's work of consolidation had been for nothing, and as the tired khaki figures struggled up the steep slopes South of the river, they could see enemy artillery and transport pouring in continuous streams down the two roads converging on Jonchery, while infantry swarmed busily across the open country. It was a sight given to gunners only in dreams, but not a gun was available."* General Grogan retreated during the afternoon and evening to the line of heights between Vandeuil and Branscourt. Three battalions of the 154th French Division, covered by their own artillery, had come into line from reserve in this vicinity and they now took up position on General Grogan's right, and also on the right of the 75th Infantry Brigade, which thus had French troops on either flank. General Grogan's left was, however, uncovered, and a gallant attempt made by the C.R.E., 8th Division (Lieut.-Colonel C. M. Browne, C.M.G., D.S.O.), to blow up Jonchery bridge had been unsuccessful.

In the meantime a great deal of pressure had been exerted during the morning against the French troops on the left of the IX Corps. Fismes had been captured and the line had been bent back considerably to the South of that place. General Grogan's left remained in the air and he was continually being outflanked, until finally at about 8 p.m. he was driven off the high ground North-West of the Savigny-Jonchery road. At nightfall, however, a French regiment, advancing from Savigny, came into line on General Grogan's left, and a sharp counter-attack, carried out principally by troops of the 2/ Devonshire, regained for us possession of the dominating ground. The 120 men of the Devons who thus restored our position had been back at transport lines when the battle opened. They worthily emulated here

* General Heneker had at this time only seven 18-pounder guns to cover his whole front.

A RESPITE

the high standard of courage and discipline which had been shown by their battalion on the previous day.

MAY 1918

Two batteries of 18-pounders, belonging to the CXII Brigade, R.F.A. (25th Division), had come up during the course of the afternoon and the artillery at the disposal of General Heneker that night was as follows:

Two 18-pounder batteries, XCV Brigade, R.F.A. (21st Division).

Two 18-pounder batteries, CXII Brigade, R.F.A. (25th Division).

One Composite 18-pounder battery (8th and 25th Divisions).

One 4·5 howitzer battery, CX Brigade (25th Division, of which one gun was 8th Divisional Artillery).

During all this period of rapid retirement and open warfare, it was naturally very difficult to co-ordinate the work of, and to group, the artillery. Superior control was almost impossible, and battery and section commanders had often, of necessity, to accept more or less roving commissions, picking up any targets which presented themselves. They worked with wonderful devotion and without cessation during all this difficult time.

In order to simplify the command of the small number of troops now remaining in the line, the G.O.C. 8th Division was instructed at 7.30 p.m. to take over command of the sector and troops of the 50th Division. He was informed that the 57th Infantry Brigade was being sent forward to his assistance from the 19th Division which, despatched in buses from the VIII Corps near Chalons, was gradually arriving behind the battle-front. The night of the 28th/29th May was fairly quiet; but General Heneker's task was not lightened by the fact that at this time the 154th French Division was intermingled with British troops all along the 8th Division line, so that there were two divisional commanders responsible for the same front. Danger, moreover, was still threatening from the left where, early in the morning of the 29th May, the enemy showed activity to the West of Lhéry. In this place the 154th French Divisional Commander had his Headquarters and, with the aid of his own troops and of British troops which had been already sent there, he soon had the situation well in hand for the time being.

Our line, indeed, remained intact until 11 a.m. on this day. At that hour, however, the enemy, covered by heavy trench-mortar fire, renewed the attack in strength and by 1.30 p.m. our troops and the French had been compelled to withdraw to the high ground which ran North-East from Faverolles to Courcelles. "This retirement was not accomplished without difficulty or casualties, but once again General Grogan by his energy and personal example extracted order out of chaos and some sort of a

THE BATTLE OF THE AISNE

line was formed." The French troops on the left about Prin had also been driven in. Fortunately, the leading battalions of the 19th Division were now at hand and came into position near Tramery, between the Faverolles heights and Lhéry. Our position on the Faverolles heights ran north of Treslon and was established on a slightly reverse slope. It had therefore the advantage of being concealed from direct enemy observation and the Germans, who had at first followed us up very closely, received such a hot reception when they attempted to cross the crest that they fell back almost at once. They were obviously uncertain as to how our exact line ran and their attempts to advance, which were not seriously pressed, were continually frustrated.

It was now but a motley crew which staved the enemy off. "The General himself*; his brigade staff officers; Smythe† the G.S.O.3, 8th Division; Major Cope of the 2/ Devonshire; Lieut.-Colonel Moore of the 1/ Sherwood Foresters, the only infantry C.O. of the division not already a casualty; two colonels of the 50th Division without a single man of the units they once commanded; a knot of machine gunners from the same division whose guns refused to function from lack of water; a woeful sprinkling of all units of the 8th and most of the 25th and 50th Divisions; in all about 200—all hungry, sleepless, dirty; many bleeding from wounds of greater or less severity. A number of French colonial troops completed the toll of men. . . . Weary and hungry as they were, the spirits of the little band were marvellous. This was largely due to the example set by the General. In a position of extreme personal and tactical danger, after three days of incessant fighting, he bumped joyously backwards and forwards along the line on a commandeered mount—his round red face wreathed in smiles, his eyes twinkling, chuckling to himself as if the whole affair were a boyish joke. His borrowed steed was quickly wounded—no matter, by this time the grooms had arrived with the brigade chargers. Mounting himself on 'Sandy'—his pet pony—the General resumed his ride in full view of the Boche, laughing and talking with the men as he passed—all the time affectionately belabouring Sandy with a great crook-handled walking stick. Yet at the same time he was perfectly conscious of the seriousness of the situation and took what immediate steps he could to avert it. A picked handful of his small command were surreptitiously withdrawn to the Bouleuse ridge to act as a covering party when the inevitable retirement should take place. An officer was also sent down to the H.Q. of a French regiment believed to be in Treslon village with a request that they should conform to these dispositions and strengthen the little force on the Bouleuse ridge."

* General Grogan. † Capt. E. H. Smythe, M.C.

BOULEUSE RIDGE

The enemy, in the meantime, despite his comparative lack of infantry activity, was not idle. He hoisted balloons close up to our line and with these, assisted by aeroplanes, he was eventually enabled to locate our positions. He was further very active in getting up trench mortars along the Jonchery–Savigny road and he began to instal them—man-handling them into position—in the valley which runs up North-East from Savigny. The Divisional Commander turned all the available guns of his small force of artillery on to this valley, but none the less the enemy was soon heavily pounding our position. "At about 3 p.m. an aimed bombardment started which in an entrenched position would have been serious enough, but which no troops, however fresh or however good their morale, could have long withstood in the open. The effect of the big minenwerfer shells on the hard soil was terrible, the tearing crash of the burst being as demoralizing as the execution wrought by the flying splinters. The little red-tiled houses in Treslon village crumbled in columns of black dust: men were torn to bleeding shreds; the line quickly thinned out. Nerves on edge before became still more jagged. . . . The pitiless bombardment continued, and in the course of it the last of the infantry C.O.'s, Colonel Moore, was killed. To complete the hopelessness of the situation, Allied guns, whether British or French is not known, began shelling the ridge. The first salvo, all too accurately aimed, burst well in the middle of the tired line, doing dreadful execution." Hurried messages were sent back to warn our guns, but meanwhile the troops on our right had already given way.

It was obvious that a crisis was impending. The enemy thickened up his firing line, brought up innumerable machine guns and heavily increased the volume of his trench-mortar and artillery fire. At about 5.45 p.m. whistles were heard all along his line and his preparations culminated in a very violent assault. Our troops, weakened as they were in numbers, were driven down to the bottom of the valley and had barely time to re-form on the further ridge North of Bouleuse, where the 2/ Wiltshire (19th Division) was already in position. All the troops here, including this battalion of the Wiltshire, were put under General Grogan's command.

The Bouleuse position was a bad one, situated as it was well down the forward slope and under close observation from our previous position. Inspired, however, by the gallant behaviour of the General* who continued to ride up and down the line on

MAY 1918

---

* General Grogan for his gallantry throughout this day received the V.C. His power of physical endurance was remarkable. Other officers at this stage had reached such a stage of physical exhaustion that not even the realization of imminent

THE BATTLE OF THE AISNE

horseback, rallying the shaken and weary, our men held their ground. Reinforcements were, none the less, urgently required and were fortunately forthcoming in the shape of seven machine guns and a composite battalion commanded by Major H. T. Forster and made up of stragglers, details, and other oddments, chiefly of the 8th Division, which General Heneker had collected together and held in Divisional Reserve at Sarcy. This force might have been available earlier, had it not been despatched to Lhéry shortly after 4 p.m., at the personal request of the Commander of the 154th French Division, who informed General Heneker at his Headquarters that the enemy had broken the line at that town with tanks. Fortunately, a British staff officer sent in advance of the battalion was able to report that no attack had taken place, the tanks, it subsequently turned out, being French armoured cars. Later in the evening two battalions of the 56th Infantry Brigade were placed by IX Corps at the disposal of the 8th Divisional Commander. These also were sent forward and, by nightfall, the enemy, who had continuously attempted to advance, ceased his attacks. Our position on the Bouleuse ridge was secure for the night, which passed quietly.

Brig.-General R. M. Heath, G.O.C. 56th Infantry Brigade, relieved Brig.-General Grogan during the night, taking over command of the Bouleuse ridge and all its troops, and at 9 o'clock in the morning (May 30th) the G.O.C. 19th Division took over the whole of the 8th Divisional command. From this time, therefore, the 8th Division, as such, ceases to have any official connection with the battle; but such of its elements as were still in line, to the number of about 800 all ranks, together with the thirteen remaining guns under Lieut.-Colonel Ballard, remained where they were and took their part in the subsequent fighting. Major G. R. P. Roupell, V.C., Major H. Ramsbotham, M.C., and Major F. C. Wallace, M.C., were attached temporarily to the 19th Division for liaison purposes. Later these troops were reinforced by an 8th Division composite battalion, consisting of three companies (each 150 strong) plus one machine-gun company, which was collected together in divisional area and sent forward under the command of Lieut.-Colonel E. M. Beall, D.S.O., on the 2nd and 3rd June. Divisional Headquarters meanwhile moved in the course of the 30th May to Villers-au-Bois, South of the Marne river and South-East of Épernay, and during the following night (31st May/1st

---

personal danger could keep them awake or stir their tired limbs. A case is recorded of one officer who in the rush which had just taken place from Treslon to the Bouleuse ridge had managed to reach the summit of the latter. Out of breath he sat down for a minute and forthwith, even while the enemy were attempting to carry the position, went sound asleep. All efforts to wake him were unavailing, and he was eventually carried off on a charger from the scene of battle still solidly sleeping.

THE ATTACK LOSES PACE

June) the divisional units, or rather the skeletons of units, followed into this area.

On the night of the 30th/31st May orders were issued by the Army Commander that the British 21st Division should be withdrawn, on relief by the 45th French Division. As a result, the British fighting troops in the line were reduced to approximately the strength of a division, and all of them had been placed under a single command, that of the 19th Division. In these circumstances, and in view of the fact that they were fighting in close combination with French divisions on either side, it was considered advisable that all the troops on this portion of the front should be placed under the orders of a French Corps Commander. At 2 p.m., therefore, on the 30th May, the command of the British troops was handed over to the G.O.C. V French Corps, who took command also of the 154th and 28th French Divisions. IX Corps Headquarters were accordingly withdrawn to Vertus, some ten miles South of the Marne river.

During the course of this day (30th May) the enemy pushed forward in the direction of Romigny and the Allied line was again forced back. The attack was, however, losing its pace, and on the 31st May it became clear that the Allied line was rapidly stabilizing. There were sectional advances by the enemy on the French front on the 1st and 2nd of June; but this latter date marked the definite limit of the enemy's forward movement. In the sector held by British troops the line became settled on the 31st May on a position extending from Aubilly South-West to Chambrecy and thence South to Boujacourt, the ridge called the Montagne de Bligny being its most important feature.

The enemy made persistent attempts to eject the British from this position. Even as late as the 6th June two determined attacks were made upon it. The first was beaten off and, though the second was temporarily successful, a brilliant counter-attack by the 1/4 Shropshire Light Infantry restored the situation. After this the enemy made no serious attempt to carry the position. The 1918 Battle of the Aisne was finally over.

What were its results? As will be seen from the map, the Germans, breaking through the Allied positions at the first onset, had thereafter advanced on their line of deepest penetration at a hitherto unprecedented rate. They had, for a time, succeeded again in substituting for trench warfare a war of movement. As a result they had bitten a huge salient out of the Allied line and they had undoubtedly scored a very substantial tactical success. But the deeper strategic aims of this offensive had by no means been fully realized. The enemy's main strategic purpose, a second advance on Paris, had been dependent upon his ability both to broaden his front and to disengage for his own use another

MAY 1918

THE BATTLE OF THE AISNE

line of lateral railway communication—a thing which was, indeed, of fundamental importance for him, as the history of the closing stages of the war clearly shows.* To establish this double purpose the capture of Rheims was essential. The intention of the attackers had been to sweep past the city to the West, and then turning East and South-East to cut it off. He would then have gained elbow room for his attack, and roads and railways to feed a further advance.† It was the IX British Corps, in conjunction with the 45th French Division, which stood heroically in the way and defeated this purpose. These last despairing attacks delivered on the 6th June against the 19th Division at the Montagne de Bligny‡ were but a final proof of the importance which the enemy attached to the accomplishment of this mission. These attacks failed and with their failure the main strategic object of the offensive remained unrealized.

They failed, but their failure had, indeed, been dearly bought. The 8th Division had once again been through the furnace, and its fighting troops had been almost entirely consumed. To quote from the Divisional Commander's report on the operations: " It may be said without exaggeration that all the gallant battalions of this division have ceased to exist as fighting units." Between the 27th and 30th May the division suffered the following casualties: Officers killed, 19; wounded, 96; missing, 251: total 366. Total casualties other ranks—7,496. Of the nine infantry battalions, not one retained either its C.O. or its adjutant. The casualties of the 2/ Devonshire and 2/ Rifle Brigade—they are merely selected as typical examples—were as follows:

	Lt.-Col.	Major.	Adjt.	Capt. or Co. Cdrs.	Lieut.	2nd Lieut.	O.R.
2/Devonshire	1	1	1	7	5	14	552
2/Rifle Bde.	1	—	1	3	1	22	744

Such figures were, indeed, only to be expected in view of the fact that so many of these battalions were, as has been revealed in the story, completely surrounded and cut off.

Let it not be considered that the loss of so many gallant officers and men was of no avail. The division had, as we have seen, played its heroic part in helping to form, in the words of General

---

* " It was a strategic disadvantage to us that we had been unable to take Rheims and get our armies further forward into the hilly country in that region."—Ludendorff: *My War Memories*, Vol. II, p. 632.

† Throughout his occupation of the Marne salient, the enemy was handicapped by the fact that the natural features of the district, and the most serviceable means of communication through it, ran transversely across rather than directly up and down the salient. Possession of Rheims, the road and rail centre of the area, would have freed him from this difficulty.

‡ The 19th Division left the line on the 19th June, and the IX Corps had finally left this area by the 6th July.

THE COUNTER-STROKE

MAY 1918

Maistre under whom the IX Corps served, "that breakwater against which the hostile waves have beaten and shattered themselves." Moreover, successful for him though it had been, it had taken generous toll of the enemy's rapidly diminishing man power and resources. The big salient was in itself a source of danger. A British officer, captured during the early stages of the battle and retained for some days near the scene of action, has described to the writer how the line of German advance was revealed to him by the semicircle, ever growing deeper and more bulging, of the German observation balloons. That great sweeping semicircle in the sky marked out the German position and suggested its dangers in an extraordinarily clear and graphic manner. The possibilities of a counter-offensive, thrusting at either angle of the bulge, was inevitably brought to his mind.

Just such a manœuvre was to be, in fact, Foch's counter-stroke. The Germans were to initiate one or two further attacks. Their last, still striving for Rheims and launched on the 15th July, drove strongly forward between the Marne and the Ardre, and gained possession of that Bligny ridge which had been so strenuously defended by the 19th Division five weeks before. But the accompanying attack East of Rheims was, on this occasion, met and crushed by the methods which General Heneker and the other Divisional Commanders of the IX Corps had recommended in vain prior to the 27th May. Three days later, Foch's counter-stroke—forerunner of a series of victories which was only to end with a complete German capitulation—was launched against the western angle of the great German salient. Foch's attack on the other angle of the salient duly followed, British troops of the XXII Corps assisting; and thus it came about that British soldiers were able to retake, on the 28th July, the Montagne de Bligny and to recapture the ground which their fellow-countrymen, a few short weeks before, had defended so stubbornly and so well.

ORDRES DU JOUR

" 2nd Battalion Devonshire Regiment.

" On the 27th May 1918, North of the Aisne, at a time when the British trenches were being subjected to fierce attacks, the 2nd Battalion Devonshire Regiment repelled successive enemy assaults with gallantry and determination and maintained an unbroken front till a late hour.

" Inspired by the sangfroid of their gallant Commander

THE BATTLE OF THE AISNE

Lieutenant-Colonel R. H. Anderson-Morshead, D.S.O., in the face of an intense bombardment, the few survivors of the battalion, though isolated and without hope of assistance, held on to their trenches North of the River and fought to the last with an unhesitating obedience to orders.

"The staunchness of this battalion permitted the defences South of the Aisne to be organized and their occupation by reinforcements to be completed.

"Thus the whole battalion—Colonel, 28 officers and 552 non-commissioned officers and men—responded with one accord and offered their lives in ungrudging sacrifice to the sacred cause of the Allies.

(signed) "BERTHELOT,
"General Commanding Fifth Army."

"5th Battery, R.F.A., on the 27th May, 1918, North of the Aisne.

"The 5th Battery, R.F.A., was subjected from 1 a.m. until 6 a.m. to a violent bombardment with heavy guns and gas shells and the battery during all these hours continued to carry out, without slackening its power, its barrage and counter-preparation with such guns as were not destroyed.

"Throughout the night, Captain John Hayman Massey, commanding the battery, continually visited the emplacements and telephone dug-outs, cheering the men and encouraging them to live up to the past tradition of the Royal Regiment and the good old 8th Division.

"Shortly after 6.30 a.m., the enemy having opened a barrage fire on the main line, delivered a flanking attack with his infantry on the positions occupied by the battery. Captain Massey with a Lewis gun and the surviving detachments with rifles at once counter-attacked, supported by Lieutenant Large, then severely wounded, who also had a Lewis gun.

"2nd Lieutenant Button, after having destroyed all maps, records and papers, also threw himself into the fight.

"Unfortunately, this gallant band was overwhelmed by vastly superior numbers. Only three gunners who were unarmed and were ordered to retire, and one with a rifle who fought his way through, survive.

"The heroic resistance of this battery had a great influence upon the issue of the battle. Its gallant conduct deserves to be mentioned as an example and does great honour to the 8th British Infantry Division.

(signed) "BERTHELOT,
"General Commanding Fifth Army."

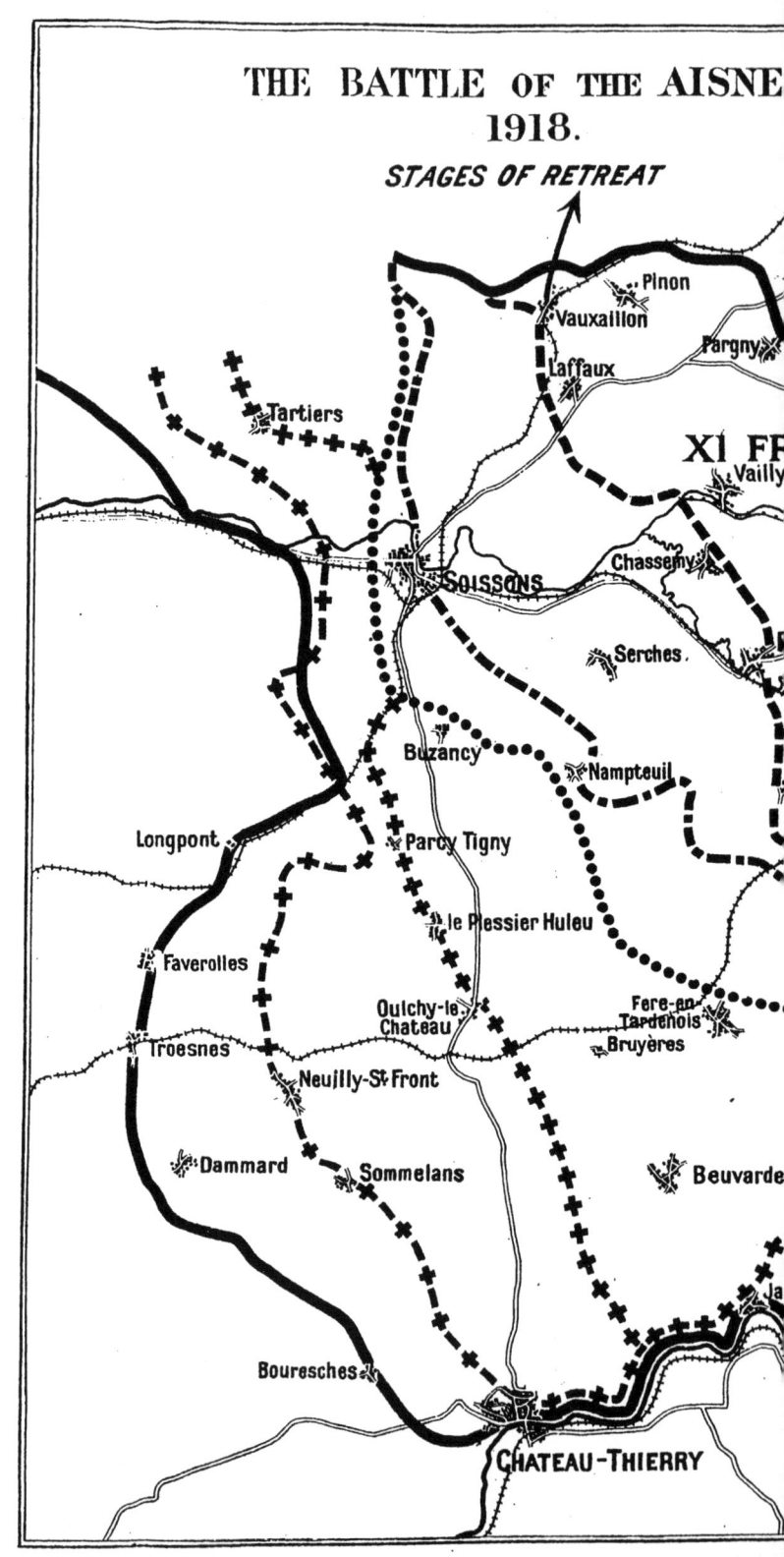

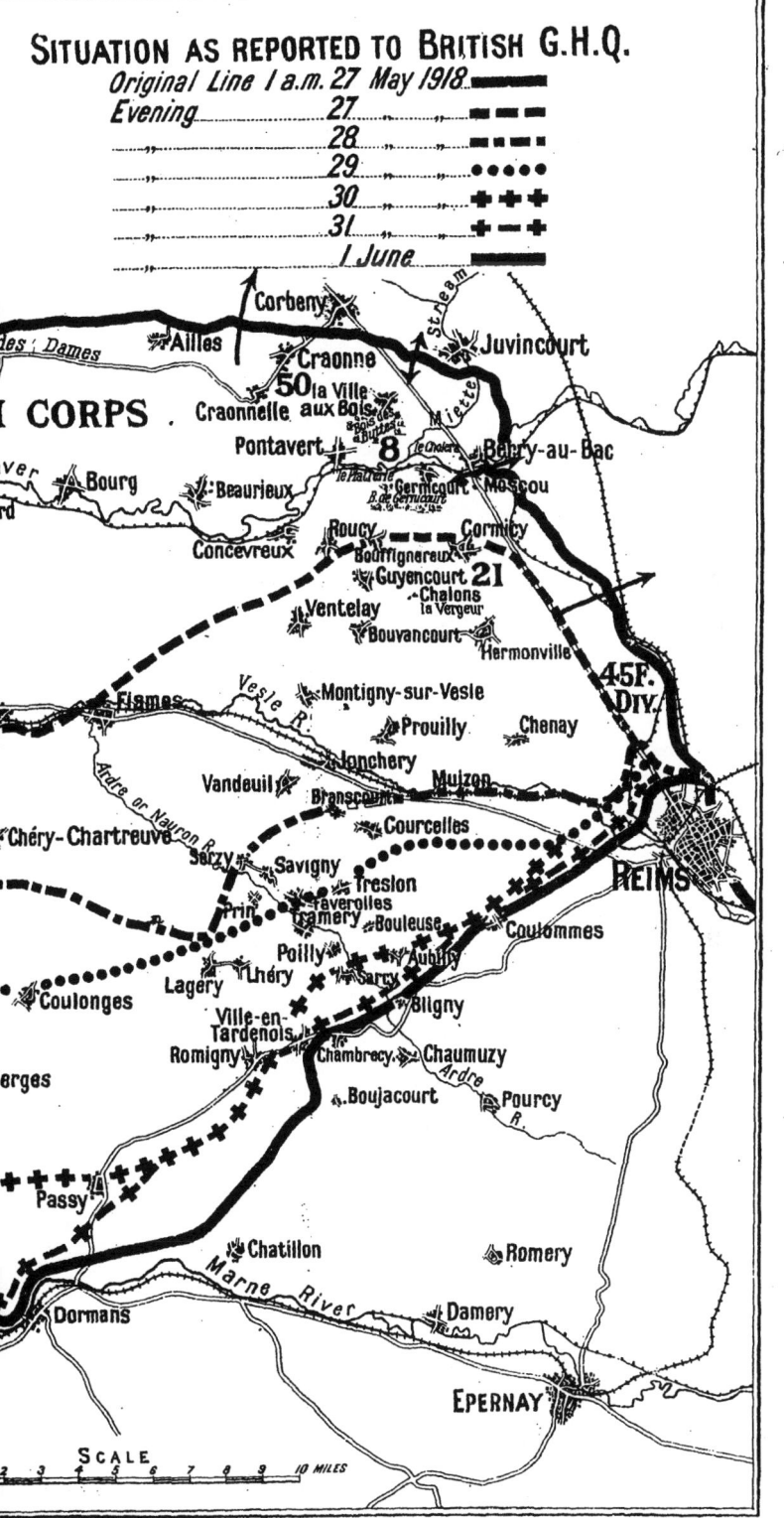

CHAPTER XV

RECONSTRUCTION

ON the 3rd June the 8th Division, which had, as will be remembered, moved into the Villers-aux-Bois area, was shifted a few miles South-East into the Bergères-lez-Vertus area and six days later moved yet further South to the neighbourhood of Pleurs.* These moves, which did not include the troops left with the 19th Division in the forward area and now formed into two composite battalions commanded by Lieut.-Colonels B. C. James and E. M. Beall, were preparatory to the complete withdrawal of the division for a comparatively long period of real rest and refitting. Training, so far as there were men to train, did, indeed, commence at once; but the numbers available were all too few and on the 12th June the welcome orders were received that the division was to leave the French area for a destination in the British zone. On the same night the 1/8th Composite Battalion, which had remained in line on the left of the 19th Division, was withdrawn and returned to its own division. The 2/8th Composite Battalion which had gone into line on the night of the 7th June did not rejoin the 8th Division till the 19th June.

Meanwhile, on the 14th and 15th June the 8th Division entrained and proceeded to the Huppy area where it came temporarily under the administrative orders of the XIX Corps, then part of General Rawlinson's Fourth Army. The rail journey of some 200 miles was made via Paris and took about twenty-four hours, the division detraining at Pont Remy, Longpré, and Hangest. Divisional Headquarters were opened at Huppy, some 7 miles South-West of Abbeville, on the following day, and on the 17th the detrainment of the division (less the 2/8 Composite Battalion) in this area was continued and completed. At noon on the 18th June the administration of the division was taken over by the VIII Corps and the troops found themselves for a few days once more under the orders of Lieut.-General Sir A. Hunter Weston.

When the 2/8th Composite Battalion had rejoined on the 19th, the division was at last collected together once more and the following days were spent by units in reorganizing and refitting, drafts arriving daily.

For the third time in little more than two months the division had suffered terrible casualties. During this period there was kept at British G.H.Q. a daily return showing for each division of the British Army the number of its losses since the 21st March. On this list the 8th Division now held the proud yet

---

* These places are all South of Epernay.

RECONSTRUCTION

unenviable position of second place, with the 50th Division less than 300 in front, and the next division more than 1,000 behind. Once again very large drafts were necessary. They came from all quarters, but they consisted chiefly of men belonging to New Army battalions which had just been disbanded. For the heavy losses of the British Army and the situation with regard to manpower had made it impossible to keep our full number of divisions on the active list. At the beginning of June, seven divisions were shown on the return above referred to as divisions which, owing to lack of reinforcements, it was not intended to make up to strength for the present. Such troops as were left to these exhausted divisions were available for the reinforcement of divisions still on the active list. It speaks well for the 8th Division that, high as it was on the list of casualty returns, it was yet kept among the number of fighting divisions. The drafting of men from one unit to another has, however, obvious disadvantages. Many of them were inclined, at first, to be discontented and to resent being posted to new battalions after having seen service with, and become proud of, their old battalions. These feelings could not be considered unnatural; but their existence necessarily added to the difficulties of re-forming the division and of renewing its old *esprit de corps*.

On the 22nd and 23rd June the division made a further small move on transfer back to the XIX Corps (Lieut.-General Sir H. E. Watts, K.C.B., C.M.G.), marching by road from the Huppy area to the Gamaches and St. Valery area nearer the coast, in order to obtain better training facilities. Divisional Headquarters were opened on the latter date at Friville; a village situated in the centre of the area and about $4\frac{1}{2}$ miles from the sea. On the same day the 1/7 Durham Light Infantry joined the division to replace the 22/ Durham Light Infantry as Divisional Pioneers. The latter battalion had done splendid service while with the division and their departure was universally regretted. Three days later a further change was made on the transfer of the XIX Corps to the 2nd Army, the XXII Corps (Lieut.-General Sir A. J. G. Godley, K.C.B., K.C.M.G.) taking over all troops then under the command or administration of the XIX Corps, including among them the 8th Division.

The process of creating the division afresh—for that is very nearly what it came to—was carried steadily on. A programme of intensive training was carefully drawn up and put into operation with great thoroughness. Combined training in the morning and specialist training, lectures, etc., in the afternoon formed the usual routine. The ranges were in constant occupation; intensive wiring and digging were frequently practised; regular attention was given to gas drill; particular stress was laid upon

NEW C.O.'S

training in manœuvre and co-operation with the artillery. Night operations and route marches took place at intervals. No one was idle, but at the same time the comfort and health of the troops were considered, and the fact that many of them had just been through a prolonged period of extreme physical and mental strain was not forgotten.

As a result of the Aisne battle every single battalion commanding officer in the division had become a casualty. During the month of June new C.O.'s were steadily arriving and before its close the division was completely re-equipped in this regard. The following were the names of the new officers, although to two of them, Lieut.-Colonel Lowry and Lieut.-Colonel Roberts, the term " new " is inappropriate, for they were returning, after temporary absence owing to wounds, to their old commands:— 2/ Devonshire, Major G. E. R. Prior, M.C.; 2/ Middlesex, Major E. E. F. Baker, M.C.; 2/ West Yorkshire, Lieut.-Colonel A. E. E. Lowry, D.S.O., M.C.; 2/ Northamptonshire, Lieut.-Colonel S. S. Hayne, D.S.O.; 1/ Worcestershire, Lieut.-Colonel F. C. Roberts, V.C., D.S.O., M.C.; 1/ Sherwood Foresters, Lieut.-Colonel J. D. Mitchell, D.S.O.; 2/ Royal Berkshire, Lieut.-Colonel A. G. F. Isaac, M.C.; 2/ East Lancashire, Lieut.-Colonel J. E. Green, D.S.O.; 2/ Rifle Brigade, Lieut.-Colonel R. H. Leyland. There were changes also in the Infantry Brigade Commands. Early in the month Brig.-General L. M. Stevens, D.S.O., took over the 24th Infantry Brigade from Brig.-General R. Haig, and Brig.-General J. B. Pollok McCall, C.M.G., D.S.O., came to take the place of Brig.-General Husey, who had been mortally wounded on the Aisne, as commander of the 25th Infantry Brigade. In the Divisional Artillery Lieut.-Colonel D. E. Forman, C.M.G., succeeded Lieut.-Colonel Fisher in command of the XXXIII Brigade, and Lieut.-Colonel C. B. Thackeray, D.S.O., succeeded Lieut.-Colonel Ballard in command of the XLV Brigade.

The infantry brigades were located in the new area as follows: The 25th Infantry Brigade had its Headquarters at Hautebut which is practically on the sea shore; the 24th Infantry Brigade was centred round Yzengremer, which is about $1\frac{1}{2}$ miles South-West of Friville; while the 23rd was in the neighbourhood of the town of Gamaches, on the Bresle river and further inland. On the 4th July the 25th and 24th Infantry Brigades changed places, thus enabling the latter also to gain a nearer taste of sea air and, on the 15th of the month, all three brigades exchanged positions by route march, the 23rd taking its turn, all too brief as the event proved, at Hautebut. Other of the divisional troops (notably the Engineers at St. Quentin) were also within easy reach of the sea. The weather during practically the whole

RECONSTRUCTION

period of the division's stay in this area was gloriously fine and full use was made of the opportunities for sea bathing. A divisional boxing tournament was held, and won by the 1/ Worcestershire whose representatives knocked out the R.A. in the final round, and in addition to this divisional event brigade and regimental sports were also organized. The 25th Infantry Brigade, in particular, held a most successful meeting on the 10th July at which the G.O.C. and his staff attended and proceedings were enlivened by the presence of the divisional band. The programme would not have been complete without a Divisional Horse Show which was duly held on the 13th and 14th of July and also proved a great success.

Fine weather, hard work and amenities such as these kept the men in good health and helped to make them contented. Despite the rigorous and comprehensive training, the division was enjoying something that was more nearly a holiday than anything it had experienced for many a month. At any rate it was at last away, for a time, from the actual fighting. Indeed, there must be many who, on looking back, will find that some of the pleasantest memories of their service with the division are bound up with the interlude, strenuous and hard-working though it may have been, which they spent during June and July in the summer sunshine and within sight of the blue waters of the Channel on that strip of Picardy coast between St. Valery and Le Tréport.

The period of training, however, gradually grew to a close. Events on the western battle-front marched on swiftly and momentously and the days of anxiety were not yet over. The three months of comparative quiet which on the British front followed the final checking of the German Lys offensive were a godsend to the British Army; but while our troops, heartened by the presence of growing American reserves behind them, were getting ready for the counter-blow, the enemy was still striking with desperate energy against the French. He was still meeting with success. The swift onrush of the May battle had carried him back to the Marne and scarce had his progress there been stayed when, on the 9th June, he struck once more on the front between Noyon and Montdidier. Again he made a deep and swift advance, filling up the gap which had existed between the two great salients in his line on the Somme and on the Aisne. Then had followed a short period of comparative quiet, broken only by the cheering news of minor British successes at Merville, the Nieppe Forest and Hamel; part of a series which showed that our recovery was proceeding steadily and well.

Yet it was known that the enemy's resources were not yet fully spent. Large German reserves were grouped in Rupprecht of Bavaria's Army opposite our Flanders front, and preparations

BACK TO THE LINE

for a German offensive there were known to be far advanced. A JULY renewal of the German attacks on the French front was expected 1918 by our Allies on both sides of Rheims. Troops were needed to meet these dangers, and at the same time to add the necessary weight to the counter-offensives for which the Allied Higher Commands were already making their arrangements. Not only had the British Army a serious danger to meet and a mighty task to provide for on its own front; but early in July it was asked to send, and did send, first four and then a second four divisions to assist in the French counter-stroke and to maintain the Allied reserves behind the point of junction of the French and British Armies.

The war, in fact, was about to pass into another, and as it proved, a final phase; and it was inevitable that the 8th Division would be called back to take its part. The summons came on the 9th July, when the division was placed in G.H.Q. Reserve and ordered to be ready to move at twenty-four hours' notice either by train or bus. A further indication of the direction in which events were moving came on the 14th July, when the division passed to the IX Corps on the transfer of the XXII Corps to the French zone. Two days later, while every one was discussing the news of the renewed attack on the French and of the crossing of the Marne at Château Thierry, directions were received by telephone that the divisional artillery was to move to the area of the First Army (General Sir H. S. Horne, K.C.B., K.C.M.G.). On the 18th a further telephone message came from the Fourth Army that the rest of the division would move by train to the First Army area on the following day.

On the 19th July, therefore, the division's " holiday " by the sea, a month that had passed all too quickly, came to an end; and, with pulses quickened by the first news of the great counterattack launched by our Allies on the Marne on the previous day, the troops entrained for the move back to the Army under which they had had their first experience of war. Detrainment took place at Aubigny, Tincques and Pernes and was not altogether without incident; for the train which carried the 2/ East Lancashires and arrived at Pernes at 5 o'clock on the morning of the 20th was machine-gunned, while in a siding, by a single-seater enemy aeroplane flying very low. No casualties, however, were caused. Divisional Headquarters closed at Friville at 9 a.m. on this day and re-opened at noon at Villers-au-Bois, about 7 miles to the North-West of Arras. A few days later it was transferred to the Château at Acq, a little to the South of Villers. The division was accommodated about Mont St. Eloy and Villers.

The division was now once more under the orders of Lieut.- General Sir Aylmer Hunter-Weston and instructions were imme-

RECONSTRUCTION

diately received from VIII Corps Headquarters for the 8th Division to relieve the 52nd Division on the right sector of the Corps front. This portion of the line was in front of Vimy and the Vimy ridge, and formed part of the ground North of the Scarpe gained in the Arras battle of the spring of 1917. It was reasonably well organized and in all respects a more comfortable sector than that in which the division had last fought under the VIII Corps. The relief was duly carried out and completed by the 23rd July, on which date Maj.-General Heneker assumed command of the sector. The division was disposed with two brigades in line and one brigade in reserve; the 4th Canadian Division was on its right, the 20th Division on its left.

The division had thus returned to the fighting line and in the fighting line it was to remain—with the exception of four days only (5th–8th November inclusive) until the Armistice. During the days that were to come it was to experience many varying types of warfare; first for a month or so the ordinary active defence of the trenches; then a period of minor operations and a gradual move forward, the loosening of the German line in this sector being a direct result of the sustained and vigorous British offensives further South; thirdly a period of attack against organized lines, a period containing some solid and stubborn, but successful, fighting; and lastly a vigorous pursuit against a beaten and broken enemy.

Which of the soldiers of the 8th Division, when they climbed into their trains at Eu, Woincourt or Feuquières to return to the front line, could have guessed that in less than four months they would be in the neighbourhood of Mons, receiving the news that an Armistice had been signed? Yet on that very day—the 18th July—on which they had received orders to move forward, the final turning point of the war, had they only known it, was reached. For it was on the 18th, as already indicated, that Foch launched his first counter-attack, and with the stroke, long and patiently awaited by the Allied High Commands, but as unexpected as it was welcome to the rank and file of the Armies, the initiative passed finally and definitely from the Germans to the Allies. "From this time onward," as a German writer[*] has said, "the German Supreme Army Command was subject to the strategical law of the enemy." On the 8th August, the "Black Day" of the German Army, as Ludendorff rightly calls it, the truth of this statement was to be even more strikingly emphasized. The battle of Amiens was opened on that day by the Fourth British and First French Armies—a secret splendidly kept. Thenceforward, that mighty and growing success was, like a stone flung in a quiet pond, to ripple its effect in ever-widening

[*] Lieut.-Colonel Wolfgang Foerster.

THE TURNING POINT

circles all the way up and down the locked trench lines of the Western Front. The development of the French battle, in which British troops had now joined, on the eastern flank of the German salient had already compelled the enemy to abandon his projected offensive in Flanders. He was now driven everywhere to a strict defensive, which he found it ever more and more difficult to maintain. With new and renewed thrusts breaking in upon him all along the line, he was to be forced into continued retreat; until finally, when the end came, it was to find him falling hurriedly back, without reserves and without coherent plan, in widespread disorder and confusion.

JULY–AUGUST 1918

In this mighty consummation the 8th Division was destined to play a worthy part.

CHAPTER XVI

THE FINAL OFFENSIVE: DOUAI

THE sector which the 8th Division had taken over, extending from opposite Fresnoy to Mericourt, was a quiet one in which the enemy's infantry, well sheltered in deep-dug trenches behind strong belts of wire, showed little enterprise.

Our own front was held by two infantry brigades, the 23rd Brigade (Brig.-General G. W. St. G. Grogan, V.C., C.M.G., D.S.O.) and the 24th Brigade (Brig.-General L. M. Stevens, D.S.O.) with headquarters in Thélus Caves and on the Vimy Ridge, and was covered by three brigades of field artillery, the XXXIII and XLV Brigades, R.F.A. (Lieut.-Colonel D. E. Forman, C.M.G., and Lieut.-Colonel C. B. Thackeray, D.S.O.) and the CCXLII Army Brigade, R.F.A. (Lieut.-Colonel L. W. La T. Cockcraft, D.S.O.) and by the XVI Brigade, R.G.A. (Lieut.-Colonel F. W. Loveday, D.S.O.). Four 15-pounder guns were specially sited along the front for Anti-Tank defence, and three groups of machine guns of one company each were placed in position after careful reconnaissance by Lieut.-Colonel J. Angell, M.C., commanding 8th Battalion Machine-Gun Corps, in conjunction with the Army Machine-Gun officer, Colonel Lindsay. From the crest of the ridge, the whole countryside as far as the Douai Canal could be seen laid out like a map, and the artillery and machine gunners had fine scope for their energies. Douai Station was steadily bombarded by the long-range guns and with such effect that it was found to be completely destroyed when later on our troops entered the town.

The division settled down into the normal routine of trench life, and there is little to record of the early days of their return to the front. An incident such as the bringing down on the 2nd August of a low-flying German aeroplane by the machine-gun and rifle fire of the 2/West Yorkshire stands out among a long series of comfortably colourless reports. The period was made notable, however, by the visit which His Majesty the King paid to the divisional area on the 8th August, a visit which must have contrasted strangely, to those of the division—if any such there were—who saw both, with that first visit of December 1914 when the division had first entered into line. During the course of this visit Brig.-General Grogan, commanding 23rd Brigade, was presented with his V.C. by His Majesty at First Army Headquarters at Ranchicourt.

Yet, if their own front produced for the moment little military incident, news now came daily from the South which acted like a tonic upon all ranks. Hopes which the 18th July had

PLATE XIV

Copyright: Imperial War Museum
OPPY WOOD FROM VIMY RIDGE

Copyright: Imperial War Museum
DOUAI: GRANDE PLACE, OCTOBER, 1918

ON VIMY RIDGE

raised the 8th August confirmed and amplified, and the troops responded eagerly when the needs of the new offensive made their first demands upon them. Every man and gun that could be spared from the defence of the less active fronts were wanted for the battle, and the troops holding the quieter sectors had perforce to do double duty.

AUGUST 1918

On the 13th August orders were received from VIII Corps that the division was to "side-step" to the South, taking over the Oppy and Willerval brigade sectors from the 52nd Division on its right, and having its own left sector relieved by the division (the 20th) on its other flank. This meant that the 8th Division was now responsible for three brigade sectors instead of two, a total front of 9,000 yards. Consequently it was necessary to have all three brigades in the line at the same time, the 24th Infantry Brigade holding the Oppy sector on the South, the 23rd Infantry Brigade the central Willerval sector and the 25th Infantry Brigade (Brig.-General J. B. Pollok-McCall, C.M.G., D.S.O.) the northern Mericourt sector. The reliefs were completed on the evening of the 16th August.

Even on a relatively quiet front, the holding of so long a line threw a great strain upon the troops. The difficulty was increased by the fact that the division was still not fully trained, and the question of training became under these conditions a problem which required solution. However, as the front was so quiet a one, it was found possible to have one battalion of each brigade right back for training, and the artillery* similarly released one battery per brigade. A divisional platoon school was organized close to Divisional Headquarters at Château d'Acq, to which platoons were sent complete in every respect. Here each platoon in turn went through a course of six days' intensive training under special instructors, and the results obtained proved of the utmost value.

However quiet a front may be and however strongly organized, the resources of modern war find means for preventing stagnation, and frequent gas discharges on either side kept both combatants constantly on the alert. On the 1st August some 20 T.M.'s bombs containing mustard gas and timed to burst in the air were fired on to the right of the right brigade, causing about 30 casualties to the 1/ Worcestershire, including the Commanding Officer, Lieut.-Colonel Roberts, his second in command, Major W. V. Franklin, and his Adjutant Capt. A. C. Owen. None of the cases, fortunately, was severe. On the

---

* The alteration in the divisional front entailed a change in the artillery arrangement also. The CCXLII Army Brigade, R.F.A., was left with the 20th Division and its place taken by the CCCXI and CCLXXVII Army Brigades, R.F.A. (Lieut.-Colonel N. P. R. Preeston, D.S.O., and Lieut.-Colonel Cochrane, D.S.O.).

THE FINAL OFFENSIVE

night of the 17th August, again, 800 gas shells were fired by the Germans into the neighbourhood of Thélus village.

Our activity in this regard was even greater. On the 2nd August 600 gas projectors were hurled into the German trenches in front of Mericourt, under cover of an artillery and machine-gun barrage, without provoking any retaliation, a fact which indicated that the discharge had been effective. On the 20th 100 drums of gas were projected North of Arleux from the centre brigade front, and a gas discharge from cylinders was carried out on the front of the right brigade. From information received on the following day it appeared that a considerable number of casualties was caused by this discharge; and on that night and the night after the centre brigade area was heavily bombarded with mustard gas in retaliation. The 2/West Yorkshire suffered considerably as the result of this bombardment, having 90 casualties. Many of these casualties were caused by liquid being evaporated by the sun on the day following the bombardment. Warned by this lesson, stringent orders were issued by the Divisional Commander that gassed areas must be immediately evacuated by all troops and no return to them permitted, until the Gas Officers and N.C.O.'s had pronounced them safe for occupation. As a result of this order, although gas shelling by the enemy continued on the divisional front and was from time to time very heavy, few further casualties were suffered from this cause.

Towards the end of August, even as the pulsing thunder of the guns drew closer and louder, the repercussion of mightier events farther to the South began to make itself more directly felt on the VIII Corps front. The magnificent advance achieved as the result of the Battle of Amiens* (8th-12th August) was followed on the 21st August and succeeding days by a second great thrust delivered by the Third Army in the area North of the old Somme battlefield between the Ancre and the Cojeul rivers. The great success achieved here allowed the flank of attack to be extended still further to the North. Accordingly, on the 26th August was begun the Battle of the Scarpe in which the Canadian Corps, on the right of the First Army, supported on its right by the XVII Corps of the Third Army and with its left flank covered by the 51st Division attacking along the northern bank of the Scarpe, drove forward strongly and successfully in front of Arras. In the opening stroke of this new battle the Canadians regained Monchy-le-Preux and its hill which, seen

---

* In this battle the Fourth Army took nearly 22,000 prisoners and over 400 guns. In the fighting between the 21st August and 3rd September the Third and First Armies captured a further 53,000 prisoners and 470 guns.

GAVRELLE

from the slopes of the Vimy Ridge, stands like a sentinel across the Scarpe Valley. On the left bank of the river the 51st Division again reached the outskirts of Roeux Village, to take which it had made so many gallant efforts in the Arras Battle of 1917, and later in the evening captured Greenland Hill.

AUGUST 1918

This was indeed bringing the battle to the very doorstep of the 8th Division, and on the same evening its three brigades were ordered to send forward patrols to test and, if possible, to occupy the German front line opposite them. By 6 a.m. next morning this was done, and in some places the forward movement had been carried to the support line. Considerable opposition was met with in Oppy Wood and the southern part of Arleux; but the 154th Infantry Brigade (51st Division) on the right had found that the ruined village of Gavrelle had been vacated and they occupied a line of trenches, Crawl, Cod and Crab, to the East of it. These trenches, however, were found to be in so bad a state of repair that they were shortly afterwards evacuated. In the meantime instructions had been received that this Gavrelle sector was to be taken over by the 8th Division, their own left brigade sector being in turn taken over by the adjoining 20th Division. The change was effected by moving down the 25th Infantry Brigade to the new sector, the 23rd and 24th Infantry Brigades being left undisturbed.

On the evening of the 28th August between 5 o'clock and 9.30 p.m. the enemy delivered three counter-attacks, one against the 25th Brigade at Railway Trench, and two in the 24th Brigade sub-sector, against the 1/ Sherwood Foresters (Lieut.-Colonel J. D. Mitchell, D.S.O.) at Blandford Trench and against the 1/ Worcestershire in Bedford Crescent. All these were beaten off; but at 9.45 p.m. the enemy again heavily attacked the two battalions of the 24th Brigade, with the result that the 1/ Sherwood Foresters were driven out of Oppy Wood and a portion of Blandford Trench. The lost ground was, however, regained by the 2/ Northamptonshire (Lieut.-Colonel S. S. Hayne, D.S.O.) on the following day, when further progress was also made by both the two other brigades.

The object of this advance North of the Scarpe, in which the 8th Division had thus taken part with the 51st Division, was to gain sufficient depth on the left bank of the river to secure from counter-attack the flank of the advance made by the Canadian Corps South of the river. This object had now been achieved, and the new line of the First Army ran back in a natural curve from the point of the Canadian advance at Eterpigny, along the western bank of the Trinquis brook to Plouvain, held by the 51st Division, Gavrelle and Oppy, to join with the old British front line of 1917 North of Arleux. There was for the

251

THE FINAL OFFENSIVE

present, no need for any further advance North of the Scarpe, and no reason to expect that the enemy would readily permit additional progress there: for he too had completed the readjustments demanded by our progress on the battle front and now held a readily defensible line.

As early as the 26th July (as soon, that is, as it had become definitely established that the initiative had once more passed to the Allies and that he could no longer hope to carry out the new Flanders offensive which he had planned for the end of July) the enemy had begun to withdraw, first stores and ammunition and then troops, from the Lys salient. The successive defeats inflicted upon him by the British Armies in August had forced him to hasten and extend this movement; but, the Lys salient once evacuated, he would have from the Scarpe to the sea a straight and well organized system of defence, to hold which he would assuredly fight hard. It was no part of the British plan to endeavour to force this line until the eastward advance of our main armies should have turned it and rendered it untenable. Accordingly, at the end of August orders were given that the gains of the 8th Division were to be consolidated and no further forward movement attempted for the present. Casualties to the division during these operations amounted to 9 officers and 182 other ranks.

During the first half of September, except for a slight advance on the 1st of the month, when the 2/ East Lancashire (Lieut.-Colonel J. E. Green, D.S.O.) reoccupied Crawl, Cod and Crab in order to improve our connection with the 51st Division, nothing of any importance was attempted on the front of the division. Conditions remained, comparatively speaking, quiet. The existing trench position, more particularly the southern portion of it, was not, however, altogether satisfactory. Our front line and the enemy's forward position now formed part of the same trench system—the old German Third Line system of 1917—and a broad No Man's Land lay on either side of it both East and West.* Should the enemy, therefore, succeed in driving us out of our part of the system, we should have to drop back across the westward No Man's Land to the front originally held by us. The converse, of course, was equally true: the enemy, if forced to retreat, would have to retire, except for isolated posts, to his main position—the Rouvroy-Fresnes line. To attack him first was the obvious inference, more particularly since the proximity of German posts to our own led to continual bombing and hand-to-hand fighting, which did not produce any definite results. Furthermore, if any offensive were to be launched on a large scale against the main German line, our chances would obviously be

* See map opposite p. 262.

A GUNNERS' RUSE

better if we could start entirely clear of this particular trench system.

SEPTEMBER 1918

General Heneker for these reasons desired to clear up the position by a local attack and the Corps Commander, Lieut.-General Sir A. G. Hunter-Weston, having given his sanction, the operation was fixed for the night of the 21st September, the 49th Division on the right co-operating. " Zero " was fixed for 11 p.m., as there was a fair moon and consolidation could be completed before daylight. The attack which was delivered on a front of 3,500 yards was completely successful and advanced our line to an average depth of 600 yards, all objectives being gained. The troops employed were the 2/ Royal Berkshire (Lieut.-Colonel A. G. F. Isaac, M.C.), on the right, the 2/ East Lancashire in the centre (both of Brig.-General J. B. Pollok-McCall's 25th Infantry Brigade), and the 1/ Worcestershire (24th Infantry Brigade, Brig.-General R. O'H. Livesay, D.S.O.), on the left. Our artillery barrage was opened by all groups at 11 p.m., in co-operation with 6-inch Newton trench mortars and machine guns, and was reported by the assaulting troops to have been excellent. The enemy's artillery fire was, on the whole, not heavy and died down by midnight. One German officer, 18 other ranks, and 2 machine guns were captured.

At 7 a.m. on the following morning, however, the enemy counter-attacked at the point of junction between the 8th and the 49th Divisions. The left battalion of the latter was forced back and as a result parties of the 2/ Royal Berkshire were taken in rear. Considerable casualties were caused, and the most southerly and advanced portion of our gains (Whine trench and most of Cheapside trench)* was recovered by the enemy.

Arrangements were immediately made for a renewed attack on our side preceded by an artillery barrage. It was launched at midnight of the 22nd/23rd September by two companies of the Berkshire and was entirely successful. By 1 a.m. all the previous night's objectives had been regained and 1 officer and 36 other ranks and 5 machine guns captured. The left battalion of the 49th division attacked also, re-establishing their posts and capturing 11 prisoners and a machine gun. The excellent co-operation of the 8th Division Artillery, under Brig.-General J. W. F. Lamont, C.M.G., D.S.O., had once more a great deal to do with our success. The gunners employed a ruse of a simple but very effective kind, putting down a series of " false " barrages at the following hours, 7–7.5 p.m., 8.10–8.20 p.m., 9–9.15 p.m., 10.50–11 p.m., and then the real one at midnight. The enemy was completely deceived, as the captured officer admitted. He stated that he had manned his parapets at 7 o'clock when the first

* See map opposite p. 262.

THE FINAL OFFENSIVE

barrage opened; but he rightly thought that the firing at 8.10 was another false alarm and did not call his men out. The third barrage, owing to its greater length of duration, was, he was convinced, the real thing and he manned his parapets again; but when once more no attack resulted he concluded that none was coming that night. Consequently he did not man his parapets when the fourth barrage was put down and so at midnight he and his men were caught in their dug-outs.

The 23rd and 24th of September were unlucky days for the division for on each of them a Battalion Commander was killed, though neither of the battalions in question was participating in the attack just mentioned. On the 23rd September Lieut.-Colonel A. E. E. Lowry, D.S.O., M.C., commanding the 2/West Yorkshire, was killed by a machine-gun bullet while visiting his outposts; at about 5 o'clock in the morning of the 24th Lieut.-Colonel R. H. Leyland, commanding the 2/Rifle Brigade, was killed by a shell while going round the line. Both were fine officers whose loss was deeply felt, not only in the battalions they commanded, but also throughout the division. Colonel Lowry had been one of the only two officers of his battalion who had survived the March battle, in which he had been captured and had escaped by the exercise of his quick wit and presence of mind, as already related. He had again distinguished himself in the Villers-Bretonneux fight when he led the remnants of his battalion in a gallant counter-attack—in which were captured, in addition to a number of prisoners, the two trench mortars now in the Regimental Mess at York—and in the Aisne battle, in which he had been wounded. Marked for a brilliant future both by his personal charm of manner and by his soldierlike qualities, his death at the age of 26 was a misfortune the extent of which was recognized by the presence at his funeral of an Army Commander, two Corps Commanders and three divisional commanders.

On the night of the 26th/27th September another attack, designed to shorten the divisional front and to complete the work that had been begun on the 21st/22nd, was carried out in cooperation with the adjoining 20th Division in the northern sub-sector of the line. The attack was launched at midnight by the following troops: 2/Devonshire (Lieut.-Colonel G. E. R. Prior, M.C.), 2/Middlesex (Lieut.-Colonel E. E. F. Baker, M.C.), and 2/Northamptonshire (all of the 8th Division) and 7/D.C.L.I. (20th Division). All objectives were gained and a total of 28 prisoners and 10 light machine guns captured. Our casualties were, however, severe, amounting to 4 officers and 94 other ranks. Following immediately upon this operation a "Chinese" attack was undertaken by the artillery at 5.30 a.m.

STROKE UPON STROKE

on the southern portion of the divisional front, dummies being SEPTEMBER
used to represent our infantry advancing. The hostile barrage, 1918
although successfully drawn, was not particularly heavy. The
object of this demonstration, with which the real attack in the
northern subsector fitted in well, was to assist larger operations
on the main battle front South of the Scarpe.

The left flank of their attack having been made secure by the
advances North of the Scarpe already described, on the 2nd
September the XVII and Canadian Corps had attacked and
broken the sector of the Drocourt–Quéant line which lay South
of the junction of the Sensée river with the Trinquis brook. This
brilliant stroke had thrown the enemy into precipitate retreat on
the whole battle front to the South of it. The troops of the
Fourth and Third British Armies had pushed on rapidly to the
outer defences of the Hindenburg Line between St. Quentin and
Havrincourt, North of which village the left of the Third Army
and the right of the First Army cleared the area West of the
Canal du Nord and South of the Sensée. The battle of Havrincourt and Epéhy (12th–18th September) had next driven the
enemy from his forward positions back to the main Hindenburg
Line, with a further loss of nearly 12,000 prisoners and 100 guns.
The stage was then cleared for the decisive battles of the 27th–
29th September in which the Third, First and Fourth British
Armies (the II American Corps acting with the latter) stormed
the Canal du Nord and broke through the formidable defences of
the Hindenburg Line South of it.

It was to assist this latter battle—or series of battles, for on
the 26th September the Americans and French had attacked in
the Argonne and on the 28th the British Second Army and the
Belgians attacked and registered a great advance in Flanders—
by extending yet further the apparent front of attack, that the
operations North of the Scarpe on the 26th/27th September
had been undertaken. The result of the new advance, however,
on the St. Quentin–Cambrai front was greatly to extend the long
northern flank of the central battle. This now stretched East
and West for a distance of some 12 miles along the Sensée and
Trinquis streams, from the neighbourhood of Aubencheul
(North-West of Cambrai) to Biache, and invited counter-attack.
It was clearly necessary to take steps to bring forward the VIII
Corps to guard against this danger and General Heneker's
proposal that he should undertake an attack was readily agreed
to by the Army Commander when the latter visited the division
on the 2nd October.

On the 3rd October, therefore, in accordance with VIII
Corps instructions the divisional boundaries were again changed.
The left (Willerval) sector of the 8th Division was handed over

THE FINAL OFFENSIVE

to the 20th Division, while two sectors (Greenland Hill and Plouvain) were taken over from the 51st Division on the other flank. The divisional right was thereby extended southwards to the Scarpe River and the total frontage was nearly 7,000 yards. The CCLXXVII Army Brigade, R.F.A., was left with the 20th Division and its place taken by the CLXXV Army Brigade, R.F.A., under command of Lieut.-Colonel W. Furnivall, D.S.O. At the same time, the XVI Brigade, R.G.A., was replaced by the XL Brigade, R.G.A., under Lieut.-Colonel W. A. Edmeades, D.S.O. The Artillery was then grouped as follows: Right Group, CXXVI Army Brigade, R.F.A., and XXXIII Brigade, R.F.A.; Centre Group, XLV Brigade, R.F.A., and two batteries of the CLXXV Army Brigade, R.F.A.; Left Group, CCCXI Army Brigade, R.F.A., and two batteries of the CLXXV Army Brigade, R.F.A. Divisional Headquarters moved to Victory Camp, on the Vimy Ridge South of Roclincourt. In its new position the division was well placed to undertake a larger operation than it had yet undertaken since its return to the line, and against a most solid obstacle—the Rouvroy-Fresnes line. Preparations for the attack on this position were at once put in hand, and the CLXIX Army Brigade, R.F.A. (Lieut.-Colonel Rainsford Hannay) was attached to strengthen the divisional artillery for this purpose.

The XXII Corps immediately to the South of the Scarpe was also endeavouring to push forward to cover the flank of the main battle and had already gained positions a considerable distance to the East of the 8th Division's right. This was a fortunate circumstance, as it made it possible to place artillery and observers South of the river and to take the enemy's lines in enfilade. Lieut.-General Sir A. J. Godley, commanding XXII Corps, was also able to accede to General Heneker's request that he should lend some heavy artillery, as well as an additional brigade of field artillery, for the operation. The batteries on this side were of great assistance in cutting the German wire, which was very thick and ran in two belts, as the guns were able to take the belts of wire in enfilade and cut them along their length. Progress was so satisfactory that it was decided to carry out the attack at dawn on the 7th October. The assault was to be launched from the South and when the southern portion of our objectives, including Biache St. Vaast, had been captured the northern portion was to be turned; a less expensive and better plan than a direct assault from the West.*

In preparation for the attack very active patrolling was carried on, brigades being ordered to push forward posts along the communication trenches which ran into the Rouvroy–Fresnes

* See map opposite p. 262.

OPPY

line from the West. A very successful and well executed operation in this connection was carried out by the 1/ Sherwood Foresters on the 6th October. Pushing eastwards along Link trench, they then turned North up the Oppy Support trench, thus practically surrounding the village of Oppy, which they entered during the afternoon. The garrison, consisting of 2 officers and 34 other ranks and 6 machine-guns, was captured.

OCTOBER 1918

At 5 a.m. on the 7th October the attack on the southern portion of the Rouvroy–Fresnes line was launched by Brig.-General Grogan's 23rd Infantry Brigade with the 2/ Middlesex and 2/ West Yorkshire (Major A. T. Champion), in line and two companies of the 2/ Devonshire in support. The 2/ Rifle Brigade under Lieut.-Colonel Hon. R. Brand, D.S.O., and the 2/ Royal Berkshire co-operated in Brig.-General Pollok McCall's adjoining 25th Brigade sector. The plan was to get through on the South and turn northwards, and it succeeded admirably. The 23rd Infantry Brigade reported that all objectives, including the village of Biache St. Vaast which was entered by the 2/ Middlesex, had been gained by 8 a.m. " A magnificent artillery barrage was put down," says the 2/ West Yorkshire official record, " and all objectives were quickly reached with but little opposition and with very few casualties. A number of prisoners were taken who all appeared very pleased to be captured." Consolidation of captured objectives proceeded without interference from the enemy.

A special feature of Brig.-General Lamont's artillery arrangements was a " criss-cross " barrage employed on Biache and its exterior defences, a novel expedient which proved most successful. The device consisted of two independent but co-ordinated barrages, " A " barrage fired from the West along the northern face of the Biache " rectangle " and " B " barrage fired from the South-East along the western face of the village.

| 1st Position. | Half-way Position. | Final Position. |

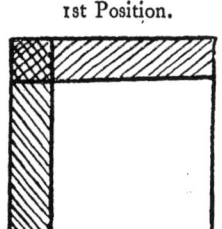 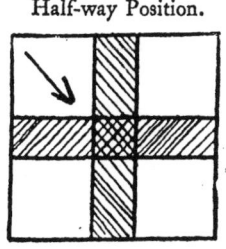 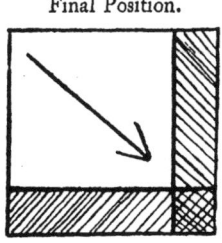

DIAGRAM TO ILLUSTRATE THE BIACHE BARRAGES.

Arrows show infantry entering behind the barrages. The rectangle represents, very roughly, the village of Biache. Barrage lines hatched.

THE FINAL OFFENSIVE

The two barrages when first laid down thus formed two sides of a square on the northern and western faces of the Biache "rectangle." As the attack progressed, "A" barrage moved due South, and "B" barrage due East, till they formed first a "St. George's Cross" through the centre of the Biache "rectangle" and later constituted the southern and eastern sides of the square. The infantry entered the Biache defences at the north-western corner behind the barrages, and following them up, gradually spread over the whole locality, with the barrages acting as protecting walls in front of them.

Three batteries of 8 machine guns each were grouped under control of a single officer, 2nd Lieut. Aspinall, in disused trenches well forward and supported the attack with overhead fire, the remaining guns of Lieut.-Colonel Angell's machine-gun battalion co-operating in the artillery barrages or going forward with the infantry.

Meanwhile the 2/Rifle Brigade and the 2/Royal Berkshire had advanced Eastward from the direction of Count Avenue. The Rifle Brigade duly reached the Rouvroy–Fresnes line, joined up with the 23rd Infantry Brigade and subsequently went right through Railway Copse. The Berkshire attacked and cleared Hollow Copse, the dug-outs in which had previously been bombarded by our heavy artillery—a delicate but successful operation—and on reaching the Rouvroy–Fresnes line, proceeded to work their way northward along it.

Farther to the North in the 24th Infantry Brigade sector the 1/Worcestershire under Lieut.-Colonel Roberts had by a well-executed operation surrounded the system of trenches, Crumb, Cruet, and Cupid, and captured 38 prisoners and 6 machine guns. It had been intended that the operation for the capture of the northern part of the Rouvroy–Fresnes line should be deferred till daylight on the following day, the attack to be preceded by an artillery barrage. Bombing was progressing so satisfactorily, however, that it was decided to carry on immediately and for as long as good progress could be made. Accordingly, the 1/Worcestershire bombed their way along Link Trench and entered the Rouvroy–Fresnes line. Thence they worked their way in each direction North and South, and to the North speedily got into touch with Lieut.-Colonel Mitchell's battalion (1/Sherwood Foresters). Southward they found progress more difficult, but went forward with great determination and after a hard fight, established touch at dawn on the 8th October with the 2/Royal Berkshire under Lieut.-Colonel Isaac. In the course of this fighting, the Worcestershire gained a mound just North of the spot where Chip Trench joined the Fresnes line,

THE ROUVROY-FRESNES LINE

whence they were able to get a direct view of the enemy both in and outside his trenches. At one spot, they caught him hung up in his own wire and were able to report "very nice shooting."

At the extreme North of the attack the Sherwood Foresters, advancing eastward with one company along Lambert Alley and another along Coke Trench, established themselves after some severe and fairly costly fighting in Chapel Trench, being in touch with the Worcestershire on their right and with the adjoining division on their left. In this way was captured the whole of the Rouvroy–Fresnes system on the divisional front, with 218 prisoners and 37 machine guns, and an important step was taken towards covering the flank of the main British thrust.

The success of the division obtained gratifying acknowledgment from the First Army Commander, General Horne, who sent the following minute, under date the 8th October, to the VIII Corps Commander:

"Please tell Maj.-General W. C. G. Heneker, C.B., D.S.O., and the 8th Division that the way in which the successful operations of yesterday were conducted reflects great credit upon all ranks.

"Since the 8th Division has occupied its present extended front I have been much impressed by the fine offensive spirit displayed."

Lieut.-General Sir A. G. Hunter-Weston in forwarding the above message to the Divisional Commander wrote as follows:

"It is with great pleasure that I forward the attached commendatory note by the Army Commander.

"I congratulate you and all officers, warrant officers, non-commissioned officers and men in the division on receiving such a high praise from a General whose opinion we all so greatly value.

"I rejoice that a division that I have had the honour of having under my command for so long a time, both in the Ploegsteert, in the Passchendaele and now in the Vimy area, should, notwithstanding its heavy losses and consequent almost complete reconstruction, exhibit now again in this recent fighting those high qualities of discipline, dash and determination which it has displayed since its first formation at the beginning of the War."

In the meantime Brig.-General Grogan's brigade had been exploiting its success. At nightfall on the 8th General Grogan had pushed forward patrols to hold the eastern exits of the crossings over Vitry Marsh and over the swamps in Gloster Wood. During the night troops were also sent forward to infiltrate between Gloster Wood and the village of Fresnes-les-Montauban,

THE FINAL OFFENSIVE

with the ultimate object of joining hands with Brig.-General Pollok McCall's brigade which was to advance South-East down Crane Trench. In this way Fresnes-les-Montauban would be surrounded and pinched out. At dawn on the 8th October accordingly, two companies of the 2/ East Lancashire (Lieut.-Colonel H. J. Miers), who had passed through the 2/ Royal Berkshire worked their way southward along Crane trench. During the day they successfully joined hands with Lieut.-Colonel Prior's battalion (2/ Devonshire) working from South to North behind the village which was thus captured. Not many prisoners were taken, however, as the enemy had evacuated the town and fled as soon as he found that his retreat was menaced. In the northern sector the 1/ Sherwood Foresters and 1/ Worcestershire continued to push forward. During the course of the day they went through the town of Neuvireuil, which also was found to be empty of Germans, and established a line East of that place.

By the morning of the 9th October our troops were well forward of the Rouvroy–Fresnes line all along its length, and during this and the following day our advancing patrols established touch with the enemy in the Drocourt–Quéant line. The village of Izel-lez-Equerchin forward of that system in the northern sector was also found to be held by the enemy and protected by very strong and thick wire. During these forward movements a few more prisoners had been captured in addition to 4 trench mortars and 7 machine guns. Casualties to the division from noon on the 6th to noon on the 10th were as follows: Killed, 4 officers, 24 other ranks; Wounded, 8 officers, 163 other ranks; Missing, 30 other ranks; Total 12 officers, 217 other ranks.

The next obstacle which faced the division—and all along its front—was the Drocourt–Quéant line. It was a formidable system; an elaborate arrangement of trenches well protected by several thick rows of wire. The artillery at the disposal of the division was not sufficient to support an attack on the whole front of 7,500 yards at the same time, and it was decided, therefore, to attack with two battalions on a selected front to the North of Vitry-en-Artois. If the enemy's defences could be pierced here, the success might be exploited and in all probability his line might be rolled up and so captured completely.

The attack was to be undertaken by General Grogan with the 2/ Devonshire and the 2/ Middlesex at 5.10 a.m. on the 11th October. The task of the artillery was made more difficult by the fact that the country about Biache, whence enfilade fire could be brought to bear upon the German wire and trenches, was extensively flooded. The inundations similarly made it impossible to get the CXXVI Army Brigade R.F.A., far enough forward South of the Scarpe for it to be used to the best effect. General

THE DROCOURT–QUÉANT LINE

Lamont's forces, too, had been lessened by the withdrawal of the CLXIX Army Brigade R.F.A. None the less, with the batteries remaining to him grouped about Biache and Fresnes, another new departure in the use of artillery in support of an attack was carried through with eminent success. The first phases of the barrage were of the normal creeping type; but two hours after "zero" it was arranged that it should fall as though for a protective barrage, and then swing northwards and move up the line of German trenches from South to North at the rate of 100 yards in 8 minutes, to allow troops of the 25th Infantry Brigade to widen the breach.

Once more the plan of attack proved immediately successful. All objectives were captured with between 50 and 60 prisoners, and as soon as there was light enough to see it became obvious that the enemy was vacating his positions all along the front and was retiring in disorder. The swinging barrage was therefore stopped and the whole division at once pushed forward. From information subsequently obtained from prisoners, it appeared that the enemy had already began to withdraw from the Drocourt–Quéant line at 3 a.m. that morning, strong rear-guards well armed with machine guns being left, however, to hold the line until attacked. Our assault caught the enemy in the midst of his withdrawal and both hastened and disorganized it.

Our troops advanced rapidly, and by 9.30 a.m. the whole of the Drocourt–Quéant line, including the village of Izel-lez-Equerchin to the North and the town of Vitry-en-Artois to the South, were in British possession. An air reconnaissance carried out by a contact aeroplane of No. 16 Squadron R.A.F. at a height of only 20 feet was of great assistance to the attack. By midday the 25th Infantry Brigade (Brig.-General Hon. R. Brand, D.S.O.) had taken the village of Quiéry-la-Motte and held the line of the railway beyond it. On the right, however, the 2/Middlesex were impeded by machine-gun fire coming from the high ground known as Hill Métier and Mont St. Georges South of the Scarpe. Information had also been received from the 1st Canadian Division on that side of the river to say that they could not get on. Accordingly, at 4 p.m. Lieut.-Colonel E. E. F. Baker detached two platoons of the 2/Middlesex to deal with this situation. The one, led by General Grogan and the battalion commander in person, crossed the Scarpe by means of the ruins of the railway bridge, taking a machine gun with it, and brought flanking fire to bear on the point of obstruction. The other crossed at Vitry village and attacked Hill Métier. The enemy at once began to retire, the hill was captured and handed over to the Canadians and both the Canadian and Middlesex were again able to get forward.

THE FINAL OFFENSIVE

The advance was vigorously exploited throughout the day and by night time it had reached 8,000 yards in the centre and about 4,000 yards on the flanks. The forward thrust in the centre was mainly due to the 2/ Royal Berkshire (Lieut.-Colonel A. G. F. Isaac) who had pushed forward patrols and followed them up with the greatest boldness. Marching along the Quiéry-la-Motte–Esquerchin high road in fours, the battalion had passed through the latter place and by 10 p.m. was occupying both Cuincy and Petit Cuincy.

The full explanation of the enemy's decision to evacuate the Drocourt–Quéant line and his subsequent withdrawals must be sought in the new series of victorious battles which, following the breaking at the end of September of the last of the enemy's fully developed field defences, were fought by the British southern armies.

"The second and concluding phase of the British offensive now opened, in which the Fourth and Third Armies and the right of the First Army moved forward with their left flank on the Canal line which runs from Cambrai to Mons, and their right covered by the French First Army. This advance, by the capture of Maubeuge and the disruption of the German main lateral system of communications, forced the enemy to fall back upon the line of the Meuse and realized the strategic plan of the Allied campaign."*

The controlling factor in the general situation on the Western Front, and the base upon which the Allied plan of campaign rested, was that the bulk of the German armies were massed South-West and West of the Ardennes† and mainly depended for supplies upon the great trunk railway line running through Namur and Liège to Cologne and the munition factories of the Ruhr. From the "Liège Gap," lying between the impracticable Ardennes mountains and forests on the one side and the projecting frontier of Dutch Limbourg on the other, branched like the ribs of a fan the roads and railways by which the German armies fronting the Allied attacks must be fed; along which, if defeated, they would have to retreat to escape disaster. This understood, a glance at the map will show at once the prime importance of the British drive. It was directed straight at the Liège Gap, and the faster and further it proceeded, the faster and the further the German forces holding the fronts to South and North would have to fall back, if they were to escape before their way of retreat was closed to them. By the breaking of the Hindenburg Line—the last and most formidable of the completed defensive systems by

---
* *Haig's Despatches*, Dent's Edition, p. 287.
† See the map inside the back cover of this book.

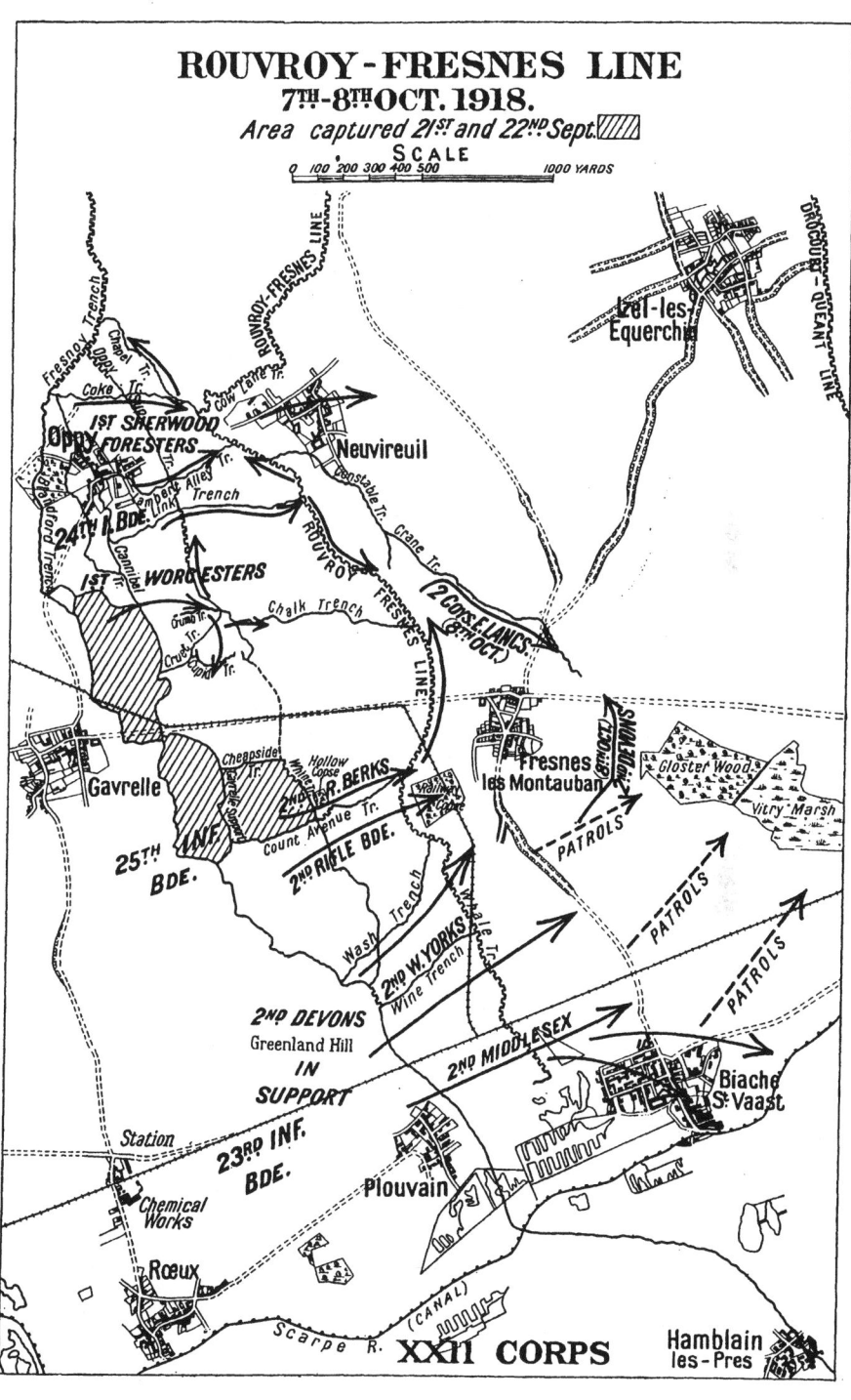

which the enemy had hoped to hold up our advance—the danger to the German armies facing the French and Americans to the South and the British and Belgians to the North became acute. It would increase every day and every hour that the British drive drew nearer to Maubeuge and Mons, where the main lateral railways serving the German southern and northern fronts linked with the trunk line running thence East to Germany.

When, therefore, on the 8th October the great advance was resumed under conditions now rapidly becoming those of open warfare, and British troops once more reached le Cateau, the enemy at once commenced a series of vast withdrawals, extending far to the South and North of the British battle area. Following upon the new advance in Flanders, he had already abandoned Lens, la Bassée and Armentières, a movement which the 8th Division had exploited by its capture of the Rouvroy–Fresnes line. He now abandoned Laon to the South, and in the North was falling back to the canal line which runs South and North past Douai to Lille.

On the 8th Division front also, progress on the scale achieved on the 11th October had definitely changed the character of the fighting into that of a war of movement. The enemy's intention to retire had been skilfully forestalled, and instead of falling back as he had meant to do in his own time and at his own pace, he was being hustled out of his positions before his preparations for evacuation were complete. Meals left half finished on the tables and valuable articles of a personal kind left behind, in addition to great quantities of stores, made it clear that the retirement had become a hurried and disorderly flight rather than a methodical retreat.

Further evidence of haste was to be seen in the fact that the destruction of many places prepared for demolition, such as road junctions, had been forgotten. This was fortunate for the division, because the question of communications was becoming a difficult one. Forward movement was necessarily dependent on good road and railway communication in rear. The belt of country over which the division had advanced had been so pounded by the guns of both sides for four years that roads and railways had ceased to exist. The main road upon which the division had to depend ran through Gavrelle and Fresnes les Montaubin to Douai, and much labour was necessary before this was able to take lorry traffic. Repairs were, however, energetically taken in hand by VIII Corps, well seconded by the Divisional Engineers under Lieut.-Colonel C. R. Brown, D.S.O., and by the 1/7 Durham Light Infantry (Pioneers), under Lieut.-Colonel B. C. James, D.S.O., and the task was accomplished with commendable speed. Railhead was advancing also and the work

THE FINAL OFFENSIVE

done on the broad gauge running through Biache St. Vaast and Vitry, as well as on the light railways joining up our system with that on the German side of the destroyed area, was magnificent.

During the whole of the advance the greatest care had to be taken in moving along roads, entering dug-outs and houses, and in touching anything left lying about. Just as had been the case in the spring advance of 1917, booby traps and mines were everywhere. Timber embedded in roads and tracks and connected to a mine which exploded if the timber was either raised or depressed was a favourite device. Fresh ruses were discovered every day and as each came to light appropriate warnings were issued to all ranks. The extent of the danger can be gauged by the fact that by the 27th October the 185th Tunnelling Company, of whom a party under Capt. G. Howatson was attached to the division, had removed no less than 1,395 mines and booby traps in the divisional area.

As the division drew nearer to the canal line, the German resistance stiffened and progress was chiefly confined to the flanks. All three brigades were in line, and each had a group of divisional artillery attached to it, under a group commander, the XXXIII Brigade R.F.A. being affiliated to the 23rd Infantry Brigade, the XLV Brigade R.F.A. to the 25th Infantry Brigade, and the CCCXI Army Brigade R.F.A. to the 24th Infantry Brigade. The CXXVI Army Brigade R.F.A. was held as a sort of roving unit, to be used where most needed. A battery of 18-pounders and a section of 4·5-inch howitzers were detailed to each battalion in front line from which sections, and even single guns, were pushed forward as required to help the infantry companies. The machine-gun companies were similarly allocated to the infantry brigades, one company being held in reserve in the hands of Lieut.-Colonel Angell. The system worked well, and the intimate co-operation between the different arms added greatly to the speed and certainty of the advance.

The 2/ West Yorkshire under Major Champion passed through Brebières on the 12th October, approaching to within 400 yards of the canal East of the village, and on the same day the 2/ Royal Berkshire under Colonel Isaac occupied Planque. On the 13th the 1/ Worcestershire under Colonel Roberts took possession of Flers. A more outstanding incident was the capture of Douai prison on the 12th October by the 2/ East Lancashire. In the course of an operation at once well planned and skilfully executed, Colonel Miers rushed light trench mortars up close to the position, and the fire of these, added to that of a section of 18-pdrs. and 2 machine-gun sections of " C " Company, 8th Machine-Gun Battalion, silenced the German machine guns, the while our infantry pushed round the left flank

CANAL DEFENCES

and surrounded the prison and its garrison. On the same day a OCTOBER
section of "A" Company, 8th Machine-Gun Battalion, under 1918
2nd Lieut. Birtles, was able to help the neighbouring 12th Division by engaging a detachment of German machine guns which was holding up the flank of that division.

By these advances the division was brought close up against the canal line which was soon found to be a very powerful defensive position. Belts of wire which in some places were of remarkable thickness protected it; while the buildings on the East bank formed admirable hiding places for light artillery and machine guns. The enemy further increased his defences in the southern sector by cutting the canal bank, the resulting floods forcing Brig.-General Grogan to withdraw the advanced forces of the 23rd Infantry Brigade to the edge of the flooded area. Hostile shelling was exceptionally heavy, the enemy being anxious, apparently, to use up surplus stores of ammunition before continuing his withdrawal. He was naturally well acquainted with the ground, and any of our batteries which attempted to take up semi-covered positions immediately came under fire. In this way on the 15th October two valuable officers, Capt. Tapson Jones and Lieut. Scott, lost their lives when an advanced section of the 3rd Battery (Major C. W. Cripps, D.S.O.) was caught in a heavy concentration.

Strong as the German defences were, the enemy were not to be left in unchallenged possession of them. On the evening of the 13th October the 1/ Worcestershire were ordered to make an attempt against the canal and to see whether a crossing could be effected. The attacking company, led by Capt. A. E. Prosser, M.C., reached the line of the canal with much difficulty, meeting not only with ordinary belts of wire entanglement but also wire fences 10 feet high fastened to the trunks of trees. The troops cut their way through, none the less, and endeavoured to dig in, but the ground was swampy and little cover could be obtained. When, therefore, at dawn the position was heavily assailed with trench mortar, artillery and machine-gun fire, and threatened in rear by the enemy debouching from the North, the remnants of the company withdrew, having suffered severely. Capt. Prosser, 2nd Lieuts. E. T. Leach and E. A. Palmer, were reported missing, the two latter wounded; and about 65 other ranks were killed, wounded or missing. This gallant attempt showed both the strength of the enemy's positions and the tenacity with which he was holding them.

During the three days following this episode not much progress was made, though on the 16th the 2/ Rifle Brigade captured the Château at Dorignies, and at other points patrols and small bodies gradually worked yet closer to the canal. To the

THE FINAL OFFENSIVE

South the Canadians were similarly held up by this obstacle. The strength of his positions along the canal was to prove, however, of little use to the enemy, save for the purposes of temporary delay. Two days before this date the advance in Flanders had been resumed. British, French and Belgian forces, following in broad outline the same plan of advance that had been contemplated in 1917, cleared the left bank of the Lys to beyond Courtrai and were thrusting north-eastwards past Roulers towards Ghent and Bruges. Next day, on the 17th October, fresh assaults were commenced on the main battle front South and North of le Cateau. The line of the Selle river was forced on both sides of the town and within a week the British front had been carried forward to the western edge of the Mormal Forest. The railway junction which in the neighbourhood of Maubeuge linked the German main lateral railways with the trunk line to Germany was under the fire of our guns.

The XXII Corps on the right of the First Army took direct part in the later stages of this fighting; but even before that occurred the renewal of the main advance, coupled with the earlier success in Flanders, had an immediate effect upon the fronts of the Canadian and VIII Corps also. The enemy's position on the canal line became a dangerous and untenable salient. He had no option but to retire, and even before the attack of the 17th October signs of his intention to do so had not been wanting. Fires had been observed in Douai, and on and after the 15th October there had been a significant change in the employment of his artillery. Fire from 4·2-inch guns and howitzers became markedly absent; practically all the shelling was done by 5·9-inch guns firing at great range.

On the 17th October reports from daylight onwards gave indications that the infantry retirement was commencing. At 8.30 a.m. two platoons of the 2/ Middlesex had reached the Scarpe and established posts on the bank without meeting any opposition; though a personal reconnaissance by Col. Roberts ascertained convincingly that German riflemen were still holding the Canal at 9.15 a.m. on the front of the 1/ Worcestershire. During the morning the 2/ Rifle Brigade heard sounds of transport moving in Douai; at 1 p.m. Brig.-General R. O'H. Livesay reported that the enemy was gradually withdrawing on the front of the 24th Infantry Brigade also. Patrols of the 2/ Rifle Brigade entered Douai at 2 p.m., and at the same hour the 2/ Middlesex led by Brig.-General Grogan and Colonel Baker, crossed the canal and took possession of the vacated town. The German flag was hauled down and the Union Jack and the regimental flag of the 2/ Middlesex were hoisted over the town-hall.

This tribute paid to British arms, on the following day the

DOUAI

French flag once more took its rightful place over a French city, flying beside the flag of the 2/ Middlesex. A document bearing the names of the advanced party which first entered the town was drawn up by Col. Baker and a copy given to every officer, non-commissioned officer and man who had formed part of it. On Sunday the 20th October the battalion held a ceremonial parade in the square at Douai and there was a short service to commemorate its entrance. A board bearing the signs of the battalion, brigade and division was also set up in the square to celebrate the capture of the town after four years of occupation by the German invaders.

OCTOBER 1918

All civilians had been evacuated and the city was empty except for a deserter from the enemy's rear-guard company. As far as the fabric of its buildings was concerned, the town was found to be fairly intact; but every building concealed a scene of utter and wanton destruction. Everything of value had been removed and such things as had been left—furniture, crockery, pictures and the like—had been smashed to atoms. The inside of the beautiful organ in the Cathedral had been torn out and its reeds lay scattered in a heap on the floor. The German, in defeat, was found to be true to his principles. Indeed, the town had probably only been saved from the systematic destruction which had previously befallen others because, for political reasons and owing to President Wilson's Note, the German High Command had issued orders that towns were not to be destroyed. It was this, no doubt, which saved Douai and accounted for the fact that no active mines were found there. Mines had been put in place, but had been withdrawn.

It was a significant admission.

CHAPTER XVII

THE FINAL OFFENSIVE: MONS

AS soon as the town of Douai had been occupied, the task of bridging the canals was immediately taken in hand by the C.R.E., Lieut.-Colonel C. Russell Brown, D.S.O., and the Royal Engineers. The first bridge to be constructed was a pontoon bridge for field guns and 1st line transport across the Haute Deule Canal at Pont d'Annoy, a few miles North of Douai. This was commenced at 10 p.m. and finished at midnight on the 17th October—a fine piece of work. Two further bridges South of the town were completed on the following day.

During the further stages of the advance the Royal Engineers had, indeed, a most strenuous time; for the country over which the division was advancing was low-lying and much intersected by streams and deep ditches full of water, all bridges over which had been destroyed. These water courses were a great hindrance, not only to the artillery and transport, but also to the machine gunners who, though they might be able to cross themselves with their guns, were frequently unable to get their ammunition limbers over. All section commanders were not able to adopt the device of 2nd Lieut. Oughton, of "B" Company, who commandeered sixteen wheelbarrows and used them throughout the advance as gun limbers. The enemy had also blown up road crossings, causing great craters which had to be filled. This work was carried out rapidly and effectively by Colonel James and the Pioneer Battalion (1/7 Durham Light Infantry) and excellent work in the repairing of roads was also done by the Royal Artillery, as well as the divisional Medical Service (Colonel A. M. McLaughlin, R.A.M.C.), throughout the whole advance. The infantry battalions in reserve likewise did their part and additional help was obtained from the voluntary assistance of liberated civilians.

Difficulties were in this way overcome and the forward movement continued. Owing to the gradual narrowing of the Allied front as it pressed eastwards, the advance of the 8th Division was now carried on on a two-brigade instead of a three-brigade front; the 25th Infantry Brigade being on the right, the 24th on the left and the 23rd in reserve. Forward reconnaissance work was much assisted by the allocation to the division of one platoon of the VIII Corps cyclists (Major J. Y. Baldwin) and of "C" Squadron 4th Hussars, Lieut. F. A. Sykes commanding, who came under divisional command on the 18th and 19th October respectively. The cavalry were given a section of field guns and were ordered forward to reconnoitre the various stages by which the infantry had been directed to advance. The cyclists were placed under the orders of the Brigadiers to whom they were

MARCHIENNES

attached. Though confined to the roads by reason of the water-intersected nature of the country, both cavalry and cyclists proved extremely useful for intercommunication and road reconnaissance.

OCTOBER 1918

Meanwhile, on the 19th October the leading infantry went steadily forward, Colonel Mier's battalion (2/ East Lancashire) moving through la Raches ahead of the 2/ Rifle Brigade. On the left, the 1/ Sherwood Foresters under Colonel Mitchell similarly took over the lead from the 1/ Worcestershire. Close touch was kept with the enemy, and by evening our line had been advanced some $12\frac{1}{2}$ miles East-North-East of Douai. The town of Marchiennes had been occupied by the 2/ East Lancashire at 1 p.m., the enemy fleeing on our approach. This town, which was full of civilians, was quite undamaged. According to the Mayor, every preparation for its destruction had been made, mines having been placed under the church, the principal buildings and the main square; but just before the Germans left the instructions for firing them were cancelled, for the political reasons mentioned above, and the mines withdrawn. The action was an acknowledgment of defeat. Everywhere our troops were received with tears of joy. Flags appeared as though by a miracle to deck the streets. Gifts of flowers were pressed upon us; but no food, for the Germans had carried off everything edible with them and the townspeople were starving.

The success which the division had been able to achieve in its long and arduous advance obtained the honour of recognition in the Commander-in-Chief's official communiqué issued on this day. The extract referring to the division was as follows:

"On the left of these troops the 8th Division has taken Marchiennes. During the past ten days troops of this division, which has been in line continuously for a long period and on a wide front, have maintained unceasing pressure on the enemy, and by the energy and activity of their pursuit have greatly harassed his retreat. In the course of an advance of over 18 miles they have captured several hundred prisoners and taken the town of Douai, besides many villages."

On the 20th, owing to the need of overcoming rationing difficulties and in accordance with VIII Corps instructions, no great advance was made. The roads were crowded by civilians released by the retreating enemy, who with the poor pitiful possessions left to them, piled on carts, hand-barrows, or carried on the owner's back, trudged wearily yet hopefully back to what might remain of their homes. The steady stream made the task of keeping up with our advanced guards well-nigh impossible; but on the 21st the cavalry and leading infantry again pushed energetically forward, driving back the enemy machine-gun posts.

THE FINAL OFFENSIVE

At noon patrols from the 2/ East Lancashire and 1/ Sherwood Foresters entered St. Amand and after some street fighting occupied the town. " A " Company 1/ Sherwood Foresters were the first to enter the town, Lieut. A. C. Willison, M.C., 24th Infantry Brigade Intelligence Officer, being the first man in. A wooden board announcing the capture of the town by this battalion was subsequently affixed to one of the buildings in the *Place*. St. Amand, too, was found to be full of civilians; not only the local inhabitants, but those also of such places as Douai which, as will be remembered, was entirely deserted when entered by our troops. Our guns, following our normal custom, had avoided firing on the town; but half an hour after our patrols had entered the enemy shelled the place heavily, using gas shell, and caused a number of civilian casualties.

To the southward and the eastward St. Amand is bounded by the River Scarpe which joins the Scheldt a little to the North of the town and, with the Forêt de Raismes South of St. Amand, forms a covering position across the deep eastward angle of the Scheldt North of Valenciennes. Since the line of the Scheldt was the next natural halting place for the enemy in his retreat, it was not a matter for surprise to find that every bridge over the Scarpe had been destroyed and that each former crossing-place was covered by machine guns posted on the further bank. Our own machine gunners were immediately sent forward to deal with the situation, two sections of " A " Company, 8th M.G. Battalion, coming promptly into action. The fire of the German guns was speedily silenced; and a small party of the 1/ Sherwood Foresters—making with planks a footway over the débris of the railway bridge—effected a crossing there during the night and established a post on the farther side. Other small parties of the same battalion then filtered across and by dawn of the 22nd October a strong bridgehead had been established. By these means the enemy was forced to withdraw and the advance was renewed, until by the evening of the 22nd the village of la Croisette and the hamlet of Cubray had both been occupied by our troops.

On the 23rd October the XLV Brigade R.F.A., and the CCCXI Army Brigade R.F.A., were grouped for convenience of the advance under Lieut.-Colonel C. B. Thackeray, the XXXIII Brigade R.F.A., and the XLVIII Army Brigade R.F.A., being retained in Divisional Reserve under Brig.-General Lamont. Progress continued towards the Scheldt; but on the 24th it was found that the enemy was holding the village of Odomez, and the high ground about it overlooking that river, in some strength. A patrol of the Cyclist Corps under Lieut. Wilson made a bold attempt to enter the village but were repulsed, and the 2/ North-

CANAL DU JARD

amptonshire (which latter battalion had come through the 1/ Sherwood Foresters) were also held up by machine-gun fire. A heavy fire from our artillery and machine guns was accordingly turned on to this position and maintained all night, and early on the following morning the 2/ Northamptonshire successfully attacked and captured the village. Patrols pushing through the village towards the river found themselves, however, everywhere held up by floods. A section of "A" Company, 8th Machine-Gun Battalion, was, none the less, moved forward at once to a position on the West bank of the canal, whence it engaged a number of targets on the further bank and made movement by the enemy difficult and dangerous.

OCTOBER 1918

It was clear that the division had again reached a position from which a further advance would be extremely difficult without assistance from beyond its own front. The advent of tanks had given a new importance to water defences, and the enemy was making full use of each successive river line which a low-lying and well-watered country provided. In the present instance, in addition to a wide flooded area, he was protected all along his front by two distinct lines of water, the Scheldt River and the Canal du Jard lying parallel with the river. It was decided, therefore, that no further advance should be attempted, until a thorough reconnaissance had been made by staff officers. This was carried out on the afternoon of the 26th, and on the same night the troops of Brig.-General Livesay's 24th Infantry Brigade in line* were relieved by Brig.-General Grogan's brigade, the 2/ Devonshire under Colonel Prior taking the place of 2/ Northamptonshire (Lieut.-Colonel S. S. Hayne) as advanced battalion. The XXXIII Brigade R.F.A., and the XLVIII Army Brigade R.F.A., replaced the XLV Brigade R.F.A., and the CCCXI Army Brigade R.F.A., in the advanced Group and "C" Squadron, 4th Hussars, were withdrawn to their own unit.

As a result of the reconnaissance above referred to, on the night of the 27th October three companies of the 2/ Devonshire attempted to cross the double obstacle of river and canal. "D" and "C" Companies met with heavy shelling and machine-gun fire and were withdrawn, but "A" Company on the right got across the river and established a post of one platoon and a machine-gun section between the river and canal. The position, however, was desperately exposed and, when at 11 o'clock on the following morning the enemy counter-attacked under cover of heavy fire, its garrison was cut off and captured. One N.C.O. (Lce.-Corporal Marchment) and 2 men, both of whom were

* Owing to its continued narrowing, the front was now held by one brigade only.

THE FINAL OFFENSIVE

wounded, succeeded in escaping; and two days later four machine gunners also got back across the river to our lines. The rest of the party, who were almost all wounded, were captured by the enemy.

The passage of the river was indeed a very difficult task to accomplish, owing to the narrowness and limited number of the approaches to the river bank and to the fact that the enemy commanded them with all his available artillery, trench mortars and machine guns. After this unsuccessful but gallant effort and a further close reconnaissance of the ground, General Grogan decided to postpone another attempt until the night of November 2nd/3rd; so as to give time for careful preparations for the making of bridges, etc. Events elsewhere, however,—on the 1st November was begun at Valenciennes the first move in the last battle of the war—made an earlier effort desirable, and on the 30th October the Divisional Commander gave orders that the river was to be crossed that evening in strength. The attempt to cross was again entrusted to the Devons and by 8.20 p.m., or soon after, two bridges constructed of Jerusalem pontoons had been thrown across the river by the Royal Engineers. Though one of these collapsed, further pontoons were put in position, and by 11.15 p.m. it was reported that three platoons were across and that the remainder were crossing fairly quickly. Ultimately three companies succeeded in establishing headquarters across the river; but hostile shell fire was severe and it was found impossible to cross the Canal du Jard.

With the morning the bombardment became intense and, as the swampy condition of the ground made proper digging-in impossible, casualties were heavy. Shelling was also severe on the western side of the river and communication with the forward troops was precarious. One message from " B " Company was brought to Battalion Headquarters at 11 a.m. by a runner who had had to swim the river and arrived without boots or coat. A previous runner had been drowned in attempting to get a message through. The situation of the three companies was becoming impossible, and when it was found that the division on the left had failed to reach the canal and that the division on the right was also unable to cross, the order was given to withdraw. By 8 o'clock in the evening the Devons had re-crossed the river, successfully evacuating all their wounded. The battalion, whose conduct all through a most difficult and dangerous operation had been splendid and heroic, had suffered about 80 casualties during this engagement; but that evening news came of the capture of Valenciennes and, though few, it may be, realized it at the time —occupied as the troops were with the concerns of their own front—the division had once more performed the useful and

BRIEF RELIEF

necessary task of occupying the enemy while victory attended British arms elsewhere.

On the 1st November Corps instructions were issued for a shifting of the divisional front, extending it on the right to Fresnes and shortening it on the left so as just to include Odomez. This new front was even more flooded than the old, and it was clear that it would not be possible to attempt to cross while the enemy continued to hold the canal in strength. Almost immediately, however, after the change over had been effected, orders were received for the division to withdraw into Army Reserve. The relief took place on the night of the 4th/5th November, when the final battle of the war had begun and our troops had crossed the Sambre river and were pushing rapidly eastward through the Mormal Forest. At 6 a.m. on the 5th command of the divisional front passed to the 52nd Division.

The division was thus released for its first rest after nearly $3\frac{1}{2}$ months in the line. In this period it had become once more a real fighting unit, capable of carrying out any operation. During the last three weeks it had moved forward with truly astonishing rapidity. In the words of the booklet subsequently issued by the First Army describing its advance: " By the 25th the 8th Division had come a distance of 30 miles in a straight line since October 7th, capturing 35 towns and many villages, freeing large numbers of civilians, capturing immense quantities of material, and inflicting heavy loss on the enemy."

The division on relief was concentrated in the Marchiennes area. Its rest was not, however, destined to be a lengthy one. The great victory of the British Armies on the Sambre had shattered the German centre and broken finally the resistance of the German armies. Our troops were at the gates of Maubeuge and the German forces to the South and North of our triumphant drive abandoned their positions without further thought of standing. " Meanwhile to the North of the Mons–Condé Canal," to quote from Lord Haig's despatch, " our success was bearing fruit. During the night 7th/8th November numerous explosions were observed behind the German lines, and on the following morning the VIII Corps . . . was able to move forward occupying Condé." The line of the Scheldt had been turned from the South.

The services of the 8th Division were required to assist in exploiting the possibilities which the great victory had opened up, and on the evening of the 8th November a wire was received from the VIII Corps ordering the division to move forward to take over once more the right of the Corps front between Condé and Hergnies. Orders were at once issued for the 23rd Infantry Brigade to move to Fresnes and Escaupont, the 24th to

THE FINAL OFFENSIVE

la Croisette and the 25th to St. Amand. Next day at noon, orders were received by wire for two battalions to proceed by motor bus from Escaupont to Thulin, whence they were to proceed on foot to relieve the Canadian infantry at Pommerœul. The buses were six hours late and the 2/ Middlesex (Lieut.-Colonel E. E. F. Baker) and 2/ West Yorkshire (Major A. T. Champion) were kept waiting for them on the roadside from 2 p.m. until 8 p.m. At 8.50 p.m. they moved off; but the night was dark and the road damaged and difficult. A broken bridge checked the column and it was not until 3 a.m. that Thulin was reached, after a cold and exhausting journey of six hours in which a distance of 15 miles had been covered. The incident serves to illustrate the enormous transport difficulties under which this stage of the advance was carried on. In the event, the Canadians at Pommerœul had already been relieved by a brigade of the 52nd Division, so the two battalions of the 8th Division sought billets in Thulin and remained there for the balance of the night.

On the following day, the 10th October, the two battalions were ordered to take over the line at Douvrain, East of Tertre, from the 157th Infantry Brigade, 52nd Division. They reached their destination at about 7 p.m.; the 2/ West Yorkshire and Brigade Headquarters remaining at Tertre, while the 2/ Middlesex took over the outpost line. At dawn on the 11th November the 2/ Middlesex resumed the advance and in co-operation with "C" Squadron of the 4th Hussars, now once more under divisional command, gained contact with weak enemy rear-guards on the railway which runs between Erbisœul and Mons. The advance, however, was not destined to outlast the day. The crumbling and shaken edifice of national resistance in Germany had finally collapsed. At 7.09 a.m. the following telegram was received at Divisional Headquarters:

"Hostilities will cease at 11.00 on November 11th aaa Troops will stand fast on line reached at that hour which will be reported to Corps Headquarters aaa Defensive precautions will be maintained aaa There will be no intercourse of any description with the enemy. "VIII Corps."

During the last remaining allotted hours, the 2/ Middlesex, with the cavalry in front of them, continued to press vigorously forward. The achievement of this battalion during these final stages was, indeed, a remarkable one. Suddenly ordered forward from the rest they had scarce begun, they had spent six hours by the roadside, followed by a dreary and fatiguing night journey by motor omnibus. Thereafter they had marched more than 27 miles, the last 7 of which were in face of the enemy whom they were driving back before them. When the end came, they were

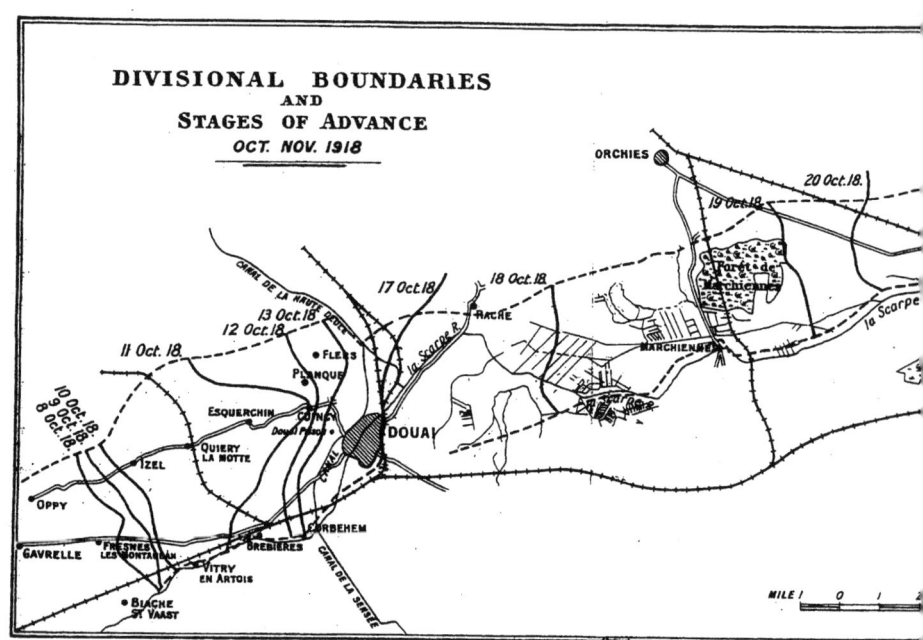

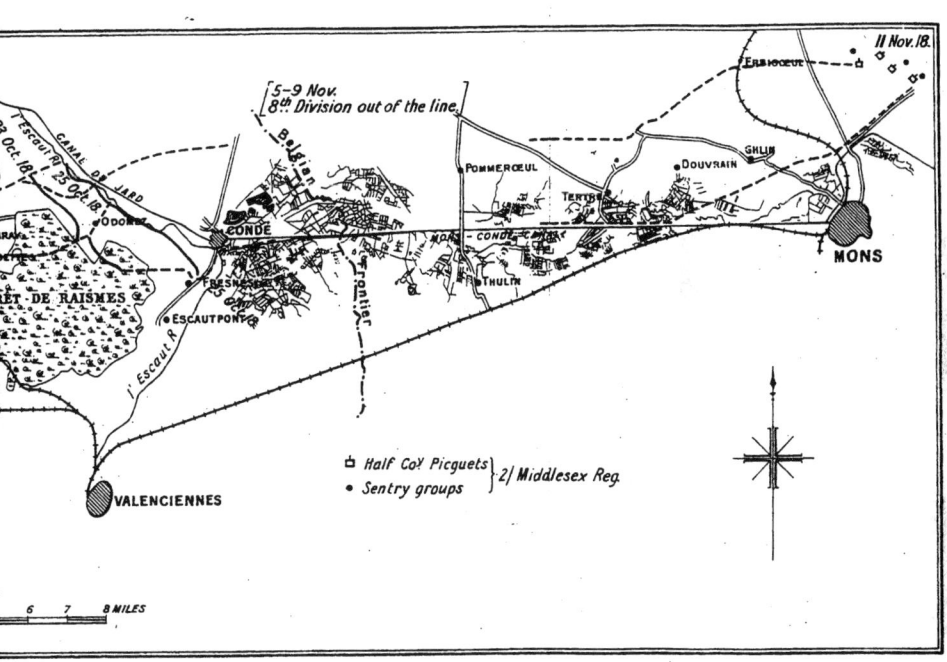

MONS ONCE MORE

occupying a position which was already forward of Mons, being actually some 3¾ miles to the North-North-East of that place.   NOVEMBER 1918

So, in the neighbourhood of a city whose name had since those early days of August 1914 been indissolubly linked in men's minds with the word "retreat," the troops of the 8th Division fired their final shots; and shots that were final only because the capitulation of the enemy was complete. The wheel had, indeed, travelled full circle.

CHAPTER XVIII

VICTORY

AT the moment when the silence of peace fell upon the British battle-front in France, the 2/ Middlesex had reached the line of the road Mons–Jurbise, with cavalry on the line of the road St. Denis–Masnuy St. Jean and in Casteau. To at least one member of the victorious army, the hour of the Armistice came with a strange physical sense of lightening and relief; but it is difficult to please everybody. Precisely at 11 a.m. the leading platoon of a company of the 2/ Middlesex found itself immediately opposite an occupied German post. The men were persuaded with difficulty to refrain from attacking it, their earnest contention being that no one need know anything about it and that it seemed a pity not to kill a few more Germans while they had the chance.

In the course of the next two hours the Middlesex took over from the cavalry, establishing half-company picquets at selected points, and at 1 p.m. the line so held was reported to VIII Corps as the official Armistice line on the divisional front. On this line the British advance was stayed for a time while transport was reorganized and, to avoid a recurrence of temptations such as that which the platoon referred to had so reluctantly withstood, a broad area of evacuated territory was established between the victors and their beaten enemy.

One incident of the final attack remains to be recorded. During the last evening of their advance the Middlesex had established posts in the village of Ghlin, and later the battalion moved into the village and spent the night there. The fact, of no particular significance in itself, has yet a curious extraneous interest. To the North of the village is situated the Château of la Verrerie, and its owner informed the men of the 2/ Middlesex that in August 1914 their colleagues of another battalion of the same regiment (the 4/ Middlesex) had been billeted there. A remarkable coincidence, but there was one still more extraordinary. For there were a number of men then in the 2/ Middlesex to whom the information was already familiar; for the very good reason that they themselves had actually been serving with the 4/ Middlesex in August 1914. These men had on the morning of the 23rd August 1914 fired the first shots of the war on the British front; on the 11th November 1918, having survived all, from the same spot they fired what may well have been the last.

During the afternoon of the 11th November, the division looked hopefully forward to the advance into Germany and orders were issued for further moves of units on the 12th, in order to close the division up ready for the march forward.

PLATE XV

Copyright: Imperial War Museum

THE KING'S VISIT, TOURNAI, DECEMBER, 1918

THE KING AT TOURNAI

Following a night of strange and unaccustomed quiet—for on the British front there were none of the *feux de joie* which a British liaison officer declared rendered his journey that night across a neighbouring Allied zone one of his most alarming experiences of the war, and a suspiciously abrupt and general shortage of strong drink made Verey-light fireworks a dull pastime—the division was collected into brigade groups about Ghlin, Ville Pommerœul and Baudour, with Divisional Headquarters at Tertre. On the 13th November the hope of taking part in the advance to the Rhine gained strength from the receipt of a warning wire from VIII Corps notifying the transfer of the division to General Butler's III Corps, of the Second Army.

The hope was to be disappointed. On the 15th November, the 8th Division was relieved in line by the 52nd Division and on the following day moved back by road and bus to Tournai where it came under the orders of the III Corps; but the III Corps was shortly afterwards transferred from General Plumer's Second Army to General Sir W. R. Birdwood's Fifth Army. With the change disappeared the chance that the sterling service and splendid spirit of the 8th Division would be rewarded by a place with the Army of Occupation.

While at Tournai the division was privileged to furnish the Guard of Honour, composed of 1914 men, on the occasion of the King's visit to that town on the 8th December. Three days earlier the Croix de Guerre won by the 5th Battery R.F.A. and the 2/ Devonshire in the Aisne battle of May 1918 had been presented by Général de Division de Laguishe in the presence of General Birdwood and General Butler at a ceremonial parade held on the 5th December on the Champ de Manœuvres, Tournai. The XLV Brigade R.F.A., the 23rd and 24th Infantry Brigades, the 1/7 Durham Light Infantry, the 1/1 Northumberland Hussars and the 18th Cyclist Battalion (the latter two units being Corps troops) attended the parade under command of General Lamont, C.R.A. 8th Division. On the same occasion the Legion of Honour was presented to General Heneker (*Commandeur*) and to General Lamont (*Officier*).

The division settled down philosophically to a period of training, recreation and education, the troops drawing what consolation they could from the thought that their departure from France and Flanders was the nearer at hand. On the 15th, 16th and 17th December the division marched to the area around Enghien and Ath, where games and education for civil employment were continued during the process of demobilization. Though, to be sure, to a Regular division the word demobilization had only a limited significance. During this period the 8th Division won the only two divisional competitions held in the

VICTORY

Fifth Army, the boxing and Rugby football competitions, and the 8th Battalion Machine Gun Corps furnished the "runner-up" team in the Fifth Army association football competition for individual units. Indeed, the division very nearly swept the board; for the 8th Battalion Machine Gun Corps team was only beaten in a replay after the first game had been drawn.

Early in the New Year, on the 29th January 1919, there took place in the grounds of the Château d'Enghien another ceremonial parade at which Général Desgoutte, commanding the Fifth French Army, accompanied by General Sir R. H. K. Butler, commanding the III Corps, presented the Croix de Guerre and Gilt Star to the 24th Field Ambulance* and the following French decorations to officers and other ranks of the division:—

Lieut.-Colonel R. Burgess, D.S.O., M.C., 24th Field Ambulance,
    Croix de Guerre and Gilt Star.
Capt. E. H. Smythe, M.C., G.S.O. III 8th Division,
    Chevalier of the Legion of Honour.
Capt. W. E. Stevens, M.C., Adj. 1/ Worcestershire,
    Croix de Guerre and Gold Star.
Lieut. W. Leslie-Carter, 490 Field Company R.E. (T.F.),
    Croix de Guerre and Palm.
Sergt. W. Millis, 5th Battery, R.F.A.,
    Croix de Guerre and Gold Star.
Gnr. R. Sowerbutts, 5th Battery, R.F.A.,
    Croix de Guerre and Palm.
Actg.-Sergt. R. Clarke, 2nd Field Company, R.E.,
    Croix de Guerre and Palm.
Sergt. J. A. Berry, M.M.P. 8th Division,
    Croix de Guerre and Bronze Star.

Two battalions of the 25th Infantry Brigade furnished the Guard of Honour, under command of Brig.-General Hon. R. Brand, D.S.O., and the 25th Field Ambulance was also on parade.

On the 15th March 1919 General Heneker left the division, on appointment to the command of the Southern Division in the Army of the Rhine. What he thought of the division he had

---

* The following translation of Marshal Petain's Order of the Day explains the circumstances in which this honour was won:

"From the 22nd to the 25th of October 1918, in a town (St. Amand-les-Eaux) violently bombarded by the enemy, all ranks of this Field Ambulance under the command of Lieut.-Colonel R. Burgess continued with unsurpassed devotion by day and by night to seek for wounded civilians in all parts of the town, to dress their wounds and administer to their comfort, and then send them back to safety. Under conditions of great difficulty they performed immediate operations in urgent cases, and in the course of their work of mercy successfully evacuated about 2,000 wounded, sick, or disabled persons, after having attended to their immediate needs.

"GENERAL HEADQUARTERS, 19 Nov. 1918."

GENERAL HENEKER'S FAREWELL

so long and ably commanded and of the quality of the troops of which it was composed can best be given in his own words:

"I have been in command of the division for nearly two years and during that time the division has passed through many vicissitudes.

"Soon after assuming command, we carried out a very successful attack at Bouchavesnes just North of the Somme, and had the good fortune to follow it up and to take part in the inspiriting advance of some 25 miles which ended in front of the Hindenburg Line East of Gouzeaucourt and Gonnelieu. Then being moved North into Second Army, we remained in Reserve during the successful operations which resulted in the capture of Messines and Wytschaete.

"Moving North again into Fifth Army, we took part in the heavy fighting of July and August about Hooge and Westhoek, where the division earned not only the thanks of the Commander-in-Chief, but also a personal visit from him.

"A short time was spent in the Ploegsteert area, and then we moved up to Ypres where we, on and off through the winter of 1917/1918, held the Passchendaele Salient.

"Pulled out for training during the month of March 1918, we were suddenly rushed South and thrown into the retreat from the Somme where the division covered itself with glory. Withdrawn to re-fit, we were sent to the Aisne for a rest, and came in for the punishing retreat on that front, where we lost very heavily. Between the 21st March and 15th June our casualties amounted to just over 17,500 all ranks.

"Finally we were fortunate in helping to push back the Germans during the operations which closed on the 11th November.

"During all this time, in offence as well as in defence, I have watched with admiration the wonderful spirit which pervaded all ranks. Neither the winter wind of the Passchendaele Salient nor the sleepless days and nights of the retreats on the Somme and the Aisne appeared able to destroy the cheerfulness, or diminish the marvellous devotion to duty which was displayed by officers and men.

"I have come out of the war with one conviction at all events, and this is that the finest man on God's earth is the British Private Soldier."

*   *   *   *   *

The long course had been run and won. If, as they waited their turn to leave the western theatre of war, any of the men of the 8th Division fought over again in mess-room or canteen the battles in which they had taken part, it must have seemed to many of them that their division had had all the worst of the

VICTORY

going. In four years of war it had always been on the outskirts of our successes, ever in the storm centre of our misfortunes. No division had seen harder or more constant fighting; none had suffered more terrific punishment, yet maintained to the final moment of victory a better discipline and more splendid fighting spirit.

It is in such a story as that which forms the record of the 8th Division in the Great War that the finest qualities of British character are best exemplified; courage and patience in adversity, an utter inability to admit defeat, a determination triumphing over every obstacle. Twice the enemy thought that he had knocked out the British Army, after Mons and after the 1918 battles of the Somme and the Lys. On both occasions he was mistaken, and the mistakes cost him the war. The marvellous resilience and recuperative power of the British soldier, which turned the scale in favour of the Allies in the battle of the Marne and drove the enemy from Amiens to Mons, is the outstanding lesson of this outline of the deeds of the 8th Division.

Let no old member of the 8th Division think, because it fell to other divisions directly to exploit the final collapse of the enemy resistance, that the efforts of his own division had no share in their success. We were engaged with a powerful and fully-organized opponent whose strength could not be broken down save by the opposition of a greater and more lasting resolution than his own. In such a war there could be no short cuts to victory. The full price had to be paid.

Neither the course of the war itself nor the splendour of the part which the 8th Division played in it can properly be understood unless the long-drawn contest is looked at as a whole. Then it can be seen that even on the days of its greatest misfortunes, such as the 1st July 1916, no less than on the days of its most glorious achievements, as in the heroic stand at Rosières, the 8th Division was helping steadily and essentially to build up the structure of our ultimate success.

" If the operations of the past four and a half years," runs Lord Haig's final dispatch, " are regarded as a single continuous campaign, there can be recognized in them the same general features and the same necessary stages which between forces of approximately equal strength have marked all the conclusive battles of history. There is in the first instance the preliminary stage of the campaign in which the opposing forces seek to deploy and manœuvre for position, endeavouring while doing so to gain some early advantage which might be pushed home to a quick decision. This phase came to an end in the present war with the creation of continuous trench lines from the Swiss frontier to the sea.

THE TRUE PERSPECTIVE

"Battle having been joined, there follows the real struggle in which the main forces of the two belligerent armies are pitted against each other in close and costly combat. . . . In this stage of the wearing-out struggle losses will necessarily be heavy on both sides, for in it the price of victory is paid. If the opposing forces are approximately equal in numbers, in courage, in morale and in equipment there is no way of avoiding payment of the price or of eliminating this phase of the struggle.

"In former battles this stage of the conflict has rarely lasted more than a few days and has often been completed in a few hours. When armies of millions are engaged, with the resources of great empires behind them, it will inevitably be long. It will include violent crises of fighting which, when viewed separately or apart from the general perspective, will appear individually as great indecisive battles. To this stage belong the great engagements of 1916 and 1917 which wore down the strength of the German armies.

"Finally, whether from the superior fighting ability and leadership of one of the belligerents, as the result of greater resources or tenacity, or by reason of higher moral, or from a combination of all these causes, the time will come when the other side will begin to weaken and the climax of the battle is reached. Then the commander of the weaker side must choose whether he will break off the engagement, if he can, while there is yet time, or stake on a supreme effort what reserves remain to him. The launching and destruction of Napoleon's last reserves at Waterloo was a matter of minutes. In this World War the great sortie of the beleaguered German Armies, commenced on the 21st March 1918, lasted for four months, yet it represents a corresponding stage in a single colossal battle.

"The breaking of such a supreme effort will be the signal for the commander of the successful side to develop his greatest strength, and seek to turn to immediate account the loss in material and moral which their failure must inevitably produce among his opponent's troops. In a battle joined and decided in the course of a few days or hours, there is no risk that the lay observer will seek to distinguish the culminating operations by which victory is seized and exploited from the preceding stages by which it has been made possible and determined. If the whole operations of the present war are regarded in correct perspective the victories of the summer and autumn of 1918 will be seen to be directly dependent upon the two years of stubborn fighting preceding them."

No troops had a larger share in the stubborn and relentless fighting, not of two years only but of nearer four, than the men of the 8th Division. Time will recognize the worth of what they

VICTORY

did. It was the fate of the 8th Division to take part in each of the early British offensives in which, during the first two years, we were learning by bitter and costly experience the art of modern war; and then in the latter and fiercer stages of the struggle to be called upon constantly to stem, with its body and blood, all the most violent and most dangerous of the final German offensives.

Only the possession of a spirit of endurance beyond the ordinary and of a high tradition and strong *esprit de corps* could have enabled the 8th Division, overwhelmed as it might seem to be time and again, to assimilate new material and continually to recreate itself anew as a first-class fighting force. Despite all its trials and vicissitudes, the 8th Division, when the war finished, was at least as efficient and formidable a unit as that which crossed the Channel on that quiet autumn night of September 1914.

In the stern years between, of no division could it be more truly said that it had proved itself able " To defy Power which seems omnipotent." No division had more surely shown that it possessed the courage

" to hope till hope creates
From its own wreck the thing it contemplates."

APPENDICES

APPENDIX I

COMPOSITION OF HEADQUARTERS

DATE OF ASSUMING DUTY

DIVISIONAL COMMANDER:

Maj.-Gen. F. J. Davies, C.B.	19th September 1914
Maj.-Gen. H. Hudson, C.B., C.I.E.	1st August 1915
Maj.-Gen. W. C. G. Heneker, D.S.O., A.D.C.	9th December 1916

INFANTRY BRIGADE COMMANDERS:

23 Infantry Brigade

Brig.-Gen. R. J. Pinney	September 1914
„ T. E. Travers-Clarke	28th July 1915
„ H. D. Tuson, C.M.G.	8th September 1915
„ E. A. Fagan, D.S.O.	27th August 1916
„ G. W. St. G. Grogan, D.S.O.	12th March 1917

24 Infantry Brigade

Brig.-Gen. F. C. Carter	September 1914
„ R. S. Oxley	16th March 1915
„ A. J. F. Eden, D.S.O.	8th July 1916
„ H. W. Cobham, D.S.O.	14th January 1917
„ R. Haig, D.S.O.	24th November 1917
„ L. M. Stevens, D.S.O.	4th June 1918
„ R. O'H. Livesay, D.S.O.	6th September 1918

25 Infantry Brigade

Brig.-Gen. A. W. C. Lowry Cole, C.B., D.S.O.	September 1914
„ R. B. Stephens	9th May 1915
„ J. H. W. Pollard, C.M.G.	1st April 1916
„ C. Coffin, D.S.O.	11th January 1917
„ R. H. Husey, D.S.O., M.C.	8th May 1918
„ J. B. Pollok McCall, C.M.G., D.S.O.	3rd June 1918
„ Hon. R. Brand, D.S.O.	9th October 1918

*70 Infantry Brigade

Brig.-Gen. L. F. Philips, D.S.O.	(In command on transfer)
„ H. Gordon, D.S.O.	8th November 1915

C.R.A.

Brig.-Gen. A. E. A. Holland, D.S.O., M.V.O.	1st October 1914
„ G. H. W. Nicholson, C.M.G.	21st July 1915
„ H. G. Lloyd, D.S.O.	3rd January 1917
„ J. W. F. Lamont, C.M.G., D.S.O.	19th March 1918

* From the 22nd October 1915 until the 16th June 1916 the 24th Infantry Brigade was transferred temporarily to the 23rd Division and its place in the 8th Division during this period was taken by the 70th Infantry Brigade.

APPENDIX I

C.R.E.   DATE OF ASSUMING DUTY

Lieut.-Col. W. H. Rotherham	November 1914
,, P. G. Grant, C.B., C.M.G.	January 1915
,, F. G. Guggisberg, C.M.G., D.S.O.	December 1915
Major A. H. Brown, D.S.O., M.C.	22nd July 1916
Lieut.-Col. C. M. Browne, C.M.G., D.S.O.	6th September 1916
,, D. S. Collins, D.S.O.	April 1917
,, C. M. Browne, C.M.G., D.S.O.	May 1917
,, C. Russell-Brown, D.S.O.	9th November 1918

G.S.O.1.

Bvt. Lieut.-Col. W. H. Anderson, *p.s.c.*	22nd September 1914
,, ,, H. Hill, D.S.O., M.V.O.	27th October 1915
,, ,, R. E. H. James	17th September 1916
Lieut.-Col. E. H. L. Beddington, M.C., *p.s.c.*	30th November 1916
,, H. S. Adair, D.S.O.	14th December 1917
Bvt. Lt.-Col. C. C. Armitage, D.S.O., *p.s.c.*	28th February 1918
Lieut.-Col. A. G. B. Bourne, D.S.O., M.V.O., *p.s.c.*	14th June 1918

G.S.O.2.

Major G. V. Hordern, *p.s.c.*	27th September 1914
Lieut.-Col. R. St. G. Gorton, *p.s.c.*	16th December 1914
Major H. A. Walker, D.S.O., *p.s.c.*	15th June 1915
,, O. H. L. Nicholson, D.S.O., *p.s.c*	22nd October 1915
,, J. C. Freeland	12th March 1916
,, D. F. Anderson, D.S.O.	15th January 1917
,, G. W. Geddes, D.S.O.	19th July 1917
Capt. J. H. T. Priestman	21st July 1917
,, R. M. Weeks, D.S.O., M.C.	24th March 1918
,, G. R. P. Roupell, V.C.	9th May 1918
Major E. O. Sewell, M.C.	30th June 1918

G.S.O.3.

Capt. H. E. R. R. Braine, *p.s.c.*	15th September 1914
,, W. W. T. Torr	23rd May 1915
,, P. Neame, V.C., D.S.O.	11th October 1915
,, G. I. Gartlan, M.C.	4th February 1916
,, A. A. H. Hanbury-Sparrow, D.S.O.	22nd May 1916
,, E. H. Smythe, M.C.	15th October 1916
,, R. W. Brooke, M.C. (T.F.)	26th November 1916
,, E. H. Smythe, M.C.	22nd April 1918

A.A. and Q.M.G.

Bvt. Lieut.-Col. A. R. Hoskins, D.S.O., *p.s.c.*	19th September 1914
Lieut.-Col. H. M. de F. Montgomery, D.S.O., *p.s.c.*	12th November 1914

APPENDIX I

A.A. and Q.M.G. (contd.)

DATE OF ASSUMING DUTY

Lieut.-Col. P. P. de B. Radcliffe, D.S.O., *p.s.c.*	22nd March 1915
Bvt. Lieut.-Col. H. L. Alexander, D.S.O., *p.s.c.*	19th July 1915
Lieut.-Col. R. Q. Crauford, *p.s.c.*	15th October 1916
„ Viscount R. E. A. Feilding, D.S.O.	25th February 1917
„ Hon. P. G. Scarlett, M.C.	3rd November 1918

D.A.A.G.

Major R. F. Uniacke, *p.s.c.*	19th September 1914
„ F. D. Logan, *p.s.c.*	2nd March 1915
Capt. Hon. P. G. Scarlett	29th August 1915
„ H. Ramsbotham, M.C.	30th August 1917

D.A.Q.M.G.

Capt. H. L. Alexander, *p.s.c.*	19th September 1914
Major A. G. Pratt	31st May 1915
„ C. J. B. Daubeny	17th April 1916
„ L. D. Luard	3rd February 1917
Capt. F. R. Burnside, D.S.O.	19th May 1917
„ E. C. Nicholson, M.C.	7th March 1918
Major D. L. Gray, M.C.	14th April 1918

APPENDIX II
ORDERS OF BATTLE*

Showing principal changes in the composition of the division.

(The absence of the name of a Commanding Officer in the date column indicates that the unit concerned did not form part of the division at that date.)

23 *Infantry Brigade.*	4th November 1914.	25th September 1915.	1st July 1916.
Commander	Brig.-Gen. R. J. Pinney	Brig.-Gen. H. D. Tuson	Brig.-Gen. H. D. Tuson
Brigade Major	Capt. L. F. Renny	Major W. B. F. Rayner	Major W. B. F. Rayner, D.S.O.
Staff Captain	Lieut. V. A. H. Daly	Capt. J. C. Blackburn	Major H. Eardley-Wilmot
2/ Devonshire	Lieut.-Col. J. O. Travers, D.S.O.	Lieut.-Col. J. O. Travers, C.M.G., D.S.O.	Lieut.-Col. A. J. E. Sunderland
2/ West Yorkshire	Lieut.-Col. G. F. Phillips	Lieut.-Col. T. P. Barrington	Lieut.-Col. L. Hume-Spry, D.S.O.
2/ Scottish Rifles	Lieut.-Col. W. M. Bliss	Lieut.-Col. V. C. Sandilands	Lieut.-Col. V. C. Sandilands, D.S.O.
2/ Middlesex	Lieut.-Col. R. H. Hayes	Lieut.-Col. R. H. Hayes, C.M.G.	Lieut.-Col. E. T. F. Sandys
1/7 Middlesex	—	Lieut.-Col. E. J. King	(to 56th Division, Feb. 1916)

23 *Infantry Brigade (contd.)*.	17th March 1917.	23rd March 1918.	11th November 1918.
Commander	Brig.-Gen. E. A. Fagan, D.S.O.	Brig.-Gen. G. W. St. G. Grogan, C.M.G., D.S.O.	Brig.-Gen. G. W. St. G. Grogan, V.C. C.M.G., D.S.O.
Brigade Major	Capt. F. C. Roberts, D.S.O.	Major P. C. Vellacott, D.S.O.	Capt. H. T. T. Harris
Staff Captain	Capt. F. A. Vernon	Capt. P. A. Ledward	Capt. H. A. Slade, M.C.
2/ Devonshire	Lieut.-Col. A. J. E. Sunderland	Major A. H. Cope	Lieut.-Col. G. E. R. Prior, M.C.

	4th November 1914.	25th September 1915.	1st July 1916.
2/ West Yorkshire	Lieut.-Col. J. L. Jack	Lieut.-Col. A. E. E. Lowry, M.C. (to 20th Division, Feb. 1918)	Lieut.-Col. A. T. Champion
2/ Scottish Rifles	Lieut.-Col. C. R. H. Stirling, M.C.	—	—
2/ Middlesex	Lieut.-Col. J. H. Hall, D.S.O.	Lieut.-Col. C. A. S. Page, M.C.	Lieut.-Col. E. E. F. Baker, M.C.

24 Infantry Brigade.

	4th November 1914.	25th September 1915.	1st July 1916.
Commander	Brig.-Gen. F. C. Carter, C.B.	Brig.-Gen. R. S. Oxley	—
Brigade Major	Capt. J. E. Turner	Major R. M. Luckock, D.S.O.	—
Staff Captain	Capt. W. V. Hume	Capt. F. St. J. Tyrwhitt	—
1/ Worcestershire	Lieut.-Col. A. E. Lascelles	Lieut.-Col. G. W. St. G. Grogan	—
2/ East Lancashire	Lieut.-Col. C. L. Nicholson	Lieut.-Col. G. E. M. Hill	—
1/ Sherwood Foresters	Col. W. R. Marshall	Lieut.-Col. R. L. Sherbrooke	—
2/ Northamptonshire	Lieut.-Col. C. S. Prichard, D.S.O.	Lieut.-Col. A. C. Buckle	—
5/ Black Watch	—	Lieut.-Col. H. F. Blair-Imrie, C.M.G. (to 51st Division Feb. 1916)	—

24 Infantry Brigade (contd.).

	17th March 1917.	23rd March 1918.	11th November 1918.
Commander	Brig.-Gen. H. W. Cobham, D.S.O.	Brig.-Gen. R. Haig, D.S.O.	Brig.-Gen. R. O'H. Livesay, D.S.O.
Brigade Major	Capt. A. Holmes-Scott, M.C.	Capt. F. C. Wallace, M.C.	Capt. F. C. Wallace, D.S.O., M.C.
Staff Captain	Capt. F. C. Wallace	Capt. T. B. J. Mahar, M.C.	Capt. N. Marshall
1/ Worcestershire	Lieut.-Col. G. W. St. G. Grogan, C.M.G.	Lieut.-Col. F. C. Roberts, D.S.O., M.C.	Lieut.-Col. F. C. Roberts, V.C., D.S.O., M.C.
2/ East Lancashire	Lieut.-Col. G. E. M. Hill, D.S.O.	(to 25th Inf. B'de, Feb. 1918)	—
1/ Sherwood Foresters	Lieut.-Col. R. L. Sherbrooke	Lieut.-Col. T. H. Watson, M.C.	Lieut.-Col. J. D. Mitchell, D.S.O.
2/ Northamptonshire	Lieut.-Col. C. C. Buckle, M.C.	Lieut.-Col. S. G. Latham, M.C.	Lieut.-Col. S. S. Hayne, D.S.O.

* For divisional commanders and staff, see previous Table, Composition of Headquarters.

25 Infantry Brigade.

	4th November 1914.	25th September 1915.	1st July 1916.
Commander	Brig.-Gen. A. W. G. Lowry Cole, C.B., D.S.O.	Brig.-Gen. R. B. Stephens	Brig.-Gen. J. H. W. Pollard, C.M.G.
Brigade Major	Capt. J. G. Dill	Capt. G. D. Pike	Capt. H. Lloyd
Staff Captain	Capt. H. E. Franklyn	Capt. E. P. Lloyd	Capt. H. N. Swann
2/ Lincolnshire	Lieut.-Col. G. B. McAndrew	Lieut.-Col. S. FitzG. Cox	Lieut.-Col. R. Bastard, D.S.O.
2/ Royal Berkshire	Lieut.-Col. E. Feetham	Lieut.-Col. G. P. S. Hunt	Lieut.-Col. A. M. Holdsworth
1/ Royal Irish Rifles	Lieut.-Col. G. B. Laurie	Lieut.-Col. R. A. C. Daunt, D.S.O.	Lieut.-Col. R. A. C. Daunt, D.S.O.
2/ Rifle Brigade	Lieut.-Col. R. B. Stephens	Lieut.-Col. F. H. Nugent	Lieut.-Col. Hon. R. Brand, D.S.O.
1/8 Middlesex	—	Lieut.-Col. E. D. W. Gregory	(to 56th Division, Feb. 1916)
1/1 London	—	Lieut.-Col. E. G. Mercer	(to 56th Division, Feb. 1916)

25 Infantry Brigade (contd.).

	17th March 1917.	23rd March 1918.	11th November 1918.
Commander	Brig.-Gen. C. Coffin, D.S.O.	Brig.-Gen. C. Coffin, V.C., D.S.O.	Brig.-Gen. Hon. R. Brand, D.S.O.
Brigade Major	Capt. N. P. Birley	Capt. B. C. Pascoe, M.C.	Capt. R. B. Stones, M.C.
Staff Captain	Capt. D. L. Gray	Capt. L. S. Greening, M.C.	Capt. H. E. Seth-Smith, M.C.
2/ East Lancashire	—	Major D. W. Hollingsworth	Lieut.-Col. H. J. Miers
2/ Lincolnshire	Lieut.-Col. R. Bastard, D.S.O.	(to 21st Division, Feb. 1918)	—
2/ Royal Berkshire	Lieut.-Col. R. Haig, D.S.O.	Lieut.-Col. C. R. H. Stirling, D.S.O., M.C.	Lieut.-Col. A. G. F. Isaac, M.C.
1/ Royal Irish Rifles	Lieut.-Col. E. C. Lloyd	(to 36th Division, Feb. 1918)	
2/ Rifle Brigade	Lieut.-Col. Hon. R. Brand, D.S.O.	Lieut.-Col. H. S. C. Peyton, M.C.	Lieut.-Col. T. R. Eastwood, M.C.

70 Infantry Brigade.	4th November 1914.	25th September 1915.	1st July 1916.
Commander	—	—	Brig.-Gen. H. Gordon, D.S.O.
Brigade Major	—	—	Major W. C. Wilson, D.S.O.
Staff Captain	—	—	Capt. E. R. A. C. Cox
11/Sherwood Foresters	—	—	Lieut.-Col. H. F. Watson, D.S.O.
8/K.O.Y.L.I.	—	—	Lieut.-Col. H. E. Trevor, D.S.O.
8/York & Lancaster	—	—	Lieut.-Col. M. L. Hornby, D.S.O.
9/York & Lancaster	—	—	Lieut.-Col. A. J. B. Addison

Mounted Troops.	4th November 1914.	25th September 1915.	1st July 1916.
Northamptonshire Yeo'ry	Lieut.-Col. H. Wickham		
"A" Squadron	Capt. G. G. Middleton	—	—
"B" Squadron	Capt. Sir C. B. Lowther, Bt. (to Corps Troops)	—	—
"C" Squadron	Capt. Miller		
Cyclist Company	Capt. R. M. Heath, D.S.O.	—	—

Artillery.	4th November 1914.	25th September 1915.	1st July 1916.
C.R.A.	Brig.-Gen. A. E. A. Holland, M.V.O., D.S.O.	Brig.-Gen. G. H. W. Nicholson, C.M.G.	Brig.-Gen. G. H. W. Nicholson, C.M.G.
Brigade Major	Capt. R. H. Johnson	Major C. R. Gover	Major C. R. Gover
Staff Captain	Capt. V. Asser	Capt. F. E. Spencer	Capt. K. S. Hunter

Artillery (contd.).	4th November 1914.	25th September 1915.	1st July 1916.
V Brigade R.H.A.	Lieut.-Col. H. C. C. Uniacke	Lieut.-Col. A. T. Butler	Lieut.-Col. A. T. Butler, C.M.G.
"G" Battery	Major H. M. Davson	(to 3rd Cavalry Division, Nov. 1914)	(to Army Brigade, Jan. 1917)
"O" Battery	Major N. E. Tilney	Major W. Stirling	Capt. J. T. Wallace
"Z" Battery	Major E. H. H. Elliot	Major E. H. H. Elliot	Major Sir T. P. Larcomb, Bt.
"D" How. Battery	—	—	—
Amm. Column	Capt. E. M. D. H. Cooke	—	Capt. H. E. Barkworth
XXXIII Brigade R.F.A.	Lieut.-Col. L. Graham	Col. L. Graham, C.M.G.	Lieut.-Col. T. St. A. B. L. Nevinson
32 Battery	Major W. Stirling	Capt. R. Archer-Houblon	Capt. R. Archer-Houblon
33 Battery	Major L. C. L. Oldfield	Major L. C. L. Oldfield, D.S.O.	Major W. V. Packe, D.S.O.
36 Battery	Major D. B. Stewart	Major C. T. S. Paul	Major C. T. S. Paul
55 Battery	—	—	Major W. E. Duncan, M.C.
Amm. Column	Capt. C. T. S. Paul	—	—
XLV Brigade R.F.A.	Lieut.-Col. A. H. S. Goff	Lieut.-Col. A. H. S. Goff, C.M.G.	Lieut.-Col. H. W. Hill
1 Battery	Major A. E. M. Head	Major A. E. M. Head	Major C. B. Rich
3 Battery	Major C. F. P. Parry	Major N. P. R. Preeston	Major M. M. Magrath
5 Battery	Major C. B. Thackeray	Major C. B. Thackeray	Major J. M. Moore
57 Battery	—	—	Major E. Sherlock
Amm. Column	Capt. R. A. Thomas	—	—
CXXVIII How. Bde. R.F.A.		Major J. O. Seagram	(broken up, May 1916)
55 Battery	—	Major H. C. Simpson	—
57 Battery	—	Major H. A. W. Webber	—

	17th March 1917.	23rd March 1918.	11th November 1918.
Heavy Artillery Brigade	Lieut.-Col. H. de T. Phillips	—	—
118 Battery	Major F. A. Twiss	—	—
119 Battery	Lieut.-Col. C. L. Hickling	—	—
Div. Amm. Column	Lieut.-Col. F. A. Elton	Col. F. W. Boteler	Col. F. W. Boteler

Artillery (contd.).	17th March 1917.	23rd March 1918.	11th November 1918.
C.R.A.	Brig.-Gen. H. G. Lloyd, D.S.O.	Brig.-Gen. J. W. F. Lamont, C.M.G., D.S.O.	Brig.-Gen. J. W. F. Lamont, C.M.G., D.S.O.
Brigade Major	Major C. R. Gover, D.S.O.	Major H. G. Lee Warner, D.S.O., M.C.	Major W. E. Duncan, M.C.
Staff Captain	Capt. K. S. Hunter	Capt. C. E. Venning	Capt. T. F. Monks, M.C.
XXXIII Brigade R.F.A.	Lieut.-Col. T. St. A. B. L. Nevinson	Lieut.-Col. H. G. Fisher, D.S.O.	Lieut.-Col. D. E. Forman, C.M.G.
32 Battery	Major T. H. Davison	Major A. G. F. Ramsden	Major H. F. Buckley
33 Battery	Major C. F. T. Lindsay	Major C. F. T. Lindsay	Major O. F. Herold
36 Battery	Major C. T. S. Paul, D.S.O.	Major N. Southern	Major J. Wedderburn-Maxwell, M.C.
55 Battery	Major W. E. Duncan, M.C.	Capt. R. L. Palmer, M.C.	Major H. T. Michelmore, M.C.
XLV Brigade R.F.A.	Lieut.-Col. C. A. H. Campbell	Major C. W. Cripps, D.S.O.	Lieut.-Col. C. B. Thackeray, D.S.O.
1 Battery	Major S. D. Bulteel	Capt. E. H. Wenham	Major H. B. Taylor
3 Battery	Major M. M. Magrath	Major D'A. V. Carden, D.S.O.	Major C. W. Cripps, D.S.O.
5 Battery	Major H. E. Barkworth	Major J. C. Griffiths, M.C.	Major J. C. Griffiths, M.C.
57 Battery	Major E. Sherlock, M.C.	Major R. M. Wilkinson-Jones, M.C.	Major H. C. Terry
Div. Amm. Column	Col. F. W. Boteler	Capt. C. E. Vivian, M.C. (acting)	Major T. H. Davison, M.C.

Trench Mortar Batteries	17th March 1917.	23rd March 1918.	11th November 1918.
Div. T.M. Officer	Capt. W. G. J. Walker, M.C.	Capt. T. Wingate, M.C.	Capt. C. G. Higgins, M.C.
Heavy			
W/8 T.M. Battery	Capt. G. H. Morris	Capt. G. R. P. Brown	—
Medium			
X/8 T.M. Battery	Lieut. R. L. C. Brown	Lieut. C. H. Haskins	Capt. R. A. Darling
Y/8 T.M. Battery	Lieut. C. Ellis	Lieut. L. F. Stamp	Capt. S. L. Bibby
Z/8 T.M. Battery	Lieut. G. R. P. Brown	Lieut. A. J. Mack	—
Light			
23rd T.M. Battery	Capt. T. B. Duncan	Capt. J. C. Holberton	Capt. H. Woodward
24th T.M. Battery	Capt. P. B. M. Powell	Capt. W. B. Greensmith	Capt. R. E. Barringer
25th T.M. Battery	Capt. A. C. Taylor	Capt. C. J. Olive	Capt. H. K. Honey

Engineers	4th November 1914.	25th September 1915.	1st July 1916.
C.R.E.	Lieut.-Col. W. H. Rotherham	Lieut.-Col. P. G. Grant	Lieut.-Col. F. G. Guggisberg, C.M.G.
2 Field Company	Major C. E. G. Vesey	Capt. A. H. Brown	Major A. H. Brown
15 Field Company	Capt. P. K. Betty	Major P. K. Betty, D.S.O.	Capt. C. V. Strong
490 Field Company	—	Major C. C. Bryan	Major C. C. Bryan, D.S.O.
8 Signal Company	Capt. O. M. T. Frost	Major O. M. T. Frost	Major O. M. T. Frost
22/ D.L.I. (Pioneers)			
	—	—	Lieut.-Col. C. B. Morgan, D.S.O.
Divisional Train	Lieut.-Col. A. K. Seccombe, D.S.O.	Lieut.-Col. C. R. I. Hull	Lieut.-Col. C. R. I. Hull

Engineers (contd.).	4th November 1914.	17th March 1917.	23rd March 1918.	11th November 1918.
C.R.E.		Lieut.-Col. C. M. Browne, C.M.G.	Lieut.-Col. C. M. Browne, C.M.G., D.S.O.	Lieut.-Col. C. Russell-Brown, D.S.O.
2 Field Company		Major A. H. Brown, M.C.	Major A. H. Brown, D.S.O, M.C.	Major J. H. F. Kendall
15 Field Company		Capt. G. Lambert, M.C.	Major R. M. Taylor	Major L. Napier
490 Field Company		Major C. C. Bryan, D.S.O.	Major D. L. Herbert, M.C.	Major L. C. Chasey, M.C.
8 Signal Company		Capt. V. A. C. Clery, M.C.	Major H. C. Crone, M.C.	Major H. C. Crone, M.C.
22/ D.L.I. (Pioneers)		Lieut.-Col. C. B. Morgan, D.S.O.	Lieut.-Col. C. B. Morgan, D.S.O.	—
1/7 D.L.I. (Pioneers)		—	—	Lieut.-Col. J. S. Turcan, M.C.
8 Battalion M.G.C.		—	Lieut.-Col. R. L. Sherbrooke, D.S.O.	Lieut.-Col. J. Angell, M.C.
Divisional Train		Lieut.-Col. C. R. I. Hull, D.S.O.	Lieut.-Col. C. R. I. Hull, D.S.O.	Lieut.-Col. C. R. I. Hull, D.S.O.

Medical Units, etc.	4th November 1914.	25th September 1915.	1st July 1916.	
A.D.M.S.	Col. J. Meek, M.D.	Col. H. N. Dunn, M.B.	Col. H. N. Dunn, M.B.	
24 Field Ambulance	Lieut.-Col. R. Pickard, M.D.	Lieut.-Col. R. Pickard, M.D.	Lieut.-Col. R. Pickard, C.M.G.	
25 Field Ambulance	Lieut.-Col. A. B. Soltau, M.D.	Lieut.-Col. A. B. Soltau, M.D.	Lieut.-Col. A. B. Soltau, C.M.G.	
26 Field Ambulance	Major A. Milne-Thompson	Lieut.-Col. A. Milne-Thompson	Lieut.-Col. A. Milne-Thompson, C.M.G.	
D.A.D.V.S.	Major P. J. Harris	Major P. J. Harris	Major P. J. Harris	
D.A.D.O.S.	Capt. E. M. De Smidt	Major E. Sigrist	Capt. K. C. Greig	
D.A.P.M.	Capt. B. Cartland	Capt. F. Fane	Capt. F. Fane	

Medical Units, etc, (contd.).	17th March 1917.	23rd March 1918.	11th November 1918.
A.D.M.S.	Col. H. N. Dunn, D.S.O., M.B.	Col. G. J. A. Ormsby, D.S.O.	Col. A. M. Maclaughlin
24 Field Ambulance	Lieut.-Col. R. Pickard, C.M.G.	Lieut.-Col. R. Burgess, M.C.	Lieut.-Col. R. Burgess, M.C.
25 Field Ambulance	Lieut.-Col. T. P. Puddicombe	Lieut.-Col. T. P. Puddicombe, D.S.O.	Lieut.-Col. T. P. Puddicombe, D.S.O.
26 Field Ambulance	Lieut.-Col. A. Milne Thompson, C.M.G.	Lieut.-Col. E. Alderson, D.S.O.	Lieut.-Col. E. Alderson, D.S.O.
D.A.D.V.S.	Major H. Bone	Major H. Bone	Major H. Bone, M.C.
D.A.D.O.S.	Capt. K. C. Greig	Capt. H. S. Chaplin	Major H. S. Chaplin
D.A.P.M.	Capt. H. S. Mortimer	Capt. H. S. Mortimer	Capt. H. S. Mortimer
Divisional Gas Officer	Capt. C. R. Stott	Capt. W. H. Perkins	Capt. L. E. Fisker

APPENDIX III

TABLE OF SECTORS, ENGAGEMENTS AND CASUALTIES

Period in Line.	Corps.	Sector.	Engagements.		Casualties.	
					Officers.	Other Ranks.
12/11/14 to 25/3/15	IV	Rue du Bois—Tilleloy	18/12/14	Operation opposite Neuve Chapelle	17	240
			10/3/15	Neuve Chapelle	218	4,616
				Casualties in line	91	3,289
27/3/15 to 29/6/15	IV Indian	Fleurbaix	9/5/15	Fromelles	192	4,298
				Casualties in line	56	1,186
30/6/15 to 24/11/15	III	Picantin—Le Bridoux	25/9/15	Bois Grenier	56	1,342
				Casualties in line	56	1,262
12/1/16 to 27/3/16	III	Fleurbaix		Casualties in line	44	728
5/4/16 to 2/7/16	II & III	La Boisselle—Thiepval	1/7/16	First Somme Battle	216	5,208
				Casualties in line	83	1,506
15/7/16 to 12/10/16	I	Cuinchy, Hohenzollern, The Quarries, Hulluch		Casualties in line	95	1,662
19/10/16 to 31/10/16	XIV	Les Bœufs—Gueudecourt	23/10/16	Le Transloy	109	2,372
8/11/16 to 18/11/16	XIV	Les Bœufs		Casualties in line	29	754
30/12/16 to 10/1/17	XV	Priez and Saillisel		Casualties in line	7	162
27/1/17 to 11/2/17	XV	Bouchavesnes and Rancourt		Casualties in line	18	232
21/2/17 to 7/3/17	XV	Bouchavesnes and Rancourt	4/3/17	Bouchavesnes	56	1,081
8/3/17 to 15/5/17	XV	Quarry Farm—Rancourt and advance to Gonnelieu		The German Retreat, 1917	89	1,786

TABLE OF SECTORS, ENGAGEMENTS AND CASUALTIES—*continued*.

Period in Line.	Corps.	Sector.	Engagements.		Casualties.	
					Officers.	Other Ranks.
15/6/17 to 11/7/17	II	Menin Road		Casualties in line	75	1,550
23/7/17 to 2/8/17	II	Menin Road	31/7/17	Ypres, 1917; Westhoek	160	3,005
12/8/17 to 19/8/17	II	Westhoek Ridge	16/8/17	Ypres, 1917; The Hanebeek	81	2,074
27/8/17 to 14/11/17	II Anzac / VIII	Ploegsteert		Casualties in line	22	345
17/11/17 to 3/12/17	VIII	Passchendaele	2/12/17	Ypres, 1917; Southern Redoubt	47	933
					186	2,444
27/12/17 to 19/1/18	VIII	Passchendaele		Casualties in line	16	283
11/2/18 to 8/3/18	VIII	Passchendaele		Casualties in line	12	379
23/3/18 to 2/4/18	XIX	Somme river	Second Somme Battle		250	4,693
20/4/18 to 27/4/18	III	Villers-Bretonneux	23/4/18	Villers-Bretonneux	133	3,420
13/5/18 to 8/6/18	IX	Berry-au-Bac		Casualties in line	7	97
			27/5/18	The Aisne, 1918	366	7,496
23/7/18 to 5/11/18	VIII	Vimy Ridge }		Casualties in line	1	34
9/11/18 to 11/11/18	VIII	Condé—Hergnies }	The Advance to Mons		139	2,454
			Total Casualties		2,927	60,931

APPENDIX IV

HONOURS AND AWARDS

(*Note.*—All possible pains have been taken to make this list, which comprises British Honours and Awards gained in service with the 8th Division, accurate and complete. Its composition, however, has entailed a search through lists containing the recommendations of all units of the British Armies in all theatres of the war, and the lists themselves disclose occasional inaccuracies. These have been checked and corrected wherever possible; but it is probable that certain of them have been passed over unobserved. The authors therefore apologise in advance for any omissions and mistakes which may be found herein.)

VICTORIA CROSS

2nd-Lieut. G. E. Cates, 2/ Rifle Brigade.
Brig.-General C. Coffin, D.S.O., R.E.
*Capt. T. R. Colyer-Fergusson, 2/ Northamptonshire.
C.S.M. H. Daniels, 2/ Rifle Brigade.
Brig.-General G. W. St. G. Grogan, C.M.G., D.S.O., Worcestershire R.
*Corpl. C. R. Noble, 2/ Rifle Brigade.
*Pte. J. Rivers, 1/ Sherwood Foresters.
Lieut.-Colonel F. C. Roberts, D.S.O., M.C., 1/ Worcestershire.
Corpl. C. Sharpe, 2/ Lincolnshire.
Capt. A. M. Toye, 2/ Middlesex.
Corpl. J. Upton, 1/ Sherwood Foresters.

KNIGHT COMMANDER OF THE BATH

Maj.-General F. J. Davies, C.B.
Maj.-General W. C. G. Heneker, C.B., D.S.O.

COMPANION OF THE BATH

Brig.-General Hon. R. Brand, D.S.O., Rifle Brigade.
Brig.-General G. W. St. G. Grogan, V.C., C.M.G., D.S.O. Worcestershire Regt.
Lieut.-Colonel R. H. Hayes, 2/ Middlesex.
Brig.-General A. E. A. Holland, M.V.O., D.S.O., R.A.
Brig.-General R. O'H. Livesay, D.S.O., R. West Surrey Regt.
Colonel J. Meek, M.D., R.A.M.C.
Brig.-General R. S. Oxley, Special List.
Lieut.-Colonel C. S. Pritchard, 2/ Northamptonshire.
Brig.-General H. C. C. Uniacke, R.A.

COMPANION OF ST. MICHAEL AND ST. GEORGE

Major H. F. Blair-Imrie, 1/5 Black Watch.
Lieut.-Colonel C. M. Browne, D.S.O., R.E.
Brig.-General T. E. Clarke, R. Inniskilling Fusiliers.
Maj.-General C. Coffin, V.C., D.S.O., R.E.
Major E. M. de Smidt, A.O.D.
Colonel H. N. Dunn, M.B., R.A.M.C.
Lieut.-Colonel C. Evans, R.F.A.
Lieut.-Colonel Viscount R. E. A. Feilding, D.S.O., Coldstream Gds.

* Posthumous.

APPENDIX IV

Lieut.-Colonel A. Fraser, 1/4 Scottish Rifles.
Lieut.-Colonel A. H. S. Goff, R.A.
Lieut.-Colonel L. Graham, R.A.
Lieut.-Colonel P. G. Grant, R.E.
Lieut.-Colonel G. W. St. G. Grogan, 1/ Worcestershire.
Lieut.-Colonel J. H. Hall, D.S.O. and bar, 2/ Middlesex.
Lieut.-Colonel M. L. Hornby, 8/ York and Lancaster.
Lieut.-Colonel G. P. S. Hunt, 2/ Royal Berkshire.
Lieut.-Colonel E. J. King, 1/7 Middlesex.
Lieut.-Colonel F. G. Lewis, 13/ London.
Brig.-General H. G. Lloyd, D.S.O., R.A.
Lieut.-Colonel E. G. Mercer, 1/ London.
Lieut.-Colonel J. D. Mitchell, D.S.O., Durham L.I.
Lieut.-Colonel A. Milne-Thompson, R.A.M.C.
Lieut.-Colonel C. B. Morgan, D.S.O., Durham L.I.
Lieut.-Colonel F. S. Penny, R.A.M.C.
Colonel H. de T. Phillips, R.A.
Lieut.-Colonel R. Pickard, R.A.M.C.
Lieut.-Colonel A. B. Soltau, R.A.M.C.
Brig.-General R. B. Stephens, Rifle Brigade.
Lieut.-Colonel J. O. Travers, D.S.O., 2/ Devonshire.
Lieut.-Colonel H. Wickham, Northamptonshire Yeo.

COMMANDER OF THE BRITISH EMPIRE

Brig.-General J. W. F. Lamont, C.M.G., D.S.O., R.A.

BAR TO DISTINGUISHED SERVICE ORDER

Lieut.-Colonel C.C.Armitage, R.A.
Lieut.-Colonel Hon. R. Brand, 2/ Rif. Brig.
Brig.-General C. Coffin, V.C., R.E.
Major C. W. Cripps, R.A.
Lieut.-Colonel G. M. C. Davidge, 1/ Worc.
Lieut.-Colonel H. G. Fisher, R.A.
Major H. T. Forster, M.C. and bar, R.A.
Major W. V. Franklin, 1/ Worc.
Brig.-General G. W. St. G. Grogan, C.M.G., Worc. R.
Lieut.-Colonel R. Haig, 2/R.Berks.
Lieut.-Colonel J. H. Hall, 2/ Midd'x.
Lieut.-Colonel A. A. H. Hanbury-Sparrow, M.C., 2/ R. Berks.
Lieut.-Colonel C. R. H. Stirling, M.C., 2/ R. Berks.

DISTINGUISHED SERVICE ORDER

Lieut.-Colonel E. Alderson, R.A.M.C.
Major H. L. Alexander, Dorset R.
Capt. G. H. G. Anderson, M.C., 2/ Rif. Brig.
Lieut.-Colonel J. Angell, M.C., M.G. Corps.
Capt. H. Archer, 2/ Devon.
Capt. R. Archer-Houblon, R.A.
Capt. J. H. M. Arden, 1/ Worc.
Lieut.-Colonel E. E. F. Baker, M.C., 2/ Midd'x.
Capt. R. Bastard, 2/ Linc.
Lieut.-Colonel E. H. L. Beddington, M.C., 16th Lancers.
Major P. K. Betty, R.E.
Capt. N.P. Birley, M.C., S. Staff. R.
Bvt.-Colonel F. W. Boteler, R.A.
Capt. R. W. Brooke, M.C., Yorks. D. Yeo.

APPENDIX IV

Major A. H. Brown, M.C., R.E.
Major C. C. Bryan, R.E.
Capt. C. B. Buckle, M.C., 2/ North'n.
Lieut.-Colonel R. Burgess, M.C., R.A.M.C.
Capt. U. B. Burke, 2/ Devon.
Major A. G. Cade, M.C. and bar, 2/ Midd'x.
Major d'A. V. Carden, R.A.
Major G. T. C. Carter-Campbell, 2/ Sco. Rif.
Capt. R. C. J. Chichester-Constable, 2/ Rif. Brig.
2nd Lieut. F. Colley, 9/ York and Lanc.
Lieut.-Colonel A. H. Cope, 2/ Devon.
Capt. E. R. C. Cox, M.G. 23rd Inf. Brig.
Capt. J. G. Dill, Leins. R.
Major C. D. Drew, 2/ Midd'x.
Bvt.-Major W. E. Duncan, M.C., R.A.
Lieut.-Colonel T. R. Eastwood, M.C. 2/ Rif. Brig.
Major J. Edwards, Sherw'd Frstrs.
Brig.-General E. A. Fagan, 36 Horse.
Capt. E. B. Ferrers, 2/ W. York.
Capt. Hon. B. M. O. S. Foljambe, 2/ W. York.
Lieut.-Colonel D. E. Forman, C.M.G., R.A.
Major J. W. Garden, M.C., M.G. Corps.
Major G. F. B. Goldney, R.E.
Major C. R. Gover, R.A.
Capt. F. R. W. Graham, R. Ir. Rif.
2nd Lieut. H. Greaves, M.C. and 2 bars, 1/ Sherw'd Frstrs.
Major J. A. A. Griffin, 2/ R. Berks.
Capt. L. A. Haldane, 2/ North'n.
Major C. C. H. Hall, 22/ Durh. L.I.
Capt. H. D. Harrington, 2/ W. York.
Capt. A. E. F. Harris, 2/ R. Berks.
Major R. L. Haynes, R.A.
Capt. E. J. Henderson, M.C., 2/ E. Lan.
Major G. E. M. Hill, 2/ E. Lan.
Lieut.-Colonel H. W. Hill, R.A.
Major E. W. Horne, 2/ Devon.
Lieut.-Colonel C. R. I. Hull, R.A.S.C.
Capt. C. H. M. Imbert-Terry, 2/ Devon.
Major P. L. Ingpen, 1/8 Midd'x.
Lieut.-Colonel N. M. S. Irwin, M.C., 2/ Linc.
Lieut.-Colonel A. G. F. Isaac, M.C., 2/R. Berks.
Major T. H. Ivey, 1/R. Ir. Rif.
Lieut.-Colonel J. L. Jack, 2/ W. York.
Capt. H. H. Jago, M.C. and bar, 2/ Devon.
Lieut.-Colonel H. St. J. Jefferies, 2/ W. York.
Major R. H. Johnson, R.A.
Lieut.-Colonel S. G. Latham, 2/ North'n.
Capt. R. B. Leslie, 2/ Linc.
Major H. Lloyd, North'n R.
Lieut.-Colonel A. E. E. Lowry, 2/ W. York.
Capt. R. M. Luckock, R. Lanc. R.
Lieut.-Colonel H. W. D. McCarthy-O'Leary, 1/R. Ir. Rif.
Capt. M. M. Magrath, R.A.
Capt. I. C. Maclean, M.D., M.C. and bar, R.A.M.C.
Major H. Maclear, 2/ E. Lan.
Capt. O. W. McSheehy, R.A.M.C.
Major A. D. N. Merriman, 1/ R. Ir. Rif.
Lieut.-Colonel H. J. Miers, 2/ E. Lan.
Capt. C. H. G. Mills, M.C. and bar, 1/ Sherw'd Frstrs.
Major J.L. Mitchell, 22/Durh.L.I.
Major L. St. H. Morley, 1/ Sherw'd Frstrs.
Lieut.-Colonel R. F. Moore, M.C., 1/ Sherw'd Frstrs.
Major C. R. Mortimer, 1/ Sherw'd Frstrs.
Major C. R. J. Mowatt, 2/ North'n.

APPENDIX IV

2nd Lieut. S. W. Murray, 2/ Rif. Brig.
Capt. P. Neame, V.C., R.E.
Lieut.-Colonel F. H. Nugent, 2/ Rif. Brig.
Major L. C. L. Oldfield, R.A.
Capt. J. B. Orr, M.C., R.A.M.C.
Lieut.-Colonel C. A. S. Page, M.C., 2/ Midd'x.
Capt. R. G. Pearse, M.C., 1/ Sherw'd Frstrs.
Lieut. D. P. Petrie, 2/ Sco. Rif.
Major A. G. Pratt, Essex R.
Major H. Price-Williams, M.C., R.A.
Capt. J. H. T. Priestman, 2/ Linc.
Lieut.-Colonel G. E. R. Prior, M.C. and bar, 2/ Devon.
Lieut.-Colonel T. P. Puddicombe, R.A.M.C.
Major W. B. F. Rayner, R. Fus.
Major A. G. F. Ramsden, R.A.
Capt. L. F. Renny, R. Dub. Fus.
Capt. F. W. Robinson, M.G. Corps.
Major C. T. Saint Paul, R.A.
Lieut.-Colonel V. C. Sandilands, 2/ Sco. Rif.
Lieut.-Colonel E. T. F. Sandys, 2/ Midd'x.
Lieut.-Colonel A. A. Sharland, 2/ E. Lan.
Lieut.-Colonel R. L. Sherbrooke, 1/ Sherw'd Frstrs.
Capt. S. A. Sherston, 2/ Rif. Brig.
Major H. C. Simpson, R.A.
Q.M. and Hon. Major E. W. Skinner, 2/ Linc.
Major D. V. Smith, 1/ Lond.
Major W. F. Somervail, M.C., 2/ Sco. Rif.
Major E. A. Steel, R.A.
Capt. N. C. Swift, M.C., 2/ E. Lan.
Major C. B. Thackeray, R.A.
Capt. B. J. Thruston, 2/ Linc.
Lieut.-Colonel A. Tillett, 2/Devon.
Capt. F. St. J. Tyrwhitt, Worc. R.
2nd Lieut. W. A. Upton, 2/ R. Berks.
Lieut.-Colonel T. H. Watson, M.C., 1/ Sherw'd Frstrs.
Lieut. (Int. Off.) A. C. Willison, M.C. 1/ Sherw'd Frstrs.
Major J. F. S. Winnington, 1/ Worc.
Capt. H. W. Wynter, R.A.
2nd Lieut. K. Young, 2/ Linc.

OFFICER OF THE BRITISH EMPIRE

Major V. E. Castellan, R.A.
Capt. and Adj. J. M. S. Coates, M.G. Corps.
Lieut.-Colonel C. R. I. Hull, D.S.O., R.A.S.C.
Q.M. and Capt. W. H. D. King, M.G. Corps.
Q.M. and Capt. E. E. L. Lawson, 1/ Sherw'd Frstrs.
Colonel A.M. MacLaughlin, M.B., R.A.M.C.
Major H. Ramsbottom, Gen. List.
Major A. L. S. Wood, R.A.S.C.

MEMBER OF THE BRITISH EMPIRE

2nd Lieut. G. W. S. Brown, 2/ Rif. Brig.
2nd Lieut. D. Uzielli, A.D.C. to G.O.C. 8th Divn.
S.S.M. W. W. Woods, M.C., R.A.S.C.

BAR TO MILITARY CROSS

2nd Lieut. G. H. G. Anderson, 2/ Rif. Brig.
Capt. L. G. Bourdillon, D.S.O., R.A.M.C.
2nd Lieut. John Brown, 1/ R. Ir. Rif.
Lieut. F. J. V. Bullen, R.E.
Capt. A. G. Cade, 2/ Midd'x.

APPENDIX IV

2nd Lieut. W. J. Cowen, 1/ Sherw'd Frstrs.
Capt. D. D. Craig, R.A.M.C.
Rev. A. S. Crawley, Army Chaplains Dept.
2nd Lieut. T. S. Dobree, R.A.
2nd Lieut. T. A. Driscoll, R.A.
Major W. E. Duncan, R.A.
2nd Lieut. E. Edwards, D.C.M., M.M., M.G. Corps.
Capt. W. Evans, 2/ Midd'x.
2nd Lieut. S. E. Farbon, 2/ North'n
Lieut. H. T. Forster, D.S.O., 2/ R. Berks.
Capt. E. S. Fox, 2/ W. York.
Lieut. O. S. Francis, 2/ R. Berks.
2nd Lieut. H. Greaves, 1/ Sherw'd Frstrs and 2nd bar.
Lieut. L. S. Greening, 2/ W. York.
Capt. H. H. Jago, 2/ Devon.
2nd Lieut. A. S. Knott, 2/ R. Berks.
Major S. G. Latham, 2/ North'n.
Capt. W. E. B. Lowe, 2/ E. Lan.
Capt. I. C. McLean, R.A.M.C.
Capt. E. H. Matheson, 2/ W. York.
Major H. T. Michelmore, R.A.
2nd Lieut. C. H. G. Millis, 1/ Sherw'd Frstrs.
Capt. R. A. O'Donovan, 1/ Worc.
2nd Lieut. J. B. Oldfield, 2/ North'n.
Capt. B. C. Pascoe, 2/ Rif. Brig.
Capt. W. Y. Paton, 2/ E. Lan.
Major A. M. Pratt, M.G. Corps.
2nd Lieut. W. Prior, 2/ Midd'x.
2nd Lieut. A. Reese, 2/ W. York.
Capt. W. F. Richmond, 2/ E. Lan.
Capt. A. H. Robson, 22/ Durh. L.I.
Capt. E. H. Smythe, Gen. List.
2nd Lieut. N. F. Spatcher, 1/ Sherw'd Frstrs., and 2nd bar.
Capt. W. C. Stevens, 1/ Worc., and 2nd bar.
Capt. N. C. Swift, 2/ E. Lan.
2nd Lieut. K. H. Thompson, 2/ W. York.
Capt. F. C. Wallace, 1/ R. Ir. Rif.
Major A. E. Wass, 2/ Rif. Brig.
Major R. M. Weeks, D.S.O., Rif. Brig.
Capt. W. Weston, D.C.M., 1/ Sherw'd Frstrs.
Lieut. A. C. Willison, 1/ Sherwd. Frstrs.
Capt. J. B. M. Young, 2/ R. Berks.

MILITARY CROSS

Capt. G. B. Adams, R.A.
2nd Lieut. G. Airth-Garth, 1/5 Black Watch.
2nd Lieut. H. P. Allaway, 2/ R. Berks.
Q.M. and Hon. Capt. H. J. Alldridge, 2/ Rif. Brig.
2nd Lieut. N. P. Ambler, 2/ W. York.
R.S.M. H. Anderson, 2/ Midd'x.
2nd Lieut. L. W. Andrews, 22/ Durh. L.I.
2nd Lieut. R. J. Andrews, 2/Devon.
Lieut. H. G. Armitage, R.A.
Capt. and Adj. K. H. L. Arnott, 2/ E. Lan.
Lieut. H. C. Asbury, M.G. Corps.
Capt. and Adj. R. St. G. Atchley, R.A.
2nd Lieut. N. F. Bacon, T.M.B.
2nd Lieut. J. M. Bailey, 2/ North'n.
Capt. G. P. Baines, 22/ Durh. L.I.
Capt. E. E. F. Baker, 2/ Midd'x.
2nd Lieut. H. L. R. Baker, 2/ Devon.
Capt. M. Balfour, R.A.
2nd Lieut. P. F. Barr, 2/ Midd'x.
2nd Lieut. A. A. Barrett, 2/ R. Berks.
Lieut. E. C. Barton, 1/ Worc.
Capt. H. Bass, R.E.
2nd Lieut. N. D. Bayley, 2/ R. Berks.
2nd Lieut. O. L. Bell, 1/ Sherw'd Frstrs.
2nd Lieut. G. A. T. Benson, 2/ Midd'x.

APPENDIX IV

2nd Lieut. F. J. Benzimra, M.G. Corps.
2nd Lieut. J. G. Berry, 2/ W. York.
Lieut. K. N. Bion, 1/ Sherw'd Frstrs.
Capt. N. P. Birley, S. Staff. R.
Capt. J. C. Blackburn, 2/ W. York.
2nd Lieut. D. Blair, R.A.
Capt. C. E. Blake, 2/ North'n.
2nd Lieut. D. J. Blake, R.A.
Capt. F. D. Blandy, R.A.S.C.
2nd Lieut. W. C. Bolton, 8/ York & Lanc. R.
Major H. Bone, R.A.V.C.
2nd Lieut. P. J. Booth, 2/ Sco. Rif.
2nd Lieut. E. N. Bostock, 2/ North'n.
Capt. J. Bourke, M.G. Corps.
Capt. G. Bowden, 2/ Midd'x.
Capt. and Adj. R. W. Bowen, 2/ Devon.
Capt. and Adj. A. H. Bower, 1/7 Midd'x.
2nd Lieut. J. H. Bowler, 2/ Rif. Brig.
Capt. W. H. Bowmer, 1/ Sherw'd Frstrs.
Capt. P. J. Bretherton, 2/ Devon.
2nd Lieut. E. H. Brittain, 11/ Sherw'd Frstrs.
2nd Lieut. A. Brodie, R.A.
Capt. R. L. Brokenshire, 2/ Devon.
Lieut. A. F. R. Brown, 2/ R. Berks.
Capt. A. Hanbury Brown, R.E.
2nd Lieut. C. Brown, 2/ R. Berks.
2nd Lieut. J. W. Brown, 2/ Linc.
Capt. G. McI. S. Bruce, 2/ Linc.
Lieut. R. Bruce, R.E.
2nd Lieut. I. M. Bruce-Gardyne, 1/5 Black Watch.
Capt. R. Burgess, R.A.M.C.
Capt. R. Burgess, R.E.
2nd Lieut. A. H. Burman, 2/ Rif. Brig.
Lieut. P. E. Burrows, 1st Sherw'd Frstrs.
Capt. J. A. Cahill, 2/ R. Berks.
R.S.M. W. Carroll, 1/ R. Ir. Rif.
2nd Lieut. A. B. Chadwick, R.A.
R.S.M. J. Chalmers, D.C.M., 2/ Sco. Rif.
Capt. C. R. Chambers, 1/ Sherw'd Frstrs.
2nd Lieut. W. F. Charter, 2/ Sco. Rif.
Lieut. M. Chennells, M.G. Corps (Cav.).
Capt. and Adj. T. F. Chipp, 1/8 Midd'x.
Lieut. H. P. Chiswell, R.E.
Capt. and Adj. A. D. Clare, 2/ R. Berks.
2nd Lieut. F. D. Clarke, 2/ Devon.
Lieut. H. C. Clarke, 1/ Sherw'd Frstrs.
Capt. B. C. Clayton, 2/ W. York.
Capt. E. W. Clayton, 2/ Midd'x.
Lieut. G. H. Clifford, 2/ Linc.
Capt. F. W. Clifton, 2/ Linc.
Lieut. F. R. Cobb, 2/ Devon.
2nd Lieut. E. A. Cobbold, M.M., 2/ North'n.
2nd Lieut. M. Cohen, R.E.
Capt. Hon. E. Coke, 13/ Lond.
R.S.M. J. Cole, 2/ W. York.
Capt. J. J. B. Cole, 2/ Rif. Brig.
Lieut. and Q.M. F. A. W. Coman, 1/ Sherw'd Frstrs.
Rev. M. W. Conran, Army Chaplains Dept.
Lieut. E. B. Conybeare, 1/ Worc.
Capt. E. R. C. Cooke, R.A.M.C.
2nd Lieut. H. L. Cooper, 1/ Worc.
Lieut. C. V. W. Court, 1/ Worc.
Lieut. G. St. J. Coventry, 8/ K.O.Y.L.I.
Lieut. E. C. Coxwell, 1/ Worc.
Capt. V. A. B. Cranwill, 2/ E. Lan.
2nd Lieut. A. M. Crellin, 1/ Sherw'd Frstrs.
Capt. E. W. Cremer, 2/ Rif. Brig.
Major H. C. Crone, R.E.
Lieut. C. H. Cropper, R.E.
Lieut. E. P. Cropper, 2/ W. York.
Capt. J. D. Crosthwaite, 2/ Linc.
2nd Lieut. G. E. Crowder, M.G. Corps.
C.S.M. G. Crump, 1/ Worc.

APPENDIX IV

Capt. A. H. Curtis, 2/ Rif. Brig.
Capt. V. A. H. Daly, W. York. R.
2nd Lieut. H. Daniels, V.C., 2/ Rif. Brig.
2nd Lieut. H. H. Darby, 2/ Rif. Brig.
Lieut. D. Davidson, R.E.
Lieut. C. Davies, 1/ Worc.
Capt. T. H. Davison, R.A.
Capt. S. F. M. Delcourt, 2/ Midd'x.
2nd Lieut. R. L. Derry, 2/ E. Lan.
Lieut. H. Dickinson, 2/ Midd'x.
2nd Lieut. B. E. C. Dixon, R.E.
Lieut. G. S. Dobbie, 1/ Sherw'd Frstrs.
Lieut. A. D. B. Don, R.E.
C.S.M. A. Dorricott, 2/ Midd'x.
Capt. J. H. M. Douglas, 1/Sherw'd Frstrs.
C.S.M. P. S. Douglas, 22/ Durh. L.I.
2nd Lieut. J. Doyle, 2/ Rif. Brig.
2nd Lieut. E. Drury, 1/ Sherw'd Frstrs.
Sergt.-Major F. Duckworth, 2/ E. Lan.
Capt. T. B. Duncan, 2/ Sco. Rif.
2nd Lieut. F. W. Dunnett, T.M.B.
Capt. J. H. Dyer, R.E.
Capt. H. P. Eames, R.E.
Capt. C. R. E. Edmundson, 8/ York and Lanc.
R.S.M. J. H. Edwards, 2/ Midd'x.
2nd Lieut. L. M. Ekin, 8/ York and Lanc.
Capt. H. H. Elliott, M.B., R.A.M.C.
2nd Lieut. W. J. R. Elliott, 1st Sherw'd Frstrs.
Major B. W. Ellis, R.A.
2nd Lieut. H. Emblem, 1/ Sherw'd Frstrs.
Capt. H. Essame, 2/ North'n.
2nd Lieut. B. S. Evans, M.G. Corps.
2nd Lieut. W. Exton, 2/ Devon.
Lieut. L. Farthing, 2/ E. Lan.
2nd Lieut. A. C. Faulkner, 2/ Devon.
2nd Lieut. M. C. Fitch, 2/ E. Lan.
Capt. H. H. Flint, 2/ R. Berks.
Capt. H. V. Forster, R.A.M.C.
Capt. C. W. Fowler, R.A.M.C.
2nd Lieut. J. E. France, M.G. Corps.
Capt. A. J. Fraser, R. Berks. R.
2nd Lieut. E. Frayne, 2/ Midd'x.
R.S.M. E. W. Frazier, D.C.M., 1/ Worc.
2nd Lieut. F. E. Frith, R.A.
2nd Lieut. J. W. Frost, 2/ North'n.
R.S.M. J. Furey, 2/ Rif. Brig.
2nd Lieut. D. M. Gall, 2/ Sco. Rif.
2nd Lieut. H. C. Garbutt, R.E.
2nd Lieut. G. I. Gartlan, 1/ R. Ir. Rif.
2nd Lieut. T. B. Gartlan, T.M.B.
2nd Lieut. A. F. Gerrard, 1/ Sherw'd Frstrs.
2nd Lieut. K. N. W. Gilbert, R.A.
Capt. A. J. Gilchrist, R.A.M.C.
Lieut. H. G. Gilchrist, R.E.
Lieut. A. S. Giles, 1/ Sherw'd Frstrs.
Capt. S. H. Gillett, 1/7 Midd'x.
Lieut. C. Gillott, 22/ Durh. L.I.
Lieut. C. B. Golding, R.A.
Lieut. B. W. Goodwin, R.E.
Lieut. A. D. Gordon, 2/ R. Berks.
2nd Lieut. G. L. Gosling, 2/ R. Berks.
Major A. W. Gossage, R.A.
Lieut. C. P. Graham, 2/ W. York.
2nd Lieut. T. E. Graham, 2/ Sco. Rif.
Capt. and Adj. T. B. Grantham, R.A.
2nd Lieut. J. A. Graves, 2/ Linc.
Capt. D. L. Gray, 2nd Sco. Rif.
2nd Lieut. V. B. Gray, 2nd Sco. Rif.
2nd Lieut. J. N. S. Green, R.A.
2nd Lieut. W. L. Green, 1/ Sherw'd Frstrs.
2nd Lieut. W. Greensmith, 1/ Sherw'd Frstrs.
Capt. F. K. Griffith, 2/ Linc.
Rev. C. Groser, Army Chaplains Dept.
Rev. St. J. B. Groser, Army Chaplains Dept.

APPENDIX IV

Capt. Hon. R. E. Grosvenor, R.A.
Sergt.-Major G. Grover, 1/ Worc.
2nd Lieut. F. B. Gunning, R. Wilts Yeo.
Lieut. W. M. Guttmann, 2/ R. Berks.
Lieut. R. Haigh, 2/ R. Berks.
Rev. J. E. Hamilton, Army Chaplains Dept.
Capt. A. A. H. Hanbury-Sparrow, D.S.O., 2/ R. Berks.
Capt. and Adj. G. A. Hancock, 1/ Sherw'd Frstrs.
2nd Lieut. F. W. L. Hardcastle, 2/ W. York.
Lieut. Hon. H. R. Hardinge, 2/ Rif. Brig.
Capt. H. T. T. Harris, 4/ Oxf. & Bucks L.I.
Capt. R. Harrison, 1/ Worc.
2nd Lieut. J. W. Hart, R.A.
Lieut. E. J. Hassard, R.A.
Capt. A. J. Hawes, R.A.M.C.
Lieut. T. M. Hawker, R.A.
2nd Lieut. S. M. Haycraft, R.E.
Capt. G. F.P. Heathcote, R.A.M.C.
Capt. D. Heaton-Ellis, 2/ Rif. Brig.
Capt. G. H. Hedley, R.E.
Capt. O. Heggs, 2/ E. Lan.
2nd Lieut. M. W. Hemingway, R.A.
Capt. E. J. Henderson, 2/ E. Lan.
2nd Lieut. P. M. Heptinstall, R.E.
Lieut. D. L. Herbert, R.E.
Lieut. T. R. Hetherington, R.A.
2nd Lieut. F. H. Hickman, R.E.
2nd Lieut. L. Hickman, 22/ Durh. L.I.
Batty. Sergt.-Major H. Higgins, R.A.
Lieut. S. G. Highmoor, 22/ Durh. L.I.
2nd Lieut. W. A. S. Hill, M.G. Corps.
Capt. Jas. Hill, M.B., R.A.M.C.
2nd Lieut. S. F. Hill, R.A.
Lieut. E. C. Hillman, R.E.
Q.M. and Hon. Capt. C. Hinchcliffe, 2/ W. York.
Lieut. A. C. Hincks, R.A.M.C.
Lieut. D. de V. Hinde, 2/ R. Berks.
Capt. R. B. Holman, 2/ Midd'x.
R.S.M. H. Holmes, 2/ North'n.
Lieut. A. H. Hornby, R.A.
Capt. B.H. Horsley, 8/ K.O.Y.L.I.
Rev. J. Howard, Army Chaplains Dept.
Capt. H. L. Howell, R.A.M.C.
Capt. and Adj. T. W. Howey, 1/7 Durh. L.I.
Lieut. J. H. Hudson, R.A.
2nd Lieut. J. W. Hudson, R.A.
2nd Lieut. A. E. T. Hunt, R.A.
2nd Lieut. H. C. Hunt, 2/ Midd'x.
2nd Lieut. M. J. Hurndall, 1/ Sherw'd Frstrs.
Capt. E. H. Impey, 2/ Linc.
Capt. H. Ingham, 2/ W. York.
2nd Lieut. A. O. Jackson, T.M.B.
Capt. A. R. Jackson, M.D., R.A.M.C.
Lieut. H. G. Janion, R.A.M.C.
2nd Lieut. J. B. Jarrett, M.G. Corps.
Lieut. J. E. Jarvis, 2/ North'n.
2nd Lieut. S. W. Jeffery, 2/ North'n.
2nd Lieut. L. Jellinek, R.A.
2nd Lieut. S. C. Johnson, 1/ Worc.
2nd Lieut. Albert Jones, M.G. Corps.
Capt. G. C. Jones, R.A.M.C.
Capt. C. H. Joyce, 2/ Linc.
Officer Interpreter H. G. L. Julitte, 23/ French Col. Inf.
Lieut. H. F. Kane, M.R.O., U.S. Army attd. 2/ Devon.
2nd Lieut. J. C. H. Kane, T.M.B.
Sergt.-Major F. C. Keightley, 2/ Linc.
Capt. J. E. Kelley, M.O.R.C., U.S. Army attd. R.A.M.C.
Lieut. C. S. C. Kennedy, R.E.
Lieut. F. R. Kennington, 2/ W. York.
R.S.M. A. Kenyon, 2/ W. York.
Lieut. L. MacG. Kerr, 2/ W. York.
R.S.M. J. B. King, 2/ Devon.

APPENDIX IV

2nd Lieut. W. Kingston, 1/ R. Ir. Rif.
Rev. S. S. Knapp, Army Chaplains Dept.
Lieut. G. Lambert, R.E.
2nd Lieut. F. G. Lancaster, 2/ W. York.
2nd Lieut. H. Lane, 2/ North'n.
2nd Lieut. R. F. Lankester, R.A.
2nd Lieut. H. R. Latimer, T.M.B.
Lieut. E. L. G. Lawrence, 1/ Worc.
Capt. E. C. Lawson, 2/ Midd'x.
Lieut. F. Lawson, 2/ R. Berks.
Capt. P. A. Ledward, Hamps. R.
Sergt.-Major G. Lee, 2/ North'n.
Lieut. E. H. Leigh, 2/ Rif. Brig.
Lieut. R. C. Lewis, 2/ R. Berks.
Capt. A. C. Lightfoot, 1/ Sherw'd Frstrs.
Capt. C. S. Linton, 1/ Worc.
2nd Lieut. H. I. Lloyd, 2/ North'n.
2nd Lieut. J. Logan, R.E.
Lieut. J. E. Lott, R.E.
Capt. and Adj. A. E. E. Lowry, 2/ W. York.
2nd Lieut. A. R. F. Lucas, R.A.
Lieut. W. C. McCauley, R.A.
2nd Lieut. M. McConville, 2/ W. York.
2nd Lieut. F. W. MacCormack, R.A.
Capt. D. A. MacGregor, 2/ R. Berks.
2nd Lieut. F. M. MacGregor, M.M., 2/ North'n.
Capt. A. H. Mackay, 2/ Midd'x.
2nd Lieut. A. J. Mackenzie, 2/ Scot. Rif.
Capt. R. W. Mackinlay, R.E.
2nd Lieut. G. E. Mahany, 2/ Midd'x.
2nd Lieut. W. S. Maitland, 1/ R. Ir. Rif.
Capt. M. Mallace, 2/ Sco. Rif.
2nd Lieut. G. W. Mant, 2/ R. Berks.
Capt. N. Marshall, E. York. R.
2nd Lieut. L. W. Martinnant, 2/ Rif. Brig.
Capt. J. H. Massey, R.A.
Q.M. and Hon. Capt. J. H. Maunder, R.A.M.C.
2nd Lieut. W. C. Maunder, M.M., 2/ Devon.
2nd Lieut. W. J. May, 2/ W. York.
Rev. A. S. Mayne, Army Chaplains Dept.
2nd Lieut. H. Meathrel, D.C.M., R.A.
Lieut. J. F. Menzies, 1/ Sherw'd Frstrs.
2nd Lieut. C. G. H. Midgley, M.G. Corps.
Capt. F. D. R. Milne, 2/ Rif. Brig.
Lieut. P. Minor, 22/ Durh. L.I.
Capt. W. S. Mitcalfe, R.A.
2nd Lieut. C. Mollet, 2/ R. Berks.
Capt. E. B. Mollett, 2/ Midd'x.
Capt. J. A. Moncrieffe, M.G. Corps (Cav.).
Capt. J. M. Monk, 1/ Worc.
Major J. M. Mood, M.G. Corps.
2nd Lieut. E. F. C. Moore, 2/ Rif. Brig.
R.S.M. G. H. Moore, 11/ Sherw'd Frstrs.
2nd Lieut. J. G. Moore, 2/ Rif. Brig.
Capt. R. F. Moore, 1/ Sherw'd Frstrs.
2nd Lieut. H. A. L. Morris, M.G. Corps.
2nd Lieut. Thos. Moss, R.A.
Capt. J. B. Mudge, 1/ Sherw'd Frstrs.
2nd Lieut. H. H. Mugford, 1/ Worc.
2nd Lieut. J. L. Muir, 1/ R. Ir. Rif.
Capt. E. V. B Murphy, 1/ R. Ir. Rif.
Lieut. P. S. Myburgh, R.A.
2nd Lieut. E. Myers, 2/ W. York.
Lieut. C. R. D. Napier, 2/ Devon.
2nd Lieut. E. J. Nicholls, 1/ Worc.
2nd Lieut. T. A. Nickalls, R.A.
2nd Lieut. W. J. Nicklin, 2/ Midd'x.
2nd Lieut. I. S. Nicol, R.A.

APPENDIX IV

Lieut. R. E. Norris, M.G. Corps.
Capt. W. M. O'Kelly, R.A.S.C.
2nd Lieut. H. Oldershaw, R.A.
Capt. M. F. O'Sullivan, A.V.C.
Capt. W. V. Packe, R.A.
Lieut. T. A. Packman, T.M.B.
Lieut. G. Paine, 2/ R. Berks.
Capt. H. L. Palmer, R.A.
Capt. F. C. Papworth, 2/ North'n.
2nd Lieut. H. Parker, 2/ Devon.
Hon. Lieut. and Q.M. S. Parker, 1/ Worc.
2nd Lieut. J. W. Pavey, 2/ R. Berks.
2nd Lieut. B. A. Peace, 2/ W. York.
Capt. G. B. Pears, R.E.
Lieut. A. C. Pearse, 2/ Midd'x.
Capt. R. G. Pearse, 1/ Sherw'd Frstrs.
Lieut. R. W. Pearson, M.D., R.A.M.C.
Capt. C. E. Pegram, 2/ Rif. Brig.
Lieut. G. C. Percy, 2/ Sco. Rif.
C.S.M. J. Pitman, 2/ North'n.
Capt. J. K. Podd, 2/ W. York.
2nd Lieut. A. S. Polhill, 2/ Midd'x.
Capt. H. W. M. Potter, 2/ Midd'x.
Capt. A. B. Pratt, 1/ Worc.
2nd Lieut. J. A. Prevel, 2/ North'n.
Capt. E. V. Price, 9/ York & Lanc.
Capt. H. R. Price, 2/ Rif. Brig.
R.S.M. W. Price, 2/ E. Lan.
Capt. J. H. T. Priestman, D.S.O., Linc. R.
Capt. I. T. Pritchard, 1/ Worc.
R.S.M. W. Pritchard, 2/ Devon.
Capt. A. E. Prosser, 1/ Worc.
2nd Lieut. A. H. Pullin, R.A.
Capt. E. F. M. Puxon, 1/ Sherw'd Frstrs.
Lieut. H. Quarry, R.A.
Capt. H. T. W. Quick, 2/ R. Berks.
Lieut. H. E. Raine, 22/ Durham L.I.
2nd Lieut. E. Rait-Kerr, R.A.
2nd Lieut. E. F. Ratliff, 2/ Rif. Brig.

2nd Lieut. J. E. R. Rayner, R.A.
Capt. C. R. Reckitt, R.A.M.C.
2nd Lieut. N. Redfern, T.M.B.
Capt. C. H. R. Reed, 1/ R. Ir. Rif.
2nd Lieut. C. H. Repton, 2/ Devon
Capt. E. F. O. Richards, 2/ Linc.
R.S.M. A. E. Richardson, 2/ Rif. Brig.
Lieut. R. C. Richardson, 2/ W. York.
Lieut. T. C. Richardson, R.E.
2nd Lieut. A. J. Riley, 8/ York and Lanc.
Lieut. M. E. Riley, 2/ E. Lan.
Lieut. A. C. G. Roberts, 2/ Devon.
Capt. F. C. Roberts, D.S.O., 1/ Worc.
Capt. F.W. Robinson, M.G. Corps.
Capt. and Adj. J. F. S. Ross, R.E.
2nd Lieut. C. R. Riddle, 2/ Sco. Rif.
Capt. A. V. Russell, R.A.M.C.
2nd Lieut. B. Russell, R.E.
2nd Lieut. S. G. Russell, 1/ Worc.
Capt. P. J. Ryan, R.A.M.C.
2nd Lieut. C. A. Samm, 2/ North'n
Capt. H. B. W. Savile, 2/ Midd'x.
Capt. B. G. H. Sawyer, 2/ R. Berks.
Capt. Hon. P. G. Scarlett, The Buffs.
2nd Lieut. W. A. Seaman, 2/ Rif. Brig.
C.S.M. C. Sexton, M.G. Corps.
Lieut. F. G. Shackle, 2/ Midd'x.
Q.M. and Hon. Lieut. J. Shaw, 2/ E. Lan.
Capt. E. Sheppard, Gren. Guards.
Capt. E. Sherlock, R.A.
Major A. Simmonds, M.G. Corps.
Lieut. R. Skelton, R.A.
2nd Lieut. S. Slade-Baker, 2/ R. Berks.
2nd Lieut. A. J. Sluman, 2/ Rif. Brig.
R.S.M. A. Smart, 2/ Sco. Rif.
2nd Lieut. R. C. Smart, 1/ Worc.
2nd Lieut. F. J. Smith, M.M., 2/ R. Berks.
2nd Lieut. F. V. Smith, Midd'x Regt.

APPENDIX IV

2nd Lieut. Leonard Smith, 1/ Worc.
2nd Lieut. L. C. Smith, 2/ Linc.
Lieut. J. A. Smithin, 1/ Worc.
2nd Lieut. S. G. Sole, 2/ Linc.
2nd Lieut. W. F. Somervail, 2/ Sco. Rif.
Lieut. F. N. Sopwith, R.A.
2nd Lieut. G. H. Southall, 2/ Rif. Brig.
Major N. Southern, R.A.
2nd Lieut. G. B. Spence, 2/North'n.
Capt. F. E. Spencer, R.A.
C.S.M. W. T. Sperry, 2/ Midd'x.
Lieut. F. P. Spooner, M.G. Corps.
Major G. S. Spurrier, R.A.S.C.
2nd Lieut. T. A. Staynes, 2/ W. York.
2nd Lieut. S. T. Stephens, 2/ Linc.
2nd Lieut. A. W. F. Stewart, 6/ Sco. Rif.
Capt. W. H. E. Stewart, R.A.M.C.
2nd Lieut. E. A. Stocken, R.A.
Capt. J. S. W. Stone, R.E.
Capt. N. H. Stone, 1/ Worc.
Capt. C. R. Stott, R.E. (Gas Off.)
2nd Lieut. F. A. Strange, 2/ R. Berks.
Lieut. C. V. Strong, R.E.
Capt. A. V. Sully, M.G. Corps.
2nd Lieut. A. Sutherland, 1/4 Sco. Rif.
Capt. E. A. Sutton, R.A.M.C.
Lieut. E. L. Taggart, 2/ Midd'x.
Rev. E. K. Talbot, Army Chaplains Dept.
Lieut. L. F. Taylor, M.G. Corps.
Lieut. R. M. Taylor, R.E.
Capt. A. E. Thompson, R.A.M.C.
2nd Lieut. G. F. Thuillier, 2/ Devon.
Capt. A. Tillet, 2/ Devon.
2nd Lieut. L. N. L. Tindal, 2/ Devon.
Lieut. J. E. Tindall, R.E.
2nd Lieut. A. E. Titley, 2/ Devon.
2nd Lieut. A. Tomlinson, 1/8 Midd'x.
Capt. W. W. T. Torr, W. York. R.
2nd Lieut. A. M. Toye, 2/ Midd'x.

Capt. and Adj. P. Triefus, R.A.
2nd Lieut. N. Tweedale, R.A.
2nd Lieut. F. Twist, M.M., M.G. Corps (Cav.).
2nd Lieut. E. A. Vansenden, 9/ York. & Lanc.
Capt. C. E. Vivian, R.A.
Capt. W. C. Wale, 8/ York & Lanc.
2nd Lieut. H. J. H. Wales, R.A.
Lieut. W. G. T. Walker, T.M.B.
Capt. J. T. Wallace, T.M.B.
R.Q.M. Sergt. F. Wannop, 2/ Sco. Rif.
C.S.M. L. Wanstall, 2/ Midd'x.
Capt. D. E. Ward, 2/ R. Berks.
Capt. J. H. Wedderburn-Maxwell, R.A.
Lieut. G. J. Wehl, 2/ E. Lan.
Capt. and Adj. T. D. Weldon, R.A.
2nd Lieut. J. L. Wenn, 2/ Midd'x.
Capt. F. C. West, R.E.
R.S.M. W. C. Weston, 2/ R. Berks.
2nd Lieut. H. J. Wheeler, R.A.
C.S.M. G. Whelan, 2/ W. York.
Capt. F. S. Whinney, 2/ Linc.
Capt. B. B. White, 22/ Durh. L.I.
2nd Lieut. W. E. White, R.A.
Capt. G. H. P. Whitefield, 1/ R. Ir. Rif.
2nd Lieut. P. Wilkins, R.E.
2nd Lieut. H. Wilkinson, 2/ E. Lan.
2nd Lieut. A. M. Williams, 2/ North'n.
Lieut. H. K. Williams, R.E.
2nd Lieut. S. J. Williams, 2/ Devon.
Lieut. W. M. Williams, 1/ Worc.
2nd Lieut. C.S. Willmer, 22/ Durh. L.I.
Capt. E. J. Willis, 2/ North'n.
2nd Lieut. W. S. Wingate-Gray, R.A.
Major A. H. Woodbridge, 1/8 Midd'x.
2nd Lieut. F. Workman, 1/ R. Ir. Rif.
2nd Lieut. C. G. Worraker, 2/ Linc.
Capt. F. C. Worster, 1/ Worc.
Capt. R. Yandle, 2/ Devon.

APPENDIX IV

BAR TO DISTINGUISHED CONDUCT MEDAL

C.S.M. J. Beaton, 2/ Sco. Rif.
C.S.M. F. Birtwisle, 2/ Rif. Brig.
C.S.M. G. Crump, 1/ Worc.
C.S.M. A. Howells, 2/ R. Berks.
Sergt. J. J. Hickman, D.C.M., M.M. and 2nd bar, 2/ Midd'x.
C.S.M. W. Lockley, M.M., 1/ Sherw'd Frstrs.
Sergt. S. Phillips, 1/ Worc. and 2nd bar.
R.S.M. F. H. Radford, 2/ Devon.
Batty. Sergt.-Major H. Seller, R.A.
Sergt. B. W. Smith, M.M, 1/ Sherw'd Frstrs.
Corpl. G. Smith, R.E.
Sergt. A. Sturgess, 2/ R. Berks.

DISTINGUISHED CONDUCT MEDAL

Pte. G. Abbott, 2/ Midd'x.
Sergt. A. Albury, 2/ R. Berks.
C.S.M. T. Alderson, 2/ W. York.
Lce.-Corporal G. Anderson, 1/5 Black Watch.
Pte. W. Anderson, 2/ Sco. Rif.
Pte. H. Andrews, 2/ Sco. Rif.
Sergt. J. Andrews, 2/ Devon.
Lce.-Sergt. B. Annes, 2/ E. Lan.
Pte. A. Applebee, 1/ Worc.
Sergt. T. Armorer, 2/ North'n.
Corpl. F. Asbrey, 2/ North'n.
Pte. W. Ashford, 2/ Linc.
Pte. C. W. Ashley, 2/ R. Berks.
C.Q.M. Sergt. A. Asplin, 2/ North'n.
Sergt. H. L. Aust, 2/ R. Berks.
S.S.M. F. C. Avis, R.A.S.C.
C.S.M. J. R. Ayres, 2/ Midd'x.
Bombdr. G. Bailey, R.A.
Lce.-Sergt. A. Baker, 1/ Worc.
C.Q.M. Sergt. H. Baker, 2/ Midd'x.
Corpl. A. Balaam, 1/ Sherw'd Frstrs.
Sergt. Arthur Ball, R.A.
Lce.-Corporal P. Ball, 2/ Rif. Brig.
Pte. H. Bamford, 2/ North'n.
Sergt. F. H. Barnsdale, M.M., T.M.B.
Pte. R. Batchelor, 1/ Worc.
Pte. F. Beaney, A. Cyclist Corps.
Pte. F. Belcher, 2/ R. Berks.
Sergt. M. Bell, T.M.B.
Bombdr. T. Bell, R.A.
Sergt. A. Bellringer, 2/ Rif. Brig.
Sergt. H. Beniams, 1/ Worc.
Sergt. H. Bennett, 2/ Rif. Brig.
C.Q.M. Sergt. J. H. Bennett, 2/ Rif. Brig.
Rfmn. H. N. Benson, 2/ Rif. Brig.
Sergt. T. M. Bentley, M.M., R.A.
Gnr. H. Binley, R.A.
Pte. R. Blakeman, 1/ Worc.
Rfmn. P. Blazeby, 2/ Rif. Brig.
Pte. G. Bloomfield, 2/ W. York.
Corpl. M. Bolton, M.G. Corps.
Sergt. W. G. Boulding, 2/ North'n.
Batty. Sergt.-Major A. Boulter, R.A.
C.S.M. J. T. Bowden, 2/ Devon.
Lce.-Corporal R. Bradshaw, 1/ R. Ir. Rif.
Pte. J. Branker, 2/ North'n.
Pte. C. Briggs, 2/ Linc.
Pte. C. Brown, M.G. Corps.
Sergt. G. V. Brown, M.M., 2/ Midd'x.
Pte. Wm. Brown, 1/ Sherw'd Frstrs.
Pte. W. T. Brown, 1/ Worc.
Corpl. J. G. Browning, M.M., 2/ Devon.
Corpl. J. Brunton, 2/ Sco. Rif.
Drummer J. Bryant, 1/ Linc.
Corpl. G. H. Budd, 2/ Devon.
Pte. A. Budworth, 2/ North'n.
Sergt. A. Bull, R.A.
Pte. G. Bullen, 2/ Devon.
C.S.M. H. Burnell, 2/ E. Lan.
Sergt. E. Burrows, 2/ R. Berks.
Pte. H. Burrows, 2/ R. Berks.
Pte. J. Butterworth, 2/ E. Lan.
Lce.-Corporal H. Cairns, 1/ R. Ir. Rif.
Pte. A. Callaghan, 2/ E. Lan.

APPENDIX IV

Sergt. B. Cannon, 1/7 Midd'x.
Lce.-Corporal H. R. Cannon, 2/ Sco. Rif.
Rfmn. J. Carton, 1/ R. Ir. Rif.
R.Q.M. Sergt. T. Carefoot, 2/ E. Lanc.
Sergt. J. Cassidy, 2/ W. York.
Corpl. J. Cassidy, M.G. Corps.
Bombdr. H. Castle, R.A.
Sapper H. Catlin, R.E.
R.S.M. J. Chance, 1/ Worc.
Sergt. W. Chart, 1/ Sherw'd Frstrs.
Pte. G. Chartman, 2/ E. Lan.
Sergt. J. Chicken, 2/ W. York.
Corpl. A. F. G. Chivers, 2/ R. Berks.
Sergt. A. Christie, 1/5 Black Watch.
Pte. W. Chumbly, 2/ W. York.
C.S.M. W. Clarke, 1/ R. Ir. Rif.
Pte. J. T. Clayton, 8/ York & Lanc.
Sergt. S. Clements, 2/ North'n.
Pte. S. Clempson, R.E.
Pte. A. Collard, 2/ E. Lan.
Corpl. C. D. Collins, R.A.
Corpl. H. R. Collins, 2/ Devon.
Sergt. J. Collins, 2/ R. Berks.
Lce.-Sergt. W. A. Connor, 2/ R. Berks.
Pte. M. Conroy, 2/ W. York.
Corpl. F. Cooper, 2/ Midd'x.
Sergt. R. Coote, 1/ Sherw'd Frstrs.
Rfmn. J. Copeland, 1/ R. Ir. Rif.
Lce.-Corporal J. L. Court, M.M. and bar, 2/ Midd'x.
Corpl. M. Coverley, 1/ Sherw'd Frstrs.
Lce.-Corporal C. Cowling, 2/ Linc.
Sergt. J. B. Cox, 1/ Sherw'd Frstrs.
Sergt. J. Coyle, 1/ R. Ir. Rif.
Corpl. J. Crisp, T.M.B.
Sergt. L. Crispin, 2/ Devon.
Sergt. W. Croft, 2/ Midd'x.
Corpl. T. J. Cronin, 2/ Midd'x.
Sergt. A. J. Cross, 2/ Rif. Brig.
Corpl. L. Crosthwaite, 2/ W. York.
Bombdr. W. Crowhurst, R.A.
Corpl. H. Croxall, M.G. Corps.
Corpl. F. Cubitt, R.A.
Lce.-Sergt. J. B. Currie, 2/ Sco. Rif.
C.S.M. A. Curtis, 2/ Rif. Brig.
Sergt. C. Dady, 1/ Sherw'd Frstrs.
Rfmn. J. Daly, 1/ R. Ir. Rif.
Lce.-Corporal J. Darcy, 1/ R. Ir. Rif.
Pte. W. Darby, 2/ Midd'x.
Sergt. C. Dark, 2/ Devon.
Sergt. E. N. Davey, R.E.
Pte. J. Davidson, 1/5 Black Watch.
Fitter J. Davies, R.A.
Sergt. E. Daykin, 2/ R. Berks.
Lce.-Corporal R. Derry, 2/ E. Lan.
Sergt. P. Devine, 1/ R. Ir. Rif.
Lce.-Corporal J. Donelly, 1/ R. Ir. Rif.
Bombdr. W. B. Doran, R.A.
Pte. H. G. Dove, 2/ W. York.
Sergt. R. Doveton, 2/ Rif. Brig.
Pte. J. Draycott, 1/ Sherw'd Frstrs.
Sergt. A. Drew, 2/ North'n.
C.S.M. J. Driscoll, 1/ R. Ir. Rif
Sergt. E. Driver, 2/ North'n.
Bombdr. G. R. Duck, R.A.
Sapper A. J. Dugdale, R.E.
Pte. C. S. Duke, R.A.M.C.
Corpl. J. Dunning, R.E.
Sergt. A. Durrant, R.E.
Sergt. D. Edgar, R.A.
Corpl. S. V. Edge, 1/7 Midd'x.
Sergt. R. E. Edgecombe, 2/ E. Lan.
Sergt. J. Egan, M.M., 1/ Worc.
Corpl. R. F. Ellingworth, R.E.
Pte. B. Ellis, 2/ North'n.
Sergt. F. Ellis, R.E.
Pte. W.H. Elliott, 9/ York & Lanc.
Pte. W. Entwisle, 2/ E. Lan.
Pte. J. L. Evans, 1/ Worc.
Sergt. A. Ewens, M.M., 2/ Devon.
Lce.-Sergt. W. Faulkner, 2/ Midd'x.
Lce.-Sergt. J. Fearn, 1/ Sherw'd Frstrs.
Drummer J. F. Ferguson, 1/7 Midd'x.
C.S.M. C. Fisher, 2/ North'n.
Pte. J. T. Fleet, 1/ Sherw'd Frstrs.
Corpl. C. Ford, 2/ Sco. Rif.
C.S.M. S. Fowles, 1/ R. Ir. Rif.
Sergt. J. F. Frankum, R.E.

APPENDIX IV

Pte. E. Fraser, 1/ Worc.
Pte. J. French, 2/ E. Lan.
Lce.-Corporal T. J. French, 1/ Lond.
Sergt. T. Fryer, 2/ W. York.
Pte. S. Fudger, 1/ Worc.
Lce.-Corporal A. Fuller, 1/7 Midd'x.
R.S.M. J. Furey, 2/ Rif. Brig.
Lce.-Corporal J. Gall, 2/ Sco. Rif.
Sergt. G. Galloway, 2/ W. York.
Pte. G. Gardiner, 2/ Sco. Rif.
Pte. C. Gardner, 2/ Sco. Rif.
Sapper R. R. Gardner, R.E.
Sergt. C. R. Garner, R.E.
Pte. H. Gates, 2/ R. Berks.
Pte. B. Gaunt, M.M., 1/ Sherw'd Frstrs.
Bombdr. W. Gibbons, R.A.
Sergt. J. W. Gibson, 2/ Rif. Brig.
Pte. A. J. Gifford, 1/ Worc.
Pte. E.E. Gilbert, 8/ York & Lanc.
Sergt. T. Giles, 1/ Sherw'd Frstrs.
Lce.-Corporal C. D. Gladwyn, M.M., 2/ W. York.
Sergt. H. Godbold, 1/ Sherw'd Frstrs.
Pte. J. Godfrey, R.A.S.C.
Sergt. A. Gould, 1/ Worc.
Pte. R. Graham, 1/5 Black Watch.
Lce.-Corporal S. Grant, 2/ R. Berks.
Pte. C. W. Graves, 2/ R. Berks.
Sergt. Geo. Gray, 2/ Sco. Rif.
Sergt. H. J. Gray, 2/ Midd'x.
C.S.M. H. Green, 2/ W. York.
Corpl. H. W. Green, 2/ North'n.
Corpl. C. Greenslade, M.M., 2/ Devon.
C.S.M. A. Gubbins, 2/ W. York.
Sergt. T. Guest, 1/ Worc.
Sergt. S. Hague, M.M., 1/ Sherw'd Frstrs.
Sergt. W. Hales, R.E.
Lce.-Corporal W. Hallam, 1/ Sherw'd Frstrs.
Sergt. J. Hamilton, 2/ E. Lan.
Batty. Sergt.-Major F. Hand, R.A.
Lce.-Corporal W. Hand, 1/ Sherw'd Frstrs.

Pte. E. Handyside, 1/7 Durh. L.I.
Lce.-Corporal S. Harley, 1/ Worc.
Sergt. R. R. Hart, 2/ Linc.
Lce.-Corporal B. W. Hawkins, 2/ North'n.
Sergt. C. Hawkins, 2/ Sco. Rif.
Pte. G. Hawley, 2/ Devon.
Pioneer A. Hawtree, R. E.
Pte. J. Hayes, 1/ Sherw'd Frstrs.
Corpl. J. Heath, 1/ Lond.
Corpl. A. Henderson, 2/ Sco. Rif.
Lce.-Corporal E. Henson, 2/ Linc.
Gnr. A. Herrington, R.A.
C.S.M. M. Hobbs, 2/ Devon.
Lce.-Sergt. T. Hole, 2/ R. Berks.
Corpl. S. Holloway, 1/ Linc.
Pte. H. Holmes, 2/ North'n.
Pte. S. Holmes, 2/ W. York.
Sergt. W. Horner, 2/ W. York.
C.S.M. F. J. Huggins, 2/ R. Berks.
Lce.-Corporal G. Hughes, 2/ Devon.
Gnr. T. Humphrey, R.A.
Pte. A. Hunt, M.G. Corps.
Sergt. G. Hunt, 1/ Sherw'd Frstrs.
Rfmn. W. Hunt, 2/ Rif. Brig.
Rfmn. W. Hunter, 1/ R. Ir. Rif.
Lce.-Corporal Wm. Hurst, R.E.
Rfmn. H. Hyde, 2/ Rif. Brig.
Lce.-Corporal E. Hyndman, 2/ E. Lan.
Pte. R. Ida, 2/ R. Berks.
Pte. A. Jackson, 1/ Sherw'd Frstrs.
Bombdr. H. James, R.A.
Sapper G. Jarvis, R.E.
Gnr. G. Jarvis, R.A.
Corpl. G. Jelly, 2/ Midd'x.
Lce.-Corporal A. C. Johns, 2/ Devon.
Pte. E. Johnson, 2/ Midd'x.
Q.M. Sergt. J. Johnson, 2/ Linc.
Sergt. W. Johnson, M.M., R.E.
Corpl. W. Johnson, 2/ W. York.
Lce.-Corporal S. Jollans, 2/ Linc.
Corpl. Thos. Jones, 2/ W. York.
C.S.M. W. S. Jones, 2/ Midd'x.
Sergt. E. Joseph, 1/ Worc.
Sapper F. Kennedy, R.E.
Pte. J. C. Kent, 2/ Midd'x.
Pte. A. King, 1/ Worc.

APPENDIX IV

C.S.M. C. H. King, 2/ W. York.
Sergt. F. King, R.A.
Corpl. G. King, M.G.C.
C.S.M. J. B. King, 2/ Devon.
C.S.M. W. H. King, 2/ Scot. Rif.
Sergt. J. Kirk, R.E.
Corpl. W. Kitchenman, 2/ W. York.
Rfmn. F. Lamb, 2/ Rif. Brig.
Batty.-Sergt.-Major E. C. Landsberger, R.A.
C.Q.M. Sergt. F. Laud, 2/ North'n
Sergt. A. Leach, 2/ Devon.
R.S.M. G. Lee, M.C., 2/ North'n.
Sergt. T. Lee, 1/ Sherw'd Frstrs.
Rfmn. W. R. Lees, 1/ R.I. Rif.
Sergt. F. Leslie, 2/ R. Berks.
Sergt. F. Lethbridge, 2/ Devon.
Sergt. J. W. Leverett, 1/ R.I. Rif.
Sergt. Geo. Lewis, 1/ Sherw'd Frstrs.
Bombdr. W. R. Lewis, R.A.
R.Q.M. Sergt. H. D. Little, 1/ Worc.
C.S.M. E. Littlewood, 2/ Devon.
Lce.-Corporal F. C. Long, 2/ R. Berks.
Pte. E. Luddington, R.E.
Pte. W. Lund, 2/ Sco. Rif.
C.S.M. T. Lunn, 1/ R. Ir. Rif.
C.S.M. J. McBeath, 2/ Sco. Rif.
Pte. H. McCabe, 2/ Sco. Rif.
Sergt. G. McCall, 2/ Sco. Rif.
Sergt. P. McGill, M.G.C.
C.S.M. F. Mackay, 2/ W. York.
Lce.-Corpl. J. McKie, 2/ Sco. Rif.
Sapper D. Macpherson, R.E.
Corpl. K. McTaggart, M.M., R.E.
C.S.M. J. Magee, 1/ R. Ir. Rif.
Sergt. T. Mallet, 1/ Sherw'd Frstrs.
C.S.M. A. Mann, 1/ Sherw'd. Frstrs.
Lce.-Corpl. J. Markland, 2/ Midd'x.
C.S.M. J. Marnie, 1/5 Black Watch.
Lce.-Corpl. A. Marr, 8/ K.O.Y.L.I.
Sergt. J. Marriott, 2/ E. Lan.
C.S.M. J. J. Marsh, 2/ W. York.
Sergt. W. Marsh, 2/ Rif. Brig.
Batty.-Q.M.-Sergt. D. Marshall, R.A.
C.S.M. C. Martin, 1/ Sherw'd Frstrs.
Driver F. Martin, R.A.S.C.
Corpl. C. Matthews, 2/ R. Berks.
Sergt. A. Maybury, 2/ R. Berks.
Sergt. P. Mayo, 2/ Sco. Rif.
Corpl. J. Meredith, M.G.C.
Corpl. P. G. Millins, 1/ Worc.
Sergt. E. Mills, R.E.
C.S.M. J. H. Mitchell, 2/ Rif. Brig.
R.S.M. F. Moore, 2/ Lin.
Sergt. W. Moore, 1/ Worc.
C.S.M. F. G. Morgan, 1/ Worc.
Bombdr. Ed. Morley, R.A.
Pte. W. Moutrie, 1/7 Midd'x.
Rfmn. S. Murphy, 1/ R. Ir. Rif.
Pte. T. Murray, 2/ E. Lan.
Sergt. T. B. Murray, R.A.
Lce.-Corporal G. Musgrove, 8/ K.O.Y.L.I.
Private H. Neal, 1/ Sherw'd Frstrs.
Drummer E. Neale, 2/ Linc.
C.Q.M. Sergt. J. W. Nicholson, 2/ E. Lan.
Pte. J. Nicoll, 1/5 Black Watch.
Sergt. T. Norsworthy, 2/ Devon.
Sergt. W. E. Oakley, 2/ R. Berks.
C.S.M. T. C. O'Brien, R.E.
Gnr. W. E. Pace, R.A.
Pte. J. Palmer, 2/ E. Lan.
R.S.M. R. Parish, 2/ Lin.
Sergt. F. Parker, 2/ R. Berks.
Sergt. T. Parker, 2/ North'n.
Pte. J. Parkes, 2/ W. York.
Sergt. S. Parr, 2/ E. Lan.
Sergt. A. H. Partridge, 2/ Devon.
Sergt. W. C. Partridge, M.M., 2/ Rif. Brig.
C.S.M. J. Pattison, Rif. Brig.
Lce.-Corporal J. W. Payne, 2/ W. York.
Sergt. J. Pearce, 2/ W. York.
Corpl. S. Pettican, 2/ W. York.
Pte. T. Phillipson, 2/ North'n.
Lce.-Corporal F. Pickard, 2/ North'n.
Sergt. W. Poole, 2/ Middx.

APPENDIX IV

Sergt. W. S. Poole, 1/ R.I. Rif.
Sergt. C. A. Powell, 2/ W. York.
R.S.M. W. Price, M.C., 2/ E. Lan.
Sergt. T. Priestley, 8/ K.O.Y.L.I.
Sergt. C. Ransted, M.M., 2/ Rif. Brig.
Gnr. J. Reece, R.A.
Sergt. H. Rees, 1/ R. Ir. Rif.
Sapper J. A. Rennie, R.E.
Sergt. J. W. Rhodes, 2/ Rif. Brig.
Lce.-Corporal C. Richards, 1/ Worc.
Sergt. E. Richardson, R.A.
C.S.M. H. W. Richardson, R.E.
Pte. A. Richmond, 9/ York & Lanc.
Sergt. A. Riddett, 2/ Rif. Brig.
Pte. F. Riggs, 1/ Worc.
Sergt. H. R. Riggs, 2/ Linc.
Pte. J. Riley, 1/ Worc.
Corpl. G. H. Robbins, M.M., T.M.B.
Pte. A. Roberts, 2/ Midd'x.
Sapper J. W. Robertson, R.E.
Lce.-Corporal W. J. Robinson, 1/ R. Ir. Rif.
Lce.-Sergt. J. Robson, 2/ E. Lan.
Lce.-Corporal W. Rogers, 2/ E. Lan.
Sergt. D. Rolfe, 1/ Sherw'd Frstrs.
Corpl. W. Russon, 1/ Sherw'd Frstrs.
Rfmn. J. Ryan, 2/ Rif. Brig.
C.S.M. E. W. Sammons, 2/ Midd'x.
Lce.-Corporal A. Sawyer, 2/ W. York.
Pte. A. Scholes, 8/ York & Lanc.
Pte. J. J. Scott, 11/ Sherw'd Frstrs.
Sergt. A. Scrimshaw, 1/ Sherw'd Frstrs.
Corpl. H. Scrivener, 2/ North'n.
Sergt. W. Scrivens, R.A.
C.S.M. W. Seale, 1/ Worc.
Lce.-Corporal W. J. F. Seall, 2/ E. Lan.
Sergt. O. Sharpe, 2/ Linc.
Sergt. H. Shaw, 2/ Midd'x.
Sergt. W. Sheffield, 2/ Rif. Brig.

C.S.M. J. A. Shelton, 1/ Sherwood Frstrs.
Sergt. J. Shortland, 1/ Sherw'd Frstrs.
Corpl. T. Shufflebotham, M.M., R.A.
C.Q.M. Sergt. H. Slater, 1/ Sherw'd Frstrs.
C.S.M. A. G. Small, 2/ Devon.
Lce.-Corporal B. C. Smith, 2/ Devon.
Corpl. R. C. Smith, 2/ Midd'x.
Lce.-Sergt. H. Souster, 2/ Rif. Brig.
Pte. J. F. Spalding, R.A.S.C.
Sergt. L. Spittall, 2/ Linc.
Corpl. C. Spurway, 2/ Devon.
Pte. E. Stockman, 2/ Devon.
Batty. Sergt.-Major F. Stonard, R.A.
Lce.-Corporal H. J. Stott, 1/7 Midd'x.
C.S.M. C. E. Stovin, 1/ R.Ir. Rif.
Rfmn. C. J. Sturch, 2/ Rif. Brig.
Sergt. W. Swain, R.E.
Sergt. J. M. Swift, 1/ Sherw'd Frstrs.
Lce.-Corporal W. J. Taylor, 2/ R. Berks.
Sergt. L. A. Titcombe, 1/8 Midd'x.
Rfmn. J. Thomas, 2/ Rif. Brig.
Pte. F. Thompson, 2/ Scot Rif.
Corpl. F. Tomlinson, M.G. Corps.
Pte. W. Tongs, 2/ Sco. Rif.
Sergt. T. W. Toop, R.A.
Pte. G. H. Toseland, 2/ North'n.
Sapper W. Towers, R.E.
Lce.-Corporal J. W. Trimmer, 2/ R. Berks.
Sergt. J. Tromans, 1/ Worc.
Pte. W. Turner, 2/ R. Berks.
Gnr. W. Turner, R.A.
Corpl. T. Turton, R.A.
C.S.M. G. G. Turvey, M.M. and bar, 2/ R. Berks.
C.S.M. C. H. Underwood, M.M., 2/ North'n.
Sergt. C. Utting, R.E.
Sergt. H. Venn, 2/ R. Berks.
Sergt. H. Vickers, M.M., 2/ E. Lan.

APPENDIX IV

Sergt. J. T. Waldron, 8/ K.O.Y.L.I.
Pte. G. Walker, 2/ E. Lan.
Pte. R. Walsh, 2/ E. Lan.
C.S.M. W. Walter, 2/ Linc.
Lce.-Sergt. W. F. Ward, 2/ Midd'x.
Lce.-Corporal C. Warner, 1/ Sherw'd Frstrs.
Lce.-Corporal H. Watson, 2/ E. Lan.
Pte. J. Watts, 2/ Linc.
Sergt. W. Weavings, 1/ Worc.
Sergt. H. Webb, 1/ Worc.
Sergt. W. J. Webb, R.A.
Sergt. J. Webster, 1/5 Black Watch.
Rfmn. J. Webster, 2/ Rif. Brig.
Lce.-Corporal W. J. Welham, 2/ E. Lan.
Sergt. G. T. Wellborn, M.M., 2/ Midd'x.
Sergt. E. West, M.G. Corps.
C.S.M. W. F. Westcott, 2/ W. York.
Pte. E. Whittaker, 1/ Sherw'd Frstrs.
Lce.-Corporal R. Widdowfield, 2/ W. York.
C.Q.M. Sergt. F. Widdowson, 1/ Sherw'd Frstrs.
Sergt. G. Willett, 2/ North'n.
Corpl. E. Williams, R.E.
Pte. W. Williams, 2/ Sco. Rif.
C.S.M. John Wilson, 2/ W. York.
Pte. I. Wood, 9/ York & Lanc.
Corpl. R. J. Wood, R.A.M.C.
Pte. T. Woodhouse, 1/ Worc.
Lce.-Corporal E. Woodward, 8/ York & Lanc.
Sergt. F. G. Wyatt, R.A.
Pte. J. Yorker, 2/ W. York.
Sapper C. Young, R.E.

BAR TO MILITARY MEDAL

Lce.-Corporal S. Abernethy, 2/ Sco. Rif.
Lce.-Corporal J. Artingstall, R.E.
Pte. A. Baker, 1/ Sherw'd Frstrs.
Pte. W. H. Barbour, 2/ Sco. Rif.
Sergt. T. Barnes, 2/ Sco. Rif.
Lce.-Sergt. J. Batty, 2/ E. Lan.
Pte. R. Black, 2/ E. Lan.
Lce.-Corporal P. Boddington, 2/ North'n.
Sergt. J. E. Brown, M.G. Corps.
Pte. S. Cauwood, 2/ W. York.
Pte. J. Clarke, 2/ Sco. Rif.
Lce.-Corporal E. Cooper, 2/ E. Lan.
Lce.-Corporal J. L. Court, 2/ Midd'x.
Sergt. A. Dale, 2/ Rif. Brig.
Sergt. H. J. Dickinson, 2/ Linc.
Corpl. E. Dodds, 22/ Durh. L.I
Gnr. J. F. Doran, R.A.
Pte. A. Dunn, 2/ Devon.
Sergt. H. Eagle, 1/ Worc.
Corpl. G. E. Fielding, 2/ E. Lan.
Sergt. J. Fowler, 2/ E. Lan.
Pte. W. Freeman, 1/ Sherw'd Frstrs.
Lce.-Corpl. A. S. Goddard, R.A.M.C.
Corpl. W. H. Green, 2/ Midd'x
Sergt. W. E. Haffenden, R.E.
Rfmn. C. F. Halcombe, 2/ Rif. Brig.
Sergt. R. C. Harman, 2/ Linc.
Sergt. F. Harrington, 2/ Midd'x.
Lce.-Corporal J. Harris, 2/ Midd'x.
Corpl. H. Healey, 2/ W. York.
Sergt. J. Henshall, R.A.
Lce.-Sergt. J. J. Hickman, D.C.M. with 2 bars, 2/ Midd'x.
Corpl. J. Hornby, 1/ Sherw'd Frstrs.
Sergt. T. G. Huggins, 2/ R. Berks.
Rfmn. H. Hyde, D.C.M., 2/ Rif. Brig.
Corpl. J. S. Joyce, M.G.Corps.
Corpl. C. V. Lane, R.A.
Corpl. J. Leach, 2/ Midd'x.
Pte. G. Lewis, 2/ Midd'x.
Pte. J. Lock, 2/ Devon.
C.S.M. W. Lockley, D.C.M., 1/ Sherw'd Frstrs.
Corpl. D. Love, 1/ R. Ir. Rif.
Sergt. R. McMahon, R.E.

APPENDIX IV

2nd Corpl. P. G. Matthew, R.E.
Lce.-Corporal H. May, 2/ Devon.
Sergt. T. E. Mead, 2/ R. Berks.
Sergt. A. J. Miller, R.E.
Sergt. W. Millins, 2/ Midd'x.
Lce.-Corporal J. Millman, 2/ E. Lan.
Sergt. J, Morgan, 2/ E. Lan.
Corpl. W. Ogie, R.E.
Sergt. W. K. Palmer, R.E.
Pte. J. Payne, 2/ North'n.
Sergt. J. Petrie, M.G. Corps (Cav.).
C.S.M. S. Phillips, D.C.M. and bar, 1/ Worc.
Lce.-Corporal E. J. Porter, 2/ Rif. Brig.
Sergt. F. Powell, 2/ R. Berks.
Sergt. W. Rice, 2/ R. Berks.
Sergt. E. Riley, 2/ E. Lan.
Pte. A. Robinson, 22/ Durh. L.I.
Sergt. J. Rotherham, R.A.
Corpl. W. H. Routledge, 2/ Midd'x.
Lce.-Corporal R. Sawyer, R.E.
S.S.M. E. G. Scott, 2/ E. Lan.
Sergt. A. Shopland, 2/ Rif. Brig.
Pte. H. Smith, 2/ E. Lan.
Corpl. H. Smith, 1/ Sherw'd Frstrs.
Rfmn. W. Smyth, 1/ R. Ir. Rif.
Rfmn. G. Stone, 2/ Rif. Brig.
Bombdr. W. T. Sweetman, R.A.
Pte. W. Tabor, 2/ Midd'x.
Pte. S. Thompson, 2/ Midd'x.
Pte. A. Turner, 2/ E. Lan.
Sergt. G. G. Turvey, 2/ R. Berks.
Pte. H. Upson, 2/ Midd'x.
Pte. G. A. Vernon, 1/ Worc.
Rfmn. J. Vince, 2/ Rif. Brig.
Corpl. J. H. Weatherley, R.A.S.C.
Sergt. T. G. Wells, R.E.
Sergt. J. Wheatley, 2/ E. Lan.
Sergt. E. Williams, 2/ Sco. Rif.
Sergt. D. J. Wood, 2/ W. York.
Lce.-Corpl. H. Wylder, 2/ Middx.

MILITARY MEDAL

Pte. J. Aaron, 8/ K.O.Y.L.I.
Pte. L. Acock, 9/ York & Lanc.
Pte. E. Adams, 2/ R. Berks.
Pte. F. Adams, 1/ Sherw'd Frstrs.
Lce.-Corporal W. Adams, 2/E. Lan.
Rfmn. A. Addison, 2/ Rif. Brig.
Sapper W. Aitken, R.E.
Sergt. C. Alexander, M.G. Corps (Cav.).
Pte. Arthur Allen, 2/ Midd'x.
Gnr. E. Allen, R.A.
Pte. W. F. Allsopp, 2/ Midd'x.
Rfmn. A. Alves, T.M.B.
Pioneer T. Anderson, R.E.
Corpl. A. Andrews, 2/ W. York.
Corpl. S. Andrews, 2/ Rif. Brig.
Lce.-Corporal A. Anthony, 1/ Sherw'd Frstrs.
Sapper E. Anthony, R.E.
Gnr. W. Appleby, R.A.
Corpl. H. Archer, 2/ W. York.
Pte. W. Arnell, 2/ E. Lan.
Sergt. B. Arnold, 2/ Linc.
Pte. R. Arnold, 1/ Worc.
Lce.-Corporal W. Ashcroft, 2/ E. Lan.
Lce.-Corporal T. Ashman, 1/ Worc.
Sapper W. Askew, R.E.
Corpl. H. Asquith, 9/ York & Lanc.
Lce.-Corporal W. Aston, 1/ Worc.
Lce.-Corporal J. T. Atkinson, 2/ W. York.
Pte. S. Atkinson, 2/ E. Lan.
Pte. G. S. Aubertin, 2/ Midd'x.
Gnr. G. G. Austin, R.A.
Lce.-Sergt. J. Austin, 2/ R. Berks.
Sergt. J. E. Austin, R.A.
Corpl. F. Axtell, 2/ Middx.
Pte. C. Axworthy, 2/ Devon.
Pioneer T. R. Aynsley, R.E.
Pte. D. Ayres, 2/ R. Berks.
2nd Corpl. W. H. Baber, R.E.
Sergt. J. Bacon, 1/ R. Ir. Rif.
Pte. T. Bacon, 2/ Linc.
Gnr. H. Bagguley, R.A.
Pte. C. J. Bailey, R.A.S.C.
Corpl. T. W. Bailey, 2/ E. Lan.
Bombdr. W. Bailey, R.A.
Gnr. J. Baker, T.M.B.
Rfmn. S. Baker, 2/ Rif. Brig.

APPENDIX IV

Corpl. A. Baldwin, 1/ Worc.
Rfmn. G. Ball, 2/ Rif. Brig.
Lce.-Corporal F. Ballard, 2/ R. Berks.
Corpl. M. Balmer, 1/ Sherw'd Frstrs.
Pte. C. M. Balson, R.A.M.C.
Pte. J. Barclay, M.G. Corps.
Sergt. T. Barclay, R.A.
Pte. A. E. Barke, 2/ R. Berks.
Rfmn. H. F. Barnard, 2/ Rif. Brig.
Sapper J. Barnard, R.E.
Corpl. A. Barnes, R.E.
Sergt. F. Barnes, 2/ Rif. Brig.
Lce.-Corporal W. Barnes, 2/ R. Berks.
Pte. A. J. Barr, 1/ Worc.
Rfmn. T. Barr, 1/ R. Ir. Rif.
Bombr. W. Barrett, R.A.
Sergt. J. Barringer, 2/ Linc.
Sergt. C. A. T. Barryman, 2/ Linc.
Lce.-Corporal C. Bartlett, 2/ North'n.
Corpl. F. J. Bartlett, 2/ W. York.
Pte. H. Bartlett, 1/ Worc.
Corpl. H. G. Bartlett, 2/ R. Berks.
Corpl. R. Bartley, R.E., attd. R.F.A.
Rfmn. J. M. Barton, 2/ Rif. Brig.
Sergt. H. Basterfield, 1/ Worc.
Corpl. E. A. Bastin, R.A.M.C.
Sergt. J. A. Batchelor, 2/ Midd'x.
Sergt. T. Bates, 2/ Sco. Rif.
Driver J. Bathgate, R.A.
Pte. W. Batley, 1/8 Midd'x.
Pte. E. Battersby, 2/ E. Lan.
Lce.-Corporal B. V. Baynham, M.G. Corps.
2nd Corporal A. W. Beacham, R.E.
Pte. A. Beaman, 1/ Worc.
Pte. E. F. Beard, 2/ Midd'x.
Pte. A. Beardsley, 1/ Sherw'd Frstrs.
Lce.-Corporal V. Beasley, 1/ Worc.
Sergt. H. Beaufoy, R.A.
Corpl. P. Beech, 8/ York & Lanc.
Pte. G. L. Beer, M.G. Corps.
Pte. J. W. Beevers, 9/ York & Lanc.

Sergt. W. J. Beland, 2/ Midd'x.
Pte. F. Belcher, 2/ R. Berks.
Sergt. F. Bell, 2/ Sco. Rif.
Pte. G. Bell, 2/ Linc.
Pte. G. H. Bell, 2/ W. York.
Lce.-Corporal K. M. Bell, R.E.
Gnr. T. Bellew, R.A.
Lce.-Corporal J. E. Bellwood, 2/ Rif. Brig.
Rfmn. A. Bennett, 2/ Rif. Brig.
Pte. A. Bennett, M.G. Corps.
Pte. J. Bennett, 1/ Sherw'd Frstrs.
Pte. S. Bennett, 2/ North'n.
Sergt. H. Beniams, D.C.M., 1/ Worc.
Lce-Corporal W. Benning, 2/ Sco. Rif.
Sergt. F. Benson, 22/ Durh. L.I.
Sergt. A. Bentley, 2/ Midd'x.
Sergt. T. M. Bently, R.A.
Lce.-Corporal A. Berris, 2/ R. Berks.
Lce.-Corporal A. Berry, 2/ Devon.
Rfmn. J. Berry, 2/ Rif. Brig.
Sergt. W. W. Beswick, R.A.
Pte. C. Betteridge, M.G. Corps.
Lce.-Corporal W. Bingham, 1/ Sherw'd Frstrs.
Corpl. A. Bird, 1/ Worc.
Corpl. S. E. Bisby, M.G. Corps.
Sergt. H. C. Bishop, 2/ Midd'x.
Corpl. J. P. Blackstock, T.M.B.
Corpl. E. Blair, 2/ W. York.
Sergt. J. Blazey, 1/ Sherw'd Frstrs.
Sergt. R. Bloodworth, 2/ Rif. Brig.
Pte. W. Blosse, M.G. Corps.
Lce.-Corporal J. Blythe, 1/ Sherw'd. Frstrs.
Lce.-Corporal E. Boame, 2/ Devon.
Sergt. W. Boaz, R.E.
Pte. M. Bond, T.M.B.
Pte. G. W. Bonner, R.A.M.C.
Pte. P. Booth, M.G. Corps.
Lce.-Corporal W. A. Booth, 11/ Sherw'd. Frstrs.
Rfmn. F. T. Boothby, 2/ Rif. Brig.
Sergt. W. Boulstredge, R.A.
Lce.-Corporal S. Boulton, 1/ Worc.
Sergt. E. Bowden, 2/ Devon.

APPENDIX IV

Sergt. J. H. Bowles, 2/ Midd'x.
Pte. W. Bowley, 1/ Sherw'd Frstrs.
Pte. W. Bowman, 2/ Sco. Rif.
Pte. J. T. Bradbury, 1/ Worc.
Lce.-Corporal H. Bradford, 8/ York & Lanc.
Pte. F. Bradley, 2/ W. York.
Pte. E. Bradwell, 2/ North'n.
Lce.-Corporal P. Brady, 2/ Linc.
Signlr. E. Brain, R.A.
Pte. E. Bramwell, 1/ Sherw'd Frstrs.
Pte. G. Bramwell, 9/ York & Lanc.
Sergt. F. A. Branch, 2/ R. Berks.
Lce.-Corporal J. W. Brant, 2/ Linc.
Pte. M. Brawman, 9/ York & Lanc.
C.Q.M. Sergt. A. E. Brewster, 2/ Linc.
Corpl. W. Bridge, 8/ K.O.Y.L.I.
Lce.-Corporal W. Bridge, 1/ Worc.
Pte. S. Briggs, 2/ W. York.
Pte. A. T. Brion, 2/ R. Berks.
Sergt. A. Bristow, 2/ Rif. Brig.
Bombdr. A. H. Britt, R.A.
Pte. C. Broadbent, R.A.M.C.
Corpl. J. Brock, 1/ R. Ir. Rif.
Corpl. S. Brock, 1/ R. Ir. Rif.
Pte. G. H. Broderick, 2/ North'n.
Lce.-Corporal A. Brooks, R.E.
Sapper J. Brooks, R.E.
Lce.-Corporal W. Brooksbank, 2/ W. York.
Pte. W. Brooksbank, 2/ W. York.
Lce.-Corporal R. Broom, 2/ Midd'x.
Pte. A. Brown, 2/ R. Berks.
Sergt. A. C. Brown, 2/ Rif. Brig.
Lce.-Corporal C. Brown, 2/ Linc.
Driver E. Brown, R.A.
Pte. G. H. Brown, 2/ W. York.
Gnr. J. Brown, R.A.
Pte. J. A. Brown, 22/ Durh. L.I.
Pte. J. W. Brown, 2/ Linc.
Sergt. R. Brown, 1/ Worc.
Lce.-Sergt. R. W. Brown, 2/ Midd'x.
Farrier-Sergt. W. Brown, R.E.
Pte. J. G. Browning, 2/ Devon.
Corpl. E. C. Brownlow, 1/ Sherw'd Frstrs.
Pte. A. R. Buckley, M.G. Corps (Cav.).
Lce.-Corporal G. Bucktrout, 8/ York & Lanc.
Lce.-Corporal F. Budd, 2/ Devon.
Sergt. W. Bull, 2/ Rif. Brig.
Lce.-Corporal H. G. Bullard, 1/ Sherw'd Frstrs.
Bombdr. R. C. Bullas, R.A.
Rfmn. H. Bullen, 2/ Rif. Brig.
Pte. J. Bullen, 9/ York & Lanc.
Rfmn. R. J. Bullock, 1/ R. Ir. Rif.
Pte. A. Bunt, R.A.M.C.
Rfmn. A. Burgess, 2/ Rif. Brig.
Pte. J. Burgess, 2/ Midd'x.
Lce.-Corporal C. Burley, R.E.
Lce.-Sergt. T. E. Burnett, 2/ W. York.
Pte. W. J. Burnett, R.A.M.C.
Pte. A. Burridge, R.A.M.C.
Pte. T. Bury, 2/ E. Lan.
Pte. F. Busfield, 2/ E. Lan.
Pte. N. Butcher, 1/ Sherw'd Frstrs.
Corpl. P. Butcher, 2/ Rif. Brig.
Corpl. E. M. Butler, 2/ Rif. Brig.
Pte. J. Butler, 2/ Linc.
Sergt. T. Butler, 2/ Midd'x.
Corpl. W. H. Butler, 2/ R. Berks.
Sergt. A. Butt, 2/ Midd'x.
2nd Corpl. C. H. Byard, R.E.
Lce.-Corporal D. Byde, 2/ R. Berks.
Lce.-Corporal J. Caine, 2/ E. Lan.
Pte. J. Cairns, 2/ W. York.
2nd Corpl. W. G. Callender, R.E.
Driver E. Calloway, R.A.
Driver F. Calloway, R.A.
Sergt. C. Campbell, 2/ Midd'x.
Rfmn. W. Canfield, 2/ Rif. Brig.
Lce.-Corporal J. G. Cannon, M.G. Corps (Cav.).
Corpl. A. Capeman, 1/ Worc.
Gnr. W. Capstick, R.A.
Bombdr. L. C. Carey, R.A.
Pte. P. Carey, 2/ E. Lan.

APPENDIX IV

Corpl. W. Carlisle, 2/ Rif. Brig.
Pte. R. J. Carnaghan, 2/ Midd'x.
Driver W. H. Carne, R.A.M.C.
Gnr. A. V. Carpenter, R.A.
Sergt. F. Carpenter, K.O.Y.L.I.
Rfmn. H. Carpenter, 2/ Rif. Brig.
Sergt. W. T. Carroll, 22/Durh.L.I.
Pte. C. Carter, M.G. Corps.
Sergt. H. Carter, M.G. Corps.
Corpl. S. Cartlidge, 1/ Sherw'd Frstrs.
Sergt. A. Cartwright, 2/ Midd'x.
Rfmn. J. Cartwright, 2/ Rif. Brig.
Pte. T. R. Casey, 2/ Devon.
Pte. J. Cashel, R. Dub. Fus.
Driver H. Castle, R.A.
Bombdr. H. Castle, D.C.M., R.A.
Sergt. W. B. G. Catchpole, 2/ Midd'x.
Pte. C. F. Cavalier, M.G. Corps.
Pte. J. Chalk, 2/ R. Berks.
Corpl. G. Chambers, 1/ Sherw'd Frstrs.
Pte. P. A. R. Chandler, 1/ Sherw'd Frstrs.
Pte. I. R. Chapman, 2/ E. Lan.
Pte. J. Chapman, 1/ Sherw'd Frstrs.
Sergt. S. F. Chapman, 2/ Midd'x.
Lce.-Corporal T. Charnick,T.M.B.
Lce.-Corporal W. E. Cheape, 2/ Midd'x.
Lce.-Corporal W. F. Christie, R.E.
Pte. N. Clare, 2/ E. Lan.
Bombdr. J. H. Clark, R.A.
Corpl. F. Clarke, 8/ York & Lanc.
Pte. J. Clarke, 2/ Sco. Rif.
Sergt. O. Clarke, 1/ Sherw'd Frstrs.
Sergt. R. Clarke, R.E.
Pte. R. Clarke, 2/ Linc.
Pte. R. Clarke, 2/ R. Berks.
Pte. R. E. Clarke, 1/ Worc.
C.Q.M. Sergt. T. Clarkson, 9/ York & Lanc.
Sergt. A. B. Claydon, 2/ W. York.
Gnr. F. G. Clift, R.A.
Bombdr. F. T. Clinch, R.A.
Pte. F. C. Clipston, 2/ R. Berks.
Pte. J. F. Clitheroe, 2/ Linc.

Lce.-Corporal E. J. Cockell, 2/ Midd'x.
Lce.-Sergt. S. B. Cockram, 2/ North'n.
Sergt. W. W. Cockram, 2/ Devon.
Pte. E. Cocks, 2/ R. Berks.
Sergt. F. C. Coffey, 2/ R. Berks.
Rfmn. J. W. Coit, 2/ Rif. Brig.
Pte. F. Cole, 11/ Sherw'd Frstrs.
Corpl. E. Coleman, 1/ Sherw'd Frstrs.
Lce.-Corporal P. Coleman, 1/ R. Ir. Rif.
Pte. R. N. Coleman, 2/ R. Berks.
Sergt. R. Coleridge, R.A.M.C.
Pte. Edward Coles, 2/ R. Berks.
Pte. E. Coles, 2/ Devon.
Lce.-Corporal S. F. Coles, 2/ Linc.
Pte. J. G. Coley, 2/ North'n.
Lce.-Corporal J. Colley, 2/ Linc.
Pte. A. Collins, 2/ Midd'x.
Pte. F. Collins, 2/ R. Berks.
Lce.-Corporal H. R. Collins, 2/ Devon.
Rfmn. J. Collins, 1/ R. Ir. Rif.
Sergt. S. Collins, R.A.M.C.
Lce.-Corporal C. Colter, 2/ Rif. Brig.
Pte. R. Coltman, 22/ Durh. L.I.
Lce.-Corporal C. H. Colton, 2/ W. York.
Lce.-Corporal R. Common, 2/ Sco. Rif.
Pte. J. W. Compton, 2/ W. York.
Rfmn. M. Condron, 1/ R. Ir. Rif.
Gnr. E. Connor, R.A.
Signlr. P. Connor, 2/ Midd'x.
Pte. R. Conway, 2/ E. Lan.
Sergt. H. Cooper, R.E.
Pte. H. Cooper, 2/ Devon.
Pte. J. H. Cooper, 2/ Lin.
Pte. J. R. Cooper, 22/ Durh. L.I.
Pte. T. Cooper, 2/ E. Lan.
Lce.-Corporal W. Cooper, 2/ Linc.
Pte. H. Copestake, 2/ Linc.
Sergt. J. Corbett, 1/ Worc.
Sergt. H. Cording, 2/ Midd'x.
Pte. G. Costello, 2/ Devon.
Lce.-Corporal J. H. Cotterell, 2/ R. Berks.

APPENDIX IV

Pte. W. Cottle, 1/ Worc.
Corpl. B. S. H. Cowdrey, R.E.
Lce.-Sergt. A. L. Cowley, 2/ North'n.
Pte. J. Cox, 1/ Worc.
Sergt. P. H. Cox, 2/ Devon.
Pte. F. J. Coxhead, 2/ R. Berks.
Rfmn. J. W. Crampton, 2/ Rif. Brig.
Pte. A. Crawford, T.M.B.
Sergt. J. F. Crawford, R.A.
Pte. J. M. Crawford, 2/ Midd'x.
Pte. J. M. Craze, R.A.M.C.
Bombdr. A. Creaser, R.A.
Pte. T. Creffield, 2/ R. Berks.
Pte. D. Crew, 2/ Linc.
Pte. F. Criddle, 2/ R. Berks.
Driver H. Criddle, R.A.
Sergt. L. Crispen, 2/ Devons.
Pte. F. A. Crispen, R.A.M.C.
Corpl. G. Crocker, R.A.M.C.
Sergt. N. Crofts, R.A.
Gnr. F. Crossley, R.A.
Corpl. W. W. Crowe, R.A.
Sergt. C. F. Crowson, 8/ York & Lanc.
Lce.-Corporal R. Cruikshanks, 2/ Sco. Rif.
Lce.-Corporal J. G. Crutchley, 1/ Worc.
Corpl. G. W. Cude, 2/ Midd'x.
Pte. W. H. Cullip, R.A.M.C.
Sergt. J. T. Cundy, 2/ Linc.
Gnr. G. Cunningham, R.A.
Gnr. J. Curran, R.A.
Sergt. R. E. L. Currell, R.A.M.C.
Pte. J. Currie, 2/ Sco. Rif.
Driver A. Curry, R.A.
Pte. G. Curtis, 2/ R. Berks.
Driver W. Cutting, R.A.
Farrier-Sergt. S. Dalton, R.A.
Pte. G. F. Damsell, 1/ Worc.
Lce.-Corporal A. G. Dance, 2/ R. Berks.
Corpl. J. Dare, R.E.
Pte. A. Darling, 1/ North'n.
Sapper G. Darling, R.E.
Pte. W. H. Darroll, T.M.B.
Lce.-Corporal H. Davey, R.E.
Corpl. W. L. Davey, 2/ Rif. Brig.

Corpl. E. J. Davidson, R.E.
Bombdr. E. Davies, R.A.
Sergt. E. Davies, R.A.
Sergt. E. J. Davies, R.E.
Sergt. John Davies, 1/ Worc.
Pte. R. Davies, 1/ Worc.
Corpl. Arthur Davis, 1/ Worc.
Corpl. F. C. Davis, R.E.
Sergt. H. Davis, R.E.
Lce.-Corporal R. T. Davis, 2/ Rif. Brig.
Pte. Wm. Davis, 2/ Linc.
Rfmn. T. Davy, 2/ Rif. Brig.
Pte. J. Deakin, 1/ Worc.
Pte. C. F. Dean, 2/ North'n.
2nd Corpl. F. Dean, R.E.
Lce.-Corporal W. Dean, 2/ E. Lan.
Corpl. A. Decort, M.G. Corps.
Pte. E. Deffee, 2/ R. Berks.
Sergt. C. Delury, 1/ R. Ir. Rif.
Driver W. Denis, R.A.
Corpl. E. Dennett, 2/ Linc.
Pte. V. Denning, 1/ Worc.
Rfmn. A. C. Dennington, 2/ Rif. Brig.
Corpl. J. R. Dennison, Cyclist Bn.
Pte. F. W. Dent, K.O.Y.L.I.
Corpl. F. Denton, 1/ Linc.
Sergt. H. Denton, 2/ North'n.
Rfmn. A. Derrington, 2/ Rif. Brig.
Lce.-Corporal P. Dewhirst, 2/ W. York.
Pte. G. Dickens, 2/ North'n.
Pte. A. G. Dickeson, 2/ Devon.
Rfmn. J. Dickeson, 1/ R. Ir. Rif.
Pte. F. W. Dicks, 2/ North'n.
Pte. J. M. Dilworth, 2/ Linc.
Sergt. A. E. Dingley, 2/ Midd'x.
Pte. F. Dinning, 22/ Durh. L.I.
Pte. W. Dinsdale, 2/ E. Lan.
Pte. A. Dixon, 8/ K.O.Y.L.I.
Sergt. C. A. Dixon, 10/ K.O.Y.L.I.
Bombdr. H. W. Dixon, R.A.
Sergt. J. Dobson, 9/ York & Lanc.
Sergt. J. P. Dobson, 9/ York & Lanc.
Pte. E. Dodsley, T.M.B.

APPENDIX IV

Sapper A. Doherty, R.E.
Sergt. J. G. Donald, 2/ W. York.
Pte. H. Dooks, 2/ W. York.
Pte. A. Douglas, R.A.M.C.
Sergt. J. Dowd, 2/ Linc.
Corpl. L. Downes, 2/ Rif. Brig.
Lce.-Corporal D. Downie, M.G. Corps.
Sapper G. H. Downing, R.A.
Driver J. Drake, R.A.
Pte. H. R. Dresser, 2/ Midd'x.
Pte. J. Drew, 2/ Sco. Rif.
Pte. W. Drew, 1/ Worc.
Pte. T. F. Drinkwater, 2/ R. Berks.
Bombdr. P. C. Drury, R.A.
Corpl. C. Duffy, 2/ Sco. Rif.
Corpl. A. J. Dugdale, R.E.
Pte. T. Duggan, 2/ E. Lan.
Pte. N. Duncan, M.G. Corps (Cav.).
Sapper F. Dunford, R.E.
Lce.-Corporal C. Dunlop, 1/ R. Ir. Rif.
Bombdr. E. Dunn, R.E.
Sergt. J. Dutton, R.A.
Sergt. S. Dyer, 11/ Sherw'd Frstrs.
Pte. A. Dyson, 8/ York & Lanc.
Corpl. J. Earle, 2/ Rif. Brig.
Rfmn. J. East, 2/ Rif. Brig.
Lce.-Corporal J. A. Eaton, 1/ Sherw'd Frstrs.
Pte. W. Eaton, 1/ Worc.
Bombdr. E. Eden, R.A.
Lce.-Corporal E. Eden, 2/ Linc.
Gnr. D. Edgar, R.A.
Pte. F. Edwards, 2/ Devon.
Pte. F. Edwards, 22/ Durh. L.I.
Pte. H. S. Edwards, 2/ Linc.
Driver L. Edwards, R.A.
Pte. T. J. Egan, 1/ Sherw'd Frstrs.
Lce.-Corporal P. A. Egre, M.G. Corps.
Pte. G. Else, M.G. Corps.
Pte. E. J. E. Elliott, 2/ North'n.
Pte. W. J. Elliott, R.A.M.C.
Pte. E. Ellis, 1/ Sherw'd. Frstrs.
Sergt. F. Ellis, R.E.
Sergt. F. J. Ellis, R.A.M.C.
Sergt. P. Ellis, 1/ Worc.
Lce.-Corporal T. Ellis, 9/ York & Lanc.
Pte. F. Ellison, 2/ W. York.
Pte. G. H. Elsey, 2/ Midd'x.
Pte. J. W. Emerson, 2/ Linc.
Sergt. W. J. Etheridge, R.A.M.C.
Pte. F. Ette, 2/ North'n.
Sergt. F. P. Evans, M.G. Corps (Cav.).
Pioneer I. Evans, R.E.
Sergt. J. T. Evans, 8/ K.O.Y.L.I.
Lce.-Corpl. W. D. Evans, 2/ Midd'x.
Corpl. W. P. Evans, R.E.
Corpl. F. Ewart, R.E.
Pte. W. Eyles, 2/ Midd'x.
Lce.-Corporal C. Fabian, 2/ Midd'x.
Pte. W. Facer, 2/ North'n.
Lce.-Corporal H. Fagence, T.M.B.
Pte. G. T. Faggetter, 2/ Midd'x.
Lce.-Corporal W. L. Fairweather, R.E.
Pte. P. Fallon, 2/ Sco. Rif.
Gnr. J. Farrell, R.A.
Rfmn. Wm. Farrell, 2/ Rif. Brig.
Corpl. G. H. Fawcett, 2/ E. Lan.
Lce.-Corpl. F. Feaviour, 2/ R. Berks.
Sapper Thos. Fergus, R.E., attd. R.A.
Sergt. G. Ferguson, 1/ Sherw'd Frstrs.
Pte. H. Ferrari, 2/ W. York.
Pte. J. Fidler, 2/ E. Lan.
Rfmn. T. Fido, 2/ Rif. Brig.
2nd Corporal Geo. Field, R.E.
Pte. A. Fillsell, 2/ North'n.
Corpl. A. F. Finch, R.A.S.C.
Pte. W. Finch, 2/ R. Berks.
Bombdr. R. Finlayson, R.A.
Rfmn. F. J. Firkin 2/ Rif. Brig.
Sapper W. Firth, R.E.
Rfmn. J. R. Fisher, 2/ Rif. Brig.
Corpl. E. Fisk, 2/ Rif. Brig.
Gnr. F. Fitzgerald, R.A.
Pte. J. J. Fitzgerald, 2/ R. Berks.
Sergt. W. Fitzgerald, 2/ Lin.
Pte. W. Fleming, 2/ Devon.

APPENDIX IV

Pte. J. Flemming, 2/ E. Lan.
Corpl. E. Fletcher, 1/Sherw'd Frstrs.
Pte. J. Fletcher M.G. Corps (Cav.).
Pte. H. Flint, 2/ W. York.
Sergt. C. H. Foster, R.A.V.C.
Sergt. E. Foster, 2/ Devon.
Pte. E. Foster, 2/ Midd'x.
Lce.-Corporal J. Fowler, 2/ Devon.
Pte. J. Fox, 2/ Sco. Rif.
Sergt. W. Frame, 1/ Sherwood Frstrs.
Gnr. A. Franks, R.A.
Pte. F. Fraser, M.G. Corps.
Sapper F. G. Freeman, R.E.
Bombdr. T. G. Fripp, R.A.
Lce.-Corporal F. Frost, 2/ North'n.
Lce.-Corporal H. Frost, 2/ Midd'x.
Sergt. W. Frost, 2/ Linc.
Pte. W. Frost, 2/ North'n.
Rfmn. C. W. Fry, 2/ Rif. Brig.
Sergt. J. F. Fryer, 2/ Midd'x.
Gnr. P. Fuller, R.A.
Bombdr. R. J. Fulliloe, R.A.
R.S.M. J. Furey, 2/ Rif. Brig.
Sergt. E. Gadd, R.A.
Sergt. W. Gaines, 8/ K.O.Y.L.I.
Pte. P. Gaitley, 2/ E. Lan.
Sergt. C. J. Gallagher, R.A.
Sergt. R. Garbutt, 22/ Durh. L.I.
Rfmn. T. Garbutt, 2/ Rif. Brig.
Sapper R. R. Gardiner, R.E.
Pte. J. S. Gardner, 11/ Sherw'd Frstrs.
Corpl. T. H. Gardner, 1/ Worc.
Sergt. H. Garley, 2/ Rif. Brig.
Corpl. C. Garner, 2/ Rif. Brig.
Pte. J. J. Garnett, 2/ W. York.
Lce.-Corporal W. Garrett, 2/ Sco. Rif.
Sergt. E. G. Garrity, R.E.
Pte. M. Garvey, M.G. Corps.
Sergt. G. H. Garwood, 1/ Worc.
Pte. J. Gaskin, 1/ R.Ir. Rif.
Sergt. A. V. Gayler, 2/ Midd'x.
Sergt. J. Gedney, R.A.
Pte. A. J. George, 2/ R. Berks.
Pte. G. George, 2/ North'n.
Lce.-Sergt. O. C. Gerrard, 2/ Rif. Brig.
Driver J. Gibson, R.A.

Gnr. J. Gibson, R.A.
Lce.-Corporal P. Gibson, 2/Midd'x.
Rfmn. T. Gibson, 2/ Rif. Brig.
Pte. W. Giddings, 2/ Linc.
Lce.-Corpl. A. Gilbert, 2/ Midd'x.
Driver C. C. Gilchrist, R.A.
Sergt. H. J. Gill, 2/ Devon.
Sergt. J. Gilliland, 2/ Devon.
Sergt. W. A. Gillingham, 2/ R. Berks.
Pte. P. Gillon, 2/ Sco. Rif.
Pte. R. T. Gladding, 2/ North'n.
Rfmn. W. G. Goddard, 2/ Rif. Brig.
Sergt. W. Golding, 2/ Devon.
Corpl. F. Goodridge, M.G. Corps.
Pte. C. Goodwin, 8/ K.O.Y.L.I.
Sergt. G. A. Goodwin, R.A.
Sergt. Wm. Goodyear, 2/ Devon.
Pte. W. H. Goosey, 2/ North'n.
Lce.-Corpl. J. Gordon, R.E.
Pte. E. Gorton, 2/ E. Lan.
Pte. T. E. Goucher, 1/ Sherw'd Frstrs.
Sergt. F. Goude, 2/ Sco. Rif.
Lce.-Corporal A. Gower, 2/ Midd'x.
Pte. G. T. Gowers, 2/ North'n.
Lce.-Corporal P. Gowland, 2/ E. Lan.
Pte. J. H. Gowling, 1/ Worc.
Pte. G. Graham, 2/ R. Berks.
Rfmn. J. Graham, 1/ R.Ir. Rif.
Pte. C. Grainger, 2/ Midd'x.
Corpl. T. H. Grainger, 2/ Devon.
Sergt. A. J. A. Grand, 1/ Sherw'd Frstrs.
Gnr. Donald Grant, R.A.
Sapper F. Grant, R.E.
Lce.-Corporal G. Gration, M.G. Corps.
Bombdr. E. C. Graves, T.M.B.
Pte. F. Green, 2/ E. Lan.
Sergt. G. E. Green, 1/ Worc.
Pte. H. W. Green, 2/ R. Berks.
Lce.-Corporal H. W. Green, 2/ W. York.
Corpl. J. Green, 22/ Durh. L.I.
Corpl. J. Green, 2/ E. Lan.
Bombdr. J. Green, R.A.

APPENDIX IV

Corpl. J. C. Green, 2/ North'n.
Sergt. J. F. Green, 2/ Linc.
Pte. P. W. Greenbury, 1/ Sherw'd Frstrs.
Gnr. F. Greenhalgh, R.A.
Corpl. C. Greenslade, 2/ Devon.
Pte. D. Greenslade, 2/ Devon.
Corpl. H. P. Greenwood, 8/ York & Lanc.
Pte. G. Gregory, 2/ Devon.
Corpl. H. Grice, 2/ R. Berks.
Lce.-Corporal J. Griffen, R.E.
Corpl. G. Griffin, 2/ Sco. Rif.
Pte. F. J. Griggs, 2/ Midd'x.
Sergt. B. Grout, 2/ Rif. Brig.
Bombdr. C. Gully, R.A.
Corpl. B. A. Gurney, 2/ R. Berks.
Lce.-Corporal A. J. Guttridge, 2/ R. Berks.
Pte. J. F. J. Guy, 1/ Sherw'd Frstrs.
Pte. F. C. Guyatt, M.G. Corps.
Sergt. A. Gyte, 1/ Sherw'd Frstrs.
Sergt. H. E. Hadley, 1/ Worc.
Sergt. C. Haigh, 2/ W. York.
Lce.-Corporal J. Hail, 1/ Worc.
Lce.-Corporal F C. Haine, 2/ R. Berks.
Bombdr. B. F. Haines, R.A.
Sergt. W. Hales, R.E.
Pte. C. Hall, 2/ Rif. Brig.
Driver Geo. Hall, R.A.
Sergt. Harry Hall, 2/ North'n.
Pte. J. Hall, D.C.M., 2/ W. York.
Sergt. S. H. Hall, M.M.P.
Driver J. Halliwell, R.A.
Corpl. H. S. Hammond, R.E.
Pte. W. G. Hands, 2/ Devon.
Pte. J. Hannaford, 2/ Devon.
Gnr. F. Hannigan, R.A.
Pte. E.J. Harcourt,10/K.O.Y.L.I.
Driver H. G. Harding, R.A.
Sergt. F. Harper, 22/ Dur. L.I.
Rfmn. A. Harrild, 2/ Rif. Brig.
Sergt. E. Harris, 2/ R. Berks.
Pte. E. J. Harris, 2/ R. Berks.
Sergt. F. Harris, R.A.M.C.
Pte. A. Harrison, 2/ E. Lan.
Sergt. D. Harrison, 2/ Sco. Rif.
Pte. F. G. Harrison, 22/ Durh. L.I.
Pte. R. Harrison, 1/ Sherw'd Frstrs.
Pte. T. Harrison, 2/ E. Lan.
Gnr. E. Harrop, R.A.
Pte. W. H. Harry, 2/ R. Berks.
Pte. A. Hartley, 2/ E. Lan.
Pte. J. W. Hartley, 2/ E. Lan.
Pte. V. Harvey, 2/ Devon.
Sergt. W. Harvey, R.E.
Pte. F. Harwood, 2/ Midd'x.
Sapper C. Hatton, R.E.
Sapper V. L. Hatton, R.E.
Driver G. T. Hayes, R.A.
Corpl. J. Hayman, 2/ Sco. Rif.
Corpl. E. W. Haynes, R.A.
Rfmn. C. Head, 2/ Rif. Brig.
Pte. W. Heafield, 9/ York & Lanc.
Pte. W. Healy, M.G. Corps.
Gnr. H Heath, T.M.B.
Lce.-Sergt. E. Heaver, 8/ York & Lanc.
Pte. T. Hebron, 2/ W. York.
Driver A. Hellbeck, R.A.
Lce.-Corporal G. Helyar, M.G. Corps.
Lce.-Sergt. J. Hemborough, 2/ Devon.
Sapper G. Hemsley, R.E.
Pte. J. W. Hemsley, M.G. Corps.
Rfmn. G. W. Hendle, 2/ Rif. Brig.
Pte. C. Henson, 1/ Sherw'd Frstrs.
Pte. E. E. Henson, 2/ Devon.
Sergt. F. J. Henwood, R.A.M.C.
Sapper A. Heppell, R.E.
Sergt. H. Hestley, 2/ R. Berks.
Sapper O. Hibberd, R.E.
Lce.-Corporal T. Hickey, 2/ Linc.
Bombdr. R. Higgin, R.A.
Lce.-Corporal T. Higgins, R.E.
Pte. J. A. Hill, 9/ York & Lanc.
Lce.-Corporal T. Hill, 2/ Midd'x.
Driver A. Hillbeck, R.A.
Gnr. J. Hilton, R.A.
Sergt. W. Hind, 2/ W. York.
Lce.-Corporal A. Hinett, 11/ Sherw'd Frstrs.
Sergt. M. Hobbs, 2/ Devon
Lce.-Corporal E. C. Hocking, 1/ Sherw'd Frstrs.
Pte. H. Hocking, 2/ Devon.
Pte. F. A. Hodgkins, 2/ Midd'x.

APPENDIX IV

Lce.-Corporal A. P. Hodgson, 22/ Durh. L.I.
Gnr. H. Hodgson, R.A.
Corpl. J. H. Hoe, 1/ Sherw'd Frstrs.
Pte. R. Hogg, 2/ R. Berks.
Sergt. S. Hoitt, 2/ W. Yorks.
Sergt. J. Holberry, 8/ York & Lanc.
Lce.-Corpl J. Holden, K.O.Y.L.I.
Pte. C. Holder, 2/ R. Berks.
Pte. C. H. Holgate, 2/ North'n.
Pte. G. Hollings, 2/ W. York.
Lce.-Corporal T. A. Hollingworth, 1/ Sherw'd Frstrs.
Pte. B. Holman, R.A.S.C.
Pte. J. F. Holman, M.G. Corps.
Lce.-Corporal. A. E. Holmes, 2/ Devon.
Pte. S. Holmes, 2/ W. York.
Corporal J. Holt, T.M.B.
Rfmn. J. Honour, 2/ Rif. Brig.
Lce.-Corporal W. C. Hook, 2/ Midd'x.
Lce.-Corpl R. Hooley, M.G. Corps.
Bugler E. Hooton, 2/ Sco. Rif.
Gnr. Robert Hope, R.A.
Corpl. S. Hope, T.M.B.
Pte. G. A. Hopkins, 2/ Devon.
Pte. R.A. Hopper, 10/ K.O.Y.L.I.
Pte. R. Hopps, 22/ Durh. L.I.
Pte. G. Horlock, 2/ Midd'x.
Corpl. R. E. Horner, 2/ North'n.
Lce.-Corporal H. Horscroft, 2/ Midd'x.
Sergt. J. Horton, 8/ York & Lanc.
Sergt. J. Hosker, 2/ E. Lan.
Lce.-Corporal J. K. Hoskings, 2/ Devon.
Sergt.-Major A. E. R. House, R.A.M.C.
Pioneer L. Houston, R.E.
Sergt. R. Houston, 1/ R. Ir. Rif.
Driver J. Howard, R.A.
Pte. W. Howard, 2/ North'n.
Corpl. Wm. Howard, 2/ North'n.
Lce.-Sergt. J. Howarth, 2/ E. Lan.
Pte. J. H. Howarth, 2/ Midd'x.
Driver H. Howe, R.A.S.C.
2nd Corporal F. Howell, R.E.
Corpl. W. J. Howell, R.A.M.C.
Sergt. J.H. Howells, 22/ Durh. L.I.
Pte. W. Howells, 2/ Devon.
Driver S. Hoye, R.E., attd. R.A.
Pte. E. Hubbock, 2/ R. Berks.
C.Q.M. Sergt. A. Huby, 2/ W. York.
Lce.-Corporal C. W. Hucklesey, 2/ Midd'x.
Gnr. H. Hudson, R.A.
Sergt. Wm. Hudson, R.A.
Gnr. W. F. Hudson, R.A.
Pte. H. Hughes, 2/ Linc.
Pte. L. S. Hughes, M.G. Corps.
Pte. F. A. Hulks, 2/ Devon.
Corpl. J. Hunter, 2/ Sco. Rif.
Corpl. J. Hunter, R.A.
Pte. E. Hurley, 1/ Worc.
Gnr. L. W. Hurst, R.A.
Pioneer W. Hurst, R.E.
Bombdr. B. Husselbee, R.A.
Rfmn. W. G. Hutchins, 2/ Rif. Brig.
Pte. W. Hutchinson, 2/ W. York.
Pte. V. G. Hutt, 2/ Devon.
Sergt. P. G. Hyde, 2/ Sco. Rif.
Lce.-Corporal P. Hyland, 1/ R. Ir. Rif.
Lce.-Sergt. E. Hyndman, D.C.M., 2/ E. Lan.
Sergt. H. Hyson, R.E.
Pte. H. Illsley, 2/ R. Berks.
Pte. R. Ingham, 2/ E. Lan.
C.S.M. T. Inwood, 2/ Rif. Brig.
Driver F. Isaacs, R.A.
Lce.-Corporal A. Isbister, 2/ Sco. Rif.
Sergt. G. A. Ives, 2/ E. Lan.
Pte. A. Jackson, 11/ Sherw'd Frstrs.
Pte. J. Jackson, 2/ E. Lan.
Sergt. A. James, 1/ Worc.
Pte. J. W. James, 1/ R. Ir. Rif.
Sergt. A. Jardine, 2/ Sco. Rif.
Lce.-Corporal A. Jarratt, 1/ Sherw'd Frstrs.
Corpl. F. Jarvis, 2/ Rif. Brig.
Pte. E. Jennings, 2/ Linc.
Bombdr. E. G. Jennings, R.A.
Corpl. W. F. Jennings, R.E.
Sapper W. F. Johncock, R.E.

APPENDIX IV

Sergt. A. Johnson, 2/ R. Berks.
Lce.-Corporal A. Johnson, 2/ W. York.
Pte. A. Johnson, 1/8 Midd'x.
Pte. G. Johnson, 9/ York & Lanc.
Lce.-Corporal J. T. Johnson, 8/ K.O.Y.L.I.
Pte. P. D. Johnson, 11/ Sherw'd Frstrs.
Sergt. W. Johnson, R.E.
Sapper W. E. Johnson, R.E.
Rfmn. W. F. Johnson, 2/ Rif. Brig.
Driver A. Johnston, R.A.
Rfmn. A. Johnston, 1/ R. Ir. Rif.
Pte. F. Joint, 2/ Devon.
Rfmn. J. Jolly, 2/ Rif. Brig.
Gnr. Alfred Jones, R.A.
Lce.-Corporal Chas. Jones, R.E.
Corpl. C. H. Jones, 8/ K.O.Y.L.I.
Sapper E. V. Jones, R.E.
Pte. G. H. Jones, 9/ York & Lanc.
Sergt. J. Jones, 2/ Rif. Brig.
Sergt. T. Jones, 11/ Sherw'd Frstrs.
Pte. Wm. Jones, 2/ E. Lan.
Lce.-Corporal J. T. Jordan, 2/ Rif. Brig.
Rfmn. L. Jordan, 2/ Rif. Brig.
Sergt. E. L. Jordon, 2/ Devon.
Sergt. E. Joseph, 1/ Worc.
Lce.-Corporal G. Joy, 2/ Midd'x.
Pte. A. Joyce, 2/ Linc.
Pte. W. B. Joynes, 2/ North'n.
Sapper E. Jukes, 11/ Sherw'd Frstrs.
Sergt. W. Justice, 2/ North'n.
Lce.-Corporal E. Kane, 2/ Sco. Rif.
Sergt. Jas. Kay, R.E.
Rfmn. J. Kearney, 1/ R. Ir. Rif.
Pte. F. Kelham, 2/ E. Lan.
Pte. J. Kelly, 2/ W. York.
Pte. A. Kemp, M.G. Corps.
Pte. A. Kemp, R.A.M.C.
Corpl. E. Kendrick, R.A.
Rfmn. A. Kennedy, 1/ R. Ir. Rif.
Corpl. R. B. J. Kerridge, R.E.
Pte. W. Ketley, 2/ Midd'x.
Pte. H. Kidd, 2/ E. Lan.
Lce.-Corporal B. W. Kidger, 2/ Devon.
Pte. A. Kilsby, 2/ R. Berks.

Pte. A. King, 2/ W. York.
Rfmn. C. King, 2/ Rif. Brig.
Sergt. H. King, 2/ York.
Rfmn. H. King, 2/ Rif. Brig.
Pte. H. King, 1/ Worc.
Gnr. J. King, T.M.B.
Sergt. Sydney King, 2/ Lin.
Sergt. G. King, 2/ Scot. Rif.
Pte. W. G. King, 2/ R. Berks.
Sapper G. L. Kirby, R.E.
Pte. J. Kirby, K.O.Y.L.I.
Pte. J. Kirby, 2/ E. Lan.
Lce.-Corporal W. Kirby, 2/ Devons
Lce.-Corporal C. Kirkland, 11/ Sherw'd Frstrs.
Pte. A. Knight, 2/ R. Berks.
Sapper P. J. Knights, R.E.
Pte. C. H. Knill, 2/ Devon.
Pte. A. Knowles, 1/ Worc.
Corpl. G. F. Lacon, 2/ Rif. Brig.
Pte. C. R. Lake, M.G. Corps.
Rfmn. H. Lane, 2/ Rif. Brig.
Gnr. J. Lane, R.A.
Pte. R. Lane, 2/ Linc.
Pte. T. Lang, 2/ W. York.
Pte. R. H. Langley, 2/ R. Berks.
Pte. F. P. Lanham, R.A.M.C.
Pte. A. Large, 2/ Linc.
Pte. W. Lauchton, 2/ Scot. Rif.
Corpl. T. Lavelle, T.M.B.
Gnr. W. J. Lavin, R.A.
2nd Corpl. F. Lawler, R.E.
Rfmn. P. L. Lawrence, 2/ Rif. Brig.
Driver R. H. Lawrence, R.A.M.C.
Pte. J. Lawton, 8/ K.O.Y.L.I.
Lce.-Corporal R. J. Lear, 2/ Devon.
Corpl. H. Leggs, R.A.
C.S.M. A. B. Leivers, 1/ Sherw'd Frstrs.
Lce.-Corporal W. Lensley, 2/ Linc.
Armr.-Staff Sergt. W. Shottlander Lesslie, R.A.O.C.
Lce.-Corporal F. Letham, M.G. Corps (Cav.).
Sergt. A. Lewin, 2/ Rif. Brig.
Pte. A. Licence, 1/ Sherw'd Frstrs.
Pte. F. Limb, 1/ Sherw'd Frstrs.
Sergt. C. Little, R.A.

APPENDIX IV

Sergt. J. Littlewood, 2/ W. York.
Corpl. C. Lloyd, R.E.
Lce.-Corporal F. Lobel, 2/ Midd'x.
Sergt. C. Lock, 2/ Devon.
Corpl. C. A. Lock, R.E.
Sergt. N. Lockley, 1/ Sherw'd Frstrs.
Pte. P. A. Lofty, 2/ Midd'x.
Pte. A. Long, 2/ R. Berks.
Sergt. W. T. R. Longhurst, R.E.
Sergt. J. Lorey, 2/ Devon.
Lce.-Corporal J. Lovell, 2/ North'n
2nd Corpl. W. R. Lovell, R.E.
Lce.-Corporal G. Lowden, 2/ Linc.
Sapper R. J. Lower, R.E.
Sapper A. Lowes, R.E.
Pte. C. E. Lucas, 2/ W. York.
Squadron Sergt.-Major E. Lucas, M.M.P.
Corpl. G. Lucas, 1/ R. Ir. Rif.
Pte. T. W. Lungley, 2/ North'n.
Lce.-Corporal G. Lyall, R.E.
Pte. T. Mabbott, 2/ Linc.
Corpl. J. McAllister, M.G. Corps.
Sergt. G. McCall, 2/ Scot. Rif.
Lce.-Corporal J. McCann, 1/ R. Ir. Rif.
2nd Corpl. P. McCann, R.E.
Lce.-Corporal G. McCartney, 2/ Sco. Rif.
Lce.-Corporal G. McCaughan, T.M.B.
Gnr. J. McCloy, R.A.
Corpl. J. McColl, R.A.
Lce.-Sergeant D. McCourt, 1/ R. Ir. Rif.
Pte. H. McDermott, 1/ Sherw'd Frstrs.
Lce.-Corporal P. Macdonal, 2/ Rif. Brig.
Sergt. A. MacDonald, 2/ Sco. Rif.
Corpl. A. MacDonald, R.A.
Rfmn. C. McDonnell, 1/ R. Ir. Rif.
Pte. H. Mace, 2/ R. Berks.
Rfmn. W. J. McEvoy, 2/ Rif. Brig.
Sapper T. McGraw, R.E.
Sergt. J. McIntosh, 2/ W. York.
Sergt. D. MacIntyre, M.G. Corps. (Cav.).

Pioneer John McKenzie, R.E.
Corpl. G. R. McLean, R.A.S.C.
Sergt. G. McLeay, 2/ Sco. Rif.
Driver A. McLeod, R.A.
Pte. H. McMorran, 2/ North'n.
Rfmn. C. McRitchie, 2/ Rif. Brig.
Sergt. J. McVee, R.E.
Sergt. G. Maddox, R.A.
Pte. R. Madigan, 2/ W. York.
Corpl. J. Magill, 1/ R. Ir. Rif.
Pte. G. H. Magnes, 2/ W. York.
Lce.-Corporal C. Maguire, 2/ Sco. Rif.
Sergt. J. F. Maguire, 2/ W. York.
Corpl. J. T. Maiden, 8/ York & Lanc.
Sapper A. C. F. Maling, R.E.
Corpl. J. Malone, 1/ R. Ir. Rif.
Lce.-Corpl. J. Maloney, R.E.
Pte. W. G. Manley, 2/ Devon.
Lce.-Sergt. J. W. T. Mann, 9/ York & Lanc.
Driver L. Manning, R.A.
Pte. J. T. Mannoch, 2/ R. Berks.
Corpl. S. Mansell, 2/ Midd'x.
Pte. R. F. Mansfield, 2/ Midd'x.
Pte. M. March, 1/ Worc.
Lce.-Corporal T. March, R.E.
Pte. F. Markham, 2/ North'n.
Lce.-Sergeant A. Marsden, 2/ R. Berks.
Sergt. F. A. Marsden, 8/ York & Lanc.
Pte. J. T. Marsden, 2/ E. Lan.
Lce.-Corporal W. Marsden, 2/ W. York.
Corpl. K. O. Marsh, R.A.
Corpl. T. Marsh, 2/ E. Lan.
Pte. H. F. Marshall, 2/ Devon.
Pte. W. Marshall, 2/ R. Berks.
Sergt. D. W. Martin, R.A.
Sergt. F. Martin, 2/ North'n.
Pte. G. Martin, 1/ Worc.
Driver H. Martin, R.A.
Sergt. H. M. Martin, R.E.
Pte. A. F. Mason, R.A.M.C.
Pte. A. J. Mason, 2/ Midd'x
Rfmn. J. T. Masters, 2/ Rif. Brig.
Corpl. S. Massey, 1/ R. Ir. Rif.
Pte. T. Massey, 2/ Devon.

APPENDIX IV

Pte. G. Masterson, 2/ E. Lan.
Pte. W. Matherick, M.G. Corps.
Sapper H. Matthews, R.E.
Lce.-Corporal H. T. Matthews, 1/ R. Ir. Rif.
Pte. F. H. W. Mattingly, 2/ Midd'x.
Sergt. F. Maydock, 2/ North'n.
Rfmn. W. Mayle, 2/ Rif. Brig.
Pte. J. Maynard, 2/ Linc.
Pte. H. Meadley, M.G. Corps.
Pte. T. Melia, 2/ E. Lan.
Sergt. E. Mellor, 2/ W. York.
Sergt. R. Melvin, R.A.
Lce.-Corporal H. H. Meyrick, R.E.
Pte. L. E. Michell, R.A.M.C.
Pte. D. T.Y. Middleton, R.A.M.C.
Pte. T. Midlane, 2/ Devon.
Pte. G. W. Miles, 2/ North'n.
Corpl. W. J. Millis, R.A.
Corpl. F. K. Mills, 2/ Devon.
Corpl. S. Mills, 2/ E. Lan.
Sergt. H. Milton, 2/ Linc.
Sergt. G. Miskimmin, 1/ R. Ir. Rif.
Sergt. A. Mitchell, 2/ Rif. Brig.
Sergt. A. F. Mitchell, R.A.
Lce.-Sergt. E. Mitchell, 2/ R. Berks.
2nd Corpl. R. Mitchell, R.E.
Corpl. R. Mitchell, 2/ Rif. Brig.
Corpl. J. G. Moore, 2/ Rif. Brig.
Corpl. R. Moore, 8/ York & Lanc.
Rfmn. W. Moore, 2/ Rif. Brig.
Sergt. C. Moriarty, 2/ R. Berks.
Pte. H. Morley, K.O.Y.L.I.
Pte. R. W. Morley, 2/ W. York.
Sergt. H. M. Morris, R.E.
Gunr. A. Morton, R.A.
Pte. H. E. Morton, 2/ Midd'x.
Pte. T. Moss, M.G. Corps.
Staff-Sergt. Farrier P. Movel, R.A.
Lce.-Corporal C. Mowat, M.G. Corps (Cav.).
Lce.-Corporal A. Mowl, 1/ Worc.
Sapper J. Munn, R.E.
Rfmn. W. Munson, 2/ Rif. Brig.
Driver G. Murphey, R.A.
Sergt. E. Murphy, R.A.
Corpl. O. Murphy, R.A.
Pte. B. Murray, 2/ Sco. Rif.
Corpl. R. Murray, 2/ Devon.
Corpl. W. Murray, R.A.
Bombdr. F. Musselbrook, R.A.
Lce.-Corporal A. H. Mutton, 2/ North'n.
Pte. A. Nancarrow, 2/ E. Lan.
Lce.-Corpl. E. W. Nash, 2/ Linc.
Pte. H. Naylor, 2/ W. York.
Sergt. S. Naylor, 2/ Linc.
Pte. F. Neale, 2/ R. Berks.
Pte. A. Neate, 2/ R. Berks.
Sergt. J. E. Needs, 2/ Midd'x.
Sapper S. Neill, R.E.
Rfmn. J. Nelson, 2/ Rif. Brig.
Rfmn. W. Nelson, 2/ Rif. Brig.
Driver G. V. Newcomb, R.A.
Sergt. G. W. Newey, 1/ Worc.
Sapper C. S. Newman, R.E.
Pte. G. Newman, 2/ Midd'x.
Pte. J. Nichol, 2/ Sco. Rif.
Pte. J. T. Nicholls, 2/ North'n.
Pte. F. Nichols, 2/ W. York.
Gnr. Geo. Nichols, R.A.
Corpl. Geo. Nicholson, 2/ W. York.
Corpl. H. Norman, R.A.
Bombdr. F. Norris, R.A.
Sergt. W. Northcote, D.C.M., R.E.
Lce.-Corpl. E. Nowell, 2/ E. Lan.
Pte. A. Oakley, 2/ R. Berks.
Pte. C. Oates, 1/ Worc.
Lce.-Corpl. G. O'Brien, 2/ Sco. Rif.
Pte. J. O'Farrell, 2/ E. Lan.
Pte. J. Ogden, 2/ E. Lan.
Corpl. W. Ogle, R.A.
C.Q.M. Sergt. J. O'Grady, M.G. Corps.
C.S.M. J. O'Hara, 2/ E. Lan.
Pte. T. O'Hara, 2/ W. York.
Sergt. G. Oldfield, 9/ York & Lanc.
Lce.-Corpl. J. Oldridge, 8/ K.O.Y.L.I.
Pte. C. O'Leary, 2/ Midd'x.
Sergt. F. Oliver, 8/ York & Lanc.
Driver F. Ord, R.A.
Pte. H. Orme, 1/ Sherw'd Frstrs.
Pte. W. Orme, 2/ North'n.

APPENDIX IV

Sapper F. Osborne, R.E.
Rfmn. W. Osborne, 2/ Rif. Brig.
Sapper T. O'Toole, R.E.
Corpl. E. Outram, M.G. Corps.
Driver T. G. B. Overy, R.A.
Sergt. A. Page, M.G. Corps.
C.S.M. E. G. Page, R.E.
Pte. F. W. Page, 2/ Sco. Rif.
Pte. R. G. Palethorpe, M.G. Corps.
Pte. E. Palmer, R.A.M.C.
Corpl. E. C. Palmer, 2/ Rif. Brig.
Corpl. W. Palmer, R.A.
Gnr. A. Pape, R.A.
Pte. A. Papworth, 2/ W. York.
Sapper A. Parker, R.E.
Driver E. H. Parker, R.A.
Pte. P. Parker, 2/ Devon.
Pte. T. Parker, M.G. Corps.
Gnr. J. T. Parkes, R.A.
Sergt. J. Parkin York & Lanc. R.
Pte. J. A. Parnell, 2/ W. York.
Pte. G. Parry, 11/ Sherw'd Frstrs.
Pioneer J. Parry, R.E.
Corpl. F. Parslow, R.E.
Pte. B. E. Parsons, 1/ Worc.
Lce.-Corporal T. Parton, 1/ Worc.
Sergt. W. C. Partridge, 2/ Rif. Brig.
Pte. L. Patnam, 2/ Linc.
Corpl. A. Patrick, 2/ Linc.
Driver F. Patrick, R.A.
Pte. W. J. Patrick, 2/ R. Berks.
Corpl. W. J. Patterson, 1/ R. Ir. Rif.
Bombdr. B. D. Paul, R.A.
Sergt. W. Pavey, 2/ Midd'x.
Pioneer A. Payne, R.E.
Sergt. R. Payne, T.M.B.
Bombdr. R. V. Payne, R.A.
Pte. J. A. Peacock, 2/ W. York.
Corpl. A. Pearce, R.A.
Rfmn. B. H. Pearce, 2/ Rif. Brig.
Pte. C. H. W. Pearce, 2/ R. Berks.
Sergt. J. Pearce, 2/ W. York.
Sergt. J. Pearson, 2/ W. York.
Corpl. H. Pegg, 2/ Rif. Brig.
Corpl. A. Pell, 2/ North'n.
Lce.-Corporal A. V. Penberthy, R.A.M.C.
Sapper T. W. Pendray, R.E.
Corpl. S. H. Peover, 2/ E. Lan.
Pte. H. Pepper, 2/ North'n.
Pte. T. Pepperell, 2/ Devon.
Sapper C. Perks, R.E.
Pte. W. F. Peters, 1/ Sherw'd Frstrs.
Pte. W. Pett, 2/ Midd'x.
Lce.-Corporal W. A. Pettit, R.E.
Corpl. A. Pettmann, R.E.
Lce.-Corporal E. Phillips, 2/ Rif. Brig.
Pte. G. H. Phipps, 1/ Sherw'd Frstrs.
Corpl. H. Pickup, R.A.
Corpl. J. Pickvance, 1/ Worc.
Pte. H. Pike, 2/ Linc.
Pte. W. J. Pike, 2/ Devon.
Lce.-Corporal W. W. D. Pilbeam, R.E.
Sergt. W. T. Pile, 2/ Devon.
Corpl. W. H. Pilton, T.M.B.
Pte. C. Pinchin, 1/ Sherw'd Frstrs.
Bombdr. B. Pinnick, T.M.B.
Corpl. L. Pinnock, 2/ Rif. Brig.
Gnr. J. Pipe, R.A.
Pte. R. J. Pitt, 2/ R. Berks.
Pte. T. Plowright, 2/ North'n.
Sergt.-Major S. C. Pocock, R.A.M.C.
Interprète Soldat 2e Classe J. Poncet, attd. 2/ Rif. Brig.
Gnr. R. H. Pond, R.A.
Pte. E. W. Poole, 1/ Worc.
Pte. H. Portas, 1/ Sherw'd Frstrs.
Pte. R. F. Porteous, 2/ Midd'x.
Lce.-Corporal E. C. Porter, 1/ R. Ir. Rif.
Corpl. E. C. Poulton, T.M.B.
Pte. J. J. G. Povey, M.G. Corps (Cav.).
Pte. W. C. Povey, 11/ Sherw'd Frstrs.
Pte. A. Powell, 2/ Devon.
Pte. C. Powell, 2/ Midd'x.
Pte. A. Pragnell, M.G. Corps.
Pte. T. Precious, 2/ W. York.
Sergt. F. Presland, R.E.
C.Q.M. Sergt. C. B. Price, 1/ Worc.
Lce.-Corpl. J. T. Pridmore, 2/ North'n.

APPENDIX IV

Sergt. A. Priestley, 2/ W. York.
Pte. J. E. Pringle, 22/ Durh. L.I.
Corpl. J. Prior, R.E.
Driver J. H. Prior, R.A.
Corpl. S. Prior, 2/ R. Berks.
Sergt. A. J. Proctor, R.A.
Corpl. T. A. Proctor, 2/ E. Lan.
Pte. J. Proufoot, 2/ Sco. Rif.
Driver C. Pugh, R.A.
Pte. R. N. Pullman, 2/ Linc.
Sergt. W. Pumpfrey, R.E.
Corpl. H. Pycock, 2/ W. York.
Pte. J. E. Quilter, 2/ Devon.
Pte. T. Ranscombe, 2/ R. Berks.
Gnr. G. W. Ransom, R.A.
Pte. W. Ransome, 22/ Durh. L.I.
Sergt. C. Ransted, 2/ Rif. Brig.
Gnr. F. Rawlings, R.A.
Pte. W. Raymont, 2/ Devon.
Sergt. J. Rea, 2/ W. York.
Rfmn. H. W. Read, 2/ Rif. Brig.
Gnr. J. Reade, R.A.
Lce.-Corporal W. Reading, 2/ R. Berks.
Lce.-Corporal F. G. Redwood, 2/ Devon.
Lce.-Corporal E. Reeves, 8/ York & Lanc.
Lce.-Corporal G. Reid, 2/ Sco. Rif.
Lce.-Corporal H. Renshaw, 2/ E. Lan.
Pte. D. Rennie, 2/ Sco. Rif.
Sapper J. Rennie, R.E.
Rfmn. T. Reynolds, 2/ Rif. Brig.
Lce.-Corporal W. Reynolds, 1/ Sherw'd Frstrs.
Gnr. W. J. Reynolds, R.A.
Sergt. G. Richards, 1/ Sherw'd Frstrs.
Pte. H. Richards, 1/ Worc.
Sergt. W. Richards, R.E.
Sergt. T. J. Richardson, R.A.
Pte. W. Richardson, 2/ North'n.
Driver J. Rigby, R.A.
Corpl. T. Riggs, 2/ Linc.
Sapper G. A. Rimmer, R.E.
Lce.-Corporal J. W. Ringrose, 2/ W. York.
Sapper E. Ringwood, R.E.
Pte. G. H. T. Robbins, T.M.B.

Sergt. C. E. Roberts, 2/ Linc.
Pte. Evan Roberts, R.A.
Gnr. Fredk. Roberts, R.A.
Corpl. J. Roberts, 1/ R. Ir. Rif.
Lce.-Corporal R. Roberts, 2/ Devon.
Corpl. W. Robertson, 2/ Sco. Rif.
Pte. H. Robinson, 2/ Linc.
Sergt. J. Robinson, 2/ W. York.
Fitter H. G. B. Robson, R.A.
Lce.-Corporal E. Roche, 2/ E. Lan.
Pte. G. Rockley, 2/ Devon.
Pte. W. Rodden, 2/ Sco. Rif.
Lce.-Corporal G. Rodgers, 9/ York & Lanc.
Pte. F. Rogers, 2/ Linc.
Pte. H. L. Rogers, 2/ Devon.
Sergt. T. Rogers, M.G. Corps.
Corpl. T. Rogers, 2/ Rif. Brig.
Pte. C. Rose, 2/ R. Berks.
Sergt. G. Rose, 2/ Rif. Brig.
Corpl. T. Ross, 2/ Linc.
Lce.-Corporal E. Rossin, 9/ York & Lanc.
Sapper Lisle Row, R.E.
Pte. F. S. Rowe, R.A.M.C.
Pte. G. F. Rowland, 2/ Midd'x.
Pte. J. Rowley, M.G. Corps.
Corpl. H. Rowse, R.A.
Lce.-Corporal A. Roy, 2/ North'n.
Sergt. N. H. Rumsey, R.A.
Pte. S. G. Rundle, 2/ Devon.
Pte. G. Rushworth, 1/ Sherw'd Frstrs.
Lce.-Corporal E. Russam, 1/ Worc.
Pte. G. Russell, 1/ Sherw'd Frstrs.
Pte. W. Russell, 2/ R. Berks.
Sergt. W. Russon, D.C.M., 1/ Sherw'd Frstrs.
Sergt. J. Ryan, 2/ E. Lan.
Pte. E. Rycroft, M.G. Corps.
Gnr. C. J. Salmon, R.A.
Lce.-Corporal H. Salter, 2/ Rif. Brig.
Pte. W. Sanderson, 2/ Linc.
Pte. W. G. Sandford, 2/ Devon.
Corpl. J. W. Satchwell, 8/ York & Lanc.

APPENDIX IV

2nd Corporal E. V. Saunders, R.E.
Corpl. H. Saunders, 1/ Worc.
Sergt. J. A. Saunders, R.A.
Corpl. J. L. Savins, R.A.
Pte. A. V. Sawyer, 2/ Devon.
Pte. C. Sawyer, 1/ Sherw'd Frstrs.
Corpl. D. Schofield, R.A.
Pte. A. Schwarzhans, 2/ E. Lan.
Driver R. Scobbie, R.A.S.C.
Pte. A. D. Scott, 2/ Sco. Rif.
Sapper Edgar Scott, R.E.
Sergt. R. Scott, 2/ E. Lan.
Pte. S. A. Scott, 2/ R. Berks.
Pte. Wm. Scott, 2/ W. York.
Lce.-Corporal A. Scriven, 2/ R. Berks.
Sergt. V. P. Scrivener, 2/ Rif. Brig.
Lce.-Corporal J. Scully, 1/7 Durh. L.I.
Sergt. W. E. Seabury, R.A.
Pte. J. Searle, 2/ Midd'x.
Lce.-Corporal H. Seddon, 2/ W. York.
Pte. J. Seeley, 2/ E. Lan.
Sergt. J. C. Seldon, 2/ Devon.
Sergt. A. Self, 2/ W. York.
Corpl. J. Sellars, 8/ York & Lanc.
Corpl. A. Sellick, R.A.M.C.
Lce.-Corporal E. H. F. Sensier, 2/ Midd'x.
Gnr. J. Shannon, R.A.
Lce.-Corporal Geo. Sharp, 2/ W. York.
Sergt. O. Sharpe, 2/ Linc.
Corpl. S. F. Sharpe, R.A.
Corpl. W. G. Sharpe, 1/ Worc.
Sapper H. Shaw, R.E.
Sergt. W. Shaxon, 2/ Devon.
Pte. J. T. Shelton, 2/ Linc.
Lce.-Corporal A. E. Shepherd, 2/ Devon.
Corpl. J. Shepherd, 2/ Rif. Brig.
Pte. W. Shepherd, R.A.M.C.
Sergt. C. Sheppard, 2/ R. Berks.
Pte. J. Sherwood, 2/ North'n.
Rfmn. P. Shiels, 1/ R. Ir. Rif.
Driver B. T. Shufflebotham, R.A.
Gnr. C. E. Sibley, R.A.
Gnr. W. Simmons, R.A.
Sergt. R. H. Simner, 1/ R. Ir. Rif.
Lce.-Corporal A. Simpson, 1/ Sherw'd Frstrs.
Lce.-Corporal Arthur Simpson, 2/ E. Lan.
Sergt. A. J. Simpson, 1/ R. Ir. Rif.
Pte. B. Simpson, 1/ Sherw'd Frstrs.
Pte. J. Sirett, 2/ Linc.
Pte. T. W. Skeggs, 2/ Midd'x.
Sergt. G. Skinner, 2/ R. Berks.
Pte. W. Skinns, 2/ Linc.
Pte. J. Slater, 2/ E. Lan.
Pte. J. Smale, 2/ Devon.
Lce.-Sergeant W. A. Small, 2/ Rif. Brig.
Corpl. A. Smalley, R.A.
Pte. F. Smallwood, 1/ Sherw'd Frstrs.
Sergt. A. Smith, 2/ Linc.
Pte. Arthur Smith, 1/ Sherw'd Frstrs.
Sergt. A. G. Smith, 2/ Rif. Brig.
Sergt. A. G. Smith, 2/ Devon.
Sergt. Bernard Smith, 1/ Sherw'd Frstrs.
Driver C. Smith, R.A.S.C.
Sergt. F. Smith, 2/ R. Berks.
Sergt. Fred Smith, M.G. Corps.
Lce.-Corporal F. C. Smith, R.A.S.C.
Gnr. G. F. Smith, R.A.
Pte. G. T. Smith, 2/ North'n.
Pte. Harry Smith, R.A.M.C.
Corpl. J. Smith, 2/ Scot. Rif.
Pte. Jack Smith, 2/ E. Lan.
Corpl. John Smith, 2/ North'n.
Pte. John Smith, 2/ E. Lan.
Pte. J. A. Smith, 2/ Midd'x.
Lce.-Corporal J. W. Smith, 2/ W. York.
Sergt. P. Smith, 1/ Sherw'd Frstrs.
Sergt. S. Smith, 2/ R. Berks.
Gnr. T. A. Smith, R.A.
Corpl. W. Smith, R.A.
Pte. W. Smith, 2/ Sco. Rif.
Corpl. Wm. Smith, 2/ Midd'x.
Corpl. W. G. Smith, 2/ R. Berks.
Pte. W. P. Smith, 2/ R. Berks.
Gnr. J. W. Smyth, R.A.
Corpl. J. Solomon, 2/ Midd'x.
Corpl. L. W. Somerwill, R.E.

APPENDIX IV

Sergt. J. Southgate, 2/ North'n.
Gnr. R. H. Sowerbutts, R.A.
Bombdr. J. Spalding, T.M.B.
Pte. W. Sparkes, 2/ Devon.
Sergt. J. Spelman, 2/ Rif. Brig.
Rfmn. J. Spence, 1/ R. Ir. Rif.
Rfmn. W. Spence, 1/ R. Ir. Rif.
Pte. C. W. Spencer, 2/ Linc.
Sergt. E. Spencer, 2/ Midd'x.
Corpl. J. Spencer, 8/ K.O.Y.L.I.
Driver J. H. Spooner, R.A.
Pte. W. Spooner, 1/ Sherw'd Frstrs.
Pte. W. A. Spooner, R.A.M.C.
Lce.-Corporal W. Spowage, 2/ North'n.
Sergt. H. R. Sprackland, 2/Rif. Brig.
Sergt. B. Spray, R.A.
Pte. W. E. J. Spurway, 2/ Devon.
Sergt. J. E. Stafford, 11/ Sherw'd Frstrs.
Lce.-Corporal T. Stainer, 2/ Rif. Brig.
Sergt. H. Stamp, 2/ R. Berks.
Sergt. F. Stanley, 2/ North'n.
Sergt. C. Stapleton, 1/ Sherw'd Frstrs.
Lce.-Corporal A. Stark, 2/ R. Berks.
Rfmn. A. G. Starling, 2/ Rif. Brig.
Pte. E. Stayton, 2/ North'n.
Corpl. J. Steed, 2/ Midd'x.
Corpl. J. Steel, T.M.B.
Sergt. E. Steele, 2/ W. York.
Bombdr. E. T. Steele, R.A.
Corpl. W. Steenkiste, M.G. Corps.
Driver A. Steggles, R.A.
Pte. W. Stephens, 2/ Devon.
Lce.-Sergeant A. L. Stephenson, 22/ Durh. L.I.
Pte. E. W. Sterrett, 2/ Linc.
Pte. F. Stevens, 2/ North'n.
Pte. H. Stevens, 2/ North'n.
Lce.-Corporal J. Stevens, 2/ W. York.
Corpl. W. E. Stevens, 2/ R. Berks.
Pte. E. Stevenson, 11/ Sherw'd Frstrs.
Sergt. F. H. Stevenson, R.A.M.C.
Sergt. A. G. Stewart, 8/ York & Lanc.
Corpl. C. Stewart, 2/ W. York.
Pte. A. W. Stobbs, 22/ D.L.I.
Driver W. J. Stocker, R.A.
Corpl. T. Stonehouse, 22/ Durh. L.I.
Gnr. F. Stopford, R.A.
Lce.-Corporal H. Stoten, 2/ Rif. Brig.
Rfmn. G. Stowe, 2/ Rif. Brig.
Corpl. P. Stratton, 1/ Sherw'd Frstrs.
Corpl. L. Straw, R.A.
Pte. A. E. Street, 2/ Devon.
Pte. H. Strevens, 2/ Devon.
Corpl. J. Strickland, 2/ E. Lan.
Pte. J. Sullivan, 22/ Durh. L.I.
Gnr. J. Sullivan, R.A.
Pte. J. Sumners, 1/ Worc.
Gnr. J. Summers, R.A.
Sergt. A. E. Sutton, R.A.
Sergt. A. F. R. Sutton, T.M.B.
Sergt. W. Sutton, 2/ Midd'x.
Lce.-Corporal E. Swaby, 2/ E. Lan.
Rfmn. T. W. Sweeting, 2/ Rif. Brig.
Pte. Fred. Sykes, 22/ Durh. L.I.
Lce.-Corporal H. Syrett, 2/ R. Berks.
Sergt. C. H. Tait, R.A.
Sergt. H. Talbot, 2/ North'n.
Pte. W. Talbot, 1/ Sherw'd Frstrs.
Sergt. W. A. Tappin, 2/ Midd'x.
Pte. G. B. Tarn, 22/ Durh. L.I.
Corpl. A. Taylor, 2/ R. Berks.
Corpl. A. E. Taylor, 2/ Linc.
Driver A. T. Taylor, R.A.
Pte. G. H. Taylor, 2/ Linc.
Sergt. H. Taylor, 1/ Sherw'd Frstrs.
Driver L. Taylor, R.A.
Lce.-Corporal P. Taylor, M.G. Corps.
Pte. R. Taylor, 2/ Devon.
C.S.M. S. H. Taylor, 2/ Devon.
Sergt. T. C. Taylor, 2/ Sco. Rif.
Lce.-Corporal W. A. Taylor, 2/ Rif. Brig.
Sergt. W. G. Taylor, 2/ Devon.
Pte. W. H. Taylor, 1/ Worc.
Corpl. S. A. Tear, 2/ North'n.

APPENDIX IV

Lce.-Corporal S. J. Tearle, 2/ Midd'x.
Sergt.-Major W. H. Teatum, R.A.M.C.
Pte. J. C. Tebbs, 2/ R. Berks.
Gnr. A. K. Tempreton, R.A.
Pte. T. B. Terry, M.G. Corps.
Pte. E. Tester, 2/ Midd'x.
Pte. A. W. Thackway, R.A.M.C.
Pte. Thos. Thomas, 1/ Sherw'd Frstrs.
Pte. A. Thompson, T.M.B.
Pte. A. Thompson, 22/ Durh. L.I.
Pte. J. A. Thompson, 2/ E. Lan.
Corpl. W. Thompson, 8/ York & Lanc.
Pte. W. Thornton, 2/ E. Lan.
Rfmn. N. Thorpe, 2/ Rif. Brig.
Col.-Sergt. E. Thurgood, 2/ Rif. Brig.
Sergt. G. Tibble, 2/ North'n.
Pte. P. W. Tighe, R.A.M.C.
Sergt. A. Tiller, 2/ E. Lan.
Lce.-Corporal J. W. Tiller, 2/ Midd'x.
Lce.-Corporal R. J. Timmings, 2/ Linc.
Rfmn. A. Tipper, 2/ Rif. Brig.
Sergt. N. Tipper, R.A.
Sergt. N. Todd, R.A.
Pte. T. Toff, 2/ Midd'x.
Driver C. J. Tomkins, R.A.
Sapper J. Tomkinson, R.E.
Driver C. Tomlinson, R.A.
Sergt. S. H. Tomlinson, R.A.
Rfmn. W. Tomlinson, 2/ Midd'x.
Pte. A. Tompkins, 2/ Midd'x.
Lce.-Corporal C. Torrington, R.E.
Lce.-Corporal C. P. Torrington, R.E.
Corpl. F. W. Tow, 2/ Linc.
Lce.-Corporal W. Towers, R.E.
Sapper E. W. Towner, R.E.
Gnr. W. Townsend, R.A.
Sergt. G. Toyne, 2/ Linc.
Rfmn. J. Tracey, 2/ Rif. Brig.
Lce.-Corporal T. Tracey, R.E.
Sergt. E. Tranter, 1/ Sherw'd Frstrs.
Gnr. E. Triggs, R.A.
Pte. H. Trundle, 2/ Midd'x.
Pte. H. T. G. Truslow, M.G. Corps.
Rfmn. H. Tumelty, 1/ R. Ir. Rif.
Driver W. F. Tunnacliffe, R.A.
Gnr. W. Turnpenny, T.M.B.
Corpl. G. Turrel, 2/ North'n.
Lce.-Corporal G. Tutty, 2/ R. Berks.
Pte. J. Twomey, 2/ R. Berks.
Sergt. W. Twomey, 8/ K.O.Y.L.I.
Sergt. J. P. Tyler, 1/ Worc.
Corpl. E. A. Tytherleigh, 2/ North'n.
Pte. T. Udoll, 1/ Worc.
Sergt. H. Unsworth, 2/ Devon.
Corpl. T. G. Upshall, 2/ Devon.
Pte. G. R. Ure, 22/ Durh. L.I.
Lce.-Corporal W. Vardey, 1/ Sherw'd Frstrs.
Pte. W. Vaughan, 8/ York & Lanc.
Pte. E. Vaux, 2/ Midd'x.
Rfmn. W. S. Veale, 2/ Rif. Brig.
Corpl. B. Veasey, 22/ Durh. L.I.
Sapper G. E. R. Venables, R.E.
Pte. W. H. Vere, R.A.M.C.
Sergt. A. E. Vickers, 2/ Rif. Brig.
Lce.-Corporal G. Vickery, 2/ North'n.
Sergt. J. Waight, R.A.
Lce.-Corporal C. W. Wakeham, 2/ Devon.
Pte. A. Wale, 2/ R. Berks.
Pte. A. P. Walker, 2/ North'n.
Pte. H. Walker, 2/ Linc.
Rfmn. H. W. Walker, 2/ Rif. Brig.
Sergt. T. Walker, R.E.
Lce.-Corporal G. A. Wallace, R.E.
Sergt. J. Walsh, 1/ R. Ir. Rif.
Sergt. E. Walters, R.A.
Sergt. I. Wanstall, 2/ Midd'x.
Pte. J. Ward, 2/ E. Lan.
C.S.M. C. Warmer, 1/ Sherw'd Frstrs.
Rfmn. W. Warner, 2/ Rif. Brig.
Pte. W. A. Warwick, 2/ Midd'x.
Pte. C. Waterhouse, 1/ Sherw'd Frstrs.

APPENDIX IV

Pte. J. Watkins, 2/ Devon.
Driver A. Watling, R.A.
Pte. F. Watling, 2/ R. Berks.
Lce.-Corporal R. Watling, M.G. Corps (Cav.).
Lce.-Corporal B. Watson, 2/ Linc.
Pte. T. Watson, 2/ Linc.
Pte. W. Watson, 22/ Durh. L.I.
Pte. W. Watts, 1/ Sherw'd Frstrs.
Pte. W. Watts, 1/ Worc.
Sergt. F. Way, 2/ Devon.
Pte. A. Weary, 2/ Devon.
Driver J. H. Weatherby, R.A.M.C.
Sergt. J. Weatheritt, R.A.
Gnr. E. F. Weavers, R.A.
Pte. E. Webber, 2/ Devon.
Lce.-Corporal J. F. Webster, 2/ Rif. Brig.
Corpl. T. Webster, R.A.
Bombdr. W. Webster, R.A.
Lce.-Corporal T. Welborn, 2/ Midd'x.
Driver G. Welton, R.A.
2nd Corporal A. W. Wenban, R.E.
Sergt. A. West, R.E.
Sergt. C. West, R.A.
Corpl. D. J. West, R.A.
Lce.-Corporal D. McW. West, R.E.
Sergt. R. E. Westlake, R.A.
Pte. C. Weston, 2/ Midd'x.
Rfmn. H. Westrop, 2/ Rif. Brig.
Bombdr. J. Whalley, R.A.
Pte. J. Whatley, 2/ W. York.
Sergt. A. Wheaton, 2/ Devon.
Pte. D. W. Wheeler, R.A.S.C.
Corpl. J. Wheeler, 2/ R. Berks.
Sergt. G. Wheeliker, 9/ York & Lanc.
Lce.-Corporal A. Wheldrake, 8/ K.O.Y.L.I.
Sergt. R. C. Wherley, 22/ Durh. L.I.
Lce.-Sergt. A. G. Whiddett, 2/ Midd'x.
Corpl. H. W. Whitaker, M.G. Corps (Cav.).
Rfmn. R. Whitaker, 2/ Rif. Brig.
Pte. W. Whitaker, M.G. Corps.
Gnr. E. S. White, R.A.

Driver G. F. White, R.A.
Corpl. G. M. White, 2/ Devon.
Pte. N. White, 2/ R. Berks.
Pte. P. R. White, 2/ Devon.
Lce.-Sergt. S. G. White, 2/ Devon.
Driver T. White, R.A.
Bombdr. W. White, R.A.
Lce.-Corporal J. Whitehead, 2/ E. Lan.
Corpl. D. Whiteman, R.A.
Lce.-Corporal J. Whiting, 2/ Rif. Brig.
Pte. S. V. Whiting, 9/ York & Lanc.
Pte. F. Whittaker, 1/ Worc.
Sergt. W. L. Whittaker, R.A.M.C.
Pte. G. Whittington, M.G. Corps.
Lce.-Corporal W. Whyman, 2/ W. York.
Pte. T. Wickham, 2/ Devon.
Pte. W. Wicks, 2/ R. Berks.
Lce.-Sergt. J. Wigham, 22/ Durh. L.I.
Pte. E. Wilcocks, 9/ York & Lanc.
Corpl. J. Wilkin, R.A.
Pte. E. Wilkins, 2/ Devon.
Pte. F. Wilkins, 1/ Worc.
Sergt. A. E. Wilkinson, 2/ Rif. Brig.
Sapper W. Will, R.E.
Corpl. A. C. Williams, R.E.
Corpl. A. J. Williams, R.A.
Pte. D. D. Williams, 2/ Devon.
Pte. T. Williams, 2/ R. Berks.
Corpl. W. H. Williams, 2/ Midd'x.
Pte. G. Williamson, 1/ Sherw'd Frstrs.
Corpl. R. Williamson, R.A.
Sergt. W. Willis, R.A.
Pte. E. Wilson, 8/ York & Lanc.
Sergt. H. N. Wilson, 2/ Midd'x.
Pte. J. Wilson, 2/ Midd'x.
Lce.-Corporal J. W. Wilson, 2/ Lin.
Sergt. R. Wilson, R.A.
Bombdr. R. Wilson, R.A.
C.Q.M. Sergt. R. H. Wilson, 2/ E. Lan.

APPENDIX IV

Corpl. P. W. Winder, T.M.B.
Corpl. J. W. Winn, R.E.
Pte. H. Winter, 2/ Midd'x.
Corpl. R. Witt, R.A.M.C.
Corpl. A. Wolstencroft, 1/ Sherw'd Frstrs.
Pte. C. S. Wood, 2/ E. Lan.
Sapper E. Wood, R.E.
Corpl. H. Wood, R.A.
Corpl. H. Wood, M.G. Corps.
Staff-Sergt. S. R. Wood, R.A.M.C.
Pte. J. T. Woodcock, 9/ York & Lanc.
Pte. R. Woodgate, R.A.M.C.
Corpl. W. Woodgate, R.E.
Signlr. J. J. Woodhead, R.A.
Sergt. F. Woods, 2/ W. York.
Pte. C. F. Woodward, 1/ Sherw'd Frstrs.
Pte. J. Woolacott, 2/ Devon.
Lce.-Corporal F. Worsdell, M.G. Corps (Cav.).
Corpl. E. J. Wotton, M.G. Corps (Cav.).
Lce.-Corporal H. Wray, 2/ W. York.
Pte. A. Wright, 2/ North'n.
Pte. F. Wright, 1/ Sherw'd Frstrs.
Sergt. J. Wright, 22/ Durh. L.I.
Pte. T. E. Wright, M.G. Corps.
Pte. W. T. Wright, 1/ Sherw'd Frstrs.
Sergt. F. Wyatt, R.A.
Corpl. W. W. Wylie, R.E.
C.Q.M. Sergt. F. W. Yokings, 2/ R. Berks.
Pte. J. Young, 2/ W. York.
Pte. J. W. W. Young, 2/ Devon.
Sergt. J. H. Yuile, R.A.

MERITORIOUS SERVICE MEDAL

Corpl. F. Aggett, 2/ Devon.
Sergt. C. Alp, 2/ Linc.
Pte. F. Andrews, 1/ Worc.
Farrier Q.M. Sergt. A. Arlett, R.E.
Sergt. W. H. Baker, 2/ Midd'x.
Sergt. C. Banstead, 2/ Rif. Brig.
C.Q.M. Sergt. A. Barnes, 2/ Sco. Rif.
Maréchal des Logis M. L. J. Bénard, 19e Escad du Train attd. 25th Inf. Bde.
Q.M. Sergt. C. E. Berbridge, R.A.S.C.
Bombdr. H. Biggs, R.A.
C.S.M. W. Birkett, R.A.S.C.
Sergt. R. Blackett, 22/ Durh. L.I.
Batty. Q.M. Sergt. K. Boggie, R.A.
Farrier Q.M. I. Brayton, R.A.S.C.
Bombdr. H. Briggs, R.A.
Pte. B. W. Bright, 2/ E. Lan.
R.Q.M. Sergt. W. M. Buck, 2/ North'n.
Mech. S. Sergt. W. T. H. Bugler, R.A.S.C.
Corpl. W. Burgess, 2/ Midd'x.
C.Q.M. Sergt. C. Butler, 2/ W. York.
Farrier S. Sergt. J. Butterworth, R.A.
Corpl. W. C. Callander, R.A.S.C.
Lce.-Sergt. F. Chambers, 1/ Sherw'd Frstrs.
Sergt. F. Chapman, 2/ R. Berks.
Q.M. Sergt. H. G. Child, 2/ R. Berks.
S.S.M. T. Chubb, R.A.S.C.
Sergt. W. W. Cockram, M.M., 2/ Devon.
Pte. D. Coldwell, 2/ E. Lan.
C.Q.M. Sergt. P. H. Coles, 2/ Midd'x.
Q.M. Sergt. L. C. Corrigan, 1/ R. Ir. Rif.
C.S.M. S. W. J. Cox, 2/ Devon.
Sergt. E. Crankshaw, R.A.S.C.
Mech. S. Sergt. W. Crook, R.A.S.C.
Lce.-Corporal R. A. J. Deamer, Labour Corps.
Sergt. J. Dymond, 2/ Devon.
C.S.M. J. Earll, R.E.
Sergt. A. E. Eastman, 2/ E. Lan.
Pte. B. E. Exley, R.A.S.C.
2nd Corpl. J. Fisher, R.E.
Pte. W. Ford, 2/ Linc.

APPENDIX IV

Sergt. A. H. Foster, 2/ North'n.
Lce.-Corporal J. Foulds, 2/ E. Lan.
C.Q.M. Sergt. O. Fox, 1/ Sherw'd. Frstrs.
Sub-Conductor P. Freck, R.A.O.C.
Corpl. W. Freeman, T.M.B.
Sergt. A. Fyfe, M.G. Corps.
Corpl. S. W. Gardiner, 2/ Midd'x.
Bombdr. J. W. Gibson, R.A.
C.Q.M. Sergt. R. Gibson, 2/ Rif. Brig.
C.Q.M. Sergt. W. Glennon, 2/ E. Lan.
R.Q.M. Sergt. C. Godfrey, 2/ R. Berks.
C.S.M. F. J. Gray, R.A.S.C.
Lce.-Corporal J.G. L. Green, R. E.
R.Q.M. Sergt. R. Gurney, 2/ W. York.
Pte. F. G. Haddock, 2/ Midd'x.
Corpl. S. Hall, 1/ Sherw'd Frstrs.
Lce.-Sergt. T. C. Halsey, 2/ E. Lan.
S.Q.M. Sergt. E. Hardy, R.A.S.C.
Sergt. A. W. Harvey, R.E.
2nd Corpl. C. W. Heald, R.E.
Sergt. W. Heggs, 2/ Linc.
Sub.-Conductor F. Highcock, R.A.S.C.
Batty. Sergt.-Major H. J. Hillyard, R.A.
Sergt. (Master Shoemaker) P. H. Humphrey, 2/ Midd'x.
Corpl. C. Hutchinson, 2/ W. York.
C.S.M. C. Huxford, R.A.S.C.
Corp. R. Imeson, 22/ Durh. L.I.
C.Q.M. Sergt. A. G. Ingram, 2/ North'n.
Sergt. T. K. Jarvis, 1/ Sherw'd Frstrs.
Pte. H. Jenkinson, 2/ W. York.
Corpl. G. J. Jestico, R.E.
Sergt. A. W. Johnson, R.A.
Lce.-Corpl. H. Johnson, 2/ North'n.
Driver E. Keen, R.A.
Sergt. T. Kelly, 1/7 Durh. L.I.
R.Q.M. Sergt. E. King, 2/ Midd'x.
Sergt. E. Labbett, 2/ Devon.
Lce.-Corporal J. W. Last, 1/ Sherw'd Frstrs.
Sergt. J. R. T. Laycock, 2/ W. York.
Sergt. J. Ledgard, M.G. Corps.
1st Class Interpreter E. Lehoucq, attd. R.A.
Sergt. T. H. Leigh, R.E.
Corpl. T. F. Lenny, 2/ Midd'x.
Sergt. G. Lewis, 1/ Sherw'd Frstrs.
Corpl. B. Lickorish, 2/ North'n.
R.Q.M. Sergt. H. D. Little, 1/Worc.
Sergt. F. H. Love, 2/ W. York.
R.Q.M. Sergt. W. Luck, M.G. Corps.
Corpl. H. MacDonald, R.E.
Sergt. P. McDonald, R.A.S.C.
S. Sergt. Artificer A. Magowan, R.A.
Sergt. J. F. Maguire, 2/ W. York.
Sergt. W. Marney, 2/ Rif. Brig.
S. Sergt. M. Marshall, R.E.
Soldat (1ère Cl.) A. Martin, French Army attd. 8th Divl. Train.
Q.M. Sergt. S. Martin, R.A.M.C.
Driver C. Metcalf, R.A.
Sergt. N. H. Michell, R.A.M.C.
Corpl. H. Millard, R.E.
C.Q.M. Sergt. G. Mills, 1st Sherw'd Frstrs.
Sergt. N. H. Mitchell, R.A.M.C.
S.S.M. W. P. Monks, R.A.S.C.
Q.M. Sergt. W. H. Moore, M.M., R.A.S.C.
Corpl. W. A. Morris, R.A.S.C.
Farrier S. Sergt. P. Mouel, R.A.
R.Q.M. Sergt. W. Moyser, 2/ Devon.
Driver J. Munns, R.A.
Sergt. R. Ness, 1/ R. Ir. Rif.
Sergt. A. Notting, R.E.
Lce.-Corporal M. F. Oliver, Labour Corps.
Sergt. Drummer A. Orme, 2/ E. Lan.
Corpl. H. E. Oxley, R.A.
Pte. H. Paine, 2/ R. Berks.
Corpl. C. G. Parish, 2/ Rif. Brig.
Sergt.-Major T. W. Parsons, R.A.M.C.

APPENDIX IV

Q.M. Sergt. A. Pattison, 2/ W. York.
Batty. Q.M. Sergt. H. Phillips, R.A.
Sergt. W. J. Pidduck, M.G. Corps.
Pte. C. J. Pinney, R.A.S.C.
C.Q.M. Sergt. W. H. Pollard, 1/ Sherw'd Frstrs.
C.Q.M. Sergt. S. M. Prudames, 2/ W. York.
Pte. A. Pulley, 2/ North'n.
Sergt. A. Randall, 2/ W. York.
Col.-Sergt. F. G. Reeves, 1/7 Durh. L.I.
Corpl. G. W. T. Roberts, R.A.S.C.
Sergt. Drummer V. Roberts, 2 Midd'x.
Conductor C. E. W. Robinson, R.A.O.C.
C.Q.M. Sergt. W. Rounds, 1/ Worc.
Sergt. E. A. Rowley, 1/ Worc.
Sergt. P. H. Ruffels, 2/ R. Berks.
Farrier S. Sergt. W. Saunders, R.A.
Sergt. J. G. Savill, 1/ Sherw'd Frstrs.
Sergt. J. L. Savins, T.M.B.
Sergt. N. Saxon, 1/7 Durh. L.I.
Sergt. F. Sharman, R.A.
R.S.M. A. Sheppard, R.E.
R.S.M. W. E. Simmons, R.A.
Sergt. Fred Smith, 2/ R. Berks.
Sergt. F. W. Smithers, T.M.B.
Sergt. F. Soley, 1/ Worc.
C.Q.M. Sergt. L. J. Spokes, 2/ Midd'x.
Sergt. A. E. Stannard, 2/ R. Berks.
Sergt. A. S. Steele, 1/7 Durh. L.I.
Sergt. H. W. Steele, 2/ Rif. Brig.
S.S.M. T. J. Stone, R.A.S.C.
Sergt. J. Strangeway, 2/ Rif. Brig.
C.Q.M. Sergt. J. Tapper, 2/ R. Berks.
Sergt. C. Taylor, 2/ R. Berks.
Driver D. R. Thomas, R.A.
C.S.M. H. T. Thorpe, R.E.
Pte. E. H. Tucker, 2/ E. Lan.
Farrier S. Sergt. A.W. Turner, R.A.
R.S.M. L. Walker, R.A.
Sergt. G. H. Ward, 22/ Durh. L.I.
Armr. Sergt.-Major C. A. Warren, R.A.O.C.
R.Q.M. Sergt. C. W. Watkins, 2/ Rif. Brig.
Sergt. H. J. Webb, R.A.V.C.
Sergt. P. Webster, 2/ E. Lan.
Sergt. H. C. Welsh, 22/ Durh. L.I.
C.S.M. J. Wilson, 2/ W. York.
R.Q.M. Sergt. J. A. Wilson, 1/7 Durh. L.I.
Pte. W. Windass, 2/ W. York.
S.S.M. W. W. Woods, R.A.S.C.
Farrier S. Sergt. Z. Wooldridge, R.A.
Pte. J. Wooley, 2/ E. Lan.
S.S.M. A. J. Yates, R.A.S.C.
Sergt. R. Young, 2/ Sco. Rif.

ALBERT MEDAL
Sergt. M. Jennings, 2/ W. York.

MENTION IN DESPATCHES (Officers)

Lieut.-Colonel A. J. B. Addison, 9/ York & Lanc.
Lieut.-Colonel E. Alderson, D.S.O., R.A.M.C.
Capt. and Adj. T. R. Aldworth, 2/ R. Berks.
Capt. A. N. Alexander, 5th attd. 1/ Worc.
Bvt. Lieut.-Colonel H. L. Alexander, D.S.O., Gen. List.
Q.M. and Major J. H. Alldridge, 2/ Rif. Brig. (3).
2nd Lieut. C. Ambler, 1/ Sherw'd Frstrs.
Capt. H. Archer, 2/ Devon.
Bvt. Lieut.-Colonel C. C. Armitage, C.M.G., D.S.O., R.A. (2).
Lieut. C. Ashby, 1/7 Midd'x.
Lieut.-Colonel H. F. Askwith, R.A.
Major V. Asser, R.A.
Lieut. D. M. Atkinson, 2/ Devon.
2nd Lieut. N. F. Bacon, T.M.B.

APPENDIX IV

Capt. P. Baden-Powell, M.G. Corps.
Lieut. C. W. H. Bailie, 2/ Rif. Brig.
Major E. E. F. Baker, M.C., 2/ Midd'x (2).
Major H. E. Barkworth, R.A.
Capt. and Adj. A. A. Barrett, M.C., 2/ R. Berks.
Lieut.-Colonel T. P. Barrington, R. Ir. Rif.
Lieut. E. I. Barrow, 2/ E. Lan.
Lieut.-Colonel R. Bastard, D.S.O., 2/ Linc.
Lieut. E. R. H. Beaman, R.E.
Lieut. F. J. Beechman, M.G.Corps.
Lieut. L. Benford, 1/ Sherw'd Frstrs.
Major P. K. Betty, D.S.O., R.E.
Major H. P. F. Bicknell, 2/ Midd'x.
Major E. B. Bird, R.A.M.C.
Capt. N. P. Birley, D.S.O., M.C., S. Staff. R.
Capt. R. P. Birtles, 1/ Worc.
Capt. A. J. Biscoe, 1/ R. Ir. Rif.
2nd Lieut. A. L. Bishop, 2/ Midd'x.
Major P. L. Blaber, R.A.M.C.
Capt. W. C. Blackham, R.A.M.C.
Capt. W. Blackwood, M.B., R.A.M.C.
Capt. D. Blyth, R.A.V.C. (2).
Capt. W. G. K. Boswell, 2/ Rif. Brig.
Bvt.-Colonel F. W. Boteler, R.A.
Capt. E. Boughton-Leigh, 2/ Rif. Brig.
Major L. G. Bourdillon, D.S.O., M.C., R.A.M.C.
Lieut.-Colonel A. G. B. Bourne, D.S.O., M.V.O., Royal Marine Arty.
Capt. and Adj. G. A. H. Bower, 1/7 Midd'x.
Capt. A. J. Bowles, 2/ R. Berks.
Major A. O. Boyd, R.A.
Capt. H.E.R.R. Braine, R. Muns. Fus.
Lieut.-Colonel Hon. R. Brand, D.S.O., 2/ Rif. Brig. (2).
Lieut. E. W. Brecken, 2/ Sco. Rif.
Lieut. W. W. Briggs, R.A.S.C.
Lieut. R. O. Bristowe, 2/ Devon.
2nd Lieut. H. A. Broadway, R.E.
Capt. R. H. Brodie, 2/ Midd'x.
Capt. A. F. Brooke, R.A.
Capt. R. W. Brooke, M.C., Yorks D. Yeo.
Lieut. C. J. Brooks, 1/ Linc.
Lieut.-Colonel C. M. Browne, D.S.O., R.E.
2nd Lieut. H. S. Bruce, 22/ Durh. L.I.
Major C. C. Bryan, R.E.
Lieut.-Colonel C. G. Buckle, D.S.O., M.C., 2/ North'n.
Major C. W. Burdon, R.A.
Lieut. W. A. Burges, 1/ R. Ir. Rif.
Lieut. R. Burgess, R.A.M.C.
Lieut.-Colonel A. T. Butler, C.M.G., R.A.
Major I. Buxton, Norf. Yeo.
Capt. J. V. Byrne-Johnson, 2/ Rif. Brig.
Capt. J. A. Cahill, M.C. (posthumous), 2/ R. Berks.
2nd Lieut. C. H. Cameron, R.A.
Lieut. J. W. Cannon, R.A.M.C.
Capt. A. G. C. Capell, 2/ North'n.
Capt. E. Carus-Wilson, M.C., R.E. (2).
Brig.-General G. T. C. Carter-Campbell, D.S.O., 2/ Sco. Rif.
Capt. J. B. F. Cartland, Worc. R.
Capt. S. E. Chamier, R.A.
Lieut.-Colonel A. T. Champion, 2/ W. York.
Rev. W. C. Charteris, Army Chaplains Dept.
Major L. C. Chasey, M.C., R.E.
Lieut. H. L. Chevens, 2/ Midd'x.
Lieut. H. P. Chiswell, R.E.
2nd Lieut. J. M. Churcher, R.A.
2nd Lieut. G. W. Coates, R.A.
Capt. and Adj. J. M. S. Coates, M.G. Corps.
Brig.-General H. W. Cobham, D.S.O., Indian Army.
2nd Lieut. M. Cohen, R.E.
Lieut.-Colonel J. H. B. Cole, M.C., 2/ Rif. Brig.

APPENDIX IV

Major J. R. Colville, R.A.
Capt. and Adj. R. A. Colvin, 2/ W. York.
Capt. A. W. H. Cooke, 22/ Durh. L.I.
2nd Lieut. E. G. W. Coward, R.A.
Lieut.-Colonel S. F.-G. Cox, 2/ Linc.
Major C. W. Cripps, R.A.
Capt. E. P. Cropper, M.C., 2/ W. York.
Lieut. J. A. Crutchley, 22/ Durh. L.I.
2nd Lieut. E. R. Culverwell, R.A.
Capt. C. E. Cumberland, 1/ Sherw'd Frstrs (2).
2nd Lieut. C. Cumming, 2/ E. Lan.
Capt. H. A. Curtis, 2/ R. Berks.
Capt. V. A. H. Daly, 2/ W. York.
Major C. J. B. Daubeny, Essex R.
Lieut.-Colonel R. A. C. Daunt, D.S.O., 1/ R. Ir. Rif.
Major H. J. N. Davis, Con. Rang.
2nd Lieut. R. A. de Stacpoole, R.A.
Capt. W. H. Diggle, G. Gds.
2nd Lieut. C. E. Dixon, R.A.
Capt. H. B. Dixon, 1/ Sherw'd Frstrs.
Capt. and Adj. R. C. Dodgson, R.A.
Lieut. N. Donaldson, R.A.
Lieut. R. B. Dorman, M.G. Corps.
Capt. and Adj. G. B. Duff, 2/ Sco. Rif.
Lieut. A. Duffy, 2/ E. Lan.
Lieut. T. B. Duncan, M.C., 2/ Sco. Rif.
Capt. W. E. Duncan, R.A. (2).
Colonel H. Dunn, R.A.M.C.
Capt. J. H. Dyer, R.E.
Capt. H. Eardley-Wilmot, 2/ Devon.
Lieut. L. W. Easman, 1/8 Midd'x.
Q.M. and Hon. Capt. G. W. Edwards, 1/ R. Ir. Rif. (3).
2nd Lieut. H. Edwards, 2/ Devon.
Lieut. L. A. Elgood, 1/5 Black Watch.
Major E. H. H. Elliot, R.A.
Capt. H. H. Elliot, M.C., M.B., R.A.M.C.
Capt. G. W. English, R.A.S.C.
2nd Lieut. H. Essame, 2/ North'n.
2nd Lieut. B. R. Everett, 2/ Rif. Brig.
Lieut. W. T. A. Everton, R.A.
2nd Lieut. C. C. Failes, R.A.
2nd Lieut. J. Ferguson, 2/ Sco. Rif.
Capt. E. B. Ferrers, 2/ Sco. Rif.
Major J. H. Fessenden, R.A.S.C.
Capt. and Adj. T. J. Fitz-Herbert-Brockholes, 2/ Rif. Brig. (2).
Capt. T. FitzJohn, 1/ Worc.
Capt. E. C. Fleming, R.A.
Capt. H. H. Flint, M.C., 2/ R. Berks.
Lieut. H. T. Forester, 2/ R. Berks.
Lieut.-Colonel D. E. Forman, C.M.G., R.A.
Lieut. H. T. Forster, 2/ R. Berks.
Capt. R. J. Foster, R.A.S.C.
Capt. and Adj. W. Foster, R.A.S.C.
Capt. W. Fotheringham, M.B., R.A.M.C.
Capt. E. S. Fox, 2/ W. York.
Capt. S. G. Francis, D.S.O., 2/ Devon.
Capt. H. E. Franklyn, York. Regt.
Major J. C. Freeland, Indian Army.
Lieut. G.R. Friendship, 2/ North'n.
Major O. M. T. Frost, R.E.
Capt. W. H. Fry, R.A.
2nd Lieut. C. H. Fuller, 2/ Midd'x.
Lieut. H. A. Fuller, R.E.
Capt. W. A. Gallagher, 2/ E. Lan.
Lieut. A. J. Gilchrist, R.A.M.C.
Lieut. H. G. Gilchrist, R.E.
Capt. W. W. Gillum, R.A.
Capt. R. B. G. Glover, 1/ Lond.
Rev. T. S. Goudge, Army Chaplains Dept.
Major P. G. Grant, R.E.
Major D. L. Gray, M.C., Sco. Rif.
Major J. C. Griffiths, M.C., R.A.
Brig.-General G. W. St. G. Grogan, C.M.G., D.S.O., Worc. R. (2).

APPENDIX IV

Capt. J. A. Grove, R.A.S.C.
Lieut.-Colonel F. G. Guggisberg, C.M.G., R.E.
2nd Lieut. R. C. Gull, 2/ Rif. Brig.
Capt. H. B. L. G. Gunn, R.A.
Brig.-General R. Haig, D.S.O., Rif. Brig.
Lieut. and Q.M. A. Hall, 1/5 Black Watch.
Capt. and Adj. C. C. H. Hall, 22/ Durh. L.I.
Lieut.-Colonel J. H. Hall, 2/ Midd'x.
2nd Lieut. T. Hall, 1/7 Durh. L.I.
Capt. H. J. Hambleton, 2/ North'n.
Capt. A. A. H. Hanbury-Sparrow, 2/ R. Berks.
Capt. J. D. Harcombe, 2/ Devon.
Major P. J. Harris, R.A.V.C.
Major C. E. Harrison, 2/ Rif. Brig.
Lieut. E. Hartley, 22/ Durh. L.I.
Lieut. C. H. Haskins, T.M.B.
Capt. A.J. Hawes, M.B., R.A.M.C.
Lieut. T. M. Hawker, R.A.
Lieut.-Colonel S. S. Hayne, D.S.O., 2/ North'n.
Major A. E. M. Head, R.A.
Capt. R. M. Heath, D.S.O., Div. Cyclist Coy.
2nd Lieut. M. F. Heath-Caldwell, R.A.
Maj.-General Sir W. C. G. Heneker, K.C.B., D.S.O.
Major G. R. Hennessy, Ches. R.
2nd Lieut. H. Hess, 2/ Midd'x.
2nd Lieut. H. Hewett, 2/ Midd'x.
Major C. L. Hickling, R.A.
Lieut. H. Higgs, R.E.
Capt. and Adj. E. D. Hill, 2/ Devon.
Bvt. Lieut.-Colonel H. Hill, M.V.O., D.S.O., R.W. Fus.
Q.M. and Hon. Lieut. C. Hinchcliffe, 2/ W. York.
Q.M. and Hon. Lieut. G. Hodgkinson, R.A.
Lieut.-Colonel A. M. Holdsworth, 2/ R. Berks.

2nd Lieut. J. M. Hood, M.G. Corps.
2nd Lieut. A. H. Hornby, R.A.
Lieut. L. G. Housden, R.A.
Lieut.-Colonel H. House, D.S.O., Indian Cav.
Lieut. E. Howard, 2/ W. York.
Capt. H. E. Howse (posthumous), 2/ R. Berks.
Capt. C. E. Hudson, 11/ Sherw'd Frstrs.
Lieut.-Colonel C. R. L. Hull, D.S.O., R.A.S.C.
Maj.-General H. Hudson, C.B., C.I.E.
Capt. J. E. Humberstone, R.A.
2nd Lieut. J. J. Huntingford, 2/ Devon.
Capt. T. C. Ibbs, 1/ Linc.
Major H. Ingham (posthumous), 2/ W. York.
Lieut. H. Ingoldsby, 2/ Linc. (2).
Lieut.-Colonel A. G. F. Isaac, M.C., 2/ R. Berks.
Lieut. C. O. R. Jacob, 2/ Devon.
Capt. R. D. Jeune, T.M.B.
Major R. H. Johnson, D.S.O., R.A.
2nd Lieut. H. T. Jones, R.A.
Major J. H. H. Jones, R.A.
Lieut. R. L. Jupp, R.A.
Major J. H. F. Kendall, R.E.
Lieut. J. P. F. Kenedy, 2/ Rif. Brig.
Lieut. C. S. C. Kennedy, R.E.
2nd Lieut. Hon. A. E. G. A. Keppel, 2/ Rif. Brig.
Lieut.-Colonel E. J. King, 1/7 Midd'x.
Major S. King, 1/7 Midd'x.
2nd Lieut. F. N. E. Kitson, 1/5 Black Watch.
Capt. J. O. Knight, M.G. Corps.
2nd Lieut. A. J. L. Knight-Bruce, R.A.
Capt. C. A. Lafone, 2/ Devon.
2nd Lieut. G. Lambert, R.E.
Lieut.-Colonel T. S. Lambert, 2/ E. Lan.
Capt. A. W. Langley, R.A.
Lieut. F. R. F. Lankester, R.A.

APPENDIX IV

Lieut.-Colonel S. G. Latham, M.C. with bar, 2/ North'n (2).
Lieut.-Colonel G. B. Laurie, 1/ R. Ir. Rif.
Capt. P. A. Ledward, Hamps. R.
Capt. R. Lee, R.A.S.C.
Major H. G. Lee-Warner, D.S.O., M.C., R.A.
2nd Lieut. R. Leetham, 2/ Rif. Brig.
Lieut. J. T. Leslie, York. R.
Capt. F. E. C. Lewis, M.G. Corps.
Major H. A. Lewis, K.O.Y.L.I.
Major C. F. T. Lindsay, R.A.
Capt. E. H. Lindsell, 2/ Linc.
Capt. and Adj. E. P. Lloyd, 2/ Linc.
Hon. Lieut. and Q.M. H. T. Lough, 1/8 Midd'x.
2nd Lieut. St. J. M. B. Low, 2/ North'n.
Capt. W. E. B. Lowe, M.C., 2/ E. Lan.
Lieut.-Colonel A. E. E. Lowry, M.C., 2/ W. York.
Brig.-General A. W. G. Lowry-Cole, Special List.
Major Sir C. B. Lowther, North'n. Yeo.
Capt. and Adj. J. G. Lowther, North'n. Yeo.
Major L. D. Luard, R.A.S.C.
Capt. H. H. W. Lydall, R.A.S.C.
Capt. C. C. Lyndon, R.A.S.C.
Capt. R. J. Lyon, 2/ E. Lan.
Lieut. R. C. Lyons, R.A.
Lieut.-Colonel G. B. McAndrew, 2/ Linc.
2nd Lieut. R. R. MacCartney, R.A.
Capt. M. H. McConnel, R.A.
2nd Lieut. W. R. McCrae, 2/ Sco. Rif.
2nd Lieut. G. MacDonald, R.A.
Lieut. R. M. MacGregor, 13/ Lond.
Capt. E. C. Mackay, R.A.M.C.
Lieut. R. J. Mackay, 2/ North'n.
2nd Lieut. C. Mackeson, 2/ Rif. Brig.
Lieut. D. L. Maclean, 2/ Rif. Brig.
Capt. J. B. McNab, 1/5 Black Watch.
Lieut.-Colonel C. C. Macnamara, 1/ R. Ir. Rif.
Lieut. R. H. Macturk, T.M.B.
Capt. and Adj. A. K. Main, R.A.
2nd Lieut. R. G. Maltby, 13/ Lond.
Q.M. and Capt. R. Mayes, 2/ North'n.
Capt. W. T. P. Meade-King, R.A.M.C.
Major A. D. N. Merriman, 1/ R. Ir. Rif.
Capt. A. T. Miller, M.C., Sherw'd Frstrs.
Lieut. E. C. Miller, R.A.
Major E. D. Miller, D.S.O., North'n. Yeo.
2nd Lieut. A. Millward, 1/Sherw'd Frstrs.
Lieut.-Colonel A. Milne-Thompson, R.A.M.C.
Lieut. P. Minor, 22/ Durh. L.I.
Lieut.-Colonel J. D. Mitchell, D.S.O., 1/ Sherw'd Frstrs.
2nd Lieut. M. E. Moir, R.A.
Lieut. W. N. Monteith, 2/ Rif. Brig.
Col. H. M. de F. Montgomery, R.A.
2nd Lieut. H. E. Moores, 2/ E. Lan.
Lieut.-Colonel C. B. Morgan, D.S.O., 22/ Durh. L.I.
Capt. H. S. Mortimer, New Armies (2).
Capt. C. D. Musgrave, R.A.S.C.
Major L. Napier, R.E.
Lieut. A. F. Nash, R.A.
2nd Lieut. J. Nettleton, 2/ Rif. Brig.
Lieut.-Colonel T. St. A. B. L. Nevinson, R.A.
2nd Lieut. F. Newhouse, R.E.
Capt. A. R. Newton, 2/ Devon.
Capt. P. W. Nickalls, North'n. Yeo.
Brig.-General G. H. W. Nicholson, C.M.G., R.A.

APPENDIX IV

Major O. H. L. Nicholson, W. York R.
Capt. W. R. C. Norgate, R.A.
Capt. F. J. O'Brien (posthumous), 1/ Worc.
Capt. A. P. O'Connor, R.A.M.C.
2nd Lieut. J. C. Oliver, 2/ Midd'x.
Colonel G. J. A. Ormsby, M.D., R.A.M.C.
2nd Lieut. A. Pace, 1/ Worc.
Lieut.-Colonel C. A. S. Page, M.C., 2/ Midd'x.
Hon. Lieut. and Q.M. G. Palmer, 2/ Devon (2).
Capt. R. A. Palmer, R.A.
2nd Lieut. G. Parker, 2/ Devon.
2nd Lieut. H. Parker, 2/ Devon.
Q.M. and Capt. S. Parker, 1/ Worc.
Capt. S. H. Parslow, R.A.S.C.
Major C. E. P. Parry, R.A.
Capt. B. C. Pascoe, M.C., Rif. Brig.
2nd Lieut. J. P. Patterson, 1/7 Durh. L.I.
Capt. C. S. Paul, R.A.
2nd Lieut. J. W. Pavey, 2/ R. Berks.
Capt. C. G. W. Peake, 2/ Linc.
Lieut.-Colonel F. S. Penny, M.B., R.A.M.C.
2nd Lieut. G. H. C. Pennycook, 2/ Midd'x.
Capt. G. H. C. Perry, 2/ W. York.
Lieut.-Colonel R. Pickard, M.D., R.A.M.C.
Capt. W. Piggott, 2/ North'n.
Capt. G. D. Pike, Ind. Army.
Lieut. T. Pilcher, 2/ Rif. Brig.
2nd Lieut. L.W. J. Pinnock, M.M., 2/ Rif. Brig.
Lieut. T. P. Pitcher, 2/ Rif. Brig.
2nd Lieut. G. A. Pocock, 2/ R. Berks.
Brig.-General J. H. W. Pollard, C.M.G., R. Sco. Fus.
Capt. H. C. M. Porter, K.R.R.C.
Rev. E. B. Potts, Army Chaplains Dept.
Lieut. C. L. G. Powell, R.A.M.C.
Capt. and Adj. H. Power, 2/ North'n.
Capt. K. E. Poyser, 8/ K.O.Y.L.I.
Lieut. A. B. Pratt, 1/ Worc.
Capt. A. M. Pratt, M.G. Corps.
Lieut. H. E. W. Prest, 2/ R. Berks.
Capt. H. R. Price, 2/ Rif. Brig.
Lieut. J. H. N. Price, R.A.M.C.
Capt. A. Prismall, 13/ Lond.
Lieut.-Colonel J. Puckle, D.S.O., R.A.S.C.
Lieut.-Colonel T. P. Puddicombe, M.B., D.S.O., R.A.M.C.
2nd Lieut. W. H. Pye, R.A.
Lieut. W. H. Radcliffe, 2/ Devon.
Capt. H. Ramsbotham, Gen. List.
Capt. J. K. Rashleigh, R.A.S.C.
Lieut. P. Rawlings, R.E.
Major W. B. F. Rayner, 1/ Lond.
Capt. J. G. G. Rea, North'd Huss. Yeo.
Capt. C. R. Reckitt, R.A.M.C.
2nd Lieut. J. W. Redding (posthumous), 2/ E. Lan.
Major L. F. Renny, D.S.O., R. Dub. Fus.
Capt. H. D. Reynolds, M.C., 2/ E. Lan.
Lieut. S. L. Ribby, T.M.B.
Major C. B. Rich, R.A. (2, 1 posthumous).
2nd Lieut. H. McA. Richards, R.A.
2nd Lieut. T. O. Richards, R.A.
Lieut. and Q.M. A. Ridley, 13/ Lond.
Lieut.-Colonel F. C. Roberts, V.C., D.S.O., M.C., 1/ Worc.
Capt. A. H. Robson, M.C., 22/ Durh. L.I.
Capt. F. Roe, 2/ Rif. Brig.
Capt. and Adj. J. F. S. Ross, R.E.
Lieut. E. Rothwell, M.G. Corps.
Maj. A. V. Rowe, 2/ North'n.
Lieut. E. B. L. Rushton, 2/ North'n.
Capt. A. W. Russell, R.A.M.C.
Capt. P. J. Ryan, M.B., R.A.M.C.
Capt. and Adj. C. Sanders, 2/ W. York.

APPENDIX IV

Lieut.-Colonel V. C. Sandilands, 2/ Sco. Rif.
Major G. H. Sawyer, D.S.O., 2/ R. Berks.
Lieut.-Colonel Hon. P. G. Scarlett, The Buffs.
Lieut. G. A. Seckham, 2/ E. Lan.
Lieut. and Q.M. J. Shaw, 2/ E. Lan.
Capt. E. Sheppard, G. Gds.
Lieut.-Colonel R. L. Sherbrooke, D.S.O., 1/ Sherw'd Frstrs. (3).
Major A. Simmonds, M.C., M.G. Corps.
Lieut. A. P. Skevington, 2/ W. York.
Q.M. and Hon. Maj. E. W. Skinner, 2/ Linc.
Major C. H. Smith, 8/ K.O.Y.L.I.
Lieut. G. S. Smith, 1/ Sherw'd Frstrs.
Major H. C. H. Smith, 2/ Sco. Rif.
Lieut. Jos. Smith, R.A.
Major S. C. M. Smith, 1/7 Midd'x.
Lieut.-Colonel E. W. Spedding, C.M.G., R.A.
Capt. F. E. Spencer, R.A.
2nd Lieut. H. M. Stanford, R.A.
Major D. B. Stewart, R.A.
Lieut.-Colonel C. R. H. Stirling, D.S.O., M.C., 2/ R. Berks.
Major W. Stirling, R.A.
Capt. N. H. Stone, 1/ Worc.
Capt. R. B. Stones, M.C., Durh. L.I.
Capt. and Adj. C. E. Stranack, R.A.
Lieut. and Adj. R. H. Stranger, 1/ Sherw'd Frstrs.
Lieut. A. V. Sully, M.G. Corps.
Lieut.-Colonel A. J. E. Sunderland, 2/ Devon (2, 1 posthumous).
Capt. H. N. Swann, Linc. R.
Capt. R. H. Tautz, M.C., 2/ R. Berks.
Capt. H. Tayler, 1/ R. Ir. Rif.
Capt. A. C. Taylor, T.M.B.
Lieut. J. G. Taylor, R.A.
Capt. T. T. Taylor, R.A.V.C.
Capt. W. C. D. Taylor, 2/ Devon.
Major H. C. Terry, R.A.
Major C. B. Thackeray, R.A.
Lieut. A. W. Thomas, U.S.A., M.R.C.
Capt. and Adj. G. Thompson, Conn. Rang.
Capt. R. Thwaites, 22/ Durh. L.I.
Major A. Tillett, M.C., 2/ Devon.
Major N. E. Tilney, R.A.
2nd Lieut. C. H. Townsend, 2/ Devon.
2nd Lieut. L. Tremellen, 2/ R. Berks.
Capt. J. E. Turner, Sco. Rif.
2nd Lieut. A.E. Turton, 2/ Midd'x.
Capt. F. St. J. Tyrwhitt, Worc. R.
Lieut.-Colonel R. F. Uniacke, R. Innis. Fus.
2nd Lieut. D. Uzielli, Corps of Interpreters.
Major P. C. Vellacott, D.S.O., Gen. List.
Capt. C. E. Vivian, M.C., R.A.
Capt. W. H. Walker, R.A.V.C.
2nd Lieut. F. C. Wallace, 1/ R. Ir. Rif.
Capt. J. T. Wallace, R.A.
2nd Lieut. E. G. Wallis, R.A.S.C.
2nd Lieut. H. G. Wedderburn-Maxwell, R.A.
Major J. Wedderburn-Maxwell, R.A.
Major A. H. D. West, R.A.
Lieut. F. C. West, R.E.
Capt. H. E. White, 2/ Midd'x.
Lieut. A. V. Whitehead, 2/ E. Lan.
2nd Lieut. A. P. Whitehurst, 1/ Worc.
Lieut. and Adj. G. H. P. Whitfield, 1/ R. Ir. Rif.
2nd Lieut. H. C. Whitley, 2/ W. York.
Hon. Lieut. and Q.M. H. A. Wiemers, 2/ Midd'x.
Capt. K. W. Wilkins, 1/ Worc.
Lieut. R. F. Wilkinson, R.A.M.C.
Capt. and Bvt. Major G. C. Williams, R.E.
Lieut. A. C. Willison, 1/ Sherw'd Frstrs.
Capt. S. Wilson, 2/ Linc.

APPENDIX IV

Capt. W. F. G. Wiseman, 2/ Linc.
Major E. C. F.Wodehouse, D.S.O., 1/ Worc.
Capt. C. W. Wolseley-Jenkins, 2/ Rif. Brig.
Major A. L. S. Wood, R.A.S.C.
Lieut. R. Woodhouse, R.A.M.C.
2nd Lieut. G. M. F. Wreford, 2/ Linc.
Capt. and Adj. A. O'H. Wright, 1/ R. Ir. Rif.
2nd Lieut. G. C. Wright, 2/Devon.
Lieut. A. W. Wylie, 2/ Linc.
Capt. and Adj. R. J. Young, 2/ Midd'x.

MENTION IN DESPATCHES (OTHER RANKS)

C.S.M. E. Addicott, 2/ R. Berks.
Bombdr. A. Ainley, R.A.
Corpl. J. E. Allsup, R.A.
Sergt. C. A. Alp, 2/ Linc.
Bombdr. T. Anderson, R.A.
Corpl. A. Andrews, 2/ W. Yorks.
R.S.M. J. H. Annetts, 2/ R. Berks.
Lce.-Corporal H. Ansell, 2/ Midd'x.
Corpl. H. Archer, 2/ W. Yorks.
Sergt. E. Archer, 2/ North'n.
Farrier Q.M. Sergt. A. Arlett, R.A.S.C.
Corpl. E. A. Armstrong, Durh. L.I.
Pte. L. R. Aspin, 2/ E. Lan.
Sergt. M. P. Austin, 1/ Worc.
2nd Corpl. W. H. Baber, R.E.
Bombdr. G. Bailey, R.A.
Pte. F. Baker, 1/ Worc.
Sgt. T. Banner, R.E.
Corpl. F. Barltrop, R.A.
Corpl. J. Barringer, 2/ Linc.
Sergt. C. H. Barrow, R.A.V.C.
Lce.-Corporal C. O. Basill, 2/ Rif. Brig.
Lce.-Corporal G. Bateman, 2/Linc.
Gnr. J. E. Bathgate, R.A.
Sergt. H. Battison, 2/ North'n.
C.S.M. J. H. Bauer, 2/ Devon.
Sergt. W. Baxter, 1/ Worc.
Sergt. A. Bennett, R.A.S.C.
Pte. A. Berry, 2/ Devon.
Lce.-Sergeant J. Betts, 1/ Worc.
Q.M. Sergt. J. J. Bicknell, R.A.M.C.
C.Q.M. Sergt. G. Bingham, 2/ Rif. Brig.
Gnr. H. G. Binley, R.A.
C.S.M. A. Blanchard, 1/ Sherw'd Frstrs.
Corpl. H. G. Blay, 1/ Worc.
Lce.-Corporal P. Boddington, 2/ North'n.
Gnr. H. Bond, R.A.
C.S.M. J. Bond, 1/ Lond.
C.Q.M. Sergt. W. Booker, 2/ R. Berks.
Lce.-Corporal J. Booth, 1/ Sherw'd Frstrs.
Sergt. B. Boult, 2/ R. Berks.
Batty. Sergt.-Major A. Boulter, R.A.
Pte. H. Boundy, R.A.V.C.
Sergt. E. A. Bowden, 2/ Devon.
Bandsman J. Bowman, 2/ Sco. Rif.
Mech. Sergt.-Major E. J. Bradford, R.A.S.C.
Sergt. T. Bradford, R.A.V.C.
C.Q.M. Sergt. J. Bradley, 2/ Sco. Rif.
Gnr. B. Braines, R.A.
Pte. J. W. Brazil, 2/ Devon.
Sergt. P. Breen, 1/ R. Ir. Rif.
C.S.M. W. Bright, 2/ E. Lan.
Pte. T. Broderick, 2/ E. Lan.
Corpl. J. Brown, 2/ Sco. Rif.
Gnr. J. Brown, R.A.
Rfmn. R. Brown, 1/ R. Ir. Rif.
Pte. S. Brown, A. Cyclist Corps.
Sergt. H. Bull, 2/ Rif. Brig.
R.S.M. G. S. Bullock, 1/7 Midd'x.
Corpl. A. Bryant, R.A.S.C.
C.Q.M. Sergt. S. A. Caleopy, 2/ Midd'x.
C.S.M. F. J. Campbell, 2/ R. Berks.
R.Q.M. Sergt. T. Carefoot, 2/ E. Lan.
Rfmn. H. Carpenter, 2/ Rif. Brig.

APPENDIX IV

C.Q.M. Sergt. S. G. Carthew, 2/ Devon.
C.S.M. R. Carwell, 2/ North'n.
Sergt. W. Caunt, 1/ Sherw'd Frstrs.
Corpl. S. Cave, 1/ Lond.
C.S.M. J. Chance, 1/ Worc.
Batty. Sergt.-Major F. Clarke, R.A.
Pte. R. Clarke, 2/ North'n.
Sergt. E. W. Clayton, 2/ W. York.
Sergt. F. Clifford, 1/ Sherw'd Frstrs.
Corpl. J. Coates, 1/7 Durh. L.I.
Pte. T. Cobern, R.A.M.C.
Sergt. G. Cole, 1/ Sherw'd Frstrs.
C.S.M. J. Cole, 2/ W. York.
C.Q.M. Sergt. P. H. Coles, 2/ Midd'x.
Pte. S. Coles, 2/ Linc.
Bombdr. F. Collett, R.A.
Corporal C. Collins, R.A.
Lce.-Corporal E. Collins, 2/ Sco. Rif.
Fitter B. Collof, R.A.
Fitter G. Cook, R.A.
C.S.M. H. Cooper, 1/ Worc.
Sergt. H. Cording, 2/ Midd'x.
Sergt. C. G. Corps, 2/ R. Berks.
R.Q.M. Sergt. L. C. Corrigan, 1/ R. Ir. Rif. (2).
Corpl. J. H. Cotterell, M.M., 2/ R. Berks.
Pte. J. Court, 2/ Midd'x.
Sergt. H. Cox, 1/ Sherw'd Frstrs.
C.S.M. S. W. J. Cox, 2/ Devon.
Lce.-Corporal E. V. Craddock, 2/ Devon.
Gnr. A. Creaser, R.A.
C.Q.M. Sergt. M. J. Crinion, 2/ E. Lan.
S. Sergt. W. Crook, R.A.S.C.
Sergt. J. Cross, R.A.M.C.
C.Q.M. Sergt. G. Crump, 1/ Worc.
Corpl. E. Cudmore, M.G. Corps.
Sergt. A. Cummins, T.M.B.
Sergt. G. Cunningham, 2/ W. York.
Pte. H. H. Cunningham, 2/ E. Lan.
Corpl. S. Cutting, R.A. (2).
Pte. D. Dambleby, 2/ Linc.
Sapper C. Darling, R.E.
C.S.M. G. Davey, M.G. Corps.
Rfmn. N. Davey, 2/ Rif. Brig.
Pte. J. Davidson, 1/5 Black Watch.
Corpl. R. Davidson, R.A.
Lce.-Corporal P. Dewhurst, 2/ W. York.
Batty. Q.M. Sergt. E. Diment, R.A.
Sergt. G. Dixon, 1/ Sherw'd Frstrs.
Pte. H. Dominy, R.A.M.C.
R.S.M. J. Doulton, 2/ Rif. Brig.
C.S.M. A. Drage, 2/ North'n.
C.S.M. J. Earll, R.E.
Pte. G. Eden, 2/ Linc.
Sergt. H. Edwards, 1/ Worc.
Pte. P. Elcock, R.A.M.C.
Corpl. G. Elsdon, 2/ Rif. Brig.
C.S.M. R. Embling, 2/ R. Berks.
Sergt. J. C. Enoch, R.A.V.C.
Lce.-Corporal A. Evans, 1/ Worc.
C.S.M. F. J. Fane, 2/ Midd'x.
Lce.-Corporal S. Fawcett, R.E.
Sergt. W. J. Fee, 1/ R. Ir. Rif.
Pte. H. Ferari, 2/ W. York.
Pte. A. Ferrier, 1/5 Black Watch.
Pte. F. Field, M.G. Corps.
Sapper W. Firth, R.E.
Corpl. F. FitzGerald, 2/ Linc.
Rfmn. H. Flight, 2/ Rif. Brig.
Pte. T. Foote, 2/ North'n.
Sergt. H. Fordham, 1/ Worc.
Drummer W. Forth, 13/ Lond.
Sergt. A. Foster, 2/ North'n.
Corpl. F. Fouracre, R.A.
Sergt. G. Fridd, R.A.
R.S.M. J. Furey, 2/ Rif. Brig.
Lce.-Corporal N. Galt, 13/ Lond.
Corpl. C. Garner, 2/ Rif. Brig. (2).
Sapper D. Giles, R.E.
Farrier Q.M. Sergt. W. Gooch, R.A.
Sergt.-Major G. Gotham, R.A.M.C.
Lce.-Corporal F. Graham, 1/7 Durh. L.I.
Pte. G. Graham, 2/ R. Berks.
C.S.M. F. J. Gray, R.A.S.C.
Sergt. C. Green, 2/ Midd'x.

APPENDIX IV

Lce.-Corporal G. Green, 1/7 Durh. L.I.
Pte. A. Greenwood, 1/ Sherw'd Frstrs.
Sergt.-Major H. W. Gregory, R.A.M.C.
Pte. D. J. Griffiths, 2/ Devon.
Lce.-Corporal J. J. Griffis, M.G. Corps.
Sergt. W. T. Haffenden, R.E.
Corpl. S. Hall, 1/ Sherw'd Frstrs.
Sergt. W. Hall, R.A.
Bombdr. W. Hammond, R.A.
Batty. Sergt.-Major F. Hand, R.A.
Pte. R. Handford, 2/ Devon.
Sergt. A. Hard, 2/ Rif. Brig.
Wheeler S. Sergt. W. G. Harding, R.A.S.C.
Pte. G. Harris, 2/ E. Lan.
Corpl. E. Harrison, R.A.
Corpl. L. Harrop, 2/ North'n.
Corpl. A. Hartell, M.G. Corps.
Sapper V. L. Hatton, R.E.
Sergt. C. J. Hawes, R.A.
2nd Corpl. W. Hawes, R.E.
Sergt. W. Hayes, 2/ Devon.
Corpl. E. W. Haynes, R.A.
S. Sergt. H. H. Hayward, R.A.M.C.
2nd Corpl. C. W. Heald, R.E.
Sergt. W. Heggs, 2/ Linc.
Pte. H. Hemus, 1/ Worc.
Sergt. J. T. Henshaw, 1/7 Durh. L.I.
C.Q.M. Sergt. T. Henson, 2/ Midd'x.
Sergt. J. Heron, 2/ E. Lan.
Pte. W. High, 1/5 Black Watch.
Rfmn. L. Hilliam, 2/ Rif. Brig.
Lce.-Corporal A. Hinett, 11/ Sherw'd Frstrs.
C.S.M. G. H. Hirst, 1/ Sherw'd Frstrs.
Sergt. J. Hodgson, 2/ Rif. Brig.
Pte. S. Holmes, 2/ W. York.
Bombdr. G. Hopwood, R.A.
Pte. T. Horry, 2/ Linc.
S. Sergt.-Major E. R. House, R.A.M.C.
Corpl. W. J. Howell, R.A.M.C.
Pte. A. Howie, 1/5 Black Watch.
Sergt. A. Hubble, M.G. Corps.
R.S.M. J. H. Hull, 11/ Sherw'd Frstrs.
Sergt. T. Hullet, R.E.
Sergt. (Master Shoemaker) J. Humphrey, 2/ Midd'x. (2).
Bombdr. Wheeler F. R. Hurd, R.A.
Sergt. J. H. Hutchinson, R.A.
C.S.M. C. Huxford, R.A.S.C.
Squad. Sergt.-Major A. J. Ingle, North'n. Yeo.
Corpl. J. Issett, M.G. Corps.
Pte. A. Jackson, 11/ Sherw'd Frstrs.
Corpl. E. Jackson, 22/ Durh.L.I.
C.Q.M. Sergt. G. Jackson, 1/ Sherw'd Frstrs.
Sptdg. Clerk M. Jackson, R.E. (2).
Batty. Sergt.-Major J. C. Jeffs, R.A.
Bombdr. J. Jenkins, R.A.
Sergt. A. Jobson, R.A.
Sergt. A. Johnson, 2/ R. Berks.
Sergt. H. H. Johnson, North'n. Yeo.
Corpl. R. C. Jolliffe, 13/ Lond.
Rfmn. E. Jolly, 2/ Rif. Brig.
Corpl. H. Jones, 2/ E. Lan.
Sergt. J. Jones, 2/ Rif. Brig.
Corpl. W/ Jones, 1/ Worc.
Sergt. W. Jones, R.A.S.C.
Corpl. C. Jordan, 1/8 Midd'x.
Sapper R. Jordan, R.E.
Bombdr. E. Joyce, R.A.
Gnr. J. C. Jupp, R.A.
Pte. E. Kane, 2/ Sco. Rif.
Corpl. J. E. Kane, 2/ W. York.
Corpl. B. A. Kavanagh, 1/ R. Ir. Rif.
Corpl. A. Kealy, R.A.
Lce.-Corporal W. Keen, 1/5 Black Watch.
Musician B. Kelly, 1/ R. Ir. Rif.
Lce.-Corporal R. L. Kelso, R.E.
Sergt. G. A. Kemp, R.E.
Corpl. B. J. Kerridge, R.E.
Rfmn. E. King, 2/ Rif. Brig.
Sergt. E. J. King, 1/7 Midd'x.
Corpl. F. King, R.A.
Lce.-Corporal B. Kingdom, 2/ Devon.

APPENDIX IV

Pte. V. O. Lander 13/ Lond.
S.S.M. A. H. Lane, R.A.S.C.
C.S.M. J. Lane, 2/ Devon.
Gnr. J. Lane, R.A.
Sergt. S. Lang, A. Cyclist Corps.
Pte. W. Larkins, 2/ Midd'x.
Sergt. A. Lawie, R.A.V.C.
Rfmn. P. Lawrence, 2/ Rif. Brig.
Sergt. A. J. Lawson, 2/ R. Berks.
Corpl. J. R. Leadbetter, R.A.M.C.
Sergt. C. R. Leeming, 22/ Durh. L.I.
C.Q.M. Sergt. E. J. Leggatt, R.E.
Bombdr. W. Lemon, R.A.
Lce.-Corporal M. Lennon, 1/ R. Ir. Rif.
S. Sergt. Artificer W. Leslie, R.A.
Sergt. G. Lewis, 1/ Sherw'd Frstrs.
Mech. Sergt.-Major J. Liddell, R.A.S.C.
Pte. J. Limerick, 1/ Sherw'd Frstrs.
Corpl. T. Lister, 2/ North'n.
Sergt. H. B. Liversedge, 2/ W. York.
Lce.-Corporal S. Lorkin, 2/ Sco. Rif.
Sergt. W. Lyall, R.E.
Sergt. B. McBeath, 2/ Sco. Rif.
Corpl. K. McCaskell, R.A.
Sapper J. McCutcheon, R.E.
Pte. J. W. McGregor, M.G. Corps.
Pte. G. McKenzie, 2/ E. Lan.
Farrier Sergt. J. McNair, R.A.
Sergt. D. McNulty, 2/ Sco. Rif.
Rfmn. C. McRitchie, 2/ Rif. Brig.
Sergt. J. P. Maguire, 1/ R. Ir. Rif.
Sergt. H. Maris, T.M.B.
Q.M. Sergt. D. Marshall, R.A.
Sergt. D. W. Martin, R.A.
Lce.-Corporal A. Martindale, 2/ Midd'x.
Sergt. F. Maycock, 2/ North'n.
C.S.M. T. A. Mayhew, 2/ North'n.
Gnr. A. Mellor, R.A.
Pte. D. T. V. Middleton, R.A.M.C.
Pte. J. Middlewick, 2/ Devon.
Lce.-Corporal W. Millins, 2/ Midd'x.
Corpl. A. Mills, 1/8 Midd'x.

Lce.-Corporal H. S. Mitchell, 2/ Midd'x.
Rfmn. J. Moncur, 2/ Rif. Brig.
C.S.M. F. Moore, 2/ Linc.
Corpl. J. G. Moore, 2/ Rif. Brig.
Sergt. J. S. Moore, R.A.M.C.
Sergt. J. Moran, R.A.
Gnr. A. Morgan, R.A.
C.S.M. F. G. Morgan, 1/ Worc.
Lce.-Corporal W. A. Morgan, R.A.S.C.
Corpl. C. T. Morris, R.A.
Sergt.-Major H. Morton, 1/ Sherw'd Frstrs.
Sergt. G. J. Mountford, T.M.B.
Lce.-Corporal A. Moxey, 1/ Worc.
Pte. A. G. Mullerhausen, 2/ North'n.
Pte. A. Munro, 1/ Lond.
Rfmn. W. Munro, 2/ Rif. Brig.
Rfmn. W. Munson, 2/ Rif. Brig.
Sergt. W. Murfitt, 1/ Sherw'd Frstrs.
R.S.M. C. E. Murien, M.G. Corps.
Sergt. W. Murray, 5/ Black Watch.
Pte. C. Newman, 1/ Worc.
C.S.M. C. Newton, 2/ Linc.
C.Q.M. Sergt. J. W. Nicholson, 2/ E. Lan.
Cpl. W. R. C. Norgate, R.A.
Pte. W. Northcott, 2/ Devon.
Pte. N. Nosworthy, 2/ Devon.
Sergt. A. Notting, R.E.
Sergt. F. Organ, 2/ E. Lan.
Bombdr. S. Osman, R.A.
Corpl. E. C. Palmer, 2/ Rif. Brig.
Corpl. W. K. Palmer, R.E.
C.S.M. A. J. Parker, R.E.
R.S.M. T. Parnell, 8/ K.O.Y.L.I.
Sergt.-Major T. W. Parsons, R.A.M.C. (2).
Lce.-Corporal W. Pavey, 2/ Midd'x.
Corpl. F. Pearce, 2/ R. Berks.
Sergt. J. Pearce, 1/ Sherw'd Frstrs.
Pte. W. Pearson, 2/ E. Lan.
Corpl. H. Pegg, 2/ Rif. Brig.
Driver G. Pegrum, R.A.
Sapper E. Pepper, R.E.

APPENDIX IV

Lce.-Corporal T. Perry, 2/ Linc.
Sergt. G. Phillips, 2/ Sco. Rif.
C.S.M. T. Phillips, 1/ Sherw'd Frstrs.
Corpl. G. H. Phipps, M.M., 1/ Sherw'd Frstrs.
S. Sergt. S. Pickering, R.A.M.C.
Corpl. H. Pickup, R.A.
C.S.M. H. L. Pike, 2/ Sco. Rif.
Corpl. L. Pinnock, 2/ Rif. Brig.
Q.M. Sergt. C. Pionchon, 2/ Rif. Brig.
S. Sergt. S. C. Pocock, R.A.M.C.
Sergt. W. Poole, 2/ Midd'x.
Corpl. J. H. Potterton, 2/ Rif. Brig.
Sergt. A. T. Price, R.A.M.C.
Corpl. J. Quinlan, 1/ R. Ir. Rif.
Sergt. F. Radford, 2/ Devon.
Sergt. W. Ragan, R.A.S.C.
Pte. T. Ranscombe, 2/ R. Berks.
Rfmn. H. W. Read, 2/ Rif. Brig.
Sergt. J. Reddin, R.E.
Pte. A. Redford, 1/5 Black Watch (2).
Pte. H. Reeks, A. Cyclist Corps.
C.S.M. W. Reeve, 1/ Sherw'd Frstrs.
Sergt. M. Reilly, 2/ Devon.
Pte. T. Revill, 2/ W. York.
Lce.-Sergeant C. F. Reynolds, 1/7 Midd'x.
Sergt. G. E. H. Rice, R.A.M.C.
Pte. W. Rice, 2/ R. Berks.
R.S.M. E. Richards, R.E.
C.S.M. A. E. Richardson, 2/ Rif. Brig.
Sergt. H. W. Richardson, R.E.
Shoeing Smith Corpl. G. T. W. Roberts, R.A.S.C.
Pte. S. Roberts, 2/ Devon.
Conductor C. E. W. Robinson, R.A.O.C.
Bandsman F. Robinson, 2/ Sco. Rif.
Lce.-Corporal J. Robinson, 2/ E. Lan.
Corpl. W. A. Robinson, 2/ W. York.
Sergt. W. Rosamond, 2/ Midd'x.

Bombdr. W. S. Rotherham, R.A.
Drummer W. Roworth, 2/ Linc.
Sergt. P. H. Ruffels, 2/ R. Berks.
Corpl.W.Russon, 1/Sherw'd Frstrs.
Bombdr. D. H. Saunders, R.A.
C.S.M. H. Scarlett, 2/ North'n.
Sergt. G. Schoales, 2/ E. Lan.
Sergt. T. Selby, 2/ E. Lan.
Sergt. A. Self, 2/ W. York.
Sergt. J. Senior, 2/ Linc.
Corpl. C. Sexton, 1/ R. Ir. Rif.
Q.M. Sergt. A. E. Sharland, R.A.M.C.
Mech. Sergt.-Major G. H. Sharp, R.A.S.C.
Corpl. O. Sharpe, 2/ Linc.
C.S.M. G. Shearstone, 2/ Midd'x.
Lce.-Corporal W. Shepherd, 2/ W. York.
Batty. Sergt. Major J. H. Sheridan, R.A.
R.S.M. W. E. Simmons, R.A.
Corpl. A. Shopland, 2/ Rif. Brig.
Sergt. H. Slate, 1/ Sherw'd Frstrs.
Pte. A. Sleete, 2/ North'n.
R.S.M. A. Smart, 2/ Sco. Rif. (2).
Pte. D. Smart, 1/5 Black Watch.
Pte. B. Smith, 2/ Devon.
Driver D. M. Smith, R.A.
C.Q.M. Sergt. F. Smith, 2/ R. Berks.
Sergt. J. Smith, 2/ North'n.
Sergt. S. Smith, 2/ R. Berks.
Pte. T. Snow, 1/ Worc.
Sergt. W. N. Snowdon, 2/ Sco. Rif.
Pte. F. Southwood, T.M.B.
Sergt. F. Sparrow, R.E.
C.S.M. H. Spencer, 2/ Rif. Brig.
Rfmn. C. A. L. Spiller, 2/ Rif. Brig.
Sergt. A. Spink, R.A.
Pte. S. J. Staples, R.A.S.C.
Sergt. H. W. Steele, 2/ Rif. Brig.
Sergt. G. Stevenson, 22/ Durh. L.I.
Lce.-Corporal E. Stewart, 2/ W. York.
Sergt. W. H. Stewart, 1/7 Midd'x.
Lce.-Corporal C. Stokes, 1/ Worc. (2).
Sergt. R. Stovin, 1/ R. Ir. Rif.

APPENDIX IV

Gnr. J. F. Stradwick, R.A.
Corpl. F. Sutton, 1/Sherw'd Frstrs.
Lce.-Corporal A. D. Swinburn, 2/ W. York.
Rfmn. S. Swinscoe, 2/ Rif. Brig.
Corpl. F. C. Symonds, 2/ Midd'x.
Pte. A. V. Tait, 1/ Worc.
Pte. E. W. A. Taylor, 1/7 Durh. L.I.
Lce.-Corporal J. Taylor, 1/5 Black Watch.
Lce.-Corporal J. Taylor, 2/ Sco. Rif.
Pte. J. Taylor, 2/ W. York.
Sergt. S. Taylor, 2/ Devon.
Pte. W. S. Thomas, R.A.S.C.
Lce.-Corporal F. G. Thompson, 2/ W. York.
Sergt. G. Thompson, 1/7 Durh. L.I.
Sergt. J. G. Thompson, 2/ W. York.
Q.M. Sergt. H. Thornhill, 2/ W. York.
Rfmn. N. Thorpe, 2/ Rif. Brig.
R.Q.M. Sergt. R. Tiernan, 2/ Linc.
Sergt. P. W. Tighe, R.A.M.C.
Rfmn. J. Traynor, 1/ R. Ir. Rif.
C.Q.M. Sergt. W. J. Trench, Divl. H.Q.
Batty. Sergt.-Major H. Troupe, R.A.
C.Q.M. Sergt. A. E. Trueman, 2/ Rif. Brig.
Pte. A. Turner, 22/ Durh. L.I.
Pte. A. C. Usher, 1/ Worc.
Sapper H. L. Vile, R.E.
C.Q.M. Sergt. F. Vokins, 2/R. Berks.
Lce.-Corporal F. Waldron, 1/ Sherw'd Frstrs.
Sergt. J. T. Waldron, 8/ K.O.Y.L.I.
Sergt. P. Walker, R.A.

Corpl. W. Wallington, 2/ E. Lan.
C.S.M. F. Wannop, 2/ Sco. Rif.
C. Sergt. C. Ward, 2/ Devon.
R.S.M. W. Ward, 1/ R. Ir. Rif.
Lce.-Corporal G. Warrener, 2/ Linc.
R.Q.M. Sergt. C. W. Watkins, 2/ Rif. Brig.
Pte. C. E. Webb, R.A.M.C.
Sergt. P. Webster, 2/ E. Lan. (2).
Corpl. T. G. Wells, R.E.
C.S.M. F. L. Wellstead, 2/ W. York.
Sergt. J. C. Welsh, R.A.S.C.
C.S.M. W. Weston, 2/ R. Berks.
C.S.M. J. West, R.A.S.C.
Pte. J. Wetton, 1/ Worc.
Lce.-Sergeant F. Whelan, Div.H.Q.
Corpl. G. White, R.A.M.C.
Gnr. S. White, R.A.
Farrier S. Sergt. W. H. White, R.A.S.C.
Corpl. J. Whittaker, R.E.
Sergt. W. A. Wilcox, R.A.
Lce.-Corporal A. Williams, 2/ Linc.
Corpl. C. Williams, R.E.
Sapper H. Williams, R.E.
Sergt. F.M.A. Williams, R.A.M.C.
Bombdr. R. Wills, R.A.
Gnr. J. Wilson, R.A.
Q.M. Sergt. E. A. Wiltshire, R.A.
Corpl. F. H. Wish, R.A.
Sergt. J. E. Wood, R.A.
Lce.-Corporal F. G. Woodason, Div. H.Q.
2nd Corpl. W. R. Woodgate, R.E.
Pte. S. Woods, 2/ Devon.
S. Sergt.-Major W. W. Woods, Div. H.Q. (2).
Corpl. H. Woolley, R.A.
Farrier Sergt. H. Worrall, R.E.
S. Sergt.-Major A. J. Yates, R.A.S.C.

INDEX

A

Abbeville, 2
Abeele, 173
Ablaincourt, 182
Adair, Lt.-Col. H. S., 167
Adam, Brig.-Gen. F. A., 1
Addison, Lt.-Col. A. J. B., 71
Air attacks, German, 94, 124, 141, 178, 245
Air Force, Royal, 70, 261
Aisne R., 216, 220–4, 227
Albert, 63
Allen, Pte., 185
Amiens, 62, 208, 213
Ancre R., 66
Anderson, Lt.-Col. G. H. G., 165
Anderson, Col. G. W. H., 40, 57
Anderson Morshead, Lt.-Col. R. H., 205, 220, 226, 240
Angell, Lt.-Col. J., 248, 258, 264
Angle, The, 53
Anzac Redoubt, 146, 147
Anzac Spur, 133, 145, 150
Arleux, 250, 257
Armentières, 3, 156
Armies :
    First, 4, 32, 43–4, 58, 79, 113, 245, 273
    Second, 119, 122, 127, 154, 277
    Third, 113, 161, 176–7, 190
    Fourth, 61, 122, 170, 216
    Fifth, 94, 99, 100, 107–8, 112, 122, 127, 135, 142, 154, 174–7, 190, 277–8
    First French, 126–7, 142
    Sixth French, 216
Armistice, 274, 276
Armitage, Lt.-Col. C. C., 171, 175, 178, 182, 187
Army Medical Corps, Royal, 4, 136, 139, 198, 268
    24th Field Ambulance, 278
    25th   ,,   ,,   231, 278
    Wessex ,,   ,,   1, 28
Arras, 112–3, 116–8, 121
Artillery, 17, 48, 53, 67, 78, 80, 85, 123, 124, 126, 136, 137, 144, 150, 159, 162, 208

Artillery, 8th Divisional, 3, 187, 227–9
Artillery, 20th Divisional, 200
Artillery, 25th Divisional, 126
Artillery reorganization, 63, 126
Artillery units :
    Ammunition Column (8th Division), 4, 63, 97, 138
    Batteries :
        "D" 63
        "O," 63
        "Z," 63
        1st, 49, 63, 227, 228
        3rd, 63, 265
        5th, 49, 63, 227–9, 240, 277
        32nd, 63, 228
        33rd, 17, 63
        36th, 63
        55th, 63
        57th, 63, 227
        104th, 37
        5th Siege, 17
    Brigades :
        V R.H.A., 63, 126
        X R.F.A., 126
        XXII R.F.A., 37
        XXIII R.F.A., 63, 97, 126, 221, 227, 248, 256, 264, 270, 271
        XXVIII R.F.A., 126
        XLV R.F.A., 63, 97, 126, 221, 227, 248, 264, 270, 271
        XLVIII R.F.A., 270, 271
        XC R.F.A., 200
        XCI R.F.A., 200
        XCV R.F.A., 233
        CX R.F.A., 221, 230, 233
        CXII R.F.A., 233
        CXXVI R.F.A., 256, 260, 264
        CXXVIII R.F.A., 63
        CLXIX R.F.A., 256, 261
        CLXXV R.F.A., 256
        CLXXXI R.F.A., 111
        CCXXXII R.F.A., 126
        CCXLII R.F.A., 249
        CCLXXVII R.F.A., 249, 256
        CCXCI R.F.A., 200

INDEX

Artillery Units :
  Brigades (contd.)
    CCCXI R.F.A., 249, 264, 270, 271
    XXIV H.A.G., 126
    LVII H.A.G., 126
    LXXIII H.A.G., 126
    LXXXVIII H.A.G., 126
    XVI R.G.A., 248, 256
    XL R.G.A., 256
Aspinall, 2/Lt., 257
Ath, 277
Athies, 175
Aubers, 34
Aubers Ridge, 18, 24, 32, 43
Aveluy Wood, 62

B

Bailey, Lt. J. M., 149
Bailey, 2/Lt. S. U., 142
Baker, Capt. E. E F., 132, Maj., 243, Lt.-Col., 261, 266, 267, 274
Baker, Maj. O. C., 19, 34
Baldwin, Maj. J. Y., 268
Ballard, Lt.-Col. J. A., 221, 227, 236, 243
Balloons, German, 70, 231, 235, 239
Bamford, Pte. H., 103
Bapaume, 84
Bargh, Maj. M. T., 227
Bassée, la, 3
Basse-ville, la, 115
Bastard, Capt. R., 20, Lt.-Col., 70, 73, 86, 115, 133, 134, 139
Bauden, Pte., 125
Baudour, 277
Bayonvillers, 190
Beall, Lt.-Col. E. M., 220, 236, 241
Beaumont Hamel, 94
Beddington, Lt.-Col. E. H. L., 97, 99, 102, 167
Bellewaarde Farm, 126
Bellewaarde Lake, 129
Bellewaarde Ridge, 128, 129, 135, 151
Belloy St. Leonard, 96, 98

Bernafay Wood, 83, 85
Berquin, 159
Berry, Sergt. J. A., 278
Berry-au-Bac, 217, 219
Bertangles, 200
Berthelot, Général, Ordres du Jour of, 239
Béthencourt, 178, 180
Bethune, 80, 83
Betty, Maj. P. K., 41
Biache Barrage, The, 257
Biache St. Vaast, 256, 257
Bird, Lt., 102, 103
Birtles, 2/Lt., 265
Biscoe, Capt., 21
Blake, Capt. C. E., 148, 149
Blaringhem, 57
Bliss, Lt.-Col. W. M., 19
Boesinghe, 127
Bœufs, les, 85, 91, 92
Bois d'Aquenne, 201, 202, 206, 207, 211, 212
Bois des Buttes, 225, 226
Bois Grenier, 45–54
Bois l'Abbé, 201
Boisselle, la, 62, 67, 68, 72, 75–8
Bombs, shortage of, 10, 15
Bombs, variety of, 51
Bomy, 125
Booby Traps, German, 264
Border Redoubt, 82
Boteler, Bvt.-Col. F. W., 60, 63, 97, 138
Bouchavesnes, 84, 96–107
Bouffignereux, 230, 231
Boulding, Sergt. W. G., 129
Bouleuse Ridge, 234–6
Bourke, Capt. J., 137
Boutillerie, la, 31
Bouvancourt, 231
Birdwood, Gen. Sir W. R., 199, 277
Brand, Capt. Hon. R., 49, Lt.-Col., 70, 86, 111, 115, 133, 140, 164, 165, Brig.-Gen., 257, 278
Brandhoek, 159
Branscourt, 231, 232
Brebières, 264
Bridoux, le, 44

348

INDEX

Bridoux Fort, 50-2
Bridoux Salient, 47, 53
Brodie, Capt., 204
Bronfay Farm, 97
Brown, Maj. A. H., 158, 191
Brown, Lt.-Col. C. R., 263, 268
Browne, Lt.-Col. C. M., 127, 138, 232
Bruay, 80
Bryan, Maj. C. C., 141
Buckle, Lt.-Col. C. G., 87, 129, 130, 139, 220, 224, 225
Bulton, 2/Lt. C. A., 228, 229, 240
Burgess, Lt., 21
Burgess, Pte., 185
Burgess, Lt.-Col. R., 278
Butler, Lt.-Col. A. T., 63
Butler, Lt.-Gen. Sir R. H. K., 277, 278
Byng, Gen. Sir J. H. G., 161

C

Cachy, 201
Cachy Switch, 205-6, 210
Caestre, 123, 154, 159
Cahill, Capt. J. A., 106, 146
Caix, 187, 190
Cambrai, 161
Camp, 34, 91, 92
Campbell, Col., 125
Campbell, Lt.-Col. C. A. H., 97
Campbell, Gen. David, 221
Canal du Jard, 271, 272
Canal du Nord, 108
du Cane, Lt.-Gen. Sir J. P., 96
Carter, Brig.-Gen. F. C., 3, 19
Cartland, Maj. J. B. F., 220, 225
Casteau, 276
Castel, 193
de Castelnau, Général, 4
Cavalry (and see Corps, Divisions), 111
  Brigades :
    5th Canadian, 110
  Units :
    4th Hussars, 208, 271, 274
    Northamptonshire Yeo., 1, 19

Cavalry :
  Units (contd.)
    1/1 Northumberland Hussars, 227
    1/1 Yorkshire Dragoons, 128
Cavan, Lt.-Gen. The Earl of, 85, 98, 159
Cavillon, 99
Cerisy, 190
Chamberlain, Sergt., 94
Champion, Maj. A. T., 257, 274
Chapigny, 28
Château d'Acq, 245, 249
Château des Près, 80
Château Wood, 129, 132
Chaulnes, 174, 178, 183, 186
Chèry Chartreuve, 216
" Chinese " Attack, 254
Chipilly, 98
Chiswell, Lt. (R.E.), 144
Christie, Brig.-Gen. H. W. A., 200
Clapham Junction, 129, 131-2, 143
Clare, Capt., 223
Clarke, A/Sergt. R., 278
Clayton, Capt., 112
la Cliqueterie Farm, 34
Cloudy Trench, 89
Cobham, Brig.-Gen. H. W., 97, 101, 127
Cochrane, Lt.-Col., 249
Cockcraft, Lt.-Col. L. W. La T., 248
Coffin, Brig.-Gen. C., 97, 101, 111, 115, 132, 134, 147-50, 170, 178, 180, 183, 187-8, 193-4
Cohen, Lt. (R.E.), 149
Coke, Maj. Hon. E., 115
Cole, Brig.-Gen. A. W. G. Lowry, see Lowry Cole
Cole, Maj. J. J. B., 143, 148
Colyer-Fergusson, Capt. T. R., 129, 130
Concevreux, 230
Condé, 273
Connaught, H.R.H. Duke of, 91
Cooper, Sir George, Bt., 1
Cope, Maj. A. H., 181, 189, 234
Corbie, 99

INDEX

la Cordonnerie Farm, 34, 80
Corner Fort, 49, 52
Corps :
  Cavalry, 3
  I, 32, 43, 79, 81
  II, 61, 123, 127, 142, 154, 163
  III, 32, 44, 59, 70, 200, 208, 277
  IV, 4, 24, 28, 34, 43
  VIII, 156–7, 163, 241, 246, 255, 263, 266, 268–9, 273, 276–7
  IX, 216, 219, 237, 245
  XI, 80
  XIV, 85, 91, 94, 98, 122, 127
  XV, 96–8, 115
  XVIII, 127, 152, 175
  XIX, 127–8, 135, 152, 174–5, 178, 182, 186, 188, 190, 241–2
  XXII, 242, 245, 256, 260
  Anzac, 156, 199
  Canadian, 142, 159, 266
  Indian, 17, 19, 20, 32, 34, 43–4
Counsell, 2/Lt. C., 229
Cox, Maj. S. FitzG., 20, 39, *Lt.-Col.*, 47, 52
Crawl, Cod, Crab Trenches, 251–2
Crawley, Rev. A. Stafford, 139
Cripps, Maj. C. W., 265
la Croisette, 270, 274
Crumb, Cruet, Cupid Trenches, 258
Cubray, 270
Cuinchy, 80
Cuincy, 262
Curtis, Capt., 144
Cyclists, 268, 270, 277

D

Daunt, Lt.-Col. R. A., 48, 70
Davidge, Lt.-Col. G. M. C., 128, 144, 205
Davies, Lt. F. F., 115
Davies, Maj.-Gen. F. S., 1, 2, 16, 23, 31, 44
Dead Dog Farm, 60
Dead End, The, 168
Defensive in Depth, The, 152–3, 160, 162

Deleval Farm, 79
Desgoutte, Général, 278
Dessard Wood, 111
Divisions :
  British :
    1st Cavalry, 178
    2nd Cavalry, 194
    Guards, 98
    3rd, 3
    4th, 85, 89, 97, 100
    5th, 3
    6th, 4, 85
    7th, 17, 19, 24, 27–8, 32, 34, 41–3
    8th, *passim*
    12th, 77–8
    14th, 167
    15th, 80, 128, 134–5
    16th, 143, 145, 152
    17th, 90–1
    18th, 128, 132–3
    19th, 76–7, 233–4, 236
    20th, 45, 55, 58, 98, 111, 113, 180, 254
    21st, 82, 220
    23rd, 56
    24th, 135, 178, 182, 186
    25th, 124, 128, 136, 142, 220
    28th, 78
    29th, 94, 170
    30th, 123, 128, 132, 134–5
    32nd, 62, 81, 163–4, 166–7
    33rd, 91, 97, 163
    34th, 59, 61, 72, 77
    35th, 61
    36th, 152
    39th, 59, 61, 80, 178, 189
    40th, 82, 98, 102, 108, 111, 115, 117, 119
    47th, 154
    48th, 111
    49th, 33, 44, 253
    50th, 176–8, 186–7, 189, 191, 220, 230, 233
    51st, 44, 251
    52nd, 273–4, 277
    55th, 123
    56th, 143, 145–7
    58th, 200, 204–6

INDEX

Divisions :
British (contd.)
  66th, 178
  2nd Australian, 157
  3rd   „   159
  4th   „   156, 213
  5th   „   200, 209, 212
  1st Canadian, 31, 261
  3rd   „   159
  Lahore, 3, 4
  Meerut, 17, 25
French :
  18th, 91
  71st, 217
  154th, 232–3, 236–7
Italian :
  8th, 198
Dobson, Cpl., 223
Dorignies Château, 265
Douai, 266–8
Douai Canal, 248
Douai Prison, 264
Douai Station, 248
Douve R., 156
Douvrain, 274
Doyle, 2/Lt. J., 206
Dreslincourt, 180, 182
Drew, Maj. C. D., 185, 203
Drocourt-Quéant Line, The, 260, 261
le Drumez, 18
Duchesnes, Général, 216
" Duck's Bill," The, 43
Duncan, Maj., 124
Duriez Farm, 157

E

Eager, Capt., 20
Eclipse Trench, 87–8, 90
Eden, Brig.-Gen. A. J. F., 87, 97
Edmeades, Lt.-Col. W. A., 256
Elliot, Brig.-Gen. H. E., 211
Ellis, Pte. B., 129
Ellis, Maj. B. W., 227
Ellis, Maj. G. M. A., 115
Enghien, 277
Engineers, Royal, 21, 63, 136–8, 144, 157, 263, 268, 272

Engineers, Field Companies, R.E., 127
  2nd Field Company, 144, 158, 186, 191
  15th Field Company, 41, 189
  490th (Home Counties), 53, 142–4, 180
Epéhy, 111
Epénancourt, 181
Equancourt, 110
Erbisœul, 274
Escaupont, 273–4
Estaires, 3, 31, 43
Essame, Capt. H., 210
Estrées, 186
Eterpigny, 178, 184
Ette, Pte., 103
Evans, Capt. W., 185

F

Fagan, Brig.-Gen. E. A., 85, 89, 110
Fauquissart, 3
Faverolles, 231, 233–4
Fay, 66
Fayolle, Général, 186
Feetham, Lt.-Col. E., 19
Ferguson, 2/Lt. J., 87
Fergusson, Capt., 103
Fergusson, Lt.-Gen. Sir C., 61
Festubert, 43
Field Companies, see Engineers, Royal
Fielding, Maj.-Gen., 98
Finch, Lt.-Col. H. W. E., 85
Fins, 110, 111
Fisher, Lt.-Col. H. G., 221, 227, 243
Fismes, 232
Flesselles, 61
Fleurbaix, 31, 59
Flint, Capt., 165
Foch, Général, 188, 190, 221, 239
Fog, favours German attacks, 176, 203, 223
Fôret de Raisnes, 270
Forman, Lt.-Col. D. E., 213, 248
Forster, Maj. H. T., 210, 236
Foucaucourt, 182

351

INDEX

Francis, Lt. O. S., 165
Franklin, Maj. W. V., 249
Fraser, Capt., 20
Fraser, Lt.-Col. A., 23
Frelinghien, 156
French, Sir John, 2, 5, 31, 43, 55, 57
Fresnes, 273
Fresnes les Montauban, 260
Fresnoy, 248
Fricourt, 91
Fritz Trench, 103, 105–6
Friville, 242
Fromelles, 31–44
Frost, 2/Lt., 130, 149
Furnivale, Lt.-Col. W., 256

G

Gall Bladder Cut, 105
Gamaches, 243
Gas, Casualties from, 201, 250
Gas Projectors, 157, 250
Gauche Wood, 114
Gavrelle, 251
Gentelles, 201
German Retreat of 1917, The, 100–20
Gernicourt, 220, 230
Ghlin, 276–7
Giddings, 2/Lt., 165
Ginchy, 92
Glasgow, Brig.-Gen. T. W., 210
Glencorse Wood, 132–3, 143
Glisy, 201
" Glory Hole," The, 62
Godley, Lt.-Gen. Sir A. J., 154, 256
Gommecourt, 65, 66
Gonnelieu, 115
Goodwyn, Maj. W. M., 10
Gordon, Lt., 20
Gordon, Lt.-Gen. Sir A. Hamilton, 216
Gordon, Brig.-Gen. H., 59, 71, 76
la Gorgue, 17, 18
Gough, Gen. Sir Hubert, 5, 123, 125, 141, 154, 174, 177
Gough, Brig.-Gen. John E., 15
Gouzeaucourt, 113

Gouzeaucourt Wood, 114
Graham, Lt., 21
Grant, Lt.-Col. P. G., 18
Gray, 2/Lt., 41
Green, Lt.-Col J. E., 243
Greensmith, Capt. W. B., 189
Gregory, Pte., 223
Gregory, Lt. G. F., 50
Griffin, Major J. A. A., 101, 194, Lt.-Col., 220, 223
Grogan, Maj. G. W. St. G., 23, 42, Lt.-Col., 87, 101, Brig.-Gen., 110, 111, 127, 178, 183, 194, 220, 227, 231–6, 248, 259, 261, 265–6, 271–2
Gueudecourt, 84–5
Guillemont, 84
Gusty Trench, 89
Guyencourt, 110

H

Haig, Sir Douglas, 4, 18, 32, 43, 57, 65, 99, 114, 125, 154, 269, 273, 280
Haig, Lt.-Col. R., 86, 101, 124, 133, 139, 167, Brig.-Gen., 178, 182, 187, 220, 225, 243
Hairpin, The, 82
Halfway House, 123
Hall, Lt.-Col. J. H., 111, 131
Hanbury-Sparrow, Capt. A. H., 106, Lt.-Col., 143, 146, 148
Hanebeek, The, 133, 141–55
Hanebeek Wood, 133, 144–6, 148
Hangard Wood, 202, 205
Harbonnières, 186–7, 189
Harington, Lt. F. J., 10
Harris, Capt., 20
Harris, Maj. P. J., 60
Hart-Synnot, Lt.-Col. A. H. S., 170
Harvey, Maj. R. P., 40
Hautebut, 243
Haute Deule Canal, 268
Havre, le, 2, 3
Hawkins, Sergt., 87
Hawley, Capt. F. H., 92
Hayes, Lt.-Col. R. H., 19, 33
Hayne, Lt.-Col. S. S., 243, 251, 271

INDEX

Heath, Brig.-Gen. R. M., 236
Hem Wood, 98
Heneker, Maj.-Gen. W. C. G., 97, 99, 113, 119, 123, 125, 136, 143, 156, 164, 174–5, 178, 180, 189, 208, 221, 231, 253, 255–6, 272–7
 Farewell Message of, 278
Henencourt Château, 62
Hennessy, Maj. G. R., 231
Herbert, Maj. D. L., 180
Hergnies, 273
High Wood, 84
Hill, Lt.-Col. G. E. M., 87, 89, 204, 220
Hill, Lt.-Col. H., 57, 81
Hill, Lt.-Col. H. W., 63
Hill Métier, 261
Hill 70, 142
Hindenburg Line, 99, 110, 112–3, 115
Hohenzollern Redoubt, 80, 82
Holdsworth, Lt.-Col. A. M., 70, 72
Holland, Brig.-Gen. A. E. A., 3, 17, 44
Hollingsworth, Maj. D. W., 180
Hooge, 123–4
Hornby, Lt.-Col. M. L., 71
Horne, Gen. Sir H. S., 245, 259
Horse Show, Divisional, 244
Hoskins, Lt.-Col. A. R., 8
Houplines, 156
Houston, Maj. S. C., 138
Houthulst Forest, 161
Howatson, Capt. G., 264
Howley, Maj. J. J., 20
Hudson, Maj.-Gen. H., 44, 47, 57, 59, 80, 85, 91, 97
Hull, Lt.-Col. C. R. I., 60, 139
Hulluch, 81
Hume Spry, Lt.-Col. L., 70
Hunt, Lt.-Col. E. P., 47, 51–2
Hunter-Weston, Lt.-Gen. Sir A. G., 156, 168, 198, 241, 245, 259
Huppy, 241
Hursley Park, 1, 2
Husey, Brig.-Gen. R. H., 219, 224, 243

I

Infantry :
 Brigades :
  2nd Guards, 98
  7th, 124
  8th, 3
  14th, 3
  17th, 183
  18th, 145
  22nd, 17
  23rd, 1, 3, 4, 6, 9, 17–9, 21–3, 25, 28, 34, 40, 42, 44, 48, 56, 59, 68, 70, 72, 76, 80, 85–7, 89, 91, 97, 98, 108, 110, 115, 117, 123, 125, 127, 130, 136, 142, 143, 150, 151, 156, 158, 159, 162, 163, 168, 170, 178, 181, 184, 186, 187, 191–5, 200, 203, 219, 220, 222, 225–7, 230, 243, 244, 248, 251, 257, 264, 265, 268, 271, 273, 277
  24th, 3, 17–9, 22, 23, 25, 27, 28, 33, 34, 40, 42, 48, 51, 56, 80, 81, 85, 87, 91, 97, 101, 108, 115, 123, 127, 131, 136, 143, 156, 158, 159, 162, 167, 170, 175, 178, 180–3, 186, 187, 191–4, 200, 203, 220, 224, 225, 227, 230, 243, 248, 249, 251, 253, 264, 268, 271, 273, 277
  25th, 3, 12, 17–9, 21–5, 27, 28, 33–5, 40, 47, 48, 53, 56, 59, 68, 70, 72, 76, 80, 85–7, 89–91, 97, 98, 101, 108, 110, 112, 113, 123, 124, 128, 132, 136, 142, 143, 149, 150, 151, 156, 158, 162–4, 167, 170, 178–83, 186, 187, 191–4, 200, 219, 220, 230, 243, 244, 249, 251, 253, 257, 261, 264, 268, 274, 278
  41st, 167

INDEX

Infantry :
  Brigades *(contd.)*
    48th, 145, 150, 151
    54th, 208, 209
    56th, 76
    61st, 98
    70th, 56, 59, 70, 73, 76, 80
    74th, 230
    75th, 230
    102nd, 59
    116th, 59
    117th, 59
    121st, 108
    146th, 43
    149th, 225, 226
    150th, 186
    154th, 251
    157th, 274
    167th, 143, 148, 149
    13th Australian, 156, 208–210, 212
    15th Australian, 209–212
    Bareilly, 21
    7th Canadian, 159
    8th Canadian, 159
    Dehra Dun, 17, 25
    Ferozepore, 4
    Garhwal, 23
    Jullunder, 4
    1 New Zealand, 156
  Brigades, Reduction of, 170
  Regiments :
    Berkshire, Royal, *2nd Bn.*, 19–21, 40, 41, 43, 47, 49–52, 68, 70, 72, 75, 86, 89, 90, 101, 106, 113, 124, 133–6, 143–6, 148, 149, 164–7, 180, 193, 194, 206, 212, 220, 223, 253, 257, 258, 262, 264
    Black Watch, *5th Bn.*, 3, 19, 31, 51
    Border, *8th Bn.*, 230
    Cameron Highlanders, *4th Bn.*, 15, 17, 19, 23, 28, 31
    Cameronians, The. *See* Scottish Rifles
    Cheshire, *11th Bn.*, 230

Infantry :
  Regiments *(contd.)*
    Devonshire, *2nd Bn.*, 3, 9, 10, 19–23, 28, 70, 71, 75, 82, 86, 110–12, 114, 126, 130, 136, 143, 162, 167, 181, 185, 189, 194, 200, 205, 206, 220, 225–6, 232, 238–9, 254, 257, 260, 271–2, 277
    Duke of Cornwall's Light Infantry, *7th Bn.*, 254
    Durham Light Infantry, *6th Bn.*, 186, 188
      1/7th Bn. (Pioneers), 184, 242, 263, 268, 277
      8th Bn., 186.
      22nd Bn. (Pioneers), 105, 138, 145, 180, 189, 209, 211–14, 220, 230, 242
    Gloucestershire, *15th Bn.*, 60
    Irish Rifles, Royal, *1st Bn.*, 19, 21, 24, 28, 34, 38, 41–2, 47, 51, 53, 62, 70, 73, 75, 86, 90, 111, 133, 135, 143–6, 151, 158, 164, 170
    King's Own Yorkshire Light Infantry, *8th Bn.*, 56, 71–4, 76
    Lancashire, East, *2nd Bn.*, 22–4, 27, 33, 35, 37, 43, 48, 87–9, 114, 132, 143, 151, 170, 180, 194, 204, 206, 220, 253, 260, 269, 270
      South, *2nd Bn.*, 230
    Lincolnshire, *2nd Bn.*, 3, 8, 19–21, 24, 39, 41, 43, 47, 50–1, 56, 70–5, 86–90, 101, 110, 115, 133–5, 143–6, 164–7, 170
    London, *1/1th Bn.*, 31, 43, 48, 50, 60
      13th Bn., 3, 19, 34, 38, 39, 40, 43
    Middlesex, *2nd Bn.*, 19, 21, 33, 70–1, 75, 86–7, 111–2, 114, 117, 131, 135–6, 141, 143, 145–8, 150–1, 171, 181, 184–5, 192,

INDEX

Infantry :
  Regiments (contd.)
  199, 203, 214, 220, 225,
  257, 261, 266, 274, 276
  4th Bn., 276
  1/7th Bn., 31, 33, 44, 60
  1/8th Bn., 44, 48, 52, 60
  Northamptonshire, 2nd Bn., 3,
  19, 24–6, 34, 37, 41, 43,
  51, 87, 101–5, 129, 131,
  144, 148–9, 151, 175, 181,
  186, 188, 195, 209–12,
  220, 224, 251, 254, 270–1
  Northumberland Fusiliers, 1st
    Service Bn., 59
    2nd Service Bn., 59
    3rd Service Bn., 59
    4th Service Bn., 59
  Rifle Brigade, The, 2nd Bn.,
    12, 19, 21, 26, 28, 34, 38,
    41–2, 47, 49–52, 56, 70,
    73, 75, 86, 88, 90–1, 111,
    113, 115, 133, 143–4, 148,
    151, 158, 164–6, 180,
    205–6, 213–4, 219, 257–8,
    265–6, 269
  Sherwood Foresters, 1st Bn.,
    24–6, 37, 43, 48, 82,
    87–90, 101, 105, 114,
    131, 144, 151, 170, 181,
    183, 189, 207, 212, 220,
    229, 251, 257, 260, 269,
    270
    11th Bn., 71, 75–6
  Scottish Rifles, 2nd Bn., 19,
    21, 28, 40, 44, 70, 72,
    75, 86–9, 110–1, 114,
    117, 131–3, 143, 145,
    150–1, 170
    6th Bn., 31
  Tyneside Scottish, see Northumberland Fusiliers
  Wiltshire, 2nd Bn., 235
  Worcestershire, 1st Bn., 14,
    23, 25–7, 40–3, 51, 87,
    101, 103, 128–30, 132,
    144, 151, 170, 180–1, 186,
    188, 194–5, 205–6, 220,
    224–5, 244, 249, 251, 253,
    258, 260, 264–6

Infantry :
  Regiments (contd.)
  York and Lancaster, 8th Bn.,
    71, 73–4, 76
    9th Bn., 71, 74–6
  Yorkshire, West, 2nd Bn., 8–
    10, 22–3, 26, 70–1, 75, 82,
    86, 89, 108, 110, 114, 117,
    126, 130–1, 136, 143–4,
    146–8, 151, 162–4, 181,
    184, 191, 194, 199, 203–4,
    212, 214, 220, 225, 248,
    250, 257, 264, 274
  Australian Infantry, 57th Bn.,
    212
  Units also referred to :
    1/8th Composite Bn., 236, 241
    2/8th Composite Bn., 241
    20th Entrenching Bn., 187–8
    11/23rd French Territorial
      Bn., 220, 230
Impey, Lt. E. H., 8
Inden Rooster Cabaret, 157
Ingham, Major H., 204
d'Ingnon, R., 178
Ingoldsby, Lt. H., 134
Ingpen, Lt.-Col. P. L., 48
Inverness Copse, 142–3, 146
Iron Cross Redoubt, 146, 148
Irwin, Lt.-Col. N. M. S., 164
Isaac, Lt.-Col. A. G. F., 243, 253, 262
Ivey, Maj. T. H., 164
Izel lez Equerchin, 260–1

J

Jabber Trench, 132, 134
Jack, Lt.-Col. J. L., 86, 93, 108, 114, 119, 130, 139
Jackson, Maj.-Gen. H. C., 221
Jacob, Lt.-Gen. Sir C. W., 123, 141, 154
Jacob Trench, 129, 130, 151
Jacquenne Copse, 111
Jaffa Trench, 131, 149
Jago, Capt. H. H., 163
James, Lt.-Col. B. C., 211, 220, 241, 263, 268
James, Lt.-Col. R. E. H., 97

INDEX

James Trench, 128
Jarvis, Lt., 102
Jeffries, Lt.-Col. H. St. J., 143
Jenkins, Capt. C. W. W., 49
Joffre, Général, 5, 8, 65, 99, 116
Johnson, Sergt. A., 50
Jonchery, 231–2
Jones, Capt. T., 265
Jumel, 192
Jurbise, 276

K

Kaiserin Trench, 81
Kay, Lt.-Col. W. M., 31
Kelly, Lt., 231
Kennedy, 2/Lt. A. J., 142
Kennedy, Brig.-Gen. H. A., 231
Kennington, Lt. R., 204
Kerr, 2/Lt. L. M., 8
Kiggell, Lt.-Gen. Sir L. E., 125
King, H.M. The, 8, 248, 277
King, Lt.-Col. E. J., 31, 33
Kit and Kat, 131, 133

L

Lafone, Capt. C. A., 9
Laguishe, Général de, 277
Lambert, Lt.-Col. T. S., 48
Lamont, Brig.-Gen. J. W. F., 221, 253, 257, 261, 270, 277
Lamotte, 159
Lane, Capt., 105
Langemarck, 152
Langley, Capt., 17
Lankester, Lt. F. R. F., 49
Lapham, Pte., 37
Large, Lt. C. E., 228–9, 240
Lassigny, 65
Latham, Maj. S. G., 144, *Lt.-Col.*, 210
Laventie, 43
Lawrie, Lt.-Col. F. G., 19
Layes, R., 32
Leach, 2/Lt. E. T., 265
Leslie-Carter, Lt. W., 278
Lewis, Lt.-Col. F. G., 19, 34
Leyland, Lt.-Col. R. H., 243, 254
Lhéry, 233, 236
Licourt, 175, 181–2

Liéramont, 110
Lihons, 186–7
Lindsay, Bt.-Lt.-Col. G. M., 248
Livesay, Brig.-Gen. R. O'H., 253, 266, 271
Lloyd, Lt.-Col. E. C., 86, 111
Lloyd, Brig.-Gen. H. G., 97, 111, 126, 144
Long Valley, 77, 79
Loos, 45
Loupart Line, 107
Loveday, Lt.-Col. F. W., 248
Lowry, Lt.-Col. A. E. E., 181, 191–2, 199, 203, 220, 227, 243, 254
Lowry Cole, Brig.-Gen. A. W. G., 3, 12, 19, 25, 33, 38–9
Lozenge, The, 50
Lynde, 57
Lys R., 156

M

McAndrew, Lt.-Col. G.B., 3, 19, 20
McCarthy O'Leary, Lt.-Col. H. W. D., 143, 147
McLaren, Maj. R. J., 130
Machine Gunners, 136–8, 150, 270
Machine Gun Companies, 102, 137–8, 144
Machine Gun Corps, 8th Bn., 220, 248, 264–5, 270–1, 278
McLaughlin, Col. A. M., 268
Maclear, Maj. H., 22, 34
McConville, 2/Lt. M., 91, 126
Maistre, Général, 239
Marcelcave, 187, 203
Marchélepot, 182–3
Marchiennes, 269
Marchmont, Lce.-Cpl., 271
Maricourt, 66
Masnuy St. Jean, 276
Massey, Capt. J. H., 228–9, 240
Mauberge, 273
Maud'huy, Général, 4
Maunoury, Général, 4
Maurepas, 84, 97
Meaulté, 90
Menin Road, 123, 126–7, 143, 157
Mercer, Lt.-Col. E. G., 31, 48

INDEX

Mericourt, 79, 248, 250
Merris, 122
Merville, 2, 17
Messines, 122
Metz-en-Couture, 113
Mezières, 191
Miers, Lt.-Col. H. J., 260, 264, 269
Miette Stream, 220, 224–6
Mild Trench, 87, 89
Millencourt, 77, 79
Millis, Capt. C. H. G., 219
Millis, Sergt. W., 278
Misery, 183
Misty Trench, 88
Mitchell, Maj. J. D., 145, 183, Lt.-Col., 243, 251, 269
Moated Grange, The, 8, 10, 19, 23
Moislains, 99, 103, 108, 119
Mollet, 2/Lt. C., 72
Mons, 274–6
Mons-Condé Canal, 273
Montgomery, Lt.-Col. H. M. de F., 8, 17
Mont St. Georges, 261
Monument Wood, 209, 213
Mood, Maj. J. M., 150
Moore, Lt.-Col. R. F., 207, 220, 234–5
Morbecque, 57
Moreuil, 191–4
Morgan, Lt.-Col. C. B., 105, 138, 180, 189
Morley, Maj. L. St. H., 37
Mormal Forest, 273
Mortimer, Lt.-Col. C. R., 24, 48
Morval, 84
Mosselmarkt, 164
Mowatt, Maj. C. R. J., 34
Murray, Pte., 87
Mustard Gas, 124, 201, 250
Myers, Lt. E., 117

N

Nash, Maj. A. F., 140
Neame, Lt. P., 8, 10
Nesle, 174–5
Neuve Chapelle, 9–12, 32
Neuve Chapelle, Battle of, 16–29
Nevinson, Lt.-Col. T. St. A. B. L., 63, 97, 126, 140

Newport, Lt., 41–2
Nicholson, Lt.-Col. C. L., 22
Nicholson, Brig.-Gen. G. H. W., 44, 63, 97
Nieuport, 122
Nivelle, Général, 99, 116
Nonne Bosschen Wood, 133, 146–8
Nugent, Capt. C., 40
Nugent, Maj. F. H., 47
Nurlu, 101, 110, 119, 121

O

Odomez, 270, 273
Oke, Capt. R., 49
Oldfield, Maj. L. C. L., 17
Omiécourt, 183
Oppy, 257
Oppy Wood, 251
Orion, 86, 89
Ormsby, Lt.-Col. G. J. A., 139
Ostend, 122
O'Sullivan, Capt. A. M., 21
Oughton, 2/Lt. H. C., 268
Ovillers, 65–79
Ovillers Post, 62
Owen, Capt. A. C., 249
Oxley, Brig.-Gen. R. S., 33, 40, 43–4, 48

P

Page, Lt.-Col. C. A. S., 171, 181, 185, 192, 199, 220
Pallas Trench, 102, 105
Palmer, 2/Lt. E. A., 265
Palmes, Capt. J. P., 115
Parapet Guns, 48
Pargny, 180
Pargny Wood, 178
Parker, Lt. O. K., 37, 41
Parker, Sergt., 105
Pascoe, Capt. B. C., 212, 224
Passchendaele, 159–67, 169
Paul, Commandant, 227
Paul, Maj. C. T. S., 140
Peake, Capt. C. G. W., 20
la Pêcherie Bridge, 225, 230
Pepper, Pte., 195
Pernes, 245
Péronne, 101, 107
Perry, Lce.-Cpl., 20

INDEX

Pertain, 180, 182
Pertwee, 2/Lt. L., 110
Petain, Général, 118, 168, *Maréchal*, 278
Petillon, 31
Peyton, Lt.-Col. H. S. C., 180
Pezière, 111
Phillips, Lt.-Col. G. F., 10
Phipps, Lt.-Col. H. R., 221
Picantin, 44
Pickard, Lce.-Cpl., 103
Pill-box, The, 145, 153, 162
Pinney, Brig.-Gen. R. J., 3, 10, 18, 22–3, 28, 34, 40–1
Pioneers, 136, 138, and *see* Durham L.I.
Planque, 264
Platrerie, la, 227
Pleurs, 241
Ploegsteert, 3, 156
Plumer, Lt.-Gen. Sir H. C. O., 159, 170, 277
Poincaré, President, 8
Pollard, Brig.-Gen. J. H. W., 70, 76, 78, 86, 89, 97
Pollok-McCall, Brig.-Gen. J. B., 243, 249, 253
Polygon Wood, 146
Pommerœul, 274, 277
Pontavert, 226
Pont d'Annay, 268
Pont Logy, 16, 17
Poperinghe, 170
Port Arthur, 16
Potsdam Redoubt, 145
Potte, 180
Pozières, 68, 78, 84
Pratt, Capt. A., 225
Pratt, Capt. A. M., 137, 144
Preeston, Lt.-Col. N. P. R., 249
Prest, Lt. H. E. W., 106
Prichard, Lt.-Col. C. S., 3, 19, 24
Prior, Maj. G. E. R., 243, *Lt.-Col.*, 271
Priez, 97
Prosser, Capt. A. E., 265
Proyart, 188
Puddicombe, Lt.-Col. T. P., 231
Pulteney, Lt.-Gen. Sir W. P., 44, 70, 76

Q
Quarry Farm, 108
Quarries, The, 81–2

R
Raches, 269
Rainsford-Hannay, Lt.-Col. F., 256
Railton, 112
Railway Wood, 151
Ramsbotham, Maj. H., 236
Ramsden, Maj. A. G., 228
Ranchicourt, 248
Rancourt, 98, 101, 108
Rawlinson, Gen. Sir H. S., 4–6, 61, 107, 113, 120, 170, 198
Reakes, 2/Lt. H., 229
Red Lamp Corner, 8
Reid, Lt.-Col. A. D., 133, 139
Relief, A., 91–4
Revelon, 111–2
Rheims, 238
Richards, Lt.-Col. E. F. O., 143
Richardson, Lt.-Col. H. S. C., 205, 220
Riley, Capt. H. L., 49, 52
Roberts, Lt. F. C., 13, *Lt.-Col.*, 180–1, 243, 249, 266
Robertson, Capt. W. E., 185
Robinson, Capt. F. W., 144
Rogerson, Capt. S., 92, 110, 217, 219
Rollo, Capt., 182
Rosières, 174, 180, 187–8, 196
Roucy, 217, 225, 230–1
Rouge Croix, 19
Rouges Bancs, 31, 38
Roupell, Maj. G. R. P., 236
Rouvrel, 193
Rouvroy-Fresnes Line, 256–9
Rue Bacquerot, 17, 19
Rue du Bois, 3, 4
Rue du Quesnes, 34
Rue du Sac, 156
Rue Tilleloy, 22
Russell, Lt. B., 50
Russell, Capt. Hon. B. J., 37

INDEX

S

Saillisel, 85, 97
Sailly, 31
Sailly Empire, The, 60
Sailly la Bourse, 80
Sailly le Sec, 98
Sailly sur la Lys, 57, 59
St. Amand, 270, 274, 278
St. Christ Bridge, 178, 181, 183-4
St. Denis, 276
St. Janshoek, 142
St. Jean, 159
St. Julien, 152
St. Omer, 2, 173-4
St. Pierre Vaast Wood, 108
Sambre, R., 273
Sandilands, Lt.-Col. V. C., 70, 86, 89, 114
Sankey, 2/Lt. D., 92
Sandys, Lt.-Col. E. T. F., 70
Sans Souci, 145
Saunders, Capt. Clive, 227
Savile, Maj. H. B. W., 71
Sawyer, Capt. G. H., 51. *Maj.*, 72
Scheldt R., 270-1, 273
Scott, Lt. (R.A.), 265
Scott, Capt. A. H., 132
Scott, Capt. V. R., 164
Scottish Camp, 124-5
Scrivener, Cpl., 195
Seely, Brig.-Gen. Rt. Hon. J. E. B., 110
Sercus, 57
Sharland, Lt.-Col. A. A., 114, 132, 144
Sherbrooke, Lt.-Col. R. L., 87, 101, 114, 131
Signpost Lane, 19-24, 26-7
Signals, 1, 136, 198
Simonds, Capt. A., 138, 144
Skett, 2/Lt. A. E., 92-3
Slee, Pte., 223
Smith, Maj. H. C. H., 151
Smythe, Capt. E. H., 234, 278
Somervail, Lt.-Col. W. F., 143
Somme Battle, The, 65-79, 84-95
Somme R., 174-5, 177, 182-3, 190
Sorel le Grand, 110-1
Southampton, 1

Southern Redoubt, 165-6
Sowerbutts, Gnr. R., 278
Soyécourt, 186-7
Steenvoorde, 136, 173
Steenwerck, 156
Stephens, Lt.-Col. R. B., 19, 34, 38-9, 41, *Brig.-Gen.*, 47, 59
Stevens, Brig.-Gen. L. M., 243, 248
Stevens, Capt. W. E., 278
Stirling, Maj. C. R. H., 114, *Lt.-Col.*, 131, 140, 164, 166, 180
Stirling Castle, 123, 140
Stone, Pte., 223
Stormy Trench, 89
Sturgess, Sergt., 125, 165
Sunderland, Lt.-Col. A. J. E., 70, 86, 111, 130, 132, 139
Sunray Trench, 89
Sykes, Lt. F. A., 268

T

Tall, Lt. E., 144
Tanks, British, 128, 134, 146, 207
  German, 203-5, 223, 225
Taylor, Maj. R. M., 189
Teale Cottage, 166, 171
Tertre, 274, 276
Tilleloy, 4
Tillet, Lt.-Col. A., 143, 167
Tilques, 173
Titley, 2/Lt. A. E., 126
Thackeray, Lt.-Col. C. B., 243, 248, 270
Thélus, 250
Thiepval, 62, 74, 76, 84
Thruston, Capt. B. J., 39, 41
Thulin, 274
Thynne, Lt.-Col. Hon. E., 111
Tortille R., 66, 84, 99
Tournai, 277
Toye, Capt. A. M., 184
Train, Divisional, 4, 139, 198
Training New Units, 56, 59
Tramways, Trench, 8
Transloy, le, 84-95
Travers, Lt.-Col. J. O., 3, 10, 20
Trench Feet, 15, 98
Trench Mortar Battery, 24th, 189

INDEX

Treslon, 234–5
Treux, 90–1
Trevor, Lt.-Col. H. E., 71
Triangle, The, 103
Triefus, Lt. P., 60
Trinder, Sergt., 223
Trônes Wood, 85
Trotter, Lt. R. H. G., 49
Tunnelling Companies, 127
185th Company, 264
Tuson, Brig.-Gen. H. D., 48, 70, 76

U

Uniacke, Lt.-Col. H. C. C., 17
Upton, Lt. W. A., 166
Uzielli, Lt. D., 34

V

Vacquerie, la, 117
Valenciennes, 270, 272
Vandeleur, Lt.-Col. C. B., 19
Vandeuil, 232
Vaux, 98
Venison Trench, 165–6
Ventelay, 231
Vermandovillers, 186–7
Verrerie Château, la, 276
Vesle, R., 231–2
Ville au Bois, 226
Villers au Bois, 236
Villers-Bretonneux, 175, 199–215
Villers Carbonnel, 175, 181
Villers Guislain, 114
Vimy, 246
Vitry en Artois, 261
Vitry Marsh, 259
Vrély, 190

W

Walker, Capt. W. G. J., 127
Wallace, Capt. F. C., 225, *Maj.*, 236
Warfusée Abancourt, 190
Warneton, 156–7
Watou, 159
Watson, Lt.-Col. H. F., 71, 75
Watson, Maj. T. H., 144, 181
Watts, Capt. G. I., 10
Watts, Lt.-Gen. Sir H. E., 174–5, 198

Weather, Influence of the, 84, 136, 142, 169
Wedderburn Maxwell, Lt. J., 49
Weeks, Maj. R. M., 189
Well Farm, 53
Well Farm Salient, 47, 52
Westhoek, 142–3
Westhoek Ridge, 121–40, 143, 145, 149, 151
Westroosebeke, 161
Wickham, Lt.-Col. H., 19
Wieltje, 159
Wilkins, Lt. (R.E.), 144
Willcocks, Lt.-Gen. Sir J., 44
Willison, Lt. A. C., 270
Wilson, Lt., 270
Winnipeg Camp, 124
Wittes, 57
Wizernes, 167, 173
Wheeler, Lt.-Col. E. L., 126
Whitfield, Capt. G. H. P., 147
Wodehouse, Maj. E., 23, 25
Wokins, R.S.M., 227
Wytschaete, 122

Y

Young, Lt. F. E., 49
Young, 2/Lt. K., 134
Ypres, 160, 168
Ypres, Canal Bank, the, 168–9
Ypres–Comines Canal, 157
Ypres Front, why selected, 121–2
Ypres Front, farewell to the, 171
Ypres Offensive, The, 121–55
Ypres Offensive, Plan of the, 122, 127, 160–1
Ypres–Poperinghe Road, 124
Ypres Ramparts, The, 123
Ypres–Roulers Railway, 135, 142–3, 157
Yzengremer, 243

Z

Ziel House, 130, 132
Zillebeke, 124
Zillebeke Lake, 123
Zenith Trench, 86, 88–91
Zonnebeke, 146
Zonnebeke Redoubt, 146–7, 151